COLLEGE LEARNING AND STUDY SKILLS

FOURTH EDITION

College Learning And Study Skills

Debbie Guice Longman
Southeastern Louisiana University

Rhonda Holt Atkinson
Louisiana State University

WEST PUBLISHING COMPANY

MINNEAPOLIS/ST. PAUL   NEW YORK   LOS ANGELES   SAN FRANCISCO

Cartoons: Richard Longman
Copyediting: Bonnie Gruen
Composition and Film: Carlisle Communications
Cover and Interior Design: Peter Thiel
Cover Image: © Bob Krist/Tony Stone Images
Index: Pat Lewis

WEST'S COMMITMENT TO THE ENVIRONMENT

In 1906, West Publishing Company began recycling materials left over from the production of books. This began a tradition of efficient and responsible use of resources. Today, up to 95 percent of our legal books and 70 percent of our college and school texts are printed on recycled, acid-free stock. West also recycles nearly 22 million pounds of scrap paper annually—the equivalent of 181,717 trees. Since the 1960s, West has devised ways to capture and recycle waste inks, solvents, oils, and vapors created in the printing process. We also recycle plastics of all kinds, wood, glass, corrugated cardboard, and batteries, and have eliminated the use of Styrofoam book packaging. We at West are proud of the longevity and the scope of our commitment to the environment.

Production, Prepress, Printing and Binding by West Publishing Company.

British Library Cataloguing-in-Publication Data. A catalogue record for this book is available from the British Library.

COPYRIGHT ©
1988, 1991, 1993   By WEST PUBLISHING COMPANY
COPYRIGHT ©1996   By WEST PUBLISHING COMPANY
                         610 Opperman Drive
                         P.O. Box 64526
                         St. Paul, MN 55164-0526

Printed in the United States of America

03 02 01 00 99 98 97 96   8 7 6 5 4 3 2 1 0

Library of Congress Cataloging-in-Publication Data

Longman, Debbie Guice.
    College learning and study skills / Debbie Guice Longman, Rhonda
  Holt Atkinson.—4th ed.
       p.   cm.
    Includes bibliographical references and index.
    ISBN 0-314-06808-2 (soft : alk. paper)
    1. Study skills 2. College student orientation—United States.
  I. Atkinson, Rhonda Holt.   II. Title.
  LB2395.L58   1996
  378.1'702812—dc20
                                                              95-24005
                                                                   CIP

To Alden J. Moe and Ray R. Buss
for your friendship and support.

Contents

PREFACE   xiv

Chapter 1:   **ENTERING THE WORLD OF HIGHER EDUCATION   1**

YOU AS CITIZEN: LEARNING STYLE ATTRIBUTES   2
Myers-Briggs Personality Types   3
Sensory Preferences   5
Brain Dominance   11
HIGHER EDUCATION CITIZENSHIP: RIGHTS AND
    RESPONSIBILITIES   15
College Catalog   15
Campus Resources   15
Academic Excellence   23
Academic Standards   27
College Faculty   29
    Your Classroom Behavior   29
    Out-of-Class Interactions with Instructors   31
A LIBERAL EDUCATION: YOUR ASSIMILATION INTO THE COLLEGE
    COMMUNITY   32
Campus Diversity   33
    Ethnically Diverse Students Minority Groups   33
    Returning Adult Students   34
    ESL Students   35
    Commuting Students   36
    Students with Disabilities   37
    Reentry Students   37
Getting Involved in the Campus Community   38
    Classroom Interactions   39
    Study Groups   40
    Campus Employment   41
    Special Interest Groups   43
    Service Organizations   43
    Social Organizations   44
GROUP LEARNING ACTIVITY   42
VOCABULARY DEVELOPMENT   49

Chapter 2:   **TIME MANAGEMENT: PUT YOURSELF TO WORK   54**

HAVING THE TIME OF YOUR LIFE: USING STYLE IN TIME
    MANAGEMENT   57
Applying Myers-Briggs Types to Time Management   57
Applying Brain Dominance to Time Management   57
Applying Sensory Preferences to Time Management   59

CONCEIVING, BELIEVING, AND ACHIEVING GOALS   61
Conceiving Goals   61
    Aptitudes   62
    Abilities   63
    Interests   63
    Needs   64
    Values   65
Believing Goals   66
    Self-Talk   66
    Visualization   67
    Action   68
Achieving Goals   69
    Specifying Goals   70
    Rewarding Yourself for Completing Goals   72
IMPLEMENTING YOUR GOALS   75
Managing a Term   75
Managing a Week   78
Managing a Day   79
    Protecting Prime Study Time   83
    Selecting a Study Site   84
    Making One Minute Work as Two   85
AVOIDING PROCRASTINATION   86
Getting Started   88
Achieving Closure   89
Avoiding Burnout   91
PLANNING FOR THE FUTURE: SCHEDULING SUBSEQUENT
    SEMESTERS   96
Full-Time versus Part-Time Status   96
Scheduling Your Class Day and Week   97
Flexibility in Scheduling   98
Undecided Majors: Exploring Institutional Options   99
MAINTAINING BALANCE   103
GROUP LEARNING ACTIVITY   106
VOCABULARY DEVELOPMENT   110

Chapter 3:   **IT'S A BREEZE: BLOWING STRESS AWAY   114**

DEFINITIONS, CAUSES, AND SYMPTOMS OF STRESS   117
Defensive Coping Mechanisms   118
Positive Coping Strategies   121
    The Power of Positive Thinking   121
    Visualization   128
    Relaxation   129
Stress Overload: Day-to-Day Crisis Situations   132
    Crisis Situations You Cannot Control   132
    Crisis Situations You Can Control   133
WELLNESS   133
Eating Right   135
R and R   139
The Role of Exercise   140
Substance Use and Abuse   140
    Alcohol   140
    Other Psychoactive Drugs   142

CONTROLLING TEST ANXIETY   145
Coping Before an Exam   145
Coping During an Exam   145
Coping After an Exam   146
  Examining Returned Exams   **146**
  Adjusting to Stress   **148**
  Makeup Exams   **150**
GROUP LEARNING ACTIVITY   152
VOCABULARY DEVELOPMENT   157

Chapter 4:   LISTENING AND NOTETAKING   164

BEFORE CLASS: PREVIEWING THE TEXT   166
Making Predictions about Content   166
Constructing a Notetaking Outline through Text Previewing   173
Using Maps to Set Your Course   175
**LISTENING IN CLASS: COMMUNICATION BETWEEN SPEAKER AND
   LISTENER   177**
Factors Affecting Your Ability to be an Active Listener   182
  Maintaining Concentration   **184**
  Recognizing Main Ideas   **185**
  Identifying Important Information   **189**
  Recall   **190**
Your Instructor, The Speaker   192
  Responding to Speaker Styles: Listening Responsibilities   **194**
  Maximizing Your Understanding of the Speaker's Message   **194**
ORGANIZING WHAT YOU HEAR IN CLASS   197
Lectures Dependent on the Text   197
Lectures Independent of the Text   198
Lectures that Include Media   198
NOTES: THE ACT IN ACTIVE LISTENING   201
Taking Notes: A Systematic Approach   201
  Your Personal Notetaking System   **202**
  Cornell System of Notetaking   **205**
  Outlining   **207**
  Taking Notes from Lecture Media   **207**
Passive Notetaking: Taped and Borrowed Notes   208
AFTER CLASS: THE FOLLOW-THROUGH   210
Post-Lecture Reading   210
Evaluating Your Notes   210
GROUP LEARNING ACTIVITY   212
VOCABULARY DEVELOPMENT   217

Chapter 5:   SQ3R: A SYSTEMATIC PLAN FOR READING TEXT
                                   CHAPTERS   220

STEP ONE: SURVEY   222
STEP TWO: QUESTION   225
STEP THREE: READ   225
Text Marking   226
Text Labeling   228
  Finding Main Ideas   **233**

Creating an Inductive Outline   **236**
Identifying Text Structure   **236**
STEP FOUR: RECITE   247
STEP FIVE: REVIEW   249
GROUP LEARNING ACTIVITY   250
VOCABULARY DEVELOPMENT   254

Chapter 6:   **SEEING WHAT YOU MEAN: LEARNING FROM AND WITH GRAPHICS   262**

GRAPHIC INFORMATION: SEEING IS BELIEVING   264
Authors' Purposes for Graphics   **264**
Organization of Information: Your Purpose for Graphics   **266**
DIAGRAMS: VISUAL REPRESENTATIONS   267
Examining Diagrams   **267**
Diagramming Processes and Objects   **269**
CHARTS: ANALYZING AND SYNTHESIZING CONCEPTS   269
Using Tables   **269**
Following Flowcharts   **273**
Reading Time Lines   **275**
Charting Information   **279**
GRAPHS: DRAWING ON DATA   280
Examining Bar Graphs   **280**
Following Line Graphs   **285**
Analyzing Circle Graphs   **286**
Graphing Data   **290**
MAPS: PHYSICAL AND MENTAL TERRITORIES   291
Reading Geographic Maps   **292**
Mapping Mental Territories   **296**
GROUP LEARNING ACTIVITY   300
VOCABULARY DEVELOPMENT   306

Chapter 7:   **MAXIMIZING MEMORY FOR TEST TAKING   308**

STAGES IN PROCESSING INFORMATION   312
Registration   **313**
Short-Term Memory (STM)   **314**
Working Memory   **315**
Long-Term Memory (LTM)   **315**
ASSOCIATION: LINKING IDEAS TOGETHER   316
Logical Links   **317**
Mental and Physical Imagery   **317**
Acronyms and Acrostics   **318**
Location   **319**
Word Games   **320**
PRACTICE EFFECTS   323
Spaced Study   **323**
Previewing   **324**
Recitation   **325**
Study Groups or Partners   **325**
Overlearning   **326**
Cramming   **327**

FORGETTING: LOSS OF INFORMATION FROM LTM   327
Interference   328
Disuse   328
GENERAL SUGGESTIONS FOR PREPARING FOR AND TAKING
     EXAMS   329
PREPARING FOR AND TAKING SUBJECTIVE EXAMS   332
PORPE: A Study Plan for Subjective Exams   332
Taking Subjective Exams   332
PREPARING FOR AND TAKING OBJECTIVE EXAMS   337
POSSE: A Study Plan for Objective Exams   338
Taking Objective Exams   340
Test of Test-Wiseness   340
Key and Test-Wise Strategies   342
TAKING SPECIALIZED EXAMS   347
Taking Open-Book and Take-Home Exams   347
Taking Final Exams   348
GROUP LEARNING ACTIVITY   349
VOCABULARY DEVELOPMENT   355

Chapter 8:   **THINKING CRITICALLY   360**

M: MATERIALS   363
Information and Concepts   364
Evaluating Information   365
     Determining Relevance   365
     Checking Credibility   366
     Identifying Facts   367
     Evaluating Opinions   368
     Noting Expert Opinions   369
     Recognizing Propaganda and Bias   370
Assumptions   375
Point of View   377
I: INQUIRY   378
The Reader's Purpose   379
The Author's Purpose   381
     Informational Writing   382
     Persuasive Writing   382
N: INTROSPECTION   384
D: DECISION   386
Decision-Making Procedures   387
     Informal Dialogue   387
     Balance Sheet   389
     Criteria Matrix   391
Enacting Your Decisions   391
APPLYING STANDARDS TO THINKING   392
Clarity   394
Accuracy, Precision, and Specificity   396
Relevance and Significance   396
Breadth, Depth, and Completeness   398
Fairness and Consistency   398
Logic and Justifiability   399

GROUP LEARNING ACTIVITY   403
VOCABULARY DEVELOPMENT   410

Chapter 9:   MAKING YOUR WAY THROUGH THE MAZE: LIBRARY
                 AND RESEARCH SKILLS   414

SOMEONE TO ASSIST YOU: THE LIBRARIAN   416
A THREAD TO GUIDE YOU: LIBRARY ORGANIZATION   419
The Card Catalog   419
The Computerized Card Catalog   421
    Searching for Authors and/or Titles   423
    Conducting a Keyword Search   423
Systems of Organization   427
A SWORD AND THE SKILL TO USE IT: A WORKING BIBLIOGRAPHY
    AND RESEARCH SKILLS   428
Creating a Working Bibliography   428
Research Skills   429
THE MAZE: VARIETY OF INFORMATION IN THE LIBRARY   434
General References   435
Specialized Content References   440
Computerized References   441
    Access to Information: On-line and CD-ROMs   441
    Information Superhighway: Internet and World Wide Web   442
RUNNING THE MAZE: THE RESEARCH PROCESS   446
GROUP LEARNING ACTIVITY   447
VOCABULARY DEVELOPMENT   451

Chapter 10:   WRITING THE RESEARCH PAPER   458

TYPES OF RESEARCH PAPERS   460
PARTS OF THE RESEARCH PAPER   461
SELECTING THE SUBJECT   463
Interest and Importance   463
Library Resource Availability   464
Narrowing the Subject   464
    Purpose   464
    Determining the Scope   465
    Writing the Thesis Statement   467
    Creating a Title   467
SYNTHESIZING SOURCES   469
Outlines   470
Charts   470
WRITING THE PAPER: THE PROCESS   479
First Draft   479
    Introduction: "Tell Them What You're Going to Say"   479
    Text: "Tell Them"   480
    Summary: "Tell Them What You Said"   481
Second Draft   481
    Elements of Style   481
    Final Revisions   483
Plagiarism   494

AVOIDING THE "I'M-OVER-MY-HEAD" FEELING: SETTING A WRITING
   SCHEDULE   496
Rationale for a Writing Schedule   497
Setting a Writing Schedule   497
NOW SHOWING: MAKING PRESENTATIONS AND SPEECHES   498
GROUP LEARNING ACTIVITY   501
VOCABULARY DEVELOPMENT   505

Sample Chapter 11:   PERSONAL VALUES, CAREER PLANNING, AND SUCCESS
                     WITH PEOPLE AT WORK   508

Supplemental Article: Wackyways to Make a Living   540

Sample Chapter 12:   THE INDUSTRIAL REVOLUTION AND ITS IMPACT ON
                     EUROPEAN SOCIETY   544

Supplemental Article: Are Americans Working Too Hard?   576

Sample Chapter 13:   An Invitation to Computers   580

Sample Short Story: Strange Inventions   598

Glossary   G–1

Index   I–1

Preface

We wrote the first, second, and third editions of *College Learning and Study Skills* to help students succeed and prosper in college. Specifically, we intended to help students develop strategies for time management, study skills, test taking, using their libraries, and writing research papers. In addition, we sought to accomplish four objectives: to provide information in a context suitable for postsecondary developmental learners; to help postsecondary developmental students become more active learners; to explain the mental processes involved in learning; and to incorporate recent theories and research into reading and study skill instruction at the postsecondary level.

We have been pleased by the response to the book. Instructors and students with whom we have spoken have felt, as we have, that *CLASS* met these objectives. An additional survey of users of *CLASS* from around the country generally agreed. We realized, however, that revisions were needed to meet the changing needs of the students for whom the book was written.

CLASS (3/E), revised using comments from users and reviewers, was enormously successful. Our goal for the fourth edition of *CLASS* is for it to also fulfill the needs of its users. In an effort to meet that goal, we again relied on information from the people who use the text—both instructors and students.

Many of the best features of CLASS (3/E) remain in this text—for example, the Write to Learn and Group Learning Activity exercises remain; so does much of the information. Nonetheless, this edition of *CLASS* contains several new features. First, each chapter of *CLASS* (4/E) continues to be refined; for example, the library chapter now contains information on the Internet and the World Wide Web. As a result, approximately 75 percent of the exercises are new. Second, the chapter on critical thinking now finds its basis in the work of Dr. Richard Paul, Director of the National Center for Critical Thinking at Sonoma State University, in Sonoma, California. Third, we overhauled the chapter on memory, adding information on test taking. New to this edition is a chapter specifically on coping with stress. Finally, three new sample chapters and articles and one short story provide reading experiences in a variety of areas.

A newly revised instructor's manual and computer program accompany this text. The computer disk, now easier for instructors and students to use, includes the following five programs: HIGH-LITE (indicating the importance of previewing and background knowledge); TESTER (reinforcing test-taking strategies); SCANNER (providing realistic practice in varying reading speed); ANALOGY (extending practice of complex word relationships); and HANGMAN (providing practice in determining the meanings of new words, using the context, and deriving meaning through structural analysis).

Although *CLASS* is designed for use in a postsecondary study skills course, it also can serve as the principal text for an advanced reading course or as a resource for English classes or learning assistance centers. It also may be used by the student independently.

The completion of any major project requires the assistance of many people. We wish first to thank our families who support and assist us in so many ways.

In addition, we wish to acknowledge the support of our colleagues at both SLU and LSU. To Doug (and Tandy) Arnold, we owe a debt of great magnitude—their work with permissions was inspired (perhaps by the desperation on our faces). We also gratefully appreciate the work of Phyllis Simpson whose tireless efforts resulted in a teachers manual for this edition. Our heartfelt thanks goes to Clark Baxter and Linda Poirier, whose support and encouragement never falter. In addition to our gratitude, Stacy Lenzen has earned our respect and friendship. Finally, we acknowledge and thank our reviewers whose efforts made this manuscript the book it is:

Dr. Jim Atkinson, Ottawa University

Dr. Barbara Blaha, Plymouth State College

Jennie L. Brown, Western Kentucky University

Dr. Henry O. Dixon, Morehouse College

Sharon Freeman, San Jacinto College/Central

Cynthia Golledge-Franz, Cleveland State Community College

Dr. Lynn McRee, Santa Fe Community College

Barbara Moore, Gulf Coast Community College

Patricia Moore, Emmanuel College

Susan J. Nunn, Abraham Baldwin College

Dolly Saulsbury, Wharton County Junior College

Cindy Thompson, Northeast Louisiana University

Suzanne G. Weisar, San Jacinto College/South

Keith B. Wilson, Brewton-Parker College

Donna Wood, State Technical Institute at Memphis

William J. Young, Jr., Wallace State Community College

Entering the World of Higher Education

OBJECTIVES
By the end of this chapter you will be able to do the following:

1. Identify your learning styles.

2. Define the rights and responsibilities of citizenship in higher education.

3. Describe ways to become assimilated into the college community.

CHAPTER MAP

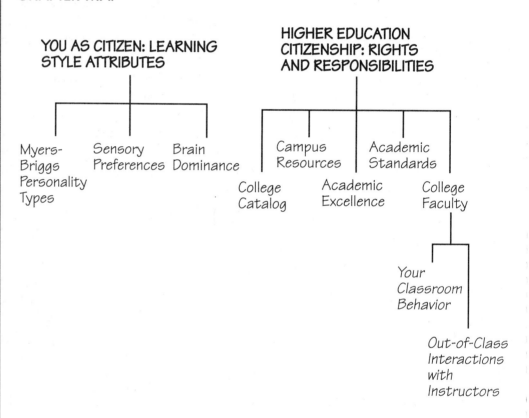

YOU AS CITIZEN: LEARNING STYLE ATTRIBUTES

- Myers-Briggs Personality Types
- Sensory Preferences
- Brain Dominance

HIGHER EDUCATION CITIZENSHIP: RIGHTS AND RESPONSIBILITIES

- Campus Resources
  - College Catalog
- Academic Standards
  - Academic Excellence
- College Faculty
  - Your Classroom Behavior
  - Out-of-Class Interactions with Instructors

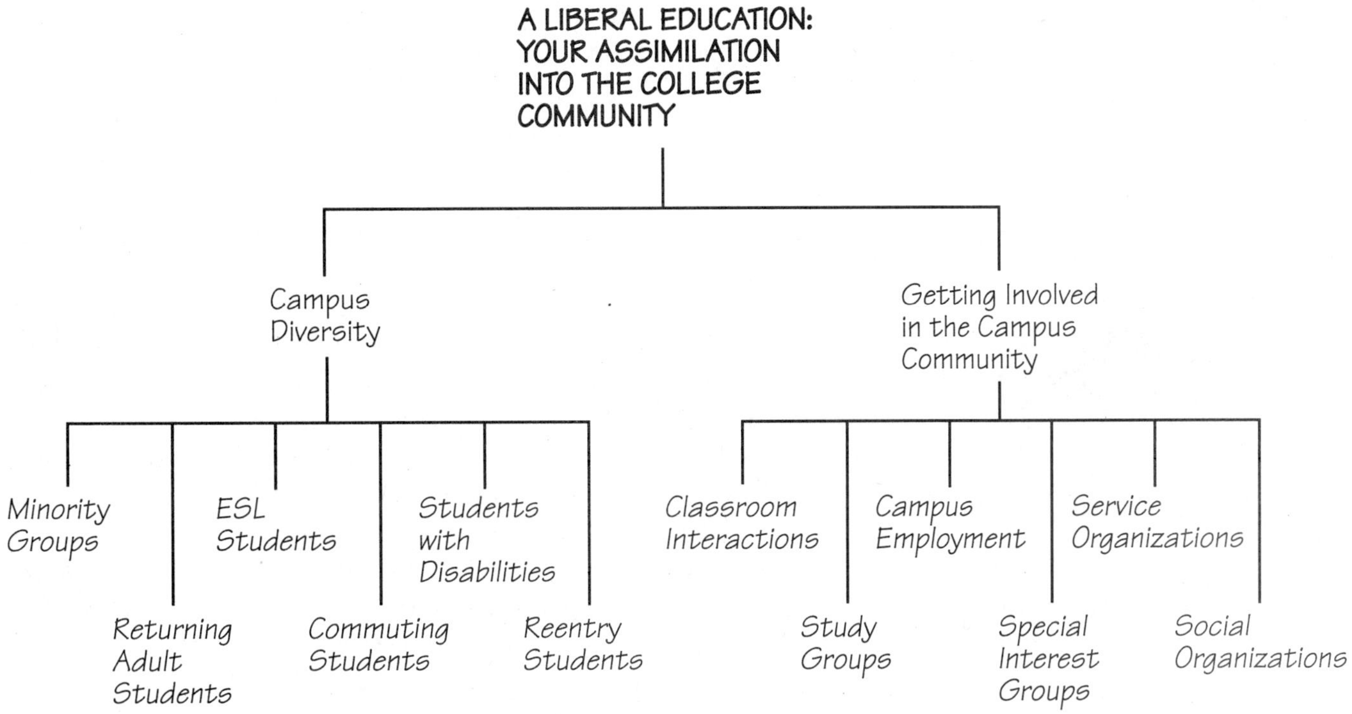

A LIBERAL EDUCATION:
YOUR ASSIMILATION
INTO THE COLLEGE
COMMUNITY

Campus
Diversity

Getting Involved
in the Campus
Community

Minority
Groups

ESL
Students

Students
with
Disabilities

Classroom
Interactions

Campus
Employment

Service
Organizations

Returning
Adult
Students

Commuting
Students

Reentry
Students

Study
Groups

Special
Interest
Groups

Social
Organizations

"Whaddaya mean it's not like bowling? Don't we get a few practice frames?"

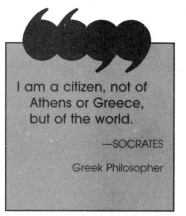

I am a citizen, not of Athens or Greece, but of the world.

—SOCRATES

Greek Philosopher

Higher education changes you in many ways; however, probably the greatest change occurs in the way you perceive yourself and the world around you. Higher education opens to you new vistas of ideas and understandings. You enter that world when you become an active participant in your quest for education and interact with others at your institution. You maximize your ability to participate actively in your educational pursuits by understanding the learning traits you possess as a citizen in higher education. Knowledge of your postsecondary institution's policies and programs helps you identify resources in higher education and its expectations of you. And understanding the diversity of experiences available in the world of higher education helps you become assimilated as one of its citizens. This chapter provides you with several ways to assess your learning style and strengths. It identifies your rights and responsibilities as a citizen in your higher education institution. Finally, this chapter describes the postsecondary experience in terms of the diversity of individuals with whom you interact and the activities in which you participate.

YOU AS CITIZEN: LEARNING STYLE ATTRIBUTES

As a citizen in the world of higher education, you interact with faculty, staff, and peers on a daily basis. You attend lectures and read course materials. Lab courses offer you hands-on experiences in everything from art to biology and from engineering to music. You'll find you have an almost instant liking for some people on campus. You'll have less in common with others. You'll enjoy some courses and dislike others in terms of their formats as well as their contents.

What you prefer says something about your **style** as well as your interests and goals. Style reveals your temperament—the mix of attributes that defines you. Thus, when you meet people or take courses you enjoy, you feel as if these things somehow fit you. You are in harmony with them. When you do activities contrary to your style, you may feel uncomfortable or dissatisfied. They create feelings of discord. As Oppenheimer notes, however, style makes it possible to act effectively, but not absolutely. This means that although your style affects the ways in which you act, you can modify your style to accommodate others. Thus, you harmonize your style with the styles of others.

Style also reflects the ways in which you learn. When you study or think in ways that match your style preferences, you learn more effectively. When you engage in learning activities opposite to your style, understanding takes longer and requires more effort. Understanding your style and modifying learning tasks to incorporate your style helps you maximize learning. Some of the styles that impact learning most involve **personality, sensory preferences,** and **brain dominance.**

MYERS-BRIGGS PERSONALITY TYPES

Based on the work of psychologist Carl Jung, Myers and Briggs developed the **Myers-Briggs Type Indicator (MBTI)** to evaluate personality type. Rather than the eight personality types described by Jung, the research of Myers and Briggs identified sixteen distinct types. Because personality type affects how you interact with people, objects, and situations in a variety of ways, you need to know more about your individual preferences. Many college counseling and academic centers administer the MBTI to students, and you would benefit from taking the entire scale. Until you do so, however, the assessment in Exercise 1.1 provides you with a quick and informal estimate of personality type. The results form a starting point for learning more about yourself, because the MBTI provides information not only about your preferences, but also about the strengths of these preferences. Your results will consist of a four-letter MBTI type. The type is derived from your dominant preferences in each of the following pairs: extraversion (E) or introversion (I), sensing (S) or intuition (N), thinking (T) or feeling (F), and perceiving (P) or judging (J).

The first letter—the *E* or *I*—indicates whether you get your energy from people (*E* for *extraverted*) or ideas (*I* for *introverted*). This preference comes to you from your parents, while other traits are learned. The second set of letters—*S* or *N*—concerns the information you have an inclination for noticing first. The *S* stands for *sensing.* If you are an *S,* you concentrate on information you acquire through tasting, touching, smelling, hearing, and feeling. The *N* derives from the word *intuition.* Information that comes to you through gut feelings or giant leaps in thought is most important to you if you are an *N*. The next set of letters (*T* and *F*) involves the process you use in making a decision. If *T* (*thinking*) is your preference, you are logical, fair, objective, and somewhat unemotional in decision making. This lack of emotion sometimes makes you appear aloof. The original Star Trek's Mr. Spock was a big-time *T*. If *F* (*feeling*) is your dominant style, you make decisions by considering how your decisions affect people and yourself. The last letter (*J* or *P*) concerns the process by which you make decisions. If your preference is *P* (*perceiving*), you like to gather information and delay making decisions. In fact, you'd probably elect not to decide at all. If your propensity is *J* (*judging*), you want to make a decision, any decision, quickly and get on with life. Like aptitudes, abilities, interests, needs, and values, each of these traits interact to form your personality. Table 1.1 provides a list of MBTI factors related to learning.

Probably no one type contains all your personality traits, and since both life changes and stress alter your personality, the personality type you show partiality for might fluctuate as your life does. Nonetheless, knowing your MBTI personality type can aid you in making all sorts of decisions, including those you make as a citizen in the world of higher education.

Exercise 1.1   Circle the letter of the phrase that you prefer. In some cases, both may seem preferable, or neither will be preferable. Still, try to make a choice between the two. Work quickly—first impressions are most likely to be correct. Total your scores for each section and record your type in the blanks below.

I prefer. . .

1. A. loud parties   OR   B. quiet gatherings of friends
2. A. working on a project   OR   B. thinking about an idea
3. A. working with others   OR   B. working alone
4. A. managing many projects   OR   B. focusing on one project
5. A. talking about an idea   OR   B. writing about an idea
6. A. discussion classes   OR   B. lecture classes
7. A. outgoing people   OR   B. reflective people
8. A. being part of a crowd   OR   B. being alone

Total A responses_____ = EXTRAVERT   Total B responses _____ = INTROVERT

I prefer. . .

1. A. practical applications of ideas   OR   B. theoretical considerations of a topic
2. A. lab courses/hands-on projects   OR   B. reading and listening

3. A. factual descriptions OR B. metaphorical descriptions
4. A. proven solutions OR B. untried solutions
5. A. to go places that I've been to before OR B. to go to new places
6. A. to attend to details OR B. to focus on main ideas
7. A. tasks in which I achieve goals quickly OR B. accomplishing goals over an extended period of time
8. A. information derived from logic OR B. information that results from conclusions

Total A responses _____ = SENSING Total B responses _____ = INTUITIVE

I prefer. . .

1. A. self-satisfaction in a job well-done OR B. appreciation of others for a job well-done
2. A. multiple-choice tests OR B. essay tests
3. A. logical arguments OR B. emotional appeals
4. A. impartial people OR B. compassionate people
5. A. rules and standards OR B. negotiation and compromise
6. A. for people to follow the rules OR B. to allow for exceptions to rules
7. A. professional expertise OR B. helpful attitude
8. A. to make decisions based on logic OR B. to let my heart influence a decision

Total A responses _____ = THINKING Total B responses _____ = FEELING

I prefer. . .

1. A. to be on time OR B. to get places when I get there
2. A. well-thought-out decisions OR B. spur-of-the-moment decisions
3. A. organization OR B. flexibility
4. A. expected activities OR B. improvised activities
5. A. structured assignments OR B. unstructured assignments
6. A. step-by-step approaches OR B. random approaches
7. A. planned parties OR B. surprise parties
8. A. serious people OR B. casual people

Total A responses _____ = JUDGING Total B responses _____ = PERCEIVING

SENSORY PREFERENCES

Sensory preferences concern the way or ways in which you like to acquire information—by seeing (**visual**), hearing (**aural**), reading/writing, or through physical experiences (**kinesthetic**). Some learning activities, for example, mapping or charting (see Chapter 6 for additional information), combine visual, reading/writing, and kinesthetic styles. The following

Table 1.1   MBTI Factors that Relate to Learning

Extraversion (E)

Likes to work with others

Relatively short attention span

Learns what instructor wants

Acts quickly, but sometimes without completely thinking a situation through

Prefers variety and active learning opportunities

Prefers many activities or ideas to in-depth treatment of one idea

Becomes impatient when working on long-term tasks

Introversion (I)

Prefers to work alone

Can concentrate for long periods of time

Sets personal standards

May delay action to think until too late to complete it

Prefers quiet, uninterrupted study site

Prefers in-depth treatment of activities or ideas

Able to follow through until completion of long-term tasks

Sensing (S)

Prefers a step-by-step approach

Oriented to the present

Likes to refine current skills

Prefers realistic application

Attentive to detail

Patient

Works steadily

Prefers goal-oriented tasks

Prefers direct experience

Prepares well for tests involving practical application

Likes audio-visuals

Prefers to involve senses (underlining, flash cards, recitation)

Needs to know rationale for a task before beginning

Prefers to study from old tests

Intuition (N)

Tends to use a roundabout approach

Oriented to the future

Becomes bored after mastering a skill

Prefers imaginative application

Attentive to "big picture"

Restless

Works in bursts of energy

Prefers open-ended assignments

Prefers reading or thinking

Prepares well for tests involving theoretical application

Likes mental visualization and memory activities

Prefers to involve right-brain strategies (mapping, drawing, charting)

Comfortable with incomplete understanding of a task; believes task will "come together" after time

Prefers to make up own questions

Table 1.1   MBTI Factors that Relate to Learning *(continued)*

Thinking (T)	Feeling (F)
Objective	Subjective
Task-oriented	Considers personal values
Firm	Flexible
Motivated by desire for achievement	Motivated by desire to be appreciated
Applies standard criteria for evaluation	Applies personal criteria for evaluation
Looks for organizational structure	Looks for personal relevancy

Judging (J)	Perceiving (P)
Goal-oriented	Self-directed
Prefers structure of deadlines	Prefers flexibility in completing tasks
Limits commitment	Tends to overcommit
Prefers to work on one task at a time	Starts several tasks at once
Prefers closure in order to make decisions	Delays closure in order to gather more information
Persistent	Distracted
Rigid	Flexible
Perfectionist	Tolerant of imperfection
Prefers to play after work is completed	Prefers to play first and work later (if time permits)
Product more important than process	Process more important than product
Enjoys planning and organizing	Enjoys thinking and adapting
Likes to know only what is needed to accomplish a task	Likes to know everything before beginning a task

exercise helps you identify your sensory preferences. Table 1.2 provides suggestions for using your sensory preferences in classroom, study, and exam situations. If you have no clear preferences for a single type, consider using a **multisensory** approach, one that combines two or more senses (for example, talking yourself through the steps in constructing a model; drawing a diagram for later visual review; talking yourself through the connections in constructing a map). Exercise 1.2 provides you with an assessment of your sensory preferences.

Exercise 1.2   Circle the answer or answers that best describe your response for each situation. Note: If a single answer does not match your perception, enter two or more choices. After you answer all questions, total your responses and compute your percentages.

1. You are about to give directions to a friend. She is staying in a hotel in town and wants to visit your house. She has a rental car. Would you
   V) draw a map on paper?
   A) tell her the directions?
   R) write down the directions (without a map)?
   K) collect her from the hotel in your car?

2. You are staying in a hotel and have a rental car. You would like to visit a friend whose address/location you do not know. Would you like him to
   V) draw you a map on paper?
   A) tell you the directions by phone?
   R) write down the directions (without a map)?
   K) collect you from the hotel in his car?

3. You have just received a copy of your itinerary for a world trip. This is of interest to a friend. Would you
   A) call her immediately and tell her about it?
   R) send her a copy of the printed itinerary?
   V) show her your route on a map of the world?

4. You are going to cook a dessert as a special treat for your family. Do you
   K) cook something familiar without need for directions?
   V) thumb through the cookbook looking for ideas from the pictures?
   R) refer to a specific cookbook that has a good recipe?
   A) ask for advice from others?

5. A group of tourists has been assigned to you to find out about national parks. Would you
   K) drive them to a national park?
   V) show them slides and photographs?
   R) give them a book on national parks?
   A) give a talk to them about national parks?

6. You are about to purchase a car. Other than price, what would most influence your decision?
   A) Talking to a friend about it
   R) Reading the details about it
   K) Driving it
   V) The car's appearance

7. Recall a time in your life when you learned how to do something like playing a new board game. (Try to avoid choosing a very physical skill, e.g., riding a bike). How did you learn best?

V) By visual clues—pictures, diagrams, charts
R) By written instructions
A) By listening to somebody explaining it
K) By doing it

8. Which of these games do you prefer?
   V) Pictionary
   R) Scrabble
   K) Charades

9. You are about to learn a new program on a computer. Would you
   K) ask a friend to show you?
   R) read the manual that comes with the program?
   A) telephone a friend and ask questions about it?

10. You are not sure whether a word should be spelled *dependent* or *dependant*. Do you
    R) look it up in the dictionary?
    V) see the word in your mind and choose the way that looks best?
    A) sound it out in your mind?
    K) write both versions down?

11. Apart from price, what would most influence your decision to buy a particular book?
    K) Using a friend's copy
    A) Talking to a friend about it
    R) Skimming parts of it
    V) It looks OK

12. A new movie has arrived in town. What would most influence your decision to go or not go?
    A) Friends talk about it.
    R) You read a review of it.
    V) You saw a preview of it.

13. Do you prefer a lecturer who likes to use
    R) handouts and/or a textbook?
    K) field trips, labs, practical sessions?
    V) flow diagrams, charts, slides?
    A) discussions or guest speakers?

TOTAL A (auditory) responses _____/ 11 = _____%
TOTAL V (visual) responses _____/ 12 – _____%
TOTAL K (kinesthetic) responses _____/ 11 = _____%
TOTAL R (reading/writing) responses _____/ 13 = _____%

SOURCE: From Neil Fleming and Colleen Mills who teach at Lincoln University, New Zealand.

Table 1.2   Applying Sensory Preferences to Classroom, Study, and Exam Situations

Visual	In class	When studying	During exams
	Underline Use different colors Use symbols, charts, arrangements on a page	Use the "In Class" strategies Reconstruct images in different way Redraw pages from memory with symbols and initials	Recall the 'pictures of the pages' Draw or sketch Use diagrams where appropriate Practice turning visuals back into words
Aural	Attend lectures and tutorials Discuss topics with students Explain new ideas to other people Use a tape recorder Describe overheads, pictures, and visuals to somebody not there Leave space in notes for later recall	May take poor notes because you prefer to listen Expand your notes Put summarized notes on tape and listen Read summarized notes out loud Explain notes to another *A* person	Listen to your inner voices and write down what you say to yourself Speak your answers Practice writing answers to old exam questions
Reading/writing	Use lists, headings Use dictionaries and definitions Use handouts and textbooks Read Use lecture notes	Write out the words again and again Reread notes silently Rewrite ideas into other words Organize diagrams into statements	Practice with multiple-choice questions Write out lists Write paragraphs, beginnings, endings
Kinesthetic	Use all your senses Go to lab, take field trips Use trial-and-error methods Listen to real-life examples Use hands-on approach	May take notes poorly because topics do not seem relevant Put examples in note summaries Use pictures and photos to illustrate Talk about notes with another *K* person	Write practice answers Role-play the exam situation in your room

SOURCE: From Neil Fleming and Colleen Mills who teach at Lincoln University, New Zealand.

BRAIN DOMINANCE

Are you right-handed or left-handed? Scientific researchers report that handedness reflects the division of labor by the brain. About 90 percent of the human population is right-handed. If you're right-handed, this means that your brain's left hemisphere is dominant in terms of motor-skills superiority although you can also perform many physical actions with your left hand.

Brain dominance goes far beyond handedness. In 1981, psychobiologist Roger Sperry won a Nobel Prize for his work on the special abilities of each half of the brain. He specialized in treating individuals with severe and almost constant epileptic seizures. To treat them, he surgically split their brains. As a result, each individual essentially possessed two distinctly separate brains. Sperry conducted a variety of experiments with these persons to see how the surgery affected their thinking.

The results indicated that language appears to be mostly a function of the **left brain.** The left brain also seems more involved in processing math and judging time and rhythm as well as speech and writing. The left brain generally analyzes information by breaking it into parts. It tends to process information in sequential, linear, logical ways.

The **right brain** controls different reasoning processes. The right brain processes information in holistic, visual forms. Thus, it prefers to synthesize, rather than analyze. Recognition of patterns, faces, and melodies, as well as other kinds of perceptual understanding, are within the domain of the right brain.

What does Sperry's work have to do with your learning? Although you combine the skills of both sides of the brain in most activities, the ways in which you study affect the two sides of your brain differently. Most information, is presented and studied in ways that appeal to the operations of the left brain—linear, verbal, text information. The kinds of formats that appeal to the right brain—visual, holistic, spatial information—are often lacking. Learning information in a variety of ways appeals to the multisensory and multifaceted ways in which the brain processes information. A summary of the functions attributed to left and right hemispheres of the brain appears in Table 1.3 with corresponding applications to learning.

Just as you have a dominant hand with which you prefer to write, you probably possess a dominant side of the brain with which you prefer to learn. The assessment in Exercise 1.3 helps you determine if you are left- or right-brain dominant.

The closer your scores are to each other, the more easily you can process either kind of information. If your score is higher on one side than the other, try to convert information into formats that your brain prefers. However, no matter your score, incorporating both right- and left-brain strategies maximizes learning because it gives you different ways to process and store information.

Table 1.3   Right and Left Brain Attributes

Left-Brain Processing	Application to Learning
Linear; sequential parts and segments	Ordered detail-by-detail understanding; notes and outlines; analysis of ideas
Symbolic	Formulas, acronyms and acrostics; algebraic and abstract math computation
Logical; serious; verifying, nonfiction; improving on the known; reality-based; replication	Factual, unemotional information; proofs of theorems; grammar; practical application of learning to known situations
Verbal; written	Notes, outlines, lectures, text information; auditory review
Temporal; controlled; planning	Structured management of time, ideas, or resources
Focal thinking	Concentration on a single issue or point of view
Objective; dislikes improvisation	Multiple-choice, true-or-false matching formats

Right-Brain Processing	Application to Learning
Holistic; general overviews	Synthesis of information; mapping; charting
Concrete; spatial	Geometry; math facts; mapping; diagrams
Intuitive; assumptions inventing the unknown; fantasy-based; fictitious	Creative writing; interpreting literature; understanding symbolism or figurative language; drawing conclusions about an issue or idea; use of metaphors and analogies; humor
Nonverbal; kinesthetic; visual	Experimentation; hands-on learning; graphics; photographs; feelings; visualizing notes or situations; drawing; mapping; charting; role playing
Random; nontemporal	Unstructured management of time, ideas, or resources
Diffused thinking	Concentration on a variety of views or issues
Subjective; likes improvising	Essay exams; short-answer questions; creative writing

Exercise 1.3   Respond to the following questions.

1. How do you prefer making decisions?
   a. intuitively   b. logically
2. Which do you remember more easily?
   a. names   b. faces
3. Do you prefer
   a. planning your activities in advance?   b. doing things spontaneously?
4. In social situations, do you prefer being the
   a. listener?   b. speaker?
5. When listening to a speaker, do you pay more attention to
   a. what the speaker is saying?   b. the speaker's body language?
6. Do you consider yourself to be a goal-oriented person?
   a. yes   b. no
7. Is your main study area
   a. messy?   b. neat and well organized?
8. Are you usually aware of what time it is and how much time has passed?
   a. yes   b. no
9. When you write papers, do you
   a. let ideas flow freely?   b. plan the sequence of ideas in advance?
10. After you have heard music, are you more likely to remember the
    a. words?   b. tunes?
11. Which do you prefer doing?
    a. watching a movie   b. working a crossword puzzle
12. Do you frequently move your furniture around in your home?
    a. yes   b. no
13. Are you a good memorizer?
    a. yes   b. no
14. When you doodle, do you create
    a. shapes?   b. words?
15. Clasp your hands together. Which thumb is on top?
    a. left   b. right
16. Which subject do you prefer?
    a. algebra   b. trigonometry
17. In planning your day, do you
    a. make a list of what you need to accomplish?   b. just let things happen?
18. Are you good at expressing your feelings?
    a. yes   b. no
19. If you are in an argument with someone else, do you
    a. listen and consider the point of view of the other person?
    b. insist that you are right?
20. When you use a tube of toothpaste, do you
    a. carefully roll it up from the bottom?   b. squeeze it in the middle?

Transfer your responses to the diagram by shading your response. The letter with the most shaded pieces indicates your preference.

HIGHER EDUCATION CITIZENSHIP: RIGHTS AND RESPONSIBILITIES

Becoming a citizen in the world of higher education requires that you recognize your citizenship and all that it includes. Citizenship in any new place includes both privileges and responsibilities. It involves understanding of the community's language and expectations as well as the resources it offers. Your **college catalog** forms a guidebook to the language and expectations of your institution. Your institution staffs a variety of campus offices that provide services and assistance to students. The faculty who teach you supply you with instruction and other academic support. Your knowledge of what each of these offers and how you can best access these services and information maximizes your success at your institution.

COLLEGE CATALOG

Your college catalog forms your contract with your institution. The catalog describes courses, degree programs, and other academic information specific to your institution. It gives you the academic rules and regulations you must follow. A catalog is not something you commit to memory. You do, however, need to be familiar with it so that you can be prepared for any eventuality—from charges of misconduct to selection of coursework and from applying for a scholarship or loan to getting involved in student organizations. Table 1.4 identifies and describes major components of a catalog. Table 1.5 provides a list of common academic terms found in college catalogs.

CAMPUS RESOURCES

Although each institution of higher education has its own campus with its own atmosphere and buildings, all share some common offices and services. Although these resources offer invaluable assistance and a wealth of information, your institution will rarely insist that you avail yourself of these opportunities for help. Your institution assumes that you will take advantage of them as needed. Knowing where each office is located and what it can do for you is both your responsibility and privilege. Table 1.6 provides a list of university offices found on most campuses and describes the functions of each one.

Table 1.4   College Catalog Components

ACADEMIC CALENDAR	Lists important dates in the academic year, including registration, first and last days to drop classes, midterm and final exam periods, and holidays and vacations.
STUDENT SERVICES	Identifies nonacademic activities and services available to students, including campus organizations, Dean of Students' Office, housing and food service information, and health services.
ADMISSIONS INFORMATION	Explains criteria for admission to the institution, regulations for the transfer of credits, and availability of special programs.
TUITION AND FEES	Lists in-state and out-of-state costs, including tuition, room and board, fee schedules, student health fees, parking fees, and lab fees. May also identify financial aid opportunities (scholarships, grants, loans, campus jobs).
ACADEMIC POLICIES AND REGULATIONS	Describes certification requirements, academic standards, and registration regulations.
ACADEMIC CLASSIFICATION	Describes how the number of completed credit-hours translates into freshman, sophomore, junior, or senior status. Credit-hour value is approximately equal to the number of hours per week of in-class instruction (lab, studio, or performance courses often involve more hours of in-class instruction than are reflected in credit-hour value). Course-load requirements describe the maximum and minimum hours required to be at full-time status.
ACADEMIC STANDARDS	Discusses the rules governing student conduct, including disciplinary sanctions, academic disciplinary actions, and appeal procedures. These rules apply in cases of academic dishonesty (cheating or plagiarism) or other institutional infractions.
COLLEGE DEGREE REQUIREMENTS	Identifies the specific and elective courses necessary for completion of a degree. These are often divided by semester/quarter or academic year.
COURSE DESCRIPTIONS	Summarizes the content of each course, which is usually identified by a number and title.

Table 1.5   Higher Education Terms and Their Definitions

Course number: Usually indicates the level of difficulty of a course; undergraduate courses range from 100- or 1000-level courses (freshman level) to 400- or 4000-level courses (senior level). Higher numbers indicate graduate courses.

Drop/withdraw: Resignation from either one course (drop) or from the university (withdraw); either process requires you follow the procedures set forth by your institution.

Electives: Courses you choose outside your major from an academic area of interest to you; some electives are required for every major; some majors limit the academic areas from which you can select.

Extracurricular activities: The nonacademic clubs and pursuits offered by your college; includes intramural sports and athletic events for students who aren't members of school-sponsored athletic teams.

Freshman: Classification of first-time college students; students generally remain freshmen until they have successfully completed thirty credit-hours.

Full-time/part-time courseload. Full-time students enroll for twelve or more credit-hours; part-time students take less than twelve credit-hours.

Juniors: Considered upperclassmen; students generally remain juniors until they have ninety hours of course credit.

Residency: Can have two different meanings: may refer to whether or not you qualify for in-state tuition or to whether or not you live on campus.

Prerequisites: Courses you must take before you can take a particular course; departments mandate the order in which you take these courses.

Semester/quarter systems: Colleges on the semester system have two regular terms (fall and spring) of about fourteen weeks each and one or more shorter summer terms; colleges on the quarter system have four terms (fall, winter, spring, and summer) of about ten weeks each.

Seniors: The final year that leads to an undergraduate degree; considered upperclassmen; students are considered seniors once they have over ninety credit-hours.

Sophomores: Students maintain sophomore status if they have between thirty and sixty hours of course credit.

Syllabus: An outline of course requirements including assignments and their due dates, exam dates, grading policies, and other information related to a specific course; at many institutions, the syllabus is seen as a contract between the professor and the student.

Transcript: Official record of the courses you completed and the grades you made in them.

Transfer credit: The number of course credits taken by a student at one college that another college accepts for credit.

Exercise 1.4   Locate the following information in your school catalog.

1. If you wish to voice a concern, who are the people you need to know? List below the chain of command (the hierarchy of positions/individuals) in the college or department in which you are majoring by name and title. If you are an undecided major, find this information for one of the areas you are considering.

_____

_____

2. Locate and record information about two scholarships/loans for which you might be eligible.

_____

_____

3. Locate the academic calendar for the current term.
   a. When is the last day to withdraw from courses?

   _____

   b. What holidays occur this term?

   _____

   c. What is the last day of classes?

   _____

   d. When do finals begin? end?

   _____

4. Locate the curriculum in which you plan to major.
   a. Compare/contrast courses suggested for your first term with those suggested for your final term. How do you account for similarities/differences?

   _____

   _____

   b. Examine the curriculum carefully. Locate two courses in your major area and read their descriptions. Which will you find more enjoyable? Why?

   _____

   _____

   c. Read the description for each of the courses in which you are now enrolled. How do the descriptions compare with the actual content of the course? What conclusion(s) might you draw about the courses and their descriptions you identified in b?

   _____

   _____

Table 1.6   Campus Resources and Services

Business Office	Also called Office of the Treasurer or the Bursar's Office. Records students' financial transactions, such as tuition, fees, fines, or other payments.
Campus Bookstore	Sells text materials for course-related topics and recreational reading, including books, magazines, newspapers, journals, and reference books. Also offers pens, pencils, notebooks, art supplies, and other materials. May carry over-the-counter drugs and toiletries as well as school-related clothing and souvenirs.
Campus Security	Also called Campus Police. Provides parking and traffic guidelines and assistance for improving your personal safety on the campus.
Career Guidance and Placement Office	Administers interest, educational, and aptitude tests to assist you in career decision making. Provides job placement information. May maintain placement files of transcripts and letters of reference that can be sent to prospective employers at your request.
Correspondence and Extension Division	Administers off-campus and independent study courses that are taken by mail.
Counseling Center	Provides personal counseling on a wide range of problems such as stress, substance abuse, sexually transmitted diseases, depression, and other sources of anxiety. Staffed by trained, professional counselors. May be called Wellness or Mental Health Center.
Dean of Students	An administrative unit that serves in an advocacy, advisory, and supervisory capacity for individual students and recognized student organizations. Also serves as a clearinghouse for student concerns and manages the college judicial system and student code of conduct.
Financial Aid Office	Also called Student Aid and Scholarship Office. Provides assistance in locating and distributing supplemental funds such as grants, loans, scholarships, and on-campus employment. Your need for financial assistance is often based on responses you provide in a written application.

Table 1.6   Campus Resources and Services *(continued)*

Job Placement Office	Maintains listing of full and part-time job openings both on and off campus. May be a part of the Career Planning or Financial Aid Office.
Learning Center	Also called Learning Resource Center, Learning Assistance Center, and Learning Lab, among other names. Offers assistance in study skills or specific content areas through workshops or individualized lessons, tutoring, and/or taped or computerized instruction.
Library	Contains materials for reference and recreation, including books, magazines, newspapers, journals, reference books, microfilms, and computerized documents. May also contain a listening room, teacher education materials, and photocopying facilities. Workshops or classes may be available to familiarize you with library services and holdings.
Registrar's Office	Also called Office of Records and Registration. Tracks courses you take and grades you receive. Evaluates advanced, transfer, or correspondence work. Provides transcripts. May have the responsibility to determine if you meet graduation requirements.
Residential Housing	Concerned with both on-campus living experiences and, in some cases, approved off-campus housing.
Student Center	Also called Student Activities Office or Union. Provides recreational activities, including short courses on crafts and other topics. Sponsors concerts, plays, and other social events. Houses student organizations. Provides meeting places for these and other groups.
Student Health Services	Provides medical assistance for students who become physically ill or injured or who have chronic health problems. May also offer mental health counseling. Services are usually free for full-time students and at a small cost for part-time students. Lab work, physical therapy, pharmaceutical drugs, emergency care, and workshops on health-related topics may also be available.

Exercise 1.5   Answer briefly but completely.

1. Complete the following chart by identifying information about resources on your campus.

	Name of office on your campus and phone number	Location	Hours open	Contact person
Career Placement Office				
Learning Center				
Campus Security				
Student Center				
Bookstore				
Library				
Correspondence/Extension Office				
Counseling Center				
Job Placement Center				
Health Services				
Registrar's Office				
Business Office				
Financial Aid Office				
Dean of Students				
Residential Housing				

2. Identify a situation in which you would need help from each of the following resources:
   a. Campus Bookstore

   _____

   _____

   b. Learning Center

   _____

   _____

   c. Library

   _____

   _____

d. Student Center

_____

_____

e. Campus Security

_____

_____

f. Career Office

_____

_____

g. Correspondence/Extension Office

_____

_____

h. Counseling Center

_____

_____

i. Job Placement Office

_____

_____

j. Student Health Services

_____

_____

k. Registrar's Office

_____

_____

l. Business Office

_____

_____

m. Financial Aid Office

_____

_____

n. Dean of Students

_____

_____

ACADEMIC EXCELLENCE

All colleges and universities set certain requirements that must be met before they grant a degree. One of the most important aspects of academia concerns the measure of your accomplishments. Thus, course grades, **grade point average (GPA),** and academic honesty are vital issues for your consideration.

Traditional grading systems consist of the letter grades *A, B, C, D,* and *F*. Other marks include *NC* (no credit), *P* (pass), *W* (withdraw), *W-grade* (withdraw with a grade), and *I* (incomplete). *NC, P, W,* and *I* grades are not used to compute your grade point average (GPA). Policies about *W-grades* vary. Some institutions use the *W-grade* in computing GPA while others do not. Check your institution's regulations to be sure.

Computation of GPA is a ratio of **quality points** earned to semester hours attempted. Quality points usually use a four point scale: $A = 4$, $B = 3$, $C = 2$, $D = 1$, and $F = 0$. Because your courses vary in credit hours, you cannot always assume that the average of an *A*, a *B*, and a *C* equals a 3.0 GPA. See Table 1.7 for an example of a GPA computation.

A college or university usually places students on **academic probation** whenever their cumulative average is ten or more quality points below a 2.0 or *C* average. Once on probation, you remain there until your cumulative average reaches 2.0 or higher.

At the end of the first and each succeeding term, the university requires that you make a 2.0. If for any reason you fail to do so, **academic action** results. Academic actions differ somewhat from one university to another. However, they generally follow the same guidelines. That is, you may remain on probation for a period of time before suspension results. The first time you get suspended it's usually for one regular term (summers usually don't count). If you have been suspended before, your second suspension spans an entire calendar year. Suspensions for universities

Table 1.7   GPA Computation

Course	Grade	Credit Hours		Point Equivalent	Total Quality Points
English 101	C	3	×	(C=)2	6
Math 104	D	4	×	(D=)1	4
Speech 130	B	3	×	(B=)3	9
Music 106	A	1	×	(A=)4	4
Biology 103	W	3			
TOTALS		11			23

QUALITY POINTS/SEMESTER HOURS ATTEMPTED = 23/11 = 2.09 GPA

Table 1.8   Formula for and Example of Calculating Needed GPA

$$NGPA = \frac{FGPA\,(TOTHRS) - (CGPA \times QHA)}{SQH}$$

where
	NGPA	stands for *Needed GPA*
	FGPA	stands for the *Final GPA* you wish to attain
	CGPA	stands for your *Current GPA*
	QHA	stands for the number of *quality hours* you have attempted; these do not include pass-fail or satisfactory/unsatisfactory hours
	SQH	stands for the sum of the number of quality hours you have left to take and the number of hours you are currently taking
	TOTHRS	stands for the sum of *QHA* and *SQH*; that is, the total number of hours you have taken, are taking, and will take before graduation

Example Calculations

$$NGPA = \frac{(FGPA \times TOTHRS) - (CGPA \times QHA)}{SQH}$$

$$NGPA = \frac{(3.3 \times 128) - (2.0 \times 45)}{83}$$

$$NGPA = \frac{(3.3 \times 128) - (90)}{83}$$

$$NGPA = \frac{(422.4) - (90)}{83}$$

$$NGPA = \frac{(332.4)}{83}$$

$$NGPA = 4.00$$

"Tell your parents you had a cumulative grade of 3.5 this semester."

other than the one you are currently attending often count in computing this formula. Any additional suspensions will also be for a whole year.

Obviously, you cannot take coursework from the suspending university during the time you are suspended. Furthermore, any courses you take from another school during the time of your suspension will not count toward your degree at your present institution. Indeed, most universities will not admit students who are under current suspension from another school.

Once your suspension ends, you need to apply for readmission to your university. Should you be suspended more than two times, however, readmission to the university holds no guarantee that you will be accepted into all professional, degree-seeking programs, which have their own admission requirements.

Once you let your GPA flounder and fall, it takes more time than you might imagine to get it soaring again. If it can be done at all and how long it will take depends on your current GPA, your future grades, and the number of semester hours you have left. For example, let's suppose you have completed forty-five hours and have a 2.0 GPA. You need eighty-three hours to graduate (including the fifteen you are taking this term) and wish to graduate with a 3.3 GPA. To reach your goal, you'll need to maintain a 4.0 for each remaining semester you are in school. Table 1.8 contains the formula for determining this figure and the computations for the preceding example.

Exercise 1.6   Compute the grade point average for the following:

1. GPA = _____

Course	Grade	Credit Hours	Point Equivalent	Total Quality Points
English 210	A	3	_____	_____
Math 103	F	5	_____	_____
Speech 102	B	3	_____	_____
History 104	C	3	_____	_____
Art 100	W	4	_____	_____
TOTALS				

2. GPA = _____

Course	Grade	Credit Hours	Point Equivalent	Total Quality Points
English 001	NC	3	_____	_____
Math 006	P	5	_____	_____
Physical Education 107	D	1	_____	_____
Word Processing 101	A	1	_____	_____
TOTALS				

3. GPA = _____

Course	Grade	Credit Hours	Point Equivalent	Total Quality Points
English 102	C	3	_____	_____
Math 200	D	3	_____	_____
Music 101	B	3	_____	_____
Nursing 100	A	3	_____	_____
Geography 102	W	3	_____	_____
TOTALS				

4. GPA = _____

Course	Grade	Credit Hours	Point Equivalent	Total Quality Points
English 101	D	3	_____	_____
Math 109	C	3	_____	_____
Geology 107	F	3	_____	_____
Physical Education 107	B	1	_____	_____
ROTC 101	A	2	_____	_____
TOTALS				

5. GPA = _____

Course	Grade	Credit Hours	Point Equivalent	Total Quality Points
English 106	F	3	_____	_____
Math 104	D	4	_____	_____
Music 105	B	2	_____	_____

Physical Education 106	A	1	_____	_____
Botany 101	C	4	_____	_____
TOTALS				

List the courses in which you are now enrolled and predict what grade you will receive in each.

6. GPA =_____

Course	Grade	Credit Hours	Point Equivalent	Total Quality Points
TOTALS				

ACADEMIC STANDARDS

Consider the following old joke: A professor comes into the classroom and says, "This exam will be conducted on the honor system. Please take seats three seats apart and in alternate rows."

In all classrooms, and particularly in testing situations, instructors trust you to act honorably. They count on you to value your moral integrity more than any grade in any course. Instructors also expect you to realize at least two other consequences of cheating. First, getting caught means a failing grade, and failing grades lower your GPA. Second, it's embarrassing and troubling for both you and your instructor.

Other than cheating on exams, the most common type of cheating in college is **plagiarism.** Plagiarism is stealing another person's work and presenting it as your own. Plagiarism comes in two forms: unintentional and intentional. Unintentional, or accidental, plagiarism occurs through inaccurate notetaking, by incorrect citing of references, and/or from poor writing ability. Intentional plagiarism is deliberate, premeditated theft of another person's work or published information. Intentional plagiarism also includes getting a paper from a friend or from a term paper service. It results from poor time management, fear of not doing well, and pure laziness. While the motives for unintentional and intentional plagiarism differ, the punishment is the same.

What happens if you're caught? In some cases, charges of plagiarism are kept between you and your instructor. You receive an *F* for the paper or test. However, if your instructor suspects that you cheated on previous papers, assignments, or tests, or if the amount of plagiarism is extreme, he/she could direct your case to a formal committee of other students, professors, and/or campus administrators. Such a committee possesses the right to suspend you for a semester or more, expel you from the university, place an academic dishonesty clause on your transcript, and/or refuse you a degree from the department. If you are not certain about the guidelines for plagiarism, you might consider taking your references and a draft of your assignment to your instructor and asking for advice.

The academic standards of your institution concern the rules governing student conduct. The standards include information on the **academic code of student conduct,** disciplinary sanctions, academic disciplinary actions, and **appeals.**

An institution's reputation depends on keeping high standards of intellectual integrity. Breaches of academic integrity consist of cheating and plagiarism. Students accused of such violations receive a hearing through the Dean of Students' Office. In this hearing, an impartial person or panel determines guilt or innocence.

If you are found guilty of academic dishonesty, disciplinary actions include probation, suspension, or expulsion. As a student, you have the right to appeal academic disciplinary actions. You also have the right to know the appeal process. If it is not outlined in your catalog, the Office of Student Affairs or another student advocacy group will assist you in making your appeal.

SOURCE: Val Cheatham.

COLLEGE FACULTY

A popular urban legend (Brunvand, 1989) tells of an instructor whose students changed his behavior. Whenever he walked to the left side of the room, they seemed to lose interest in what he said. They yawned, wrote notes, whispered, and paid little or no attention. When he moved to the right, they sat up straight. They made a point to listen carefully, take notes, and ask questions. The instructor soon began to lecture only from the right side of the class.

Like the students in the story, you, too, can influence the behavior of your instructors. Instructors try to be fair and impartial, but they are people, too. Think about the people you've met in your life. Some had qualities that made you want to know them better. Others had characteristics that made you happy to see them leave. Instructors feel the same way about students. Each semester, they meet a new group of people. They react to and with each one. Your behavior determines if their reactions to you are positive or negative. You control whether or not you are a student worth knowing better.

SOURCE: Reprinted by permission of Glen Dines and *Phi Delta Kappan*.

Your Classroom Behavior

To obtain and maintain an instructor's goodwill, you must be polite and respectful. If you arrive on time and dress appropriately, you make a good first impression. Your prompt and consistent attendance proves your diligence and commitment to the course. The quality of your work also shows your regard for the instructor and the course. Your work is, after all, an extension of you. Only work of the highest quality in content, form, and appearance should be submitted to an instructor.

Sitting near the front of the room in about the same seat for each class gives the instructor a visual fix on you. Although the instructor may not keep attendance records, he or she will subconsciously look for you and know you are there. Sitting near the front of the room also helps you maintain eye contact with the instructor.

Your apparent interest in the lecture is enhanced when your body language also shows your interest. Facial expressions and movements (smiling, nodding your head, raising your eyebrows) and body language (sitting straight, facing the instructor, arms uncrossed) indicate your openness and desire to learn.

The opposite of this is also true. Nonverbal responses of skepticism or boredom are clear in body language and facial expressions (yawning, reading the newspaper, sighing, looking out the window, rolling your eyes). Body language is especially important when you read your instructor's comments on returned assignments in class. Constructive criticism is part of the learning process and should be a learning experience. An instructor's critical comments are not a personal attack. Your body language should reflect your ability to accept those comments in the spirit in which they are given.

Some students fear speaking in class. Often they are afraid that their questions will sound "dumb" to either the instructor or other students. Sometimes the class is a large one with several hundred students. Maybe past experiences led to embarrassing results. Generally, however, if something in the lecture confused you, it confused others, too. Many times others are waiting for someone else to make the first move. That person needs to be you. All you have to fear is fear itself, to paraphrase President Franklin Roosevelt.

Speaking in class is less stressful if you know how to phrase your questions or comments. Questions and comments must be relevant and respectful. Nothing frustrates an instructor more than rude questions; long, unrelated stories; or questions whose answers were just discussed. Preceding your questions with what you do understand helps the instructor clarify what confuses you. By briefly stating what you think was just said, you aid the instructor in finding gaps in your knowledge. Another way to help an instructor help you is to be exact about the information you need.

Active participation in class discussions proves your interest. If you ask questions or make comments about the lecture topic, you signal your desire for understanding. However, if you feel you simply cannot ask a question in class, then see your instructor before or after class or make an appointment.

WRITE TO LEARN

Do you ask questions or make comments in class? On a separate sheet of paper, identify why you are or are not vocal in class. If you tend to be silent on some (or all) occasions, describe how you can overcome or compensate for it.

Out-of-Class Interactions with Instructors

Getting to know an instructor personally involves special effort. Smiling and saying hello when you see an instructor outside of class is a friendly opening gesture. Positive, sincere feedback about lecture topics, the instructor's lecture style, and so on often opens lines of communication. Visiting an instructor's office often and for long time periods also affects how an instructor feels about you—but, unfortunately, the effect is negative. Instructors have office hours so students who have valid problems can contact them. They also use that time to grade papers, complete paperwork, and conduct research. Thus, many instructors resent students who—without reason—constantly visit them.

This does not mean that instructors do not like to talk to you and other students. They do. Talking to you helps them understand your problems and learning needs. It gives them an opportunity to interest you in their content areas.

There are several good reasons to visit an instructor's office. Questions about course content or test items should be asked politely and intelligently. Previous suggestions for asking questions in class also apply here. Appealing a poor grade is another reason for seeing an instructor. Having some viable options to present strengthens your appeal. Indicate that you are willing to write a research paper, do extra reading, take a makeup exam, or work extra problems. That you have thought of these options proves you realize your grade is your responsibility. Whether or not you are allowed to make up work is at the discretion of the instructor. If your instructor refuses to allow you this concession, you need to smile, say "Thank you," and take the grade you've earned. Another legitimate reason for seeing an instructor is to ask for an incomplete grade. Usually students who have valid reasons and the proper attitude have few problems with getting extra time to complete work.

If you discuss your grade with an instructor and feel you have been unfairly treated, you have the right to an appeal. This appeal involves, first, meeting with the instructor and attempting to resolve your problem. During the second step of the appeal process, you write a letter to the head of the department in which the course was taught asking for a meeting with that person and your instructor. If you are not satisfied with the results of this hearing, you may appeal to the dean of the department in which the course was taught. If you are firmly convinced that you are in the right, your final appeal is made to the head of academic affairs at your institution.

"Never be late, never call your instructor at home after midnight, and, whatever you do, never let 'em see you sweat."

There are three "nevers" in getting along with instructors: never miss class, never be inattentive or impolite, and, if you miss class, never say, "I missed class today. Did we do anything important?" Instructors never feel they are teaching unimportant information.

It is possible to win grades and influence instructors. You can do it by remembering the Golden Rule and treating them as you want them to treat you.

A LIBERAL EDUCATION: YOUR ASSIMILATION INTO THE COLLEGE COMMUNITY

The word *liberal* comes from the Latin word *liber* meaning *free*. Robert Maynard Hutchins believed that the concept of education was more than learning a trade. He was a staunch supporter of academic freedom and a liberal education. While you may think that your education is confined to the walls of your classrooms or laboratories and prepares you for the world of work, a truly liberal education comes from your interactions with other students and your assimilation into the college community. It prepares you for life. Your institution offers you a variety of formal and informal opportunities to meet and become part of the college community.

A liberal education . . . frees a person from the prison-house of class, race, time, place, background, family, and even nation.

—ROBERT MAYNARD HUTCHINS

Twentieth Century American Educator

CAMPUS DIVERSITY

Since the late 1960s, postsecondary education has changed. Before then, typical students came from college preparatory schools and had similar economic and/or social backgrounds.

Today, diversity characterizes the typical postsecondary campus. Students come from a variety of academic backgrounds. Age, ethnic identity, and socioeconomic levels vary. Students with learning and other disabilities all find a place on the college campus. International students from a variety of countries and U.S. students from a variety of states may attend the same institution. Students from rural communities and those from metropolitan areas share classrooms and ideas.

Some groups need additional help during their entry into the confusing realm of higher education. Special programs provide chances for personal enrichment and improvement of learning skills. The campus learning center provides academic assistance, tutoring, and a variety of self-help materials.

Minority Groups

Minority groups are groups of people who, because of their perceived physical and cultural differences from the dominant group, tend to be treated unequally (Knox, 1990). Minority groups may be defined by race, ethnicity, religion, sex, and age characteristics.

What is college life like if you are a member of a minority group? You may experience some form of prejudice—a learned tendency to think negatively about a group of people—directed toward you. The social outlets available to other students may seem more limited to you. As a result, you may feel isolated and uncomfortable. Involvement, then, is critical for you. Student groups (for example, Society of Women Engineers, Black History Association, Returning Adult Coalition) provide opportunities to network and retain contacts within your minority group.

Membership in other campus groups and associations (for example, music groups, athletics, study groups, dorm groups, professional organizations) provide you with opportunities to become more involved in the campus community, learn more about other cultures, and create new relationships of support. These involvements will help you down the road, when you enter the majority-dominated workforce.

You may also face differences in the academic arena. You may have been actively recruited prior to enrollment only to feel virtually alone once you arrive on campus. Such changes in institutional attitude sometimes result in your having increased feelings of isolation. In addition, faculty may expect more—or, perhaps, less—of you if you are a minority student. Both attitudes present problems in achievement. As a result, you may feel threatened or insulted. Again, your campus connections and networks may be able to help you resolve such problems. You can also confer with minority faculty members and alumni or departmental counselors and administrators. In addition, you should seek the supports available to all students—library services, career planning and placement, counselors, tutors, campus employment, and so on. These, too, provide insights into academia and assist you in becoming more involved in campus life.

Returning Adult Students

If you are an older adult student, you possess some advantages over more traditional students. College attendance is your goal, not that of your parents, teachers, or peers. Your life experiences provide a greater background for learning new information. You are sometimes more motivated than younger students. Your maturity and commitment provide you with the will needed to face the problems of an older adult student.

The first problem many adult students face is the red tape that holds together higher education. Particularly trying is registration, a confusing process for anyone. Adults often think that younger students are more experienced and knowledgeable about registration. If registration is computerized, you may feel even more a victim of time. However, no one is ever totally prepared for registration no matter how it's done. If the registration schedule conflicts with your work or household commitments, you may be able to negotiate night registration or registration by mail. If you are a returning student, you have successfully navigated the registration channels at least once already. If you still feel confused about the process, have an experienced friend walk through it with you.

Transferring credits from other institution poses another problem for returning students. This procedure is handled by the admissions office. Most problems can be avoided by having transcripts sent to the school you are currently attending as soon as possible. This gives the institution time to evaluate your academic work and make decisions before you register.

As an older adult student, you feel the same pressure to perform that other college students feel. In addition, you face the stress of being in a new situation. Employers, friends, or family may add to this stress by not fully supporting your educational goals. You also may feel the stress of trying to balance academics, work, and personal commitments.

Time probably seems your enemy—an opponent that beats you by moving faster than you can. You combat this problem by being more organized. Like the straw that broke the camel's back, going to school is an overwhelming burden to people who cannot eliminate—without guilt—nonessential responsibilities. Asking friends and family for help involves them in your education. Time is your most valuable resource. You must evaluate each minute you spend. You need to become a careful consumer of it.

A course or workshop in stress management may help you cope with returning to school. Another way to decrease stress is to take a reduced course load during your first term. This acclimates you to academic demands and the concessions and responsibilities they involve. Involvement in extracurricular activities is another way to adjust to higher education. These activities provide new friends and interests. Your interactions with them give you a recreational outlet. They also break barriers between you and traditional students and build ties between you and other nontraditional students.

Your institution probably offers services designed to meet your particular needs. A day-care center, financial aid, counseling services, and so on may be available to assist you. In addition, most institutions offer educational courses designed to improve academic skills. You need to find out how to locate these services and courses—either through the catalog, from instructors, or from administrative personnel. You need not be afraid or embarrassed to use them.

Working, being part of a family, and going to school are difficult in and of themselves. Doing all three is, at best, a juggling act.

ESL Students

You, as one of many ESL (English as a second language) students, face a unique situation. You are not only learning new subjects, but you also may be learning a new culture and language.

Like other nontraditional students, improving your study skills is important. Some special learning suggestions may aid your understanding. First, preview your text before class to help you predict the information the lecture will contain. This allows you to avoid misunderstanding the instructor. Second, watch successful American classmates and copy what they do. Your classmates can provide you with models for notetaking and interacting with instructors and other students. Watching other students helps you identify the behaviors American students consider appropriate. Third, study with a native student to practice your English and acquire information. Fourth, many institutions provide special classes and workshops to aid you in perfecting your learning skills. Designed expressly for ESL students, they give you a chance to discuss problems and interact with others who are also new to American culture. These programs are well worth your time and investigation.

Overcoming cultural and language differences involves an open mind and varied experiences. Being here is a novelty for you. Meeting you is a novelty for most Americans. The most valuable way for you and natives to learn from one another is for you to become involved with an American family. Your institution's international office or a local church probably keeps lists of families who will invite you into their homes and their lives. Listening to American radio and television and going to movies are also ways of learning about American customs and language. Visiting shopping centers, museums, and restaurants can increase your knowledge of life and language in the United States. Reading newspapers, magazines, and books is also valuable.

One problem for many ESL students that the English they learned in their native countries is British English. Americans and Britons speak different forms of the English language. Although the grammatical structures are the same, there is sometimes a variation in vowel sounds and word usage. In addition, the rhythm, speed, and slang of American English with its regional differences may be new for you. Your understanding of the language will improve as you hear more of it.

Commuting Students

If you are a commuting student, you may not think of yourself as a nontraditional student. However, if you commute to an institution where the majority of students reside on campus, you face unique problems. Often you may find that courses are available only at inconvenient times. In addition, schedule conflicts may cause you to miss speeches, study sessions, research opportunities, and other learning experiences that enrich academic life. Next, as a commuting student, you are part of a group often called "suitcase" students. With no dorm room or office to serve as a base, you often find that the materials you need are at home, in your car, or at your job. Finally, traveling back and forth limits your contact with others. This often leads to a feeling of alienation and a lack of true assimilation into the institution.

Rural parking . . . Urban campus

Each of these problems requires creative coping. Solving scheduling problems, for example, involves effective time management. Often each minute you stay on campus needs to be stretched to two. You can stretch time through careful organization and planning. Having the library run a computer search while you attend a study session is an example of such planning. Another way to cope is to find and use alternative resources. Your neighborhood library or videotaped lectures provide reasonable options to supplement what you miss on campus. Using the time you spend commuting to your advantage is another way you can manage more effectively. Listening to audio tapes, memorizing and rehearsing information, or discussing information with others in your car pool, for example, help you learn while you travel.

To avoid misplacing important materials, you need to be organized and prepared. You become a suitcase student in fact as well as name. To do so, you use a backpack or a briefcase to hold all the books and papers you use each day. By organizing your pack or case each night, you know you're ready for the next day.

Last, you avoid feeling separated from others on campus by consciously attempting to make yourself a part of the school. Reading the campus newspaper, talking with others before and after class, and exchanging phone numbers with classmates decreases your feelings of alienation.

Students with Disabilities

If you are disabled in any way, you know that you encounter challenges usually not faced or even considered by others. You may have a chronic (that is, permanent physical or learning disability) or temporary (due to an illness, accident, or surgery) disability. Whatever the case, federal law protects your rights as a student and mandates that appropriate and reasonable accommodations be made for you. It is your responsibility to determine what services you need for academic success and ensure that you receive them.

To locate services, you first contact the admissions office. Its staff should be aware of the services that your institution offers and where to find them. In addition, your college catalog probably lists and describes these services in detail. The academic and student affairs departments, as well as your dean's office, should also provide you with information and assistance.

Reentry Students

If you are a reentry student, you are someone who previously entered the institution, left it, and is now returning. The key to your success often lies in the reasons for your previous withdrawal from academic life. You may have run out of money and left school to work until you were once again solvent. Personal problems may have caused you to withdraw. Maybe you weren't ready for college when you first began. Perhaps you lacked the academic goals and desire required for success, and you flunked out. Identifying your reason(s) for "stopping out" is critical in helping you avoid old habits and the same mistakes.

If you previously lacked financial resources, you now have a better idea of what it costs—both in time and effort—to stay in school. If you have not already done so, talk to staff members of the financial aid department. They can help you apply for grants and loans. They also place students in work-study jobs and sometimes maintain lists of off-campus employment opportunities. Second, examine your college catalog for scholarships and requirements for application. Many of these specify degree programs, academic classification, and other criteria required for selection. You may be the person who fits the bill. Finally, look for creative ways to cut expenses and make money. Perhaps a faculty or staff member could use a baby-sitter or chauffeur for their children. Maybe they need a responsible person to house-sit while they're on sabbatical leave. Such services could be exchanged for a salary or for room and board.

The types of personal problems that contributed to your previous withdrawal from school span a great range from caring for family members to succumbing to peer pressure. Whatever the cause, determine if the problem is truly resolved, both in your mind and the minds of others. If the problem is not resolved, you must be prepared to handle it, if and when it resurfaces. This may involve examining alternatives personally or with those affected by the problem. You also may need to seek professional counseling or other objective viewpoints to assist you in coping.

Some reentry students are more serious and determined, whereas others seem to fall into the same habits that caused their earlier failures. If you now believe that you are ready for learning and to make commitments for success, you must be especially wary. Examine your previous course loads and content; evaluate how you spent your time. Prepare to readjust. Take advantage of the learning assistance services, workshops, and tutorial programs that are available on your campus. Time management and study strategies will be especially relevant for you this second time around.

GETTING INVOLVED IN THE CAMPUS COMMUNITY

One of the goals of your institution is retention. That means your institution wants you to stay in school until you complete your degree or other educational goal. What motivates a person to remain in school? Courses, curricula, and faculty all play a role in whether or not a student stays enrolled. However, research indicates that the key to retention is how involved a student is in the institution. The student who feels a part of the campus is more likely to stay than the student who merely attends classes on the campus. In addition, job recruiters and employers often seek candidates who are well rounded with a variety of interests. They want to see students who can handle a diversity of activities while remaining academically successful.

What group should you join? Again, your needs, values, and interests determine which groups suit you best. In general, it really doesn't matter which group you choose, as long as you become involved in campus life.

Classroom Interactions

Each class in which you enroll becomes a group with whom you associate. Your interactions with the group depend on you and your behavior as well as on the other members of the class and how they act. You choose whether simply to come to class, take notes, and leave, or to become part of the class through your interactions.

The first impression you make on your classmates sets the tone for your interactions with them. Probably the first thing they will notice is your appearance. Although how you dress shouldn't matter, it does. It's true that you can wear almost anything in today's classrooms. However, clothes sometimes form barriers between you and others. Overly expensive or outlandish costumes can alienate or intimidate. Your best bet is clothing that reflects your style and personality but does not draw too much attention to you.

The first day of class is often as unsettling as the first day in a new school or on a new job. You may be eager to meet others but hesitant about taking the first step. One initiative may be taken at any time during the term. It involves smiling and saying hello. Finding out the names of people who sit around you is a second step. To start conversation, you might ask other students if this is their first class, where they're from, or what courses they are taking. In addition to making new friends, knowing the people who sit around you and exchanging phone numbers with them is good insurance for absences. You'll know whom to contact for assignments or notes.

The way you treat your classmates directly corresponds to how they will treat you. Several things can almost guarantee that you will be someone others won't want to know. First, consistent late arrivals or noisiness during lectures distracts people around you. Second, telling numerous personal stories bores everyone. In addition, monopolizing class discussions or asking frequent irrelevant questions annoys others who also wish to contribute. Third, if you show disapproval or voice sarcasm when others make comments, you'll alienate everyone. Your body language often speaks for you, too. What it says may surprise you. The way you sit, move your eyes, or place your arms can signal your disinterest or disapproval.

In every classroom, you are in one of two situations. You either do or do not know about the topic under discussion. If you know, you can make friends by finding classmates who do not know about the topic and helping them learn. Offering help without judging or boasting can be tricky, but it is essential to interaction with others. If you do not know the topic, you need to find someone who does and who is willing to help you. Asking for help gives classmates chances to feel knowledgeable and needed. Sometimes asking for help is just as hard as giving it. You may fear wasting other students' time or making a poor impression. A couple of ways to overcome this fear are to form a study group or ask several students to join you for coffee to discuss class material.

Study Groups

Studying in groups gives you a practical reason to interact with other students on an informal basis. In addition, research indicates that study groups provide optimum learning opportunities. Students who participated regularly in a study group (Shanker, 1988) understood and scored better than those who studied independently. When independent learners formed study groups, their grades improved to the level of those already involved in group study. Work at Harvard University (Light, 1990; 1992) found that in every comparison, working in small groups (three to five people) was superior to another format. Small group learning showed better outcomes than working in large groups, independent study, or—in some cases—one-to-one tutoring from a faculty member. And while changes in grades were modest, student involvement in a course, enthusiasm for the course, and pursuit of topics to higher levels increased. Students felt that working within groups taught them valuable strategies for working with others, strategies that they would have had no other chance to develop.

What is a study group? A study group is a collection of two or more persons whose contact, proximity, and communication produce changes in each other. As part of the group, you interact with and influence other students. The purpose of your group is the active discussion of information. Therefore, your group needs to have appropriate communication skills, a common purpose, the ability to set tasks, and the skills to accomplish those tasks. The creation and maintenance of such a group is often easier said than done. Guidelines for establishing and maintaining a study group appear in the following group learning activity.

What advantages do study groups have over independent study? When you study alone, you have only your skills and strategies at your disposal. Group study allows you to see, hear, and practice a variety of problem-solving, communication, and learning skills. You learn more actively because you participate more fully than in individual study. Group study often helps focus attention and efforts. You have more opportunities to see, hear, verbalize, and otherwise come in contact with the information you study. Group study also increases the ways in which you think about a subject. Other members of the group contribute their perspectives, cognitive processing styles, and insights about a concept. You have not only your own ideas, but the ideas of others from which to draw.

Group study provides psychological as well as cognitive benefits. Your commitment to others in the group enhances your study. While you may be prone to break study dates with yourself, you'll be more likely to prepare if you know others depend on you. In addition, participation in a study group gives you support. Knowing that others are having difficulty or have been successful at a task lessens your anxiety and provides encouragement. Group members provide an empathetic network for the academic, personal, time, and financial problems of the higher education student.

While group learning certainly has many advantages, study groups have one potential disadvantage. Group study focuses on verbal exchange of information and often fails to provide practice in generating the kinds of answers needed for essay exam questions. And, while some students can explain information verbally, they may not perform as well when asked to provide a written answer. If you have difficulty composing written responses to test items, you need to include writing in your study strategies.

Campus Employment

Campus employment is one of the most lucrative ways for students to get involved in campus life. While student wages are often minimal, employment offers many other benefits. First, campus employers understand that a student's real job is school. Such employers are willing to let you work around class schedules and often rearrange work hours to accommodate special projects or tests. Campus employment often offers you the opportunity to work within your field of study in such positions as a lab assistant, office worker, tutor, and so on. Even if your campus job is not in your area of interest, it may provide you with experiences relevant to your career or lead you to an entirely new field of interest. Finally, campus employment gives you additional opportunities to meet and know students, faculty, and staff.

GROUP LEARNING ACTIVITY
GUIDELINES FOR ESTABLISHING ACTIVE STUDY GROUPS

A group consists of two or more persons whose contact, proximity, and communication produce changes in each other. As part of the group, you interact with and influence other students. The purpose of your group is the active discussion of information. Therefore, your group needs to have appropriate communication skills, a common purpose, the ability to set tasks, and the skills to accomplish those tasks. Unfortunately, acquiring these is easier said than done. The following guidelines can help you establish an effective study group.

1. *Select group members who have the academic interest and dedication to be successful.* Your friends do not always make the best study partners. Study group members must be prepared to discuss the topic at hand, not what happened at last night's party. You may not know which students in the class are interested in forming a group. Ask your instructor to announce the formation of a study group in class or place a sign-up sheet on a nearby bulletin board.

2. *Seek group members with similar abilities and motivation.* The group functions best when each member of the group contributes to the overall learning of the group, and no one uses the group as a substitute for personally learning the information.

3. *Limit group size to five or fewer students.* You don't want to restructure your entire class into a study group. Five or fewer members is more manageable in arranging schedules and setting goals. Larger groups also decrease the amount of time each member has to actively participate in the group.

4. *Two heads are better than one.* Although a group can consist of as many as five members, it can also contain just two. Lack of interest on the part of other committed members, lack of similar goals, or scheduling problems may preclude your participation in a larger study group. Work or other time commitments also limit the times at which you can meet on a regular basis. Two schedules generally have more in common than five.

5. *Identify the purpose and lifetime of the group.* Are you looking for a term-length group for in-depth study in a difficult course? Do you need pretest meetings to exchange ideas? Specific goals help prospective members decide if their investments of time will serve their purposes.

6. *If possible, schedule regular group meetings at the same place and time.* Group members can plan accordingly if they know that their study group meets every Tuesday afternoon at 2:00. If the group meets less frequently, members may forget which week the group meets. If you meet at different locations, members may forget where to go.

GROUP LEARNING ACTIVITY
GUIDELINES FOR ESTABLISHING ACTIVE STUDY GROUPS *(continued)*

7. *Get acquainted.* You will be investing a great deal of time and effort with these people. Although you don't need to know their life histories, you do need to know something about their level of ability in the course (have they had six chemistry courses and this is your first?), their current time commitments (do they have jobs, family, social, or other activities that affect the times at which they can and cannot meet?), and their expectations of the group. At the very least, you need to exchange names and phone numbers so that you can contact members in case of an emergency.

Application

Form a study group for this class. Establish a purpose for the group and set a schedule for out-of-class meetings. As a group, create a checklist or survey to help you get acquainted with each other. Include questions that help you determine if group members have similar academic interests and levels of dedication. Make copies and exchange your group's checklist or survey with other groups in the class. Compare and determine which features are most appropriate.

Special Interest Groups

Special interest groups are based on the notion that "birds of a feather flock together." Interest groups develop around a variety of topics from academic interests (for example, Accounting Society, Philosophy Club, College Choir, Pre-Law Association, Marching Band) to those which are simply for fun (Frisbee Club, Chess Club, intramural sports, Science Fiction Association, computer user groups). Groups may reflect political affiliation (College Republicans), sexual orientation (Gay and Lesbian Alliance), ethnic membership (Arab Students' Association), or religious belief (Inter-Varsity Christian Fellowship). Such groups may be formal or informal. Some are honorary and base membership on academic criteria. Joining these groups gives you opportunities to meet others with similar interests or to develop new interests.

Service Organizations

Service organizations provide various opportunities to work for the common good of your institution or community. These groups include any organization in which you volunteer your time for the benefit of others. Student government associations and residence hall associations represent students in a variety of ways. They organize to further the desires and needs of students they represent. The students who staff campus newspapers and yearbook offices often volunteer to gain experience in journalism and production. Many interest groups have a service organization that provides tutoring, advice, and support to its members. Finally, some organizations (for example, Gamma Beta Phi) provide more traditional forms of service (Big Buddy programs, literacy tutors, drives for food or blood banks).

Why should a busy student devote time to service projects? First, some people believe additional education confers additional responsibility as a citizen. Second, service provides valuable experience in working on committees and projects to accomplish specific goals and tasks. Third, experience with such projects may result in leadership positions in which you can develop additional skills.

Social Organizations

Some groups form for strictly social reasons. Like many other campus groups, their purpose is to connect you to other people within the institution. Greek groups have national affiliations and a long tradition. Some students join because their parents, grandparents, or siblings were members. Thus, the networks within such groups are often far ranging and well connected. While Greeks are often known for their ability to party, many also focus on academic standards and community service.

A group need not be affiliated with Greeks to be social in nature. Many other groups provide opportunities for interacting with other students. First, students may join an **intramural sports** group, which organizes athletic events and services for students who are not part of a school-sponsored athletic team. These activities focus on competition that encourages fair play, leadership, health, and fun. Second, students interested in the same subject often form a club through the student affairs office. This helps them develop friendships with others. Third, students might join other clubs on campus that involve individuals with similar interests or hobbies. Membership often depends on grade point average or other criteria. Finally, leisure or other noncredit courses also provide opportunities for you to meet others. While fun is the immediate goal, the long-range effect is friendship and greater assimilation into the institution.

WRITE TO LEARN

On a separate sheet of paper or in your journal, identify 3 of the ways you could become more involved in your campus community. Are these groups described in your text? If so, how? Explain how your needs, values, and interests contribute to the suitability of these groups for you.

Exercise 1.7   Use Sample Chapter 11 (Personal Values, Career Planning, and Success with People at Work) to respond to the following questions.

1. Read the section "Another Look: Which corporate culture fits you?" (pp. 533–535). Describe how specific MBTI attributes relate to preference to belong to an "academy," a "fortress," a "baseball team," or a "club."

_____

_____

_____

_____

2. Read the section "What organizations expect of management employees" (pp. 479–482). Consider the campus resources available on your campus. Create a chart in which you identify the kinds of things companies expect from their management employees and specific ways in which faculty and staff on your campus fulfill each one.

_____

_____

_____

_____

_____

WRITE TO LEARN

Read the sample short story, "Strange Inventions." Based on what you've learned from this chapter, identify John Muir's probable MBTI, sensory, and brain preferences. Justify your choices. Write your response on a separate sheet of paper or in your notebook.

SUMMARY OF MAIN POINTS

1. Studying and thinking in ways that complement and employ your learning style (personality, sensory preferences, and brain dominance) maximizes understanding.

2. The Myers-Briggs Temperament Indicator provides information about personality in terms of eight factors: extravert/introvert, sensing/intuitive, thinking/feeling, judging/perceiving.

3. Sensory preferences include learning through visual, aural, kinesthetic, and reading/writing modalities as well as a multisensory approach.

4. Brain dominance reflects differences in right-brain and left-brain processing of information.

5. The rights and responsibilities of higher education citizenship include understanding information in your college catalog, using campus resources and services, striving for academic excellence, maintaining academic standards, and interacting with college faculty.

6. A liberal education involves getting to know members of the diverse groups of individuals found on higher education campuses as well as getting involved in campus life through interactions with other students, employment on campus, and membership in student organizations.

CHAPTER REVIEW

Answer briefly but completely.

1. How does identification of MBTI personality factors, brain dominance, and sensory preferences affect learning? What might be the effect of a failure to understand these traits in terms of learning?

_____

_____

_____

_____

_____

2. Choose any five components of a college catalog as identified in Table 1.4. Describe a specific purpose you might have for using each one you choose.

_____

_____

_____

_____

_____

3. Categorize the higher education terms found in Table 1.5 according to the following categories:

TERMS

Terms appear in the order in which they occurred in the chapter.

style
personality
sensory preferences
brain dominance
Myers-Briggs Type
    Indicator (MBTI)
visual
aural
kinesthetic
multisensory
left brain
right brain
college catalog
grade point
    average (GPA)
quality points
academic probation
academic action
plagiarism
academic code of
    student conduct
appeals
intramural sports

Terms related to students	Terms related to courses	Terms related to students and courses

4. What is the relationship between academic standards and academic excellence?

5. What is the relationship between grade point average and quality points?

6. What aspects of classroom behavior also apply to communicating with faculty in out-of-class interactions and office visits?

7. Which of the diverse groups discussed in this chapter (for example, ESL students, students with disabilities) do you find to be most prevalent on your campus? What services are available for that group on your campus?

8. Compare involvement in campus activities via classroom interactions with involvement in campus activities via study groups.

_____

_____

_____

_____

_____

9. Identify five places where students work on your campus and the kinds of work experiences available at each location.

_____

_____

_____

_____

_____

10. Compare the number and type of service organizations with the number and type of social organizations on your campus.

_____

_____

_____

_____

_____

Vocabulary Development   Terminology: The Language of College Courses

Becoming a citizen in the world of higher education involves setting your own goals, as well as meeting those that your institution sets for you. It means knowing the people who work, teach, live, and study at school with you. Most of all, higher education provides you with opportunities—to assess yourself, enhance current abilities, learn new ideas, and grow in ways you've never even thought of. These changes will necessitate changes in your vocabulary to accommodate the new ways in which you think and communicate. From *academic year* to *astronomy*, from *GPA* to *Greek affairs*, from *provost* to *political science*, from *residential housing* to *religion*, you'll encounter new terminology in the world of higher education.

Since words are the currency of thought, the more words you master, the richer become your thought processes.

Joseph Bellafiore, 1968

Words are the medium of exchange for the subjects you study. Without them, you can neither buy new ideas nor spend them in the form of written or verbal transactions. Just as sound financing forms the basis of any business, a sound understanding of course vocabulary underlies the business of learning that subject.

Just as your profession affects the terminology you use, the language of the courses in which you enroll varies according to the course. Basically, college courses fall into four categories: humanities, social studies, sciences, and applied or technical courses (see Table 1). The kinds of terms you encounter and the way in which you meet them vary according to the course type.

Course vocabulary generally takes three forms: **technical vocabulary, specialized vocabulary,** and **general vocabulary** (see Table 2). Your mastery of the vocabulary in a specific course depends on your prior knowledge of the course's content, the stages of your vocabulary development, and the depth of understanding required by the course.

Your knowledge of a word can range from no knowledge to the ability to use the word. Edgar Dale (1958) theorized four progressive stages of vocabulary development (see Table 3). In stage one, you have no knowledge of the word's meaning. You only realize that the word you encounter is new. At the second stage, you believe that the word is one you've seen or heard. However, you possess no real knowledge of its meaning. In stage three, you associate the word with a very general concept. For example, suppose you encounter the word *Protista* in biology class. You associate it with classifications of life. Further, you believe it to be a fairly simple

Table 1   Academic Disciplines and Subjects of Study

Humanities

Art	English	Journalism
Music	Philosophy	Classical languages
Speech	Religion	Foreign languages

Natural Sciences

Biological	*Mathematical*	*Physical*
Biology	Computer science	Astronomy
Botany	Mathematics	Chemistry
Marine science		Geology
Microbiology		Physics
Zoology		Physical science

Social Sciences

Anthropology	History	Psychology
Economics	Sociology	Political science
Geography		

Technical or Applied

Engineering	Education	Allied health
Agriculture	Physical education	Social work
Business	ROTC	

Table 2   Course Vocabulary

Type	Description	Frequent College Contexts	Examples
Technical	Specific to the course	Science Applied/Technical	ion lactose
Specialized	General vocabulary used in new or unfamiliar ways	Humanities Social studies Science	base core cell family rotation
General	Common words unfamiliar to you	Humanities Social studies	euthanasia laconic icon collate

Table 3   Stages of Vocabulary Development

1. You know that a word is new to you. You have no prior knowledge of the word.
2. You recognize a word but are unsure about its meaning or any general associations with it.
3. You recognize a word but have only vague associations with general concepts.
4. You recognize a word and can use it in the context of the course.

form of life. Beyond that general concept, you have no clear understanding. At stage four, you attain an understanding of the word in terms of the course and the manner in which it used. You know that *Protista* is a kingdom of single-celled organisms of such diversity that they include both plants and animals.

Making an effort to stop and learn the terminology in a course affects the depth of your understanding of the course. One way to estimate your understanding of a course is to identify the levels at which you understand its terms. Such identifications serve several functions. First, when you identify a word that you don't know, you focus your attention on it. This increases your chance of knowing the word in later encounters. Then, by attempting to determine the meaning, you increase your recall through association and active learning. Finally, the more you relate terms and ideas, the more effective you are at making future associations.

Activity 1
Words Can Make You Rich!

An exercise used with high school and college students for a number of years with interesting reactions is included here. The tongue-in-cheek idea is that you may determine your salary level based on your age and the number of words you can identify correctly. The terms come from a wide field.

1. Did you see the *clergy*?   a. funeral   b. dolphin   c. church members
   d. monastery e. bell tower

2. Fine *louvers*.   a. doors b. radiators c. slatted vents
   d. mouldings. bay windows

3. Like an *ellipse*.   a. sunspot b. oval c. satellite d. triangle e. volume

4. *Dire* thoughts.   a. angry b. dreadful c. blissful d. ugly e. unclean

5. It was the *affluence*.   a. flow rate b. pull c. wealth d. flood e. bankruptcy

6. Discussing the *acme*.   a. intersection b. question c. birthmark
   d. perfection e. low point

7. How *odious*.   a. burdensome b. lazy c. hateful d. attractive
   e. fragrant

8. This is *finite*. a. limited b. tiny c. precise d. endless e. difficult

9. Watch for the *inflection*. a. accent b. mirror image c. swelling d. pendulum swing e. violation

10. The *connubial* state. a. marriage b. tribal c. festive d. spinsterly e. primitive

11. See the *nuance*. a. contrast b. upstart c. renewal d. delinquent e. shading

12. Where is the *dryad?* a. water sprite b. fern c. dish towel d. chord e. wood nymph

13. Will you *garner* it? a. dispose of b. store c. polish d. thresh e. trim

14. A sort of *anchorite*. a. religious service b. hermit c. marine deposit d. mineral e. promoter

15. *Knurled* edges. a. twisted b. weather beaten c. flattened d. ridged e. knitted

16. Is it *bifurcated?* a. forked b. hairy c. two-wheeled d. mildewed e. joined

17. Examining the *phthisis*. a. cell division b. medicine c. misstatement d. dissertation e. tuberculosis

18. *Preponderance* of the group. a. majority b. heaviness c. small number d. foresight

19. Ready to *expound*. a. pop b. confuse c. interpret d. dig up e. imprison

20. Starting at the *relict*. a. trustee b. antique table c. corpse d. widow e. excavation

SOURCE: Marian J. Tonjes and Miles V. Zintz *Teaching Reading Thinking Study Skills in Content Classrooms.* (2E). © 1987, Wm. C. Brown Communications, Inc. Dubuque, Iowa. All rights reserved. Reprinted by permission.

Score your responses using the key that follows the references in this chapter. Now, based on your raw score, find your salary level.

	Age 17–20	Number Correct Age 21–29		Age 30 and up	
20–15	$40,000 and up	20–17	$40,000 and up	20–19	$35,500 and up
14–13	32,000–$40,000	16–15	32,000–$35,500	18–17	32,000–$35,500
12–11	28,000–32,000	14–13	28,000–32,000	16–15	28,000–32,000
10–9	25,000–28,000	12–11	25,000–28,000	14–13	25,000–28,000
8–7	20,000–25,000	10–5	20,000–25,000	12–11	20,000–25,000
6–3	15,000–20,000	Below 5	Under 15,000	10–7	15,000–20,000
Below 3	Under 15,000			Below 7	Under 15,000

Activity 2

On a separate sheet of paper, copy the list of terms from Sample Chapter 11 in this text (found at the end of the chapter) and from any chapter from a course in which you are now enrolled. Identify which are specialized, technical, or general terms. Then based on Dale's ranking system, identify your level of knowledge of each.

REFERENCES

Brunvand, J.H. (1989). *Curses! Broiled again!* New York: W.W. Norton & Co.

Dale, E. (1958). How to Know More Wonderful Words. *Good Housekeeping, 146,* 17+.

Knox, D. (1990). *Sociology.* St. Paul, Minn.: West Publishers.

Light, R.J. (1990). *The Harvard assessment seminars: First report.* Harvard University Graduate School of Education and Kennedy School of Government: Cambridge, Mass.

Light, R.J. (1992). *The Harvard assessment seminars: Second report.* Harvard University Graduate School of Education and Kennedy School of Government: Cambridge, Mass.

Shanker, A. (Fall 1988). Strength in numbers. *Academic Connections,* 12.

ANSWERS TO ACTIVITY 1

1. C	11. A
2. C	12. E
3. B	13. B
4. B	14. B
5. C	15. D
6. D	16. A
7. C	17. E
8. A	18. A
9. A	19. C
10. A	20. B

CHAPTER 2

Time Management: Put Yourself to Work

CHAPTER MAP

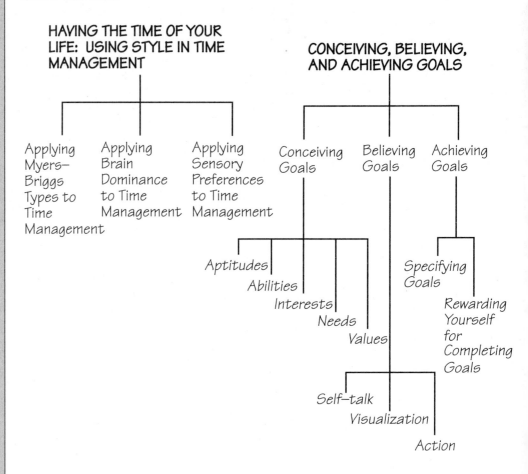

HAVING THE TIME OF YOUR LIFE: USING STYLE IN TIME MANAGEMENT

CONCEIVING, BELIEVING, AND ACHIEVING GOALS

Applying Myers-Briggs Types to Time Management

Applying Brain Dominance to Time Management

Applying Sensory Preferences to Time Management

Conceiving Goals

Believing Goals

Achieving Goals

Aptitudes

Abilities

Interests

Needs

Values

Self-talk

Visualization

Action

Specifying Goals

Rewarding Yourself for Completing Goals

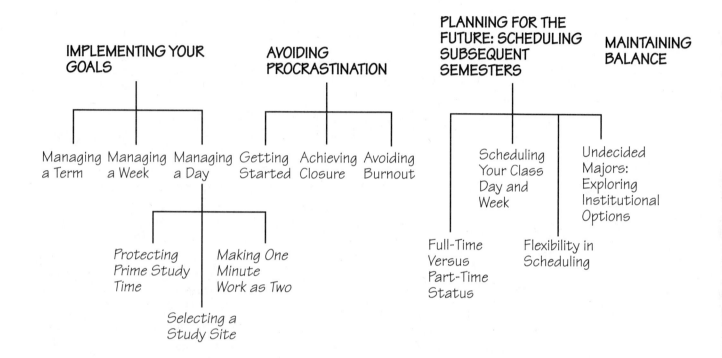

Source: Ziggy. Copyright © 1990 Ziggy & Friends, Inc.
Distributed by Universal Press Syndicate. Reprinted with
permission. All rights reserved.

Ziggy's dilemma—things to do today versus things due today—actually represents differing time-management styles. Some students work methodically on projects and finish them ahead of schedule. They organize papers and other materials and store them in files or other containers. Other students wait until the last minute to begin projects and work in energetic, high-pressure spurts. They place papers and other materials in numerous stacks around a room. Or, a student may fall somewhere in between, carefully organizing some activities and completing others in a more flexible fashion.

Whatever the case, the way you organize time affects the way you work. The same personal attributes that affect your learning style also affect your time-management style. Recognizing how they affect time management helps you maximize your strengths and, when necessary, modify your style to accomplish what you need to do in a timely fashion. This chapter describes how to incorporate personality, brain dominance, and sensory preferences into a time-management system. It shows you how to create term, weekly, and daily time-management plans. It helps you identify how you can use your goals to maintain your focus on current tasks. This chapter also provides suggestions for overcoming procrastination, scheduling classes for subsequent semesters, and maintaining balance as a postsecondary student.

HAVING THE TIME OF YOUR LIFE: USING STYLE IN TIME MANAGEMENT

To have the time of your life means to have a wonderful time. Indeed, it means to have the best experience of your life. When you use your personal style (see Chapter 1) in managing time, every day can be the time of your life ... as long as what you do in life has the same expectations of time as you have. Unfortunately, life and the demands of life do not always exist on your terms. You must not only understand your style in terms of time, but you must also accommodate your style to meet the expectations and needs of others.

APPLYING MYERS-BRIGGS TYPES TO TIME MANAGEMENT

Your personality type indicates you have a propensity for the characteristics and behaviors in that type. (See Exercise 1.1 to determine your type.) However, according to Lawrence (1987), as you solve problems, interact with others, or analyze situations, you use all of the dimensions to some degree. For example, you might use sensing *(S)* to collect ideas relevant to a paper while remaining open to new angles on the topic *(N)*. At some point, you begin to use logic *(T)* to analyze the information although you consider your personal priorities *(F)* as you do so. You could approach your paper in an orderly way *(J)* and yet retain some flexibility *(P)*. You take time to explore a variety of ideas that interest you *(I)*, yet you keep the deadline for completion of the paper in mind *(E)*. Your personality type determines, to some degree, the level to which you let one dimension override another. For example, if your type includes *I* rather than *E*, you may spend so much time exploring ideas that you miss the deadline for completion of the paper.

How do the dimensions of your type relate to time management? Table 2.1 categorizes factors involving time management by type.

APPLYING BRAIN DOMINANCE TO TIME MANAGEMENT

If you're a left-brain dominant individual (See Exercise 1.3 and Table 1.3), you'll probably find yourself agreeing with Dr. Bennett. You are the kind of person who favors traditional time-management principles. You feel comfortable with calendars, planners, and lists. You're analytical and detail oriented. You complete tasks on time and in an orderly manner. Your work space is organized with a place for everything and everything in its place. You clean off your desk and put materials away neatly each day. Maintaining a schedule gives you a feeling of control. Interruptions

Don't try to do two or more things at once. Set priorities so that you are not worrying about something else while you are attending to the task at hand. Arrange your work space so that your eyes aren't drawn to other jobs that need to be done. The time you invest to organize your space will be paid back with improved efficiency.

WILLIAM BENNETT

Twentieth Century American Secretary of Education

Table 2.1   MBTI Factors that Relate to Time Management

Extraversion (E)
Likes to work with others
Relatively short attention span
Learns what instructor wants
Acts quickly
Tolerates interruptions
Prefers many activities or ideas to
   in-depth treatment of one idea

Introversion (I)
Prefers to work alone
Can concentrate for long periods
   of time
Sets personal standards
May delay action
Prefers quiet, uninterrupted study
   site
Prefers in-depth treatment of ac-
   tivities or ideas

Sensing (S)
Prefers a step-by-step approach
Oriented to the present
Likes to refine current skills
Prefers realistic application
Attentive to detail
Patient
Works steadily
Prefers goal-oriented tasks
Prefers direct experience

Intuition (N)
Tends to use a roundabout ap-
   proach
Oriented to the future
Becomes bored after mastering a
   skill
Prefers imaginative application
Attentive to ``big picture''
Restless
Works in bursts of energy
Prefers open-ended assignments
Prefers reading or thinking

Thinking (T)
Considers logical outcomes
Objective
Task-oriented
Firm
Motivated by desire for achieve-
   ment

Feeling (F)
Considers feelings of self and
   others
Subjective
Considers personal values
Flexible
Motivated by desire to be appre-
   ciated

Judging (J)
Goal-oriented
Prefers structure of deadlines
Limits commitment
Prefers to work on one task at a
   time
Maintains a time-management
   plan
Prefers closure in order to make
   decisions
Persistent
Uncomfortable with unplanned
   events
Rigid
Perfectionist

Perceiving (P)
Self-directed
Prefers flexibility in completing
   tasks
Tends to overcommit
Starts several tasks at once
Prefers unstructured time
Delays closure in order to gather
   more information
Distracted
Comfortable with spontaneous
   events
Flexible
Tolerant of imperfection

annoy you because they get you off your schedule. You like to get things done. You may already consider yourself a good manager of your time.

If you're a right-brain dominant individual, you probably feel a little less enthusiastic about Dr. Bennett's suggestions. As a right-brain individual, you have the capability to work on a number of tasks, more or less simultaneously. As a result, you feel comfortable shifting from project to project. You feel less comfortable with deadlines and prefer to work in a more self-paced, flexible, and energetic manner. You find interruptions stimulating and interesting. Others may watch you and think you're doing nothing, but you know you are thinking about your project. You tend to organize spatially and like to see everything around you. You prefer to leave projects in progress spread out on your desk until their completion rather than putting things away at the end of each day. When you finish a project, you may find you feel a little unsettled. You may like to use term planners to get an overview of an entire semester and concept maps (see Chapter 6) to organize. Because you don't adhere to traditional time-management plans, you may feel that you lack time-management skills.

Unless you are an extremely unusual individual, you probably find that you have both right- and left-brain attributes rather than only one or the other. The key to time management—like the key to learning—involves balancing the two and using the strengths of one side of the brain to offset the weaknesses in the other. Table 2.2 identifies some right- and left-brain problems in time management and provides suggestions for solving each one. Because left-brain individuals possess more attributes compatible with traditional time-management practices, most problems occur when right-brain strengths affect organizational needs.

APPLYING SENSORY PREFERENCES TO TIME MANAGEMENT

While sensory preferences have less impact than personality factors and brain dominance, you can still use them to enhance your time-management strategies. For example, if you prefer to learn visually, you could use color coding to indicate task priorities or visualization to sequence activities. Aural learners might use answering machines to their advantage by calling and leaving themselves verbal messages about tasks to accomplish or deadlines to meet. Small tape recorders might also be used for such purposes. Kinesthetic learners might find arranging activities, times, and due dates on a bulletin board or magnetic board provides them the physical activity needed to structure time. If your preference involves reading and writing, traditional time-management principles probably work well for you with few adaptations.

Table 2.2   Time-management Problems Associated with Brain Dominance

Left-Brain Problems	Suggestions for Solution
Overemphasis on detail; spending more time on a project than it warrants; inability to judge when enough is enough.	Set priorities. Determine the grade or amount of effort required. Set time limits for completion.
Impatience with effort or time required to complete a task.	Set realistic expectations.
Inability to handle interruptions.	Determine the best use of your time for a particular moment. You may need to strengthen assertive skills in communicating your needs to others. Consider closing the door to your room or going to a less distracting place to work.

Right-Brain Problems	Suggestions for Solution
Inability to decide what project to begin first.	Use term and weekly planners to set daily to-do list priorities. Visualize each step of your project from beginning to end before starting the project.
Disorganization of papers and other materials; inability to find things.	Use spatial organizers (e.g., boxes, baskets, peg boards, bulletin boards, open shelves). Cluster items by their use (e.g., art cluster, English cluster, math cluster). Color-code information and files and store the ones you use most often in a graduated vertical file on your desk or shelf.
Inability to stay on task; boredom and restlessness with concentrated effort.	Allow yourself to take frequent breaks after working for a set period of time; force yourself to return to the task after a specified (short) period of time or switch tasks to maintain concentration.
Inability to meet deadlines.	Break down large jobs into smaller tasks. Set intermediate goals and deadlines for completing projects. Work with a more left-brain individual and follow his or her timetable.

WRITE TO LEARN

On a separate sheet of paper or in your journal, explain how you manage your time in terms of your MBTI, sensory, and brain preferences. What aspects of your time-management style surprised you? Why? What did not? Why?

CONCEIVING, BELIEVING, AND ACHIEVING GOALS

(Today's students) can put dope in their veins or hope in their brains. . . . If they can conceive it and believe it, they can achieve it. They must know it is not their aptitude, but their attitude that will determine their altitude.

—REVEREND JESSE JACKSON

Twentieth Century American politician

Jesse Jackson's comment applies not only to students but to everyone regardless of age or occupation. The goals you set for yourself determine, in part, where you end up in life. Barbara Sher, author of *I Could Do Anything If I Only Knew What It Was* (1994), believes that goals express only hopeful predictions rather than concrete realities. So, if you might not achieve your goals, why even have any? Sher responds that goal setting and planning for the future gets you going in a definite direction. If you set a goal and start trying to achieve it, your life will definitely change as a result. Will you reach that goal? Maybe, but maybe not. You may not reach your specific goal, but you could end up someplace better—someplace you never imagined or could have reached if you weren't already on your way to something and somewhere.

Active and enthusiastic pursuit of your goals often puts you in the path of opportunity. To assure that you head in the right direction, Sher suggests you consider whether a choice will take you closer or farther from what you really want and always choose the action that takes you closer to your goals. For example, your goal may be to become a doctor. You get an opportunity to take a job in sales, which will help you make a lot of money but you must quit school to do it. Or you could take a lesser-paying job as an orderly at a hospital, which would allow you to continue school part time. The first choice has immediate but short-term results. The second choice has more potential for the future because it allows you to stay in college and gain experiences and make connections that could help you get into a medical school.

CONCEIVING GOALS

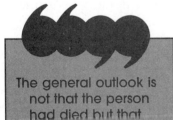

The general outlook is not that the person had died but that the person has lived.

—WILLIAM BUCHANAN ON OBITUARIES

Twentieth Century American politician

How do you want to be remembered when you're gone? Loyal friend? Loving spouse/parent/child? Successful business owner? Professional musician? World traveler? Social activist? The list has endless possibilities.

Your goals form the answers to the question, "What do you want to do, have, or be at the end of your life? You derive your goals from a combination of factors that contribute to your point of view—your **aptitudes, abilities, interests, needs,** and **values** (see Figure 2.1).

Figure 2.1   Factors That Contribute to Point of View

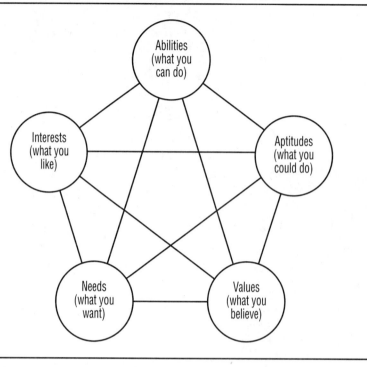

Aptitudes

Aptitudes reflect what you could do—your potential. These natural or inborn traits precede ability. They may be visible or hidden. Visible traits are ones you already recognize and have developed. Hidden traits are parts of your personality you have not yet explored. For example, you may have an aptitude for music. If you grew up in a home where you took music lessons or went to concerts, then your aptitude for music is more likely to be developed. If you grew up in a home where music interest was not fostered, then your aptitude for music may be hidden.

One way to learn more about your hidden aptitudes is to take aptitude tests. General aptitude tests estimate such abilities as verbal skills, numerical skills, spatial skills, motor coordination, and manual dexterity. More specialized aptitudes, such as music and art, are not evaluated by general aptitude tests.

The counseling or placement center at your college probably administers aptitude tests to aid in setting goals and making career choices. Discovering your aptitudes is important in the goal-setting process because awareness of your visible and hidden traits helps you identify areas of interest and clarify career directions.

Abilities

Abilities are what you can do—your capabilities. They result from aptitude combined with experience. Abilities are not constant. They increase with practice and decrease with disuse.

Unlike aptitude, which is estimated, ability is measured by performance in two ways: formal tests and informal assessment. Formal tests generally do not measure specific skill areas. Instead, they measure generalized areas, such as intelligence and achievement. Because they measure broad skills, they do not identify specific strengths and weaknesses. Thus, informal assessment often forms a better means of measuring ability. Informal self-assessment occurs when you look at those areas in which you excel, examine your past performances, and recall comments others have made about your skills.

Such assessments may be misleading, however. First, time is a necessary consideration. In other words, suppose you and a friend each work a set of math problems equally well. However, you finish in one hour while your friend takes all day. Your ability in math, then, is probably greater than your friend's. In addition, ability differs in quality or kind. For example, math ability could mean solving complex equations or simply balancing a checkbook.

How do assessments of ability affect your academic goals? They help you identify your subject-area strengths and weaknesses. Knowing these helps you better determine those courses you're ready for and those in which you may need tutoring or other assistance. In addition, knowledge of your abilities helps you plan time and energy commitments needed for academic success.

Interests

Your interests are what you like. How interests develop has never been completely understood. Your experiences with situations and people create some of your interests. The sources of other interests may not be as easily identified.

Interests can and do change. The things that interested you as a child may not interest you now. The things that interest you now may not interest you in the future. Changes in your life cause changes in your interests. College life, for example, contributes to changes in your interests as you are exposed to new ideas and experiences.

Prior to college, your academic experiences and interests were probably limited to courses available at your high school (English, math, some science and social science subjects). Part-and full-time employment also may have shaped your interests. Postsecondary education now opens realms of information that were previously unavailable to you—for example, anthropology, philosophy, music history, Japanese, and robotics. Your first reaction to such courses might be disinterest. However, what you perceive as disinterest may actually be unfamiliarity. In contrast, you may find courses that you thought would be interesting are not. You may find such changes in interest frustrating in that you may question your major, your values, and even your reason for being in college. Remember that such changes in interest should be an expected part of the postsecondary education process. Postsecondary education provides you with opportunities to rethink and redefine your interests—and yourself—in the process.

Changing interests do, and should, affect your choice of major and goals. While it would be nice if these changes occurred in your first semester or two, often they do not. You may find yourself interested in another major in your junior or senior year. Several options should be considered. First, can you pursue this interest as a variation of your current major? If so, completing your current degree program with additional electives may suffice. Obtaining advanced degrees or certifications after you complete your undergraduate degree might also help you meet your goal. You may find, however, that only an entirely different course of study will meet your needs. For example, you may pursue a degree in business and later find your interests are in medicine. This change may cause you a loss of applicable credits and require additional time. While you may wonder if this extra time and effort is worth it, you should consider that time you will spend in your career will be far longer than the additional time you will spend in school.

You determine your interests in several ways. Some of your current interests are topics you like or activities you enjoy. You discover these by looking at past experiences and preferences. You find other, new interests by trying out new activities and by talking to others. You also might identify new interests by taking a standardized interest inventory. Interest inventories identify your preferences by assessing broad areas of interest or by comparing your responses with those of people in various occupations. Your college counseling center or placement office probably gives vocational interest tests.

High scores in specific areas of an interest inventory should not be the sole factor in academic goal setting. Sometimes an area of interest indicates a hobby, or avocational interest. For example, suppose your score indicates a high interest in art. You may not paint well enough to major in art, but you can enjoy painting as a hobby or you might choose to be an art historian.

Needs

A. H. Maslow (1954) developed a hierarchy of needs (Figure 2.2). He theorized that your lowest needs concern your physical well-being and

Figure 2.2   Maslow's Hierarchy of Needs

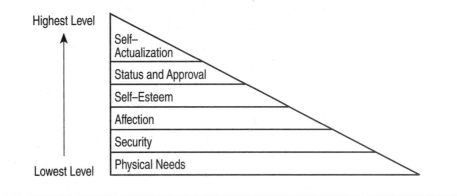

safety. Unless these basic needs are met, higher-level needs are never realized. Your need for affection involves interpersonal relationships with others. Self-esteem and independence needs affect your feelings of worth and ability. Your concern for the opinions and approval of others influences your status and approval needs. Self-actualization, the highest level, occurs when you are motivated to be your best for yourself.

Although these needs develop from lowest to highest levels, once developed, they interact. Thus, your needs exist at many levels. They direct and motivate your actions in setting goals. No one level or factor determines what your goals should be. The needs important to you and your choice of goals are unique to you. Thus, the ranking Maslow theorized differs for each person.

Values

Values result from your experiences. You derived some of your values from your family and friends. Your thoughts and reactions to situations and people formed other values. Events and people you learned about through television, literature, and other media also shaped them.

Just as new courses shape your interests, new ideas shape your values. High school instructors generally hold the same principles and values as the communities in which they teach. Postsecondary faculty represent a greater diversity of geographical regions, ideas, interests, and, therefore, values. In fact, you may feel as though you have stepped into a wind tunnel of contradictory viewpoints and cultures: animal rights, pro-choice, anti-abortion, liberal, conservative, atheist, Christian, Muslim, vegetarian, politically correct, pacifist, pro-union, and so on. Exposure to these perspectives is part of the postsecondary educational process. Indeed, many college instructors see their role as being academically free to pursue intellectual inquiry and research, ask or stimulate the asking of questions, and/or raise controversial issues. As you encounter more and different views, your ability to listen, read, and think critically about information grows. The opinions, attitudes, and influences of others will have less and less impact as you learn to analyze information and judge for yourself. As a result, professors who require you to choose a position and defend it are generally less interested in your opinion than in your ability to logically support your argument in written or oral form. Helping you define your personal values in this way is also a role of the college instructor.

Why are values important? Values help you rank your needs. Because values vary, you must examine your needs in terms of what you value most. Your academic goals affect study and time commitments, course selection, career orientation, and personal and professional associations. Pursuing your goals—what you value in life—is essential in achieving life satisfaction.

> **WRITE TO LEARN**
>
> On a separate sheet of paper, respond to the following: What is your major? How do your interests and values support that choice? How have your postsecondary experiences affected your interests, values, and choice of major?

BELIEVING GOALS

As Jesse Jackson noted, it's your attitude and not your aptitude that determines your altitude. What you believe about yourself impacts your life more than any other factor. You develop your belief in your ability to achieve goals through self-talk, visualization, and action.

Self-Talk

In a variation of Eric Berne's (1966) concept of transactional analysis, Karen Coltharp Catalano at the U.S. Military Academy in West Point, New York, suggests that your inner dialogue affects your beliefs in what you can do. She suggests that when you talk to yourself, you often function in the role of a **child** (the part of you that wants to have fun) or a **critic** (the part of you that denounces you), each of which negatively affects your ability to achieve your goals. Recognizing these roles and the kinds of self-talk each uses are the first steps to controlling them and regaining your ability to think and act in the role of the **adult,** one who thinks analytically and solves problems rationally. Table 2.3 provides some typical comments for each role in terms of goal-setting and achievement.

Table 2.3   Self-talk of the Child, Critic, and Adult

Child Comments

I don't see the point of the goal.

The things I have to do to reach the goal aren't always going to be fun.

I'm too tired to work toward my goal.

I think I'll skip this next class. The professor is dull.

I wish I were doing something else.

Critic Comments

This is too hard/too much for me.

I don't know how to get started on something like this.

Nobody in my family has succeeded, so why do I think I will?

Everyone else can do this. There must be something wrong with me.

I didn't think I could succeed at that.

I'll never make it.

Adult Comments

This is difficult, but I have a plan.

I didn't do as well as I wanted on that activity, but I know what to do

differently next time.

Other people have succeeded at this and I can too.

This isn't very interesting, but I know I still need to do it to achieve my goals.

This is hard, but I've learned/accomplished hard things before.

Visualization

Linda Allred of Conextion Therapeutic Center in Baton Rouge, Louisiana, described the effect of the mind on the body in a recent news report. She said that Dr. Dabney Ewin, a surgeon and clinical hypnotherapist at Turo Hospital in New Orleans, Louisiana, uses visualization to enhance the recovery of burn patients who have second and third degree burns all over their bodies. If Dr. Ewin can work with a patient within the first two to four hours after the burn occurs, he tells them that happy, relaxing, enjoyable thoughts will help release their healing energy. He uses the "laughing place" from the children's story of Brer Rabbit as an example. Using guided imagery, he asks his patients to visualize a place where they feel safe, peaceful, pleasant, happy, and free from responsibility. Once the patients visualize the "laughing place," he tells them that it is also a place where all of their injured areas will feel cool and comfortable. Dr. Ewin helps them go to their "laughing places" frequently in the healing process. The doctor's patients heal within two weeks and experience no pain or scarring.

Visualization has just as much effect on achievement of goals as it has on achievement of physical health. Albert Einstein often thought in images rather than words and conducted what he called "thought experiments." He sometimes imagined himself riding beams of light. From these imaginings, he eventually developed his theory of relativity. Unfortunately, people often picture the worst. They see themselves failing exams, losing athletic events, and blowing important opportunities. They actually visualize themselves failing to reach their goals. In her book *The Empowered Mind* (1994), Gini Graham Scott suggests that you repeatedly visualize and affirm what you want as if it has already occurred. She recommends that you close your eyes and imagine the future as clearly as if it were projected on a movie screen. You put yourself in the picture as you plan, execute, and realize the success of your goals. Steps to use for visualization appear in Table 2.4.

Action

You may have heard the old adage, "Actions speak louder than words." In other words, what you actually do often overrides what you say you

---

Table 2.4   Steps for Visualization

1. **Reduce outside interference.** Find a place where you can be quiet and relaxed. Eliminate outside noise as well as inner distractions and worries. Close your eyes and look through your inner eye.

2. **Create a screen.** As you create images, project them on a movie screen in your mind. You can watch them almost as if you were watching a TV program or movie.

3. **Evolve the image.** Move from the part you see initially to the whole picture, or from the whole to the part. Fill in the details. Picture each step you need to take to reach your goal. Look for logical consequences of your actions. Visualize different options and settle on the one you want to occur. Picture the success of your goal and imagine your feelings of success.

5. **Transfer the image.** Convert your visualization into reality step by step. Externalize your inner view.

SOURCE: Steps adapted from K. Hanks and J. Parry (1993), *Wake up your creative genius*, (Menlo Park, Calif.: Crisp Publications).

will do. Controlling negative self-talk and visualizing help you focus on the possibility of successfully achieving your goals. Action translates that talk into reality.

What if you aren't sure if you really believe that you can achieve your goals? Gini Graham Scott (1994) and Barbara Sher (1994) both suggest *acting as if* as a mechanism for building confidence when you have personal doubts. *Acting as if* involves pretending that you have the traits or capabilities you need before you have proof of their existence. Thus, if you apply for a job and lack confidence, you act as if you were a confident individual. If you feel nervous about taking a test, you act as if you were calm. Sher suggests that *acting as if* benefits you in several ways. It helps you think in successful ways, improves your self-image, invites good luck in the form of information or opportunities, and sharpens your instincts.

ACHIEVING GOALS

According to time-management consultant Stephen Covey (1994), traditional time-management approaches generally focus on control, independent effort, efficiency, and chronological time. He identifies eight basic approaches to time management. The getting organized approach focuses on order. The warrior approach focuses on survival and independent production. The goal approach focuses on achievement. The ABC approach focuses on values identification and prioritization. The magic tool approach focuses on the use of planners, calendars, and other technology. The time-management courses approach focuses on the development of new skills. The go-with-the-flow approach focuses on harmony and natural rhythms. The recovery approach focuses on self-awareness of time-management flaws and dysfunctions. However, the title of Stephen Covey's book—*First Things First*—says it all. Time management isn't a search for a perfect system to run your life. Time management is your life and what you believe is important. Reconsider William Buchanan's quote about obituaries at the beginning of the section on conceiving goals. He said that the focus should be on a person's life, not his or her death. Your goals reflect what you believe is important in life, whether it is making friends, developing personal integrity, supporting a family, completing your education, increasing your professional expertise, and so on.

You've examined your aptitudes, interests, values, abilities, and needs. You've decided what's important to your life—what you want to do, have, or be. You've visualized success. All you need to do now is make it happen. How do you do that? Specifying the steps needed to reach your goal helps you determine how to achieve it. Rewarding yourself for completing these steps helps you maintain your motivation to continue toward your goals.

Specifying Goals

Lifetime goals cannot be achieved overnight. You reach your goals in small steps. Analysis of what you need to do to reach the goal forms your first step. For example, one of your lifetime goals might be to have your own business. The steps toward achieving that goal might include taking economics, accounting, and management courses to prepare you for business ownership; gaining work experiences in similar businesses; and making contacts with individuals who might provide advice, finances, or other support to you in starting a business.

The steps in achievement of goals range from large to small commitments and from **long-term goals** to **short-term goals.** Long-term goals usually extend through a semester (for example, making the dean's list, completing all assignments on schedule) or even through an academic career (for example, finishing with a B average). Short-term goals usually span a day or a week (for example, writing an English paper or reading an assigned text). You usually use them to reach long-term goals. Setting achievable goals is no easy task. To be useful, a goal must describe specific measurable outcomes. Your goals need to measure observable, concrete facts, rather than your good intentions. Specific deadlines help you meet your goals and thus avoid procrastination. They offer you the inspiration to get to work.

Consider the following long-term goals:

• Study harder.

• Attend class more regularly.

• Take better notes in class.

Such goals are too abstract to be useful. You have no way of knowing if and when you achieve them. You make these goals achievable by adding measurable outcomes and deadlines as follows:

• Raise my grade point average by 0.2 by the end of the semester.

• Attend class each time it meets for the next quarter.

• Attend a notetaking seminar this term.

Your goals are best when they depend on you alone. "Practice vocal music twice a week with a quartet of singers" and "Complete assigned lab experiments with a partner" sound like achievable goals. However, because they rely on others' actions (and inactions), your goals may be sabotaged when others fail to do their parts or do not show up.

To know if a goal is achievable, ask the following questions:

• How will I know if I attain this goal?

• When will I attain this goal?

• On whom do I depend to complete this goal?

Evaluation helps you determine where you may have gone wrong and how you can improve future goal setting. To do this, ask the following questions:

- What obstacles delayed the accomplishment of this goal?
- Who or what was responsible for these obstacles?
- How can these obstacles be eliminated in the future?

Exercise 2.1   Use this key to describe each of the following goals. If a goal is **not** satisfactory, more than one letter may apply. Then list five goals of your own and evaluate them.
S—Satisfactory goal
M—Measurable outcomes lacking
D—Deadline lacking
O—Others needed to achieve goal

_____ 1. Define each biology term by the first exam.

_____ 2. Know all math formulas by the end of next month.

_____ 3. Appreciate art more fully as the result of visiting an art gallery.

_____ 4. Identify the handouts that will be covered on the final exam by Tuesday.

_____ 5. Learn more about construction engineering.

_____ 6. Become a better reader.

_____ 7. Improve my English grade by one quality point by participating in a group study project before the end of the term.

_____ 8. Complete all assigned history readings by next Wednesday.

_____ 9. Read geography notes immediately following each class in order to make additions and corrections.

_____ 10. Improve my tennis grade by ten points from midterm to final by practicing with another student three days per week for the rest of the quarter.

_____ 11. _____

_____

_____

_____ 12. _____

_____

_____

_____ 13. _____

_____

_____ 14. _____

_____

_____

_____ 15. _____

_____

_____

_____

Rewarding Yourself for Completing Goals

Imagine the following: You stand in a line in the rain for several hours. You pay money for the privilege of pushing your way into a crowded room. For the next two hours, you hear loud sounds and screams. It takes you twice as long as usual to get home because of traffic jams. Would you undergo such an experience? Yes, if the event were a concert you really wanted to attend. What makes you undertake such hardships? Motivation, either internal or external. Motivation is an extension of the needs described by Maslow's hierarchy (see Figure 2.2). Motivation at each level is based on an internal and/or external reward structure (see Figure 2.3).

Internal motivation comes from within you. It is your desire to accomplish a task. It is more powerful than other forms of motivation. Perhaps your goal is to graduate and attend law school. The good grades you get when you finish a project affect your grade point average. Higher grades improve your chances of getting into law school. Internal motivation, then, corresponds to Maslow's levels of self-esteem or self-actualization.

But what if you're not interested in attending the previously described concert? You may attend to please a date or other friend. Responding to **external motivation** is working for a reason other than yourself. Responding to such needs and desires of others corresponds to Maslow's levels of approval or affection. You might also devise artificial reasons for completing your goals. These might range from getting a candy bar for completing a math assignment to a new car for finishing your degree. These correspond to Maslow's lower physical and security needs.

Behavior modification is one way to use external motivation in the form of **rewards.** To be effective, the reward should be something you really enjoy or want (for example, an ice cream cone, a movie, a walk). Thus, you substitute desire for the reward for the dread of the task.

Figure 2.3   Internal and External Rewards in Terms of Maslow's Hierarchy.

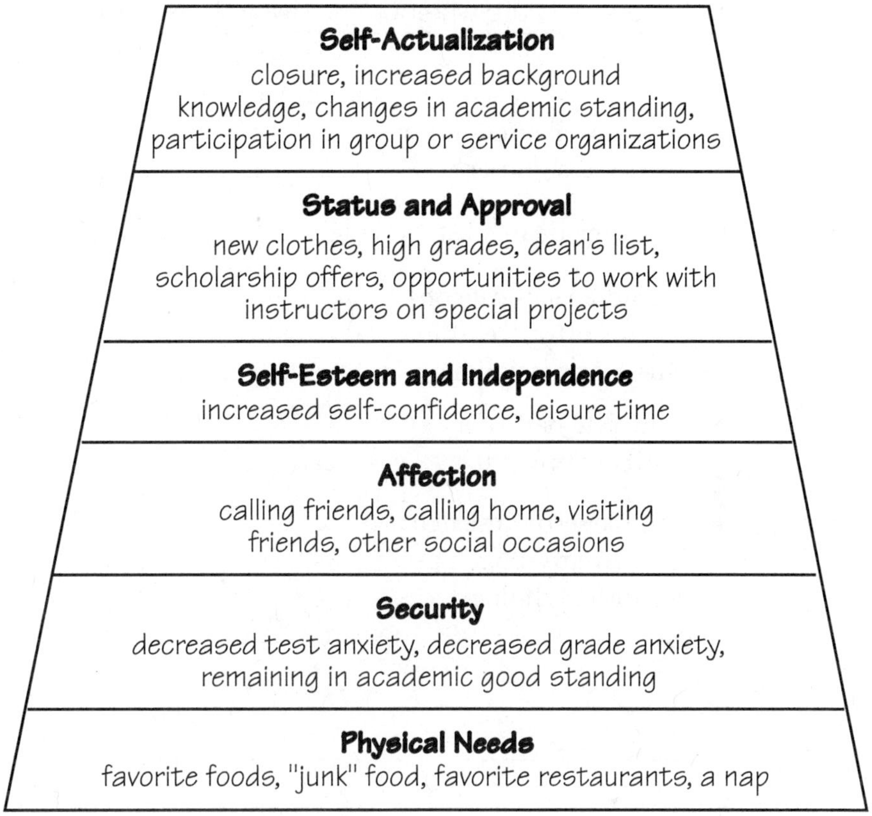

Self-Actualization
closure, increased background
knowledge, changes in academic standing,
participation in group or service organizations

Status and Approval
new clothes, high grades, dean's list,
scholarship offers, opportunities to work with
instructors on special projects

Self-Esteem and Independence
increased self-confidence, leisure time

Affection
calling friends, calling home, visiting
friends, other social occasions

Security
decreased test anxiety, decreased grade anxiety,
remaining in academic good standing

Physical Needs
favorite foods, "junk" food, favorite restaurants, a nap

However, the reward needs to fit the task. For example, if you have a 500-page novel to read for English, your reward should be great enough to make yourself complete the book (for example, a movie). If your task is to summarize a three-page article, an ice cream cone may be sufficient.

Other types of external motivation include **peer pressure** and punishment. By telling a friend you plan to accomplish a certain task by a certain time, you pressure yourself to perform. If you do not complete the task, you face your friend's disapproval, as well as your own. A final form of external motivation is punishment. Here, you take privileges (for example, going out with friends, having dessert, attending a ball game) from yourself if you fail to finish a task. This form of external motivation is generally ineffective and is not recommended. Unless you're a masochist, you won't punish yourself.

Exercise 2.2 Decide whether each of the following tasks is a short- or long-term goal. Identify an appropriate reward for each task. Indicate whether the reward is external or internal. Then identify five tasks that you need to complete. Identify an appropriate reward for each task. Indicate whether the reward is external or internal.

Task	Short-/Long-Term Goal	Reward	Internal/External Motivation
1. Read six chapters for a history assignment	_____	_____	_____
2. Make the dean's list	_____	_____	_____
3. Attend a classical concert for extra credit in Music Appreciation	_____	_____	_____
4. Complete half of a math assignment	_____	_____	_____
5. Complete the research for a twenty-page paper for psychology class	_____	_____	_____

Your Tasks

1. _____	_____	_____	_____
2. _____	_____	_____	_____
3. _____	_____	_____	_____
4. _____	_____	_____	_____
5. _____	_____	_____	_____

IMPLEMENTING YOUR GOALS

Examine the chart below. It contains the numbers one through eighty. Giving yourself one minute, circle in numerical order as many numbers as you can.

76	4	48	28	64	5	77	33	53	45
56	32	16	44	72	17	37	69	29	1
20	36	8	24	52	21	61	13	57	49
68	60	12	80	40	9	41	65	25	73
3	67	47	79	23	70	22	38	14	54
19	31	55	51	71	6	62	2	46	50
59	7	63	27	39	74	10	42	66	26
35	75	15	43	11	78	18	34	30	58

How many numbers did you circle?

Now examine the next figure. It is the same as the preceding figure except that it has been divided into four quadrants. The number *1* can be found in the upper right quadrant, the number 2 in the lower right, the number *3* in the lower left, the number *4* in the upper left, and so on.

Now, giving yourself one minute, circle in numerical order as many numbers as you can.

76	4	48	28	64	5	77	33	53	45
56	32	16	44	72	17	37	69	29	1
20	36	8	24	52	21	61	13	57	49
68	60	12	80	40	9	41	65	25	73
3	67	47	79	23	70	22	38	14	54
19	31	55	51	71	6	62	2	46	50
59	7	63	27	39	74	10	42	66	26
35	75	15	43	11	78	18	34	30	58

How many numbers did you circle?

Knowing the plan in which the numbers are arranged aided you in your second attempt. Having a plan and implementing it is equally important in managing a term, a week, or a day.

MANAGING A TERM

The first thing to do to manage a school term is to get a calendar for the months during that term and a college catalog. The purpose of setting up this calendar is to get an overview of long- term goals and commitments. This aids you in planning your short-term and daily activities. Your calendar should include recreational as well as serious commitments. Table 2.5 provides steps for constructing a term calendar.

Table 2.5   Steps in Completing a Term Calendar

1. Obtain a college catalog for the current term, a monthly calendar, and course outlines.

2. Use the catalog to do the following:
   a. Record any holidays, school vacations, or social commitments.
   b. Record midterm and final exam dates.
   c. Record dates for dropping and adding courses, and so on.

3. Use your course outlines to complete the following:
   a. Record test dates.
   b. Record due dates for papers or other projects.
   c. Set up deadlines for completing phases of lengthy projects.

4. Record important extracurricular and recreational events (for example, athletic events, concerts).

Exercise 2.3   Using a calendar for this year, label the months and days for the term in which you are currently enrolled on the following blank calendars. Using the process outlined in Table 2.5, construct a term calendar.

Monday	Tuesday	Wednesday	Thursday	Friday	Sat/Sun

Month of _____

Monday	Tuesday	Wednesday	Thursday	Friday	Sat/Sun

Month of _____

Monday	Tuesday	Wednesday	Thursday	Friday	Sat/Sun

Month of _____

Monday	Tuesday	Wednesday	Thursday	Friday	Sat/Sun

Month of _____

Monday	Tuesday	Wednesday	Thursday	Friday	Sat/Sun

Month of _____

MANAGING A WEEK

The span of time covered by a term calendar makes it unwieldy to use on a weekly or day-to-day basis. Thus, you need to review your commitments on a weekly basis. This helps you form weekly plans for managing the term.

A weekly plan consists of a weekly calendar of events and a daily to-do list. As a student, you have much to remember: course information, due dates for assignments, class meetings, appointments, and so on. Your weekly calendar of events helps you keep track of your fixed commitments. It also helps you find the most important items to record on your to-do list. Table 2.6 helps you set up your weekly calendar.

MANAGING A DAY

In managing the day, you attempt to add hours through effective time management. After you complete your weekly calendar, construct a to-do list. Then organize your goals for each day. You need to remember two

---

Table 2.6   Steps in Constructing a Weekly Calendar

1. List fixed commitments first. This includes classes, meals, sleep, travel time to class, and so on. Allow a realistic amount of time for each activity. For example, daily travel times differ according to time of day, amount of traffic, and route taken. The time it takes to get to campus during rush hour may be very different from the time it takes to get home in the middle of the afternoon.

2. Set aside a few minutes before each class to review your notes and preview that day's topic. Leave a few minutes following each class to correct and add to your notes.

3. Identify blocks of free time.

4. Look for ways to group activities and schedule these in the blocks of free time. For example, if you have two papers to write, you can complete all your library work at once and avoid making two trips.

5. Plan to complete activities before the due date to allow for unexpected delays.

6. Schedule recreational breaks.

7. Schedule time for studying. Two hours of out-of-class study for every hour of in-class time is often advised. However, this rule varies according to your expertise in the subject and the course demands of the subject. Scheduling this much study time may be difficult for someone who works full-time and/or has family commitments. If you are such a student, you need to be careful not to overburden yourself. If you see you don't have enough time, you may need to drop one or more classes.

things when setting up your daily schedule. The first is that you don't have to plan each minute of each hour of each day. The second is that you don't have to stick to your schedule like glue. Be reasonable. Allow yourself the flexibility to relax and enjoy life.

Exercise 2.4   List the courses you want to take next term in the margin and plan a schedule.

	SUN	MON	TUES	WED	THUR	FRI	SAT
6–7							
7–8							
8–9							
9–10							
10–11							
11–NOON							
NOON–1							
1–2							
2–3							
3–4							
4–5							
5–6							
6–7							
7–8							
8–9							
9–10							
10–11							
11–MIDNIGHT							
MIDNIGHT–1							
1–2							
2–3							
3–4							
4–5							
5–6							

Exercise 2.5   Develop a weekly plan for next week and a to-do list for Monday.

Weekly Planner   Week beginning_____

MONDAY _____

AM _____

_____

_____

Noon _____

_____

_____

PM _____

_____

_____

_____

TUESDAY _____

AM _____

_____

_____

Noon _____

_____

_____

PM _____

_____

_____

_____

WEDNESDAY _____

AM _____

_____

_____

Noon _____

_____

_____

PM _____

_____

_____

_____

THURSDAY _____

AM _____

_____

_____

Noon _____

_____

_____

PM _____

_____

_____

_____

FRIDAY_____

AM _____

_____

_____

Noon _____

_____

_____

_____

PM _____

_____

_____

_____

SATURDAY   **SUNDAY**_____

AM _____   _____

_____   _____

_____   _____

Noon _____   _____

_____   _____

_____   _____

PM _____   _____

_____   _____

_____   _____

_____   _____

TO DO

_____

_____

_____

_____

_____

_____

_____

_____

_____

_____

_____

_____

_____

_____

_____

_____

_____

_____

Your items on the to-do list consist of that day's commitments transferred from your weekly calendar and any items left over from the previous day. You add other items as you think of them. Your next step is to rank the items on your to-do list by numbering each item in order of its importance. Chances are you won't get to the end of your to-do list by the end of the day. That's okay. If you placed your commitments in their order of importance, then you finished the most important goals first. To obtain closure, at the end of each day update that day's to-do list and construct a new list for the next day.

Protecting Prime Study Time

Prime study time is the time of the day when you are at your best for learning and remembering. This time differs from person to person. Your best time may be early in the morning, or you may learn more easily in the afternoon or at night. You determine your prime study time by observing when you get the most accomplished, when your studying results in higher grades, or when you feel most alert and able to concentrate.

Your best time of the day should be spent either in your hardest classes or on the class work that is more important or requires the most effort. Working on the hardest or most urgent task first allows you to work on that problem when you are most alert and fresh. Your one or two most important assignments should be scheduled for this time. By completing the hardest task first, one built-in reward is that you soon get to do an easier task.

Threats to prime time include mental distractions. You may find yourself thinking of other tasks you need to do. If so, keep a pad and pen

handy to make a list of your concerns as you think of them. By doing so, you literally put your problems aside until you are free to think about them. If you find yourself daydreaming, force your mind back to the task at hand.

Physical needs also affect prime study time. If you are too hungry or too full, concentration may be affected. If this occurs, you need to study at a different time. Fatigue is another factor that hinders study. A short nap often restores your stamina and memory. In addition, a well-balanced schedule that provides adequate time for sleep or rest limits fatigue.

Some threats to prime study time are less easily controlled. For example, you may find it difficult to rid yourself of friends concerned with your social life. All too often, invitations to go out with the gang come at prime study times. The solution, although simple, is a hard one to implement. It involves saying "no" in such a way that you offend no one yet make your point clear. Sometimes it's easier just to be unavailable. Taking the phone off the hook or closing the door to your room limits your availability. Another way to solve this problem is to hang a "Do Not Disturb" sign on your door. You can get one from a motel (usually free of charge), buy one at a card or stationery store, or make your own. A final option is to hide in the library or some other out-of-the-way place. You will probably never rid yourself of all interruptions during prime study time, but you can reduce them.

Selecting a Study Site

Managing your day involves more than recognizing your best time of day. You must also manage your surroundings to maximize your study time.

The first thing you do is choose a place to study. Where you study needs to be environmentally comfortable. The temperature, furniture, and lighting should match your physical needs. If they don't, these factors will affect the quality of your work.

Where you study also should be free of distractions. It should be conducive to work, not relaxation or fun. For example, you may think the student center or your living room is a good place to review. However, if remembering information—not talking to others or watching TV—is your goal, you may be disappointed with the amount you recall later. In addition, the place you study should not hinder your alertness. Studying in bed may be comfortable but make you sleepy. Using music or television as a background for study sometimes affects your recall. If you find yourself singing along with a song or a television commercial, then your concentration leaves something to be desired.

The place you study should be free of clutter but should contain all the materials you need. Clutter affects your concentration because your eyes are drawn away from your notes. It also results in your feeling disorganized and overwhelmed. Your desktop should contain what you are studying, and nothing else. You need to distinguish between clutter and essentials, such as your text, notes, and so on. All study materials should be organized and within reach to make the best use of your prime study time.

Making One Minute Work as Two

On any one day, you may find yourself with spare minutes before you attack your next major goal. You might be waiting for the library to open, for class to begin, or for the bus to come. These spare minutes seem few when looked at separately. But when you add them up, they total more time than you would guess. Because you can't squeeze these minutes together, you need to do the next best thing. You need to develop a "quick-fix" for your free time. Table 2.7 lists some quick fixes for five-, fifteen-, and thirty-minute time periods. Once you get the idea, you'll think of others.

Table 2.7   Quick Fixes for 5-, 15-, and 30-minute Time Periods

If you have a spare five minutes, you can:
Review notes.
Update your schedule or calendar.
Skim newspaper headlines.
Make a telephone call.
Do a few sit-ups or other exercises.

If you have a spare fifteen minutes, you can:
Straighten a room.
Pay bills.
Take a walk to relax.
Survey a chapter.
Read a magazine.

If you have a spare thirty minutes, you can:
Run errands.
Begin initial library research.
Go to the grocery store.
Brainstorm and/or outline a paper.
Write a letter.

WRITE TO LEARN

Your younger brother is a junior in high school. He almost never completes assignments on time and crams for most of his exams. You think the information you've learned about managing a term and day could benefit him. On a separate sheet of paper, explain what suggestions you would give him for getting organized.

Exercise 2.6   Answer briefly but completely. Then categorize each one as five-, ten-, or fifteen-minute fixes.

1. List three times you have available for quick fixes.

_____

_____

_____

_____

2. Identify several tasks you can accomplish during these times.

_____

_____

_____

_____

_____

_____

AVOIDING PROCRASTINATION

> Putting off an easy thing makes it hard, and putting off a hard one makes it impossible.
>
> —George H. Lorimer
>
> Twentieth Century American magazine journalist

You've identified your time-management style. You've targeted the goals you want to reach. You've made a term planner, weekly schedule, and daily to-do list. Now is the time, in the words of sports company Nike, to "Just do it!" So, why **procrastinate** (put off activities until later)?

The truth is that everybody—at one time or another—procrastinates, even in light of the knowledge that doing so only makes things worse. So, why do we procrastinate? What is our motive?

Students—and others—procrastinate for a variety of reasons. One of the most common misconceptions about procrastination is that it is caused by laziness. Generally, if you've had enough drive and ambition to get to a postsecondary institution, laziness is not your problem.

In many cases, the same negative child and/or inner critic self-talk that influenced your belief in your goals also makes you procrastinate. When the child within you gains control, you avoid those tasks that seem dull, boring, or too difficult. When your inner critic gains control, you doubt your abilities, goals, and yourself. Either way, procrastination results.

The adult in you provides the voice of reason and logic. The adult knows that some tasks are no fun but that they must be completed. The adult then musters the internal motivation to begin dull and distasteful tasks and see them through. The adult must also be able to outtalk the inner critic in a stronger voice. "Yes, this is difficult, but I've been successful before." "I lack experience in this particular area, but I have similar experiences upon which I can draw." "I don't have the right background, but I can learn it." "Others have been successful, and I can be, too."

Functioning in the role of the child, the critic, or the adult affects the way you work, as well as the ways in which you perceive problems. The child's primary behavior is lack of productive activity. Conversing with friends, partying, and doing other leisure activities prevent the child from ever getting to the business at hand. Worry is the critic's chief activity. Instead of studying, the critic worries about studying. This includes such self-questioning as "Can I learn this? What if I don't? If I don't, I may fail. What if I fail? What will I do?" and "What will other people think?" Problem-solving is the adult's forte. When the adult must study, the adult thinks, "What do I have to learn? What would be the best way to learn this? Am I learning it? If not, how can I rethink my understanding?"

Finally, the adult may appear to procrastinate at times. Weighing priorities and making choices about when and what to accomplish may seem like procrastination. The difference is in the motive. If your reasoning for putting off something is sound and appropriate, it may be the best plan of action. For example, you may be considering whether or not to drop a course after the first month of class. You've regularly attended class, and you have a good grade in it. However, your financial status indicates that you need to increase your work hours. Logically, you decide that you cannot do justice to the course and work more hours. What appears to be procrastination is actually a logical decision based on the reality of the situation.

GETTING STARTED

Sometimes it is hard to get started on a project or an assignment, and this leads to procrastination. This problem surfaces in several ways, and each way requires its own solution. First, if a project seems too large or complex, you should cut it down to size. For example, you might have to design a school as a project for an architecture class. As a whole, the project might overwhelm you until you divide it into manageable parts. This might consist of researching the needs of the school, determining the price limitations, drawing a bubble diagram, and so on. In other words, use time management to locate the overall goal of the project and the steps needed to complete it. Second, you may not think of yourself as good at thinking of ideas for creative assignments (like speeches, and English themes). Brainstorming with others, asking your instructor for suggestions, or researching several topics to find one of interest often solves this problem. A final reason for procrastination is that the assignment may be beyond your skills in the subject. This occurs for any one of several reasons. You may have been ill or absent from class. Your high school preparation in the subject may have been inadequate. In any case, you can cope with this lack in skills by going to the campus learning lab, arranging for tutoring, or contacting your instructor.

Exercise 2.7   Think of the last major assignment you completed. List below any problems you faced getting started, how you solved these problems, and other solutions you could use in the future when similar problems arise.

Type of assignment: _____

_____

Problems getting started: _____

_____

_____

_____

_____

_____

Solutions: _____

_____

_____

_____

_____

_____

Other alternatives: _____

_____

_____

_____

_____

_____

ACHIEVING CLOSURE

Closure is the positive feeling you get when you finish a task. Lack of closure results in the panicked feeling that you still have a million things to do.

One way to obtain closure is to divide a task into manageable goals, list them, and check them off your list as you finish them. For example, suppose your history teacher assigns three chapters to be read. If your goal is to read all three chapters, you may feel discouraged if you don't complete the reading at one time. A more effective way to complete the assignment is to divide the reading into smaller goals by thinking of each chapter as a separate goal. Thus, you experience success as you complete each chapter. Although you failed to complete the overall goal, you know you've progressed toward it.

"I think Harry's taking this concept of closure too literally."

A second block to obtaining closure is unfinished business. You may have several tasks with the same deadline. Although changing from one task to another serves as a break, changing tasks too often wastes time. Each time you switch, you lose momentum. You may be unable to change mental gears fast enough. You may find yourself thinking about the old project when you should be concentrating on the new one. In addition, when you return to your first task, you have to review where you were and what steps were left for you to finish.

Often you solve this problem by determining how much time you have free to work. If the time available is short (that is, an hour or less), you need to work on only one task. Alternate tasks when you have more time. Completing one task or a large portion of a task contributes to the feeling of closure.

Sometimes, when working on a long-term project, other tasks take precedence before the first one is completed. If this occurs, take time to write a few notes before moving on to the new task. Your notes could include the goal of the task and a list of questions to be answered or objectives to be completed. References, papers, and other materials concerning the task should be stored together, so you know where to begin when you return to it.

WRITE TO LEARN

``25 OR 6 TO 4''

Waiting for the break of day,
Searching for something to say,
Flashing lights against the sky,
Giving up, I close my eyes.
Sitting cross-legged on the floor,
Twenty five or six to four.
Staring blindly into space,
Getting up to splash my face,
Wanting just to stay awake,
Wondering how much I can take.
Should I try to do some more,
Twenty five or six to four.
Feeling like I ought to sleep,
Spinning room is sinking deep,
Waiting for the break of day,
Searching for something to say,
Twenty five or six to four;
Twenty five or six to four.
—ROBERT LAMM

Copyright © 1970 Lamminations Music and Aurelius Music. Printed with permission. All rights reserved.

Robert Lamm's song ``25 or 6 to 4'' tells of the plight of a person facing a deadline for writing music lyrics. The narrator faces a dilemma common to many college students. Should he continue working? Should he give up and get some sleep? Working against the clock often results from poor time management. Effective time management usually prevents a last-minute race with deadlines.

On a separate sheet of paper, write a song or poem similar to ``25 or 6 to 4'' describing a situation in which you are writing a paper or studying for a test. Include information on procrastination, motivation, and closure.

AVOIDING BURNOUT

Sometimes you procrastinate because you are burned out. **Burnout** results when you work without breaks. Burnout is unusual in that its causes are the same as its symptoms. Fatigue, boredom, and stress are all signs of burnout.

A balance between break time and work time helps you avoid burnout. Therefore, you need to plan for breaks, as well as study time. A break does not have to be recreational. It simply can be a change from one task to another. For example, switching from working math problems to reading a book for English relieves boredom. Such planning also decreases interruptions during prime study time.

"Another classic case of student burnout."

Another way to avoid burnout is to leave flexibility in your daily schedule. If you schedule commitments too tightly, you won't complete your goals and achieve closure. This defeats you psychologically because you fail to do what you planned.

Excerpt 2.1   Overcoming the Deadline Dodge by Barbara Smalley

- George, a junior at Queens College, rarely takes tests on time. Instead he invents a different excuse for each exam and begs for a second chance.

- Jim, a graduate student at the University of California at Berkeley, hasn't been seen on campus for months. "I'm avoiding my adviser," he explains, "because of all the outstanding commitments to him that I have."

- Kevin, a recent graduate of the City University of New York, is washing dishes because he has postponed making a career choice. "I always thought choosing a career would just happen, and I was having too much fun in school to think about it. One of these days I'll take a career- planning seminar," he vows.

Sound familiar? After teaching and counseling students for more than a decade, William Knaus, psychologist and author of *Do It Now: How to Stop Procrastinating,* estimates that a whopping 95 percent of college students put things off to some degree. And of that number, he says, some 25 percent are *chronic* procrastinators. "These are the ones who end up dropping out. Others finish school but begin postponing assignments when they're out on their own and no longer have the structure of college to rely on."

Procrastination on campus usually means that you delay doing a task that you have agreed to complete. Although the casual procrastinator postpones tasks *sporadically* and the chronic one does so *habitually,* Knaus points out that the differences between the two are not just a matter of degree. "Hard-core procrastinators usually have anxiety problems, may be depressed, or may suffer from acute self-doubt." And though casual delayers may start by putting off tasks now and then, many soon find themselves with a serious procrastination problem. "It's like being on a vicious merry-go-round," he explains, "because postponing tasks, even occasionally, can cause anxiety, self-doubt, and depression, which in turn provide the victim with even greater reasons to procrastinate."

Why You Put Off Projects

Procrastination can be remedied, but the cure often lies in first figuring out exactly why you are unable to complete your projects on time.

Are You Just Plain Afraid?

Fear and anxiety cause many students to dodge deadlines. "Ask me to give a speech, and I'll do fine," says Luann Culbreth, a graduate student at Georgia State University, "but I'm so intimidated by grammar that I can't seem to get started on a writing assignment."

Actually, procrastinators often spend more time worrying about tasks than they would actually use completing them, reports Knaus. Thus the trick to breaking through the anxiety barrier is to stop worrying and start working. Practicing Knaus's "five-minute plan" is a good way to begin. It requires that you commit five minutes to a task that you have been putting off. When the time is up, decide if you can handle another five minutes of it. Chances are that you will have built up enough momentum to forge ahead.

Do You Feel Overwhelmed?

You have to take a biology test, turn in a history paper, and give a speech during the same week, but you are so behind that you don't know where to begin. Knaus advises setting mini-goals and deadlines for each project. "The satisfaction of accomplishing each small step should keep you going." The same principle holds if you are faced with a single but colossal project. First slice the task into more manageable pieces, then set up a schedule of clear and achievable goals.

Are You a Perfectionist?

Surprisingly, perfectionists are especially vulnerable to procrastination. "They are terrified of getting anything less than 100 percent, because the tiniest flaw means an entire assignment is no good," claims Dr. David Burns, author of *Feeling Good: The New Mood Therapy* and *Intimate Connections.* Some perfectionists have trouble starting projects because they have set impossibly high standards. (Their rationale: "If I don't start, I can't fail.") Others refuse to recognize when a task is complete.

Burns concedes that if you are a perfectionist, you may require counseling to change, but he suggests that you try this introspective exercise in an attempt to do so on your own: "Make a list of the pros and cons of behaving flawlessly. Though there may be some pluses to being perfect, those are likely to be outweighed by a host of disadvantages that prevent you from growing and experimenting both with your schoolwork and in your personal life." The standards you have set for yourself, after all, are *guidelines* and not absolutes.

Are You Unable to Concentrate?

The environment in which you work can have an enormous effect on both your attitude and your productivity. Thus it pays to analyze *where* you typically study. "Students who work on cluttered desks and in areas open to a mass of interruptions are particularly prone to procrastination," says Knaus. He suggests that you choose a quiet workplace with room to spread out, stock it with reference materials you use regularly, and spend a few minutes setting goals. "Most people don't want to waste time getting organized, but spending 10 to 15 minutes a day doing so will save you hours of frustration later."

Do You Feel Indecisive?

Sometimes an uncertainty about your major or a strong desire to do something other than attend college can cause apathy, indecisiveness, and in turn, procrastination. When offered a one-month professional directing job, Natasha Shishkevish quit school 11 credits short of receiving her theater degree from Towson State University. "I fully intended to resume my studies afterward, but I just never got around to it."

Shishkevish has since held enough low-paying and unchallenging jobs to motivate her to return to college. "I'm finally happy with my career choice, and now that I've seen what work is like, I think I can discipline myself to do well in school."

But the transition between college and career may not be that easy for those whose habitual tardiness stems from a desire to be noticed. "I get more attention from professors when I have an excuse for being *late* with assignments than I do when I turn them in on time," admits one student. Although professors who accept excuses from students are merely reinforcing such behavior, students who squeak by on professorial pardons in school won't function well on the job. "Unless a company rides on you and your abilities," reports Knaus, "it simply won't put up with procrastination that causes a work slowdown."

When Postponing Isn't a Problem

Because setting priorities requires postponing activities and assignments, in some cases procrastination makes sense. "If you truly work better in spurts of massed time," admits Knaus, "holding off to do a term paper in the last week of a semester may work fine. Or if you forget things quickly, last-minute cramming rather than studying for days or weeks in advance of an exam may save you time and trouble."

How then can you tell when your stalling is "legit?" Knaus advises that you learn the difference between procrastination and a "strategic delay." Kim Bogert, for example, has purposefully put off taking freshman English in her first year at Northern Virginia Community College. "It's my worst subject," she explains, "and knowing that adjusting to college would be difficult in itself, I figured, why add more pressure up front?"

Because Bogert's postponement is not a cover-up for something like a fear of failure, Knaus believes her actions qualify as a sound strategy. "In each case you need to apply the definition of procrastination—putting off a relevant activity that *can* be and properly *should* be done today," he says. "Also, since most procrastinators tend to be self-cons, you should always be on the alert for irrational excuses."

New York career counselor and management consultant Janice LaRouche provides another clue. "Procrastination is a problem when you know you'll end up paying a high price as a result." For some, experiencing feelings of guilt for turning in mediocre work is too costly; others balk at receiving "incomplete" or failing grades.

Help Is on the Way

If you're prone to needless procrastination, psychologists and counselors suggest practicing these techniques:

- *Pinpoint where your delays typically start.* "Most procrastinators follow a pattern," Knaus reveals. Determine whether you put off beginning a project, fizzle out at the halfway point, or fade in the homestretch. After examining your behavior, become totally committed to altering it.

- *Discipline yourself to use your time wisely.* "Procrastinators are very bad at telling time," says Dr. Richard Beery, a procrastination workshop leader at the University of California at Berkeley. Most underestimate the time it takes to complete an assignment. Successful time management involves setting realistic deadlines, allowing extra hours for the unexpected, learning to use bits of time, and sticking steadfastly to your timetable.

- *Set priorities by making a list.* Force yourself to devote most of your efforts to the number-one task on that list. "Most procrastinators go to the bottom of the list," claims Knaus. "They'll have a history test and study biology instead."

- *Set a deadline and ask someone to hold you accountable for it.* In tight situations, promise to give up something meaningful if you fail to meet your goal. Pledging your front-row concert tickets to your roommate, for instance, might bring newfound motivation.

- *Beware of the inaction-exertion-inaction cycle.* Don't postpone a task and then become so immersed in playing catch-up that you become burned out and postpone your next assignment. Alternate periods of work with stretches of rest and recreation to prevent this vicious circle.

- *Don't wait until you finish a project to reward yourself.* "Most procrastinators value only the finished product," says Dr. Beery. "People need to realize that intermediate steps are also accomplishments."

Most important, says Knaus, procrastinators must learn that it's *not* terrible to feel uncomfortable. "There are a lot of unpleasant things in life that must be done," he stresses. "The more people are willing to tackle those tasks, the more those jobs become less bothersome—and more routine."

SOURCE: Smalley, Barbara S. (1985, December–January). ``Overcoming the Deadline Dodge.'' *Campus Voice*, pp. 55–56.

WRITE TO LEARN

Read the preceding essay by Barbara Smalley entitled ''Overcoming the Deadline Dodge.'' On a separate sheet of paper, respond to the following question. How do Knaus's five reasons for why you put off projects and six techniques identified in the section ''Help Is on the Way'' relate to Catalano's description of the child, critic, or adult?

PLANNING FOR THE FUTURE: SCHEDULING SUBSEQUENT SEMESTERS

If what you want out of life requires postsecondary coursework, certification, or a graduation diploma, you will probably remain in a postsecondary institution for several terms or years. The way you organize your subsequent semesters affects the success you achieve in them. Enrollment as a full- or part-time student, organization of your class day and week, and your need to explore institutional options are factors for you to consider as you make your scheduling decisions for the future.

FULL-TIME VERSUS PART-TIME STATUS

You have the choice of being a **full-time student** or a **part-time student.** Full- time enrollment usually means twelve or more hours in a quarter or semester system. This seems like a ridiculously short amount of time to be in class if you're used to a full-time 40-hour work week or a traditional high school schedule. The difference lies in where your work—in this case, your learning—is accomplished. Most high schools and employers expect you to work during class or on the job. In postsecondary education, most of the work you'll accomplish occurs on your own, after you leave the classroom. Some people say you should spend two hours out of class for every hour you are in class. Thus, for a fifteen-hour schedule, you spend thirty hours in study. Fifteen plus thirty equals forty-five hours per week, more than a full-time job. Of course, such estimates are just that—estimates. Perhaps you love math and finish an assignment in twenty minutes. On the other hand, you may be less proficient in English and spend six hours writing a two-page paper. The time you spend in learning must match your strengths and weaknesses, as well as your goals and priorities. Still, a full-time class schedule is generally a full-time job and should be approached in that manner.

Whether you enroll full time or not depends on your other commitments. If you work, have family responsibilities, or are involved in other fixed activities, then the number of courses you can successfully complete may be limited. Course difficulty also affects the total number of hours you schedule. If courses are less difficult, more can be scheduled. Another factor to consider is how experienced you are in a given subject or as a postsecondary student. A French course will be easier for students who have had previous course work in French or previous postsecondary experience.

SCHEDULING YOUR CLASS DAY AND WEEK

In the fifth century B.C.E., Solon, a wise lawmaker said, "Nothing in excess." That philosophy holds true for many experiences. Overwork leads to exhaustion. Overspending results in high bills. Too much food causes a stomachache. Even too much information is hard to digest at one time.

College classes often cause such information overloads. Because much of your learning occurs outside of class, the time you spend in class is especially valuable. Your professors may highlight only the most important concepts. They might elaborate on information found in assigned readings. They may shape and refine your understanding. They may focus on application, analysis, and synthesis of ideas. No matter how they approach their courses, they generally have one thing in common. They concentrate the information presented in class. The information you add through more reading, study, and thought dilutes it for your understanding. Because the concentration of information is so strong, packing idea upon idea often results in forgetfulness and confusion. After three classes in a row, you may find it hard to recall what occurred in the first. As a result, you spend additional time outside of class trying to figure out just what went on. Filling your class weeks and days often helps you solve information overload problems.

Some institutions schedule classes on alternating days so that a class meets two or three days per week. Some students think that by scheduling courses for only two or three days a week, they have time for concentrated study. Often this results in their being overworked and burned out on class days. They spend free days recuperating, rather than studying. If you do not work or have other fixed commitments, you should schedule your classes throughout the week.

A good schedule fills the day as well as the week. Time between classes gives you opportunities to consciously and subconsciously reflect on information. Reviewing information as soon as possible after class provides you with time to think through a lecture while the information is still fresh. Connections among information can be made before you have to go to another class and listen to another concentrated lecture.

Your most difficult courses should be scheduled during the times you are most alert. If you like getting up early, then morning is the time for your most difficult course. If you do your best work after lunch, then schedule your most difficult classes at that time. If you schedule classes on alternating days, consider the level of difficulty or your interest in a course. These factors affect the length of time you can concentrate. If you are very interested in a course or if a course is easy for you, then you can schedule it for longer time periods.

FLEXIBILITY IN SCHEDULING

The old adage "First things first" doesn't always apply to choosing your classes. Of course, certain courses must be taken in sequence. Some are prerequisites for courses that you'll need in the future. Few curricula, however, are completely rigid. Generally, the outline of courses in a catalog is just a suggested way to divide coursework into years or terms (semesters or quarters), rather than a requirement. Thus, you have a great deal of flexibility in choosing when to take many of your courses.

While it would be wonderful if you liked and wanted to take every course in your curriculum, that is rarely the case. No matter what your major, you'll probably take some courses in which you feel you have little initial interest. In addition, based on your aptitudes and abilities, some courses will be more difficult for you than others. Too many difficult courses often overwhelm even the best students. Courses that you perceive as uninteresting may lead you to the conclusion that higher education as a whole is not worth the effort. Scheduling flexibility forms the solution to both problems. Your schedule should include courses that you look forward to attending, as well as those in which you have less interest. You should also balance difficult with easier coursework.

Changes in your personal life can change your scheduling priorities. Perhaps you are an athlete. You may want to schedule more difficult classes during the terms in which your team is less active. Maybe you know that a family member will have surgery during a particular term so you adjust your schedule accordingly. You might have a job, hobby, or other interest with predictable highs and lows in effort during the year. You can accommodate such changes through flexible scheduling and thus affect how well you manage your time during the term.

Finally, flexibility in scheduling helps you choose from whom, as well as when, you will take a course. Interactions with faculty form one of the greatest benefits of a college career. Upper-class students often provide insights into who is considered to be the most outstanding teacher in the field. In addition, many student government associations monitor faculty performance and make the results available to students. These two sources provide you with views of how a professor is seen by other students. Once you decide whom you want for a specific course, you must determine when that person teaches that course. Faculty course loads vary by term. Although a specific instructor may or may not teach the same courses each term, course assignments are usually made a term, and sometimes a year, in advance. Thus, you can often find out when a specific person will be teaching and take advantage of the best that your institution has to offer.

UNDECIDED MAJORS: EXPLORING INSTITUTIONAL OPTIONS

If you have not decided on a major, you may fear that your indecision will be costly in terms of time (and money). This does not have to be the case. In most **curricula,** the first year consists of general coursework. Even in more specialized curricula, if you carefully select your courses, you can avoid wasting time. Thus, through careful scheduling you can maintain academic progress while keeping all your options open.

For example, consider Fred. Fred is undecided whether to major in business administration, chemical engineering, or criminal justice. Using the curriculum guides suggested in Table 2.8, Fred plans to take English 101, Math 121, Chemistry 101, Speech 161, and Geography 100. All of the courses Fred selected apply to any of the three majors he is considering.

All three curricula require English 101. Business administration and criminal justice require Math 121. It is also the prerequisite math course needed in engineering. Engineering requires chemistry, whereas the other two accept any science course. Both business and criminal justice require Speech 161. Which is an elective in engineering. Geography is required for criminal justice. It is a general elective in the other two.

One way you make more informed choices about a major is to take trial courses. Such introductory courses provide an overview of the subject area. They consist of general information about many related topics. These courses, if in a general field of study, can often be used as **free elective** credits. If more specialized, they can be considered as an investment in your career choice.

Table 2.8   Curriculum Guides

Business Administration	Chemical Engineering	Criminal Justice
Business 101	Chem. 101; 102; 121	Geog. 100 or Hist. 103
English 101; 102	English 101; 102	Crim. Justice 107
Math 121; 122	Math 155; 156***	Math 115 or 121
Science Electives*	Physics 121	Science Electives*
Speech 161 or 162	General Electives**	English 101; 102
General Electives**	Engineering 104	Speech 161

*Choose from Biology, Physics, Botany, Zoology, Chemistry
**Choose from Art, Foreign Language, Geography, History, Music, Speech
***Prerequisite courses are Math 121, 122

Again consider Fred. Fred can find out more about his chosen fields by taking trial courses. Taking Business 101, Engineering 104, or Criminal Justice 107 would help Fred learn about each career. However, if Fred takes too long or takes too many trial courses, he will hinder his academic progress. Thus, he needs to take these courses within the first year or so.

Many undecided students delay making career decisions because they mistakenly think that their majors must exactly match the career they desire. That's true for some careers. If you want to be a druggist, you must major in pharmacy. If you want to be a librarian, you need to major in library science. If you want to be a chemist, you need to major in chemistry. On the other hand, some jobs do not require specific majors. You can major in English or business and still be a lawyer, a journalist, or a secretary. Your career decision then, although important, is not a decision that cannot be changed.

Every day, someone makes a career move—to a different job, to a related career, or to an entirely different field. Changing majors may ultimately result in your spending an additional semester or two in school. In comparison to the twenty to forty years you will spend in the work force, this time becomes a very brief investment in your future.

If you have not declared your major, you need to learn more about your goals and explore various career options. When you use your time learning about yourself, taking advantage of campus resources, and finalizing a career decision, your time is well spent.

Excerpt 2.2   Majors Just Don't Matter That Much   By William Raspberry

---

Soon to every fledgling student comes the moment to decide. But since Angela's a freshman, my advice is: Let it ride.

WASHINGTON—With apologies to James Russell Lowell, that is pretty much my counsel to my daughter, who is about to begin her first year in college. Soon enough, she'll have to face the sophomore necessity of choosing a major—whether or not she's decided on a career. In the meantime, I tell her, don't worry about it.

A part of the reason for my advice is the memory of my own struggle to decide on a major. I eventually had four of them, none of them related to what was to become my career.

But the more important reason is my conclusion, regularly reinforced, that majors just don't matter that much.

The latest reinforcement is from John Willson, a history professor at Michigan's Hillsdale College, who, having heard once too often the question "But what do I do with a history major?" has decided to do what he can to put his students at ease.

"Every sophomore has a majoring frenzy," he wrote in a campus publication. "It is typical for sophomores to say, 'I want to be an anchorman. Therefore I will major in journalism. Where do I sign up?.' They act like they have had a blow to the solar plexus when I say, a) Hillsdale has no major in journalism, and b) if we did, it would no more make you an anchorman than a major in English makes you an Englishman."

But rather than simply repeating what professionals already know, or urging colleges to dispense with the requirement for declaring a major, Willson has reduced his advice to a set of rules and principles.

The first, which college students often find incredible, is that aside from such vocational courses as engineering or computer science, any relationship between majors and careers is largely incidental. Physics majors are hardly more likely to become physicists than business majors to become entrepreneurs. The rule that derives from this principle:

If you wanted your major to be practical, you should have gone to the General Motors Institute.

The second principle is that students (and colleges) should delay the necessity of choosing for as long as practicable. "Most students (and even more parents) have rather vague notions of what the subject of any given subject is. . . . Talk with your parents, but don't let parents, teachers, media experts, television evangelists or fraternity brothers pressure you into a majoring frenzy before you know what the major is all about." In short:

All things being equal, it is best to know what you are talking about, which may even prevent majoring frenzies.

The third is a quote from the Rev. James T. Burtchaell (writing in "Notre Dame" magazine): "Pick your major on the pleasure principle, for what you most enjoy studying will draw your mind in the liveliest way to being educated."

The rule: People do not get educated by hitting themselves over the head with hammers.

It's good advice, and not only for students at small liberal-arts colleges. A few years ago, the University of Virginia published a booklet, "Life after Liberal Arts," based on a survey of 2,000 alumni of its college of arts and sciences.

The finding: 91 percent of the respondents not only believe that liberal arts prepared them for fulfilling careers but would not hesitate to recommend liberal-arts majors to students considering those same careers.

Those who responded to the survey included a biology major who later earned a master's of business administration and became president of a bank, a psychology major who was a well-paid executive, and English majors whose careers embraced television sales, editorial production, systems analysis and law.

The "winning combination" derived from the Virginia survey: a liberal-arts foundation, complemented with career-related experience and personal initiative. Colleges aren't assembly lines that, after four years, automatically deposit students into lucrative careers. What is far likelier is a series of false starts followed by the discovery of a satisfying career. In the Virginia survey, for example, only 16 percent reported being happy with their first jobs.

Willson's advice, the results of the University of Virginia survey, and my advice to Angela come down to the same thing: Major in getting an education.

SOURCE: Reprinted by permission of Washington Post © 1990.

WRITE TO LEARN

Read the essay by William Raspberry. On a separate sheet of paper, respond to the following: What three principles does he give for declaring a major? What is your opinion concerning the validity of these principles? Would you follow them? Why or why not? Explain the meaning of the phrase "Major in getting an education." Do you agree? Why or why not?

Exercise 2.8   Below are curricula guides for the freshman year (fall and spring semesters). Unless otherwise stated, assume that all courses are three-hour credit courses and that specific subject area courses must be taken in sequence (e.g., English 101 before 102). Use the curricula to answer the questions that follow.

PRE-MED
English 101, 102
Chemistry 100, 110
Chemistry lab 105, 115 (1 credit hour)
Zoology 101, 102 or Biology 101, 102
3 hours of any foreign language
Any 100-level history course
Math 121, 122

MUSIC
English 101, 102
Approved science electives*
Music Theory 170
Approved math electives**
   (6 credit hours)
Music History 101, 110
Approved general electives***
   (6 credit hours)

COMPUTER SCIENCE
English 101, 102
Approved science electives*
   (6 credit hours)
Math 121, 122
Approved general electives***
   (6 credit hours)
6 hours of any foreign language

ELEMENTARY EDUCATION
English 101, 102
Biology 101, 102 or Zoology 101, 102 or Botany 101, 102
History 101, 103
Math 109, 110, or any higher-level course
Education 101
Speech 100
Psychology 105

HOME ECONOMICS
English 101, 102
Chemistry 100, 110
Chemistry lab 105, 115 (1 credit hour)
Home Economics 101, 102
Math 114, 115 or Math 121, 122
Speech 100
Psychology 105

BUSINESS (Pre-Law Option)
English 101, 102
Approved science electives*
   (6 credit hours)
Math 121, 122
Approved general electives***
   (6 credit hours)
Speech 101
History 101, 103

*Approved science electives: Choose from Biology 101, 102; Botany 101, 102; Zoology 101, 102; Chemistry 100, 110; Geology 105, 110; Astronomy 111, 112

**Approved math electives: Choose from Math 109, 110, 121, 122, 155, 157

***Approved general electives: Choose any art, foreign language, music, psychology, sociology, history, geography.

1. You want to major in music or computer science. You have a job and will only be taking nine hours this semester. What schedule would give you coursework that will apply toward either major?

    _____

    _____

    _____

2. You are a transfer student with credits in English 101 and 102, Math 121, and Speech 101. You want to take fifteen to sixteen hours this semester. You want a pre-law or a pre-med degree. What should you take?

    _____

    _____

    _____

3. You plan to major in home economics, elementary education, or music. You want to take twelve hours. What could you take that would apply to all three programs?

    _____

    _____

    _____

4. You are completely undecided about a major. Which of these freshman-level courses could apply to any of the curricula?

    _____

    _____

    _____

5. Which of the courses apply only to the curriculum in which they are found?

    _____

    _____

    _____

MAINTAINING BALANCE

You're doing it all: full-time student, fraternity member, part-time employee, participant in intramural sports, scholarship student, president of a service organization, and member of the debate team. How do you do it?

You're doing it all, too: full-time student, full-time parent, part-time employee, active member of a church or synagogue, scholarship student, treasurer of the Spanish Club, and member of a student Union committee. How do you manage everything?

Most students feel overwhelmed by the number of roles they hold. The truth is, you can't do it all and do it well. At some point, you must reevaluate your goals and reset priorities according to what's important to you. Your goal is to achieve balance . . . not lose your balance!

Unrealistic expectations may contribute to your situation. Perhaps you plan to finish your coursework in four years or graduate with a 4.0 average. If you are a traditional freshman student who begins college at age seventeen or eighteen, this means that you will finish at age twenty-one or twenty-two. And then what? You get to work for the rest of your life! If you work until you're sixty-five, this means you will be working for the next forty-three or forty-four years. If you get involved in a wide range of campus activities, you gain valuable experience although your stay in postsecondary education lengthens. An extra year means you still get to work for the next forty- two or forty-three years. In terms of grades, some goals (for example, professional postgraduate programs and fellowships) require a show of academic excellence. While grades are important, many employers prefer to see a prospective employee that can handle a variety of tasks other than academic pursuits. Whatever your goals, consider them in terms of your life goals. If additional postsecondary experiences enhance your life and your chances of gaining employment after you graduate, they may be a trade-off well worth your consideration.

Exercise 2.9   Use Sample Chapter 11 (Personal Values, Career Planning, and Success with People at Work) to respond to the following questions.

1. Read the section "Key Idea 1: Career Planning" (pp. 510–514). How do the components involved in career planning (goals, self-evaluation, vision, and occupational information) relate to the factors involved in conceiving goals?

   _____

   _____

   _____

   _____

   _____

2. Read the section "Key Idea 4: Managing Yourself" (pp. 524–531). What aspects of this section reinforce the information about implementing goals presented in this chapter? What additional ideas does the sample chapter present that you can apply to postsecondary time management?

_____
_____
_____
_____
_____

3. Read the sections "A Case in Point: Bridget Goes Bananas" and "A Case in Point: George Landen's Short Career" (pp. 538–539). What aspects of style (personality, brain dominance, or sensory preferences) do you find in Bridget and George? How does this affect their on-the-job performance? What kind of postsecondary students do you think they would be?

_____
_____
_____
_____
_____

CHAPTER SUMMARY

1. Myers-Briggs type, brain dominance, and sensory preferences interact and affect the ways in which you manage time.

2. Goal achievement is based on first setting goals and then believing those goals are attainable.

3. The goals you set depend on your aptitudes, abilities, interests, needs, and values.

4. You develop your belief in your ability to achieve goals through positive self-talk, visualization, and action.

5. Term calendars, weekly schedules, and daily to-do lists are tools that help you implement your goals.

6. Avoiding procrastination involves positive self-talk as well as strategies for getting started, achieving closure, and avoiding burnout.

7. Factors that affect scheduling in subsequent semesters include full-time versus part-time status, the way you schedule your day and week, flexibility in scheduling, and the degree to which you explore institutional options.

8. Maintaining balance is the key to successfully managing your time and your life.

GROUP LEARNING ACTIVITY
BILL OF RIGHTS FOR GROUP MEMBERS

Time-management strategies make or break study groups. Indefinite goals contribute to group, as well as individual, procrastination. Although the group should have a long-range purpose, it should also have effective short-term goals that result in feelings of accomplishment and closure. The following bill of rights for group members requires commitment of both time and effort on the part of each person.

Bill of Rights for Study Groups

1. You have the right to limit group membership to no more than five and to dismiss members who consistently fail to meet their commitments as group members.

2. You have the right and responsibility to select a study site and time that are mutually beneficial to all members.

3. You have a right to contribute to the formation of group goals that have measurable outcomes and deadlines.

4. You have the responsibility to be an active participant, not a passive receiver, in the group process, and you have a right to expect active participation from other group members.

5. You have the right to have meetings begin and end promptly and to have study sessions without needless interruptions.

6. You have the right to participate in a group that is free from arguing and competition.

7. You have the right to expect that the group will stay on the task it sets for itself and the responsibility for helping the group do so.

8. You have the right to take a break after an extended study session as long as the group resumes its study after the break.

9. You have the right to ask group members to limit socialization or discussion of off-the-subject topics to before and after study sessions.

10. You have the right to feelings of accomplishment at (1) the end of each study session and (2) the end of the group's life span.

SOURCE: Reprinted by permission of Longman, D. L., and Atkinson, R. H. (August, 1992). *The Teaching Professor.* 2718 Dryden Dr, Madison, WI: Magna Publications.

Application

In your class study group, identify additional rights that you expect in the study group. Are there any occasions for which you might give up your rights? Which ones and why?

Application

Maintain a log of all your academic and nonacademic activities for a week. In your study group, compare logs and identify ways in which group members could use their time more effectively.

TERMS

Terms appear in the order in which they occurred in the chapter.

aptitudes
abilities
interests
needs
values
child
critic
adult
long-term goals
short-term goals
internal motivation
external motivation
behavior
   modification
rewards
peer pressure
prime study time
procrastinate
closure
burnout
full-time student
part-time student
curricula
free elective

CHAPTER REVIEW

Answer briefly but completely.

1. Describe how MBTI type, brain-dominance, and sensory preferences interact to affect time-management strategies.

   _____

   _____

   _____

   _____

   _____

2. How do aptitudes, abilities, interests, needs, and values contribute to goal formation?

   _____

   _____

   _____

   _____

3. Identify and provide an explanation of the three ways to impact your belief in your ability to achieve goals.

   _____

   _____

   _____

   _____

   _____

4. What does goal specification involve?

   _____

   _____

   _____

   _____

   _____

5. What is the relationship between Maslow's Hierarchy of Needs and internal/external motivation?

   _____

   _____

   _____

   _____

6. Describe the relationship between goal setting, term calendars, week schedules, and daily to-do lists.

_____

_____

_____

_____

_____

7. How can you avoid procrastination?

_____

_____

_____

_____

8. How can effective scheduling in subsequent semesters improve your ability to manage time? What time-management problems could arise from an ineffective semester schedule?

_____

_____

_____

_____

9. What are the advantages of being an undecided major? What are the disadvantages?

_____

_____

_____

_____

10. What does it mean to you to maintain balance as a postsecondary student?

_____

_____

_____

_____

REFERENCES

Berne, E. (1966). *Principles of group treatment.* New York: Oxford Press. New York: Simon & Schuster (2nd ed.).

Lawrence, G. (1987). *Personality types and tiger stripes* Gainesville, Fla.: Center for Applications of Psychological Type.

Maslow, A. H. (1954). *Motivation and personality.* New York: Harper & Row.

Scott, G. G. (1994). *The empowered mind.* Englewood Cliffs, NJ: Prentice Hall.

Sher, B. (1994). *I could do anything if I only knew what it was.* New York: Delacourte Press.

Vocabulary Development   Learning the Lingo with a Single Flame

The same time-management principles you need for success in higher education aid you in vocabulary development. Modifications of the suggestions for avoiding procrastination and implementing your goals result in vocabulary development without cramming or burnout.

Learning the lingo—the language of the courses you take—is an overwhelming task. You might be tempted to "burn the candle at both ends." Aside from a little more light, you won't accomplish much, and you'll run the risk of burning out twice as fast. How can you learn it all? Consider the following suggestions for managing your vocabulary development. Carrying out each individual suggestion requires relatively little time.

1.   **Preview the text glossary before attending the first class.** Invest ten or fifteen minutes in getting a sense of the language of the course. Determine whether the words seem to be general, specialized, or technical terms. (See Vocabulary Development section in Chapter 1.) Rate your general understanding of the vocabulary. Are the words all new to you? Do you recognize some words? Can you form general associations? Are you able to use any of the words?

2.   **Preview key terms before reading a text assignment.** Texts vary in the way they highlight important terms. These terms may appear in a list at a chapter's beginning or end, in a special typeface (for example, bold-face or italics), or as marginal notations (sometimes with definitions). Again, check to see if they seem to be general, specialized, or technical in nature. Consider if you've already heard the terms in a lecture. Do you have any associations with

"Frankly, aside from a little more light, I don't see what they get out of it."

SOURCE: Reprinted by permission of Bill Maul. *Phi Delta Kappan,* October 1986.

the words? How do you think they will fit into the content of the chapter?

3.   **Review key terms and concepts as soon as possible after each lecture.** After each lecture (and at least within twenty-four hours), review notes to identify key terms. How

did the terms relate to each other? How would you define the terms in your own words? How did they relate to the content of the lecture and/or reading assignment?

4. **Process terms weekly.** Recognition and memorization provide the raw materials for learning. Learning at these levels often results in a false sense of security because you think you know the information. In order to understand the language more fully, you must convert information to a form that you can use and understand. Such processing helps you become an owner, rather than a renter, of what you know. Effort forms the key. Such learning in-volves more than looking at words. It consists of active strategies to integrate information. These include mapping, charting, and creating note cards (see Chapter 6).

5. **Use terms in speaking and writing.** The old adage, "If you don't use it, you lose it" applies to vocabulary development. The words you use are those that you will retain.

6. **Don't be fooled.** Some students get misled by course content. Just because you've already had a biology class doesn't necessarily mean you already know the vocabulary as it will be applied to another biology course.

Activity 1

Using the following glossary, preview the terms and determine if they appear to be general, specialized, or technical in nature. How would you evaluate your overall understanding of these terms?

Example of a Glossary

Interpreter A high-level language translator that evaluates and translates a program one statement at a time; used extensively on microcomputer systems because it takes up less primary storage than a compiler.

Interrecord gap (IRG) A space that separates records stored on magnetic tape; allows the tape drive to regain speed during processing.

Interrupt A condition or event that temporarily suspends normal processing operations.

Inverted structure A structure that indexes a simple file by specific record attributes.

K (kilobyte) A symbol used to denote 1,024 (2^{10}) storage units (1,024 bytes) when referring to a computer's primary storage capacity; often rounded to 1,000 bytes.

Key The unique identifier or field of a record; used to sort records for processing or to locate specific records within a file.

Keypunch A keyboard device that punches holes in a card to represent data.

Keypunch operator Person who uses a keypunch machine to transfer data from source documents to punched cards.

Label A name written beside a programming instruction that acts as an identifier for that instruction; also, in spreadsheets, information used to describe some aspect of the spreadsheet.

Large-scale Integration (LSI) Method by which circuits containing thousands of electronic components are densely packed on a single silicon chip.

Laser printer A type of nonimpact printer that combines laser beams and electro-photographic technology to form images on paper.

Laser storage system A secondary storage device using laser technology to encode data onto a metallic surface; usually used for mass storage.

Librarian The person responsible for classifying, cataloging, and maintaining the files and programs stored on cards, tapes, disks, and diskettes, and all other storage media in a computer library.

Librarian program Software that manages the storage and use of library programs by maintaining a directory of programs in the system library and appropriate procedures for additions and deletions.

Light pen A pen-shaped object with a photoelectric cell at its end; used to draw lines on a visual display screen.

Linear structure A data structure in which the records in a computer file are arranged sequentially in a specified order.

Link A transmission channel that connects nodes.

Linkage editor A subprogram of the operating system that links the object program from the system residence device to primary storage.

LISP (LISt Processing) A high-level programming language commonly used in artificial intelligence research and in the processing of lists of elements.

Local system Peripherals connected directly to the CPU.

Logical file The combination of data needed to meet a user's needs.

Activity 2

Copy the terms from Sample Chapter 11, Personal Values, Career Planning and Success with People at Work. What associations do you have with these words? How do you think they fit into the chapter's content?

It's a Breeze:
Blowing Stress Away

OBJECTIVES
By the end of this chapter, you will be able to do the following:

1. Distinguish between positive and negative ways to manage stress.

2. Identify factors in maintaining wellness.

3. Identify strategies for managing test anxiety.

CHAPTER MAP

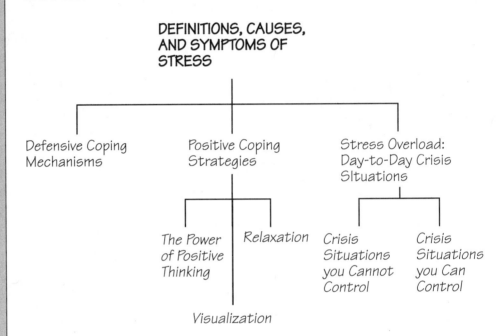

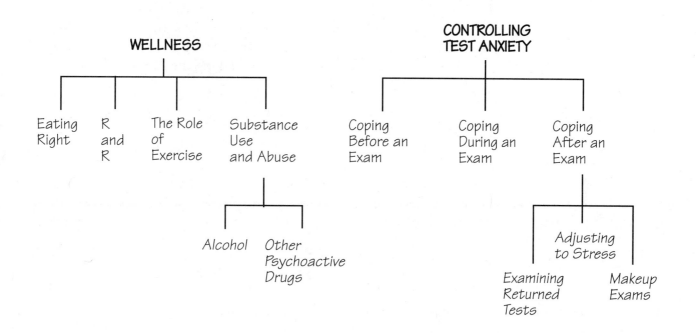

A maiden at college, Ms. Breeze,
Weighted down by B.A.s and Ph.Ds,
Collapsed from the strain.
Said her doctor, "It's plain
You are killing yourself—by degrees!"

I f like Ms. Breeze, you feel the **stress** of college life, you're not alone. Changes in your life, as well as ongoing events and activities, affect the manner in which you manage stress. The strain of getting a college degree affects all students at one time or another. You can determine how well your lifestyle protects you from stress by taking the inventory in Exercise 3.1.

Exercise 3.1   Respond to each of the following on a scale of 1 (almost always) to 5 (never), according to how much of the time each statement is true of you.

POINTS

1. I eat one hot, balanced meal a day. _____

2. I get seven to ten hours sleep at least four nights a week. _____

3. I give and receive affection regularly. _____

4. I have at least one relative or friend within fifty miles on whom I can rely. _____

5. I exercise to the point of perspiration at least twice a week. _____

6. I smoke less than half a pack of cigarettes a day. _____

7. I take fewer than five alcoholic drinks a week. _____

8. I am the appropriate weight for my height. _____

9. I have an income adequate to meet basic expenses. _____

10. I get strength from my religious beliefs. _____

11. I regularly attend club or social activities. _____

12. I have a network of friends and acquaintances. _____

13. I have one or more friends to confide in about personal matters. _____

14. I am in good health (including eyesight, hearing, teeth). _____

15. I am able to speak openly about my feelings when angry or worried. _____

POINTS

16. I have regular conversations with the people I live with about domestic problems (e.g., household responsibilities, money, and daily living issues).   _____

17. I do something for fun at least once a week.   _____

18. I am able to organize my time effectively.   _____

19. I drink fewer than three cups of coffee (or tea or cola) a day.   _____

20. I take quiet time for myself during the day.   _____

TOTAL POINTS   _____

Subtract 20   _____

FINAL SCORE   _____

SCORING: You obtain your total "stress audit" score by adding your individual scores and subtracting 20. Your lifestyle is not having a negative effect on your stress tolerance if your score is below 30. If it is between 50 and 75, you are not doing all you can for yourself to help reduce your vulnerability to stress, and you may want to consider some fine tuning. The behaviors on this questionnaire help increase stress tolerance through basic physical and emotional health and fitness; if your score is over 75, you may want to consider some substantial changes.

SOURCE: Reprinted from "Vulnerability Scale" from the *Stress Audit,* developed by Lyle H. Miller and Alma Dell Smith. © 1983, Biobehavioral Associates, Brookline, MA 02146.

DEFINITIONS, CAUSES, AND SYMPTOMS OF STRESS

You know stress by many names—pressure, worry, concern, anxiety, and nervousness, to name a few. These words probably have negative connotations to you. That's because stress hurts more often than it helps. Such stress is called **distress.** It results from many causes and includes many symptoms (see Tables 3.1 and 3.2). Nevertheless, some stress is positive. Positive stress, or **eustress,** is the energy that drives you to be your best. This happens on the playing field, in a performance, or in the classroom. Here, stress motivates and helps you to think clearly and decisively. For example, healthcare professionals face stressful emergency situations as part of their jobs. These professionals use stress to help them perform faster and better. You can harness its power to help you make better grades by using positive **coping strategies** and avoiding defensive coping mechanisms. Coping positively is a more difficult but longer-lasting and more effective solution to stress.

Table 3.1   Common Sources of Stress

Classification	Explanation
1. Intrapersonal conflict	The turmoil within you that concerns which paths to take in life including goals, values, priorities, and decisions.
2. Interpersonal relationships	Stress resulting from interaction with others (outside your family). Friends or peers are common sources of stress as you deal with the differences between you and learn to communicate and compromise.
3. Family	Although a major source of support, the family is also a source of stress because of the strength of the emotional ties among the people involved. Also, interaction among family members is more frequently of a judgmental nature.
4. Work and school demands	Stress resulting from your satisfaction with your work and meeting standards expected of you.
5. Money concerns	Always with you, especially as college students, money problems are usually not a matter of having enough to survive (although it may seem like that at times) but how to prioritize how you spend your income.
6. Global instability	In the United States, we are more isolated from the type of regional war that occurs in many other parts of the world, but conflict in another part of the globe can have immediate, deleterious effects here, particularly to students who are immigrants from that area, who are members of the armed forces, or who are related to people in the armed forces.-

---

WRITE TO LEARN

Examine the physical and psychological signs of stress in Table 3.2. On a separate sheet of paper, respond to the following: Which do you experience? How could you cope with these in the future? Which have you observed in others? What would be your advice to them?

DEFENSIVE COPING MECHANISMS

Withdrawal tends to block behaviors needed for facing and overcoming stress. You remove yourself from stressful situations by either physically or psychologically withdrawing. You can physically withdraw from

Table 3.1   Common Sources of Stress *(continued)*

Classification	Explanation
7. Environmental abuse	Stress which can come in the form of pollution (e.g., smoking in classrooms, trash in common areas), crowding (e.g., in classrooms, cafeterias, and parking lots), crime both on- and off-campus, overstimulation (especially by the media), and ecological damage.
8. Technology	Advances such as the computer are stressful because they require adaptive change and speed up the pace of life.
9. Change	Any sort of change is a source of stress, although certain changes are clearly more stressful than others. College students experience more change than do most other people. The more changes present in your life and the faster these changes come about, the greater the stress you will encounter.
10. Time pressure	Time pressures can cause stress brought on by other factors. Many students are not instinctively effective at time management.
11. Spiritual issues	Coming to terms with discovering meaning in codes of ethical and moral behavior can be stressful, especially if it involves rejecting previously held beliefs.
12. Health patterns	Illness, injury, dietary imbalances, exposure to toxic substances, and the like are fairly obvious forms of stress. The physiological stress response is often more clearly seen in these instances than in situations involving social and psychological stress.

SOURCE: Reprinted with permission from *Health Dynamics* by Boskin, Graf, and Kreisworth. Copyright © 1990 by West Publishing Company. All rights reserved.

school by dropping a class or dropping out of school, and sometimes withdrawal seems the only solution. But since you can't physically withdraw every time you face stress, you might tend to withdraw mentally or emotionally from academic stress. This psychological withdrawal constitutes a normal, and to some degree unconscious, reaction to stress. It is your psyche's attempt to soften the blow of a stressor. Such withdrawal takes place in one of several ways (see Table 3.3). Blocking the cause of stress from your memory is one way you withdraw from anxiety. Called **repression,** this method involves your doing nothing to solve the problem. You think about more pleasant things instead of whatever bothers you. **Denial** also provides a way to withdraw. Again, you fail to prepare. By denying the test's existence or its importance to

Table 3.2 Signs of Stress

Physical Signs	Psychological Signs
Pounding of the heart, rapid heart rate	Irritability, tension, or depression
Rapid, shallow breathing	Impulsive behavior and emotional instability, the overpowering urge to run and hide
Dryness of the throat and mouth	Lowered self-esteem, thoughts of failure
Raised body temperature	Excessive worry, insecurity
Decreased sexual appetite or activity	Reduced ability to communicate with others
Feelings of weakness, light-headedness, dizziness, or faintness	Increased awkwardness in social situations
Trembling, nervous tics, twitches, shaking hands and fingers	Excessive boredom, unexplained dissatisfaction with job or other normal conditions
High-pitched, nervous laughter	Increased procrastination
Stuttering and other speech difficulties	Feelings of isolation
Insomnia—that is, difficulty in getting to sleep, or a tendency to wake up during the night	Avoidance of specific situations
Grinding of teeth during sleep	Irrational fears (phobias) about specific things
Restlessness, an inability to keep still	Irrational thoughts, forgetting things more often than usual, mental ``blocks,'' missing of planned events
Sweating (not necessarily noticeably), clammy hands, cold hands and feet, chills	Guilt about neglecting family and friends, inner confusion about duties and roles
Blushing, hot face	Excessive work, omission of play
The need to urinate frequently	Unresponsiveness and pre occupation
Diarrhea, indigestion, upset stomach, nausea	Inability to organize oneself, tendency to get distraught over minor matters
Migraine or other headaches, frequent unexplained earaches or toothaches	Inability to make decisions, erratic, unpredictable judgment making
Premenstrual tension or missed menstrual periods	Decreased ability to perform different tasks
More body aches and pains than usual, such as pain in the neck or lower back or any localized muscle tension	Inability to concentrate
Loss of appetite, unintentional weight loss, increased appetite, sudden weight gain	General (``floating'') anxiety, feelings of unreality
Sudden change in appearance	A tendency to become fatigued, loss of energy, loss of spontaneous joy
Increased use of substances (tobacco, legally prescribed drugs such as tranquilizers or amphetamines, alcohol, or other drugs)	Feelings of powerlessness, mistrust of others
Accident proneness	Neurotic behavior, psychosis
Frequent illness	

SOURCE: Reprinted with permission from *Essential Life Choices* by Whitney and Sizer. Copyright © 1989 by West Publishing Company. All rights reserved.

Table 3.3	Examples of Defensive Withdrawal
Method of Withdrawal	**Typical Withdrawal Statements**
REPRESSION	''Oh, that test is next week. I'll study after my date Saturday. Where can we go? I know! We'll go see that new movie. Then, we'll eat dinner at . . . ''
DENIAL	''I'm not worried about my grade in that course—it's only an elective.''
PROJECTION	''Sure, I made a 55 percent! What did you expect? You know she gives the hardest exams in the entire math department—well, she grades the hardest anyway.''
RATIONALIZATION	''Well, I didn't have time to study for my history exam because I was so busy volunteering at the hospital. My work with disabled children is so much more rewarding than a good grade in one history course.''

you, you withdraw from the stress it creates within you. Another way to avoid stress is **projection.** Here you blame someone or something else for your failure. You refuse to accept responsibility for your actions and project that responsibility onto someone else. A fourth way to withdraw from stress is to **rationalize** for being unprepared or not making the best grade possible. Here you identify a reasonable and acceptable excuse for failure and exchange it for the more distasteful truth. Withdrawal techniques work—at best—as only a temporary check on stress.

POSITIVE COPING STRATEGIES

Fast food . . . microwaved meals . . . fax machines . . . faster computers . . . e-mail . . . cellular phones . . . beepers . . . on-line access to libraries. . . . A multitude of services and devices make our lives more efficient and provide us with instant results. Unfortunately, there is no miracle cure for stress that provides instant relief. Stress management requires a combination of effort and time. You must find personal stressors and figure out which positive coping strategies will help you manage them (see Table 3.4).

The Power of Positive Thinking

Humorist Steven Pearl once said, "I phoned my dad to tell him I had stopped smoking. He called me a quitter." For some reason, humans most often remember and believe the worst rather than the best about themselves and others. You, too, might find yourself dwelling on past

Table 3.4   Coping with Personal Stressors

Stressor	Solution
Information overload (class assignments: the number and size of them, workload, spacing of exams, assignment due dates)	• Reevaluate time-management plan. • Consider reducing course load. • Form a study group for support and assistance.
Mismatch of instructor/student learning styles	• Form a study group.
Stress carriers (peers who are also overstressed)	• Find more supportive and positive friends. • Seek out counseling services.
Self-doubts (own high expectations, family pressures, concerns about career choices, class presentations, low exam grades, academic competition)	• Practice test taking. • Avoid cramming. • Take stress-management course. • Practice relaxation exercises. • Seek counseling services. • Hire a tutor.
Interpersonal relationships (family conflicts, love decisions, social pressures, family responsibilities, sexual pressures/fears, religious conflicts, job conflicts)	• Seek counseling services. • Talk to family and friends. • Examine values and priorities.
Intrapersonal conflicts (social anonymity, loneliness, depression, anxiety)	• Seek counseling services. • Attend campus activities. • Join postsecondary organizations. • Volunteer your services.
Financial concerns	• Investigate campus loans, grants, and scholarships. • Share expenses. • Cut current expenses. • Seek additional employment.

embarrassments, problems, and failures. In similar situations, you think that the same disasters will recur. Your anxiety mounts, you lose confidence, and the cycle repeats itself.

Anxiety about coursework is one of these cyclical processes. When prompted, you feel pressure from within and without. You lack the confidence to succeed. Voices echo in your mind. Examples of this **self-talk** (see Chapter 2) include statements like "I must pass, or I'll never get into medical school." "What if I freeze up?" "I must, I must, I must." "I can't, I can't, I can't."

The secret to combating anxiety is twofold. First, you figure out what stresses you and why. Is the voice you hear that of your own feelings? Is it a ghost from your past? Can you believe what is being said? Is it true? Have you *never* performed well under pressure? Have you *never* been able to recall dates? What is reality? What is not?

Second, you replace negative messages with positive ones. Consider the coach of a team sport. The coach doesn't say, "Well, our opponent is tough. I don't see any way we can win." No, the coach acknowledges the opponent's worth. Then he or she says, "Well, our opponent is tough. But, we've practiced hard all week. I know we're prepared. Do your best. That's all I ask, and all we'll need."

The coach's talk before a game motivates players to excel even in stressful situations. Table 3.5 contains steps to follow in fighting a negative mindset. The success messages it contains help you motivate yourself to succeed. Remember, however, the best messages are those you create for yourself. Such statements are personal and, thus, more meaningful. They help you prepare for visualizing success. To be effective, you need to repeat them only once a day—once a day, every day, all day long.

Table 3.5   Self-talk Success Messages

1. *Prepare for an anxiety-producing situation.*
   - What is the question I have to answer?
   - What is the problem I face?
   - I know information about it.
   - Don't worry. Worry won't help.

2. *Confront and handle the situation.*
   - I can answer this question.
   - I can do this.
   - One issue at a time, I can handle this.
   - I won't think about fear—just about what I have to do.

3. *Avoid feeling overwhelmed.*
   - Keep focused. What is the first question I need to answer? What is the major issue I must face?
   - This will soon be over.
   - This is not a life-and-death issue.
   - Life will continue.

4. *Reinforce your coping strategy.*
   - It worked! I answered every question asked of me. I faced the problem with courage.
   - It wasn't as bad as I feared!
   - Me and my imagination! When I control it, I control my stress.

SOURCE: Reprinted with permission from ''The clinical potential of modifying what clients say to themselves,'' by D. H. Meichenbaum and R. Cameron, in M. J. Mahoney and C. E. Thorensen (Eds.), *Self-control: Power to the person.* Copyright © 1974 by Brooks/Cole.

WRITE TO LEARN

Your best friend is afraid of flying. You think self-talk can help him overcome this fear. On a separate sheet of paper, explain self-talk to him. Then provide examples of statements he might use to combat his fear.

Exercise 3.2 Identify one situation in which stress is a problem for you. Then create three self-talk statements you could use to combat this stress.

SITUATION: _____

_____

_____

SELF-TALK COMMENTS:

1. _____

_____

_____

_____

2. _____

_____

_____

_____

3. _____

_____

_____

_____

Exercise 3.3 Think about the ways you view your academic self. What negative messages do you hear? What are their sources? Complete each of the following sentence fragments. Mark the source of each. Then provide examples of messages you tell yourself. Mark their sources.

1. I can't_____

_____

SOURCE: Message comes from me? _____   from others? _____

2. I always_____

_____

SOURCE: Message comes from me? _____   from others? _____

3. I never_____

_____

SOURCE: Message comes from me? _____   from others? _____

4. I don't_____

_____

SOURCE: Message comes from me? _____   from others? _____

5. My friends think I_____

_____

SOURCE: Message comes from me? _____   from others? _____

Exercise 3.4   Create three positive messages for each of the following general situations.

1. Writing a paper

a. _____

_____

b. _____

_____

c. _____

_____

2. Solving a problem

a. _____

_____

b. _____

_____

c. _____

_____

3. Taking a final exam

a. _____

_____

b. _____

_____

c. _____

4. Taking an unannounced quiz

   a. _____

     _____

   b. _____

     _____

   c. _____

5. Reading a chapter

   a. _____

     _____

   b. _____

     _____

   c. _____

     _____

6. Taking notes

   a. _____

     _____

   b. _____

     _____

   c. _____

     _____

7. Being called on in class

   a. _____

     _____

   b. _____

     _____

   c. _____

     _____

8. Managing time

   a. _____

     _____

   b. _____

     _____

   c. _____

     _____

9. Choosing a major

   a. _____

   _____

   b. _____

   _____

   c. _____

10. Getting back a test with a poor grade

   a. _____

   _____

   b. _____

   _____

   c. _____

   _____

Exercise 3.5   Create a positive message for each of the following scenarios. Then provide examples of situations you have faced or will face this semester. Create a positive message for coping with these.

1. You enter a class in a subject you know little about. The other students appear much older (or younger) than you.

MESSAGE: _____

_____

2. You have an excellent GPA and plan to go to law school. Now the time has come to take the LSAT—the Law School Admissions Test.

MESSAGE: _____

_____

3. You are a learning-disabled student. You fear explaining to your instructor that you need special accommodations.

MESSAGE: _____

_____

4. You are in a speech class. Your first speech in front of the large class is tomorrow. You are well prepared but afraid.

MESSAGE: _____

_____

5. Although you have done well on all math homework assignments, a surprise quiz has just been passed to you.

MESSAGE: _____

_____

6. You just got back an English paper. There is no grade on it, but the instructor has written a note. The note asks you to make an appointment to discuss the paper.

MESSAGE: _____

_____

7. SITUATION: _____

MESSAGE: _____

_____

8. SITUATION: _____

MESSAGE: _____

_____

9. SITUATION: _____

MESSAGE: _____

_____

10. SITUATION: _____

MESSAGE: _____

_____

We (Americans) suffer primarily not from our vices or our weaknesses, but from our illusions. We are haunted, not by reality, but by those images we have put in place of reality.

DANIEL J. BOORSTIN

Twentieth century American Historian

Visualization

As Boorstin noted, our imaginations either free or bind us. **Visualization** takes positive messages one step further. It uses imagination to put positive messages into action. Thus, instead of imagining the worst and seeing yourself fail, you imagine success. Just as you sometimes embellish the worst with all the gory details, you now imagine the best in all its splendor. See Table 2.4 for steps in visualization.

WRITE TO LEARN

Using any one of the scenarios in Exercise 3.5, create a visualization to help you imagine success.

Relaxation

"Relax, you won't feel a thing," many doctors say right before they give you an injection. And, while you're sure to feel the needle going in, it really does hurt less if you can ease the tension in your body. Similarly, relaxation eases stress. Even in the throes of a stressful situation, relaxation occurs. How long it takes for you to relax depends on the time you have available and the way you relax.

Early humans responded to threats by either fighting or fleeing. Contemporary life is not that simple, but people still maintain this fight or flight instinct. As a result, our muscles often respond to stress even when these options are not available. Steps for progressively relaxing your mind and muscles appear in Table 3.6. You can also relax your muscles by doing a physical body check. Whenever you feel tense, stop and see if any muscles are involved that really don't need to be. For example, suppose you feel your shoulders tense as you read. Since shoulder muscles play little part in reading, you need to make a conscious effort to relax them. Conscious deep breathing also relaxes the body.

Taking a vacation also relaxes you. Of course, if you're enrolled in school, you can't go to Nassau for the weekend. A mental vacation serves the same purpose as a real one. It's just not as much fun! Mental vacations, however, are fast and inexpensive. To take one, you simply close your eyes. You visualize your favorite vacation spot. Or, you see a

---

Table 3.6	**Steps for Muscular Relaxation**
	1. Sit or lie in a comfortable position with your eyes closed.
	2. Picture yourself in a quiet place in which you felt relaxed in the past (the beach, the forest, a park, your backyard, your room, or elsewhere). Imagine that you're there once more.
	3. Breathe deeply, hold for one count, and breathe out. Repeat the word *calm* each time you inhale. Repeat the word *down* each time you exhale.
	4. Beginning with your toes, flex, then relax those muscles. Progress to the foot, ankle, leg, and so on.
	5. Let your thoughts drift. Allow them to come and go without intervention.
	6. Remain calm and quiet. If possible, remain in this state for at least twenty minutes.
	7. Open your eyes and remain quiet. Enjoy the feeling of relaxation.

place where you wish to vacation. You don't always have to picture quiet, relaxing places. You can imagine yourself shopping, sightseeing, playing sports, or whatever you like to do. Another type of vacation also serves to relax you. Simply changing the way you do things is a kind of vacation. For example, try going to class by a different route, eating in a different location, or shopping at a different grocery. These simple changes of pace are refreshing.

Laughter releases tension, too. It often allows you to put things into perspective. If you have time, you can watch a favorite comedy. If not, listening to a radio station that tells jokes and plays upbeat songs yields the same effect. Print cartoons and funny stories also entertain and relieve stress. Browsing through the greeting card section of a store also relaxes you through humor.

Meditation is yet another form of relaxation. It involves narrowing your conscious mind until anxiety wanes. Several types of meditation exist, but all forms share common features. One is the changing of the normal person-environment relationship through passive observation. A second is the lowering of anxiety levels by focusing on peaceful, repetitive stimuli. A third is the repeating of **mantras,** relaxing words or sounds. The steps in meditation are outlined in Table 3.7.

Table 3.7   Steps in Meditation

1. Begin by meditating once or twice daily for ten to twenty minutes.

2. What you *don't* do is more important than what you do do. Adopt a passive, ``what happens, happens'' attitude.

3. Create a quiet, nondisruptive environment. Don't face direct light.

4. Don't eat for an hour beforehand. Avoid caffeine for at least two hours beforehand.

5. Assume a comfortable position. Change it as needed. It's okay to scratch or yawn.

6. For a concentrative device, you may focus on your breathing or seat yourself before a calming object such as a plant or burning incense. Benson (1975) suggests ``perceiving'' (rather than ``mentally saying'') the word *one* on every outbreath. This means thinking the word but ``less actively'' than usual (good luck!). You could also think or perceive the word *in* as you inhale and *out,* as you exhale.

Table 3.7   Steps in Meditation (continued)

7. If you are using a mantra, you can prepare for meditation by saying it several times. Enjoy it. Then say it more and more softly. Close your eyes and think only the mantra. Allow the thinking to become passive so that you sort of perceive, rather than actively think, the mantra. Again, adopt a passive, ``what happens, happens'' attitude. Continue to perceive the mantra. It may grow louder or softer, or disappear for a while and then return.

8. If disruptive thoughts come in as you are meditating, allow them to ``pass through.'' Don't get wrapped up in trying to stop them or you may raise your level of arousal.

9. Above all, take what you get. You cannot force the relaxing effects of meditation. You can only set the stage for it and allow it to happen.

10. Allow yourself to drift. (You won't go far.) What happens, happens.

SOURCE: Reprinted with permission from *Adjustment and Growth*, 5th ed. by Rathus, S. A., & Nevid, J. S. Copyright © 1991 by Harcourt Brace Jovanovich. All rights reserved.

Exercise 3.6   You need to practice relaxation at least once each day. This is the general order of muscle groups to be relaxed. Do each exercise twice, concentrating on the difference between tension and relaxation. First, tense up muscles in the area mentioned and then relax that area as completely as possible.

1. Relax your hands and arms by
   a. making a fist with your right hand and then releasing it.
   b. making a fist with your left hand and then releasing it.
   c. bending both arms at elbows, making a muscle, then straightening both arms.

2. Relax your neck, shoulders, and upper back by
   a. wrinkling your forehead and releasing.
   b. frowning and creasing your brows and releasing.
   c. closing your eyes tightly and then opening them.
   d. clenching your jaws, biting your teeth together, and releasing.
   e. pressing lips tightly and releasing.
   f. pressing back of neck down against a chair and releasing.
   g. pressing chin against your neck and releasing.
   h. shrugging shoulders.

3. Relax your chest, stomach, and lower back by
   a. holding breath for a period of time, then exhaling.
   b. tightening and releasing stomach muscles.
   c. pulling stomach muscles in and releasing.

4. Relax your hips, thighs, and calves by
   a. tightening your buttocks and thighs and releasing.
   b. straightening your knees, pointing feet and toes downward away from your face.
   c. bending your feet toward your face and releasing.

5. Relax as you imagine a calm scene by closing your eyes and visualizing a quiet, relaxed outdoor setting. Pay attention to the sounds and sights in this scene. Try to feel the breeze; try to see the sun, clouds, birds, and trees; try to hear the birds, water, and wind.

Exercise 3.7   Listen as your instructor plays a relaxation tape, and follow the directions it gives. After the tape is completed, record your responses to the following questions on a separate sheet of paper or in your journal.

1. How did you feel as you began listening to this tape?
2. How did you feel at the end of this tape?
3. To what factor(s) do you contribute changes in your feelings, if any?
4. Would you be willing to try this method on your own? Why or why not?
5. Consider your campus. From what sources might relaxation tapes be available?

STRESS OVERLOAD: DAY-TO-DAY CRISIS SITUATIONS

> There cannot be a crisis next week. My schedule is already full.
>
> HENRY KISSINGER
>
> Twentieth century Secretary of State

As Kissinger noted, there is never a good or convenient time for crisis situations to occur. They always seem to come at the worst possible time, thus causing stress overload. You can't schedule family problems, financial concerns, illnesses, and interpersonal dilemmas when you want. You must be prepared to handle them when they occur.

How do you define crisis? In his April 12, 1959, address, John Kennedy said, "When written in Chinese the word 'crisis' is composed of two characters—one represents danger and the other represents opportunity." The word "crisis" comes from the Greek word *krisis*, which means "decision." A crisis is, then, a juncture—another opportunity for you to make decisions that will affect you both personally and academically. Crises come in two forms, those you cannot control and those you can.

Crisis Situations You Cannot Control

Death . . . illness . . . family problems . . . accidents . . . crimes . . . These are all situations that are outside of your control. How do decision-making skills aid you in coping with such events?

You need to clarify the situation and identify the options available to you. Your goals and values (see Chapter 2) factor into your decision. For example, perhaps, due to no fault of your own, you become seriously injured in an accident. You are hospitalized for several weeks and come back to school determined to finish. You discover that you cannot catch up, but you feel that resigning is a cop-out. However, when you reexamine your goals, you realize that your goal is to finish and do well—not finish in a hurry. Death of a close family member may also cause you to focus on family needs. Once the immediate concerns of the funeral arrangements are concluded, you assess your situation. Should you withdraw from school and return home to care for family business? How much of the term remains? Can you delay your return until then, or would it be better to go home now? Again, your goals and values direct your decision. You may choose to compromise and return home on weekends until you straighten things out. Or you may resign with firm intentions to return to school the following term.

You may find that you can't change the problem—your parents divorce, someone steals your car, or you become chronically ill. In such cases, you may need to alter the way you view the problem—your thoughts, attitudes, and resulting behavior. When problems are outside of your control, the most important thing you can do is come to that realization and let go of the problem. Table 3.8 provides some suggestions for doing so.

Crisis Situations You Can Control

Sometimes what seems like a crisis is actually an opportunity to learn and grow. Lack of money, disagreements with others, difficult children or other family members, poor performance in courses, job losses, and other problems often seem devastating at the time. Once the issue is resolved, life continues, for the most part, the same as it did before. You may also need to improve your life skills in a variety of ways. Table 3.9 lists some common controllable crisis situations and some ways to solve them.

Table 3.8   Coping with Problems Outside Your Control

1. *24-hour rule.* Letting go doesn't mean that you don't cope with the problem. You must. Living each day one day at a time is a first step. Problems that might overwhelm you in a lifetime can be handled for twenty-four hours.

2. *Talk it out.* Talk to others. Friends, mentors, family, and others can advise you, support you, and listen to you. Problems that seem insurmountable appear less difficult when someone else shares them with you.

3. *Run away.* While you can't run away forever, you can escape for a while. This takes you away from the problem and helps you regain perspective. If you can't physically leave town for a day or two, escape to a movie, a new place to eat, a park, or a different place to study.

Table 3.8   Coping with Problems Outside Your Control (continued)

4. *Act normal.* Do something you normally do. A crisis is an abnormal event. Simple, everyday activities like grocery shopping, taking a walk, or studying can take the edge off and regulate the situation.

5. *Busybody.* Regular physical activity (e.g., exercise, building, cleaning, etc.) burns excess energy. Mental activity (e.g., reading, studying, solving puzzles) occupies your mind and prevents you from worrying.

6. *Make time for fun.* Schedule time for recreation. Recreation literally means to re-create or renew. Like an escape, it breaks the tension and provides a vacation from the problem at hand. Laughter improves any situation.

7. *Golden rule.* Do something nice for yourself or for others. You deserve it and they probably do too.

Table 3.9   Crisis Situations You Can Control

Crisis	Alternatives for Control
Communication problems (e.g., assertiveness, parenting skills, personal relationships)	1. Course in interpersonal communication 2. Counseling 3. Self-help books
Money management	1. Share expenses 2. Seek financial aid 3. Work part-time 4. Economize 5. Assess priorities 6. Create a budget
Study skills/time management	1. Counseling 2. Campus learning assistance center 3. Study skills/orientation course 4. Campus seminars
Job loss	1. Campus career center 2. Retraining 3. Activate network of support (faculty, friends, other employees) to help locate job options

WELLNESS

How can you keep yourself fit and ready to cope with stress? Baseball pitcher Satchel Paige offers the following suggestions:

- Avoid fried foods, which angry up the blood.
- If your stomach disputes you, lie down and pacify it with cool thoughts.
- Keep the juices flowing by jangling gently as you move.
- Go very light on the vices, such as carrying on in society. The social ramble ain't restful.
- Avoid running at all times.
- Don't look back. Something might be gaining on you.

And while Paige's suggestions seem light-hearted, they contain good advice for meeting your physical needs and staying well. Maslow's Hierarchy of Needs (see Figure 2.2) theorizes that physical needs must be satisfied before other needs can be met. Thus, lifestyle factors like nutrition, rest, exercise, sexual activity, and drug use affect how well you cope with stress. They also have bearing on whether or not you reach self-actualization, the top of your mental and emotional health ladder.

EATING RIGHT

Students at Columbia University's College of Physicians and Surgeons try to reduce stress in all the same ways you do. One place they frequent to relax is Coogan's, a beer and sandwich shop on Broadway in Manhattan. To help students cope with the stressors of academic life, Coogan's publishes a brochure that includes a stress diet (see Table 3.10).

Perhaps you've tried diets like Coogan's to cope with stress. Lots of students do, and they find them just as successful as Coogan's expects you to find theirs—which in a word is *NOT*.

If Coogan's diet relieves any stress, it does so through humor, not by its nutritional suggestions. Nutrition, however, really is a serious subject. It affects your physical well-being. It also impacts your study habits and grades. What you eat affects your stamina and behavior. It's a subject that cannot be avoided, even if you've heard it before. A balanced diet (see Figure 3.1) supplies the nutrients you need. It serves as the basis of good health. It helps you store energy. Unfortunately, in college, what and when you eat is not always in your control. Classes, work, and study play havoc with regular mealtimes. Thus, you need a plan for getting nutrition even when you miss meals. For example, suppose a class extends past the hours the cafeteria serves lunch. Eating a later breakfast or an earlier dinner helps you cope. Or, your college cafeteria might prepare a sack lunch for you. You could carry some fruit or cheese in your backpack for a between class snack, if all else fails. The Eating Smart Quiz in Exercise 3.8 provides a way for you to measure your own dietary habits.

Table 3.10   Coogan's Stress Diet: Rules and Sample Menu

1. When you eat something and no one sees you eat it, it has no calories.

2. If you drink a diet soda with a candy bar, the calories in the candy bar are canceled out by the diet soda.

3. When you eat with someone else, calories don't count if you do not eat more than they do.

4. Foods used for medicinal purposes NEVER count, such as hot chocolate, toast, and Sara Lee Cheesecake.

5. If you fatten up everyone around you, then you look thin.

6. Movie-related foods (such as Milk Duds, buttered popcorn, Red-Hots, and Tootsie Rolls) do not have additional calories because they are part of the entire entertainment package and are not part of your personal fuel.

7. Cookie pieces contain NO calories. The process of breaking (cookies into pieces) causes calorie leakage.

8. Things licked off knives and spoons have no calories if you do so in the process of preparing something. Examples: peanut butter knife while making a sandwich and ice cream spoon while making a sundae.

9. Foods that have the same color have the same number of calories. Examples: spinach and pistachio ice cream, mushrooms and white chocolate. Note: Chocolate is a universal color and may be substituted for any other color.
   Sample Daily Menu
   BREAKFAST
       1 grapefruit
       1 slice whole wheat toast, dry
       3 oz. skim milk
   LUNCH
       4-oz. lean broiled chicken breast
       1 cup steamed spinach
       1 cup herb tea
       1 Oreo cookie
   MID-AFTERNOON SNACK
       Rest of Oreos in the bag
       2 pints of rocky-road ice cream
       1 jar hot fudge sauce
       Nuts, cherries, and whipped cream
   DINNER
       2 loaves garlic bread with cheese
       Large sausage-mushroom and cheese pizza
       3 Milky Way candy bars
   LATE EVENING SNACK
       Entire frozen cheesecake eaten directly from freezer

SOURCE: Reprinted with permission of Coogan's; New York, NY.

Figure 3.1   The Food Pyramid

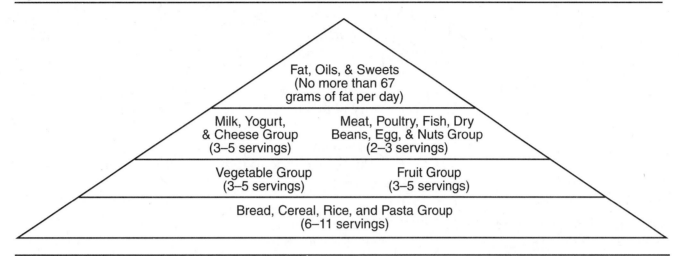

WRITE TO LEARN

On a separate sheet of paper, explain the role nutrition and a steady, balanced diet play in maintaining your grades. Then identify five ways (other than those mentioned in the text) for finding time for meals within a hectic class schedule.

Exercise 3.8   Read each group of three items, and select the number (0, 1, or 2) that best describes your own eating habits. Write that number in the blank space in the Points column. Then add up the points and write that number in the ``Total'' space at the end of the quiz. Finally, interpret your score according to the key at the end of the chapter.

THE EATING SMART QUIZ

Oils and Fats		Points
butter, margarine, shortening, mayonnaise, sour cream, lard, oil, salad dressing	I always add these foods in cooking and/or at the table.	0
		1
	I occasionally add these to foods in cooking and/or at the table.	2 _____
	I rarely add these to foods in cooking and/or at the table.	
	I eat fried foods three or more times a week.	0
	I eat fried foods one to two times a week.	1
	I rarely eat fried foods.	2 _____

Dairy Products

I drink whole milk.	0
I drink 1%-2% fat-free milk.	1
I drink skim milk.	2 _____
I eat ice cream almost every day.	0
I eat ice milk, low-fat frozen yogurt & sherbet.	1
I eat only fruit ices, seldom eat frozen dairy dessert.	2 _____
I eat mostly high-fat cheese (jack, cheddar, colby, Swiss, cream).	0
I eat both low- and high-fat cheeses.	1
I eat mostly low-fat cheeses (pot, 2% cottage, skim milk mozzarella).	2 _____

Snacks
potato/corn chips, nuts, buttered pop-corn, candy bars

I eat these every day.	0
I eat some occasionally.	1
I seldom or never eat these snacks.	2 _____

Baked Goods
pies, cakes, cookies, sweet rolls, doughnuts

I eat them five or more times a week.	0
I eat them two to four times a week.	1
I seldom eat baked goods or eat only low-fat baked goods.	2 _____

Poultry and Fish*

I rarely eat these foods.	0
I eat them one to two times a week.	1
I eat them three or more times a week.	2 _____

Low-fat Meats*
extra lean hamburger, round steak, pork loin roast, tenderloin, chuck roast

I rarely eat these foods.	0
I eat these foods occasionally.	1
I eat mostly fat-trimmed red meats.	2 _____

High-Fat Meat*
luncheon meats, bacon, hot dogs, sau-sage, steak, regular & lean ground beef

I eat these every day.	0
I eat these foods occasionally.	1
I rarely eat these foods.	2 _____

Cured and Smoked Meat and Fish*
luncheon meats, hot dogs, bacon, ham & other smoked or pickled meats and fish

I eat these foods four or more times a week.	0
I eat them one to three times a week.	1
I seldom eat these foods.	2 _____

Legumes
dried beans & peas: kidney, navy, lima, pinto, garbanzo, split-pea, lentil

I eat legumes less than once a week.	0
I eat these foods one to two times a week.	1
I eat them three or more times a week.	2 _____

Whole Grains and Cereals

whole grain breads, brown rice, pasta,   I seldom eat such foods.   0
whole grain cereals   I eat them two to three times a day.   1
   I eat them four or more times daily.   2 _____

Vitamin C-Rich Fruits and Vegetables

citrus fruits and juices, green peppers,   I seldom eat them.   0
strawberries, tomatoes   I eat them three to five times a week.   1
   I eat them one to two times a day.   2 _____

Dark Green and Deep Yellow Fruits and Vegetables**

broccoli, greens, carrots, peaches   I seldom eat them.   0
   I eat them three to five times a week.   1
   I eat them daily.   2 _____

Vegetables of the Cabbage Family

broccoli, cabbage, brussels sprouts,   I seldom eat them.   0
cauliflower   I eat them one to two times a week.   1
   I eat them three to four times a week.   2 _____

Alcohol

   I drink more than 2 oz. of 80 proof liquor daily.***   0
   I drink alcohol every week but not daily.   1
   I occasionally or never drink alcohol.   2 _____

Personal Weight

   I'm more than 20 lbs. over my ideal weight.   0
   I'm 10 to 20 lbs. over my ideal weight.   1
   I am within 10 lbs. of my ideal weight.   2 _____

TOTAL SCORE

---

*If you do not eat meat, fish or poultry, give yourself a 2 for each meat category.
**Dark green and yellow fruits and vegetables contain beta carotene, which your body can turn into vitamin A, which helps protect you against some types of cancer-causing substances.
***Alcohol Equivalents: 2 oz. of 80-proof liquor = 6½ oz. wine *or* 18 oz. beer or 25 oz. 32 beer.

SOURCE: Used with permission. Copyright © 1987. American Cancer Society, Inc.

R AND R

In addition to nutritious food, you need adequate rest. What's adequate? It depends on two factors: your physical condition and the tasks you undertake. High degrees of fitness, interest, or skill help you achieve more with less fatigue. Methods of avoiding fatigue vary in quality and effectiveness. Sleep is the most obvious way to become rested. It is, however, not your only choice. Changing activities—for example, studying different subjects—also rests your mind. Recreational activities help you relax. These might include listening to music, talking to friends, or reading a book. Study time is the only price you pay for these activities. This price, however, seems too steep to some students. Such students bypass natural methods of avoiding fatigue. They rely on tranquilizers to relax. They use amphetamines to increase productivity. Other students use alcohol or tobacco to cope with stressful situations. These artificial means are quick, costly, and only temporarily effective (if at all). They can create dependencies and serve as study crutches, not study supports.

THE ROLE OF EXERCISE

Exercise also plays a role in reducing stress. It enables you to work off excess adrenaline and energy. You rid your body of these before they make you tired or sick. Paradoxically, exercise also increases your energy level. When this happens, you better cope with stress because you no longer feel exhausted or overwhelmed. It's not surprising, then, that exercise also decreases fatigue. This is particularly true when you use it as an alternative to challenging mental processes. For example, jogging for thirty minutes breaks the intensity of a long study session. Another benefit of exercise is that it tends to have a positive effect on your lifestyle. That is, if you exercise regularly, you'll probably find yourself drinking, smoking, and/or overeating less often. This, in turn, causes you to feel and look better. If you worry about your appearance often, as do many people, exercise eliminates this potential stressor as well. Exercise affects your long-term health. It increases strength and flexibility while it decreases your chances of cardiovascular or skeletal-muscular problems. Finally, exercise tends to slow the natural aging process.

SUBSTANCE USE AND ABUSE

Substance use and abuse alters your attention span, memory, judgment, self-control, emotions, and perceptions of time and events. Why, then, do people use drugs? Table 3.11 provides a classification of drug-taking behaviors.

Alcohol

Which of the following contains the most alcohol?

a. a 4-ounce glass of white wine

b. a 10-ounce wine cooler

c. a 12-ounce draft beer

d. 1 ounce of whiskey

Water taken in moderation cannot hurt anybody.

—MARK TWAIN

Nineteenth century American author

Table 3.11   Classification of Drug-taking Behaviors

Classification	Reason for Use	Duration	Quote Associated with Classification
Experimental	Curiosity	Short-term	"But I didn't inhale. (Bill Clinton)"
Social-recreational	Pleasure, relaxation	Occasional	"'I only drink at parties."
Situational	Cope with a problem	Occasional	"Drink today and drown all sorrow." (John Fletcher)
Intensive	Avoid withdrawal; beginning dependence	Daily	"I'm no good until I get my morning coffee."
Compulsive	Avoid withdrawal; dependence	Daily	"Smoking is, if not my life, then at least my hobby. I love to smoke. Smoking is fun. Smoking is cool. Smoking is, as far as I am concerned, the entire point of being an adult." (Fran Lebowitz)

The answer? Each of these contain about the same amount of alcohol, the most widely used drug on any campus. College students use alcohol to celebrate, reduce tension, relieve depression, intensify pleasure, enhance social skills, and change experiences for the better (Brown, 1985). Moderate amounts of alcohol work well in doing all of these. Larger amounts tend to decrease its benefits, however.

How much is moderate? How much is too much? No one really knows. That's because the amount varies from person to person, depending on genetics, health, sex, weight, and age. Nonetheless, most people agree to define moderation as no more than two drinks per day for an average-sized man or no more than one drink per day for an average-sized woman.

As the drug of choice of most college students, it's not surprising that alcohol takes a direct route (no detours) to your brain. This means that an empty stomach absorbs 20 percent of alcohol molecules almost immediately. One minute after taking a drink, then, and particularly on an empty stomach, you feel the buzz you associate with alcohol.

If all goes according to plan, the route alcohol takes through your brain is orderly and well-timed. When alcohol reaches your brain, it first sedates the reasoning part of your brain. Thus, judgment and logic quickly fall prey. This is the reason that when you drink, you find yourself in situations you'd ordinarily avoid or doing things you would not normally do. Next, it affects your speech and vision centers. Third, it attacks your voluntary muscular control, sometimes causing you to stagger or weave as you walk. Loss of vision and voluntary muscular control can cause dire consequences when drinking and driving. Finally, it strikes respiration and cardiac controls. Eventually, the brain is completely conquered, and you pass out before you drink a lethal amount. If you drink so fast that the effects of alcohol continue after you are no longer conscious, you die. It is for this reason that you sometimes hear of students dying during drinking contests.

Suppose you avoid drinking contests. What's the worst that could happen to you? Guilt, shame, poor grades, addiction? Yes, all are possible. And, just as possible if you drink sensibly, none of these. Table 3.12 contains suggestions for helping you drink intelligently.

Other Psychoactive Drugs

Use of **psychoactive drugs** often results in either physical addiction or psychological dependence. Addiction happens most often with drugs that cause withdrawal symptoms like vomiting, diarrhea, chills, sweating, and cramps. In addition to alcohol, such drugs include tobacco, amphetamines, barbiturates, heroin, and cocaine. All psychoactive drugs can lead to psychological dependence, the feeling that you need a drug to stay "normal" or "happy." Table 3.13 lists psychoactive drugs and their classifications, medical uses, dosages, effects, duration of effects, long-term symptoms, and potential for dependence and organic damage.

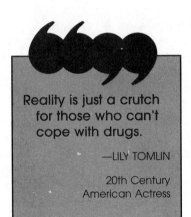

Reality is just a crutch
for those who can't
cope with drugs.

—LILY TOMLIN

20th Century
American Actress

Table 3.12   Suggestions for Drinking Sensibly

1. Sip drinks with food or eat a good meal before you drink.

2. Limit your ready (refrigerated) supply of alcohol.

3. Alternate between alcoholic and nonalcoholic beverages.

4. Switch to beverages with a lower-alcohol content.

5. Avoid situations in which you'll be expected to drink heavily.

6. Choose a designated driver.

7. Respect other people's decisions not to drink.

8. Act responsibly if you are hosting a party.

9. Set a limit to the amount you will drink and stick to it.

10. Space your drinks—it takes about an hour and a half for your body to metabolize a drink.

11. Sip, don't gulp.

12. Identify your reasons for drinking—get help if you need it.

Table 3.13   Comparison of Psychoactive Drugs—Continued

Effects Sought	Long-Term Symptoms	Physical Dependence Potential	Psychological Dependence Potential	Organic Damage Potential
Sense alteration, anxiety reduction, sociability	Cirrhosis, toxic psychosis, neurologic damage, addiction	Yes	Yes	Yes
Alertness, activeness	Loss of appetite, delusions, hallucinations, toxic psychosis	Yes	Yes	Yes
Anxiety reduction, euphoria	Addiction with severe withdrawal symptoms, possible convulsions, toxic psychosis, addiction	Yes	Yes	Yes
Wakefulness, alertness	Insomnia, heart arrhythmias, high blood pressure	No	Yes	Yes
Excitation, talkativeness	Depression, convulsions	Yes	Yes	Yes
Euphoria, prevent withdrawal discomfort	Addiction, constipation, loss of appetite	Yes	Yes	No
Euphoria, prevent withdrawal discomfort	Addiction, constipation, loss of appetite	Yes	Yes	No*
Insightful experiences, exhilaration, distortion of senses	May intensify existing psychosis, panic reactions	No	No?	No?
Relaxation; increased euphoria, perceptions, sociability	Possible lung cancer, other health risks	No	Yes	Yes
Insightful experiences, exhilaration, distortion of senses	May intensify existing psychosis, panic reactions	No	No?	No?
Prevent withdrawal discomfort	Addiction, constipation, loss of appetite	Yes	Yes	No
Euphoria, prevent withdrawal discomfort	Addiction, constipation, loss of appetite	Yes	Yes	No*
Insightful experiences, exhilaration, distortion of senses	May intensify existing psychosis, panic reactions	No	No?	No?
Alertness, calmness, sociability	Emphysema, lung cancer, mouth and throat cancer, cardiovascular damage, loss of appetite	Yes	Yes	Yes

(Question marks indicate conflict of opinion. It should be noted that illicit drugs are frequently adulterated and thus pose unknown hazards to the user.)

*Persons who inject drugs under nonsterile conditions run a high risk of contracting AIDS, hepatitis, abscesses, or circulatory disorders.

SOURCE: Reprinted with permission from *Essentials of Psychology Exploration and Application* by D. Coon. Copyright © 1994 by West Publishing Company. All rights reserved.

Table 3.13   Comparison of Psychoactive Drugs—Continued

Effects Sought	Long-Term Symptoms	Physical Dependence Potential	Psychological Dependence Potential	Organic Damage Potential
Sense alteration, anxiety reduction, sociability	Cirrhosis, toxic psychosis, neurologic damage, addiction	Yes	Yes	Yes
Alertness, activeness	Loss of appetite, delusions, hallucinations, toxic psychosis	Yes	Yes	Yes
Anxiety reduction, euphoria	Addiction with severe withdrawal symptoms, possible convulsions, toxic psychosis, addiction	Yes	Yes	Yes
Wakefulness, alertness	Insomnia, heart arrhythmias, high blood pressure	No	Yes	Yes
Excitation, talkativeness	Depression, convulsions	Yes	Yes	Yes
Euphoria, prevent withdrawal discomfort	Addiction, constipation, loss of appetite	Yes	Yes	No
Euphoria, prevent withdrawal discomfort	Addiction, constipation, loss of appetite	Yes	Yes	No*
Insightful experiences, exhilaration, distortion of senses	May intensify existing psychosis, panic reactions	No	No?	No?
Relaxation; increased euphoria, perceptions, sociability	Possible lung cancer, other health risks	No	Yes	Yes
Insightful experiences, exhilaration, distortion of senses	May intensify existing psychosis, panic reactions	No	No?	No?
Prevent withdrawal discomfort	Addiction, constipation, loss of appetite	Yes	Yes	No
Euphoria, prevent withdrawal discomfort	Addiction, constipation, loss of appetite	Yes	Yes	No*
Insightful experiences, exhilaration, distortion of senses	May intensify existing psychosis, panic reactions	No	No?	No?
Alertness, calmness, sociability	Emphysema, lung cancer, mouth and throat cancer, cardiovascular damage, loss of appetite	Yes	Yes	Yes

(Question marks indicate conflict of opinion. It should be noted that illicit drugs are frequently adulterated and thus pose unknown hazards to the user.)
*Persons who inject drugs under nonsterile conditions run a high risk of contracting AIDS, hepatitis, abscesses, or circulatory disorders.

SOURCE: Reprinted with permission from *Essentials of Psychology Exploration and Application* by D. Coon. Copyright © 1994 by West Publishing Company. All rights reserved.

CONTROLLING TEST ANXIETY

"Just a test" and "only one research paper" don't seem like major stressors. However, they become so when placed in the context of your daily personal and academic life. Two Australian researchers (Sarros and Densten, 1989) identified the causes of stress felt by most college students (see Table 3.14). Which ones pose stressors for you?

COPING BEFORE AN EXAM

Generally speaking, coping before an exam involves keeping yourself physically fit through adequate rest and nutrition. Specifically, it means getting sleep the night before an exam and not skipping meals or eating too much the day of the test. Your body needs to be ready to face whatever an exam has in store for you. Being exhausted from study or partying and/or hungry or stuffed to oblivion serves to focus your attention on you rather than the questions whose answers you know. Exercise, too, helps you prepare physically for an exam. After you have tended to your physical needs, you need to consider your emotional needs. Mental preparation takes the forms of study, positive thinking, visualization, and relaxation.

Simply put, coping before an exam involves knowing and practicing the coping strategies discussed in this chapter.

COPING DURING AN EXAM

During an exam, you can manage stress by pausing for about fifteen seconds and taking a few deep breaths. You need to force your breathing to flow smoothly and slowly. Breathe as described in step 3 of Table 3.6. This calms your nerves and steadies your mind. A second way to manage stress while taking a test is to use test-wise strategies. For example, first answering questions you know and making notes of information you're afraid you might forget eases stress. A third way to reduce stress during an exam is to ask your instructor for help if the way a test is constructed or the wording of a question causes you stress. Fourth, the positive self-talk that helped you control stress before the exam works equally well during the test.

Worry about your grade, indecision among possible answers, concern with the physical symptoms of stress, and anxiety about the consequences of failing the test can cause negative self-talk during an exam. To fight a negative mindset during an exam, follow the suggestions outlined in Table 3.5. These suggestions can help free your mind from worry and help you concentrate on test.

Table 3.14   Top Ten Stressors of College Students

1. Number of assignments	6. Class presentations
2. Taking course exams	7. Course work load
3. Size of assignments	8. Own expectations
4. Low grade on the exam	9. Spacing of exams
5. Assignment due dates	10. Class assignments

SOURCE: Sarros and Densten. (1989). Undergraduate student stress and coping strategies *Higher Education Research and Development 8,* 1.

COPING AFTER AN EXAM

Once the test is over, it's over. Waiting for your grade, receiving it, and living with it are the next problems you face. How you manage this time affects your future performance in both your courses and in college.

Examining Returned Tests

What do you do when a test is returned to you? Do you throw it away? Do you file it carefully, never to look at it again? Or do you examine it carefully? A review of your test provides information about both your study and test-taking skills. It helps you decide which of your study and test-taking strategies work and which do not. You use this information to improve future test performance and reduce the stress of taking another exam in the same course.

Table 3.15 provides a form for examining your test paper. To complete this worksheet, you list each item you missed in the first column. Then you mark an *X* under the description that best explains why you missed a question. Sometimes you will mark more than one reason for a question. Next, you add the number of *X*'s under each reason. These numbers indicate the areas of study and test-taking strategies that need more attention.

After you determine or obtain as much information as you can about your study and test-taking habits from the exam, you look for information about how your instructor constructs exams. You look for patterns in the types of questions asked. You see if your instructor emphasized text or lecture information. You determine grading patterns. This information helps you prepare for the next exam. Being so prepared reduces stress.

Another way to acquire information after the exam involves asking your instructor for information. You need to make an appointment and ask you instructor to read over your exam with you. This helps you determine why you got credit for some answers and not others.

Table 3.15   Examining Returned Tests

Test Item Missed	Insufficient Information						Test Anxiety					Lack of Test-Wisdom						Test Skills					Other		
	I did not read the text thoroughly.	The information was not in my notes.	I studied the information but could not remember it.	I knew main ideas but needed details.	I knew the information but could not apply it.	I studied the wrong information.	I experienced mental block.	I spent too much time daydreaming.	I was so tired I could not concentrate.	I was so hungry I could not concentrate.	I panicked.	I carelessly marked a wrong choice.	I did not eliminate grammatically incorrect choices.	I did not choose the *best* choice.	I did not notice limiting words.	I did not notice a double negative.	I changed a correct answer to a wrong one.	I misread the directions.	I misread the questions.	I made poor use of the time provided.	I wrote poorly organized responses.	I wrote incomplete responses.			
Number of Items Missed																									

• *Every student knows that examination time can be a source of great stress. In the following article, Professor John J. Chiodo of Clarion University describes some truly extraordinary effects of exam-related stress and suggests a variety of ways in which faculty members can help to alleviate the problem.*

I entered the ranks of academe as well prepared as the next fellow, but I was still unaware of the threat that midterm exams posed to the health and welfare of students and their relatives. It didn't take long, however, for me to realize that a real problem existed. The onset of midterms seemed to provoke not only a marked increase in the family problems, illnesses, and accidents experienced by my students, but also above-normal death rates among their grandmothers.

In my first semester of teaching, during the week before the midterm exam, I got numerous phone calls and visits from the roommates of many of my students, reporting a series of problems. Mononucleosis seemed to have struck a sizable portion of my class, along with the more common colds and flu.

A call from one young woman awakened me with the news that her roommate's grandmother had died, so she (my student) would be unable to take the exam. I expressed my condolences, and assured the caller that her roommate would not be penalized for such an unexpected tragedy.

Over the next few days I received many more calls—informing me of sickness, family problems, and even the death of a beloved cat. But the thought of three grandmothers passing away, all within the short exam period, caused me a good deal of remorse. But the term soon ended and, with the Christmas break and preparations for the new semester, I forgot all about the midterm problem.

Eight weeks into the second semester, however, I was once again faced with a succession of visits or phone calls from roommates about sick students, family problems, and, yes, the deaths of more grandmothers. I was shaken. I could understand that dorm meals and late nights, along with "exam anxiety," might well make some students sick, but what could account for the grandmothers? Once again, though, other things occupied my mind, and before long I had stopped thinking about it.

I moved that summer to a large Midwestern university, where I had to reconstruct my teaching plans to fit the quarter system. I taught three classes. By the end of the first midterm exams two of my students' grandmothers had died; by the time the year was over, a total of five had gone to their reward.

I began to realize the situation was serious. In the two years I had been teaching, 12 grandmothers had passed away; on that basis, if I taught for 30 years 180 grandmothers would no longer be with us. I hated to think what the universitywide number would be.

Adjusting to Stress

Once you've examined your test and learned all you can from it, you need to adjust your thinking to help prepare for future exams in that same course. There are four ways you can prepare. First, you might see your instructor and ask for suggestions. Your instructor can make study recommendations that will aid you in future study. Second, you might change your appraisal of the situation. All too often the pressure you put on yourself results in the most tension. You can decide that a *B* or *C* is the best you can do in a course, and that your best is the most you can

I tried to figure out the connection. Was it because grandmothers are hypersensitive to a grandchild's problems? When they see their grandchildren suffering from exam anxiety do they become anxious too? Does the increased stress then cause stroke or heart failure? It seemed possible; so it followed that if grandmothers' anxiety levels could be lowered, a good number of their lives might be prolonged. I didn't have much direct contact with grandmothers, but I reasoned that by moderating the anxiety of my students, I could help reduce stress on their grandmothers.

With that in mind, I began my next year of teaching. On the first day of class, while passing out the syllabus, I told my students how concerned I was about the high incidence of grandmother mortality. I also told them what I thought we could do about it.

To make a long story short, the results of my plan to reduce student anxiety were spectacular. At the end of the quarter there had not been one test-related death of a grandmother. In addition, the amount of sickness and family strife had decreased dramatically. The next two quarters proved to be even better. Since then, I have refined my anxiety-reduction system and, in the interest of grandmotherly longevity, would like to share it with my colleagues. Here are the basic rules:

- Review the scope of the exam.

- Use practice tests.

- Be clear about time limits.

- Announce what materials will be needed and what aids will be permitted.

- Review the grading procedure.

- Review the policies on makeup tests and retakes.

- Provide study help.

- Make provision for last-minute questions.

- Allow for breaks during long exams.

- Coach students on test-taking techniques.

I have been following these rules for 13 years now, and during that time have heard of only an occasional midterm-related death of a grandmother. Such results lead me to believe that if all faculty members did likewise, the health and welfare of students—and their grandmothers—would surely benefit.

SOURCE: Morris, C. G. (1988). *Psychology: An Introduction.* Englewood Cliffs, N.J.: Simon & Schuster.

---

demand of yourself. Removing the self-imposed goal of *A*-level work lessens stress. Third, you can change your response to the situation. This means you avoid stress by replacing anxiety with activity. For example, instead of staying awake and worrying about a grade you made, spend the evening either playing tennis or preparing for the next class meeting. Either way, you gain. If you play tennis, you get needed exercise. You will also probably become physically tired enough to sleep. If you study, you gain the confidence of knowing you're prepared for class. This, too, helps you sleep. That's because you know that whatever happened on the last test, you've taken positive steps toward the future. Fourth, you can change the situation or take a strategic retreat. This means you can drop a course if it gives you too many problems. A strategic retreat is just that—a logical and temporary step back. Such a maneuver gives you time to reflect on yourself, your goals, and academic realities. This does not mean you won't ever pass the course. It simply means you will take it again at a better time.

Makeup Exams

As a student, you may feel that instructors do not care how well you do in class. This misconception can prevent you from seeking the help you need to be successful. This is particularly true when it comes to asking for makeup exams.

It is true that instructors hear all too often, "I was too ill to take the exam" or "My Great-aunt Wilma is sick, and I have to leave campus immediately." On the other hand, sometimes illness, family, or job pressures cause you to miss an exam. Perhaps your first idea is to simply skip class and confront the instructor later. Contacting the instructor as soon as possible, preferably before the exam, is a better alternative. Making this special effort shows your concern for your grade. It also indicates your respect for the instructor. Arranging for makeup work at this time decreases stress. That's because you'll know if and when you'll be able to make up work. If you are ill for a period of time, you need to talk with your instructor about receiving an incomplete or "I" grade. This enables you to complete the work when you recover.

College instructors care. Give them an opportunity to do so.

"Let me get this straight. You flunked English because your electric typewriter broke down, you flunked Math because your electric calculator broke down, and you flunked everything else because the electrical system in your car broke down and you couldn't get to your classes."

SOURCE: Button, Ford. *Phi Delta Kappan.*

WRITE TO LEARN

Your roommate experiences test anxiety. On a separate sheet of paper, leave your roommate a note which describes ways to cope with stress before, during, and after an exam.

Exercise 3.9   Read "Another Look: Choosing to be a top performer" on pages 536–538 from Sample Chapter 11. Then answer the questions below.

1. Explain the relationship between the information in this section and stress.

_____

_____

_____

_____

_____

_____

_____

2. Create an analogy that compares and/or contrasts *react, respond, positive coping strategies,* and *defensive coping strategies.*

_____

_____

_____

_____

_____

_____

_____

3. What role would each positive coping strategy play in this author's life?

_____

_____

_____

_____

_____

_____

_____

GROUP LEARNING ACTIVITY
MAKING IT UP

Seeing professors about makeup work is stressful for many students. On the other hand, students often give little thought to the feelings of the instructor with whom they're meeting. To help you and fellow group members overcome anxiety, complete the following activity:

1. Write each of the following on a separate, unlined piece of paper:
   a. You are student who has been seriously ill for several weeks. You have a doctor's note and your hospital bill. You meet with your professor to schedule makeup work.
   b. You are student who consistently skips class. It's near final exam time, and you have become worried about your grade. You meet with your instructor to schedule makeup work and exams.
   c. You are student who has missed only one class the entire semester. Your clock battery died in the night, and you overslept. Unfortunately, your instructor assigned a major homework assignment for the next class. You meet with your instructor to get the assignment.

2. Write each of the following on a separate lined piece of paper:
   a. You are a professor who always attempts to be fair. However, it's been a bad semester, and you've given more makeup work than anything else. You are tired of grading late work and hope you never see another student asking for makeup work.
   b. You are professor who never allows student to make up work unless they have documentation from a doctor or a police officer.
   c. You are professor who has no clear-cut makeup policies. As such, it is difficult for students to pin you down as to what work you will let them make up.

3. Fold the pieces of lined and unlined paper in fourths and place them in a container.

4. Divide the group into sets of partners.

5. Have each partner select a different kind of paper. (One partner gets lined paper, the other gets unlined paper.) Partners do not tell anyone the role they've drawn.

6. Allow each partner a few minutes to think about his or her role.

7. Have each set of partners role-play a meeting between the two characters they've drawn.

8. After five minutes of role playing, have other group members try to guess what kind of student/instructor pair they just observed.

9. Let the next set of partners begin their role play.

CHAPTER SUMMARY

1. Stress management involves both defensive and positive coping techniques.

2. Among the positive coping strategies are positive thinking, visualization, and relaxation.

3. Managing stress also involves knowing what crisis situations you can and cannot control.

4. Physical wellness, mental preparation, exercise, and the avoidance of substance abuse also aid in coping with stress.

5. Controlling test anxiety before, during, and after an exam also alleviates stress.

6. After an exam, you need to examine returned tests, adjust stress levels, and use appropriate mechanisms to schedule makeup exams.

CHAPTER REVIEW

Answer briefly but completely.

1. Compare and contrast positive and negative ways of coping with stress. Which positive method most benefits you? Which negative method causes you the most grief? How can you maximize the positive and lessen the negative?

    _____

    _____

    _____

    _____

    _____

2. Consider the last crisis situation you encountered. Evaluate how well you coped by using information in this chapter. How would you cope with a similar situation if it occurred now?

    _____

    _____

    _____

    _____

    _____

3. How do you cope with stress before, during, or after an exam? Explain one method you will add to your coping repertoire for handling stress before, during, and after tests.

_____

_____

_____

_____

_____

4. List two specific situations about which you are concerned, and develop three positive messages for each one.

_____

_____

_____

_____

_____

_____

5. Describe in three to five sentences the quiet place you go to relax and ten specific features you plan to use in creating a relaxation visualization of that location.

_____

_____

_____

_____

_____

_____

6. Perform an after-exam survey of your last test in each of your classes. What is your most common mistake? How can you solve this problem?

_____

_____

_____

_____

_____

7. A student applies for a job but fails to get it. Create three positive and three negative forms of self-talk that the student might use in this situation.

_____

_____

_____

_____

_____

8. What effect would adjusting to stress after an exam have on future self-talk? Give three examples to illustrate this effect.

_____

_____

_____

_____

_____

9. Consider the stressors discussed in this chapter. Which cause the most trouble for you? Why is this so?

_____

_____

_____

_____

_____

10. Develop a plan for coping with the stressors you identified in the previous question. Use strategies discussed in this chapter.

_____

_____

_____

_____

_____

REFERENCES

Benson, H. (1975). *The relaxation response.* New York: Morrow.

Brown, S. A. (1985). Expectancies versus background in the prediction of college drinking patterns. *Journal of Consulting and Clinical Psychology,* 53, 123–130.

Sarros, J. C., & Densten, I. L. (1989). Undergraduate student stress and coping strategies. *Higher Education Research and Development,* 8, 1.

Vocabulary Development   Structural Analysis: Words in Your Pocket

Test taking requires a calm hand and a cool wit. It calls for strength and perseverance. It takes steady nerves and courage. But, most of all, it requires knowledge and the words that reflect that knowledge. Sometimes knowing a part of a word's meaning allows you to eliminate distractors on exams. Other times, it helps you understand words in questions that seem tricky or ambiguous. Knowledge of word parts, then, aids you in determining correct answers on exams and in showing the knowledge you have gained in a course.

A word is not the same with one writer as with another. One tears it from his guts. The other pulls it out of his overcoat pocket.

—CHARLES PEGUY
Twentieth Century French poet

Using the parts of words to determine meaning is called structural analysis. Parts of a word fit together much as parts of a car do. As with a car, some parts are essential to the functioning of a word. Called bases, these word parts give you an overall meaning. Affixes (prefixes and suffixes) accessorize the word and affect the overall meaning. Prefixes occur at the beginning of words. Suffixes are found at their ends.

Affixes sometime help identify the subject area of a word. They can also help determine the part of speech or use. The following charts show common roots (Table 1), prefixes (Table 2), suffixes (Table 3), and math and science roots (Table 4). Knowing how word parts fit together saves your guts and puts words in your pocket.

Table 1   General Roots

Root	Example	
script (write)	manuscript	_____
vert (turn)	convert	_____
ject (throw)	eject	_____
port (carry)	transport	_____
vis/vid(see)	video	_____
rupt (break)	interrupt	_____
dict (say)	dictionary	_____
aud (hear)	auditory	_____
cede (go)	recede	_____
junct (join)	junction	_____

Table 1   General Roots (continued)

| pseudo (false) | pseudonym | _____ |
| mem (mind) | memory | _____ |

Table 2   Prefixes

Prefix	Example	
be (by)	beloved	_____
pre (before)	prehistoric	_____
de (away, from)	detract	_____
inter (between)	intervene	_____
ob (against)	obstruction	_____
in, il, ir (not)	illegible	_____
a (not)	asexual	_____
un (not)	unconnected	_____
ad (to, toward)	adhere	_____
contra (against)	contraband	_____
en, in (in)	encapsule	_____
com/col/con/co (together, with)	coauthor	_____
non (not)	nonexistent	_____
auto (self)	autonomy	_____
ex (out of)	exist	_____
re (again)	repeat	_____
pro (forward)	proponent	_____
homo (same)	homogeneous	_____
hetero (different)	heterosexual	_____
dis (apart from)	disjointed	_____
over (above)	overwhelm	_____
super (above)	superscript	_____
sub (under)	subscript	_____
mis (bad, wrong)	mistaken	_____
trans (across)	transfer	_____

Table 3   Suffixes

Prefix	Example	
Noun		
ane/ine/ene (forms a name of a chemical)	butane	_____
ade (act of; result or product of)	blockade	_____
age (state or condition of)	blockage	_____
arch/archy (rule)	monarchy	_____
ard/art (one who does something not admirable to excess)	braggart	_____
arian (age, sect, or social belief; occupation)	agrarian	_____
asis/osis/ysis (condition character-ized by)	paralysis	_____
tion (state of being)	elation	_____
cide (kill)	homocide	_____
ory (place or state of; ability in)	laboratory	_____
ster (one who is or does)	youngster	_____
wright (one who builds or makes)	playwright	_____
hood (state of being)	statehood	_____
ship (state of being)	leadership	_____
ance/ence (state of being)	absence	_____
Root	**Example**	
ism (state of being)	communism	_____
ness (state of being)	kindness	_____
sion (act of)	conversion	_____
ation (act of)	jubilation	_____
ity/ty (state or condition)	creativity	_____
ist (one who does)	journalist	_____
or/er (one who)	inventory	_____
mont (action or state of)	government	_____
Adjective		
able (able to/capable of being)	remarkable	_____
ible (able to)	divisible	_____
ful (full of)	beautiful	_____

Table 3   Suffixes (continued)

Prefix	Example	
ous (having)	advantageous	_____
ive (having the quality of)	creative	_____
al (pertaining to)	comical	_____
ic (pertaining to)	academic	_____

Verb

en (belonging to/cause to be)	roughen	_____
ize (to become/to make)	maximize	_____
fy (to make)	unify	_____

Adverb

ly (in the manner of)	carefully	_____

Table 4   Math and Science Roots and Affixes

Root	Example	
mono (one)	monograph	_____
aqua (water)	aquatic	_____
hydro (water)	hydrolic	_____
hemi (half)	hemisphere	_____
semi (half)	semicircle	_____
equi (equal)	equidistant	_____
tele (far off)	telescope	_____
some (body)	chromosome	_____
sphere (ball, globe)	biosphere	_____
quad (four)	quadrant	_____
bi (two)	bisect	_____
geo (earth)	geology	_____
micro (small)	microscope	_____
onomy (science of)	astronomy	_____
ology (study of)	biology	_____
uni (one)	universe	_____
tri (three)	triangle	_____

Table 4   Math and Science Roots and Affixes (continued)

octa (eight)	octagon	_____
dec (ten)	decimal	_____
centi (hundred, hundredth)	centigrade	_____
milli (thousand, thousandth)	millimeter	_____
bio (life)	biology	_____
astro (star)	astronomy	_____
thermo (heat)	thermal	_____
meter (measure)	kilometer	_____
ped/pod (foot)	arthropod	_____
kilo (thousand)	kilogram	_____
botan (plant)	botanist	_____
cyto (cell)	cytoskeleton	_____
lymph (water)	lymph nodes	_____

Structural analysis is an important tool in preparing for and taking a test. Because it is an active process, it stimulates you to use what you know to analyze new words and understand familiar words more fully.

When preparing for a test, you may be struggling with learning the meanings of a large number of words. Structural analysis helps you connect and organize meaning. For example, consider the following words and meanings:

macrophage—a cell derived from the white blood cells called monocytes whose function is to consume foreign particles, such as bacteria and viruses.

monocyte—one type of white blood cells; produces macrophages

lymphocyte—white blood cell produced by the lymphatic system.

lymphatic system—the system that helps protect the body against infection and returns excess fluid to the blood circulatory system.

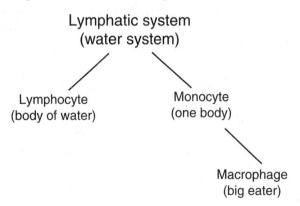

At first glance, they may seem a bit confusing. Consider the following map with meanings (in parentheses) derived from structural analysis:

Now you see the relationships. The lymphatic system produces both lymphocytes and monocytes. Monocytes produce macrophages, which "eat up" foreign bodies in the body.

How does structural analysis aid you in test taking? Consider the following test questions:

1. Which of the following is a *pseudopod?*
    a. amoeba
    b. horse
    c. spider
    d. anteater

2. Unlike in the aristocracies of Europe, the founders of the United States believed that all humans are of the same worth. As a result of this _____ philosophy, anyone can rise to power.
    a. egalitarian
    b. diversify
    c. coordinator
    d. unification

Your recall of word parts aids you in answering question 1. But if you cannot think of a specific meaning of a word part, you can attempt to think of other words that contain that particular part. So, if you couldn't think of the meaning of *pseudo* or *pod,* you might think of such words as *pseudonym* or *tripod.* From this, you might generalize that *pseudo* means *false* and that *pod* means *foot.* Thus, *pseudo pod* means "false foot." Since spiders, horses, and anteaters all have some sort of foot, the answer must be *a*, amoeba.

In question 2, the correct answer depends on two factors. First, the word that fits in the blank must modify the noun *philosophy.* Thus, it must be an adjective. Second, you must recall how suffixes change part of speech. If you recall that *tion* and *or* indicates nouns and that *ify* indicates verb forms, then answer *a* is the correct choice. This will be verified when you recall that some adjectives end in *ian.*

Activity

Fill in the blanks in Tables 1, 2, 3, and 4 with your own examples of words with these parts.

Key For Eating Smart Quiz

How do you rate?

0–12: A Warning Signal
Your diet is too high in fat and too low in fiber-rich foods. It would be wise to assess your eating habits to see where you could make improvements.

13–17: Not Bad! You're Part-way There

You still have a way to go. Review figure 3.1 and look for ways to make improvements in your diet.

18–36: Good for You! You're Eating Smart!

You should feel very good about yourself. You have been careful to limit your fats and eat a varied diet. Keep up the good habits and continue to look for ways to improve.

Note that a poor score on the quiz does not guarantee that you will get cancer, and a high score does not guarantee that you will not. However, your score will help you assess the risks of your current dietary habits, and the guidelines will suggest ways in which you can reduce your risk of cancer.

The American Cancer Society notes that "This eating quiz is really for self-information and does not evaluate your intake of essential vitamins, minerals, protein or calories. If your diet is restricted in some ways (i.e., you are a vegetarian or have allergies), you may want to get professional advice" (1987).

The American Cancer Society provides guidelines for dietary habits that may help prevent cancer of the mouth, larynx, throat, esophagus, stomach, bladder, colon, rectum, lungs, breast, prostate, and uterus:

- Maintain a desirable body weight.
- Decrease your total intake of fats.
- Eat more high-fiber foods, e.g. whole grain cereals, legumes, vegetables, fruits.
- Eat a varied diet.
- Include a variety of both vegetables and fruits in the daily diet.
- Limit consumption of salt-cured, smoked, and nitrite-cured foods.
- Limit consumption of alcoholic beverages, if you drink at all.
- The society's Eating Smart Quiz can help you assess whether your own dietary habits are consistent with the society guidelines.

Listening and Notetaking

1. Construct a notetaking outline or map through text previewing.

2. Identify factors that affect your ability to listen.

3. Organize notes from various types of lectures.

4. Develop a systematic notetaking approach.

5. Complete notes using an effective post-lecture process.

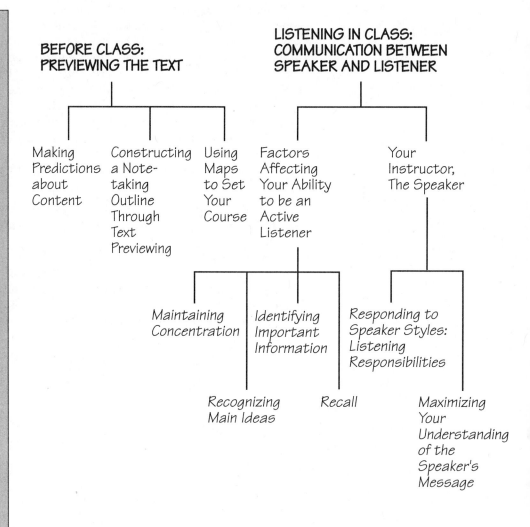

BEFORE CLASS: PREVIEWING THE TEXT

- Making Predictions about Content
- Constructing a Note-taking Outline Through Text Previewing
- Using Maps to Set Your Course

LISTENING IN CLASS: COMMUNICATION BETWEEN SPEAKER AND LISTENER

- Factors Affecting Your Ability to be an Active Listener
  - Maintaining Concentration
    - Recognizing Main Ideas
  - Identifying Important Information
    - Recall
- Your Instructor, The Speaker
  - Responding to Speaker Styles: Listening Responsibilities
  - Maximizing Your Understanding of the Speaker's Message

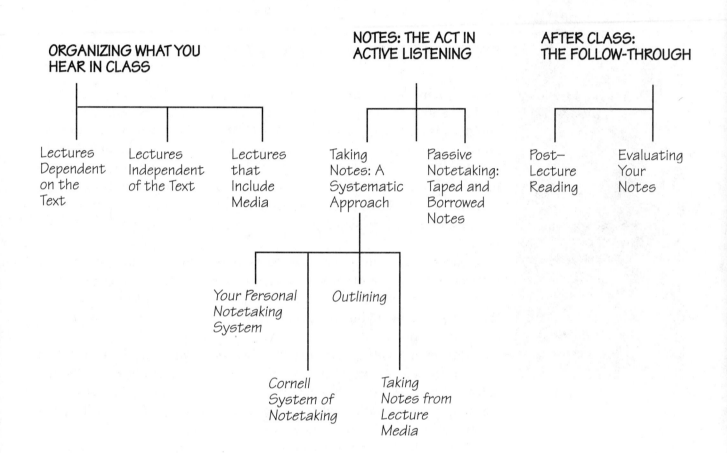

Plutarch spoke of a problem your instructors face each day. That problem is students who are not prepared and not ready to learn. Chapter One helped you idenify your place in a post-secondary community. Chapter Two showed you ways to manage time, and Chapter Three provided you with specifics for effectively managing stress. Thus you are now ready to confront a college classroom. To do so, you need strategies for studying and learning. Just as an instructor is responsible for preparing a lecture, you are obliged to be ready to process lecture information.

BEFORE CLASS: PREVIEWING THE TEXT

Your enjoyment and understanding of an activity often depend on your **background knowledge.** For example, most people who know nothing about sports fail to enjoy sporting events. Most people who know nothing about music fail to enjoy classical concerts. The same is true of academic activities. If you know nothing of a subject, you often fail to enjoy and understand that subject. On the other hand, the more background knowledge you have, the more easily you will enjoy and learn from lectures. One way to increase your background knowledge is to interact with the text.

Luckily for you, a process exists that helps you predict chapter information and then regulate or control your understanding of lecture content. Just as you examine the sky and check the wind for clues about the weather, **previewing,** or surveying, entails examining text features for clues about content.

Previewing is the first interaction between you and the text. When you survey before class, you think about what you already know about a subject. This lets you make the best use of background knowledge in learning and integrating what you hear in class. This information then can be related to what you know about the topic.

Previewing helps you create a mental outline for what the chapter contains. Once you get an overall picture of a chapter, you can see how details relate to major points. Previewing also improves your recall of what you read. This occurs because, rather than reading material that's unfamiliar to you, you read information you've seen before. Finally, previewing helps you set the speed at which you will later read and process information. The steps in previewing appear in Table 4.1.

MAKING PREDICTIONS ABOUT CONTENT

The most basic way to begin reading a chapter is to make predictions about what each section contains. This helps you interact more actively with the text. Instead of "just reading," you look for specific information. Predicting chapter content also helps you increase your understanding of lectures.

Table 4.1   Steps in Previewing

1. Read the title. What is the chapter about? Recall what you already know about the topic.

2. Read the introduction or first paragraph. The main idea of the chapter is usually found here.

3. Read the boldfaced headings throughout the chapter.

4. Read the first paragraph or sentence under each heading. This gives you an overview of each section.

5. Look at accompanying graphs, charts, and pictures. Visual aids usually emphasize main points. They also summarize details.

6. Note any typographical aids (boldface, underlining, italics). In the body of the text, these aids highlight important terms. When found in the margins, they may outline important facts.

7. Read the last paragraph or summary. This often gives the main points or conclusions.

8. Read the objectives at the beginning of each chapter. Objectives help you set goals and purposes. Such goals help you determine what you should know or be able to do at the end of each chapter.

9. Read the vocabulary terms at the beginning or end of each chapter. You may recognize some of the terms. However, they may have specialized meanings for that topic.

10. Read the purpose-setting or review questions that accompany the chapter. These focus on key concepts.

Table 4.2 Questioning Words for Main Ideas and Details

Questioning Words for Main Ideas

IF YOU WANT TO KNOW . . .	THEN ASK . . .
a reason	why?
a way or method	how?
a purpose or definition	what?
a fact	what?

Questioning Words for Details

IF YOU WANT TO KNOW . . .	THEN ASK . .
a person	who?
a number or amount	how many/how much?
a choice	which?
a time	when?
a place	where?

You can predict content in one of several ways. One way is to examine the chapter objectives provided by the author(s). Objectives specify what you should be able to do or understand after you read the chapter. Examining these objectives helps you set learning goals and compare chapter content to what you already know.

Another method is to preview the chapter summary or review questions. This helps you identify important information that forms the basis of the chapter.

A third method is to change headings and subheadings into questions. Certain questioning words help in identifying main ideas, and others help in locating details. Table 4.2 provides a key to these questioning words. In addition, the headings and subheadings guide your understanding of how information fits together. Perhaps in your psychology text, for example, the subheadings "Physical" and "Psychological" come under the heading "Stressors." Already, you know that there are two kinds of stressors, physical and psychological. As such, you know that you can compare and contrast the two. You do not know, however, if one causes the other to occur. You should expect the text to define and describe physical and psychological stressors and give examples of each.

Exercise 4.1   The boldfaced headings from Sample Chapter 11, "Personal Values, "Career Planning, and Success with People at Work" follow. Preview Sample Chapter 11, then write a purpose-setting question for each heading. Describe the connections you find for the headings and subheadings.

Heading	Question
1. **KEY IDEA 1: CAREER PLANNING**	
2. **Developing Personal Goals: Start with a Dream List**	
3. **Conducting a Self-Appraisal**	
4. **Creating a Vision**	
5. **Gathering Occupational Information**	
A: **Connections**	
6. **KEY IDEA 2: CLARIFYING EXPECTATIONS**	
7. **What Organizations Expect of Management Employees**	
8. *Representation of the Company*	
9. *A Desire for Success*	
10. *A Professional Business Appearance*	
11. *Time Spent on the Job*	
12. *Some Creativity*	

13. *A Long-Term Commitment*

_____

14. Customer Service

_____

15. What Companies Do Not Expect from a
New Manager

_____

16. What Management Employees Can Expect from the Company

_____

17. *Openness and Honesty in the Recruiting
Process*

18. *Appropriate and Adequate Training*

_____

19. *Reasonable Compensation and Benefits*

_____

20. *Performance Reviews and Periodic Raises*

_____

21. *A Good Working Environment*

_____

B: Connections_____

_____

_____

_____

_____

_____

22. **KEY IDEA 3: MANAGING YOUR
BOSS**

_____

23. **Resolving Key Issues**

_____

24. *Clarifying Job Content*

_____

25. *Taking Initiative*

_____

26. *Keeping the Boss Informed*

_____

27. *Asking for Help*

_____

28. Developing Trust with the Boss

_____

29. *Accessibility*

_____

30. *Availability*

_____

31. *Predictability*

_____

32. *Loyalty*

_____

C: Connections _____

_____

_____

_____

_____

_____

33. KEY IDEA 4: MANAGING YOURSELF

_____

34. Identifying Time-Saving Techniques

_____

35. Time and Task Management Tools and Skills

_____

36. The Nuts and Bolts of Time and Task Management

_____

_____

_____

37. *Step 1. Develop a Priority Task List for Each Day*

_____

_____

_____

38. *Step 2. Assign a Letter Priority to Each Item on Your List*

_____

_____

_____

39. *Step 3. Assign a Number to Your Task*

_____

_____

40. *Step 4. Use Completion Symbols: The Payoff*

_____

_____

_____

41. Incorporating Goals and Values in Your Daily Planning

_____

_____

_____

42. *Blocking Out Time Wasters*

_____

_____

43. Delegating to Save Time

_____

_____

_____

44. *Why Some Managers Hesitate to Delegate*

_____

_____

_____

45. *Why You May Not Delegate*

_____

_____

46. *How Delegation Can Sometimes Go Wrong*

_____

_____

_____

D: Connections_____

_____

_____

_____

_____

_____

_____

CONSTRUCTING A NOTETAKING OUTLINE THROUGH TEXT PREVIEWING

Previewing to construct a **notetaking outline** before class (see Table 4.3) also provides you with the basics needed for understanding the lecture. Making a notetaking outline gives you a chance to locate what appear to be important terms, concepts, and dates before the lecture. It helps you predict the content of the lecture. Figure 4.1 shows a notetaking outline, before and after the lecture.

Table 4.3   Constructing a Notetaking Outline through Text Previews

Before beginning the previewing process, divide each page for your notes vertically into sections, with one third on the left and two thirds on the right. Record the following in the left-hand section as indicated:

1. Survey the physical characteristics of the chapter (that is, length, text structure, visual aids, or term identification).

2. Record the chapter title. Think about what you know about this topic. Consider how this information relates to the course content.

3. Read the chapter introduction or first paragraph. This gives you the overall main idea of the chapter.

4. Read and record each major and minor heading or subheading. Major headings express main ideas. Subheadings provide details to support major headings.

5. Estimate the amount of space for each section and skip lines accordingly.

6. Survey graphs, maps, charts, diagrams, and so on. These summarize details, emphasize main points, and highlight other important information.

7. Look for typographical aids (boldface, underlining, italics). In the body of the text, these highlight important new terms. In the margins, they outline important ideas. Record terms.

8. Read the last paragraph or summary. This generally reviews the main points or conclusions of the chapter.

Figure 4.1   Example of a Notetaking Outline: Before and after the Lecture

Headings before

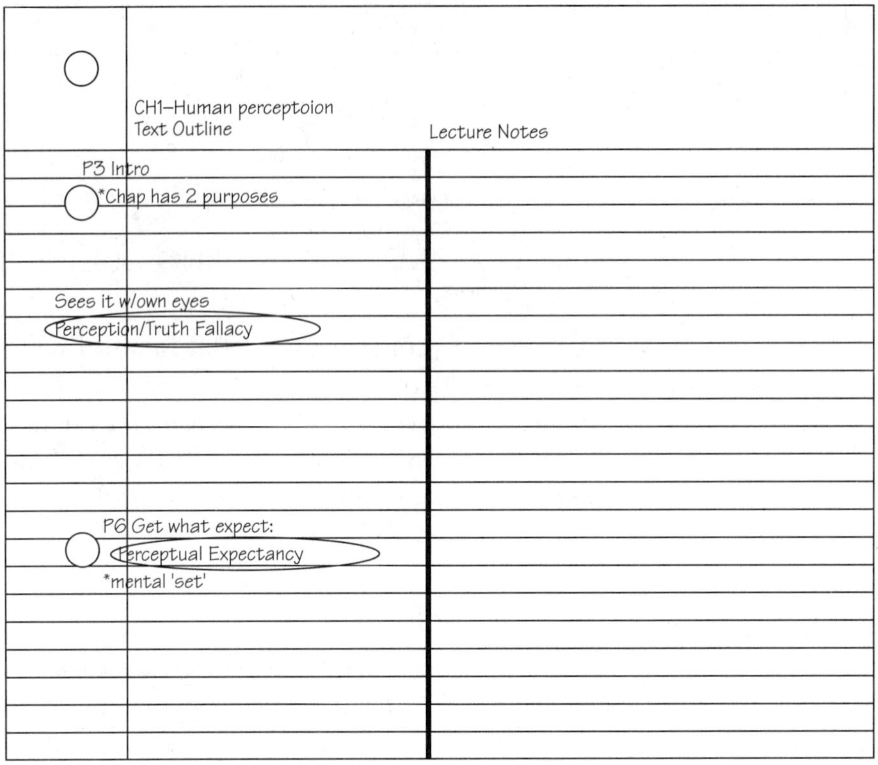

	CH1—Human perceptoion Text Outline	Lecture Notes
P3 Intro		
*Chap has 2 purposes		
Sees it w/own eyes		
Perception/Truth Fallacy		
P6 Get what expect:		
Perceptual Expectancy		
*mental 'set'		

Headings after

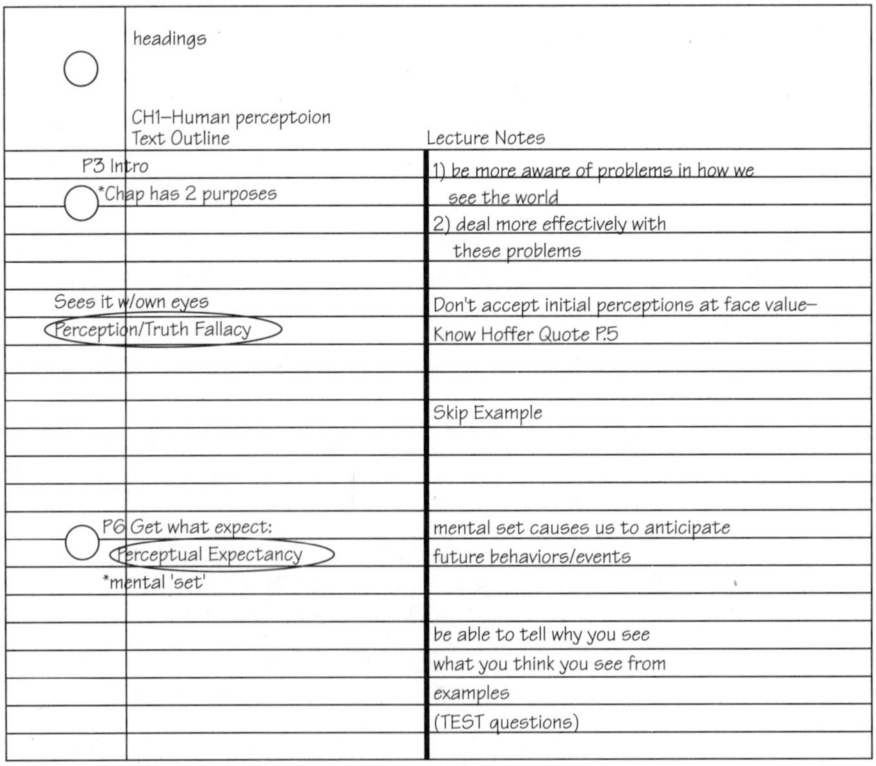

headings

	CH1—Human perceptoion Text Outline	Lecture Notes
P3 Intro		1) be more aware of problems in how we see the world
*Chap has 2 purposes		2) deal more effectively with these problems
Sees it w/own eyes		Don't accept initial perceptions at face value— Know Hoffer Quote P.5
Perception/Truth Fallacy		
		Skip Example
P6 Get what expect:		mental set causes us to anticipate future behaviors/events
Perceptual Expectancy		
*mental 'set'		
		be able to tell why you see what you think you see from examples (TEST questions)

Some text readings provide general background information, rather than a framework for the lecture information. Notetaking outlines, then, lose effectiveness for lectures that are less dependent on information in your textbook. In these cases, skimming the chapter in its entirety or reading it more thoroughly may be needed.

Exercise 4.2   Preview Sample Chapter 13, ``An Invitation to Computers.'' On a separate sheet of paper, create a goal-setting outline based on the headings and subheadings in the sample chapter. Then read the chapter summary points and respond to the goal-setting questions based only on that information.

''I think the artist's left brain overpowered his right brain.''

USING MAPS TO SET YOUR COURSE

Research in the functioning of the brain indicates that its two halves process information differently. The left half of the brain tends to think in analytical, logical, linear, and verbal terms. The right brain prefers holistic, nonverbal, and visual images.

Doonesbury

BY GARRY TRUDEAU

Chapter maps help you set your course with information for both sides of your brain. They provide verbal information in the context of a visual arrangement of ideas. They show relationships among concepts and express an author's patterns of thought. Each chapter of this text begins with a map for just these reasons.

Table 4.4	Steps in Constructing a Chapter Map

1. Turn a sheet of paper horizontally.

2. Write the first major heading in the top left corner.

3. Place the next-level headings (if any) underneath the major heading with lines showing their relationship to the major heading.

4. Place the next-level heading(s) (if any) underneath the second-level heading(s).

5. Continue the pattern until you come to the next major heading.

6. Repeat the process until the end of the chapter.

You construct a chapter map by using headings and subheadings in a family tree-style branching format. Table 4.4 provides steps in constructing a chapter map. After you create your map, formulate some questions that analyze the links between information and synthesize the chapter as a whole. Figure 4.2 shows how these steps would be used to create the map for Sample Chapter 13.

LISTENING IN CLASS: COMMUNICATION BETWEEN SPEAKER AND LISTENER

Classroom communication takes place between your instructor, the speaker, and you, the listener. In the preceding *Doonesbury* cartoon, the cartoon's professor and his students are communicating at opposite ends of the continuum of listening (See Table 4.5). The students apparently are listening at the lowest end of the spectrum, the attention level. The lecturer tries desperately without success to entice them to evaluate what he says. Little communication occurs, no matter how hard the speaker tries.

Listening, then, is more difficult than it looks. It appears easy because it's something you've been doing all your life. It requires only the equipment you have with you, and you can use it in all of your classes and at any time. One problem with learning from verbal information is your lack of training in being a good listener in the classroom. Educators take for granted that you know how to learn from lectures. That, however, is seldom the case. Since listening is a seemingly passive activity, you can appear to know how to listen even when you don't. You can appear to listen, even when you aren't. Listening, however, is not an all-or-nothing proposition. The level at which you listen depends on your background knowledge, the difficulty of the concepts, and your purpose in listening.

Figure 4.2   Chapter Map of Sample Chapter 13

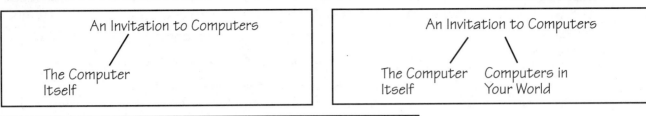

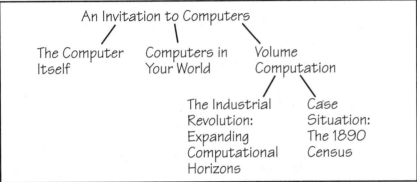

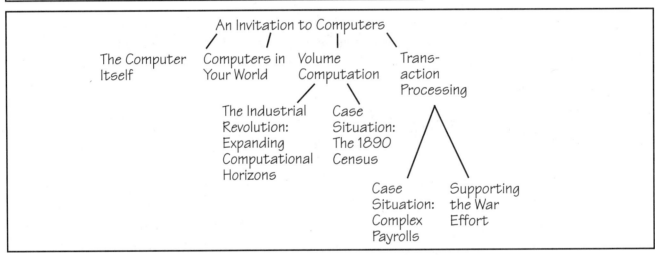

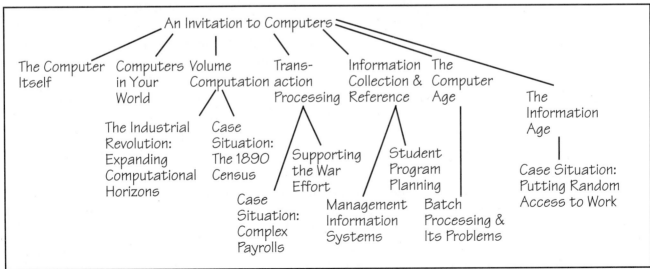

Figure 4.2   Chapter Map of Sample Chapter 13 *(continued)*

Questions

1. What role did the Industrial Revolution play in the development of computers?

2. How does the methodology for collecting the 1890 census compare with today's methodology?

3. How did transaction processing affect the war effort?

4. What is the relationship between the computer age and the information age?

5. What components define the computer itself?

Table 4.5   Continuum of Listening

EVALUATION	Judging information in terms of accuracy and relevance
APPLICATION	Applying information to personal experience; using information in new situations
IMPLICATION	Drawing conclusions
INTERPRETATION	Synthesizing information; putting information into your own words
INTEGRATION	Relating new information to old learning
DEFINITION	Lowest level of active listening; giving meaning to isolated facts and details; no overall organizational plan
ATTENTION	Listening passively; no effort to relate or understand what is being said
RECEPTION	Hearing without thought

Exercise 4.3   Using Figure 4.2 as a guide construct a chapter map of Sample Chapter 11 and create corresponding questions.

For most students, listening to lectures involves following a linear sequence of one idea after another. Like the students in the *Doonesbury* cartoon p. 181, they tend to take at face value what is being said. They passively accept any statement, evaluating little of what they hear. What a speaker says should elicit mental comments, if not spoken comments and questions. These comments should question what is said as well as what and how you think about it. In essence, you should always be asking, "What?" "So what?" and "Now what?" Table 4.6 modifies the continuum of listening to include the kind of mental comments that might be appropriate at each level.

> **WRITE TO LEARN**
>
> Examine Table 4.5. Compare your behavior in your favorite and least favorite classes. Consider the amount of time each of these classes lasts. On a separate sheet of paper, determine when and for how long you might be at each level of listening in each of these classes. What factors contribute to the level at which you listen and for how long you remain at a level in each class? Are there any differences? Why?

Doonesbury

Table 4.6   Mental Comments for the Continuum of Listening

Level	Comments
EVALUATION	Do I agree with . . . ? What information supports . . . ? Is this true and accurate? Why would . . . be so?
APPLICATION	How would . . . be used? How would . . . differ if one of its components changed? What situation would show . . . ?
IMPLICATION	What would be the result of . . . ? What would cause . . . ? So if . . . is true, then . . . follows.
INTERPRETATION	In other words, . . . To summarize, . . . That means . . . . .
INTEGRATION	Then . . . relates to . . . . is part of . . . process. . . . could be organized like . . . . could be classified as . . . .
DEFINITION	The meaning of . . . is . . . .
ATTENTION	Sure looks like a nice day outside.
RECEPTION	?????

FACTORS AFFECTING YOUR ABILITY TO BE AN ACTIVE LISTENER

The student who spoke in the second *Doonesbury* cartoon demonstrates the alert and active process of listening. He related what the instructor said to what he already knew. He took advantage of this knowledge by communicating with his instructor. He maintained eye contact and gave a thoughtful response. He seemed interested. As a result, the instructor took an interest in him and wanted to get to know him better.

You, too, should be like this *Doonesbury* student. By combining what you learn from the instructor with what you know about yourself and the world, you become an active listener. Active listening occurs when you consciously monitor your listening and use preplanned strategies for improving and maximizing these listening skills.

Are you an effective listener? Do you know what factors affect listening skills? The personal profile found in Exercise 4.4 helps you rate your abilities as a listener.

Exercise 4.4   Rate yourself as a listener. There are no correct or incorrect answers. Your responses, however, will extend your understanding of yourself as a listener and highlight areas in which improvement might be welcome . . . to you and to those around you.

When you've completed the tests, examine the Profile Analysis to see how your scores compare with those of thousands of others who've taken the same tests.

Quiz #1

1. Circle the term that best describes you as a listener.
   Superior
   Excellent
   Above Average
   Average
   Below Average
   Poor
   Terrible
2. On a scale of 0-100 (100 = highest), how would you rate yourself as a listener?

Quiz #2

Check (✔) how frequently (almost always, usually, sometimes, seldom, almost never) you do the following listening behaviors:

LISTENING HABITS	FREQUENCY					SCORE
	Almost Always	Usually	Sometimes	Seldom	Almost Never	
1. Call the subject uninteresting	_____	_____	_____	_____	_____	_____
2. Criticize the speaker's delivery or mannerisms	_____	_____	_____	_____	_____	_____
3. Get overstimulated by something the speaker says	_____	_____	_____	_____	_____	_____
4. Listen primarily for facts	_____	_____	_____	_____	_____	_____
5. Try to outline everything	_____	_____	_____	_____	_____	_____
6. Fake attention to the speaker	_____	_____	_____	_____	_____	_____
7. Allow distractions to interfere	_____	_____	_____	_____	_____	_____
8. Avoid difficult material	_____	_____	_____	_____	_____	_____
9. Let emotion-laden words arouse personal antagonism	_____	_____	_____	_____	_____	_____

LISTENING HABITS	FREQUENCY					SCORE
	Almost Always	*Usually*	*Sometimes*	*Seldom*	*Almost Never*	
10. Daydream while the speaker is talking	_____	_____	_____	_____	_____	_____

TOTAL SCORE _____

KEY

For every "Almost Always" checked, give yourself a score of	2
For every "Usually" checked, give yourself a score of	4
For every "Sometimes" checked, give yourself a score of	6
For every "Seldom" checked, give yourself a score of	8
For every "Almost Never" checked, give yourself a score of	10

Profile Analysis

This is how other people have responded to the same questions that you've just answered.

Quiz #1

1. 85% of all listeners questioned rate themselves as Average or less. Fewer than 5% rate themselves as Superior or Excellent
2. On the 0-100 scale, the extreme range is 10-90; the general range is 35-85; and the average rating is 55.

Quiz #2

All these habits get in the way of effective listening. Therefore, the higher your score (the more you *don't* fall into these habits), the better listener you are.

The average score is 62 . . . 7 points higher than the average of 55 in Quiz #1. This suggests that when listening is broken down into specific areas of competence, we rate ourselves better than we do when listening is considered only as a generality.

Of course, the best way to discover how well you listen is to ask the people to whom you listen most frequently—your spouse, boss, best friend, and so on. They'll give you an earful.

Maintaining Concentration

Inactive listening results from **distractions.** These draw your attention from the subject being discussed. Some of these factors are beyond your control and others are not. All prevent you from fully focusing on the topic at hand.

Distractions beyond your control include traffic noises; sounds within the classroom, such as whispering, papers rattling, people moving, or hall noises; and other environmental interruptions. Your instructor's mannerisms pose another distraction you cannot control. Often an instructor's dialect, speech rate, and body language affect your concentration. Because you have no control over these distractions, you must learn to cope with them.

One way to cope is to increase your interest in the subject. You can try to become so interested in what is being said that you ignore what is bothering you. Another way to reduce environmental distractions is to move to a different seat. You may need to move away from a door or window. If you are in a large lecture class, moving closer to the instructor helps you hear better and focuses your attention.

Sometimes distractions are within you. These also prevent you from concentrating on the topic. Such distractions include physical discomforts, personal concerns, and daydreams. It is difficult to think when you are hungry, tired, or sick. Proper nutrition, rest, and exercise get rid of these physical distractions. Personal concerns, no matter how large or small, cannot be solved during a class. If your problem is a large one, consulting a counselor or talking with a friend before or after class may help reduce your anxiety. Worry about small problems (getting your laundry done, meeting a friend, running errands) can be handled by listing them on a page in your notebook. Then you can forget about them until the end of class. Daydreaming is another common distraction. **Self-talk** can be used to force yourself back to attention. Self-talk involves your interrupting your daydream with a strong internal command like, "STOP! Pay attention now. Think about this later." Finally, you must maintain your stamina in listening to lectures. In general, students tend to take fewer and less comprehensive notes as a lecture progresses. Active listening and continued mental questioning helps you remain focused and attentive.

Recognizing Main Ideas

Every lecture has a plan, purpose, and structure that indicate the main idea of the talk. Learning to recognize the various patterns that lectures follow helps you distinguish between main ideas and details. It also aids you in recognizing examples and understanding the reasons for anecdotes.

Lectures follow five basic patterns. Instructors either: 1) introduce new topics or summarize information; 2) list or rank details; 3) present two (or more) sides of an issue; 4) identify cause(s) and effect(s) or problem(s) and solution(s); or 5) discuss concepts with supporting details. These patterns vary as the instructor's purposes change in the course of a lecture. Identifying your instructor's mix of the patterns helps you predict the direction of the lecture. Signal words and other verbal markers help you identify the flow and content of these lecture patterns.

Listening for these signals makes you a kind of word detective. A detective follows a suspect, predicting where he or she will go based on clues left behind. You follow an instructor's lecture and predict the lecture's direction by identifying the **transition words** your instructor uses. These words also mark the end of a lecture. This is important because instructors often restate main ideas in their summaries. Becoming familiar with transition words helps you organize lecture notes and listen more actively. Table 4.7 compares transition words with **lecture patterns.**

Table 4.7   Lecture Patterns and Corresponding Signals

Pattern	Description	Signal Words
Introduction/Summary	Identifies main points	Identified by location, either at the beginning or end of a discussion of a topic; or by such words as: *in summary, in conclusion, as a review, to summarize, to sum up*
Enumeration/Sequence	Lists or orders main points or presents a problem and steps for its solution	*First, second, third, next, then, finally, in addition, last, and, furthermore, and then, most important, least important*
Comparison/Contrast	Describes ways in which concepts are alike or different or presents two or more sides of an issue	Comparison—*similarly, both, as well as, likewise, in like manner* Contrast—*however, on the other hand, on the contrary, but, instead of, although, yet, nevertheless*
Cause/Effect	Shows the result of action(s) or explains a problem and its solution	*Therefore, thus, as a result, because, in turn, then, hence, for this reason, results in, causes, effects*
Subject Development/ Definition	Identifies a major topic and describes or develops it through related details	Identified by terms denoting definition; types or kinds; characteristics, elements, and other kinds of supporting details

> **WRITE TO LEARN**
>
> On a separate sheet of paper, identify the lecture pattern in each of your classes today and tomorrow. Also list three to five of the signal words that your instructor(s) used to help you determine this pattern.

Exercise 4.5   Underline the transition words found in each lecture excerpt. Use the following key and write the lecture type in the space below the excerpt.
I/S: Introduction/summary
C/E: Cause/effect
E/S: Enumeration/sequence
C/C: Comparison/contrast
SD/D: Subject development/definition

1. Regardless of cultural or socioeconomic background, socialization has several common goals. The first goal is basic discipline of the individual. This discourages behaviors deemed unwanted by the group. Second, socialization inspires aspiration. In order for the group to prosper, people must continue to grow. Next, socialization forms identities. Who you are is often determined by how you fit into the context of the group. Fourth, social roles are learned from socialization. This includes external actions and internal values. Finally, socialization teaches skills necessary for the person to fit into the group.

   Lecture type: _____

2. In this case, both evaporation and condensation occur in the closed container. Condensation is an exothermic process. This means that it liberates heat. Condensation occurs when a gas or vapor is converted to a liquid or solid. Evaporation is, on the other hand, an endothermic process. In this process, heat is absorbed. Also called vaporization, evaporation occurs when particles leave the surface of a material. Equilibrium exists when two such opposing processes occur at equal rates.

   Lecture type: _____

3. In this problem, we are attempting to show the rate of growth for investments based on five-year intervals. As class ended last meeting, we had completed the majority of this programming example. Today, we will look at how to determine if a year is divisible by five. One way to accomplish this is to use the truncation property of integer division. If an integer is exactly divisible by a second integer—in this case, five—then the quotient times the second integer will produce the first as its value. If

the value of the final result is not equal to the first integer, then the year is not divisible by five.

Lecture type: _____

4. Clinical observation is what most of us think of as the case study method. This model comes from medicine. It is the foundation of the majority of the most popular and influential personality theories. The foremost strength of the clinical observation method is its great depth. The amount of time a clinical observer devotes to each case possibly accounts for this advantage. A second strength is its realism, its lack of artificiality. Despite its popularity, however, clinical observation has its weaknesses. First, there is a possibility of observer bias. A second factor to consider is that clinical observation offers no possibility of replication. Should two observers agree on what they have seen, there is no way to duplicate the same set of circumstances for further study. Finally, there is a problem of sample bias. If observers see a sample of people not representative of the rest of humanity, then the observer finds information not generalizable to others.

Lecture type: _____

5. How does stress affect you physiologically? When you sense danger, your brain sends a message to the adrenal gland to secrete catecholamines, epinephrine, and norepinephrine into the bloodstream. This causes the liver to release glucose, which gives you more energy. It also decreases blood loss by increasing clotting time. It conserves fluid in the kidneys. Blood moves from the extremities of the body to the vital organs and legs. You breathe faster, which brings in more oxygen and allows you to rid yourself of carbon dioxide more quickly. Your heart rate also increases to provide more nutrients and oxygen to the body via the blood stream.

Lecture type: _____

6. Money and position affect lifestyles in various ways. Upper-middle class females have more career opportunities. Wealthy women are more likely to combine marriage and work because of a commitment to their careers than are poorer women, who work out of necessity. Poorer families generally maintain the traditional division of labor within their household. Middle-class families exhibit more equal relationships between husbands and wives. Middle-class parents tend to be less strict than working-class parents. Thus, people in higher and lower socioeconomic classes act and react in different ways.

Lecture type: _____

7. Using statistics from law enforcement agencies across the nation, the Uniform Crime Reports (UCR) program provides assessments of crime in the country. Law enforcement agencies make these assessments by measuring the number of crimes that come to the attention of the police. The program's main goal is to generate reliable criminal statistics for use in law enforcement administration, operation, and management. Criminal justice professors, legislators, and scholars also use this data. The UCR also provides information to the public about levels of crime.

Lecture type: _____

8. Before we begin a discussion of the Basque language, you need to realize how few people actually speak it and why that number is so small. Only one language currently spoken in Europe, the Basque language, came there before the Indo-European invasion. Basque is spoken by about 2 million people in northern Spain and southwestern France. The uniqueness of the language reflects the isolation of the Basque people in their mountainous homeland.

Lecture type: _____

Identifying Important Information

Identifying important information is a third factor that contributes to your ability to be an active listener. Although instructors emphasize main points differently, there are some common ways that they let you know what's important. Instructors often use one or more kinds of emphasis. Careful observation of your instructor helps you know when your instructor is stressing a main idea.

First, some instructors write key information on the chalkboard. They often place lecture outlines on the board before class begins. Instructors also write **terms** or key points on the board as they lecture. Copying this outline or list of terms aids learning in three ways. Initially, you learn as you write. Next, copying the outline gives you an idea of the lecture's topic. Finally, the outline serves as a guide for study.

A second way an instructor stresses a point is by providing "wait time." When an instructor speaks more slowly, you have more time to write what is being said. Hesitations and pauses are forms of "wait time." In addition, you are given "wait time" when your instructor repeats information.

Third, your instructor may change tone of voice when stressing an important point. An instructor's voice could also change in volume or intensity. You need to listen for these changes.

A fourth way instructors emphasize main points is through body language. If your instructor pounds on the desk, moves closer to the class, or makes some other gesture to stress a point, it is often one essential to your understanding.

The next way instructors explain main ideas is by using visual aids. Films, overhead transparencies, videotapes, or other audiovisual materials signal important topics.

Sixth, some instructors refer to specific text pages. Information an instructor knows by page number is worth noting and remembering.

Finally, instructors stress information by referring to that information as a possible test question. Your instructor might say, "You may see this again," or "This would make a good test question."

Exercise 4.6   Listen to the instructor on the videotape provided by your instructor. Write down the main points. Following each point, list the cue used to emphasize the information.

_____
_____
_____
_____
_____
_____
_____
_____
_____
_____
_____
_____
_____
_____
_____
_____
_____

Recall

Sometimes a lecture is like a television movie that's continued for several nights. Often an instructor doesn't finish discussing a topic during one class. He or she begins with that same topic the next class meeting. You need a review, similar to the "scenes from last night's exciting episode." Without this review, you forget what happened in the notes, just as you might forget what happened in the movie. In either case, you lose continuity and interest. Recall is diminished.

Frequent reviews aid recall by transferring information from short-term to long-term memory (see Chapter 5). The more often you hear or read something, the easier it is to remember. The "Ebbinghaus curve" or **curve of forgetting** (Figure 4.3) shows the relationship between recall of information without review and time since presentation. The numbers along the left of the graph indicate the amount of material forgotten. The numbers along the bottom show the number of days since the material was presented. Note that on the basis of one exposure, most information is lost within the first twenty-four hours. This curve explains why you are sometimes confused by notes that seemed clear when you took them. Reviewing your notes within twenty-four hours after taking them slows down your curve of forgetting.

Reviewing your notes is your responsibility. After each day's class, reread your notes. Before the next class, review your notes again. Try to anticipate what the instructor will say next. This provides background information for you to use when listening to your class lecture. It helps you relate information and remember more. In addition, it refreshes your memory of content you found confusing. You can begin the class by asking the instructor to clarify this material before he or she continues with the topic.

Figure 4.3   Curve of Forgetting

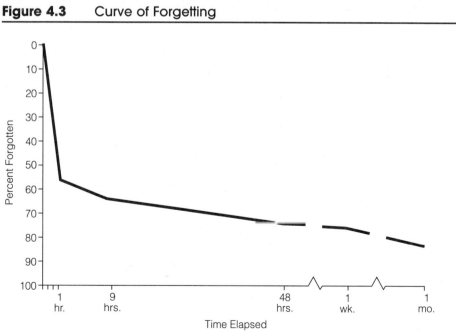

YOUR INSTRUCTOR, THE SPEAKER

The job of your instructor, the speaker, is to provide you, the listener, with information. College faculty spend their lives learning about their areas of expertise in order to share that information with you. As such, they are interested in talking about their topics and hope that you are interested in listening to what they have to say.

Instructors, like any other group, vary in ability. Some are excellent speakers. Others are mediocre at best. They vary in the ways in which they pace information. Some speak very rapidly, others more slowly. Information delivered at breakneck speeds often results in your feeling frustrated and lost. Information delivered too slowly tends to bore and therefore lose you.

Unlike a text, a lecture often shifts between major and minor topics with few cues concerning which is which. Previewing the text chapter, having some ideas about how the content is organized, and recognizing signal words help you determine a lecture's organization.

In general, your ability to distinguish good speakers from poor ones improves with practice. A rating system like the one in Table 4.8 helps you determine how effective your instructor is and how much you need to work to compensate. The more *A's* your instructor receives, the more effective that instructor is.

Table 4.8   Rating checklist for Instructors

Indicate how often your instructor does each of the following by marking either A—Always; S—Sometimes; U—Usually; or N—Never.

DOES YOUR INSTRUCTOR . . .	A	S	U	N
1. Explain goals of the lecture?				
2. Review previous lecture material before beginning the new lecture?				
3. State main ideas in introduction and summary of lecture?				
4. Provide an outline of the lecture?				
5. Provide ``wait time'' for writing notes?				
6. Speak clearly with appropriate volume?				
7. Answer questions without sarcasm?				
8. Stay on topic?				
9. Refrain from reading directly from the text?				
10. Emphasize main points?				
11. Use transition words?				
12. Give examples to illustrate difficult ideas?				
13. Write important words, dates, etc. on board?				
14. Define important terms?				
15. Use audiovisual aids to reinforce ideas?				
Totals				

Responding to Speaker Styles: Listening Responsibilities

How determined you need to be as an active listener depends in part on the effectiveness of your instructor. If your instructor is well organized and knows the subject, the amount of work you need to do lessens. Think again of the continuum on which listening takes place. With an effective instructor, you need only focus on the information that's presented. If, however, your instructor is less effective, then your responsibilities as an active listener increase. It becomes necessary for you to define, integrate, and interpret information. In addition, you must draw conclusions for yourself. Finding applications for information and judging its value become your job. The main way that you can cope with ineffective lecturers is to compensate for their deficiencies (see Table 4.9).

Maximizing Your Understanding of the Speaker's Message.

The speaker controls what is said and how it is organized. To be sure you "realize that what you heard is what is actually meant," you need to control the way you listen to get the most from the lecture. You need to use what you know to interpret, organize, and store what you hear. Such information is then available for later retrieval and use. Whatever the lecture ability or style of your instructor, you need a way to understand and remember information. Table 4.10 shows a plan for maximizing your understanding of what you hear.

I know that you believe you understood what you think I said, but I am not sure you realize that what you heard is not what I meant.

QUOTE FROM THE '60s

"I've spotted a Professor Emeritus—you can tell one by its tufted crown, bulging eyes, pointed beak, and garish plummage."

Table 4.9   How to Compensate for an Ineffective Lecturer

If Your Instructor Fails to . . .	Then You . . .
1. Explain goals of the lecture	Use your text and syllabus to set objectives
2. Review previous lecture material before beginning new lecture	Set aside time before each class to review notes.
3. State main ideas in introduction and summary of lecture	Write short summaries of the day's lecture immediately after class.
4. Provide an outline of the lecture	Preview assigned readings before class or outline notes after class.
5. Provide ``wait time'' for writing notes	Politely ask instructor to repeat information or speak more slowly.
6. Speak clearly with appropriate volume	Politely ask instructor to repeat information or speak more loudly or move closer to him or her.
7. Answer questions without sarcasm	Refrain from taking comments personally.
8. Stay on topic	Discover how anecdotes relate to the topic or use anecdotes as a memory cue.
9. Refrain from reading directly from the text	Mark passages in text as instructor reads or summarize or outline these passages in text margin.
10. Emphasize main points	Supplement lectures through text previews and reading.
11. Use transition words	Supplement lectures through text previews and reading.
12. Give examples to illustrate difficult ideas	Ask instructor for a clarifying example, discuss idea with other students and/or create an example for yourself.
13. Write important words, dates, etc. on board	Supplement notes with terms listed in text and highlight information contained in lecture and/or text.
14. Define important terms	Use text glossary or a dictionary.
15. Use audiovisual aids to reinforce ideas	Relate information to what you know about the topic or create a clarifying example for yourself.

Table 4.10   Method for Maximizing Your Understanding of the
Speaker's Message

1. Have a purpose for listening.

2. Pay careful attention to the instructor's introductory and summary statements. These usually state main points.

3. Take notes.

4. Sit comfortably erect. Slouching makes you sleepy and indicates to your instructor your disinterest.

5. Look attentive. Show your interest by keeping your eyes on your instructor.

6. Concentrate on what the instructor is saying. Try to ignore external distractions. Try to eliminate internal distractions.

7. Think of questions you would like to ask or comments you want to make.

8. Listen for transition words that signal main points.

9. Mark words or references you don't understand. Do not attempt to figure them out now—look them up later.

10. Be flexible—adjust your listening and notetaking to the lecture.

11. If the instructor speaks too quickly or unclearly, then

    a. Ask the instructor to speak more slowly or to repeat information;

    b. Leave plenty of white space and fill in missing details immediately after class;

    c. Exchange copies of notes with fellow classmates;

    d. Ask the instructor for clarification after class; and

    e. Be sure to preview lecture topic before class.

12. Avoid being a distraction (keep hands still, wait your turn in discussions, avoid whispering, etc.).

Exercise 4.7   The instructions for this activity will be read aloud by your instructor. Listen and follow each instruction carefully. Do not begin until you are told to do so.

_____

_____

_____

_____

_____

_____

_____

_____

_____

_____

_____

_____

_____

_____

_____

_____

ORGANIZING WHAT YOU HEAR IN CLASS

In learning, it is said that "we hear and we forget; we see and we remember; we do and we understand." Because this is true, you need to apply active listening techniques and take effective notes during class. These processes aid you in collecting information for later learning. They allow you to store data for future recall and use. They provide the oral and visual stimuli you need for remembering and understanding.

Lectures follow three general formats. In the first, lecture content corresponds closely to assigned textbook chapters. In the second, the content of the lecture is not necessarily contained in the text. Rather, the text provides additional information to help you better understand the subject. The third type can be either text-dependent or text-independent. It differs in that media is used to focus and enhance the delivery of information.

LECTURES DEPENDENT ON THE TEXT

When lectures are text-based, the way you use your text during the lecture depends on your preclass preparation. If you read the chapter in its entirety before class, you can record notes and instructions emphasized during the lecture directly in your textbook. As your instructor speaks, you can highlight or underline these items. You can cross out information your instructor tells you to omit and note important information in the margins of the chapter.

If you constructed a notetaking outline through text preview, you respond differently during the lecture. Using this method, you record class notes and instructions directly on your outline. You highlight important information and cross out sections that your instructor tells you to omit. You make notes in the larger section of your notetaking outline. When the instructor refers to specific graphics or quotations, you underline or mark these in your text.

LECTURES INDEPENDENT OF THE TEXT

When instructors lecture on information not contained in the text, your responsibility for taking notes increases. Because you do not have the text to use as a backup source, you need to be an especially active listener. After the lecture, you need to discover the plan of the lecture and outline or map its content. Your class notes and syllabus aid you in this attempt. Also, setting study objectives for yourself will help you create a purpose for learning and increase recall. To be sure you have fully grasped the content, discuss your notes with another classmate or do supplemental reading. Finally, when lectures are independent of the text, they are based on what your instructor feels is most important about the subject. For this reason, your instructor is a good source for clarifying confusing points. Feel free to ask questions.

LECTURES THAT INCLUDE MEDIA

Instructors use a variety of media—handouts, films, slides, models, and so on—to stimulate your visual and auditory senses during lectures. When the instructor selects media from published resources, the information tends to be more general. When an instructor creates the media, the information it contains is more course-specific. It corresponds closely to what you need to know for an exam.

Instructors use media to add knowledge and information, arouse emotion or interest, and increase skills and performance. Your responsibility is to recognize your instructor's purpose for using media and judge its worth in meeting your learning needs. For instance, suppose a psychology instructor shows a film introducing the concept of classical conditioning. How carefully you attend to the film depends on your prior knowledge of the topic. If you have extensive knowledge about classical conditioning, then the film serves only as a review for you. If classical conditioning is a new topic for you, then the film serves to build background knowledge. Table 4.11 is a list of media types and the corresponding purposes for their use.

Table 4.11   Media Types and Corresponding Purposes for Their Use

Purposes for Media	Media Types					
	Chalk-board	Trans-paren-cies	Hand-outs	Audio-tapes	Films, Slides, Television	Models
To provide examples	X	X	X	X	X	X
To list characteristics	X	X	X	X	X	
To describe or define concepts	X	X	X	X	X	
To summarize notes	X	X	X			
To supplement information	X	X	X	X	X	X
To arouse emotion or interest				X	X	X
To document proof			X	X	X	X
To aid recall	X	X	X	X	X	X
To reinforce ideas	X	X	X	X	X	X
To provide back-ground information	X	X	X	X	X	X
To provide a vicarious experience				X	X	X
To demonstrate a process				X	X	X
To introduce new concepts	X	X	X	X	X	X

Exercise 4.8   Circle the item that best answers or completes each of the following questions or statements.

1. An English literature professor begins a unit on Shakespeare by showing a film of life in sixteenth-century England. The purpose of this use of media is
   a. to provide contemporary examples of Shakespearean plays.
   b. to list characteristics of Shakespearean plays.
   c. to summarize notes.
   d. to provide background information about life in Shakespearean England.
2. A political science instructor wants to arouse interest in the development of political parties in the United States. Which of the following types of media could be used for this purpose?
   a. Transparencies
   b. Handouts
   c. Chalkboard presentations
   d. Audiotapes

3. A biology professor brings to class a model of the human heart. Which of the following is *least* likely to be a purpose for the use of this lecture media?
   a. To arouse emotion or interest in the processes of the human heart.
   b. To supplement information about the human heart and its processes.
   c. To aid recall of the human heart.
   d. To demonstrate how the human heart processes blood.

4. As a review, a history professor provides a handout of a timeline that includes all important events during the first twenty years of the American colonial period. The purpose of such a handout is most likely
   a. to arouse emotion.
   b. to provide a vicarious learning experience.
   c. to demonstrate a process.
   d. to summarize notes.

5. A mathematics professor shows how to work a complicated algebraic equation using a transparency. The purpose of the transparency is
   a. to describe concepts.
   b. to list characteristics.
   c. to provide an example.
   d. to provide background information.

6. A music history instructor provides tapes of Gregorian chants. The purpose of the tapes is least likely to be
   a. to summarize notes.
   b. to aid recall.
   c. to provide examples.
   d. to supplement information.

7. A chemistry instructor wants to teach a class the properties of solids. To ensure that each student has a complete summary of notes, the instructor provides which of the following?
   a. A film
   b. Models of solids
   c. A simulation of chemical processes
   d. A handout

8. A zoology professor asks students to view a public television special on primates. Which of the following would *not* be a logical purpose for such an assignment?
   a. To aid recall.
   b. To provide background information.
   c. To reinforce ideas.
   d. To summarize notes.

9. An education instructor demonstrates the use of a braillewriter in a class on teaching the visually impaired. The purpose of this activity is
   a. to list characteristics of visually impaired students
   b. to document proof.
   c. to supplement information.
   d. to provide a definition of visually impaired.

10. An astronomy professor wants to provide students with the experience of visiting the moon. Because he can't send them there, his next best opportunity for doing so is
   a. a handout describing the moon's rocks and craters.
   b. an example of a moon rock.
   c. a film of astronauts on the moon.
   d. a transparency of the solar system.

NOTES: THE ACT IN ACTIVE LISTENING

One of Aesop's fables tells of a blacksmith and his dog. The blacksmith, unhappy about the dog's laziness, said, "When I work, you sleep; but when I stop to eat, you want to eat, too." The moral of the fable is "Those who will not work deserve to starve." This moral holds true for notetaking. While the instructor "works," many students "sleep," passively receiving lecture information. Others actively take notes.

Notetaking supplements **active listening** in several important ways. First, some information in the lecture may not be found in the text or handouts. The lecture may be the only source for certain facts. Second, the information emphasized in a lecture often signals what will be found on exams. Next, class notes serve as a means of external storage. As a busy college student, it is impossible for you to remember everything you hear accurately. Thus, notes serve as an alternative form of memory.

The process of notetaking adds to learning independent of review. Notes often trigger your memory of the lecture or the text. Review, however, is an important part of notetaking. In general, students who review notes achieve more than those who do not (Kiewra, 1985). Researchers found that if important information was contained in notes, it had a 34 percent chance of being remembered (Howe, 1970). Information not found in notes had only a 5 percent chance of being remembered.

TAKING NOTES: A SYSTEMATIC APPROACH

Peper and Mayer (1978) discuss three theories about notetaking: the attention theory, the effort theory, and the generative theory. The attention theory suggests that, by taking notes, you pay more attention and become more familiar with new material. The effort theory is based on the idea that notetaking requires more effort and thought than reading. The generative theory states that, as you take notes, you paraphrase, organize, and understand information. To do so, you relate this new information to your background knowledge. These three theories regard notetaking as an active process that results in learning. This process requires you to become an active listener. To do so, you need a plan. This plan can be an original creation or it can be a combination of parts of other plans.

Your Personal Notetaking System

Active listening requires more than passive reception of the speaker's voice. It is enhanced by action. Active listening requires you to recognize important concepts and supporting details. One way to make your listening active is by taking notes (see Table 4.12).

As a knowledgeable notetaker, you need to selectively record only important information. What information is recorded is your choice. You make this decision based on what you know about the lecture topic, what subject you are studying, and what facts your instructor stresses. If you are familiar with a topic, your notes need not be as detailed as when you are less familiar with a subject. Active listening helps you find important information. Now you must get it written down.

Notes are not like a theme you turn in for a grade. They need not be grammatically correct. They don't even have to contain complete words. In fact, as a good notetaker, you need to develop your own system of shorthand to record your notes. In developing your system, you need to limit the number of symbols you use. After you thoroughly learn a few symbols, you can add others. Table 4.13 gives some rules for developing your own shorthand system.

Table 4.12   Suggestions for Taking Notes

1. Date each day's notes. The date serves as a reference point if you need to compare notes with someone or ask your instructor for clarification. If you are absent, the missing date(s) identifies which notes you need.

2. Develop a system for taking notes that best fits your learning style and course content.

3. Keep all notes together. You accomplish this in one of two ways. You can purchase a single spiral notebook or ring binder for each class. Or, you can purchase two multiple-subject notebooks or loose-leaf binders, one for your classes on Monday-Wednesday-Friday, and one for your classes on Tuesday-Thursday. This way you carry only one notebook each day. Notebooks with pockets are useful for saving class handouts.

4. Bring all necessary materials (notebooks, pencils and pens, text) to each class.

5. Develop a key for your symbols and abbreviations until you are comfortable using them. Without this, you may be unable to decode your notes.

Table 4.12   Suggestions for Taking Notes *(continued)*

6. Try to group and label information to aid recall.

7. Write down all terms, dates, diagrams, problems, etc. written on the board.

8. Use white space. Skip lines to separate important groups of ideas.

9. Write on only the front of your paper. This seems wasteful but makes reading your notes easier.

10. Write legibly. Notes are worthless if you can't read them.

11. If your instructor refers to specific text pages, turn to those pages and mark the information in your text rather than trying to duplicate information in your notes. Record in your notes the corresponding numbers of text pages.

12. Underline or mark important ideas and concepts with a different color ink than the one you used to take notes.

13. Compress your notes as you study. Underline or mark key words and phrases with a different color ink than the one you used to write the shorthand version.

14. Read over notes as soon as possible after class and make connections and additions. If you have any gaps, check with another student, your instructor, or the text.

15. While you wait for class to begin, review notes to set up a framework for new material.

Table 4.13   Rules for Developing a Shorthand System

1. Limit the number of symbols you create.

2. Use the beginning letters of words
   Examples   assoc/associated
   w/with
   geog/geography
   hist/history
   info/information
   intro/introduction

3. Use standard symbols
   Examples   &/and
   #/number
   %/percent
   $/money, dollars
   ?/question
   +/plus
   ×/times, multiply
   < or > /less than or greater than

Table 4.13   Rules for Developing a Shorthand System *(continued)*

---

4. Use traditional abbreviations but omit periods.
   Examples   lb/pound
                  ft/foot
                  wt/weight
                  mi/mile
                  Dec/December
                  US/United States

5. Omit vowels and keep only enough consonants to make the word recognizable.
   Examples   bkgd/background
                  mxtr/mixture
                  dvlp/develop

6. Drop endings that do not contribute to word meaning.
   Examples   ed
                  ing
                  ment
                  er

7. Add ``s'' to show plurals.

8. Omit *a, an, the,* and unimportant verbs and adjectives.
   Example   Cause of CW = slavery. Instead of: A cause of the Civil War was the issue of slavery.

9. Write out terms and proper names the first time. Show your abbreviation in parentheses after the term or name. Then use the abbreviation throughout the rest of your notes

10. Indicate dates numerically.
    Example   12/7/42 instead of December 7, 1942

11. Use common misspellings of words.
    Examples   thru/through
                   nite/night
                   rite/right

12. Express numbers numerically.
    Examples   1/one
                   2/two
                   1st/first
                   2nd/second

Exercise 4.9   Use your personal shorthand system to transcribe the paragraphs in Exercise 4.5.

1. _____

   _____

2. _____

   _____

3. _____
_____

4. _____
_____

5. _____
_____

6. _____
_____

7. _____
_____

8. _____
_____

Cornell System of Notetaking

One system of notetaking that works well for students was developed at Cornell University. Because the system is not difficult, it saves time and effort. The step-by-step process brings efficiency to your notetaking. Walter Pauk (1984), director of the Reading Study Center at Cornell, identified five stages in notetaking. They are record, reduce, recite, reflect, and review. Notes in Figure 4.4 are written according to the Cornell system of notetaking.

Stage 1 is to record. You prepare for this stage by drawing a vertical line about 2½ inches from the left edge of your paper. This column is your recall column. You leave it blank until Stage 2. During the lecture, you listen actively. You write in paragraph or outline form as much information as you think is important in the second, larger column.

Reduce is the key word in Stage 2. As soon after class as you can, you condense your notes and write them in the recall column. Your promptness in doing this is important because it helps you decrease your curve of forgetting. To condense notes, you omit adjectives and adverbs and leave nouns and verbs intact. It's important to use as few words as possible. If you wish, you can transfer these cues to index cards and carry them with you for quick and efficient review. The reduction stage increases your understanding and recall.

Recitation is Stage 3. During this stage, you cover your notes and try to say what's in them in your own words. You use the recall column to cue your memory. Then, you uncover your notes and check your accuracy. This review also aids in decreasing your curve of forgetting.

Stage 4 is reflect. After reciting your notes, you give yourself some "wait time." Then, you reread your notes and think about them. Next,

Figure 4.4   Notes Written Using the Cornell Notetaking

	Shelters topic
	Shelters are more efficient made of natural (raw) materials
Tropical shelters	Tropical Dwellers
list types	1) Frequent rainfall
& quantities	2) Bamboo — made of
	3) Roof sloped for run off
	4) Floor raised for dryness
	Grassland Dwellers
Grassland Dwellers	1) Winds, cold nights, & severe winters
Types of weather	2) Use animal hides stretched over wood
cond. materials.	3) These tents are portable
	Desert Dwellers
Desert Dwellers	1) Use mud masonry
Types & quantities	2) Mud added to wood dries like brick
of materials	3) Mud insulates from severe climate changes (hot day— cool nights).
	4) Most are farmers or nomadic.
	5) Some dried brick shelters have lasted 1000 yrs.
Summary	Shelters are more efficient made of raw materials. There are 3 main types or areas where shelters are built. Tropical, Grassland & Desert regions.

SOURCE: Courtesy of Greg Jones, Metropolitan State College, Denver, Colorado.

you read your text to supplement and clarify your notes. You use your text and notes to discover the causes and effects of issues, define terms, and relate concepts. You make generalizations and draw conclusions. This helps you become a more active thinker.

Review is the goal of Stage 5. Briefly reviewing your notes several times a week helps you retain what you have learned. This distributed review keeps information fresh, provides repetition, and decreases your chances of forgetting what you've learned. (Chapter 7 discusses various memory techniques for rehearsing information.)

WRITE TO LEARN

On a separate sheet of paper or in the appropriate notebook, take notes in your next lecture using the Cornell system. Bring your notes to the next class for evaluation and discussion.

Outlining

The most common way to organize information you hear is through **outlining.** In this sequential process, you record major concepts and supporting details, examples, and other information in the same order as they appear in your text or the lecture. The disadvantage of this system is that you may record information without thought. Because you do not synthesize or relate the information you are writing, your understanding of key concepts remains superficial.

When the lecture is independent of the text, you combat this problem by active listening strategies. If the lecture reflects text content, your notetaking outline gives you a framework for recording information. With this framework, in-class notetaking becomes more active as you listen for details within subheadings.

Outlines use either formal or informal formats (See Figure 4.5). The formal format uses roman numerals (I, II, III, etc.) placed on the left side of the page or margin to note major concepts. You indent ideas that support the major concepts. You indicate these secondary points with capital letters. You show lesser supporting details with indented Arabic numerals (1, 2, 3).

Because notes are for your personal use, they need not be formally outlined. The key to an outline is to visually highlight information in some manner. For the sake of consistency, informal outlines retain the indented format of formal outlines. To make informal outlines clearer, you separate major headings and entire sections with a blank line. To construct informal outlines, you use symbols, dashes, various print types or other means of identifying differing levels of information.

Exercise 4.10   Take notes from the videotape shown by your instructor. Use either a formal or informal outline approach to do so.

Taking Notes from Lecture Media

You take notes from lecture media (for example, handouts, chalkboard, transparencies) in much the same way you take notes from lectures. You can do this because instructors control the pace of presentation and content. Conversely, taking notes from films, slides, or television differs from traditional notetaking in several ways. First, you may associate such formats with entertainment and fail to realize the importance of remembering the information they provide. Second, such media types take place in semidarkened rooms which some time encourage naps, rather than attention. Third, the fast pace and continuous action found in these formats often provide few pauses for taking notes. For this reason, taking

Figure 4.5   Formal and Informal Outline Formats

```
Formal Outline
1. Personality theorists
   A. Psychodynamic
      1. Freud
      2. Jung
      3. Erickson
   B. Behavior
      1. Skinner
      2. Bandura
```

```
Informal Outline with Dashes
Personality Theorists
–Psychodynamic
   –Freud
   –Jung
–Behavioral
   –Skinner
   –Bandura
```

```
Informal Outline with Symbols or Print Style Differences
*PERSONALITY THEORISTS
Psychodynamic
   Freud
   Jung
   Erickson
Behavioral
   Skinner
   Bandura
```

notes immediately following the presentation sometimes provides the best alternative for recording new information.

PASSIVE NOTETAKING: TAPED AND BORROWED NOTES

In his poem "The Courtship of Miles Standish," Henry Wadsworth Longfellow tells of Miles Standish's courtship of a woman named

Priscilla. Because Miles was such a shy man, he asked his friend John Alden to talk to Priscilla for him. John did so. During John's attempts to convince Priscilla of Miles's worth, Priscilla fell in love with John. John, however, was unaware of this. One night when he was trying to tell Priscilla of Miles's love of her, she said, "Speak for yourself, John." John did. Soon he and Priscilla were married, much to Standish's dismay.

Longfellow's poem shows that there are some tasks in life a person must do without help from others. For Miles Standish and John Alden, that task was love. For you, it's notetaking. Borrowed or purchased notes reflect the person who took them. They require no effort or action on your part. Thus, they are not part of active listening. The most effective notes are personal and reflect your background knowledge and understanding.

. . . and as time passed, technology overtook culture and culture became extinct.

Likewise, using a tape recorder to take notes seems a good solution. After all, a recorder copies every word the instructor says. A recorder doesn't become bored, daydream, or doodle. It appears to be the perfect notetaking solution. On the other hand, using a tape recorder—like letting someone else speak for you—has drawbacks. First, listening to tapes is too time consuming. Transcribing them in their entirety contributes little to understanding the lecture's main ideas. Similar to underlining too much on a text page (see Chapter 5), writing each word the lecturer says decreases your ability to highlight important information. Second, because a tape recorder only records auditory information, your notes lack diagrams, terms, and other information that the instructor might have written on the board. Third, technical difficulties sometimes arise. Problems like dead batteries or missing tapes sometimes prevent you from getting the notes you need. Fourth, the use of tape recorders sometimes offends or intimidates instructors. Therefore, if you want to record notes, you need to get your instructor's permission before recording any lecture. Fifth, your reliance on recorders keeps you from learning good notetaking skills. The sixth and most important drawback is that, as with using borrowed notes, you are a passive listener.

There is a place for borrowed or taped notes, however. If you are ill or unavoidably absent from class, having someone else take or tape notes for you is better than not having notes at all. Another acceptable use of taped notes is to record the lecture while you take notes. Taped information allows you to fill gaps during review. Thus, this method is especially helpful if your instructor speaks rapidly. Like the telephone, taped notes are the next best thing to being there.

AFTER CLASS: THE FOLLOW-THROUGH

It is said that in the classroom there is more teaching than learning. Outside the classroom there is more learning than teaching. In class, you receive information from the instructor. After the lecture, your goal is to process that information. Thus, learning is not simply recording what you've seen or heard during the lecture. It's assimilating what you've seen and heard after the lecture. As a result, what you learn becomes a part of you. Post-lecture reading and evaluating your notes are the follow-through that allows you to truly assimilate course information.

POST-LECTURE READING

After the lecture, you actually have been exposed to information on the lecture topic twice. First, you either previewed or read the chapter. Your second exposure was during the lecture. Post-lecture reading helps you focus on the information emphasized in the lecture. If you previewed the text before the lecture, this final reading provides details, explanations, and examples to support the main ideas of the lecture. If you read the chapter in its entirely before the lecture, you should focus on the areas that confused you or that were emphasized in class. In both cases, post-lecture reading fills the gaps in your understanding.

EVALUATING YOUR NOTES

Notes organize the information you hear in a lecture—information that presumably will be the basis of a test. As a result, your notes need to be the best they can be for each course you take. Table 4.14 can be used to evaluate your notes—the higher the number, the better. Assess your notes for each course you take. Notetaking ability varies according to the content and demands of the class.

Table 4.14   Notes Evaluation Criteria

Value points and descriptors of notetaking habits

FORMAT	4	3	2	1	0
Use of ink	I use my pen consistently.		I use pen and pencil.	I use pencil.	
Handwriting	Others can read my notes.		Only I can read my notes.	I can't read my notes.	
Notebook	I use a looseleaf binder.		I use a spiral notebook.	I don't use a notebook.	
Use of page	I leave enough space for editing.		I leave some space for editing.	My notes cover the page.	

ORGANIZA-TION	4	3	2	1	0
Headings	I use new headings for each main idea.		I use headings inconsistently.	I don't use headings for changes in main ideas.	
Subtopics	I group subtopics under headings.		I don't indent subtopics under headings.	My subtopics are not grouped.	
Recall column	I use cue words and symbols to make practice questions.		I use cue words in a recall column.	I do not use a recall column.	
Abbreviation	I abbreviate whenever possible.		I use some abbreviation.	I don't abbreviate.	
Summaries	I summarize lectures in writing.		I write a list of summary lecture topics.	I don't summarize.	

MEANING	4	3	2	1	0
Main points	I identify main points with symbols and underlining.		I list main points.	I don't list main points.	
Supporting details	I show the relationships between main ideas and details.		My notes list details.	I don't list details.	
Examples	I list examples under main points.		I list some examples.	I don't record examples.	
Restatement	I use my own words.		I use some of my own words.	I use none of my own words.	

SOURCE: Reprinted with permission of Norman A. Stahl and the International Reading Association.

GROUP LEARNING ACTIVITY
EFFECTIVE NOTETAKING—GOOD STUDENTS, TAKE NOTE!

Effective notetaking requires active listening. Active listeners know how to control their attention to avoid classroom daydreaming. Here's a listening/notetaking plan that works for many students. The important steps are summarized by the letters LISAN, pronounced like the word listen (Carman & Adams, 1985).

L = *Lead. Don't follow.* Try to anticipate what the instructor is going to say. Try to set up questions as guides. Questions can come from the instructor's study guides or the reading assignments.

I = *Ideas.* Every lecture is based on a core of important ideas. Usually, an idea is introduced and examples or explanations are given. Ask yourself often, "What is the main idea now? What ideas support it?"

S = *Signal words.* Listen for words that tell you the direction the instructor is taking. For instance, here are some groups of signal words: *There are three reasons why* . . . Here come ideas, *Most important is* . . . Main idea, *On the contrary* . . . Opposite idea, *As an example* . . . Support for main idea, *Therefore* . . . Conclusion.

A = *Actively listen.* Sit where you can hear and where you can be seen if you need to ask a question. Look at the instructor while he or she talks. Bring questions you want answered from the last lecture or from your reading. Raise your hand at the beginning of class or approach your instructor before the lecture begins. Do anything that helps you to be active.

N = *Notetaking.* As you listen, write down only key points. Listen to everything, but be selective and don't try to write everything down. If you are too busy writing, you may not grasp what is being said. Any gaps in your notes can be filled in immediately after class.

Here is something more you should know: A revealing study (Palkovitz & Lore, 1980) found that most students take reasonably good notes—and then don't use them! Most students wait until just before exams to review their notes. By then, the notes have lost much of their meaning. This practice may help explain why students do poorly on test items based on lectures (Thielens, 1987). If you don't want your notes to seem like hieroglyphics or "chicken scratches," it pays to review them *on a regular basis.* And remember, whenever it is important to listen effectively, the letters LISAN are a good guide.

SOURCE: Coon, D. (1989). *Introduction to Psychology, Exploration and Application.* St. Paul: West Publishing.

Application

Use LISAN in the next lecture for this class or ask your instructor to give a brief sample lecture. In your study group, compare answers to the following questions:

1. What did you do to lead? What questions did you have? Where did you get your questions?

2. What was the core of the lecture's content? What details supported that idea?

3. What signal words were used in the lecture?

4. What did you do to actively participate in the lecture? Did other group members take note of your active participation?

5. Are you satisfied with your notes? What, if any, gaps occurred? What precipitated these gaps? What could you do differently?

CHAPTER SUMMARY

1. Strategies for previewing the text prior to class help you build background knowledge for course content. These include making predictions about content, constructing a notetaking outline through text previewing, and using chapter maps to direct your learning.

2. Several factors affect your ability to listen actively in class and communicate effectively with your instructor, the speaker. These include the abilities to maintain concentration, hear main ideas, identify important information, and recall what you hear. Although your listening responsibilities vary according to the speaker's style, you can develop a plan for maximizing your understanding of the speaker's message. As an active listener, you control the learning process and integrate what you already know with what you hear.

3. Lectures formats vary according to whether they are text-dependent, text-independent, or include media.

4. Taking notes enhances active listening. Your systematic approach to notetaking could be based on your personal system, the Cornell system, or another system. Taking notes from lecture media requires some modification of your notetaking strategy. Passive notetaking methods are less effective because they fail to reflect your own background knowledge and purposes for learning.

TERMS
Terms appear in the order in which they occurred in the chapter.

background
    knowledge
previewing
notetaking outline
chapter maps
distractions
self-talk
transition words
lecture patterns
terms
curve of forgetting
active listening
outlining

5. The follow-through for notetaking occurs after class when you begin to assimilate information through post-lecture reading. Periodic evaluation of your notes for all your classes helps you assess weaknesses and formulate strategies for improvement.

CHAPTER REVIEW

Answer briefly but completely.

1. Examine the textbooks you use for each of your classes (or the sample chapters in this text). How do factors within the text impact your choice of previewing strategy for making predictions about content?

    _____

    _____

    _____

2. Compare and contrast Table 4.1, *Steps in Previewing,* with Table 4.3, *Constructing a Notetaking Outline through Text Previews.* How are the tables alike? How are they different? What accounts for their similarities and differences?

    _____

    _____

    _____

    _____

    _____

3. Explain how differing lecture formats (text-dependent, text-independent, with media) might affect left- and right-brain learning.

    _____

    _____

    _____

4. How do the listening habits in Quiz #2 of Exercise 4.4 affect your ability to understand and process a class lecture? Why?

    _____

    _____

    _____

5. What is the relationship between the factors affecting your ability to be an active listener and the items in Table 4.8, *Rating Checklist for Instructors?*

_____

_____

_____

6. Which of Peper and Mayer's three theories of notetaking do you feel best supports the Cornell system of notetaking? Why?

_____

_____

_____

7. How do formal and informal outline formats (see Figure 4.5) affect right- and left-brain learning? Why?

_____

_____

_____

8. A notetaking service has just opened near your institution. It sells copies of the entire set of notes for each of the classes in which you are now enrolled. What might be the advantages of having these copies? What would be the disadvantages?

_____

_____

_____

9. How does the after-class follow-through affect the curve of forgetting (Figure 4.3)?

_____

_____

_____

10. Give a specific example of how course content and demands affect notetaking ability.

_____

_____

_____

REFERENCES

Howe, M. J. (1970). Notetaking strategy, review and long-term relationships between notetaking variables and achievement measures. *Journal of Educational Research, 63:* 285.

Kiewra, K. A. (1985). Investigating notetaking and review: A depth of processing alternative. *Educational Psychologist* 20(1): 23–32.

Pauk, W. (1984). *How to study in college.* Boston: Houghton Mifflin, pp. 127–29.

Peper, R. J., and Mayer, R. E. (1978). Notetaking as a generative activity. *Journal of Educational Psychology 70(4):* 514–22.

Williams, T. H. (1969). *Huey Long.* New York, NY: Alfred A. Knopf, pp. 262–63.

Vocabulary Development   Integrating Listening and Notetaking: Connecting What You Learn with What You Know

Consider Legos. Some people think of college vocabulary development as a building process much as children build with Legos. They think words are like blocks that can be placed one on top of the other. Words, however, connect to each other in a variety of ways with many connections or only a few. The way you think about information and the connections you make affect what you hear and how you note it. Vocabulary development increases when you connect what you learn with what you know.

Background knowledge forms your personal set of mental Legos for connecting new information with what you already know. You make these connections as you listen to a lecture. You use the words you hear to cue the information you know. The information you know helps you make sense of and learn more about the topic. Vocabulary development is more efficient because learning something you already know about is easier than learning something you know nothing about. Notes that reflect your reactions, feelings, and connections, as well as lecture content, help you integrate new information more fully.

Background knowledge consists of everything you know about a topic. It is your knowledge of language and the world. Your knowledge of language consists of two areas: vocabulary and grammar.

Your vocabulary contributes to your knowledge of language. Your personal vocabulary consists of four subsets: listening, speaking, writing, and reading. Your listening vocabulary consists of words you understand when you hear them. Your speaking vocabulary includes words you use in talking, just as your writing vocabulary contains words you use in writing. Finally, the words you know when you see them comprise your reading vocabulary.

These four types of vocabulary can be divided into two groups, according to their use. The first group consists of those words you deposit in memory through listening and reading. The second group encompasses those words you use in speaking and writing (see Figure 4.6). You increase your listening vocabulary, the largest of the four types, with the least effort. Anything you hear (television, radio, teachers, friends, and so forth) enlarges your listening vocabulary. Similarly, your reading vocabulary increases each time you find the meanings of new words. Both reading and listening involve actively receiving new information. Speaking and writing are the ways you use the words you learn. If you make no deposits, you have no words to use.

The second area of language knowledge is grammar. Even if English isn't your favorite subject, you possess much knowledge about the English language. Your knowledge of words and their functions in sentences allows you to find meaning.

Figure 4.6 Four Types of Vocabulary

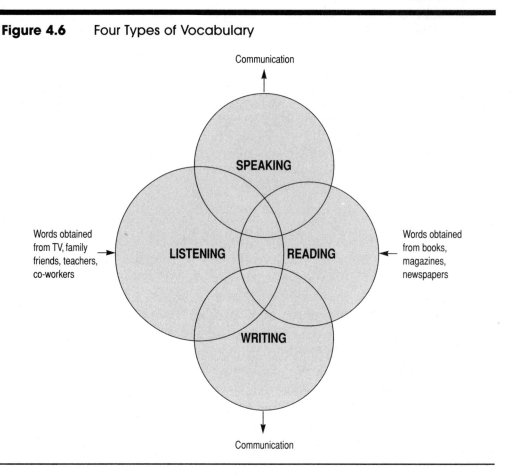

Your knowledge of punctuation also helps you find meaning. This process is cyclical. The more you know about how language functions, the more you are able to learn. The more you are able to learn, the more you know. Knowledge of language aids you in becoming a more active listener. Active listening, in turn, helps you increase your language knowledge.

World knowledge comes from the sum of your experiences. It consists of what you know about the way people, places, things, and concepts work and relate to each other. It includes facts, opinions, inferences, and other information you get through direct experience or through vicarious learning.

For example, it's one thing to go to France. It's another to read about going to France. Although both provide you with information about the country, the direct experience of traveling to France provides you with more complete and direct information. The sights, sounds, and feelings you experience are your own. However, time, money, or other factors may keep you from taking such a trip. You can still learn about France vicariously through reading, television, movies, travel brochures, conversations with people who have been there, and so on. The quantity and quality of the information you get depends on the viewpoints, experiences, and perceptions of your sources. Active listening also increases your store of world knowledge.

Activity

In the space below, list the things you associate with the phrase

"Every man a king but no one wears a crown."

Now read the following passage from a biography of Huey Long, Louisiana governor in the 1930s (Williams, 1969). After reading, add to your list above in ink. On a separate sheet of paper, respond to the following question: How did the passage affect your consideration of the topic? What accounts for the differences in before and after reading? What happens when you connect what you learn with what you know? What happens if you fail to connect what you learn with what you know?

Above the platform stretched banners proclaiming the Long slogan: "Every Man a King, But No One Wears a Crown." John H. Overton presided and introduced the dignitaries on the platform, among whom were John P. Sullivan and Swords Lee, and the candidate who was also the speaker of the evening. Huey gave the same kind of speech that he had given in launching his campaign four years before. . . . He wanted to make Louisiana into "a progressive, educated and modern commonwealth." He promised free textbooks, free bridges, surfaced roads ("practically every public road" should be surfaced), improved state hospitals and other institutions, natural gas for New Orleans and other cities, state warehouses to aid farmers in marketing their crops, vocational training for the deaf, dumb, and blind, and an expanded court system. He strongly implied that the state should supply financial assistance to local school units (every boy and girl should be able to live at home and have access to an education) and to students of poor families who wished to attend higher institutions. He denied that he was hostile to corporations. He had opposed only the evil ones, but he thought that all the big ones should bear a higher and fairer burden of taxation.

SQ3R: A Systematic Plan for Reading Text Chapters

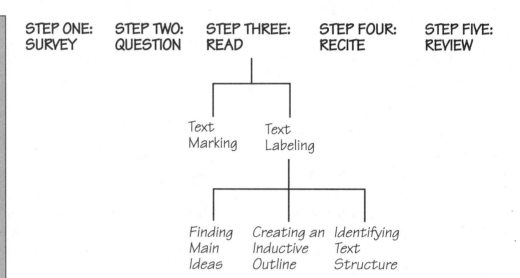

STEP ONE: SURVEY   STEP TWO: QUESTION   STEP THREE: READ   STEP FOUR: RECITE   STEP FIVE: REVIEW

Text Marking   Text Labeling

Finding Main Ideas   Creating an Inductive Outline   Identifying Text Structure

The president was introducing the commencement speaker and Kate forced herself to concentrate. A plump woman in her fifties took the podium. Her plain, stern-lipped face was hazily familiar as that which in photographs of feminist rallies, usually appeared just behind that of Friedan or Steinem.

"I envy you women," she was saying. "The path is so clearly marked for you. There will be no need for you to repeat the mistakes of my generation. The obstacles that blocked us now exist only for you to hurdle. You will be free to go out and have anything and everything you want!"

Kate listened attentively. The message was clear: go out and do something and be sure that it is creative and meaningful, that it gives you power and above all makes you a success. But now the speaker was retiring from the podium. Wait! Kate shrieked silently. Don't go yet! You haven't told us what that something is, nor shown us how to get it. The path isn't clear . . . no, not clear at all.

SOURCE: Reprinted with permission from *Everything We Wanted* by Lindsay Marcotta. Copyright © 1984 by Lindsay Marcotta. Used by permission of Crown Publishers, Inc.

As a student, you face a challenge in each class you take. Like Kate, you know what is expected of you—good grades, a degree, a new job. You probably have a general idea of what you need to do to meet your goals. You know that studying and preparing for class lead to success. Also like Kate, you may feel that you have no specific plan to help you accomplish the necessary tasks (reading texts, reviewing information) for achieving your goal.

Such a plan exists for using information from texts. Developed by Frances Robinson, the SQ3R study system has been used by countless students to help them read and recall text information. SQ3R involves five steps: *survey, question, read, recite,* and *review.* Table 5.1 defines all steps of the SQ3R process. It also provides a quick index of where additional information about each step is found.

STEP ONE: SURVEY

Surveying, or previewing, is the first step in your interaction with the text. Surveying before reading accomplishes two goals. First, it makes reading an active, rather than a passive, process. It requires you to think about the topic of the chapter before you begin reading. Second, it provides you with an opportunity to connect what you already know about the topic, your background knowledge, with the new information you will be learning. How does your background knowledge affect your understanding? Read the passage below and answer the accompanying questions.

Table 5.1	Steps in SQ3R	
SQ3R Step	**Definition**	**Process Used**
Survey	Previewing to find main ideas or get the gist of a chapter.	Previewing. See Table 4.1.
Question	Predicting chapter content or setting purposes for reading.	Making predictions about content. See Table 4.2.
Read	Checking your predictions through literal and inferential comprehension.	Reading or processing text and scanning. See Tables 5.3, 5.4, 5.5, and 5.6 and Figure 5.3.
Recite	Checking your understanding of the text.	Monitoring understanding. See Table 5.9.
Review	Transferring information from short-term to long-term memory.	Rehearsal through practice, organization, and association. See Chapter 7.

The procedure is actually quite simple. First you arrange things into different groups. Of course, one pile may be sufficient depending on how much there is to do. If you have to go somewhere else due to lack of facilities that is the next step; otherwise, you are pretty well set. It is important not to overdo things. That is, it is better to do too few things at once than too many. In the short run this may not seem important but complications can easily arise. A mistake can be expensive as well. At first the whole procedure will seem complicated. Soon, however, it will become just another facet of life. It is difficult to foresee any end to the necessity for this task in the immediate future, but then one can never tell. After the procedure is completed one arranges the materials into different groups again. Then they can be put into their appropriate places. Eventually they will be used once more and the whole cycle will then have to be repeated. However, that is part of life.

SOURCE: Reprinted with permission from Contextual Prerequisites for Understanding: Some Investigations of Comprehension and Recall. By Bransford, J. D., and Johnson, M. K. Copyright © 1972 by *Journal of Verbal Learning and Verbal Behavior* 2:6. All rights reserved.

1. What is the topic of this passage?

2. What do you know about this topic?

3. In the first sentence, what procedure is being referred to?

4. How did you identify this procedure?

5. The passage states that after putting things into different groups, you might have to go somewhere else due to lack of facilities. What place does "somewhere else" refer to?

6. How do you recognize the location of "somewhere else?"

7. The passage states that mistakes could be expensive. What does that mean?

8. Why is there no foreseeable end to this procedure?

The topic of the passage is identified on the bottom of the last page in this chapter. After you have checked the topic, answer questions 2 through 8 again.

How was your understanding improved by knowing the topic? Although the passage contained no more information than when you first read it, you—the learner—provided the details needed to understand it. Before you knew the topic, you had no way to interact with the information. Without information supplied by you, it made no sense.

When you learn, information comes from two sources: one external, the other internal. The text is an external source of information. You, the learner, are the internal source.

Many students learn without making the most of the interaction of internal and external sources. Because you are a less obvious source of information, you may not have thought of yourself as a source.

The survey step in SQ3R allows you to maximize yourself as a source of information in learning. Surveying usually is part of your before-lecture preparation. As such, surveying, or previewing, was described in Chapter 4, Table 4.1.

WRITE TO LEARN

Consider the preceding cartoon. It shows how different people would define the word *score* based on their differing backgrounds. On a separate sheet of paper, write how the word *set* would be defined by each of the following: (1) a mathematician, (2) a jeweler, (3) a china salesperson, (4) a tennis pro, and (5) a cook. What accounts for differences among the definitions?

STEP TWO: QUESTION

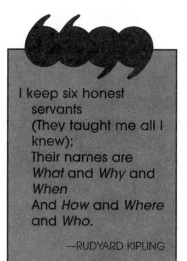

I keep six honest
servants
(They taught me all I
knew);
Their names are
What and *Why* and
When
And *How* and *Where*
and *Who.*

—RUDYARD KIPLING

For many students, the goal of reading is to finish. Whether or not they learn anything is beside the point as long as they meet their goal.

Your goals for learning should be part of a quest for knowledge. Employing Kipling's six servants assists you in your quest by helping you set goals for understanding what you read. Although you set your goals by asking questions as part of the before-lecture process as described on pp. 193 in Chapter 4, you find the answers to your questions through reading—Step 3 of the SQ3R process. Table 5.2 summarizes the kinds of information that each of your "honest servants" helps you find.

STEP THREE: READ

If you have ever bought a product marked "REQUIRES ASSEMBLY," you know how vital it is to preview the diagrams and read all of the directions before beginning. This thorough reading, in combination with your preview, provides you with all available information before you tackle your task.

Table 5.2   Question Words and Corresponding Indicators

If your question begins . . .	Look for . . . when you read.
Why?	Words such as *because, for that reason, consequently, as a result*
How?	A sequence; a list; or words such as *by, through, as a result of*
What?	Nouns; linking verbs; punctuation symbols (commas, dashes, parentheses); words such as *involves, consists, includes*
Who?	Capitalized words or names of groups; nouns
How many? How much?	Numbers (written or Arabic)
Which?	Nouns and adjectives
When?	Capitalized words such as days, months, or other time periods; time of the day (written or Arabic); numerical symbols for months, days, and years; words like *before, during, after, soon, later, prior*
Where?	Capitalized places (cities, states, countries); addresses; words such as *behind, across, near, next to*

Similarly, reading a chapter in its entirety before class helps you glean all important details and main ideas for use during class. Rather than encountering new ideas in the lecture, you affirm what you read and clarify misconceptions. Your background knowledge enables you to grasp new ideas more quickly and firmly.

To get the most from reading you must do more than simply sit and stare at a text. In the second step of SQ3R, you posed questions. Now you need to actively seek their answers. This means that you look for patterns, or connections, among information. You consider the meanings of terms in their surroundings. You try to summarize main ideas. You draw conclusions. You attend critically to the information in the text. One way to assure that you read actively is to mark your text as you read. Table 5.3 summarizes the reading process.

TEXT MARKING

Text marking sounds simple. You find important information and mark it. You highlight or underline what you want to remember. But what exactly do you mark? How do you know what is really important? How do you know what to "overlook?"

First, what you mark depends on how much you already know about the topic. Consider what might happen if you were studying about the settlement of Salt Lake City. If you're from Salt Lake City, you'd probably mark less. This is because you might already know some of the

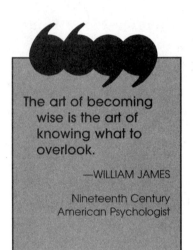

The art of becoming wise is the art of knowing what to overlook.

—WILLIAM JAMES

Nineteenth Century American Psychologist

Table 5.3   Steps in the Reading Process

1. Keeping your purpose-setting question in mind, read the paragraph or passage.

2. Identify the topic by looking for the repetition of key words and phrases. If the main idea is unstated, identify the topic by retrieving background knowledge that seems appropriate until details confirm or disprove your choice.

3. Retrieve the background knowledge necessary to understand the text.

4. Based on elements in the text and your background knowledge, identify stated details and make inferences about new terms or concepts.

5. Make inferences about unstated details or the text pattern of the main idea.

6. Restate the main idea through paraphrasing, summarizing, or synthesizing.

7. Determine if the main idea answers your purpose-setting question.

information. In contrast, if you know little about Salt Lake City, you'll probably mark more. In general, the less you know, the more you mark. The more you know, the less you mark.

Second, if you previewed and asked content-predicting questions, what you mark should answer your questions. As a result, you mark the information that highlights terms and main ideas.

You might also include other details that support your answers to your questions. These could be the steps in a sequence or other kinds of lists, reasons, conclusions, and so on. Knowing which and what kind of details your instructor deems most important helps you choose what to mark.

The difficulty of text language is a third factor to consider in text marking. Although how difficult you find a topic to be depends on your familiarity with that topic, its difficulty also depends on how it is written or presented. Such factors as subject depth, number of details, and vocabulary affect the ease with which you understand.

As you read the following excerpts, note their differing lengths. Although both passages concern the same topic, their content differs. The second passage includes more details and provides more information about the subject. In addition, the vocabulary (see bold-faced italicized words) is much more difficult.

PASSAGE 1

Babbage did not give up, however. In 1833 he developed a plan for building an ***analytical engine.*** This machine was to be capable of addition, subtraction, multiplication, division, and storage of intermediate results in a memory unit. Unfortunately, the analytical engine was also too advanced for its time. It was Babbage's concept of the analytical engine, though, that led to the computer more than a hundred years later. This earned him the title of "the father of modern computers."

SOURCE: Reprinted by permission from *Introduction to Computers and Basic Programming* by Brenan and Mandell. Copyright © 1984 by West Publishing Company. All rights reserved.

PASSAGE 2

One reason Babbage ***abandoned*** the Difference Engine was that he had been struck by a much better idea. Inspired by Jacquard's punched-card-controlled loom, Babbage wanted to build a punched-card-controlled calculator. He called his proposed automatic calculator the *Analytical Engine.*

The Difference Engine could only compute tables (and only those tables that could be computed by successive additions). But the Analytical Engine could carry out any calculation, just as Jacquard's loom could weave any pattern. All one had to do was to punch the cards with the instructions for the desired calculations. If the Analytical Engine had been completed, it would have been a nineteenth-century computer.

But, alas, that was not to be. The British government had already sunk thousands of pounds into the Difference Engine and had received nothing in return. It had no intention of making the same mistake with the Analytical Engine. And Babbage's ***eccentricities*** and ***abrasive*** personality did not help his cause.

Looking back, the government may have even been right. If it had *financed* the new invention, it might well have received nothing in return. For, as usual, Babbage's idea was far ahead of existing mechanical technology. This was particularly true because the design for the Analytical Engine was *grandiose.* For example, Babbage wanted his machine to do calculations with fifty-digit accuracy, an accuracy far greater than that found in most modern computers and far more than is needed for most calculations.

What's more, Babbage often changed his plans in the middle of a project, so that everything done previously had to be abandoned and the work started anew. How *ironic* that the founder of operations research, the science of industrial management, could not manage the development of his own inventions.

Babbage's *contemporaries* would have considered him more successful if he had stayed with his original plan and constructed the Difference Engine. If he had done this, however, he would have earned only a footnote in history. It is for the Analytical Engine he never completed that we honor Babbage as "the father of the computer."

Your goal should be to mark amounts of information that are "just right." Consider the two examples of text marking found in Figure 5.1. In the first example, the student marked too much information to be useful for study. Remember that the purpose of text marking is to tell the difference between important and unimportant information. Here, there is no difference. Even if you know nothing about a subject, you should be marking half or less of the information.

In the second example in Figure 5.1, the student marked too little information. This could mean that the student already felt confident about understanding the information. It also could signal a lack of attention, poor understanding, or a lack of knowledge about what to mark.

Now consider the text marked in Figure 5.2. It shows the "just right" amount of text marking. Remember, while the amount you mark depends on what you know about the topic, the difficulty of the text, the goal-setting questions you posed, and what you think your instructor will ask questions about, overmarking results in nothing gained but a neon-colored page.

TEXT LABELING

Imagine that you take a trip and have gotten lost. When you ask for directions, a friendly citizen gets a map and highlights the route you should take. Thanking your new friend, you start off once more. However, when you look at the map, you find no names for streets, buildings, or other locations. Although you may be able to reach your destination, it will take more effort to get there.

Figure 5.1   Overmarking and Undermarking Text

ORGANIZING COURSE CONTENT TO SET READING GOALS

Think again about how you best learn information (see Chapter 1). Outlines and maps help you predict and organize information while surveying. This is particularly true if you rephrase headings and subheadings into questions or connect chapter titles with headings and subheadings to questions. Questions require you to look for answers and thus, make reading more active. You read to answer *what, how, when, who, which, where,* and *why.* (see Table 2.3). When previewing, you will normally be looking for main ideas. Thus, *why, how,* and *what* questions will form the basis of your previewing outline. Question outlines and maps make previewing less covert and more concrete. They help set goals for reading.

ORGANIZING THROUGH OUTLINING

An outline consists of a written collection of ideas ranked according to importance. Every idea is subordinate to or summarized by another idea. Thus, an outline forms an ordered picture of information. You determine importance based on the ways in which ideas fit together.

One way of organizing information in a chapter is outlining it. The subject of the chapter serves as the subject of your outline. The question you created from each major heading in the chapter is a major heading in your outline. Each question you formed from a subheading becomes a minor heading. Information found under subheadings becomes questions about supporting details.

Outlines can be formal or informal formats (see Table 2.4). The formal format uses Roman numerals (I, II, III) placed on the left side of the page or margin to note major concepts. You indent ideas that support the major concepts. You indicate these secondary points by capitalizing them. You show lesser supporting details by indented Arabic numerals (1, 2, 3). You note details that refer to these third-level facts with lowercase letters (a, b, c).

Informal outlines look much like formal outlines. The key difference is that they don't follow the Roman and Arabic numeral format. Instead, white space or other symbols identify major and minor points. The purpose of the outline is to organize ideas, and the structure of the outline adds little to understanding. Informal outlines are just as useful as formal outlines.

ORGANIZING THROUGH MAPPING

Maps provide a quick means for determining the plan of a chapter. They form pictures that show relationships among concepts. In addition, they express patterns of thought. You sketch a map by using headings and subheadings in a combination boxed-branching format (see Table 2.5 and Figure 2.1). You place each question you created from major headings in separate boxes horizontally (from left to right) in the order in which they appear in the chapter. You then arrange questions about subheadings in a branching formation within the box.

Figure 5.1   Overmarking and Undermarking Text *continued*

ORGANIZING COURSE CONTENT TO SET READING GOALS

Think again about how you best learn information (see Chapter 1). Outlines and maps help you predict and organize information while surveying. This is particularly true if you rephrase headings and subheadings into questions or connect chapter titles with headings and subheadings to questions. Questions require you to look for answers and, thus, make reading more active. You read to answer *what, how, when, who, which, where, and why* (see Table 2.3). When previewing, you will normally be looking for main ideas. Thus, *why, how, and what* questions will form the basis of your previewing outline. Question outlines and maps make previewing less covert and more concrete. They help set goals for reading.

ORGANIZING THROUGH OUTLINING

An outline consists of a written collection of ideas ranked according to importance. Every idea is subordinate to or summarized by another idea. Thus, an outline forms an ordered picture of information. You determine importance based on the ways in which ideas fit together.

One way of organizing information in a chapter is outlining it. The subject of the chapter serves as the subject of your outline. The question you created from each major heading in the chapter is a major heading in your outline. Each question you formed from a subheading becomes a minor heading. Information found under sub-headings becomes questions about supporting details.

Outlines can be in formal or informal formats (see Table 2.4). The formal format uses Roman numerals (I, II, III) placed on the left side of the page or margin to note major concepts. You indent ideas that support the major concepts. You indicate these secondary points by capitalizing them. You show lesser supporting details by indented Arabic numerals (1, 2, 3). You note details that refer to these third-level facts with lowercase letters (a, b, c).

Informal outlines look much like formal outlines. The key difference is that they don't follow the Roman and Arabic numeral format. Instead, white space or other symbols identify major and minor points. The purpose of the outline is to organize ideas, and the structure of the outline adds little to understanding. Informal outlines are just as useful as formal outlines.

ORGANIZING THROUGH MAPPING

Maps provide a quick means for determining the plan of a chapter. They form pictures that show relationships among concepts. In addition, they express patterns of thought. You sketch a map by using headings and subheadings in a combination boxed-branching format (see Table 2.5 and Figure 2.1). You place each question you created from major headings in separate boxes horizontally (from left to right) in the order in which they appear in the chapter. You then arrange questions about subheadings in a branching formation within the box.

Figure 5.2   Text Marking

ORGANIZING COURSE CONTENT TO SET READING GOALS

Think again about how you best learn information (see Chapter 1). Outlines and maps help you predict and organize information while surveying. This is particularly true if you rephrase headings and subheadings into questions or connect chapter titles with headings and subheadings to questions. Questions require you to look for answers and, thus, make reading more active. You read to answer *what, how, when, who, which, where,* and *why* (see Table 2.3). When previewing, you will normally be looking for main ideas. Thus, *why, how,* and *what* questions will form the basis of your previewing outline. Question outlines and maps make previewing less covert and more concrete. They help set goals for reading.

ORGANIZING THROUGH OUTLINING

An outline consists of a written collection of ideas ranked according to importance. Every idea is subordinate to or summarized by another idea. Thus, an outline forms an ordered picture of information. You determine importance based on the ways in which ideas fit together.

One way of organizing information in a chapter is outlining it. The subject of the chapter serves as the subject of your outline. The question you created from each major heading in the chapter is a major heading in your outline. Each question you formed from a subheading becomes a minor heading. Information found under subheadings becomes questions about supporting details.

Outlines can be in formal or informal formats (see Table 2.4). The formal format uses Roman numerals (I, II, III) placed on the left side of the page or margin to note major concepts. You indent ideas that support the major concepts. You indicate these secondary points by capitalizing them. You show lesser supporting details by indented Arabic numerals (1, 2, 3). You note details that refer to these third-level facts with lowercase letters (a, b, c).

Informal outlines look much like formal outlines. The key difference is that they don't follow the Roman and Arabic numeral format. Instead, white space or other symbols identify major and minor points. The purpose of the outline is to organize ideas, and the structure of the outline adds little to understanding. Informal outlines are just as useful as formal outlines.

ORGANIZING THROUGH MAPPING

Maps provide a quick means for determining the plan of a chapter. They form pictures that show relationships among concepts. In addition, they express patterns of thought. You sketch a map by using headings and subheadings in a combination boxed-branching format (see Table 2.5 and Figure 2.1). You place each question you created from major headings in separate boxes horizontally (from left to right) in the order in which they appear in the chapter. You then arrange questions about subheadings in a branching formation within the box.

Much the same problem occurs in text marking. Many students read and mark information, just to find themselves somewhat "lost" when they have to study. Only with effort can they reconstruct why they marked their texts as they did.

Consider again the marked text in Figure 5.2. Most students would agree that, just by looking, it appears to be appropriately marked. However, reviewing for a test several weeks later, you might forget how the information relates. You would need to reread most of what you marked to reconstruct your thoughts.

Text labeling helps you identify relationships and summarize information. It does not replace text marking. Instead, you use it in addition to text marking. Text labeling forms a kind of index to help you locate information more quickly. You also use it to write yourself notes for later review.

Text marking and labeling require several steps (see Table 5.4). First, you read and mark your text. Then you look for patterns, main ideas, and ways to summarize information. Once you've thought of one or two summary words, you write them in the column next to that information.

Table 5.4   Guidelines for Marking and Labeling Text

1. Read a paragraph or section completely before marking anything.

2. Mark those points that comprise the answer to your purpose-setting question.

3. Number lists, reasons, or other items that occur in a series or sequence.

4. Identify important terms, dates, places, names, and so on.

5. Be selective in marking. If you identify every line as important, you lose the benefit of text marking. If you are not good at being selective, mark your textbook in pencil first. Then, go back with a colored pen or highlighter and selectively mark important information.

6. Write main idea summaries, questions, or other comments in the margins.

7. Put a question mark beside unclear or confusing information.

8. Put a star or exclamation point beside information your instructor emphasizes in class, possible test questions, or what seems to be extremely important information.

9. Write comments on the table of contents or make your own table of contents of important topics inside the front cover or on the title page of the text.

10. When buying a used text, never choose one that's been underlined by another student.

Finally, you include any notes to yourself about how and what to study (see Figure 5.3).

Finding Main Ideas

Every chapter and every paragraph of a text has a main idea, a central thought. The main ideas and supporting details of each paragraph support the key concept of the chapter. Sometimes, but not always, a topic sentence tells you the main idea; this sentence usually appears at the beginning or end of the reading but may appear anywhere. To answer your goal-setting questions and understand how information in a section relates to the chapter, you must locate and label main ideas.

Look at the paragraph below.

TWO THEORIES OF POWER

The two major *theories of power* are *pluralism* and *elitism*. According to the *theory of pluralism*, decision-making is the result of competition, bargaining, and compromise among diverse *special interest groups*. In this view, *power* is widely distributed throughout a *society* or *community*. On the other hand, according to the theory of *elitism*, a *community* or *society* is controlled from the top by a few individuals or organizations. *Power* is said to be concentrated in the hands of an *elite* group with common interests and background.

SOURCE: Reprinted with permission from *Sociology*, 2d ed., by Shepard. © 1984 by West Publishing Company. All rights reserved.

To find the main idea of the preceding paragraph, you first create a purpose-setting question from the heading. Here, the question might be "What are two theories of power?" Then you read the paragraph to identify key words and phrases. (Italics highlight key words for you in the example.) You now look to see what idea the sentences share (that is, two theories of power—elitism and pluralism—affect societies and communities). Next, you decide if the key concept answers your purpose-setting question. Yes, your prediction is verified. Now, you create a label that states the key concept. In this case, your label might read: *Two theories of power—elitism and pluralism—affect societies and communities.*

Now consider the following paragraph:

THE FIRST BUG

The first "bug" was found in the summer of 1945. The Mark II computer used by the Department of Defense suddenly stopped functioning. Routine checks found no problems. The search continued until a moth, which became stuck in one of the computer's relays, was located. Since then, the term has come to mean any hardware malfunction or software error which affects the ability of the computer to run.

Figure 5.3 Text Labeling

ORGANIZING COURSE CONTENT TO SET READING GOALS

Think again about how you best learn information (see Chapter 1). Outlines and maps help you predict and organize information while surveying. This is particularly true if you rephrase headings and subheadings into questions or connect chapter titles with headings and subheadings to questions. Questions require you to look for answers and, thus, make reading more active. You read to answer *what, how, when, who, which, where,* and *why* (see Table 2.3). When previewing, you will normally be looking for main ideas. Thus, *why, how,* and *what* questions will form the basis of your previewing outline. Question outlines and maps make previewing less covert and more concrete. They help set goals for reading.

Outlines/Maps = ways to organize info. (Stated Information)

ORGANIZING THROUGH OUTLINING

An outline consists of a written collection of ideas ranked according to importance. Every idea is subordinate to or summarized by another idea. Thus, an outline forms an ordered picture of information. You determine importance based on the ways in which ideas fit together.

Main Ideas = why, how, what (Translation)

maps/outlines also used for test preparation?? (Application)

Heading questions: focus attention (Conclusion)

One way of organizing information in a chapter is outlining it. The subject of the chapter serves as the subject of your outline. The question you created from each major heading in the chapter is a major heading in your outline. Each question you formed from a subheading becomes a minor heading. Information found under subheadings becomes questions about supporting details.

Outlines can be in formal or informal formats (see Table 2.4). The formal format uses Roman numerals (I, II, III) placed on the left side of the page or margin to note major concepts. You indent ideas that support the major concepts. You indicate these secondary points by capitalizing them. You show lesser supporting details by indented Arabic numerals (1, 2, 3). You note details that refer to these third-level facts with lowercase letters (a, b, c).

comparison/contrast of outline formats (Analysis)

Informal outlines look much like formal outlines. The key difference is that they don't follow the Roman and Arabic numeral format. Instead, white space or other symbols identify major and minor points. The purpose of the outline is to organize ideas, and the structure of the outline adds little to understanding. Informal outlines are just as useful as formal outlines.

ORGANIZING THROUGH MAPPING

Maps provide a quick means for determining the plan of a chapter. They form pictures that show relationships among concepts. In addition, they express patterns of thought. You sketch a map by using headings and subheadings in a combination boxed-branching format (see Table 2.5 and Figure 2.1). You place each question you created from major headings in separate boxes horizontally (from left to right) in the order in which they appear in the chapter. You then arrange questions about subheadings in a branching formation within the box.

Good idea! (Comment)

Mapping process (Stated Information)

Maps: right-brain learning Outlines: left-brain learning (Synthesis)

Before reading, your purpose-setting question probably was "What was the first bug?" Perhaps you then inferred that the paragraph would have something to do with insects. Thus, you chose that background to use in understanding the text. As you read, you quickly found that you lacked details to support that topic. The second sentence probably led you to retrieve knowledge related to computers. Based on text elements and your knowledge about computers, you understood references to terms such as *hardware, software, computer relays,* and *run.* You inferred that the people who located the moth coined the term *bug,* filling that element by default. Therefore, you conclude that the main idea is that the first bug in computer technology was a moth and that the term *bug* became synonymous with a computer malfunction. This inferred main idea answers the question "What was the first bug?" Your label for this paragraph might read: *The first computer bug was a moth that caused trouble; now* bug *refers to a part of the computer process that causes trouble.*

The examples of labels for these paragraphs are complete sentences. When you label your text, often there is not room in the text or time in your life to write complete sentences. Then, you identify the main idea and abbreviate your main idea statement. For example, an abbreviation of the last example could be as follows: 1st computer bug = moth →TROUBLE—now "computer bug" = TROUBLE.

A list of some simple shorthand symbols and their meanings appears in Table 5.5. This list changes depending on your needs and the course you take. Be careful not to abbreviate too much. You need to be able to decode your labels when studying.

Table 5.5	Shorthand Symbols for Text Labeling
Symbol	Meaning
Ex	Example or Experiment
FORM	Formula
Conc	Conclusion
MI	Main idea
! or *	Important Information
→	Results, Leads to, Steps in a Sequence
(1),(2),(3)	Numbered Points—Label What Points Are Important
circled word	Summarizes Process
?	Disagree or Unclear
TERM	Important Term
SUM	Summary
{	Indicates that Certain Pieces of Information Relate
OPIN	Author's Opinion, Rather than Fact

> **WRITE TO LEARN**
>
> Consider again the quote by William James that accompanies the section on text marking: "The art of becoming wise is the art of knowing what to overlook." On a separate sheet of paper, explain this quote in light of what you have learned about text marking and labeling.

Exercise 5.1   Read, mark, and label each paragraph of Sample Chapter 11 in your notebook or in the margins.

Creating an Inductive Outline

Have you ever heard the expression, "He's on a fishing expedition?" It dates back to 1682 and literally refers to a long sea voyage. Today, it implies someone who possesses little information that a wrongdoing has occurred but who still looks carefully for evidence of it. When you create an **inductive outline** to locate main ideas, you go on a fishing expedition, with one notable difference. You know there's a main idea lurking in the content from which you fish.

When you make an inductive outline, you reduce information from major concepts to specific main ideas. To do so, you follow the steps outlined in Table 5.6. An example of an inductive outline is found in Table 5.7. Notice that if you read from right to left, you see a traditional outline form. The difference is that instead of outlining major concepts first (and then finding supporting details), you outline supporting details and generalize major concepts.

Exercise 5.2   Create an inductive outline for Sample Chapter 13 in your notebook.

Identifying Text Structure

Text structure consists of how the vocabulary and topic of a text are organized. The patterns in which ideas, or details, are structured include introduction/summary, subject development/definition, enumeration/sequence, comparison/contrast, and cause/effect. Recognizing how ideas fit together helps you relate information more easily. Instead of having to recall isolated details, you fit them into an organized pattern. This helps you recall categories or blocks of information more easily within paragraphs, sections, and entire chapters.

Table 5.6   Steps in Creating an Inductive Outline

1. Write the title of the chapter in the center of your notebook page.

2. Indicate the page number of the piece of text you are summarizing. Be sure to show when this page number changes on your outline.

3. Create three vertical columns in your notebook. Label the first column, *What are the facts?* Label the second column, *What is their immediate significance?* Label the third column, *What is their larger significance?*

4. Take notes *in your own words* on the first paragraph of the text, noting italicized words and definitions, lists, steps, and so forth. Be sure to number each paragraph in consecutive order.

5. Complete the entire section of text before you proceed to the second column.

6. Reread your notes in the first column. What do you see as the overall significance of these notes? Do you detect a trend? Are any concepts repeated? Can you group any of the notes together? Summarize and record these, labeling them consecutively as *A, B, C,* and so forth.

7. Complete the entire section of text before you proceed to the third column.

8. Reread your notes in the second column. Locate and summarize related concepts to find their overall significance or the big picture. Label your summary statements consecutively as *I, II, III,* and so forth. This completes your inductive outline.

Because text structure varies according to the topic and the author's purpose, there is seldom one single pattern. Features of various types of text structure usually are combined, with one predominant type. For example, a cause/effect passage may enumerate causes or effects. Nonetheless, patterns of text structure do exist, and identifying them aids you in reading and understanding texts. Special words signal the way the text is structured. These words show the direction and organization of the ideas being presented. Signal words within the passage, if present, help you draw conclusions and find main ideas. Table 5.8 gives a short description of each of the text structure types and lists examples of signal words. If no signal words are present, you determine structure by examining how the information is discussed.

Introduction/summary text structures differ from other text structures in that they are identified by their physical placement in a chapter

---

Table 5.7 Example of an Inductive Outline

Chapter IV. "Reading Effectively"

What are the facts?	What is their immediate significance?	What is their larger significance?
1. Mathematics Chemistry History English	A. Different courses require varying amounts of reading.	
2. Arnold reports 7% of college group below 8th- grade norm in reading comprehension.		
3. Pressey reports 20% of freshman class were less efficient than 8th-grade pupils.	B. Ability in reading varies with individuals.	I. Reading ability is an important factor in academic success.
4. U. of M. ``How to-Study'' classes: less than half of 272 students equaled median of high school seniors in reading comprehension.		

SOURCE: Byrd, C. (1927). *Effective Study Habits.*

or by headings such as "Introduction" or "Summary." Introduction/ summary text paragraphs also may be found at the beginning or end of major sections. Once you have discovered the placement and identification of these passages in a textbook chapter, you probably will find them in the same place with the same identification throughout the other chapters of that text.

The content of an introduction or summary contains features of other structure types and aids you in choosing the information you need to retrieve from memory. Many readers skip these sections, but they often concisely identify the main points of a chapter. To use an introduction/ summary text structure, you identify the placement of introductory and summary passages and the major points in the chapter or section. Figure 5.4 provides an example of this structure type.

Table 5.8   Text Structure Patterns and Signal Words

Pattern	Description	Examples of Signal Words
Introduction/ Summary	Identifies main points	Identified by location, either the beginning or end of a discussion of a topic, and by such words as *in summary, in conclusion, as a review, to summarize, to sum up*
Subject Development/ Definition	Identifies a concept and describes, develops, or explains it	Linking verbs, lists of facts related to the topic but unrelated to each other
Enumeration/ Sequence	Lists or orders main points or presents a problem and steps for its solution	*First, second, third . . ., first, next, then, finally, in addition, last, and, furthermore, and then, most important, least important*
Comparison/Contrast	Describes ways in which concepts are alike or different or presents two or more sides of an issue	Comparison—*similarly, both, as well as, likewise, in like manner* Contrast—*however, on the other hand, on the contrary, but, instead of, although, yet, nevertheless, distinguish, alternative*
Cause/Effect	Shows the result of action(s) or explains a problem and its solution	*Therefore, thus, as a result, because, in turn, then, hence, for this reason, results in, causes, effects, leads to, consequently*

Subject development/definition text structure identifies a concept and lists its supporting details. Such paragraphs are usually found at the beginning of major sections.

A subject development/definition passage describes or explains a topic by providing a definition and/or listing characteristics. Often these facts relate to the topic but have little or no relationship to each other. To

Figure 5.4   Examples of Introduction and Summary Structures

Introduction Passage

The way anthropologists approach the study of humanity has undergone many changes since the discipline originated in the nineteenth century. Some ideas held by most scholars a century ago have been discarded today; others are still with us. In this chapter, we discuss some of the important scholars and schools of thought that shaped the way modern anthropologists approach their studies. For each approach, we emphasize its assumptions, its basic questions, its errors, and its contributions to the theoretical ideas of modern anthropology.

Summary Passage

In this chapter we have reviewed the functions of society, the ways in which societies are organized around food, the basis of social structure, and the process of social interaction. We have learned that society is an exceedingly complex phenomenon with its inner workings hidden from the casual view.

Individuals in every society must be socialized to behave in ways that are beneficial for that society. In the next chapter, we examine the process of socialization and consider how both the individual and society benefit from such socialization.

locate subject development/definition passages, you look for a key concept and details that describe, develop, or explain it. Figure 5.5 provides an example of this structure.

Enumeration/sequence text structure lists major points. Although you may not be told initially how many points will be discussed, words such as "first, . . . second, . . . third" or "first, . . . next, . . . finally" often signal the number of points under discussion. The points are a list of equivalent items (enumeration structure) or a list of items in a progression (sequence structure). Such lists include information arranged alphabetically or in order of importance, direction, size, time, or other criteria. This structure also describes solutions to problems, answers to questions, or proofs of thesis statements. To use the enumeration/sequence text structure, you look for the overall concept, procedure, or problem; the total number of items in the list or steps in the sequence, whenever possible; the signal words that indicate the points in the list; and the relationship of items in the list or steps in the sequence. Figure 5.6 provides an example of this structure.

Figure 5.5   Example of Subject Development Structure

SLUMP. A slump is the intermittent movement of a mass of earth or rock along a curved slip-plane. It is characterized by the backward rotation of the slump block so that its surface may eventually tilt in the direction opposite the slope from which it became detached. Slumps are most likely to occur on steep slopes with deep, clay-rich soils after a period of saturation by heavy rains. The movement generally takes place over a period of days or weeks and is nearly impossible to control or halt once it has begun.

Slumps are common along the California coast, where slopes have frequently been oversteepened by wave undercutting. They also occur along the sideslopes of river gorges in various parts of the western United States. Small slumps capable of blocking traffic frequently occur on steep roadcuts following heavy rains.

Figure 5.6   Examples of Enumeration and Sequence Structures

Enumeration Passage

Nerve cells can be categorized by structure or function. For our purposes, a functional classification is more useful. According to this system, nerve cells fall into three distinct groupings: (1) sensory neurons, (2) interneurons, and (3) motor neurons.

Sensory neurons carry impulses from body parts to the central nervous system, transmitting impulses from sensory receptors located in the body. Sensory receptors come in many shapes and sizes and respond to a variety of stimuli, such as pressure, pain, heat, and movement.

Motor neurons carry impulses from the brain and spinal cord to effectors, the muscles and glands of the body. Sensory information entering the brain and spinal cord via sensory neurons often stimulates a response. A response is brought about by impulses transmitted via motor neurons to muscles and glands of the body. In some cases, intervening neurons—called interneurons or associated neurons—are present. Interneurons transmit impulses from the sensory neurons directly to motor neurons and may also transmit impulses to other parts of the central nervous system.

Sequence Passage

OUTPUT

Once processing is complete, the results are available for output. There are three steps involved in the output phase of data flow. In retrieving information, the computer pulls information from storage devices for use by the decision maker. By converting information, the computer translates information from the form used to store it to a form understandable by the user (such as a printed report). Finally, communication occurs when the right information is in the right place at the right time.

Figure 5.7   Example of Comparison/Contrast Structure

A fault takes the form of a two-dimensional plane that typically extends from the earth's surface downward to a variable but often considerable depth. The trace of the fault on the surface is termed the fault line. Fault lines may extend for hundreds of miles, but lengths of a few tens of miles are more common. Most faults are nearly straight. This linearity, which results from the tendency of rock to fracture along straight lines, contrasts markedly with the irregularity of the features produced by most other geomorphic processes.

Geologists recognize four general categories of faults according to the nature of the displacements that occur; these are termed normal, reverse, transcurrent, and thrust faults. Relative motion is more vertical than horizontal, and an expansionary component is present, so the opposing sides also move apart, resulting in crystal extension. Normal faults are usually produced by broad regional arching in areas of tetonic stress.

Reverse faults are so-named because the movement of the opposing sides is reversed from that of normal faults. Like normal faults, reverse faults have deeply dipping fault planes and undergo predominantly vertical motion. Unlike normal faults, though, reverse faults are produced by regional compression. Crystal shortening results, and a net uplift of the surface normally occurs.

Transcurrent faults undergo a predominantly horizontal offsetting of their opposing sides. They are most frequently located along transform plate boundaries, where the relative motions of the opposing plate boundaries are essentially parallel. Most transcurrent faults are located on the floors of oceanic plates and are produced by seafloor spreading movements, but some, like California's San Andreas Fault, occur on land.

Thrust faults result from the extreme compression of rock strata produced by lisopheric plate collisions. The relative movements of the opposing sides is similar to that of a reverse fault. Relative motion, however, is predominantly horizontal, as one side is thrust over the other, sometimes for considerable distances.

SOURCE: Reprinted with permission from *Essentials of Physical Geography,* by Scott. Copyright © 1991 by West Publishing Company. All rights reserved.

Comparison/contrast text structures express relationships between two or more ideas. Comparisons show how ideas are alike, whereas contrasts show how they differ. Signal words indicate whether likenesses or differences are being shown. Both comparisons and contrasts may be included, or the structure may consist of only comparisons or only contrasts. To use this type, you look for the items that are related and the signal words that indicate comparison and/or contrast. Figure 5.7 provides an example of this structure.

The **cause/effect** text structure shows an idea or event resulting from another idea or event. It describes what happens (the effect) and why it happens (the cause). To use this type of text structure, you look for the effect and the cause(s) of the effect. Figure 5.8 provides an example of cause/effect structure.

Figure 5.8   Example of a Cause/Effect Structure

Chemical weathering processes are considerably hampered by a lack of water in arid regions. As a result, the aridsols are shallow, stony, and mineralogically immature, with poorly developed horizons. Soil textures are generally coarse and sandy, leading to water retention ability even when water is available. The humus content is low to completely absent because of the sparseness of vegetation.

An important characteristic of the *aridisols* is their high alkalinity. Evapotranspiration exceeds precipitation, producing a surfaceward movement of ground water and dissolved minerals. Well-drained soils typically experience an accumulation of calcium carbonate and other soluble bases at the site of water evaporation, normally a few inches below the surface. Frequently, this produces a duricrust layer. In poorly drained depressions, the salinization process results in conditions toxic for most vegetables.

Exercise 5.3   Circle the signal words, if any, in the following paragraphs. Then identify the predominant text structure (introduction/summary, subject development/definition, enumeration/ sequence, comparison/contrast, cause/effect) of each passage. Write your answer in the corresponding blanks below.

1. _____
2. _____
3. _____
4. _____
5. _____
6. _____
7. _____
8. _____

1. The duties of the bailiff vary. As sergeant-at-arms within the courtroom, he or she keeps watch over defendants and suppresses disorderly behavior among spectators. He or she summons witnesses when they are called to testify and maintains the legal proprieties pertaining to the actions of jurors and witnesses. When the jury is sequestered on the order of the judge, the bailiff accompanies the jurors and guards to prevent violations of trial secrecy—such as making unauthorized phone calls, reading an unedited newspaper, or listening to accounts of the trial on the radio or television. It is also the bailiff's job to see that the jury is suitably housed and fed during a trial.

2. But today's union member seeks satisfaction on a wider range. Money or safety is no longer the dominant reason for joining a union. Most people earn a livable wage and work under reasonable conditions. Today, the need to join a union often stems from a higher level. Labor relations professors Arthur A. Sloane and Fred Witney tell us that "research suggests that dissatisfaction with the extent of gratification of (1) safety, (2) social, (3) self-esteem needs—in approximately that order—has motivated many workers to join unions. To a lesser extent, status and self-fulfillment needs have also led to union membership."

3. Let us start with the religion most familiar to North American readers, Christianity. Christianity has approximately 1 billion adherents in the world, more than any other religion, and is the predominant religion in North America, South America, Europe, and Australia. In addition, countries with a Christian majority can be identified on every other continent. No other religion has such a widespread distribution.

4. Whether using the topical or regional approach, geographers can select either a descriptive or systematic method. Again, the distinction is one of emphasis, not on absolute separation. The descriptive method emphasizes the collection of a variety of details about the characteristics of a particular location. This method has been used primarily by regional geographers to illustrate the uniqueness of a particular location on the earth's surface. The systematic method emphasizes the identification of several basic theories or techniques developed by geographers to explain the distribution of activities.

5. Victims of crime and their relationships with criminals were briefly explored in this chapter. Beginning with a historical sketch of the ways in which various societies in the past have dealt with the victim of crime, the pioneering work of Hentig and Mendelsohn in the development of victim typologies was discussed and some consideration was given to the issue of victim compensation and restitution. Models for the delivery of victim services were also examined briefly. Victimization surveys and their significance for the assessment of crime were treated in some detail, and the chapter concluded with several observations on the bystander who remains a passive witness to someone else's victimization.

6. Three major aspects of communication must be understood for anyone to be an effective communicator: (1) people, (2) messages, and (3) the environment. In communication, the person, or both *people,* is the focus of understanding. Communication really represents people in transaction. Second, although the people are of primary importance in a study of communication, *messages* mediate their transactions. Through sending or receiving messages, people make sense of one another. Third, communication takes place in a social environment. An organization where one works can be a major environment in which one communicates. How does this environment affect communication?

7. Fear is a basic ingredient of any psychological or social reaction to crime. It is a gut reaction that produces marked changes in individual behavior. The most intense fear is of the crimes least likely to occur: murder, assault, and forcible rape. Ironically, the perpetrator in such crimes is often a family member, close friend, or personal acquaintance. Nevertheless, what people fear most is violence at the hands of a stranger. Fear of an unknown assailant is prominent in both individual and collective responses to crime. Fear of strangers generalizes to fear of strange places, and people eventually see even public streets as unsafe. When fear of public places peaks, people avoid areas perceived as potentially hazardous. Consequently, normal activity is interrupted in various areas, removing one deterrent to criminal activity. Areas thus avoided are then increasingly frequented by persons bent upon crime.

8. **Modern Romance Languages.** The five most important contemporary Romance languages are Spanish, Portuguese, French, Italian, and Romanian. A reasonably close fit exists between the boundaries of these languages and the modern states of Spain, Portugal, France, Italy and Romania. An examination of a physical map of Europe provides ample evidence for the development of separate Romance languages, because the Spanish, Portuguese, French, and Italian language regions are separated from each other by mountains—the Pyrenees between France and Spain and the Alps between France and Italy. Romania is isolated from the other Romance language regions by Slavic-speaking people. Mountains serve as a strong barrier to communications between people living on opposite sides. Languages evolve over time. The distinct Romance languages did not suddenly appear. Instead, numerous dialects existed within each province, many of which still exist today. The creation of standard national languages, such as French and Spanish, was relatively recent.

Exercise 5.4   Read each of the following paragraphs and identify its text structure.

1. Paragraph 2, page 511 of Sample Chapter 11, beginning with the words "Goals should be . . . "

TEXT STRUCTURE _____

2. Second full paragraph, page 513 of Sample Chapter 11, beginning with the words "In the book . . . "

TEXT STRUCTURE _____

3. Paragraph 2, page 518 of Sample Chapter 11, beginning with the words "Regardless of . . . "

TEXT STRUCTURE _____

4. Paragraph 5, page 525 of Sample Chapter 11, beginning with the words "A planner needs . . . "

TEXT STRUCTURE _____

5. Paragraph 4–8, page 529 of Sample Chapter 11, beginning with the words "Delegating work to others . . . "

TEXT STRUCTURE _____

6. Paragraph 3, page 545 of Sample Chapter 12, beginning with the words "Although the . . . "

TEXT STRUCTURE _____

7. Third full paragraph, page 549 of Sample Chapter 12, beginning with the words "The new boost . . . "

TEXT STRUCTURE _____

8. First full paragraph, page 546 of Sample Chapter 12, beginning with the words "Although the . . . "

TEXT STRUCTURE _____

9. Second full paragraph, page 523 of Sample Chapter 13, beginning with the words "Computers collect . . . "

TEXT STRUCTURE _____

10. Paragraph 3, page 581 of Sample Chapter 13, beginning with the words "In today's . . . "

TEXT STRUCTURE _____

Exercise 5.5   Examine the text structures in Figures 5.4, 5.5, 5.6, 5.7, and 5.8. Identify the words that signal each particular type of text structure by circling them.

Exercise 5.6   Reread each paragraph in Exercises 5.1 and 5.3. Mark and label each one.

STEP FOUR: RECITE

If, at the end of each section of a chapter, you recite correct answers to your purpose-setting questions, then you continue reading.

What if you cannot completely answer your questions? One of two things has happened. Either you have asked the wrong questions or you have not understood what you read.

You decide where the problem lies by looking at your questions in light of the content of the passage. Does the content answer your questions? If not, you asked the wrong ones. Your skill in developing purpose-setting questions improves with practice.

Recitation becomes easier and more active when you study with someone. This helps you see how others develop questions and find answers. You can also practice by using a tape recorder. First, you record your purpose-setting questions. Then you read and record your answers. When you play your tape, see if your questions were appropriate and if your responses answered the questions correctly. Another way to practice involves writing your questions on index cards. Again, after reading, determine if your questions were appropriate. Then, write your answers on the back of the card.

If you find your questions are inappropriate, you form new questions and reread. If you still have problems understanding, you need to assess your reading in terms of the passage at hand. Do you know the terminology? Are you confused by the author's writing style? Table 5.9 provides a list of common comprehension obstacles and solutions.

Evaluating your text marking also helps you increase your understanding. If you marked too much, you may not be able to separate important from unimportant information. If this is a common problem for you, you need to use a pencil while marking and labeling. This allows you the freedom to rethink your notations. If you overmark only on occasion, you can remark text with a contrasting ink or highlighter. If you marked too little, you may not have enough information to comprehend fully. Thus, you need to reexamine the text and make more explicit notations. You need to be sure you have labeled all text markings. If you have done so, you can see at a glance where important information lies. If your labels are vague, then reread and relabel your text. Labels should concisely, yet completely, summarize what you've marked.

Table 5.9   Reasons and Solutions for Comprehension Failure

Reasons	*Solutions*
	FAILURE TO ASK RIGHT QUESTION
Lack of experience in questioning	Practice with index cards by putting a question on one side and the answer on the other.
	Practice with tape recorder.
	Practice with study partner.
	Review types of questioning words.
	FAILURE TO UNDERSTAND TEXT
Lack of concentration	Avoid external distractions.
	Study in short blocks of time over a longer period.
	Use a study system.
	Set learning goals.
	Keep a ``worry list.''
Unfamiliar terms	Use context and structural analysis to decode unknown terms.
	Use the text's glossary.
	Find the word in a dictionary or thesaurus.
	Actively consider new terms in context.
Lack of understanding	Reread or skim for main ideas.
	Scan for specific information.
	Verbalize confusing points.
	Paraphrase, summarize, or outline main ideas.
	Consult an alternate source.
	Reset learning goals.
Speed	Adjust speed to purpose.
	Take a speed-reading course.
	Use a study system.
	Practice with a variety of materials.
	Read recreationally.
Failure to identify text structure	Examine transition words as you reread.
	Outline the paragraph or passage.
Failure to locate main idea	Label the main idea of each paragraph.
	Identify text structure.
	Outline details.
	Summarize the main idea in your own words.
Insufficient background knowledge for understanding	Find alternative sources of information.
	Obtain tutoring
Inability to set appropriate purpose-setting questions.	Practice with a tape recorder.
	Practice with a friend.
	Reset learning goals.

STEP FIVE: REVIEW

At this point in the SQ3R process, review seems redundant. You've already seen the information four times. You previewed the chapter to get the big picture. You began your analysis of content by asking questions. You examined each section by reading. You checked understanding. The review stage brings you full circle by allowing you to synthesize the chapter's meaning as a whole, see how information relates, and begin studying information for recall.

While Chapter 7 will provide many memory and study techniques, three strategies are immediately available to you as part of SQ3R. First, many chapters begin with objectives; you surveyed them during the first step of SQ3R. One way to review is to determine if you met all the objectives. A second way to review involves answering, without referring back to the text, any pre- or postchapter questions posed by your author; these, too, should have been identified during your initial survey of the chapter. Both of these review strategies rely on the good graces of the text's author. Chapter objectives and questions may or may not be part of the text you are reading. The third review strategy depends solely on you. For this review, you return to the outline or map you created during the second stage of SQ3R and answer your goal-setting questions.

Any of these three study strategies—indeed, all three—allow you to test your recall and determine where you have memory deficits. This provides you with information about what and how much you need to study to complete the learning process.

Exercise 5.7   Survey, question, read, recite, and review Sample Chapter 12. You may use either text marking and labeling or an inductive outline to do so. Record your notes on a separate sheet of paper or in your notebook.

GROUP LEARNING ACTIVITY
READING STRATEGIES FOR GROUPS

An important phase of reading and learning information is monitoring. This stage helps you determine when you know information or when you need to reflect and review. However, many students lack the self-awareness to differentiate between when they know information from when they don't know it. The following group reading strategy helps you learn to monitor learning as well as practice summarization and memory skills. The group's goal is to master text information. This strategy incorporates visual, verbal, and aural components. It provides group members with opportunities to see how others identify, organize, and learn important information.

The following steps, based on cooperative learning instructions (Larson and Dansereau, 1986), can be used in your in-class study group:

1. Select and study a limited amount of text information. Initially, or when reading complex or unfamiliar information, this might be as little as a section in a chapter introduced by a minor subheading. It never should be more than two or three pages.

2. Each group member should practice appropriate marking and labeling strategies in reading the information.

3. Members continue to study and reflect on the information until everyone has completed the task.

4. Select one person to recall and summarize the information *without looking at the text*. That person should include important terms and ideas in the summary, describing mnemonic devices, analogies, charts, drawings, or other visuals to reinforce and clarify information.

5. As the recaller summarizes information, group members *using their texts* check the accuracy and completeness of the summary. Group members correct errors and supply or elaborate on information following the summary, again using any mnemonic devices (see Chapter 7), analogies, charts, drawings, or other visuals to reinforce and clarify information.

6. The group then discusses the information, continues to clarify information, and suggests ways to consider and remember concepts.

7. During discussion, each person should notate important information, terms, visuals, or other information for later individual study.

8. Repeat the process with another member of the group serving as the recaller until all the information has been studied or all the members have had the opportunity to serve as recallers. To be most effective, group members need to actively facilitate the understanding of the recaller and themselves through questioning, elaborating, and otherwise amplifying information.

Application

Using the same text material, use the cooperative learning activity in your group. Then, compare notes with other groups in the class, focusing on how others identify important information and facilitate learning.

CHAPTER SUMMARY

1. SQ3R is a systematic reading plan for studying text chapters. Its steps include *survey, question, read, recite,* and *review.*

2. Surveying, or previewing, is a strategy often used before attending a lecture. It helps you be an active learner and connect what you know with what you are learning.

3. The questioning stage concerns setting goals for reading.

4. Reading a chapter involves finding and recording main ideas.

5. When you recite information, you check your understanding and use strategies to solve comprehension problems, if they exist.

6. In the review stage, you attempt to see and remember how all information in the chapter relates. Additional strategies for learning information are included in Chapter 7.

CHAPTER REVIEW

Answer briefly but completely.

1. Complete the following analogy:

   goal: objective:: survey:_____

2. Which of Kipling's questioning words (*What, Why, When, How, Where,* and *Who*) might elicit main idea responses? Which would require details for answers?

   _____

   _____

   _____

   _____

   _____

3. Create a drawing that shows the role of *topic, main ideas,* and *details* in a paragraph or passage.

   _____

   _____

_____

_____

_____

4. Think of the following subjects in light of the factors to be considered when marking text. Which factor might be most important to you in each area?

  a. Freshman-level chemistry _____

  b. Music appreciation _____

  c. European history _____

  d. Junior-level trigonometry _____

  e. Introduction to computer science _____

5. Create a cardinal rule for text marking that explains how much information should be marked.

_____

_____

_____

_____

6. Locate examples in this chapter for any three different types of text structure.

  a. *Type:* _____

     Page: _____ *Paragraph:* _____

  b. *Type:* _____

     Page: _____ *Paragraph:* _____

  c. *Type:* _____

     Page: _____ *Paragraph:* _____

7. What are the functions of signal words?

_____

_____

8. Compare/contrast inductive and deductive outlines.

_____

9. Examine Table 5.9. Which of these comprehension obstacles, if any, do you feel you experience most often and why?

_____

_____

_____

_____

10. How do the three review strategies discussed in this chapter allow you to evaluate recall? What might you do if you find your recall failing in a given area?

_____

_____

_____

_____

REFERENCES

Larson, C. O., and Dansereau, D. F. (1986). Cooperative learning in dyads. *Journal of Reading 29*: 516–20.

Vocabulary Development   Context: Time Flies versus Fruit Flies

Look around you. Are you in your room? Your car? A bus? A classroom? Outside? Your surroundings are your current context. What you see in that context often depends on those surroundings to make sense. The kind of seat you find in a car or bus differs from that found in a classroom or living area. Similarly, words differ according to the context in which they are found. Context helps you make sense of the new words you encounter when you read and forms a means of developing vocabulary.

> Time flies like an arrow.
> Fruit flies like a banana.
> —Lewis Grizzard
> Twentieth Century American Humorist

What does *flies* mean in each of the sentences above? The meaning of many words changes according to the words that surround them. These words—called context—give you the meaning and usage of the word in a realistic setting. For example, in psychology, the word *set* means orientation, as "mind set." In math, *set* refers to a group of things. *Set* refers to scenery in drama. As a result, context forms one of the most valuable aids to vocabulary development. Context consists of both stated and unstated clues to meaning.

While context is your first best choice in defining words you do not know, it is not foolproof. Sometimes authors embed words in weak context. That means, they provide too little information for you to identify the meaning of a new term. When that happens, your

"Sure I've seen a good play . . . in the game on Sunday."

only alternative is to consult a dictionary or glossary. Then you need to reconsider the word in its original context.

STATED CONTEXT CLUES

Stated context clues consist of various punctuation marks and key words that signal meaning (see Table 1). In addition, they rely on your language knowledge to help you define unknown words. For example, punctuation clues actually identify appositives, words or phrases that restate or modify an immediately preceding term.

Definition clues link nouns with describing or renaming words. Other clues indicate both synonymous (comparison and example) and antonymous (contrast) relationships among ideas within a sentence or paragraph. Finally, meanings may be located in other sentences.

Table 1   Types of Stated Context Clues

Stated Types	Stated Clues	Examples
Punctuation	commas ,,, parentheses ( ) dashes — brackets ( )	He also distinguished between *social statics*—the study of stability and order—and *social dynamics*—the study of change.[1]
Definition	*is, was, are, means, involves, seems, is called, that is, i.e., which means, resembles*	One of his enduring contributions is the idea that sociology should rely on *positivism;* that is, it should use observation and experimentation, methods of physical sciences, in the study of social life.[2]
Comparison	*similarly, both, as well as, likewise*	Similar in function to the parity bit is the *check digit.* Like a parity bit, a check digit is used to catch errors.[3]
Example	*such as, such, like, for example, e.g., other*	Have you ever watched people's eyes closely when they read? Their eyes don't flow smoothly over the words; instead they skitter or jump across the letters. Such motion is called *visual saccade.*[4]
Contrast	*however, on the other hand, on the contrary, while, but, instead of, although, nevertheless, yet*	Participants in an artificially created situation in a laboratory may not behave as they would in a real-life situation. In contrast, the *natural* experiment takes place in a real-life situation that is not totally created or controlled by the experimenter.[5]

[1] Reprinted with permission from *Sociology*, 2d ed., by Shepard. Copyright © 1984 by West Publishing Company. All rights reserved.

[2] Reprinted with permission from *Sociology*, 2d ed., by Shepard. Copyright © 1984 by West Publishing Company. All rights reserved.

[3] Reprinted with permission from *Understanding Computers*, by Hopper and Mandell. Copyright © 1984 by West Publishing Company. All rights reserved.

[4] Reprinted with permission from *Introduction to Child Development*, 2d ed., by Dworetzky. Copyright © 1984 by West Publishing Company. All rights reserved.

[5] Reprinted with permission from *Sociology*, 2d ed., by Shepard. Copyright © 1984 by West Publishing Company. All rights reserved.

UNSTATED CONTEXT CLUES

Unstated context clues require the use of your background knowledge to infer meaning. Key words and phrases identified within the text provide you with the clues necessary for decoding meanings. For example, consider the word *elite* in the paragraph below:

> The existence of a surplus food supply explains why cities were able to develop but does not explain why people were attracted to them. Cities tended to attract four basic types of people: *elites,* functionaries (officials), craftsmen, and the poor and destitute. For elites, the city provided a setting for consolidating political, military, or religious power. The jewelry and other luxury items found in the tombs of these elites symbolize the benefits that this small segment of the population gained from their consolidation of power and control. Those who lived in cities as political or religious officials received considerably fewer benefits, but their lives were undoubtedly easier than those of the peasant-farmers in the countryside. Craftsmen, still lower on the stratification structure, came to the city to work and sell their products to the elites and functionaries. The poor and destitute, who were lured to the city for economic relief, were seldom able to improve their condition (Gist and Fava, 1974).
>
> SOURCE: Reprinted with permission from *Sociology,* 2d ed., by Shepard. Copyright © 1984 by West Publishing Company. All rights reserved.

The text does not define *elite* for you or provide stated clues. The words *power, jewelry, luxury,* and *benefits* help you know that *elite* describes a wealthy class of people. In addition, by process of elimination, you may realize that a wealthy class of people is the only class that the text fails to mention.

Activity 1

Define any ten of the following words in context from Sample Chapter 13 "An Invitation to Computers." Then identify the type of context clue that helps you determine the word's meaning. Words appear in boldface in the chapter in the same order as they appear in the activity.

1. Information society

   *Definition:*_____

   _____

2. computer

   *Definition:*_____

   _____

3. programs

   *Definition:*_____

   _____

4. input

   *Definition:*_____

   _____

5. output

   *Definition:*_____

   _____

6. microprocessors

   *Definition:*_____

   _____

7. transaction

   *Definition:*_____

   _____

8. number crunching

   *Definition:*_____

   _____

9. abacus

   *Definition:*_____

   _____

10. double-entry bookkeeping

    *Definition:*_____

    _____

11. Industrial Revolution

    *Definition:*_____

    _____

12. difference engine

    *Definition:*_____

    _____

13. looping

    *Definition:*_____

    _____

14. Boolean algebra

    *Definition:*_____

    _____

15. census

    *Definition:*_____

    _____

16. punched card

    *Definition:*_____

    _____

17. payroll

Definition:_____

_____

18. system

Definition:_____

_____

19. information resources

Definition:_____

_____

20. unit record

Definition:_____

_____

21. batch processing

Definition:_____

_____

22. sequential file

Definition:_____

_____

23. magnetic tape

Definition:_____

_____

24. random access

Definition:_____

_____

25. magnetic disk drive

Definition:_____

_____

26. read/write head

Definition:_____

_____

27. track

Definition:_____

_____

28. model

Definition:_____

_____

Activity 2

Provide a definition for each of the words below prior to reading the chapter. Then identify the meanings of these words from context from Sample Chapter 13, the section entitled "Issue: Who's in Control?" The words appear in the boldface italicized typeface in the same order as they appear in the activity.

1. will
    Your definition:_____

    _____

    Definition in context:_____

    _____

2. traces
    Your definition:_____

    _____

    Definition in context:_____

    _____

    _____

3. discounted
    Your definition:_____

    _____

    Definition in context:_____

    _____

4. wholesale
    Your definition:_____

    _____

    Definition in context:_____

    _____

5. measures
    Your definition:_____

    _____

    Definition in context:_____

    _____

6. issue
    Your definition:_____

    _____

    Definition in context:_____

    _____

7. fired
Your definition:_____
_____
Definition in context:_____
_____

8. replete
Your definition:_____
_____
Definition in context:_____
_____

9. point
Your definition:_____
_____
Definition in context:_____
_____

10. power
Your definition:_____
_____
Definition in context:_____
_____

KEY

The topic of the passage is "Washing Clothes."

CHAPTER 6

Seeing What You Mean: Learning from and with Graphics

OBJECTIVES

1. Contrast authors' purposes for graphics with your purposes for using graphics to organize information.

2. Examine text diagrams and diagram processes and objects.

3. Use different kinds of charts to analyze and synthesize concepts.

4. Use different kinds of graphs to analyze and organize data.

5. Use maps to understand physical representations of locations and to map mental territories.

CHAPTER MAP

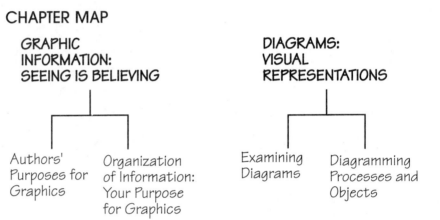

GRAPHIC INFORMATION: SEEING IS BELIEVING
- Authors' Purposes for Graphics
- Organization of Information: Your Purpose for Graphics

DIAGRAMS: VISUAL REPRESENTATIONS
- Examining Diagrams
- Diagramming Processes and Objects

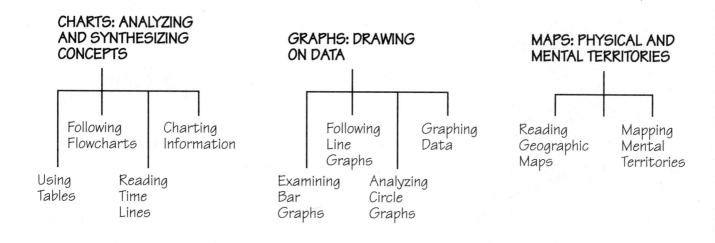

CHARTS: ANALYZING AND SYNTHESIZING CONCEPTS

Following Flowcharts

Charting Information

Using Tables

Reading Time Lines

GRAPHS: DRAWING ON DATA

Following Line Graphs

Graphing Data

Examining Bar Graphs

Analyzing Circle Graphs

MAPS: PHYSICAL AND MENTAL TERRITORIES

Reading Geographic Maps

Mapping Mental Territories

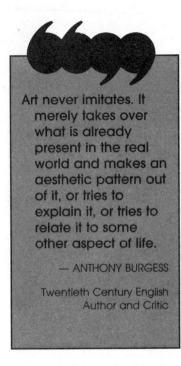

Before the development of written language, ancient people communicated through pictures they carved or painted. These pictures helped Egyptians, Aztecs, Native Americans, and other early societies express ideas and concepts. Today, both words and pictures express and relate ideas and concepts.

In much the same way, **graphics** never imitate. They merely take over what is already present in written form. They organize it, or try to explain it, or try to relate it to some other piece of information. This chapter provides information about different kinds of graphics and shows you how to apply them to learning situations.

GRAPHIC INFORMATION: SEEING IS BELIEVING

In 1918, sports cartoonist Robert Ripley published his first sketches of "Believe It or Not!" in the *New York Globe.* This feature depicted such unlikely events as men who won races by running backward or fish that walked on land. Encouraged by an enthusiastic readership, Ripley pursued his quest for oddities. "Believe It or Not!" was eventually carried by over 300 newspapers in thirty-eight countries. His readers evidently subscribed to the notion that seeing is believing.

Graphics provide ways to see what you or an author believe about information. Graphics refer to visual representations such as diagrams, charts (tables, flowcharts, and time lines), graphs (bar, line, and circle), and maps (general reference, special purpose, and idea). The type of information determines the graphic format to some degree. For example, a chart or graph summarizes or classifies data whereas diagrams illustrate complex ideas. You and authors use graphics, therefore, to exemplify, clarify, organize, and illustrate key ideas.

AUTHORS' PURPOSES FOR GRAPHICS

Authors often use graphics to illustrate complex information. Many students conclude that the graphics, too, must be complex--probably too complex to understand. Once you learn how to decipher graphics, you will find that reading them is actually faster and easier than understanding written information. This is because graphics focus attention and provide visual reinforcement. Graphics give authors ways to make abstractions more real. Table 6.1 summarizes purposes of graphics by type.

As a reader, you view these graphics carefully in an attempt to see why the author included them. Your goal is to find their main ideas. Your success depends on the information in them and your store of background knowledge. Much like the title, headings, and subheadings of a

Table 6.1   Purposes of Text Graphics

	Diagram	Table	Flow-chart	Time Line	Bar or Line Graph	Circle Graph	Map
Summarize	X	X	X	X	X	X	
Organize		X	X		X	X	
Illustrate	X		X	X	X	X	
Demonstrate	X		X				
Compare		X	X	X	X	X	
Contrast		X	X	X	X	X	
Show parts of a whole	X		X	X		X	
Sequence	X		X	X			
Depict location	X						X

chapter, the title of a graphic identifies its subject and, thus, the information you need to draw from your background to understand it. Authors usually identify the purpose and subject of untitled graphics in the text. Because you must recognize and evaluate this information for yourself, processing untitled graphics requires higher-level thinking and the ability to draw conclusions.

Understanding graphics helps you learn information in another way. Your brain consists of two halves. One side, the left side, processes text and data in a logical, systematic fashion. The other side, the right side, processes information that has a more artistic, visual nature. Graphics appeal to the right side of your brain. By attending to both text and graphic information, you use both sides of your brain to aid learning and memory. (See Chapter 1 for more information about brain dominance and learning style.)

You process graphic information through an overt action—writing. Taking notes from text graphics involves six steps. First, you decide why you think the author included a graphic. Because publishers pay illustrators or others for permission to print graphics, if it's there, it's there for a reason. Second, you identify important details or features of the graphic. From these, you determine the graphic's main idea. In other words, you summarize the information the graphic includes. Then you note your summary in the margin beside the graphic. The fourth step is to draw conclusions about the importance of the graphic to your overall understanding. Next, you check your understanding of the graphic with information presented in the text or emphasized in class. Sixth, you record in your notes where important text graphics are located.

ORGANIZATION OF INFORMATION: YOUR PURPOSE FOR GRAPHICS

Picasso, Monet, Rembrandt, Michelangelo
Donatello, Michaelangelo, Raphael, Leonardo
John, Paul, George, Ringo
Matthew, Mark, Luke, John
Cecil, Katy, Isaac, Regina

Everything is organized in some way. Each of the lines above contains members of specific sets of information. The sense you make of each line depends on whether you can discern what concept organizes that set. Your ability to do so depends on your background knowledge. In analyzing line 1 you may realize that Picasso, Monet, Rembrandt, and Michelangelo are all artists. Michaelangelo, Raphael, Leonardo, and Donatello are the names of the Teenage Mutant Ninja Turtles, as well as artists. John, Paul, George, and Ringo were members of a musical group called the Beatles. Matthew, Mark, Luke and, John were apostles in the New Testament. Your analysis of the last line may not provide you with a single organizational format that includes all the names. Nothing in your background knowledge seems to fit. Indeed, the last line consists of names of pets of the authors of this text. So background knowledge forms one key to organizing information for learning. When you lack sufficient background knowledge, analysis of text organization or lecture content often provides you with the connections you need to categorize and organize new information.

Lecture notes, text chapters, and other materials provide a variety of details about new information you need to learn. Deciding what information you have forms the first step in creating your own graphics. Once you identify the information, you organize it by analyzing how the details relate to each other. For example, your details might consist of dates in history, ways to solve a physics problem, or processes in cell replication. You then decide which graphic fits your needs. The arrangement that best suits your needs depends on learning goals, course emphasis, and course content. Sometimes an instructor suggests organizational structures by identifying types of information to remember (dates, names, places). An instructor might also provide the general categories of information you need to know. Other times, you need to do this for yourself. Like many other memory aids, the most effective organizational structures are those you make for yourself. In the example above, a time line could depict historical sequences of events, a chart could be used to compare ways to solve problems, and a diagram or flowchart could be used to show cellular processes. With the exception of mapping, you use the same purposes for text graphics that authors use (see Table 6.1). While maps enable you to show relationships among physical locations, they also help you visually represent mental relationships.

Just as understanding graphics requires both right- and left-brain processing (See Chapter 1), creating graphics that represent text information utilizes both sides of the brain. This, too, aids learning and memory.

DIAGRAMS: VISUAL REPRESENTATIONS

A dignified old lady, attending a contemporary art exhibition, was caught staring at a painting by its artist. "What *is* it?" she inquired. The artist smiled condescendingly.

"That, my dear woman, is supposed to be a mother and her child."

"Well, then," asked the lady, "why isn't it?"

Often you encounter **diagrams** in texts that make you, like the woman in the story, wonder, "What is it?" That's because diagrams often depict complex concepts. They explain as well as represent relationships. Authors use them to help you picture events, processes, structures, relationships, or sequences described in the text.

EXAMINING DIAGRAMS

Diagrams often require both the written description and the visual picture for understanding. The written description often explains the connections and relationships among the parts shown on the diagram. The title of the diagram and labels on it help you identify concepts important to your understanding. Consider the following description of the visual cliff:

The visual cliff—a tool for studying depth perception—consists of a center board on top of a glass table. On one half of the board, a patterned surface is directly below the glass, whereas on the other half of the board the patterned surface is several feet below the glass table. This gives the illusion of a cliff.

This somewhat confusing description makes it difficult to understand the concept of the visual cliff (unless you are already familiar with it). Now, consider the diagram in Figure 6.1. The precision with which the diagram has been drawn and labeled allows you to better understand the concept of the visual cliff.

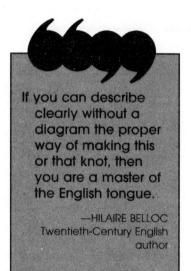

If you can describe clearly without a diagram the proper way of making this or that knot, then you are a master of the English tongue.

—HILAIRE BELLOC
Twentieth-Century English
author

Exercise 6.1   Use Figure 1-2 (page 587) and ``Case Situation: The 1890 Census'' ( page 586) in Sample Chapter 13, ``An Invitation to Computers'' to answer the following questions:

1. What object is diagrammed in Figure 1-2?

2. You want to punch * # $. In what columns would these symbols possibly be found?

_____

_____

3. What are the upper and lower limits for the columns that identify the alphabet? How many numbers are included in this range? What is the significance of that number?

_____

_____

4. Which corner is cut? What might be the value of that?

_____

_____

5. What prompted the invention of punched cards? What might have been the implications for other kinds of data collection and processing?

_____

_____

Figure 6.1   Example of the Use of a Diagram

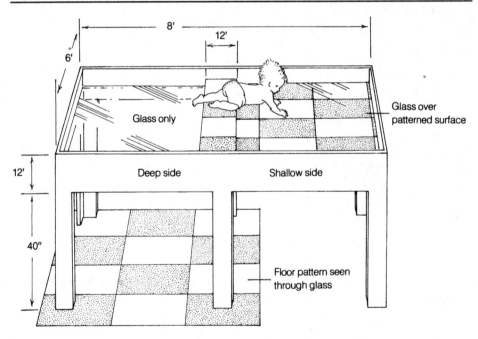

SOURCE: Reprinted with permission from *Introduction to Child Development*, 2d ed. by Dworetzky. Copyright © 1984 by West Publishing Company. All rights reserved.

DIAGRAMMING PROCESSES AND OBJECTS

If you like to doodle, you probably like to diagram ideas. You use diagrams for the same purposes as authors—to represent and explain complex text concepts. You can also use them as right-brain mnemonic devices (see Chapter 7).

To create a diagram, you first identify the concept you want to depict. Second, you list the parts of the concept you want to include. Third, you identify relationships among the parts. Finally, you create a drawing that represents and explains the concept. In diagramming information, artistic ability is helpful, but not necessary. The key to understanding the process of the diagram comes from your analysis of the relationships and from the cognitive rather than the aesthetic quality of your conceptual synthesis.

> **WRITE TO LEARN**
>
> Using Sample Chapter 11, ``Personal Values, Career Planning, and Success with People at Work,'' review the third paragraph in the section on ``Time and Task Management Tools and Skills,'' (page 525) beginning with the sentence, ``A planner needs. . . .'' On a separate sheet of paper, create a diagram that depicts the pages and/or formats you need to incorporate those features into a planner.

CHARTS: ANALYZING AND SYNTHESIZING CONCEPTS

Like diagrams, **charts** show information too complex to be easily understood in written or oral forms. Charts condense and simplify information. They aid in comparison of like and different attributes. They organize information by order or time. They emphasize important points. Common types of charts include **tables, flowcharts,** and **time lines.** Examples of common charts include class schedules and academic calendars.

USING TABLES

Tables indicate relationships among pieces of information. To permit direct comparisons, tables organize information into rows and columns. A row runs horizontally across the page (left to right). A column runs vertically down the page (up to down). Headings or labels identify rows or columns.

A special type of table shows the presence or absence of common features for the items being analyzed (see Figure 6.2). If a feature is possessed by an item, a mark fills the box or space where the item and feature intersect or meet. If the feature is not possessed by that item, the box or space is left blank. This type of table is called a **feature analysis table.** This chart allows you to find details related to the items being compared, infer unstated information, and summarize.

A second kind of table shows the amount or quality of the items being compared (see Figure 6.3). This table allows you to locate details about each item or feature, infer unstated information, and identify **trends** (directions in which features change). Such a chart is called a **quality table.**

Table 6.2 lists steps in reading both feature analysis and quality tables.

Figure 6.2   Example of a Feature Analysis Table

Comparison of Programming Languages

Feature	Assembly Language	Fortran	COBOL	PL/I	Rpg	BASIC	PASCAL	APL
Strong math capabilities	X	X		X		X	X	X
Good character manipulation capabilities	X		X	X		X	X	X
English-like			X	X		X	X	
Available on many computers	X	X	X		X	X	X	
Highly efficient	X							
Standardized		X	X	X		X		
Requires large amount of storage			X	X				X
Good interactive capability						X	X	X
Procedure oriented		X	X	X		X	X	X
Problem oriented					X			
Machine dependent	X							

Figure 6.3   Example of a Quality Table

Mean Annual Income by Sex, Race, and Education

Demographic Group	Overall Median Income	YEARS OF SCHOOLING*					
		7 or Less	8	9-11	12	13-15	16 or More
White males	$16,267	$7,004	$8,948	$12,053	$16,622	$18,574	$23,556
Black males	10,109	4,686	6,623	9,172	12,074	13,803	16,811
White females	5,487	3,425	3,820	4,233	5,774	7,342	10,813
Black females	5,338	2,963	3,423	4,282	6,856	8,910	13,767

Note: These figures include the total money income of full-time and part-time workers, ages twenty-five and over, as of March 1981.
*In terms of highest grade completed.
SOURCE: U.S. Department of Commerce, Bureau of the Census, *Money Income of Households, Families, and Persons in the United States: 1980,* Current Population Reports, Series P-60, No. 132 (Washington, D.C.: U.S. Government Printing Office, 1982), pp. 174, 178.

Table 6.2   Steps in Reading Tables

1. Read the title. This tells you the subject or general content of the table.

2. Identify the type of table. This helps you determine the kind(s) of information given. A table shows the presence or absence of a feature, or it shows the quantity or quality of a feature.

3. Look at the labels or headings in the table. These tell you what items are being compared and what features are being used to compare them. You need to keep the items and features in mind to recognize when and how the relationships change.

4. Note any general trends.

5. If you are looking at a table as part of a chapter survey, stop your examination of this graphic. Continue previewing the chapter.

6. When you reach the section of the text that refers to the table, identify the purpose before turning to the table. Does the author want you to note specific facts, generalizations, or trends?

7. Turn back to the table. Use the purpose set in the text to look at specific areas of the table.

8. Reread the section of the text that referred to the table. Make sure you understand the points and relationships noted by the author.

Exercise 6.2   Examine Table A on page 273 taken from a nutrition text to answer the questions below.

1. How many vitamins are fat soluble? How many are water soluble? Explain the difference between the two types.

_____

_____

_____

2. Which vitamins are still under intense study?

_____

_____

_____

3. Which vitamins are co-enzymes in energy metabolism?

_____

_____

_____

4. Which vitamins are widely distributed in foods?

_____

_____

_____

5. What are the effects of taking too much pantothenic acid and biotin?

_____

_____

_____

6. A patient exhibits upset stomach. What might be the cause?

_____

_____

_____

7. You eat a salad of lettuce only. What vitamins are you most likely to get?

_____

_____

_____

8. How is vitamin D acquired?

_____

_____

_____

Table A

VITAMIN	MAJOR DIETARY SOURCES	MAJOR FUNCTIONS	SIGNS OF SEVERE, PROLONGED DEFICIENCY	SIGNS OF EXTREME EXCESS
Fat soluble				
A	Fat-containing and fortified dairy products; liver; provitamin carotene in orange and deep green produce	Component of rhodopsin; still under intense study	Keratinization of epithelial tissues including the cornea of the eye (xerophthalmia); night blindness; dry, scaling skin; poor immune response	From preformed vitamin A: damage to liver, kidney, bone; headache, irritability, vomiting, hair loss, blurred vision. From carotene: yellowed skin.
D	Fortified and full-fat dairy products; egg yolk	Promotes absorption and use of calcium and phosphorus	Rickets (bone deformities) in children; osteomalacia (bone softening) in adults	Gastrointestinal upset; cerebral, CV, kidney damage; lethargy
E	Vegetable oils and their products; nuts, seeds; present at low levels in other foods	Antioxidant to prevent plasma membrane damage; still under intense study	Possible anemia	Debatable; perhaps fatal in premature infants given intravenous infusion
K	Green vegetables; tea, meats	Aids in formation of certain proteins, especially those for blood clotting	Severe bleeding on injury; internal hemorrhage	Liver damage and anemia from high doses of the synthetic form menadione
Water soluble				
Thiamin (B-1)	Pork, legumes, peanuts, enriched or whole-grain products	Coenzyme used in energy metabolism	Beriberi (nerve changes, sometimes edema, heart failure)	?
Riboflavin (B-2)	Dairy products, meats, eggs, enriched grain products, green leafy vegetables	Coenzyme used in energy metabolism	Skin lesions	?

FOLLOWING FLOWCHARTS

Flowcharts diagram the sequence of steps in a complex process. Arrows show the route through the procedure. Circles, boxes, or other shapes tell what should be done at each step. Flowcharts also depict ordered associations among elements. In such an arrangement, a ranking of information shows superior, equal, and lesser relationships. Some flowcharts show both sequence and hierarchical relationships. The flowchart in Figure 6.4 indicates the process for advancement in the field of law enforcement and the progressive ranks in law enforcement. Table 6.3 depicts the steps in following a flowchart.

Figure 6.4   Example of a Flowchart

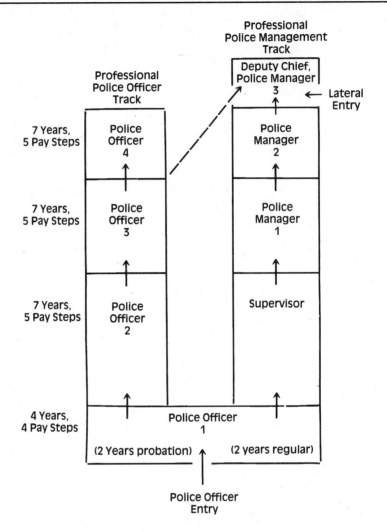

Table 6.3   Steps in Reading a Flowchart

1. Look at the caption to determine the subject of the flowchart.

2. Note the beginning and ending points on the flowchart.

3. Infer trends and/or any breaks in trends by identifying the regularity or irregularity of steps.

4. If you are looking at a flowchart as part of a chapter preview, stop your examination of this graphic. Continue previewing the chapter.

5. When you reach the section of the text that refers to the flowchart, determine the author's purpose before turning to the flowchart. Does the author want to emphasize specific facts, generalizations, or trends?

6. Turn to the flowchart. Use the purpose set by the author to look at specific areas of the chart.

7. Reread the section of the text that referred to the flowchart. Make sure you understand the information noted by the author.

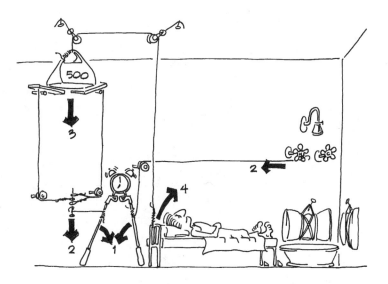

READING TIME LINES

Suppose that a local radio station intends to spotlight musical acts from the fifties, sixties, and seventies—one act per night. Its advertisement of this musical revival is a series of posters, each with a rebus indicating the band that will be featured that night. Because the posters appear in chronological order, they form a sort of time line of music. Can you decipher the rebuses in the cartoon above to determine who has been chosen to perform? (The answers appear on the last page of this chapter.)

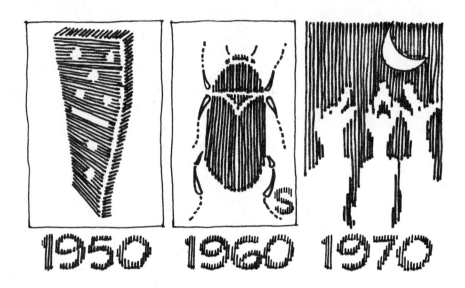

A time line is a graphic **chronology** (time-ordered sequence) or outline of important dates or events. It relates these features to the overall time frame in which they occur. Thus, time lines indicate order. Table 6.4 lists the steps in reading a time line. A time line, like the one in Figure 6.5, describes the history of a topic or the sequence in which things happen.

Table 6.4   Steps in Reading a Time Line

1. Look at the caption to determine what time period is being covered.

2. Note the beginning and ending points on the line.

3. Infer trends and/or any breaks in trends by identifying the regularity or irregularity of events.

4. If you are looking at a time line as part of a chapter preview, stop your examination of this graphic. Continue previewing the chapter.

5. When you reach the section of the text that refers to the time line, determine the author's purpose before turning to the time line. Does the author want to emphasize specific facts, generalizations, or trends?

6. Turn to the time line. Use the purpose set by the author to look at specific areas of the chart.

7. Reread the section of the text that referred to the time line. Make sure you understand the points and relationships noted by the author.

Figure 6.5   Example of a Time Line

The Evolution of Life

Number of Years Ago	Evolutionary Advances
3.6 billion	Primitive one-celled organisms that obtained energy through the method of fermentation
3 billion	Sulfur bacteria that used hydrogen sulfide to conduct photosynthesis Single-celled organisms able to use water in photosynthesis instead of sulfur. These were the ancestors of the blue-green algae and green plants
2 billion	Oxygen atmosphere
1.6 billion	Bacteria able to use nonsulfur photosynthesis and oxygen in respiration. These bacteria could extract 19 times more energy from food than could the first primitive bacteria
1.3 billion	Cells with nuclei evolved
1 billion	Multicelled organisms. Plant and animal kingdoms divide
500 million	Many marine animals, corals, clams, and fish
300 million	Amphibians, ferns, spiders, insects, and first reptiles (over 800 species of cockroach)
150 million	Dinosaurs and reptiles rule the land, sea, and air First birds evolve from smaller dinosaurs Modern insects (bees, moths, flies)
70 million	Dinosaurs extinct Marsupials and primitive mammals Flowering plants Deciduous trees Giant redwoods 50 percent of North America under water; Rocky Mountains are formed
50 million	Modern birds The early horse (only 1 foot high) The ancestors of the cat, dog, elephant, camel, and other mammals Seed-bearing plants and small primates
40,000	Modern man

SOURCE: Reprinted from *Introduction to Child Development*, 2d ed., by Dworetzky. Copyright © 1984 by West Publishing Company. All rights reserved.

Exercise 6.3 Use ``Countdown to Computing—A Time Line'' in Sample Chapter 13, ``An Invitation to Computers'' (pages 588–590) to answer the following questions:

1. What time span does the time line cover?

   _____

   _____

2. According to the time line, what decade or decades experienced the most development in computing?

   _____

   _____

3. According to the time line, what decade or decades experienced no development in computing?

   _____

   _____

4. Identify the time spans covered by the first, second, third, and fourth generations of computers.

   _____

   _____

5. What is the relationship between 1945 and 1988?

   _____

   _____

6. Identify one of the years in which computer languages were developed. Which language was developed that year?

   _____

   _____

7. What happened in 1977 to revolutionize the computing industry?

   _____

   _____

8. What was the impact of the introduction of IBM's Personal Computer in 1981?

   _____

   _____

Table 6.5   Steps in Creating Timelines and Flowcharts

1. Make a vertical list of the items you want to show.

2. Determine if the list follows a linear or multilevel order.

3. If items are linear, arrange according to time or order.

4. If items are multilevel, organize by levels before arranging according to time or order.

CHARTING INFORMATION

What you understand about the relationships among ideas can be indicated by charting. Thus, charting information organizes information. It helps you compare information according to specific factors or traits. It allows you to classify information and look for trends across time. It enables you to sequence processes, events, and ideas.

Listing the information you have forms the first step in creating a chart. Once you create a list, you analyze it to identify relationships within it. For example, information could relate according to time, common trait, spatial proximity, causation, result, order, or other attribute.

Once you determine how ideas relate, you determine which kind of chart best fits your needs. Time lines are most suitable for information that occurs in a linear time order or linear sequence. Flowcharts apply to processes that flow in more than one direction or that have multiple simultaneous steps. Tables best organize like information that compares in more than one way. Table 6.5 provides steps in creating time lines and flowcharts. Table 6.6 lists the steps involved in creating tables. Figure 6.6 gives examples of organizational formats for tables.

WRITE TO LEARN

On a separate sheet of paper use the section entitled ``The Spread of Industrialization,'' pages 553–557, in Sample Chapter 12, ``The Industrial Revolution and Its Impact on European Society,'' to create a chart that compares British and continental industrialization.

Table 6.6   Steps in Charting Information

1. Make a vertical list of the items you want to compare.

2. List horizontally the factors you want to know about each item.

3. Draw a grid by sketching lines between each element and each factor.

4. Locate and record the information that fills each box of the grid.

Figure 6.6   Synthesis Charts

CHARTS FOR TERMS IN ANY SUBJECT

TERM	DEFINITION	CONNOTATION	PERSONAL EXAMPLE/ASSOCIATION

CHART FOR ARTISTS AND AUTHORS IN HUMANITIES CLASSES

TITLE	AUTHOR/ ARTISTS	THEME	SETTING	DESCRIPTION OF ACTION	MAIN CHARACTERS

CHARTS FOR DISCOVERIES IN APPLIED AND SOCIAL SCIENCES

WHO ?	FROM WHERE ?	WHAT ?	WHEN ?	HOW ?

Painting can illustrate,
but it cannot inform.

—SAMUEL JOHNSON

Eighteenth Century
English Author

GRAPHS: DRAWING ON DATA

Graphs both illustrate and inform. They allow large amounts of information to be organized into a more manageable form. **Graphs** show quantitative comparisons between two or more sets of information. Bylooking at comparable amounts or numbers, you determine relationships. The most common types of graphs are **bar graphs** (or **histograms**), **circle graphs,** and **line graphs.** Table 6.7 lists the steps in analyzing graphs.

EXAMINING BAR GRAPHS

Bar graphs (see Figure 6.7) compare and contrast quantitative values. They show the amount or quantity of an item. Although the units in which the items are measured must be equal, they can be of any size and can start at any value. If the units are large, the bar graph may show approximate rather than exact amounts.

Table 6.7 Steps in Analyzing Graphs

1. Read the title, heading, or caption to identify the general group of objects being compared.
2. Note labels or headings for each item or unit to identify the specific objects being compared or contrasted.
3. Determine the units used to measure the items in a bar or line graph. Identify the number that each symbol represents in a symbol graph.
4. Note any general trends.
5. If you are looking at a graph as part of previewing a chapter, stop your examination of this graphic. Continue previewing the chapter.
6. When you reach the section of the text that refers to the graph, identify the text's purpose before turning to it. Does the author want you to note specific facts, generalizations, or trends?
7. Turn to the graph. Use the purpose set by the author to look at specific areas of the graph.
8. Reread the section of the text that referred to the graph. Make sure you understand the points and relationships noted by the author.

Figure 6.7 Example of a Bar Graph

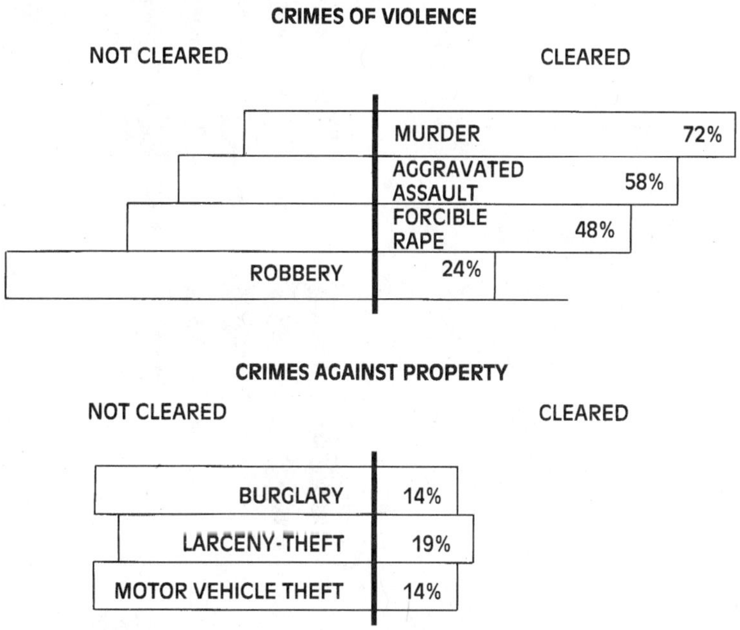
CRIMES OF VIOLENCE
NOT CLEARED
CLEARED
MURDER
72%
AGGRAVATED ASSAULT
58%
FORCIBLE RAPE
48%
ROBBERY
24%
CRIMES AGAINST PROPERTY
NOT CLEARED
CLEARED
BURGLARY
14%
LARCENY-THEFT
19%
MOTOR VEHICLE THEFT
14%

SOURCE: Note: Crimes cleared by arrest, 1981. Data from Federal Bureau of Investigation, crime in the United States, FBI Uniform Crime Reports (Washington, D.C.: U.S. Government Printing Office,) p. 152. Reprinted with permission from *Crime and Justice in America: A Human Perspective,* by Vetter and Territo.

Symbol or **pictorial graphs** (see Figure 6.8) are specialized types of bar graphs. They use **symbols** to show quantitative amounts. A key or legend tells what each symbol represents. You multiply the number of symbols by the value of the symbol to determine totals.

Figure 6.8   Example of a Symbol Graph

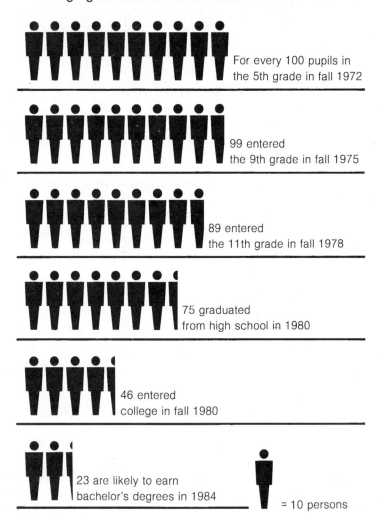

Estimated retention rates, fifth grade through college graduation: United States 1972 to 1984

For every 100 pupils in the 5th grade in fall 1972

99 entered the 9th grade in fall 1975

89 entered the 11th grade in fall 1978

75 graduated from high school in 1980

46 entered college in fall 1980

23 are likely to earn bachelor's degrees in 1984

= 10 persons

SOURCE: Reprinted with permission from *Reading Enhancement and Development,* by Atkinson and Longman. Copyright © 1985 by West Publishing Company. All rights reserved.

Exercise 6.4   Answer these questions about the bar graphs that follow.

1. Without reading the caption, define *total engagement* and *caregiving.*

_____

_____

_____

_____

2. Now read the caption and define *total engagement* and *caregiving.* How closely did your definitions resemble the ones used in the caption?

_____

_____

_____

_____

3. After reading the caption, explain what the two graphs indicate.

_____

_____

_____

_____

4. Who tends to spend most time with an infant? Do you find this surprising or not surprising in today's society? Why or why not?

_____

_____

_____

_____

5. What trend occurs in the father's total engagement time as the child grows older? In his caregiving time? What might account for these trends?

_____

_____

_____

_____

6. What trend occurs in the mother's behavior as the child grows older? What might account for this trend?

_____

_____

_____

_____

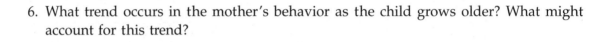

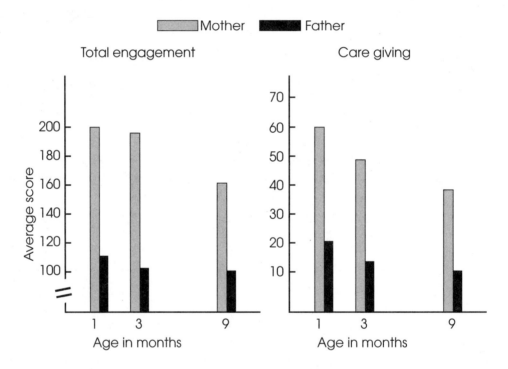

Mother-infant and Father-infant interactions. These graphs show what occurred on routine days in a sample of 72 American homes. The graph on the left records the total amount of contact parents had with their babies, ... The graph on the right shows the amount of care-giving done by each parent.

FOLLOWING LINE GRAPHS

Line graphs (see Figure 6.9) show quantitative trends for an item over time. Each line on the graph represents one item. When one or more lines are shown, a **key** or **legend** tells what each line represents. Lines show increases, decreases, or no directional changes. Line graphs often are thought to be more accurate than bar graphs because they represent amounts more precisely.

Figure 6.9   Example of a Line Graph

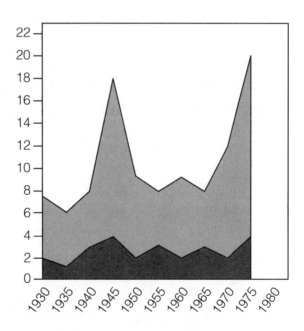

Annual divorce rate for the United States
Source: National Center for Health Statistics.
Advance Report: Final Divorce Statistics. 1975.
May 1977 (Vol. 26, No. 2, Supplement 2).

Figure 6.10 Example of a Circle Graph

Types of Study Habits

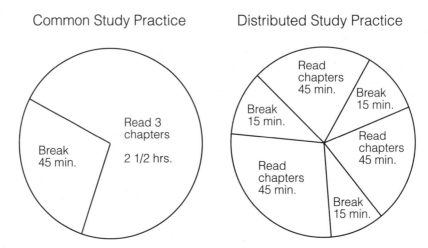

Common Study Practice

Break 45 min.

Read 3 chapters 2 1/2 hrs.

Distributed Study Practice

Read chapters 45 min.

Break 15 min.

Break 15 min.

Read chapters 45 min.

Read chapters 45 min.

Break 15 min.

ANALYZING CIRCLE GRAPHS

Probably the most common circle graph resembles something you may have had for lunch today—a pizza. Because circle graphs so closely resemble pies, they often are called pie charts.

A circle graph (see Figure 6.10) represents only one unit. It shows the relationship of parts of one unit to the whole of that unit. Because all of

the parts equal the whole unit, or 100 percent of the unit, percentages and/or fractions measure the parts of the graph. Contrasting colors or shading often denote these components in pie-shaped wedges.

Circle graphs deal with fractions of a whole, instead of units on a continuum. Thus, the steps involved in reading them differ somewhat from those for reading other kinds of graphs. Table 6.8 lists the steps in reading circle graphs.

Exercise 6.5   Answer these questions using the circle graphs that follow.

1. What is the title of the graph on the left? On the right? From what source did the information in each originate?

_____

_____

_____

_____

2. In what specialty do most psychologists study? In what specialty does the smallest percentage of psychologists study?

_____

_____

_____

_____

3. Where do most psychologists work? Where does the smallest percentage of psychologists work?

_____

_____

_____

_____

4. Compare the percentage of psychologists who specialize in school and educational psychology with the percentage of those who work in academic settings. How might you account for the disparity in these figures?

_____

_____

_____

_____

5. Compare the percentage of psychologists who specialize in counseling with the percentage of those who work in private practice. In what other area(s) might psychologists who specialize in counseling work?

_____

_____

_____

_____

(a)

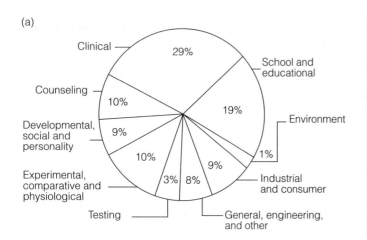

(b)

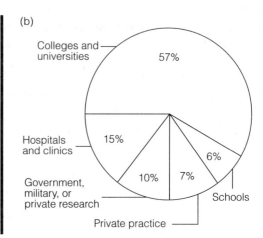

SOURCE: Reprinted with permission from *Introduction to Psychology* by Coon. Copyright © 1989 by West Publishing Company. (a) Specialties in psychology. Percentages are approximate (from Howard et al., 1986). (b) Where psychologists work (from Pion, 1986).

Table 6.8   Steps in Reading Circle Graphs

1. Read the title, heading, or caption. These identify the whole unit whose parts are being shown and compared.

2. Look at the labels for each part of the circle.

3. Identify the general sizes for each of the parts. Note relationships between and among the parts.

4. Note any general trends.

5. If you are looking at a circle graph as part of a chapter preview, stop your examination of this graphic. Continue previewing the chapter.

6. When you reach the section of the text that refers to the graph, identify the text's purpose before turning to the graph. Does the author want you to note specific facts, generalizations, or trends?

7. Turn to the graph. Use the purpose set by the text to look at specific areas of the graph.

8. Reread the section of the text that referred to the graph. Make sure you understand the points and relationships noted by the author.

Exercise 6.6   Use the line graph to answer the questions that follow.

FIGURE 12–6 ■ Number of Highway Fatalities by Day of Week, Time of Day, and Alcohol Involvement, 1981.

SOURCE: Fifth Special Report to the U.S. Congress on Alcohol and Health, U.S. Department of Health and Human Services, December 1983.)

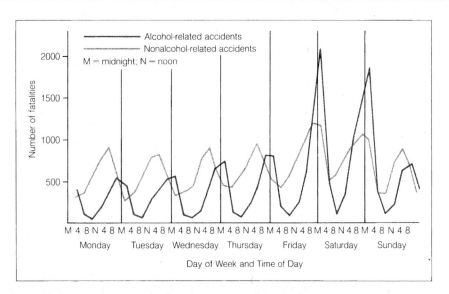

More than half of all highway deaths—approximately 25,000 each year—are related to drinking and driving (see Table 12–4). Although, in most states, it takes a BAL of 0.10 percent for a person to be considered legally drunk, many people are not capable of driving a car with far less alcohol in their bloodstreams. At a BAL of 0.10 percent, a driver is ten times more likely to have an accident than a nondrinker. At a BAL of 0.15 percent, the likelihood of an accident increases by twenty-five times and at 0.20 percent by one hundred times. Most drunk-driving accidents occur at about midnight on weekdays and at about 2 A.M. on Friday and Saturday nights (see Figure 12–6). Beer is the beverage most frequently associated with drinking and driving. Accidents not involving motor vehicles are also significantly higher when alcohol is involved.

1. What is the time span covered in the figure in hours? In days?

_____

_____

2. What is the significance of the time of day and day of week when the incidence of alcohol-related accidents is greatest?

_____

3. Explain the horizontal labels on the graph (M, 4, 8, N, 4, 8).

_____

_____

4. What BAL is considered to mean that one is legally drunk? What level is considered lethal?

_____

_____

_____

GRAPHING DATA

Graphing allows you to organize quantitative information in order to visually show relationships and trends. Like creating a chart, graphing begins with a collection of information. Although you can use charts to organize quantitative information (e.g., grades in a gradebook), the resulting table often contains too much data for quick analysis. Graphing forms a synthesis in that it allows you to show numerical changes for individual items. Each line, bar, or circle represents quantitative changes for a particular item or class of items. Thus, when you want to show what happens to a class of quantitative information as well as organize it, graphs are a better choice than charts.

Once you collect data, you organize according to the attributes of the data that you want to examine. For example, your data might consist of scores on tests for students in a class. You might arrange the data by students, by range of grades (e.g., number of people whose scores fall between 90 and 100), by exam, and so on. Once you choose the attributes, you select the upper and lower limits for comparison. For example, in terms of grades, 0 to 100 is the range for most exams. Using appropriate labels, scale the range along the horizontal or vertical side of your graph (e.g., 10, 20, 30, and so on). Again, using labels, list the items being compared across the remaining side of the graph. Finally, you plot the score for each item on the graph. If you construct a bar graph, you create bars that extend from the lower limit of your range to the point you plot. If you construct a line graph, you connect the points as they change.

Just as reading circle graphs differs from reading line or bar graphs, creating circle graphs differs from creating line or bar graphs. Because circle graphs represent segments of a whole, the first step in creating a circle graph is determining what unit represents the entire circle. The second step is converting the data to fractions or percentages. The final step is sketching the parts and labeling accordingly.

WRITE TO LEARN

On a separate sheet of paper, use the following information to construct a line graph, a bar graph, and a circle graph.
Students at Northeast College:

Freshmen	3500
Sophomores	2500
Juniors	2000
Seniors	1500
TOTAL	9500

MAPS: PHYSICAL AND MENTAL TERRITORIES

"You want to know how to get to the library? Well, first you go past Jones Hall, or is it Smith? Anyway, then you pass three, or maybe four more buildings, turn right, go straight for another two buildings, and turn left. You can't miss it."

If you've ever received directions like these, you probably wished you had a map. **Maps** provide information about places and their characteristics in a two-dimensional format. Because they often depict places you haven't physically seen, maps often—as Lawrence notes—appear more real to us than the lands they show.

Most commonly found in geography or history texts, maps are sometimes found in science, math, or literature texts and recreational reading books. Map-reading skills add to your understanding of the text by giving you visual representations of what's been written.

Unless you're giving directions to someone, map-making may seem like an unlikely study strategy. However, in terms of learning, maps refer to physical representations of connections among mental concepts. Like geographical maps, these maps show the location of ideas in relation to one another. They provide an overview of mental territory and help you analyze and synthesize relationships.

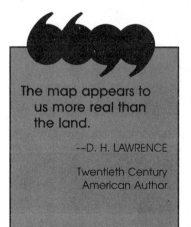

The map appears to us more real than the land.

--D. H. LAWRENCE

Twentieth Century American Author

WRITE TO LEARN

On a separate sheet of paper or in your journal, select a graphic of your choice and use it to demonstrate a feature of your class (for example, number of males to females, students by major, hair color, eye color, and so forth).

*"I think it's a bad omen to take a test on Friday
the thirteenth on a chapter whose map looks like this!"*

READING GEOGRAPHIC MAPS

The **general reference map** and the **special purpose map** (also known as
a **thematic map**) are the most common types found in texts. The general
reference map (see Figure 6.11) gives general geographical information.
This includes surface features (rivers, plains, mountains), places and their
distances from each other, political data such as boundaries between
states or countries, and urban population data. Special purpose or
thematic maps (see Figure 6.12) highlight a particular feature of a
geographical region. They show variations among other regions with
respect to this feature. Such maps include information on scientific data
(for example, ocean currents and climate), social or cultural data (people
and customs), political data (boundaries, governments), and economic
data (expenditures and finances).

General reference and thematic maps come in two types: physical—
showing the natural features of an area—and political—indicating
human-made features of an area. City, state, or national boundaries
comprise the only political information found on physical maps. Mountains or major bodies of water (rivers, oceans) comprise the only physical
information found on political maps.

Special characteristics of maps include a **scale of distance,** symbols,
and keys or legends. Although these may seem to add to the complexity

Figure 6.11   Example of a General Reference Map (Political)

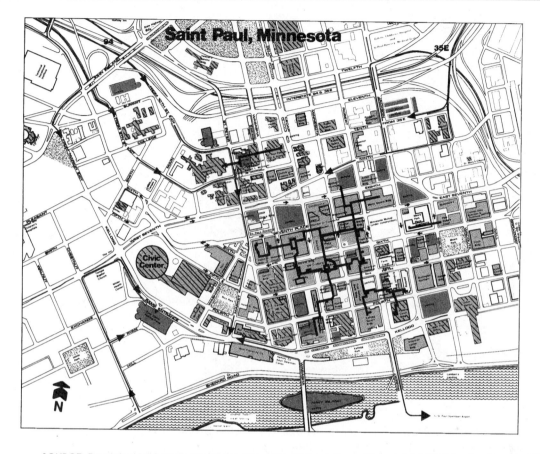

SOURCE: Reprinted by permission of the University of Illinois Press. Copyright © 1979 by the Board of Trustees of the University of Illinois.

of maps, such devices let authors provide vast amounts of information concisely. They also help you recognize the features highlighted by maps and make comparisons among these.

Because it would be unrealistic to make a map the actual size of the area it represents, **cartographers** (mapmakers) draw maps according to a set scale. A scale of distance, found on most maps, shows the relationship between distances on a map and distances in real life. Scales can be shown in the following three ways:

Fraction	1″ : 50 miles
Written Statement	1 inch equals 50 miles
Graphic Scale	

/		/	/	/
0		50	100	150

Figure 6.12 Example of a Special or Thematic Map (Physical)

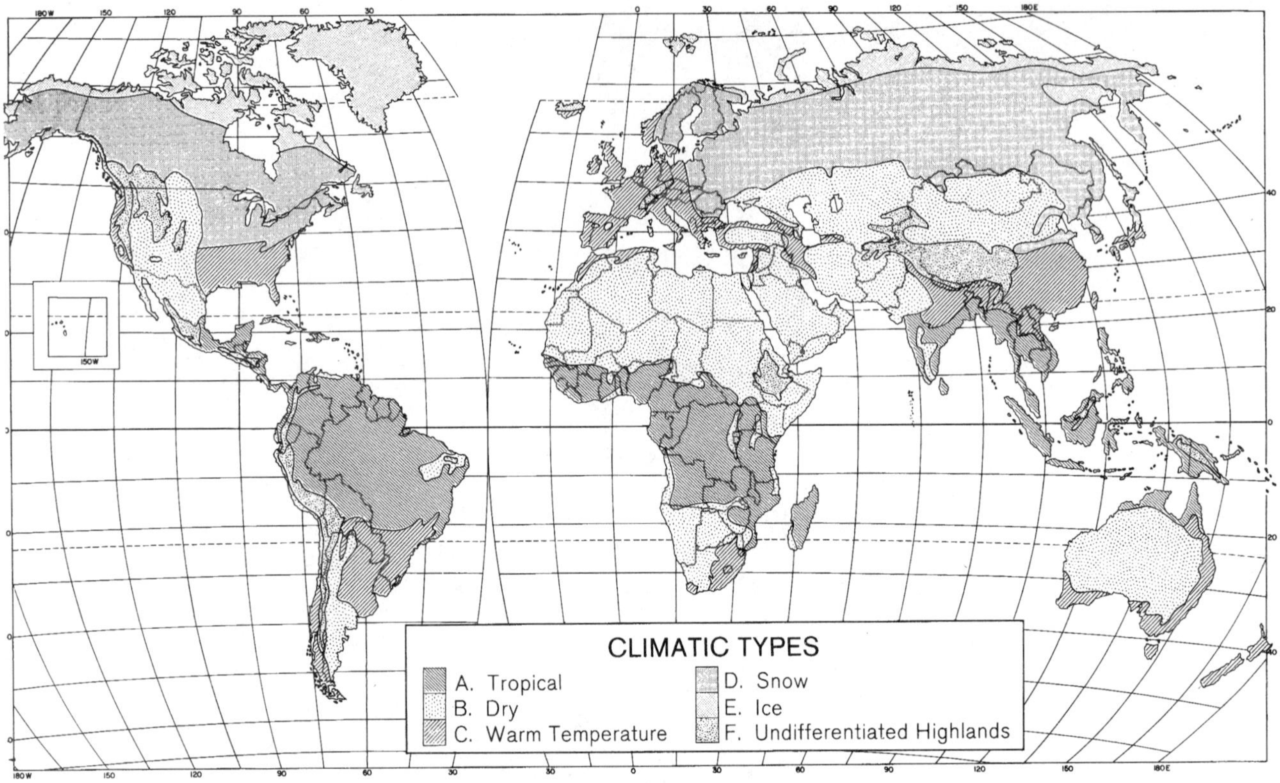
CLIMATIC TYPES
A. Tropical
B. Dry
C. Warm Temperature
D. Snow
E. Ice
F. Undifferentiated Highlands

SOURCE: Reprinted with permission from *The Cultural Landscape*, by Rubenstein and Bacon. Copyright © 1983 by West Publishing Company. All rights reserved.

Symbols, contrasting colors, or shading represent natural or human-made details. Thorough reading of a map depends on a thorough understanding of the ways in which features are represented. This understanding is accomplished with the aid of a key or legend that shows each symbol, color, or shade used on a map and its corresponding explanation. Figure 6.12 shows a key ("Climatic Types") on a thematic map. Steps for reading maps appears in Table 6.9.

WRITE TO LEARN

A friend of yours needs directions from your house to the nearest grocery store. On a separate sheet of paper, provide: 1) written directions and 2) a map (including landmarks, scale of distance, and key). Compare the two. Which provides the clearest instruction? Why? Which type of map did you draw? How is this type different from the other type?

Table 6.9   Steps for Reading Maps

1. Locate and read the title, heading, or caption. This identifies the geographical area represented by the map.

2. Read the key or legend to identify symbols that are used on the map. Check the scale to get an idea of how much area the map covers.

3. If you are looking at a map as part of a chapter preview, stop your examination of the map. Continue previewing the chapter.

4. When you reach the section of the text that refers to the map, identify the text's purpose before turning to the map. What information does the map illustrate?

5. Turn to the map. Use the purpose set by the text to look at specific features of the map.

6. Reread the section of the text that referred to the map. Make inferences about information provided by the map and the text.

Exercise 6.7   Use Maps 21.1 (page 546) and 21.2 (page 555) in Sample Chapter 12, ``The Industrial Revolution and Its Impact on European Society,'' to respond to the following questions.

1. Are the maps physical maps, political maps, or both? Cite map features that support your response.

_____

_____

2. What are the scales for the maps? Which map shows the most territory?

_____

_____

3. What is the relationship between the subjects of the two maps?

_____

_____

4. Identify three political features on each map.

_____

_____

_____

5. Identify three physical features on each map.

_____

_____

_____

_____

6. According to Map 21.1, what major industries do you find in Great Britain?

_____

_____

7. According to Map 21.2, identify three major cities in 1820 and three major cities in 1850.

_____

_____

8. Other than Great Britain, in what other European country would you find silk or textile industries?

_____

_____

9. Other than Great Britain, in what other European country would you find coal mining or iron industry?

_____

_____

10. Using Map 21.1, identify three towns with a population of 400,000.

_____

_____

11. Using Map 21.2, identify two countries that did not emancipate peasants prior to 1848.

_____

_____

MAPPING MENTAL TERRITORIES

Throughout history, individuals explored new territories. As they did so, they created maps to show where they had been. Their maps represented the synthesis of their background knowledge about a particular place. Mapping mental territories serves somewhat the same purpose as mapping physical territories. Often called a **concept** or **idea map,** a map represents the synthesis of relationships about a topic in graphic form. Because the visual representation of ideas impact a different area of the brain than words (see Chapter 1), concept maps provide another way for you to encode and recall information. Taking an active part in organizing and creating the map helps you remember more with less effort.

Visual representations of information include idea or concept maps and word maps. Some kinds of representations are more appropriate for certain kinds of information than others. Determining the graphic you need depends on the content of the information and your skill in representing ideas visually.

Idea or concept maps are pictures that show relationships among concepts. They express patterns of thought. Idea maps can be used to organize or condense text chapters or lecture notes. Because concepts and ideas are related in various ways, maps differ. Thus, you can be somewhat creative in your mapmaking. The text structure you've identified from the lecture or text (See Chapter 4 and 5) helps you decide what concepts to map (see Table 6.10). In addition, if your instructor or text specifies elements or relationships, your map should reflect these.

Idea maps relate information to a central topic. They indicate major, minor, and equal relationships among details. Such maps show rankings of details by branching out from the central topic (see Figure 6.13). This text uses idea maps at the beginning of each chapter to show the relationship between chapter headings and subheadings. Another way idea maps show how details relate to a topic is by showing a progression of steps or chronological order of events or historical periods. Such maps show the logical flow of information (see Figure 6.14). The idea map you choose to use depends on the type of information you diagram and your

Table 6.10   Structure Patterns and Corresponding Elements in Idea Maps

Pattern	Examples of Elements	
Introduction/Summary	main ideas supporting details	
Subject Development/Definition	definitions supporting details examples	characteristics types or kinds elements
Enumeration/Sequence	main points details steps	elements procedures
Comparison/Contrast	similarities differences	pros cons
Cause/Effect	problems solutions elements	reasons procedures

Figure 6.13   Example of a Web Idea Map

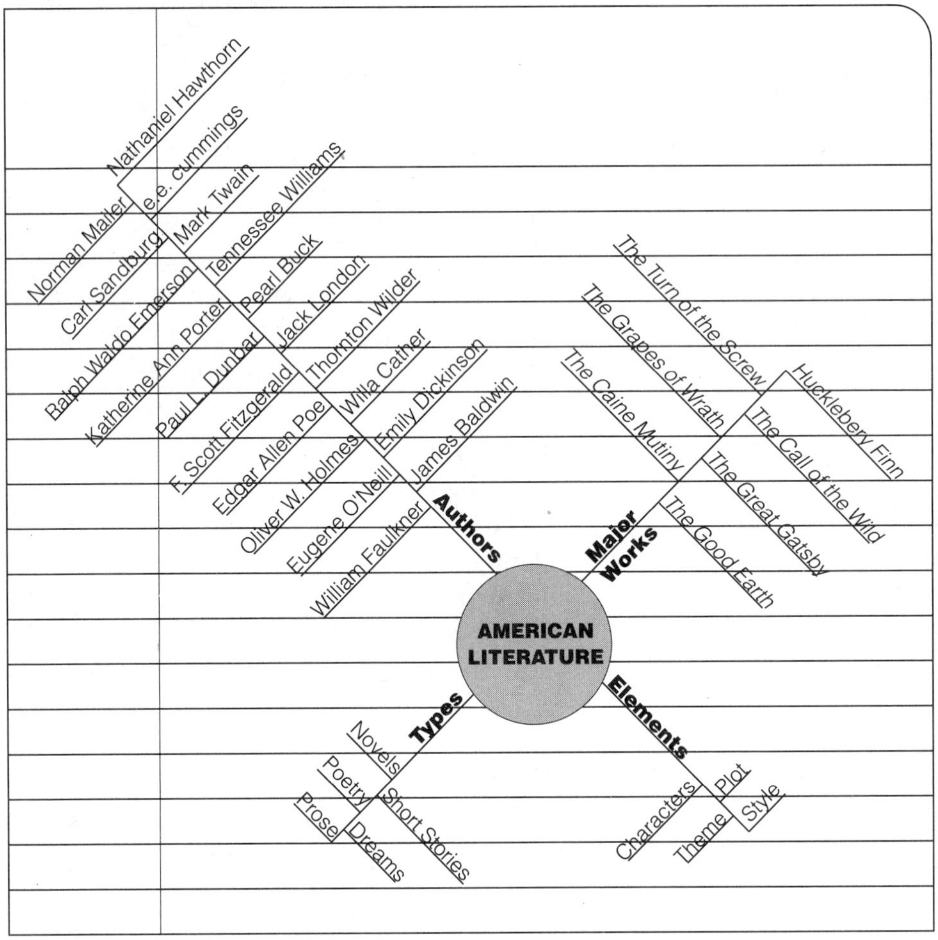

preference (see Figure 6.15). Table 6.11 explains the steps in drawing an idea map.

Another way to map concepts is to draw or map the terms in a particular chapter. You do this by identifying general headings under which terms might fall. Then you draw a map showing these headings. Under each heading, you list the appropriate terms. Then you draw two

WRITE TO LEARN

On a separate sheet of paper, briefly explain the differences between outlines and graphic representations of information. Which appeal to you? Why?

Figure 6.14 Example of a Branching Idea Map

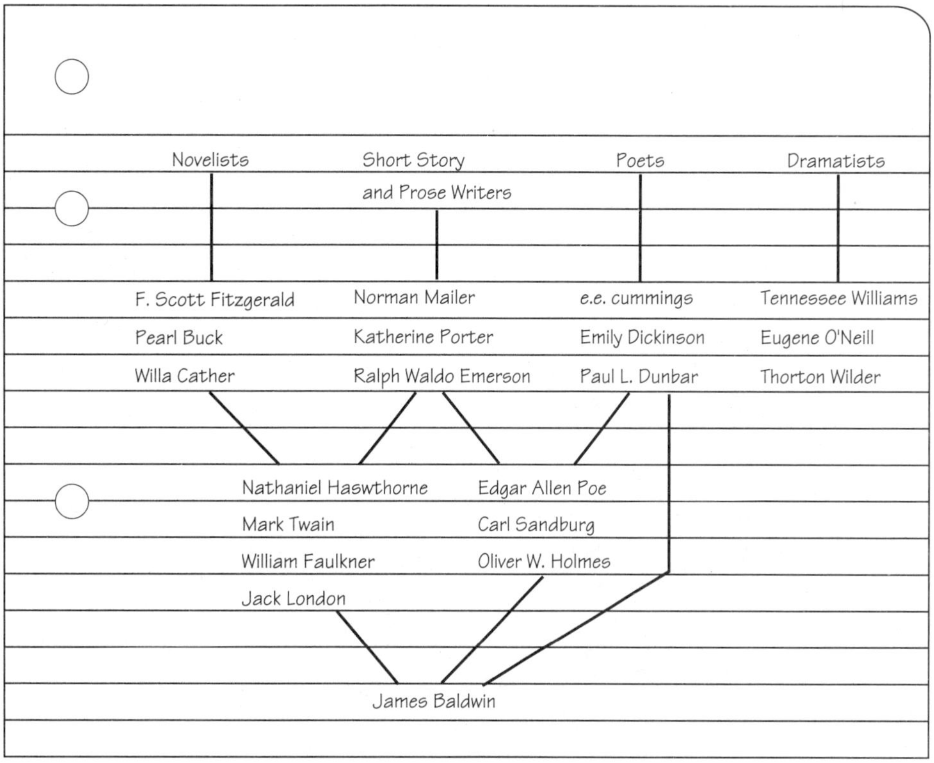

lines under each term. On the first line, you draw a picture that you associate with the term and/or its meaning. On the second line, you write the term's meaning in your own words. Figure 6.16 provides an example of a word map.

When studying terms, you cover the information below the term. Then you try to remember the term's meaning. If you are not successful, you reveal the picture. Seeing your drawing should cue recall. If not, you uncover the definition. Your final step in using this memory technique is to spend a few seconds studying the term and recalling why you drew the picture you did.

WRITE TO LEARN

Create an idea map to reflect the content of ``Key Idea 3: Managing Your Boss'' in Sample Chapter 11, ``Personal Values, Career Planning, and Success with People at Work.''

Figure 6.15   Map Structures

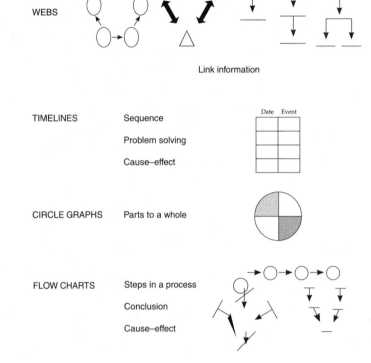

GROUP LEARNING ACTIVITY
A PICTURE OR 1,000 WORDS

Consider again the job of cartographers. They observe, plot, survey, photograph, and otherwise describe the locations of places by measuring distances, directions, and elevations. The maps they draw contain lines, words, symbols, and colors that describe new places to us or help us move from place to place.

The following activity provides you with the opportunity to create a map and interpret both written and graphic information.

Application

Step one: Create a map of a mythical country. Include information about the size and shape of the country; number and location of large cities; descriptions of natural formations; and names, sizes, and shapes of border

Table 6.11   Steps in Constructing Idea Maps

1. Choose a word or phrase that represents the topic you wish your map to cover. This word could be the chapter title, a purpose-setting question, a heading, an objective, a term, or any other major concept.

2. Write this concept at the top of your notebook page.

3. List information about the concept. This could include descriptive details, definitions, functions, reasons, or any other listing of facts.

4. Examine the elements to determine how they relate to one another. Identify any associations between elements (least to most, largest to smallest, nonequivalent or nonsequential details, cause-to-effect, problem-to-solution, etc.).

5. Choose the type of idea map that can best represent the relationships you've identified.

6. Sketch the map.

7. Draw lines or arrows to indicate relationships among details and between the topic and details.

8. Judge the usefulness of your map by answering the following questions:
   a. Does the word you used to label the map accurately define the concept?
   b. Do the terms and ideas adequately support and describe the concept?
   c. Is the map logically organized?
   d. Is the map easy to read?

countries and their locations. Select your own symbols for major highways, cities, natural formations, and so forth.

Step two: Pass your map to the person on your left and take the map from the person on your right. Write a one- to two-paragraph description of the mythical country based on this map.

Step three: Give this description to the person on your left and take the description from the person on your right. Now draw a map of the country that person has described.

Step four: Return the maps and accompanying descriptions to the original owners. Provide time for each person to compare his or her map with the corresponding description and map.

Step five: Discuss as a group how people interpret written and graphic material.

Figure 6.16   An Example of a Word Map

Government and Politics

Development of Government

Early Forms of Government

GOVERNMENT

Body of people and institutions that regulate society

AUTOCRATIC

Characteristic of a monaach or another person with unlimited power

AUTOCRACY

State where one person has unlimited political power

DIRECT DEMOCRACY

Form of government in which people have power and use it directly

TERMS

Terms appear in the order in which they occurred in the chapter.

graphics
diagrams
charts
tables
flowcharts
time lines
feature analysis
   table
trends
quality table
chronology
graphs
bar graphs
histograms
circle graphs
line graphs
symbol graphs
pictorial graphs
symbols
key
legend
maps
general reference
   map
special purpose
   map
thematic map
scale of distance
cartographers
concept map
idea map

CHAPTER SUMMARY

1. Graphics provide ways to see what you or an author believes about information and how each of you organizes it to exemplify, sort, and clarify key concepts.

2. Graphic information helps you process and remember information more effectively because it involves both sides of the brain.

3. Diagrams provide visual representations of events, processes, structures, relationships, or sequences.

4. Charts (time lines, flowcharts, and tables) organize, condense, and simplify information so that you can analyze and synthesize concepts more easily.

5. Graphics (bar graphs, circle graphs, and line graphs) enable you to interpret or organize two or more sets of quantitative information.

6. Maps provide information about physical locations or mental relationships in visual form.

CHAPTER REVIEW

Answer briefly but completely.

1. Examine Table 6.1. Which type of text graphic is most versatile? Least versatile? Why is this so?

_____

_____

_____

_____

_____

2. How do graphics enhance your ability to process and recall information?

_____

_____

_____

_____

_____

3. What is the process for taking notes from text graphics?

_____

_____

_____

_____

4. How do feature analysis tables differ from quality tables? How are they alike? How do you use purpose to identify the type you need?

_____

_____

_____

_____

5. In what ways are tables, flowcharts, and time lines alike? How do they differ? How do you use purpose to identify the type you need?

_____

_____

_____

_____

6. In what ways are bar graphs and line graphs alike? How do they differ? How do you use purpose to identify the type you need?

_____

_____

_____

_____

7. How do circle graphs differ from bar or line graphs?

_____

_____

_____

_____

8. What is the difference between general reference and special purpose maps?

_____

_____

_____

_____

_____

9. Compare physical and political maps.

_____

_____

_____

_____

_____

10. What is the purpose of keys or legends in reading graphs or maps?

_____

_____

_____

_____

_____

REFERENCE

Wittrock, M.C. (1977). The generative processes of memory. In M.C. Wittrock (Ed.), _The Human Brain._ Englewood Cliffs, N.J.: Prentice-Hall.

Vocabulary Development   Right-Brain Note Cards: Picture This!

Think of your instructor for this course. Did you think of a name or a face? Authors know that verbal and visual information impacts learning and memory differently. A combination of text and graphic information provides you with stimuli for both kinds of understanding. Similarly, vocabulary development can be enhanced through the use of visual as well as verbal information.

> One picture is worth ten thousand words.
> —FREDERICK R. BARNARD

In many ways, Barnard's view of pictures has been scientifically validated by the work of Nobel prize winner Roger Sperry (See Chapter 1).

Wittrock (1977) put Sperry's findings to work in a study of memory and learning. He found that students remembered vocabulary words better when they drew pictures to represent them than when they read and wrote the words and the definitions. Tracing a picture of a definition resulted in better recall than writing the definition. Creating a personal visual image for the word proved to be more effective than tracing.

The work of Sperry and Wittrock has clear implications for college vocabulary development. Pictures capture the attention of the right brain. The left brain focuses on the words. Like text graphics, pictures impact your brain, your learning, and your memory differently than do words alone. Using both sides of the brain—instead of relying only on the left side—increases your potential for learning. While your pictures may not be worth ten thousand words, they will help you picture—and learn—the words you need.

Use the following suggestions and Figure 6.17 to picture words with note cards that appeal to the right brain.

1. Write the word on the front of the card.
2. On the front of the card, draw a picture that represents its meaning. Form personal associations. Use humorous or outrageous images. Use common symbols.
3. Write the word's meaning on the back of the card.
4. Use the front of the card for recall. If you cannot recall the meaning, look at your drawing. Try to remember why you drew what you did. If you still cannot recall the meaning, refer to the definition.

Activity

Choose any five of the terms on pages 531-532 in Sample Chapter 11, ``Personal Values, Career Planning, and Success with People at Work,'' and create right-brain note cards for them.

Figure 6.17   Example of a Right-Brain Note Card.

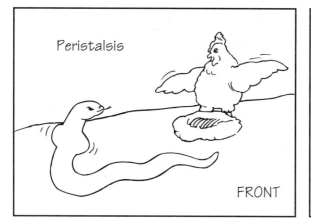

Peristalsis

FRONT

Involuntary contraction of the muscular wall of the esophagus to force food to the stomach and propell waste through the rest of the digestive tract.

BACK

KEY

The singers and/or groups in the time line are Fats Domino, the Beatles, and Three Dog Night.

Maximizing Memory for Test Taking

CHAPTER MAP

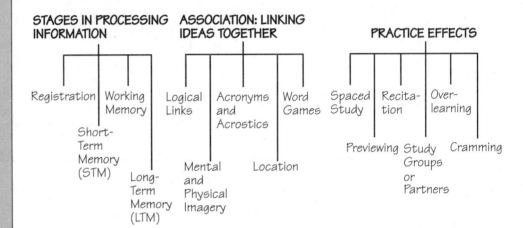

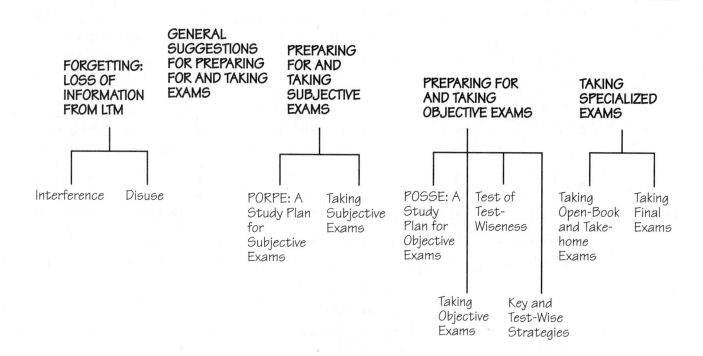

A learned fool is one who has read everything and simply remembered it.

—Josh Billings

Nineteenth century American humorist

The process of learning is far more than memorization. Memorization, or recall, is the lowest level of understanding in Bloom's taxonomy, a system developed in 1956 to describe levels of difficulty, sophistication, and thoroughness in thinking and reading (see Figure 7.1). Indeed, you can memorize information and not understand it at all. In memorization, what you "learn" is all there is. In general, you have no way to use the information other than the form in which you learned it.

That's why many students who had very good high school grades discover that the learning and memory strategies they used in high school often result in less-than-satisfactory grades in college courses. After studying for tests, they can define or recite almost any fact from the text or lecture; however, they often lack the ability to make important connections among information. This is a problem of depth. How deeply you process information impacts how well you understand it. The more you know about a concept, the better you can relate it to other ideas. This

---

Figure 7.1   Bloom's Taxonomy of Thinking

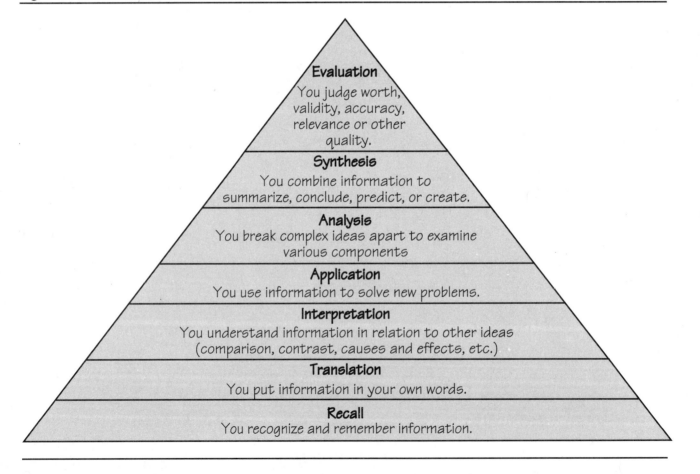

requires a deeper understanding. In high school, you are most often asked to think in words; in college, you must think in concepts.

Processing depth varies for a number of reasons. The strength of your interest in a subject and the amount of desire you have for learning affect how deeply you process information about the subject. Intense interest or desire causes you to process more thoroughly. Negative attitudes often result in superficial processing. Purpose and intention also influence depth of processing. Like setting purposes for reading, determining the level of understanding you need gives you a goal. In addition, how well you concentrate affects how deeply you process information. When you concentrate well, you make stronger and more numerous links among facts and ideas in the information for future applications. Finally, relating information to what you know—your background knowledge—affects processing. It allows you to form more connections between new information and what you already know.

For instance, consider what you know about Abraham Lincoln (sixteenth president of the United States) and Andrew Johnson (seventeenth president of the United States). If you are like most people, you can visualize Abraham Lincoln (tall, thin, bearded, black top hat). You associate several ideas with him (Civil War, Gettysburg Address, assassination, lawyer, log cabin). However, like most people, you may find that you recall little about Andrew Johnson, other than his name and that he succeeded Lincoln as president. What you recall about each man reflects, to some extent, depth of processing. Because you know more about Lincoln and connect him to other concepts, you possess a deeper understanding of him. In contrast, if you know few details about Andrew Johnson, you make few connections between him and what you know. Your understanding of Andrew Johnson is shallowly processed.

As you use the various rehearsal techniques in this chapter to help you process information, you also must consider how you associate and organize information. Doing this allows you to develop the necessary links among information, thus increasing your ability to apply what you've learned.

For example, in a psychology course, you may be learning about the biological bases of behavior. As you study, you memorize the parts of the forebrain—thalamus, hypothalamus, limbic system, corpus callosum, cerebrum. You also learn a definition for each and can identify its function. With this information stored, you can answer questions, such as the following:

1. *What is the thalamus?*

2. *What part of the brain regulates autonomic functions?*

However, on the test you find the following questions:

1. *A classmate experiences memory lapses. Which part of the forebrain is most likely to contribute to this problem and why?*

2. *Hypothesize a time line for the development of forebrain structures and provide a rationale for the order of development.*

3. *As a research psychologist, devise a research question that you want to investigate for each of the components of the forebrain.*

4. *Which of the components of the forebrain have the most impact on the acquisition of knowledge for elementary school students?*

To answer the second set of questions, you must not only know the information but also be able to apply that knowledge to different situations. It requires you to have a deeper understanding of the biological bases of behavior.

Processing depth varies from person to person and from subject to subject. The way you practice, organize, or associate information depends on your personal learning preferences and goals, what your instructor emphasizes, and the content information and requirements.

Learning, then, involves a process or action that results in a product—knowledge. This process depends on your prior knowledge of the material, your reason for learning, and the level of understanding you need as well as the kind of material to be learned. You, the learner, control the process by understanding how memory enables you to select, assimilate, retrieve and use information.

STAGES IN PROCESSING INFORMATION

Do you ever wonder why you remember some things and not others? Because you store memories in different ways and forms, you remember some things more easily or clearly.

You probably cannot recall your first birthday. Two factors account for this lapse of memory. First, the brain structures used for remembering don't fully develop until you are about two years old. Second, because you had not learned to speak at one year old, you could not store information in words the way you do now. Thus, although that information is still stored in your brain, you cannot access it.

You remember your first kiss, as opposed to your fifth, tenth, and twelfth kisses, because the first kiss was a new event that caused a new category to be formed in your memory. With each subsequent kiss, more information was added to that category, and kisses became less unique.

You probably don't recall where you found your keys the last time you lost them because you have no single specific place where lost keys are found. Because you have no general category for "lost keys" in memory for you to search, you don't recall where you found them.

Thus, how our memories work determines what we remember and what we forget. Because school courses require you to remember vast

Do you remember . . . your first birthday? your first kiss? where you found your keys the last time you lost them?

amounts of information, you need to understand the stages involved in processing information. These stages are **registration, short-term memory, working memory,** and **long-term memory** (see Figure 7.2).

REGISTRATION

Just as your first interaction with college classes is registration, your first interaction with information involves its registration. In this initial stage, you receive information but not necessarily understand it.

Next, depending upon your background knowledge, you perceive information. For example, suppose you visit a foreign country whose language you do not speak. When you see signs and billboards there, you receive stimuli and recognize the symbols on them as words. However, you do not understand their meanings. This is similar to what happens when you first encounter information. If you do speak that country's language, however, you understand their meanings. Thus, **reception** leads to **perception.**

The final phase of registration involves **selection.** What you select depends on you and the material at hand. Your purpose for learning and

Figure 7.2   A Model of Memory

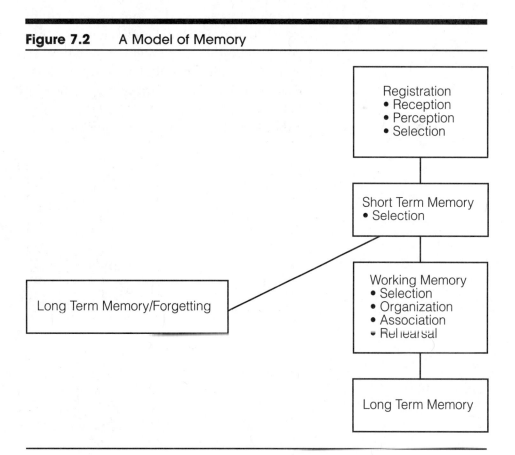

your background knowledge help you decide what to select. The content and difficulty of the information, as well as the way it is organized, also play a part in what you select. For example, suppose you need a place to sleep in the country you're visiting. As you look at the signs and billboards, you ignore ones advertising restaurants, tours, or shops. You concentrate on those for hotels. You selectively ignore or process depending on your purpose. You quickly forget what's ignored. The information you choose is transferred into your short-term memory—the second stage of memory processing.

SHORT-TERM MEMORY (STM)

All information you plan to remember goes through short-term memory (STM). When you try to remember a telephone number until you dial it, you use your STM. Its stay there is brief, lasting perhaps as little as fifteen seconds. This short duration results from the limited capacity of STM. This capacity resembles a library shelf that holds only a certain number of books. Miller (1956) found that STM could hold seven plus or minus two **chunks** of information. This varying capacity depends on how well or how poorly you "chunk," or group information for easier recall. The meaningfulness of the information chunks also affects capacity. For example, suppose you try to remember the numbers 1-8-6-0-1-8-6-4. If you chunk those numbers into dates—1860–1864—the numbers are easier to recall. This allows more memory space for other information. Factors such as age, maturation, practice, and the complexity of information also affect the size of STM. From its short stay in STM, information is either forgotten or moved to working memory.

"Come on, Harold! The sign says 'Girls! Girls! Girls! but it's not the bathroom!"

WORKING MEMORY

Thinking takes place in working memory—the third stage of memory processing—through selection, association, organization, and rehearsal. Learning about working memory, then, helps you understand how and what you think about information.

Working memory is like a worktable on whose surface are the tools and materials you need. The tools and materials in your working memory include your intent for learning, your skills in processing information, relevant STM and background data, and the choices you make concerning how to process information. Thus, you take STM and background information, decide what you want from it, inventory your choices about how you could process the information, and choose the most appropriate one.

For example, you may need to evaluate various perspectives on U.S. foreign policy since World War II. You get your notes, text, and so on for reference and consider the background knowledge you already have. Then, you consider the ways in which you might process the information through association or organization. You decide to organize information so that you can identify the patterns of the perspectives and their effects in order to judge their worth. Rehearsal strategies help you encode the information—or place it in memory—more fully. How rehearsal takes place depends on the type of information to be learned and your strategies for organizing and associating it with other information. The amount of time you spend rehearsing information is less important than what you do during that time.

Like any worktable, working memory has a limited amount of space. Just as you clear table space to work on a project, you clear memory space to process information. And just as you lose items on an overloaded table, memory processing becomes confused and information is lost when you think about too many ideas at one time or fail to clear memory space. For example, in learning a poem or in understanding U.S. foreign policy, you may find the information as a whole too complicated or unwieldy to think about at once. You need to divide the information and process a bit at a time.

LONG-TERM MEMORY (LTM)

If a library shelf represents STM, then the entire library corresponds to LTM. Following rehearsal, information enters LTM. It stays there until consciously or unconsciously recalled to working memory. Information in LTM is organized and stored for long periods of time. How long information remains there depends on how deeply you processed or learned it and factors relating to forgetting. The apparent permanence of LTM is somewhat misleading, although the actual loss of information is slow. This loss results from variations in processing depth or forgetting.

WRITE TO LEARN

Two actors of the sixteenth century, Samuel Foote and Charles Macklin, reportedly argued about who had the better facility for learning lines. Macklin boasted that he could learn a speech after hearing it once. Foote then asked Macklin to repeat the following, "So she went into the garden to cut a cabbage leaf to make an apple pie; and at the same time a great she-bear, coming up the street, pops its head into the shop—What! No soap? So he died and she very imprudently married the barber; and there were present the Picninnies, the Joblillies, and the Garyalies, and the grand Panjandrum himself, with the little round button at top." Macklin could not remember the speech and was defeated. On a separate sheet of paper, explain how the factors that contribute to the process of learning—prior knowledge, intent, level at which information is to be learned—affected Macklin's inability to remember the speech.

ASSOCIATION: LINKING IDEAS TOGETHER

John Gilbert, an early twentieth-century actor, was once called upon at the last minute to play the role of the heroine's father. He succeeded in learning his lines but had great difficulty in remembering the name of the character he played—Numitorius. A fellow actor helpfully suggested that he associate the name with the Book of Numbers in the Bible. Confidence renewed, Gilbert rushed on stage and delivered his opening line, "Hold, 'tis I, her father—Deuteronomy."

Association forms links between familiar items and the items you want to remember. Once established, the links become automatic. Recalling a familiar item cues recall of the other item. Unfortunately for John Gilbert, he associated what he had to learn with the wrong book of the Bible.

This familiar mechanism is one you use every day. For example, perhaps you associate a certain song with a particular time, event, or person in your life. Hearing the song cues that memory. In much the same way, you form conscious associations between something familiar to you and the information you need to recall. Thus, to be effective, associations must be personal.

Logical links, mental imagery, physical imagery, acronyms and acrostics, and word games connect information. The effectiveness of the various techniques depends on the type of information you need to learn and, most important, on you. Table 7.1 lists questions to help you choose the most appropriate technique.

Table 7.1   Questions for Developing Associations

1. Does the item remind you of anything?
2. Does the item sound like or rhyme with a familiar word?
3. Can you visualize something when you think of the item?
4. Can you rearrange any letters to form an acronym?
5. Do you know of any gimmicks to associate with the item?
6. Can you draw a picture (mnemonigraph) to associate with the item?
7. Can you associate the item with any familiar locations?
8. Can you form logical connections among concepts?

LOGICAL LINKS

Sometimes the logic or meaning of the information lends itself to memory. In this case, the whole may, indeed, be greater than the sum of its parts. For example, you may need to learn about the following aspects of aging: nutritional implications of aging, the effect of loneliness on nutrition, financial worries associated with aging and nutrition, assistance programs, and preparing for the later years. Such concepts would be difficult to learn in isolated parts. The sense of the concept as a whole forms the key. Consider the logic that links these ideas: What one eats (nutrition) impacts aging. Loneliness and lack of finances affect nutrition. Assistance programs provide adequate nutrition. One can prepare for aging if one knows what to expect and what assistance is available.

Understanding how concepts connect facilitates learning through the elaboration of ideas. Elaboration allows you to reframe information in terms of what you already know from experience. You provide the logic from your background knowledge of how information fits together.

MENTAL AND PHYSICAL IMAGERY

When you picture something in your mind, you experience mental imagery. Mental imagery is a natural occurrence because you often think in pictures, rather than words. For instance, think of an ice cream cone. Do you think i-c-e/c-r-e-a-m/c-o-n-e, or do you picture how an ice cream cone looks, smells, or tastes? This use of your visual and other senses aids your recall of both the familiar and unfamiliar. In addition, pictures are stored differently in the brain than words (See Chapter 1). Imagery

Table 7.2   Suggestions for Maximizing Mental Imagery and Examples

GOAL: To remember the four of the food groups: milk, meat, fruit and vegetables, and breads and cereals.

Suggestion	Example
1. Use common symbols, such as a heart for *love* or a dove for *peace*.	A cornucopia overflowing with cheese *(milk)*, sausages *(meat)*, fruits, and breads
2. Use the clearest and closest image.	Your family sitting at your dining table and eating fully loaded *cheeseburgers* (bread, meat, cheese, lettuce, tomatoes, onions, and so forth)
3. Think of outrageous or humorous images.	A *milk* cow *(meat)* eating a banana *(fruit)* sandwich *(bread)*
4. Create action-filled images.	See 2 and 3 above

provides an additional way to encode information. Table 7.2 lists suggestions for creating effective mental images.

Such mental associations link concrete objects with their images (for example, a picture of an apple with the word *apple*) or abstract concepts with their symbols (for example, a picture of a heart with the word *love*). Mental imagery also links unrelated objects, concepts, and ideas through visualization. For example, suppose you want to remember the name of the twenty-first president of the United States, Chester Arthur. You visualize an author writing the number *21* on a wooden chest. This mental picture helps you associate chest, author, and 21 to recall that Chester Arthur was the twenty-first president.

If you draw your mental image on paper, you make use of another sense, your **kinesthetic perception.** This type of memory aid is called a **mnemonigraph.** By actually making your mental image a physical one, you provide yourself with a form of repetition that reinforces your memory. Drawing or diagramming information also helps in another way. Rather than learning a list of details, you sketch a picture that includes all the details you need to learn. For instance, suppose you need to remember the parts of an eye. Drawing and labeling the parts aid your recall.

ACRONYMS AND ACROSTICS

Forming **acronyms** and/or **acrostics** is most helpful for recalling lists of information (for example, the bones in the body). Acronyms are words created from the first letter or the first few letters of the items on the list. *Roy G. Biv,* one of the most commonly used acronyms, aids you in recalling the colors of the rainbow in order (red, orange, yellow, green, blue, indigo, and violet). *HOMES,* another common acronym, cues your memory of the names of the Great Lakes (Huron, Ontario, Michigan, Erie, and Superior). Another acronym that aids your recall of the Great Lakes might be "Sho' me." Acronyms, then, need not be real words. Like others mnemonics, they work best when you create them for yourself.

"If only the test were just ten questions long!"

Acrostics are phrases or sentences created from the first letter or first few letter of items on a list you need to remember. For example, "George eats old gray rat at Paul's house yesterday" helps you spell "geography" correctly. Note that to be used as an acrostic, sentences need not be grammatically correct. They need only make sense to you. Thus, an acrostic ("Hot oatmeal makes eating sensational") cues your memory for the Great Lakes just as the acronym *HOMES* does.

LOCATION

The location method of mnemonics dates back to a gruesome event in ancient Greece. According to Cicero (Bower, 1970), Simonides, a Greek poet, had just finished reciting a poem when a messenger asked him to step outside the building. Just as he left the building, the roof collapsed. Everyone inside was killed. The guests' bodies were so mangled that they could not be identified. Simonides identified the corpses by remembering where each guest sat. Similarly, location memory occurs when you associate a concept with a place. This includes where you were when you heard the concept, how it looked in your notes, which graphics were on the page containing the information, and so on.

You can create location memory artificially as well. To create a memory map, you think of a familiar place. You associate the facts you need to know with features of that location. Then, you visualize yourself either walking around the place or looking at each feature of it. As you "see" the features, you recall the topic you've associated with it. For instance, suppose you want to learn a list of chemical elements. You choose a familiar route, like the route from the college bookstore to your math class. As you pass each building along the way, you assign it a chemical element. Later, in your class, you visualize your route. As you "see" each place, you recall the element it represents.

This same type of system works through visualizing a closet that contains many pegs or hooks for clothes. You "hang" information on each hook and then recall what's on each one.

WORD GAMES

Some memory aids involve what amounts to playing games with information. Such techniques aid your memory in two ways. First, they require you to actively think about the information in order to create the game. Second, they provide clues that entertain you and stimulate your recall. Diverse in nature, word games can be both easy and difficult to create.

Advertisers realize the value of rhymes and jingles in making their products memorable. Rhymes and jingles can make what you need to learn memorable as well. A common rhyme or jingle that aids recall of a spelling rule is "*I* before *E* except after *C* or when sounded like *A,* as in *neighbor* or *weigh.*"

Puns and **parodies** are humorously copied common words, poems, stories, or songs. A pun is the humorous use of a word or phrase to suggest more than one meaning. Parodies copy serious works or phrases through satire or burlesque. The humor of puns and parodies also brings cognitive benefits. Like other mnemonics, they make studying more imaginative and entertaining. For instance, suppose you want to learn the meaning of *numismatist* (a coin collector). You might parody the children's nursery rhyme "Four and Twenty Blackbirds." Instead of the king being in his counting house, counting all his money, you change the rhyme to "The numismatist was in his counting house, counting all his money." Or, you might make a pun to help you recall the definition. This could be something like "two numismatists getting together for old 'dime's' sake."

Many people create other memory tricks to aid recall. Many such tricks have been created to teach the basics of common concepts. A good example of this is a trick for remembering the multiplication tables for

Table 7.3   Memory Trick for Multiplying by Nine

1. List the numbers 0 to 9 in a column.

    0
    1
    2
    3
    4
    5
    6
    7
    8
    9

2. List the numbers 0 to 9 in a column beginning from the *bottom* beside the numbers you've already listed. Your combined columns form the products derived from multiplying 9 times 0, 1, 2, 3 . . . 9. (i.e., 9 × 0 = 00, 9 × 1 = 09, 9 × 2 = 18 . . .)

    09
    18
    27
    36
    45
    54
    63
    72
    81
    90

3. Note also that if you add the two digits in each product, you get 9. For example,

    9 × 1 = 09 (0 + 9 = 9)
    9 × 2 = 18 (1 + 8 = 9)
    9 × 3 = 27 (2 + 7 = 9)

nine (Table 7.3). Others you devise for yourself. For example, one student—needing to know the difference between *skimming* and *scanning*—decided to use the letters in the word to signal its purpose. The *mi* in *skimming* cued the purpose of finding main ideas. The *an* in *scanning* cued the purpose of finding specific answers.

WRITE TO LEARN

On a separate sheet of paper, select one of the association techniques to help you remember the names of each of your instructors. Explain how and why the technique cues your memory.

Exercise 7.1   Respond to each of the following:

1. Create an acronym or acrostic to help you remember the eight broad categories people value that are listed in Sample Chapter 11 (p. 512).

_____

_____

_____

_____

_____

2. Create a word game to help you remember the difference between time and/or task management as described on page 525 of Sample Chapter 11.

_____

_____

_____

_____

_____

3. Create and draw a physical image to help you recall the concept of corporate culture as described on pages 533–535 of Sample Chapter 11.

_____

_____

_____

_____

_____

4. Create an acronym or acrostic to help you recall four conditions for trust as described on page 522 of Sample Chapter 11.

_____

_____

_____

_____

_____

_____

5. Create and describe a mental image to help you describe what new businesses do not expect from a new manager as described on page 518 of Sample Chapter 11.

_____

_____

_____

_____

_____

_____

PRACTICE EFFECTS

When the Polish pianist Ignacy Paderewski played before Queen Victoria, she said, "Mr. Paderewski, you are a genius!" Paderewski replied, "Perhaps, Your Majesty, but before that I was a drudge."

Learning is less genius and more drudgery. But rather than practice making perfect, as it does in music, practice makes permanent in learning. Practice aids storage in LTM. In addition, practice helps make retrieval from LTM into working memory more automatic.

You practice information visually, auditorily, or semantically. **Visual practice** usually involves the silent reading of information. Such practice often takes place in frantic, last-minute cramming sessions. **Auditory practice** occurs when you repeat information aloud or discuss it with another student. You practice information semantically when you write or diagram it. Both auditory and **semantic practice** yield better results because they involve active processes. And, as with any learning process, the more actively you are involved, the more learning takes place.

Practice methods assume many forms. They vary in amount of time involved, depth of learning, and manner in which information is learned. When you choose a practice method, you should consider your purpose for learning the information and the way you learn most effectively. No matter which method you choose, you will be repeating information in some way.

SPACED STUDY

Spaced study consists of alternating short study sessions with breaks. This method is also known as **distributed practice.** You set study goals by time (for example, fifteen minutes) or task (for example, three pages) limits. After reaching these goals, you allow yourself a short amount of free time. You could take a walk, have a soft drink, or call a friend. This method helps you process information into LTM.

Spaced study works for many reasons. First, spaced study rewards hard work. This form of study involves **behavior modification.** This type of learning is based on research by B. F. Skinner, an American psychologist. In his studies with animals, Skinner found that they respond best when rewarded with food. The breaks in spaced study serve as your reward for completing a set amount of study. Second, because you work under a deadline of time or task limits, you complete quality work. Knowing you have a certain amount of time or work to study motivates you. Third, because working memory has limited capacity, breaks provide time for information to be absorbed into LTM. Fourth, when studying complex, related information, study breaks keep you from confusing similar details. Avoiding this **interference** is best accomplished by sleeping between study sessions. It is for this reason that cramming seldom works well as a form of practice.

"A score of 7.5 isn't earth shattering unless I grade it on the Richter scale."

PREVIEWING

As discussed in Chapters 4 and 5, many study strategies suggest that you preview information before reading a text or hearing a lecture. The primary purpose of previewing is to access what you already know about a topic. Previewing also provides a form of practice, because it requires you to analyze information before you read or study it. As a result, you increase the amount of details you can later recall.

RECITATION

Recitation involves silent, oral, or written repetition of the answers to study questions. These questions can come from the text, the instructor, or yourself. Thus, the first step of recitation is to locate or create study questions. Next, you read or study information to answer these questions. Third, you recite answers. Fourth, you use your text or notes to check the accuracy of your answers. This process keeps information in your working memory. Repeated recitation transfers information to LTM.

STUDY GROUPS OR PARTNERS

The old saying "Two heads are better than one" describes the purpose of study groups or partners. The purpose of such groups is discussion of information. Therefore, learning becomes an active, rather than passive, process. In a group, members explain and listen to explanations from each other, which allows them to use their auditory, visual, and physical senses. Combining these sensory impressions not only enhances the active learning process but also helps transfer information to LTM. Finally, group discussions motivate members. This happens because members make commitments to prepare for and come to study sessions.

Study groups learn a variety of information. Group members provide drill in learning **verbatim information,** such as definitions of terms

The more we study,
the more we know.
The more we know,
the more we forget.
The more we forget,
the less we know.
The less we know,
the less we forget.
The less we forget,
the more we know.
So why study?

or lists of names or dates. In addition, group members practice skills, such as solving math problems or learning foreign languages. Analysis and organization of complex or confusing information enhances the understanding of group members. Finally, creating and discussing test questions provides practice of test-taking skills and reduces test anxiety.

One note of caution concerns the way in which groups practice. Because most groups discuss information orally, members may neglect practicing their writing skills. If you have difficulty composing written responses to test items, you also need to practice your skills in putting information on paper.

OVERLEARNING

Overlearning, most appropriate for verbatim information, consists of overlapping study. This form of practice continues to reinforce information after you've first seen it (Tenney, 1986). For example, suppose you need to learn a list of forty terms for a history course. You can overlearn the list in one of two ways as described in Table 7.4.

Table 7.4   Methods of Overlearning

Method I	Method II
1. List each item separately on note cards.	1. Divide the list into manageable units (three to five items per unit, depending on the difficulty of the material).
2. Learn the first three cards.	2. Learn one set by practicing it orally.
3. Add one card.	3. Add another set.
4. Practice all four cards orally.	4. Practice all sets orally.
5. Add one card.	5. Repeat steps 3 and 4 until you know all the items.
6. Practice all five cards orally.	
7. Delete the card from the original set that you know the best and add one new card.	
8. Practice with all five cards.	
9. Repeat steps 7 and 8 until you know all the items.	

CRAMMING

It's the night before the test. You have twelve chapters left to read. You missed the last week of classes but borrowed a friend's notes. Unfortunately, your friend doesn't take very good notes.

What to do? Cram for the exam! **Cramming** involves frantic, last-minute (and sometimes all-night) memorization. Such learning rarely results in complete success. Such learners have no time to learn information. They simply try to memorize everything. As a result, they become renters, rather than owners, of information. Short-term benefits rarely translate into long-term results. Since students fail to really learn the information, they must memorize it over and over. Cramming, then, is one of the least effective means of study.

But, what if it *is* the night before the exam and you really do have twelve chapters left to read? Your best bet is to use parts of the SQ3R process to maximize your efforts. You begin by reading all chapter introductions and summaries. These provide you with the most basic condensation of information. Then you construct chapter maps or outlines. These show you the connections among ideas. Finally, you examine the terms to see how they support chapter concepts. These measures will not ensure a good grade. They only represent a more informed means of cramming.

FORGETTING: LOSS OF INFORMATION FROM LTM

Once information is processed, it may or may not remain in LTM. You, too, may wonder "why study?" When you lose information from LTM, more commonly known as forgetting, you do so because of interference and/or disuse. Which of these two occurs more often depends on four factors: your interest in learning, your purpose for learning, the frequency you use information, and the number of connections you make with other information. For instance, suppose you hear a funeral home ad the same day you meet an attractive member of the opposite sex. Whose name are you more likely to recall? Because you have greater interest in meeting new people than in visiting funeral homes, your recall of the person's name is stronger. If you plan to contact the person at a later date, your purpose for remembering also strengthens recall. If you date the person often, remembering the person's name becomes automatic. This is because you use it so frequently. As you learn more about the person, you associate these additional bits of information in your background knowledge with the person. This, too, strengthens recall.

*"If she can remember our credit card number,
looks like she could remember our phone number."*

INTERFERENCE

Have you ever been listening to your favorite radio station when another station broke into your station's frequency? That's called **interference**. This happens in your memory, too. Interference occurs because new, conflicting information affects background knowledge. It hinders memory for specific details more often than it does memory for main ideas.

Interference occurs for two reasons. Either new information confuses existing knowledge or existing knowledge confuses new learning. For example, suppose you are taking courses in both sociology and psychology. Because the content of these courses is somewhat alike, interference is more likely to occur. As previously stated, interference is best avoided by alternating study periods with at least a short nap.

DISUSE

"Who was President Carter's vice-president?" "What does M*A*S*H* mean?" "How do you write fifty-one in Roman numerals?" Part of the fun and frustration in answering these and other trivia questions is remembering information learned long ago. The answers to such questions depend on your ability to recall seldom-used information. Such information is sometimes difficult (or even impossible) to locate in memory because you have not used it for a long time. Because of its disuse, you no longer remember where the information is stored. Or you forgot many of the details concerning it. In a way, "use it or lose it" applies to memory.

GENERAL SUGGESTIONS FOR PREPARING FOR AND TAKING EXAMS

Successful test taking involves what someone once called "that old *ABC*—ability, breaks, and courage." Luckily, you can acquire these. Successful test-taking abilities include knowing about kinds of tests, various memory strategies, and how to alter your studying to make the most of the two. Being test-wise means that you take advantage of breaks and avoid any pitfalls you might encounter during a test. Having the courage you need to be a successful test-taker means identifying and effectively managing the stress that comes with exams. Just as the *ABCs* are the basics of language, these *ABCs* are the basics you need to maximize your test performances.

Tests consist of two types: **subjective** and **objective.** Subjective tests require you to supply the answers in your own words. They measure your recall of information, your skills in organizing and expressing yourself, and your ability to relate ideas. Types of subjective test questions include short-answer, essay, and fill-in-the-blank (see Table 7.5). Objective tests involve your choosing among provided answers. Instructors frequently give objective exams because they allow for the quick testing of a large amount of material and are easy to grade. Types of objective test questions include multiple-choice, matching, and true-false (see Table 7.6). Some students think objective tests are a fairer judge of their abilities because these exams are free from grader bias.

"Now, let's see. Tomorrow, I'll put D for #1, A for #2, and E for #3!"

Table 7.5   Subjective Test Formats

Example of an essay question:
  Compare and contrast Emily Dickinson's ``Because I Could Not Stop for Death'' with Hilda Doolittle's ``Evening.''

Example of a short-answer question:
  Briefly describe the hydrologic cycle.

Example of a fill-in-the-blank question:
  A _____ is a form of figurative language in which two dissimilar objects are compared using the words *like* or *as.*

Table 7.6   Objective Test Formats

Example of a true-false question:
  T   F   Soil fertility depends upon relative amounts of gravel, sand, silt, and clay.

Example of a multiple-choice question:
  Sources of vitamin A include all of the following except
  a. dark green leafy vegetables.
  b. yeast.
  c. fish liver oils.
  d. yellow and orange fruits.

Example of matching questions:
  1. Johannes Guttenberg   _____ Electric self-starter
  2. Guglielmo Marconi   _____ Mimeograph machine
  3. Charles F. Kettering   _____ Printing press
  4. Thomas Edison   _____ Wireless telegraph

To prepare for a test, you need to know what to expect from it. Because most exams are written by the instructor, the instructor is a prime source of information about them. Most instructors want you to do well. Thus, they are willing to answer questions about test content and format. Instructors can tell you if a test is **comprehensive** (covering all material presented since the beginning of the term) or **noncomprehensive** (covering only that information presented since the last exam).

Extensive preparation alone is not all you need to pass an exam. Special test-taking skills enhance your carefully acquired knowledge. No matter how well you are prepared, you should use the following general suggestions for taking exams (see Table 7.7).

All exams test the way you process information. Some questions ask you to define or remember information exactly as it was presented in your text or the lecture. Other questions demand you link information to form conclusions about a topic. You may also be asked to use information in a new way. Questions that ask you to think critically require you to analyze, synthesize, and evaluate information. Both subjective and objective exams often test your ability to remember and manipulate concepts in a variety of ways. The kinds of knowledge required for different kinds of questions appear in Figure 7.1, Bloom's Taxonomy at the beginning of this chapter.

Table 7.7   Steps in Taking Exams

1. Bring the appropriate materials for the test (pencil, paper, blue book, calculator).

2. Arrive at the test on time.
   a. If you are early, do not discuss the test with other students. Their concerns and worries will increase any anxieties you have.
   b. If you are late, you may miss important verbal directions. Arriving late also makes you feel rushed and anxious. If you do arrive late, take a minute to relax and organize your thoughts. Ask your instructor for clarification if you feel confused.

3. If you are trying to keep a difficult formula or process in mind, jot it down after you get your test paper.

4. Preview the test. Note the total number of items. Identify variations in point values. Estimate the amount of time to spend on each item. Spend the most time on questions receiving the most credit.

5. Read all directions slowly and carefully. When given a test, many students ignore the directions. However, directions often state information you need to receive full credit. They also provide information about the way answers should be marked. Although you may have all the right answers, selective instructors may not give full credit when responses are not correctly marked.

6. Underline key terms and steps in the directions.

7. Answer the easiest questions first. This builds your confidence and triggers your memory for other information. Also, if you run out of time before you complete the test, you will have answered the questions you knew.

8. Expect memory blocks. Mark difficult questions, but skip them and go on. Return to these questions, if time permits.

9. Answer every question, if possible. If incorrect answers are not penalized, guess at all objective and subjective questions.

10. Make your responses as neat and legible as possible.

11. Work at your own pace. Do not be concerned when other students finish and leave before you.

12. If time permits, review questions and answers. Be sure you understood the question and marked the correct response. Some students think it is better to always stay with their first answer. You can determine what's best for you by examining some of your old tests. Count the number of questions you changed to correct answers. Compare that total with the number of those you changed to incorrect answers.

PREPARING FOR AND TAKING SUBJECTIVE EXAMS

"Writing is hell," someone once said. This certainly seems true to many students who face subjective exams. These exams require you to understand major concepts and describe them in a coherent written form. Your essay must state main points and contain the facts that support the ideas you express. It must show your analysis and/or synthesis of ideas and application of knowledge. Taking such exams requires careful preparation and confidence in your test-taking skills.

PORPE: A STUDY PLAN FOR SUBJECTIVE EXAMS

Often students fear subjective exams because they are uncertain of their writing skills. A study plan exists that helps you become a better writer by asking you to practice writing. This plan, PORPE, consists of five stages: Predict, Organize, Rehearse, Practice, and Evaluate (Simpson, 1986). When put into motion at least three days before an exam, PORPE helps you predict possible essay questions, organize your thoughts, and find strategies for recalling information.

Even if your predicted questions never appear on the test, PORPE will not be a waste of time for several reasons. First, your predicted questions will probably reflect the content, if not the wording, of the test. Second, you often can use the information you rehearsed and practiced in answering questions you may not have predicted. Third, the practice you give yourself in writing increases not only your self-confidence but also your writing ability. Remember the quote from Epictetus that began this discussion of PORPE: "If you wish to be a writer, write." To follow the stages in PORPE, you answer a series of questions and complete the steps at each stage (Table 7.8).

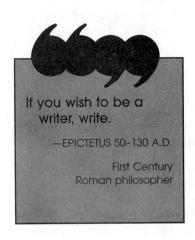

If you wish to be a writer, write.

—EPICTETUS 50-130 A.D.

First Century
Roman philosopher

TAKING SUBJECTIVE EXAMS

> Freshmen who are preppies have a great advantage.... They ... arrive at college well-versed in the techniques of the essay question, and could pad their paragraph with such useful phrases as "from a theoretical point of view," or "on first inspection we may seem to discern a certain attitude which may well survive even closer scrutiny," and so forth. This sort of wind can sail you halfway through an hour test before you have to lay a single fact on paper.

The great advantage that Segal describes is part of what preppies learn at college-preparatory schools. They learn the art of taking subjective tests—a skill you, too, can learn.

Essay exams require special test-taking considerations. Because answering them is much like writing short papers on assigned topics, there is more work involved. The procedure outlined in Table 7.7 is important to follow, but other steps are also necessary (see Table 7.9). The wording of essay questions helps you organize and write your answers (see Table 7.10).

Table 7.8   Stages of PORPE

Three days before the exam:

PREDICT
Predict information about the test by answering these questions:
  What does the test cover?
  Is the test comprehensive or noncomprehensive?
  How many questions will the test contain?
  Will the test require me to apply information?
  How much does this test count in my final course grade?
  When is the test?
  Where will the test be given?
  What special material(s) will I need to take the test?
Predict essay test questions by answering the following questions:
  What information did the instructor stress during the lectures?
  What information did the text emphasize?
  What questions appeared in both my initial preview and the chapter's
    review or study guide?
  What terms did the instructor emphasize during the lectures?
Predict at least three times as many questions as your instructor has
indicated will be on the exam.

Two days before the exam:

ORGANIZE
Organize information by answering the following questions:
  What type of text structure will best answer the questions I set
    (cause/effect, subject development, enumeration/sequence,
    or comparison/contrast)?
  What is the best way to organize this information (outline, idea map,
    note cards, chart)?
  What information is essential for answering this question?
  What information adds relevant, supporting details or examples?
  What is the source of this information:
    textbook?
    handouts?
    lecture notes?
    supplemental readings?

Table 7.8   Stages of PORPE *continued*

REHEARSE

Lock information into your memory by answering these questions:

What mnemonic techniques (acronyms, acrostics, word games, etc.) can I use to practice this information?

How much time each day will I study?

When will I study?

How will I distribute my study time?

Where will I study?

If necessary, when will my study group/partner and I meet?

What obligations do I have that might interfere with this study time?

Construct mnemonic aids.

Use overlearning to help you practice mnemonic aids overtly (writing or speaking them).

One day before the exam:

PRACTICE

Practice writing your answers from memory.

EVALUATE

Judge the quality of your answer as objectively as possible by answering the following questions:

Did I answer the question that was asked?

Did my answer begin with an introduction?

Did my answer end with a conclusion?

Was my answer well organized?

Did I include all essential information?

Did I include any relevant details or examples?

Did I use transition words?

Is my writing neat and easily read?

Did I check spelling and grammar?

If you answered any of these questions negatively, you need to continue practicing your answers. Repeat the final four stages of PORPE until you answer all of these questions positively.

After the exam has been returned, read your instructor's comments and compare them with the last evaluation you made during your study sessions. Look for negative trends you can avoid or positive trends you can stress when you study for your next exam. File your PORPE plan, course materials, study aids, and evaluation data for future reference.

Table 7.9   Taking Essay Exams

1. Choose a title. Even though you won't necessarily entitle your paper, a title helps you focus your thoughts and narrow your subject.

2. Outline your response or list main points before you begin. This keeps you from omitting important details.

3. Have a beginning, a middle, and an end. Topic and summary sentences are important in making your answer seem organized and complete.

4. Use transitional words. The key words in each question help you identify the transitions you need for clarity.

5. Attempt every question. If you run out of time, outline the remaining questions. This shows your knowledge of the content. Partial responses often result in partial credit.

6. Proofread your answers. Check spelling, grammar, and content.

Table 7.10   Key Terms in Essay Questions

If You Are Asked To . . .	Then . . .
compare or match,	identify similarities.
contrast or distinguish,	identify differences.
discuss or describe,	provide details or features.
enumerate, name, outline, or list,	identify major points.
sequence, arrange, trace, or rank,	list information in order.
explain, defend, or document,	give reasons for support.
relate or associate,	show connections.
summarize, paraphrase, or compile,	provide a short synopsis.
outline,	list major points.
apply,	show use for.
construct, develop, or devise,	create.
criticize or analyze,	review features or components.
demonstrate, illustrate, or show,	provide examples.

The wording you use to answer the questions determines the quality of the responses. Figure 7.3 shows examples of good and poor responses to an essay question. How do they differ?

The good response begins with an introductory sentence that identifies the three symptoms of Parkinson's disease. The second sentence identifies early symptoms of the disease. Sentences 3 and 4 identify and describe the first major symptom. Sentences 5 and 6 identify and describe the second major symptom. The next three sentences identify

Figure 7.3   Examples of an Essay Question and Responses

QUESTION: *Identify and describe the symptoms of Parkinson's disease.*

RESPONSE 1

Parkinson's disease is a neurological disease characterized by gradual changes in three fundamental symptoms: tremor, rigidity, and bradykinesia. Although the onset of this disease is so gradual that neither the patients nor the people close to them notice it, early symptoms include fatigue and complaints of mild muscular aches. Tremor is often the first real symptom to appear. Conspicuous, but rarely disabling, tremor usually begins in one hand and occurs when the limb is at rest. Rigidity, the second major symptom, is muscular stiffness. This results in slow movement, muscle cramps, and resistance against passive movement. The most disabling symptom is bradykinesia. This describes slowness and poverty of voluntary movements. It also leads to difficulty in performing rapid or repeated movements. It underlies facial masking and involuntary hesitations. Variations in these three symptoms cause the variety of disabilities associated with Parkinson's disease.

RESPONSE 2

Parkinson's disease was first described by Dr. James Parkinson, an English physician. Parkinson wrote an essay entitled, "Essay on the Shaking Palsy," which described the symptoms he saw in six patients. He described the three primary symptoms as involuntary shaking movements of the limbs, muscular stiffness, and slowness and poverty of movement. Because the entire body was involved, Dr. Parkinson theorized that it was a mental illness resulting from a dysfunction in the brain. Parkinson's disease can affect anyone—men, women, children. Various theories account for the symptoms, including genetic links, viral causation, stress, neurotransmitter damage, and environmental causes.

RESPONSE 3

Parkinson's disease is a terrible disease. It affects millions of people. Parkinson's disease has many symptoms. One symptom is shakiness. Some people become very shaky. Their hands shake most. This makes it difficult to pick up things or hold things. Another symptom is that you can't move very well anymore. You have difficulty climbing stairs or walking. So, these symptoms are very terrible.

and describe the third major symptom. The last sentence summarizes the effects of variations in these symptoms.

At first glance, the second response appears to be a good one. It is well written and appropriate in length. It appears to be the work of a student who knows something about Parkinson's disease, but it lacks the specific information required for a correct response to this question. Closer inspection reveals several weaknesses. Sentences 1 and 2 could be considered introductory sentences; however, sentence 3 is the only sentence that identifies (and not by correct terminology) and describes the three major symptoms of Parkinson's disease. Sentence 4 incorrectly identifies the disease as a mental, rather than a neurological, illness. Sentence 5 describes who is affected by Parkinson's disease. The last sentence—an attempt at a summary—actually lists the theories that account for the symptoms.

The last example, another poor response, is more clearly identifiable as such. The writer uses the word *symptom* frequently to disguise the fact that he or she really has little understanding of what the symptoms are. Sentences 1, 2, and 3 are feeble introductory attempts. Sentence 4 identifies one symptom as shakiness, without using the appropriate terminology. While the writer apparently knows that the hands are often affected, he or she does not realize that this occurs most often when the limb is at rest. Sentences 8 and 9 identify mobility impairments and their effects. The reader cannot tell if this refers to the symptom of rigidity or that of bradykinesia. The last sentence attempts to conclude the paragraph by restating the main idea of sentence 1.

PREPARING FOR AND TAKING OBJECTIVE EXAMS

Find a perfect star in the pattern below. As you look for it, try to be aware of the search strategies you use.

SOURCE: Reprinted with permission from *A Kick in the Seat of the Pants* by Roger von Oech. Copyright © 1986 by Harper Collins Publishers. All rights reserved.

Did you find the star? If not, reexamine the lower-right quadrant. If you did, how did you go about finding it? (A key appears at the end of this chapter.) According to Roger von Oech, who originated this exercise in his book *A Kick in the Seat of the Pants*, the point of the exercise is that you have to know what you're looking for in order to find it. To locate the star, you first have to determine what kind of star you're seeking. The star could be a regular five-pointed star, a Star of David, a seven-pointed sheriff's star, or the Chrysler star. It could be large or small. It could be composed entirely of white pieces, black pieces, or a combination of both. In other words, to locate the star, you need the ability to recognize it when you see it. You also need a strategy for finding it.

The same is true when preparing for and taking objective exams. When you take an objective exam, your job is to search among the answers provided by the instructor for the correct one. If you've studied carefully and are more than familiar with the information covered on the exam, you are able to focus on the one or two choices that are most appropriate. Test-wise strategies aid you in making the best choice possible.

POSSE: A STUDY PLAN FOR OBJECTIVE EXAMS

In preparing for an objective test, you need to know the harbor you are making for and how you intend to get there. POSSE (Plan, Organize, Schedule, Study, and Evaluate) is a system to help you identify your study goals and make plans for achieving them. To follow the stages of POSSE, you answer a series of questions and complete the steps at each level (Table 7.11). Responding to the questions in written form forces you to concentrate on each question. It also keeps you from inadvertently omitting one. You will obtain many answers from either your syllabus, your instructor, or your experience in the class. Other questions, however, will force you to examine your study strengths and weaknesses. Your success on your upcoming test depends on your honesty in dealing with such issues. It is also important that you begin the POSSE process at least a week before the test is scheduled. If you work through POSSE with care and determination, you will make the best of your study time and efforts.

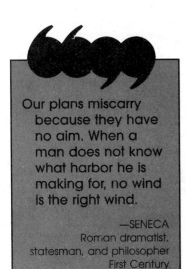

Our plans miscarry because they have no aim. When a man does not know what harbor he is making for, no wind is the right wind.

—SENECA
Roman dramatist, statesman, and philosopher
First Century

Table 7.11   Stages of *POSSE:* Questions to Be Answered

PLAN
Answer these questions:
  What does the test cover?
  Is the test comprehensive or noncomprehensive?
  Will the test questions be multiple-choice, true-false, and/or matching?
  How many questions (of each type) will the test contain?
  In what ways will the test require me to apply information or think critically?
  How much does this test count in my final grade?
  When is the test?
  Where will the test be given?
  What special material(s) will I need to take the test?

Table 7.11   Stages of *POSSE:* Questions to Be Answered *continued*

ORGANIZE

Answer these questions:

What information do I predict will be on the test?

What materials do I need to study:

textbook?

handouts?

lecture notes?

supplemental readings?

old exams?

What study and memory methods will work best with this material?

Can I find a partner or group to study with?

Gather materials together.

Construct study and memory aids.

SCHEDULE

Answer these questions:

How much time do I have before the exam?

How much time will I need to study for this test?

How much time each day will I study?

When will I study?

How will I distribute my study time?

Where will I study?

When will my study group/partner and I meet?

What obligations do I have that might interfere with this study time?

Construct a time schedule.

STUDY At the end of each study session, answer these questions:

Am I studying actively, that is, through writing or speaking?

Am I distributing my study time to avoid memory interference and physical fatigue?

Am I following my schedule? Why or why not? What adjustments do I need to make?

Am I learning efficiently? Why or why not? What adjustments do I need to make?

EVALUATE

After the test has been returned, complete the worksheet in Table 3.15.

Answer these questions:

What pattern(s) emerge(s) from the worksheet?

What type of questions did I miss most often?

What changes can I make to my study plan to avoid these trends in the future?

File your POSSE plan, course materials, study aids, exam, worksheet, and evaluation for future reference.

When to elect
    There is but one,
    'Tis Hobson's choice,
    take that or none.

—THOMAS WARD

TAKING OBJECTIVE EXAMS

"Hobson's choice" refers to Tobias Hobson, a stablekeeper who made his customers take whatever horse was nearest the door when they came into his stable. Hobson's choice, then, refers to the only choice possible. In taking objective exams, your goal is to find Hobson's choice among the answers provided by the instructor. You seek to locate the one alternative that answers the question completely. Even when you've adequately prepared for the test, finding Hobson's choice isn't always easy. You need test-taking tips to help you find the correct answer among the alternatives. The following Test of Test-Wiseness shows you these strategies.

TEST OF TEST-WISENESS

The test below measures your test-wiseness. Little content knowledge is required and the answers to all questions can be determined through test-taking skill.

After finishing the exam, score it using the key that follows Specific test-taking strategies are explained there. Follow specific directions given for each section.

Multiple-Choice Questions

Credit: 2 points each
Circle the correct answer for each multiple-choice question.

1. SQ3R is
    a. a study plan.
    b. a kind of test.
    c. a course number.
    d. none of the above.
2. The first thing you should do when taking a test is
    a. has a sharpened pencil.
    b. looks over all questions.
    c. read the directions.
    d. asks the teacher for clarification of directions.
3. Which of the following is true of standardized reading exams?
    a. Standardized reading tests require no special test-taking skills.
    b. A score on a standardized reading test may equal the number of right answers minus a percentage of the number of wrong answers.
    c. Always guess on standardized tests.
    d. Standardized tests are never timed tests.

4. If you do not understand a question during a test, you should
   a. ask a friend to explain it to you.
   b. skip that question.
   c. look it up in your textbook.
   d. ask the instructor for clarification.

5. Response choices are found on
   a. an objective test.
   b. a multiple-choice test.
   c. an essay test.
   d. all of the above.
   e. a and b only.

6. All of the following are parts of a study plan *except*
   a. reviewing information frequently.
   b. copying another person's notes.
   c. surveying a chapter.
   d. reading assignments.

7. Which of the following should *not* be done before taking a final exam?
   a. Review study notes.
   b. Find out when and where the test will be given.
   c. Determine if the test will be comprehensive or noncomprehensive.
   d. Become anxious.

8. An illusion is
   a. something that is not really there.
   b. an allusion.
   c. the same as elusive.
   d. another word for illustration.

9. The capital of Canada is
   a. New York City.
   b. Paris.
   c. Ottawa.
   d. Dallas.

10. The SQ3R study plan was developed in the 1940s by
    a. Francis Robinson.
    b. George Washington.
    c. Michael Jackson.
    d. Christopher Columbus.

11. The chemically inactive substances used in experiments to determine drug effectiveness are _____.
    a. prescription medications
    b. federally controlled pharmaceutical products
    c. similar to physician-prescribed drugs
    d. placebos

12. Who was the third president of the United States?
    a. Lyndon Baines Johnson
    b. Franklin Delano Roosevelt
    c. Rutherford B. Hayes
    d. Thomas Jefferson

True-False Questions

Credit: 5 points each
Respond to each question by writing the word *true* or *false* in the blank.

_____ 1. You should always answer every question on every test.

_____ 2. All exams are comprehensive.

_____ 3. Never study with a partner.

_____ 4. Some tests are too lengthy to complete in the allotted time.

_____ 5. A test may not be without poorly worded questions.

_____ 6. Following directions is not unimportant.

Matching Questions

Credit: 4 points each
Write the letter of the correct answer in the blanks. Answers may be used more than once.

_____ 1. George Washington   a. a study plan

_____ 2. SQ3R   b. multiple-choice

_____ 3. example of a objective test   c. essay

_____ 4. example of a subjective test   d. president

_____ 5. a written theme

Math Questions

Credit: 10 points each
Write your answers in the blanks.

_____ 1. A container holds 20 gallons. It is ⅗ full. How many gallons do you need to fill the container?

_____ 2. 20,819 + 74,864 =
    a. 10,993
    b. 95,683
    c. 95,666
    d. 85,333

KEY AND TEST-WISE STRATEGIES

The Test of Test-Wiseness helps you examine your test-taking skills. When taking any test, it is important that you preview the test and carefully follow directions. If you previewed this test, you probably realized that the test contained more multiple-choice questions than any other type. However, the multiple-choice questions received the least amount of credit. If you spent too much time on these questions, you might have failed to complete questions with higher point values.

Directions had to be followed exactly. If you failed to underline answers to the multiple-choice section, count them as incorrect. If you responded to the true-false questions with letters instead of the entire word, count them as incorrect. All other answers should have been written in the blanks to the left of the questions for you to receive credit.

Responses on any test often are designed to be similar and confusing. Whenever possible, after you read the question, you should answer it in your own words without looking at the responses given. Then, you should search for a response that matches your answer.

The following test-wise principles are no substitute for study and preparation. They can, however, help you eliminate choices and make educated guesses. The principle to remember is italicized.

Multiple-Choice Questions

Question 1
If you don't know an answer, skip it and go on. Don't waste time mulling over an answer. Go on to the questions you know. Sometimes a clue to the answer you need is found elsewhere in the test. In this case, the clue is in question 10. The answer is *a*.

Question 2
Eliminate grammatically incorrect responses. Sometimes, questions are poorly worded. The only grammatically correct choice in this question is answer *c*. Misuse of *a* or *an* is also a common grammatical error found in test questions.

Question 3
Often the longest choice is correct. For a correct answer to be absolutely clear, a response may need to be lengthy. The correct answer is *b*.

Questions 4 and 5
Be sure the right choice is the best choice. At first glance, answer *b* seems correct for question 4; however, further examination of choices reveals that answer *d* is a better choice. Watch for "all of the above," "none of the above," and paired choices. Answer *d* is the correct answer for question 5.

Questions 6 and 7
Read questions carefully. Not and except are small words, but they completely change the meaning. The careless reader might interpret question 6 as asking for a part of a study plan. Such a reader might also interpret question 7 as asking for a procedure to be done before taking a final exam.

"You may be wise to the test, but is this test-wise?"

The correct response for question 6 is *b*. The correct response for question 7 is *d*.

Question 8
Responses that look like the word to be defined are usually incorrect. Allusion, elusive, and *illustration* all resemble the word *illusion*. These are called "attractive distractors" because they look so appealing. Attractive distractors are almost always poor choices. The answer, therefore, is *a*.

Questions 9 and 10
If you do not know what the answer is, determine what the answer is not. Eliminate silly choices and use common sense. You may not know the capital of Canada. However, you should realize that New York City and Dallas are in the United States and Paris is in France. Only answer *c* remains. For question 10, answer *c* is silly. Answers *b* and *d* are wrong because neither Christopher Columbus nor George Washington was alive in the 1940s. Answer *a* is correct.

Question 11
Watch for responses that are essentially the same. A careful reading of choices *a, b,* and *c* reveals that they restate the same idea in a variety of ways. In this case, a physician-prescribed drug is a prescription medication. It is also federally controlled and a pharmaceutical product. Because these answers are synonymous, none of them can be the correct answer. The correct answer is answer *d*.

Question 12
Use what you know to analyze and make decisions about information. At first glance, you may not recall who the third U.S. president was. And, unlike the responses in questions 9 and 10, all of the men identified in the

responses have served as president of the United States. But when were their terms of office? You reflect on what you know about each man. You might think of Lyndon Baines Johnson as a recent president, perhaps recalling that he took office after the assassination of John F. Kennedy and that the nation was involved in the Vietnam War during his presidency. Clearly a president of the twentieth century, he could not have been the third president. You might associate Franklin Delano Roosevelt with the Great Depression and World War II. Thus, he, too, was also a relatively modern president. You might have little knowledge about Rutherford B. Hayes, so you go on to Thomas Jefferson. You recall that he signed the Declaration of Independence and visualize him in colonial-era clothing. Logically, then, *d* is the correct choice.

True-False Questions

Questions 1, 2, 3, and 4
Look for words that determine limits. Words such as *always, never, none, every,* and *all* place no limitations on meaning. Words such as *some, few, often, many,* and *frequently* limit meaning and are better choices. If you can think of one example that contradicts an unlimited meaning, then it is false. For example, the answer to question 1 is false. This is because you wouldn't answer every question if a percentage of wrong responses were to be subtracted from the total of correct choices. The answers to questions 2 and 3 are also false. The answer to 4 is true.

Questions 5 and 6
Watch for double negatives. Just as multiplying two negative numbers equals a positive number, two negative words in a sentence indicate a positive relationship in standard English usage. In question 5, *not* and *without* cancel each other. The gist of the sentence is that a test may have poorly worded questions. The answer to question 5, then, is true. In question 6, the word *not* and the prefix *un-* cancel each other. The gist indicates that following directions is important. The answer to question 6 is true.

Matching Questions

Matching sections are somewhat like multiple-choice tests. Thus, the same principles apply. However, there are some special strategies for matching sections.

Often the two items being matched rely on an implied rather than a stated association. These relationships include a word and its definition, a person and a noted accomplishment, a step in a process and the process from which it comes, and so on. As with other test questions, complete items you know first. Use the side with the longer responses as your question side. This keeps you from repeatedly reading through numerous lengthy responses. When responses are used only once, do not blindly fill in the last question with the only remaining choice. Check to make sure it fits. If not, recheck all answers.

The answers to the matching section are as follows: question 1, *d;* question 2, *a;* question 3, *b;* question 4, *c;* and question 5, *c.*

Math Questions

Many good math students have difficulty with word problems. Panic prevents them from translating a word problem into a numerical one. Thus, the first step in solving math problems is to remain calm and avoid negative thinking. Second, visualize the problem. This allows you to determine what the question asks. Next, identify your facts and the processes required. If possible, estimate the response. Work the problem and check it against your estimate. Recheck if necessary.

Problem 1
Picturing the problem reveals an everyday situation. You have a container that is partially filled, and you want to know how much more is needed to fill it. You have the following facts: a 20-gallon container that is ⅗ filled. You will need to multiply ⅗ and 20 to find out how much is in the container. Then you subtract that amount from 20 to find out how much more can be put in the container. You know that the container is more than half full but less than ¾ full; ½ of 20 is 10 and ¾ of 20 is 15. The container holds between 10 and 15 gallons now. Subtracting those amounts from the total results in an estimate of 5 to 10 gallons. The problem is worked in the following manner:

$$⅗ \times 20 = 12$$
$$20 - 12 = 8$$

The answer is 8; 8 is within the estimated range.

Problem 2
Standardized math tests provide a choice of answers. You can save time by estimating answers and eliminating responses. In this problem, adding the final digits (9 + 4 = 13) indicates that the response must end in 3. This eliminates answer *c.* Rounding off the two figures results in 21,000 and 75,000. The sum of the rounded figures is 96,000. The answer that is closest to the estimate is answer *b.*

WRITE TO LEARN

On a separate sheet of paper or in your notebook, create five subjective questions and five objective questions that cover information discussed in Sample Chapter 12, ``The Industrial Revolution and Its Impact on European Society.''

TAKING SPECIALIZED EXAMS

Marathon runners often talk about "hitting the wall." This happens when runners get to the point where they feel they can no longer keep going. While some runners may routinely cover several miles each day with ease, the length or difficulty of some race routes can sometimes seem insurmountable.

You, too, may feel like you've "hit the wall" when it comes to taking specialized exams. The strategies you successfully use in subjective and objective tests are not sufficient. Just as runners develop specialized techniques to help them pass "the wall," you need special strategies for specialized tests, open-book, take-home, and final exams.

TAKING OPEN-BOOK AND TAKE-HOME EXAMS

Open-book and take-home tests are types of finals that sound too good to be true. You might think that these tests require no study at all. In fact, they require as much studying as any other exam. Such tests are easier when you have the appropriate strategies for taking them (see Table 7.12).

An open-book exam tests your ability to locate, organize, and relate information quickly. Such tests also measure how quickly you can read and process information. Thus, the open-book test may be biased toward well-prepared students. This is another reason why you need to study thoroughly before taking this type of exam. Next, insufficient studying results in your wasting test time while you decide what the question means or where to find the answer.

A take-home exam also evaluates your ability to locate, organize, and relate information. Because you are not expected to take the test

Table 7.12   Steps in Taking Open-Book and Take-Home Exams

1. Familiarize yourself with your text. Tab sections of the text that deal with major topics or contain important formulas or definitions.

2. Organize your notes. Mark them in the same way you tabbed your text.

3. Highlight important details in both your text and notes.

4. Know how to use the table of contents and index to locate information quickly.

5. Paraphrase information. Unless you are quoting a specific source, do not copy word-for-word from your text.

6. Use other applicable test-taking strategies.

during class, it measures your knowledge more fairly, although spelling and neatness generally count more. In most cases, a take-home test allows you to avoid the stress associated with in-class exams. On the other hand, setting your own pace has drawbacks, particularly if you tend to procrastinate. Waiting until the last minute to begin working on such a test results in the same stressful feelings you get during an in-class test. Such scheduling also results in work of lesser quality.

"Did your instructor say to take home the library, too?"

TAKING FINAL EXAMS

You might not believe it, but in many ways a final exam is just like all the other tests you take. However, finals usually are longer than regular exams. In a way, this works to your advantage. Longer exams cover more information. You get a better chance to get answers correct because there are more questions to attempt. The same strategies and suggestions for taking other tests apply to final exams (see Table 7.7).

Finals are often given in places and at times that differ from your regular class schedule. Final exam locations and schedules are printed in campus newspapers, posted in each department, and announced by your instructor. If more than two of your exams occur on the same day, you can sometimes ask to reschedule one of them. Procedures for such requests vary. Seeing your advisor is the first step in the process.

GROUP LEARNING ACTIVITY
MEMORY DETECTIVES

You may not think of yourself as a "memory detective," but active probing often helps improve recall. A case in point is the *cognitive interview*, a technique used to jog the memory of eyewitnesses. The cognitive interview was created by R. Edward Geiselman and Ron Fisher to help police detectives. When used properly, it produces 35 percent more correct information than standard questioning (Geiselman et al., 1986).

By following four simple steps, you can apply cognitive principles to your own memory. The next time you are searching for a "lost" memory—one that you know is in there somewhere—try the following search strategies.

1. Say or write down everything you can remember that relates to the information you are seeking. Don't worry about how trivial any of it seems; each bit of information you remember can serve as a cue to bring back others.

2. Try to recall events or information in different orders. Let your memories flow out backward or out of order, or start with whatever impressed you the most.

3. Recall from different viewpoints. Review events by mentally standing in a different place. Or try to view information as another person would remember it. When taking a test, for instance, ask yourself what other students or your professor would remember about the topic.

4. Mentally put yourself back in the situation where you learned the information. Try to mentally re-create the learning environment or relive the event. As you do, include sounds, smells, details of weather, nearby objects, other people present, what you said or thought, and how you felt as you learned the information (Fisher & Geiselman, 1987).

These strategies help re-create the context in which information was learned, and they provide multiple memory cues. If you think of remembering as a sort of "treasure hunt," you might even learn to enjoy the detective work.

Application

As a preexam activity, use the preceding strategies to assist recall when you or another member of your study group becomes stumped on a question. Compare memories among group members. Once you learn to use these strategies, you can use them to aid recall on exams.

SOURCE: Reprinted with permission from *Introduction to Psychology, Exploration and Application* by Coon. Copyright © 1989 by West Publishing Company. All rights reserved.

SUMMARY

1. The process of learning includes the ability to evaluate, synthesize, analyze, apply, interpret, and translate, as well as recall, information.

2. The stages of processing information are registration of information, transference to short-term memory, manipulation in working memory, and transference to long-term memory.

3. Logical links, mental and physical imagery, acronyms and acrostics, location, and word games are associational techniques for linking ideas.

4. Information can be organized into lists or visual representations, such as idea maps, charts, and word maps.

5. Rehearsal occurs through practice strategies, such as spaced study, previewing, recitation, study groups or partners, and overlearning. Cramming is also a way of rehearsing information, but it is not as effective as other means.

6. Forgetting, or the loss of information from long-term memory, results from interference and/or disuse.

7. All exams require certain test-taking strategies (getting to the test on time, reading the directions, and so on).

8. Because subjective exams require you to provide your own answers, you need to be well-versed in the subject matter and skilled in writing.

9. Objective exams force you to select an answer from a set of instructor-made choices. Your selection needs to be based on both your knowledge of content and test-wise strategies.

10. Finals are longer forms of subjective and objective exams; they require no special test-taking strategies, unless they are open-book or take-home exams.

CHAPTER REVIEW

TERMS

Terms appear in the order in which they occurred in the chapter

registration
short-term memory
working memory
long-term memory
reception
perception
selection
chunks
kinesthetic
   perception
mnemonigraph
acronyms
acrostics
puns
parodies
visual practice
auditory practice
semantic practice
spaced study
distributed practice
behavior
   modification
recitation
verbatim
   information
overlearning
cramming
interference
subjective
objective
comprehensive
noncomprehensive

Answer briefly but completely.

1. Using the levels of understanding in Bloom's taxonomy (Figure 7.1), determine the level for each of the following sample questions:

   a. State exactly the meaning of *secondary reinforcer*.

   _____

   b. Compare your text definition of visual thinking with that of the supplemental reading.

   _____

   c. You are an advisor to the president. After considering the four futures of U.S. foreign policy identified in my lecture, what other future would you conceptualize?

   _____

2. Choose any two courses in which you are not enrolled. Compare the depth at which you have processed information for each. How do you account for these differences?

   _____

   _____

   _____

   _____

   _____

3. Organize the following list of locations for recall: Las Vegas, Brazil, Alabama, Utah, Canada, Greenland, Connecticut, London, and Munich.

   _____

   _____

   _____

   _____

4. Locate a list of information you need to remember for a course you are taking. Devise and show an acronym or acrostic to aid you in recalling this list.

   _____

   _____

   _____

   _____

5. In what ways are visual representations of ideas improvements on lists?

    _____

    _____

    _____

    _____

6. Describe the differences between objective and subjective tests. Which kind do you personally find easier to prepare for and take? Why?

    _____

    _____

    _____

    _____

7. Create a chart for practice strategies (spaced study, previewing, recitation, study groups or partners, overlearning, and cramming) and give examples of how they can include visual, auditory, and semantic practice.

    _____

    _____

    _____

    _____

    _____

    _____

    _____

    _____

    _____

8. Identify the reason why each of the following people forgot information:
    a. Meguami cannot remember the name of the person who sat behind her in first grade.

    _____

    b. Mrs. Johnson cannot recall if the education department's number is 757-0349 or 759-0346.

    _____

    c. Kate has difficulty remembering the difference between inductive and deductive reasoning.

_____

    d. Lee failed to remember what he received as graduation gifts.

_____

9. Relate time management to the use of PORPE and POSSE.

_____

_____

_____

_____

_____

10. Identify what the text describes as the *ABCs* of successful test taking. Which one(s) do you possess? Which one(s) do you need to improve? Give examples of each for a specific course in which you are enrolled.

_____

_____

_____

_____

REFERENCES

Bower, G. H. (1970). Analysis of a mnemonic device." *American Scientist* 58:496.

Bryson, B. (1990). The mother tongue and how it got that way. New York: W. Morrow.

Miller, G. A. (1956). The magical number seven, plus or minus two: Some limits on our capacity for processing information. *Psychological Review* 63:81–97.

Shanker, A. (1988, Fall). Strength in numbers. *Academic Connections*, p. 12.

Simpson, M. L. (1986). "PORPE: A writing strategy for studying and learning in the content areas. *Journal of Reading* 29:407–14.

Tenney, J. (1986, March). Keyword notetaking system. Paper presented at the nineteenth annual meeting of the Western College Reading Association, Los Angeles.

von Oech, R. (1986). *A Kick in the Seat of the Pants.* New York: Harper and Row.

Key to Star puzzle.

Vocabulary Development   Word Histories: Using the Results of Reasoning, Belief, Action, and Passion

Numerous supermarket tabloids appeal to the public's desire for gossip. ``Is Elvis still alive?'' ``Was there a conspiracy to assassinate Kennedy?'' ``Are aliens living and working in the United States?'' The stories are often more interesting, and therefore memorable, than the people they describe. And so it goes with words. Word histories provide you with many of the same sort of stories. They whet your interest and help you remember the meanings of the words you encounter.

> What is all knowledge too but recorded experience,
> and a product of history; of which, therefore,
> reasoning and belief, no less than action and passion,
> are essential materials.
>
> Thomas Carlyle
> Nineteenth century Scottish essayist

Knowledge springs from a variety of sources. According to Carlyle, reasoning, belief, action, and passion form the essential materials for its development. The words that define and describe that knowledge also find their roots in these essential materials. And just how do these materials create words? *The Mother Tongue: English and How It Got That Way* (1990) provides some answers. According to Danish linguist Otto Jespersen, people form words by adding or subtracting from current words, by making them up, or by attaching new meanings to them. Bill Bryson, the book's author, adds two other ways words are developed: we borrow them from other languages and create them by accident.

And so it goes throughout history. People acted and reacted according to their thoughts, beliefs, and passions. The names of some of these people became so intertwined with their actions that they now refer to that action. For example, Vidkun Quisling was a leader of Norway in 1940. He undermined his country by collaborating with the Nazis during World War II. Today, *quisling* means "traitor." Josh Billings, a humorist in the 1800s, popularized a bantering comedy style now known as joshing.

Words from other countries also contribute to the English language. For example, the meaning of *calculate* dates back to ancient Rome. Romans often hired carts to take them where they wanted to go. The cart was equipped with a kind of taxi meter. A cylinder filled with pebbles was attached to the wheel. Each time the wheel turned, a pebble dropped through a slot into a separate container. The fare was computed based on the number of pebbles that fell into the container. The

Roman word for pebble was *calculus.* Thus, calculate means to count. As a second example, in the 1812 campaign against Napoleon's armies, Russian soldiers got as far as Paris. They patronized sidewalk cafes and shouted "Bistro!"—or "hurry up"—to the slow-moving waiters. Today, *bistro* is a synonym for a sidewalk cafe.

Words often reflect current interests, trends, and innovations. These include such words as *feminist, New Wave, planned parenthood,* and *rap music.* New products of technology also result in new words. These include *astronaut, lunar module, user-friendly, byte, nylon, yo-yo,* and *trampoline.*

Words also come from abbreviations when the abbreviation is commonly used as the word itself. These include *IQ* (intelligence quotient), *TV* (television), and *CD* (compact disk). Words also come from acronyms (words formed from the first letter or first few letters of several words). The word *posh* originally stood for "port outbound, starboard home." Passengers traveling through the Suez Canal in the 1800s ordered cabins on the left side of the ship for the trip out and ones on the right for the return trip. This kept their staterooms in the shade both ways. Records for these very desirable accommodations noted them as "P.O.S.H."

The creation and development of a word is its etymology—the word's history. Found in dictionary entries, etymologies tell information about a word's evolution, how it was first used, and how it is used now. Knowing a word's etymology serves as another mechanism to expand your connections with and understanding of that word.

Activity

Look up the etymology of the boldface words in a large collegiate dictionary. Describe the history or origin of each. Then define it. In the sample dictionary entry, the history of the word has been underlined.

hip-po-pot-a-mus (hip -a -pat' -a mas) *n.* a very large pachydermatous African quadruped frequenting rivers. *-pl.* -es or hippopotami (hip a pat' a mi) (Gr. *hippos,* a horse; *potamos,* a river).

1. Convert 45° on the Celsius scale to its **Fahrenheit** equivalent.

   etymology_____

   definition _____

2. **Gremlins** are fictitious creatures.

   etymology_____

   definition _____

3. Prisoners who **escape** are generally recaptured within a short period of time.

   etymology _____

   _____

   definition _____

   _____

4. **Radar** enables ships to navigate treacherous seas.

   etymology _____

   _____

   definition _____

   _____

5. Few people know what **RSVP** means.

   etymology _____

   _____

   definition _____

   _____

6. **Luscious** fruits come from tropical regions.

   etymology _____

   _____

   definition _____

   _____

7. The owner of the company was a **shyster.**

   etymology _____

   _____

   definition _____

   _____

8. The **Miranda warning** must be given to each suspect.

   etymology _____

   _____

   definition _____

   _____

9. **Sequoya** forests flourish in California.

   etymology _____

   _____

   definition _____

   _____

10. Oil **derricks** dotted the countryside.

    etymology _____

    _____

    definition _____

    _____

Activity

Read the following essay, "A Few Famous Trips of the Tongue," by Jack Smith. On a separate sheet of paper, describe the histories of each of the following words: *spoonerism, sandwich, boycott, wellington, cardigan, raglan,* and *bowdlerize.* Identify the dictionary definition and check the history for each one. Give one of Smith's examples of a spoonerism. Create a spoonerism of your own to help you remember any concept from one of the sample chapters.

Excerpt 7.1   A Few Famous Trips of the Tongue   by Jack Smith

---

For no discernible reason other than sheer whimsy, John Liddle of San Diego has sent me a London-dateline story from the Los Angeles Times of Sept. 11, 1977, about the inimitable Rev. William Archibald Spooner (1884–1930).

No reason other than whimsy prompts me to recall that otherwise extraordinarily dull man's one endearing service—his gift to the English language of that slip of the tongue known, in his honor, as a spoonerism.

Thus, Spooner joins the small company whose names, usually because of some personal quirk or invention, have become common nouns. It was John Montagu, 4th Earl of Sandwich (1718–1792), who invented the sandwich to avoid having to leave the gaming tables, and hence gave his name to that handy meal.

Boycott comes from Capt. C. C. Boycott (1832–1897), an Irish land agent who was boycotted by his tenants when he refused to lower their rents in 1880.

Wellingtons are the boots named after Arthur Wellesley, 1st Duke of Wellington (1769–1852), who bested Napoleon at Waterloo—and wore that type of boot.

Cardigan—a long-sleeved, collarless knitted sweater that buttons down the front—was named after James Thomas Brudenell, 7th Earl of Cardigan (1797–1868), a vainglorious martinet who led the foolhardy charge of the Light Brigade at Balaklava, in which Errol Flynn was a film hero. A notorious dandy, Cardigan evidently favored that garment.

Raglan, an overcoat or topcoat with sleeves that continue in one piece to the collar, was named after FitzRoy James Henry Somerset, 1st Baron Raglan (1788–1855). He was the British commander in chief during the Crimean War who issued the ambiguous order sending Cardigan on his disastrous charge.

And a verb:

Bowdlerize, to damage a literary work by censoring lines that one finds offensive, comes from an English editor, Thomas Bowdler (1754–1825), who had the effrontery to publish an expurgated Shakespeare.

Spooner's gift was his habit of transposing the initial or other sounds of words. For instance, it is said that Spooner once referred to Queen Victoria as "the queer old dean," when he meant to say "the dear old Queen."

Spooner's slips were never deliberate, though they brought him a strange sort of fame. He lived in dread of making the next error and remained modest about his accomplishment.

Finding his name in a newspaper, he noted, "But of course they thought me most famous for my spoonerisms, so I was not greatly puffed up."

For 60 years Spooner was a member of New College, Oxford, and served as its warden from 1903 to 1924. He was a small man and colorless, in fact an albino, and had cruelly been called "this shrimp-like creature."

That this remarkably unprepossessing Anglican clergyman should be remembered with such reverence today is owed entirely to his oral lapses.

He was likely to drop them in church and once assured his flock that "the Lord is a shoving leopard." Also, he once announced that the next hymn would be "Kinkering Kongs Their Titles Take."

It is said that he once told a lady, "Mardon me, padam; this pie is occupied; allow me to sew you to another sheet," but that sounds too contrived to be authentic.

Perhaps his most famous was a quadruple—a prodigious accomplishment even for the gifted Spooner. While lecturing a delinquent undergraduate, he is said to have told him: "You have tasted a whole worm. You have hissed my mystery lectures. You were fighting a liar in the quadrangle. You will leave by the town drain."

The complexity of that quadruple suggests that it was invented by one of Spooner's contemporaries or perhaps even put together from remarks Spooner made to different students at different times. But there is evidence that Spooner himself was capable of such an achievement.

This is one of my favorite spoonerisms, perhaps because it was spoken during World War I, when the dean was getting on in years, and it suggests that age had not diminished his powers.

When Brits were fighting across the channel, he told the Home Front: "When the boys come back from France, we'll have the hags flung out." Typical of the kind of British spunk that helped them survive the deaths and mutilations of two world wars.

Perhaps Spooner hoped wistfully to be eulogized for a more scholarly skill. "We all know what it is," he once told his flock, "to have a half-warmed fish within us."

CHAPTER 8

Thinking Critically

OBJECTIVES

By the time you finish this chapter you should be able to do the following:

1. Identify materials used in critical thinking.

2. Describe how the purposes and questions created as part of inquiry into a topic or problem affect critical thinking.

3. Determine how introspection results in inferences and interpretations in critical thinking.

4. Describe how materials, inquiry, and introspection help you arrive at logical decisions.

5. Apply standards of thought to the processes of thought.

CHAPTER MAP

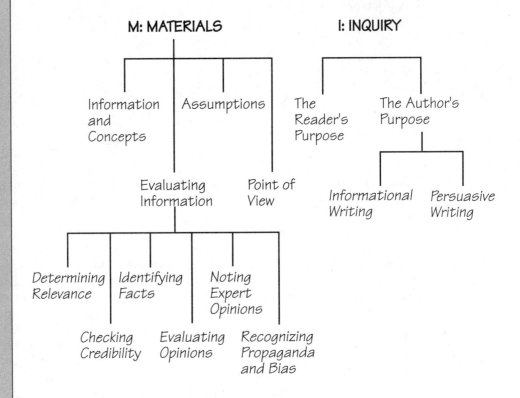

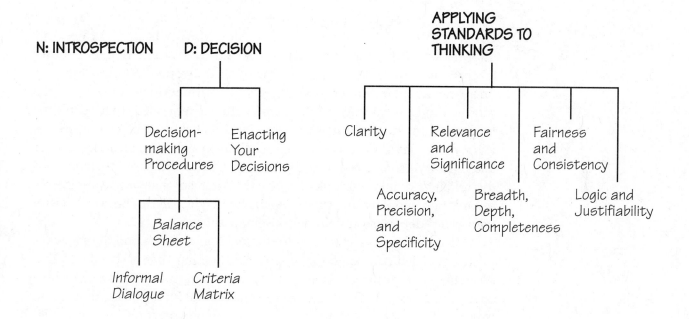

N: INTROSPECTION

D: DECISION

Decision-
making
Procedures

Enacting
Your
Decisions

Balance
Sheet

Informal
Dialogue

Criteria
Matrix

APPLYING
STANDARDS TO
THINKING

Clarity

Relevance
and
Significance

Fairness
and
Consistency

Accuracy,
Precision,
and
Specificity

Breadth,
Depth,
Completeness

Logic and
Justifiability

Imagine yourself sitting in an introductory zoology class. Your instructor's first lecture concerns the cattywampus. She describes it as an ill-adapted and nocturnal animal that became extinct during the Ice Age. She notes that no traces of it remain. Using an overhead projector, she shows a diagram of the animal's skull. Dutifully, you—and the rest of your classmates—take notes. At the end of the class, your instructor gives you a quiz. Confidently, you record your answers. To your surprise and dismay, you—and the rest of your classmates—fail the test.

What happened? Your experience was the same as that of David Owen (1990). The best teacher he ever had, Mr. Whitson, fabricated this information about the cattywampus to make a point; that is, neither teachers nor textbooks are perfect. Mr. Whitson wanted his class to avoid uncritical acceptance of spoken or printed information. In the case of the cattywampus, if no trace of the extinct animal remained, there could be no physical evidence of its skull nor could its behavior be characterized. What made David Owen describe Mr. Whitson as the best teacher he ever had? Mr. Whitson introduced the class to **critical thinking,** the ability to discipline and take control of your thinking so that you can process information more easily (Paul, 1990). How you discipline and control your mind depends on your purpose and subject.

Your professors expect you to think at higher levels and in new ways in college. Each course you take requires thinking that is specific to that discipline. For example, rather than simply memorizing facts in a history course, you need to think like a historian: to look for causes that led to events, effects of those events, implications of one person's influence over another, what-if situations, and ways to prevent repetitions of disastrous historical events. While the prospect of thinking like a historian, biologist, mathematician, or professional in whatever subject you take may seem overwhelming, you possess a wealth of personal background for doing just those kinds of thinking. When you decide not to invite someone to a party because that person ruined the last party you gave, you think historically in order to avoid repeating a disastrous event. Likewise, you think historically when you try to predict how your relationship with someone would change if you got married by considering the implications of your influence over one another. When you develop your ability to discipline and take control of thinking, you think more effectively and efficiently. The discipline involved in thinking critically requires an orderly and careful way of thinking about issues, people, and problems. However, the control you exert over the process depends on your ability to think about your own thinking. Using the acronym **MIND** helps you systematically work through the process of critical thinking. Figure 8.1 identifies the components in the MIND process. The circle reminds you that there is no one magical starting or ending place to insure critical

Figure 8.1   MIND Components

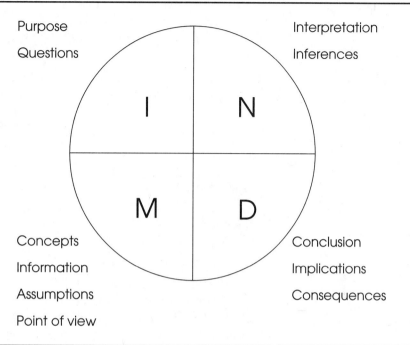

thinking. Indeed, you may examine your thinking by starting at any point as long as you cover all components. For example, if you are a college student in California considering a job offer in West Virginia, you might start by examining your assumptions about the people and climate of that state. Or, you might start with the information on salaries in that state or the cost of living there. Your conclusion could even be to get more information or to test the validity of your assumptions. Regardless of where you begin the critical thinking process, you fail to logically cover the issue unless you consider all components.

Some aspects of critical thinking fit together because of their relationships to each other. For example, if your purpose for thinking about a possible job change is to decide how you feel about it, you will almost immediately identify a question that you want to answer about that topic. That question might be, "Should I take the job?" or "Will my family be better off in another state?"

M: *MATERIALS*

Quick, can you trace the following spiral to the center of the whirlpool? (Answer appears on the last page of this chapter.)

The results of your thinking depend on the materials you use. You get materials from two sources. First, materials come from outside of you in the form of **information** and **concepts.** In terms of learning, these include things you see (e.g., words and pictures), things you hear (e.g., words, music, or other sounds), and things you experience (e.g., situations, activities, experiences). The materials with which you work also come from within you—your **assumptions** and **point of view.**

The preceding figure provided you with information in the form of a visual figure and the verbal concepts of *spiral, center,* and *whirlpool.* Your point of view was probably that of a learner or competitor—one who was to follow directions quickly in order to complete a task. If you checked the answer at the end of the chapter, you found that the design and wording of the information and concepts affected your assumptions about the figure. You assumed that the figure was as stated—a spiral—and responded accordingly.

INFORMATION AND CONCEPTS

Information comes from the data you acquire from life—what you see, hear, smell, taste, touch, and feel. As you gather information, you categorize and organize it to form concepts or ideas. This forms the basis of your background knowledge and the concepts you understand. You might think of a concept as a connected and organized network or web of information. For example, as a resident of the United States, your concept of money includes information like penny, dime, dollar, and so on. However, while you may understand the concept of money in terms of foreign currency, you probably lack detailed information for a specific country (e.g., Japan and the yen). In other words, while you understand that other countries have units of money with which you buy and sell merchandise, you probably don't know the names of the units or their worth.

When you think critically about a subject, you consider the information and concepts that concern that subject. A different subject may or may not result in different concepts. For instance, choosing the right major requires that you consider the concepts of *interest, marketability,* and *personal aptitude.* Without considering these concepts, you might choose a major because your best friend likes it or because your parents urge you to select it. Since concepts form interconnected, organized webs or networks, they are empty terms without data or information to fill and support them.

EVALUATING INFORMATION

Gathering and evaluating information often seems like the easiest aspect of thinking critically about an issue. However, inaccurate, incorrect, insufficient, or irrelevant information affects your ability to think critically about its content. Think about the effects of trash being dumped next to the river. Suppose organic insecticide in the trash kills only mosquito larvae. In this case, dumping may do area residents a service rather than harm. However, normally dumping trash supports the concepts of toxicity and environmental imbalance and is considered a problem, not a benefit.

What information is relevant? What does lager-beer and pumpkins have to do with a doctor's case? What's credible? Can doctors who discuss such things instead of patients be trusted? What information is provided without bias? As twentieth-century novelist Anthony Burgess once said, there is as much sense in nonsense as there is nonsense in sense. For the critical thinker, separating the nonsense from the sense is sometimes difficult.

Determining Relevance

Relevance involves determining what you need to solve a particular problem or answer a particular question. Your role in determining relevance is to separate similar pieces of information into those you need and those you do not need. The way you think of the problem determines what you perceive to be relevant. In addition, what is relevant in one situation may or may not be relevant in another.

Anderson and Pichert (1978) conducted a research study in which they examined the effect of point of view on recall. They asked students to read a passage about what two boys did at one boy's home when playing hooky from school. Some readers were asked to read as if they were burglars. Others were asked to read as if they were home buyers. A third group read from no particular point of view. Researchers found that the reader's point of view affected what was relevant and later recalled. For example, those who read as burglars were more likely to recall where the money was kept. That's what was relevant to them. Readers who read as home buyers recalled more about the home's landscaping. That's what was relevant to them. Determining the relevance of information, then, depends on your purpose, the question at issue, and your point of view.

Now when a doctor's patients are perplexed,
A consultation comes in order next—
You know what that is?
In a certain place
Meet certain doctors
To discuss a case
And other matters,
Such as weather, crops,
Potatoes, pumpkins, lager-beer, and hops.

—WENDELL HOLMES

Nineteenth century American author

Exercise 8.1   Respond to the following using Sample Chapters 11, 12, and 13 as sources.

1. You must write a paper on the industrial revolution. Which chapter or chapters are relevant to this purpose? What specific sections within the chapter(s) could you use?

_____

_____

2. You are preparing for midterm exams and want to review terms in assigned materials. Which chapter or chapters are relevant to this purpose? Where would you find that information within the chapter(s)?

_____

_____

3. You are writing a paper on inventions of the nineteenth century. Which chapter or chapters are relevant to this purpose? What specific sections within the chapter(s) could you use?

_____

_____

4. You are making a speech on the contributions of women to business and industry. Which chapter or chapters are relevant to this purpose? What specific sections within the chapter(s) could you use?

_____

_____

5. You want to compare management practices in the nineteenth century with management practices in the twentieth century. Which chapter or chapters are relevant to this purpose? What specific sections within the chapter(s) could you use?

_____

_____

Checking Credibility

What is truth? What is real? Who can you trust? P. T. Barnum, owner of a circus show he billed as "The Greatest Show on Earth" is often thought to have said, "There's a sucker born every minute." He often used exaggeration and deception to create interest in his circus shows; thus, logically, he might have thought and even said that a sucker is born every minute. In reality, however, no record exists of Barnum making this statement. In fact, in Barnum's time, the word *sucker* was not used in this context. And so, what is truth? What is real? Who can you trust?

In a free country like ours, almost anything anyone thinks can be spoken or printed. Whether those thoughts begin as fact or not, distortions occur. You are responsible for determining if information is fact or opinion, and if opinion, whether or not to give credence to that opinion. You evaluate **credibility.** You control whether you exist as a critical judge of information or just another sucker.

Identifying Facts

Witnesses sworn in during trials promise to tell all the **facts** they know about a crime. Their opinions are immaterial, or not important. The judge wants to hear what the witnesses know to be true. Thus, they describe what they actually saw or heard. They cannot add to, subtract from, or change the facts in any way. It is the judge and jury's job to determine how closely each witness sticks to the facts.

What are facts? A fact is a statement of reality. For example, there are seven days in a week. That's a fact. Canada is north of most of the United States. That's also a fact. Facts also exist in the form of events known to have occurred. For instance, George Washington was the first president of the United States. The bombing of Pearl Harbor occurred on December 7, 1941. These are facts. Facts are truth.

When you evaluate information, you act as judge and jury to decide if the information is factual. Facts are based on direct evidence or on actual observation or experience. The sources of this information are called **primary sources.** Primary sources consist of original documents or first-person accounts of an event.

Secondary sources also provide facts. They interpret, evaluate, describe, or otherwise restate the work of primary sources. Because

"But how will we footnote this source?!"

information may be altered or lost in translation, primary sources provide more accurate information.

Qualitative words describe facts. They give details but are not judgmental. They express absolutes and represent concepts that can be generally agreed upon. Words like *dead, freezing,* and *wet* are examples of such words.

Other words, sometimes called **weasel words,** limit a statement of fact. Weasels are animals with keen sight and smell that are known for their quickness and slyness. Because of these characteristics, words that show the possibility of other options and lack exactness are called weasel words. Information is given but not guaranteed. For example, look at the difference between these two statements: "I make *A*'s and *B*'s." "In some courses, I make *A*'s and *B*'s." The words *in some courses* limit the truth of the first sentence. Words like *frequently, occasionally,* and *seldom* are examples of such words.

Evaluating Opinions

Like facts, **opinions** are also a form of truth. The difference between the two lies in whose reality is being represented. Facts belong to everyone; they are the same for everyone; they are universally held. An opinion belongs to one person.

An opinion is what you think about a subject. It is a belief or judgment. Opinions reflect attitudes or feelings. Words describing opinions are interpretive.

Consider again the topic of grades. Suppose instead of saying "I make *A*'s and *B*'s," you say, "I make *good* grades." How is *good* defined? What you consider to be "good grades," someone else might consider to be inferior grades. Other students might consider them to be excellent grades, ones they could not achieve in a lifetime of effort. *Good* is a qualitative descriptor and, as such, depends on what you think for its definition. Its meaning is strictly your opinion. When you assume everyone defines qualitative words the same way you do, you make a **definitional assumption.**

Because opinion is biased, you need to be objective as you consider it. Objectivity refers to your skill in reporting facts without including personal opinions, definitional assumptions, feelings, or beliefs. Inclusion of such material in critical thinking undermines the validity and value of the conclusions you reach.

Noting Expert Opinions

The background of the person giving an opinion affects the value of the opinion. Anyone can give an opinion, but some people have the qualifications necessary to give **expert opinions.** For example, suppose a freshman tells you, "Take Sociology 421—my friend Jana said it's a great course." Now suppose your academic advisor says, "Take Sociology 421—with your background, you'd really enjoy it and learn a lot!" Which person would you trust to know more about Sociology 421?

An expert opinion depends on many factors. First, you need to evaluate an author's or speaker's educational and professional background. An author's or speaker's background affects point of view, what is said about a topic, and the way in which facts are reported. You find background information about an author in the preliminary or concluding statements of an article or book. A biographical dictionary or an encyclopedia also contains such information about authorities in a vast number of fields. You also gain knowledge though discussions with others in the same area of expertise. You judge where the author or speaker works and the reputation of that institution.

You also judge the reputation of the author or speaker. However, this works both as an advantage and disadvantage. People who are well-known authorities in one field might write or speak below their standards in another. As a critical thinker, you need to know the difference.

Sometimes information about the author's or speaker's credentials is missing. You then need another way to judge information. For example, suppose an article in *Today's Science* compares the incidence of cancer in the United States with that of France. The author, who is unknown to you, concludes that the air in France is cleaner than the air here and that this keeps the French in better health. Since you have no information about the author's background, you cannot evaluate his or her qualifications or **bias.** In this case, you judge the standards and credibility of the journal containing the article.

> Advertisements are now so numerous that they are very negligently perused, and it is therefore become necessary to gain attention by magnificence of promises, and by eloquences sometimes sublime and sometimes pathetic.
>
> —SAMUEL JOHNSON
>
> Eighteenth century English author

WRITE TO LEARN

On a separate sheet of paper, respond to the following: In your American history class, a graduate student in history guest lectures. She asserts that Grover Cleveland was the most effective president. Do you consider hers an expert opinion? Justify your answer.

Recognizing Propaganda and Bias

The magnificent promises and sublime and pathetic words advertisers use to sway our minds are forms of **propaganda.** Propaganda provides faulty information in that it is one-sided; it tells only one side of an issue to make you believe that side is the right one. It is used to try to make you think a certain way or believe or desire a certain thing.

Advertisers have used propaganda to convince you to buy their products since perhaps even before the eighteenth century. Politicians often use propaganda to convince voters to vote for them. Even authors and speakers slant the meaning of text, or bias it, both knowingly and unknowingly, through propaganda. Likewise, people around you use propaganda, both consciously and unconsciously, to persuade you to form opinions that conform with their own; that is, to bias your beliefs.

Exercise 8.2   Locate ten facts and ten opinions from ``Another Look: Choosing to be a Top Performer'' on pages 536-538 of Sample Chapter 11 ``Personal Values, Career Planning, and Success with People at Work.''

FACTS	OPINIONS
1. _____	_____
2. _____	_____
3. _____	_____
4. _____	_____
5. _____	_____
6. _____	_____

7. _____   _____

_____   _____

8. _____   _____

_____   _____

9. _____   _____

_____   _____

10. _____   _____

_____   _____

11. How do you recognize facts? How do you recognize opinions? What makes one different from the other?

_____

_____

_____

_____

_____

_____

Propaganda and bias affects the accuracy and objectivity of information. You can be wary of its effect by knowing what it is (see Table 8.1).

In addition to propaganda, authors and speakers use **euphemisms** and **loaded words** to sway beliefs. The word _euphemism_ comes from two Greek word parts—_eu_, which means _good_, and _pheme_, which means _voice_—which translate literally into "good voice." Euphemisms substitute "good" or pleasant phrases for "bad" or unpleasant phrases. Authors and speakers use them to soften the reality of negative statements or to disguise the truth. For example, describing a fellow instructor as being _careful with details_ sounds better than saying the person is _picky_.

Loaded words, on the other hand, make people, issues, and things appear worse than they might really be. Because of the definitional assumptions carried by loaded words, a word that seems okay to you may trigger an emotional response in another. For example, examine these terms from criminal justice class, _accused murderer_ and _convicted felon. Accused murderer_ has a different impact than _convicted felon_ because you have more definite feelings about murder and less definite ideas about felonies. Because the way speakers and authors use words affects what you hear and believe, you need to be a critical evaluator of all you read and hear.

Table 8.1   Types of Propaganda and Bias, and Definitions

Types of Propaganda	Definitions
Image advertising	Associates a person, product, or concept with certain places, sounds, activities, symbols, or people in order to create a positive mental image of the initial person, product, or concept.
Bandwagoning	Implies that you must conform to the wishes or beliefs of a particular group in order to be right; suppresses individual rights.
Testimonial	Suggests that when a famous person or authority on a subject says a product, person, or idea is good, you must believe it.
Plain folks	Attempts to make you feel that ordinary, everyday people like yourself approve of the person, product, or idea.
Ad hominem (name-calling)	Forms unfair comparisons between two persons, products, or ideas by using unpopular or unflattering language about the competition.
Strawman	Shows an opposing person, product, or idea in its weakest form.

WRITE TO LEARN

On a separate sheet of paper, create or think of an example for each of the types of propaganda listed in table 8.1.

Exercise 8.3   Read ``Who's in Control?'' from Sample Chapter 13, ``An Invitation to Computers.'' Examine each of the italicized words below which come from this chapter. Identify the image each word evokes. Determine if each is used either as a euphemism or a loaded word. Identify why the author chose to use this word in this way.

   a. . . . movies that *conjure* up images of *world-class* destruction brought on by computers that break their *"fail-safe"* traces.

   1. *conjure*
      MEANING: _____

      _____

      IMAGE EVOKED: _____

      _____

EUPHEMISM OR LOADED WORD? _____

WHY WORD IS USED THIS WAY: _____

_____

2. *world-class*

MEANING: _____

_____

IMAGE EVOKED: _____

_____

EUPHEMISM OR LOADED WORD? _____

WHY WORD IS USED THIS WAY: _____

_____

3. *fail-safe*

MEANING: _____

_____

IMAGE EVOKED: _____

_____

EUPHEMISM OR LOADED WORD? _____

WHY WORD IS USED THIS WAY: _____

_____

b. . . . *wholesale* death . . .

4. *wholesale*

MEANING: _____

_____

IMAGE EVOKED: _____

_____

EUPHEMISM OR LOADED WORD? _____

WHY WORD IS USED THIS WAY: _____

_____

c. *Fantasy?* There was no fantasy to the real-life dread of Russian missiles. . . . There was no fantasy about the situation . . . when . . . Flight 007 . . . was shot down. . . .

5. *fantasy*

MEANING: _____

_____

IMAGE EVOKED: _____

_____

EUPHEMISM OR LOADED WORD? _____

WHY WORD IS USED THIS WAY: _____

_____

d. Is there real danger that computers can run *amok* . . .

6. *amok*
   MEANING: _____

   _____

   IMAGE EVOKED: _____

   _____

   EUPHEMISM OR LOADED WORD? _____

   WHY WORD IS USED THIS WAY: _____

   _____

e. . . . development of military systems that have been called *"doomsday machines."*

7. *doomsday machines*
   MEANING: _____

   _____

   IMAGE EVOKED: _____

   _____

   EUPHEMISM OR LOADED WORD? _____

   WHY WORD IS USED THIS WAY: _____

   _____

f. The question cannot be avoided: Are world leaders wise enough to avoid *unleashing* the potential *"overkill"* possible in a world replete with weapons of atomic and chemical warfare?

8. *unleashing*
   MEANING: _____

   _____

   IMAGE EVOKED: _____

   _____

   EUPHEMISM OR LOADED WORD? _____

   WHY WORD IS USED THIS WAY: _____

   _____

9. *overkill*
   MEANING: _____

   _____

   IMAGE EVOKED: _____

   _____

EUPHEMISM OR LOADED WORD? _____

WHY WORD IS USED THIS WAY: _____

_____

g. Part of the planning for development and use of any computer system should include creation of scenarios that picture potential failures. This process has been called *"constructive worrying."*

10. *constructive worrying*

MEANING: _____

_____

IMAGE EVOKED: _____

_____

EUPHEMISM OR LOADED WORD? _____

WHY WORD IS USED THIS WAY: _____

_____

WRITE TO LEARN

On a separate sheet of paper or in your journal, discuss the role of propaganda in national and international politics. Is it ever appropriate to use propaganda? Why or why not?

ASSUMPTIONS

As detailed in Ann Lander's advice column on August 22, 1994, Morty Storm of Brooklyn, New York, wrote a humorous story called "A Dog Named Sex". In this story, the narrator describes several ways in which his dog's name, Sex, resulted in confusion. For example, when he went to get the dog a license, he said, "I want a license for Sex." The clerk replied that she wanted the same thing. He told the clerk that he had had Sex since he was nine years old, and the clerk said, "You must have been quite a kid!" When he took the dog on his honeymoon, he told the manager that Sex kept him awake at night, and the manager said he had the same problem. After a number of similar experiences, the narrator said that Sex ran away from home one evening, and he spent several hours looking for him. When a cop asked him what he was doing on the streets at four o'clock in the morning, he said that he was looking for Sex. The narrator concluded the story by saying that his court case was coming up next Friday.

The humor of the preceding story depends on assumptions embedded in the concept of *sex*. Assumptions consist of the beliefs and expectations you take for granted about a situation. They come from your actual and/or vicarious background experiences. Identifying your assumptions helps you analyze your interpretation of a situation. In this story, the people the narrator met assumed that Sex referred to something other than a dog; however, the narrator assumed that people understood he was talking about a dog when he talked about Sex. These assumptions resulted in a variety of misunderstandings.

Identifying assumptions in your own thinking as well as in the thoughts of others is no easy task for several reasons. First, assumptions are somewhat hidden. They reside below the surface of any thought or argument. Second, because assumptions arise from background knowledge, they are second nature to you. You unconsciously think them. Third, because you may have held certain assumptions for so long, you do not recognize them as assumptions—you see them as truth or fact.

Ironically, actively attacking or defending an alternative argument helps you identify the underlying assumptions in any situation. For example, suppose, in discussing a psychology chapter your instructor says, "To remove the burden from a family of a terminally ill patient, euthanasia is the best course of action." How can you recognize the assumptions your instructor is making? If you can identify and defend another alternative, like hospices, you will recognize the instructor's assumption—the patient's death will help the family.

Another way of identifying the assumptions of others involves identifying qualitative terms, those words whose definitions vary from one person to another. Likewise, these words seem most persuasive in leading you toward one idea over another. Think again of your instructor's statement: "To remove the burden from a family of a terminally-ill patient, euthanasia is the best course of action." Which words seem less clear in definition and, thus, leave room for argument? *Terminally-ill, patient,* and *euthanasia* seem exact enough, but what about the words *burden* and *best*? Their definitions differ qualitatively from one person to another, one situation to another. Locating these words helps you identify and clarify definitional assumptions.

Exercise 8.4   In each of the following situations, identify the common assumption that led the individuals to react the way they did.

1. Gerald is going out with his friends. He tells his parents he will be home about midnight. His friends want to stop by a club where a new band is performing. The

band will not perform until 11:45. One of Gerald's friends offers to take him home before the performance. Gerald's response: "No problem. I won't be more than one hour late."
Assumption:_____

_____

_____

2. Several of Jennifer's professors will be absent next Friday because of a professional conference. Her professors have asked graduate assistants to cover their classes. Jennifer decides to go home for the weekend on Thursday.
Assumption:_____

_____

_____

3. Jack is driving down the highway. As he glances in the rear-view mirror, he sees a highway patrol car rapidly approaching. Jack curses and pulls over.
Assumption:_____

_____

_____

4. Jenny sees a dog running across a busy highway. The dog has a collar and tag. She captures the dog and calls the vet.
Assumption:_____

_____

_____

_____

POINT OF VIEW

Point of view involves perspective—the position from which you view or evaluate things. Just as an astronaut's view of earth from the space shuttle differs from your view of earth from your window, your perspective affects how you see things. Gender, ethnicity, educational background, personal experience, or other concepts form perspective, which affects a person's point of view. For example, a Hispanic male who graduated from Harvard ten years ago probably has a different point of view of the university experience than a Hispanic female high school student who is applying for admission to Harvard this year. Recognizing point of view helps you understand why you or someone else takes a particular position about an issue.

Consider the story about the dog named Sex again. It contains several points of view. First, the narrator's point of view was that of a typical dog owner. Everything he tried to do was perfectly normal. The clerk's perspective was sympathetic because she assumed a license for "Sex" sounded like a good idea. According to this clerk's point of view, the narrator must have been quite a kid because he had had "Sex" since he was nine. Another clerk with a different point of view might have been horrified at such an idea. The hotel manager also had a sympathetic point of view because he thought that he and the narrator shared common sleepless experiences with "Sex." Finally, from the cop's point of view, anyone who was looking for "Sex" at 4 A.M. probably ought to be arrested for something.

Exercise 8.5   Answer the following.

1. I am _____ years old.
2. My ethnic background is _____.
3. I am _____.
   a. male
   b. female
4. My political views would best be described as _____.
   a. conservative
   b. moderate
   c. liberal
5. I would characterize my religious beliefs in the following way:
   a. devoutly _____ (religious affiliation)
   b. _____ (religious affiliation)
   c. agnostic
   d. atheist
6. The place I grew up would best be characterized as which of the following?
   a. rural
   b. urban
7. What is your MBTI personality style? (see Chapter one) _____ _____ _____ _____

WRITE TO LEARN

On a separate sheet of paper or in your journal, write a brief description of yourself using the information in Exercise 8.5. This forms the foundation of your perspective. Your assumptions about any given topic form the remainder of your perspective and, thus, vary from subject to subject.

I: INQUIRY

A popular supermarket tabloid uses "Inquiring minds want to know" as their slogan. Why? Their writers know that people want the scoop on a story: what happened and why. As a critical thinker, you, too, need the scoop on the subjects about which you think. Identifying a **purpose** for thinking and **questions** to answer helps you achieve that goal.

Consider the following example. You are reading the newspaper. You turn to the sports page and begin to read an article about your favorite professional basketball team. Your *purpose* is to find out what happened at the game. The primary *question* at issue for you might be, "Did they win?" Your roommate, who heard the score on the radio, enters the room and reads over your shoulder to answer the *question*, "Who scored the winning basket?" At this point, you should realize that two people could have the same purpose but a slightly different question at issue.

Thus, your goal for thinking and/or reading is the same as your purpose. To benefit from thinking or reading you must have a reason for doing it. If no reason exists, you probably won't get any results or satisfaction from the activity. What you want to know about the topic results in the question at issue. When you read or think critically, you need to clarify or refine your purpose by identifying a problem you need to solve or question you want to answer.

THE READER'S PURPOSE

Just as you have a purpose for the thinking that you do, you also have a purpose for the reading that you do. For all too many students, that purpose is to finish as quickly as possible. This purpose requires no critical thought and results in little understanding. In fact, one basic difference between critical and uncritical readers is that critical readers delineate a clear and specific purpose for their reading.

The actual purpose of your reading varies from one situation and its materials to another (see Table 8.2). Whatever your purpose, knowing it helps you become a more active and involved reader. Reading that's active is far more interesting and results in critical thinking and efficient learning. Asking questions, making predictions, and identifying problems to be solved all are ways to set purposes in thinking and reading.

Table 8.2   Purposes for Reading

1. To answer questions

2. To confirm data

3. To get an overview of a topic

4. To identify an author's point of view

5. To check predictions

6. To enjoy reading by reading recreationally.

Questions for reading arise from a variety of sources. Instructor questions often help you set purposes for your reading. You might find these questions written on an overhead transparency or chalkboard or as part of your course syllabus or other course materials. Whatever the case, they provide you with a means for identifying information you need to know. Questions also come from the author of the text itself. How? Authors often provide pre- or postchapter exams for your use in evaluating your understanding (see Chapter 4). Questions also occur as a result of your interactions with author-provided information. For example, the use of a study system like SQ3R mandates that you set your own questions as part of an initial skimming of the title, headings, subheadings, and terms (see Chapter 5). If the title, headings, and/or subheadings are ambiguous or missing, then the first sentences of sections often provide information on which you can base your questions.

Making predictions goes hand-in-hand with asking questions. That is because when you ask a question, you are in fact predicting that its answer appears in the section or chapter you are about to read. Thus, asking questions is one way to make predictions. Another way involves examining illustrations and guessing their importance to the information in the text. Based on the extent of your background knowledge, you may be able to make predictions by summarizing a chapter before reading it. Corrections to or elaborations on the content of this summary after reading provides an effective study aid. Making predictions increases your curiosity, a kind of motivating force, and provides an additional purpose for reading: learning how accurate your predictions are.

A final way to set purposes for reading involves your linking text information with yourself. If you identify how the text relates to a problem you or someone you know faces or how information in it connects with what you wish to do when you graduate, you have identified a purpose for reading.

Creating and pursuing questions are both the rigor and the passion of critical thinking and reading. Making predictions allows you—the critical reader or thinker—to be curious and creative in approaching information. Linking the text with yourself encourages individuality.

WRITE TO LEARN

On a separate sheet of paper or in your journal, write a short paragraph about a homework assignment that you recently completed. What questions do you have about that assignment? What questions do you think your instructor had that led to making the assignment? Were you able to answer all of your questions before you completed the assignment? How did the questions and the answers affect the quality of your completion of the assignment?

THE AUTHOR'S PURPOSE

Every term, college instructors ask the routine question: "Why did you come to college?" Traditionally, the answers seem as cliché as the question itself. Nonetheless, the question remains a valid one. That's because everyone has a purpose, a goal they mean to achieve, for everything they do.

Authors are no different. In most cases, they consciously decide to write with a specific objective or purpose in mind. While some, like poets, artists, or composers may create for the joy of artistic expression, other authors write to influence your understanding, emotions, beliefs, and actions.

Because writing is purposeful, an author seeks to obtain a desired response from you. For example, if an author writes to inform, then you should expect to acquire information you have not known before or review knowledge you already possess. If an author writes to persuade, then you should expect to examine your beliefs in light of the information the author provides. If an author writes to entertain, you should expect to feel amused or interested. These, then, comprise the three purposes authors have when writing: to inform, persuade, or entertain.

Although one purpose may be foremost in mind, an author sometimes mixes in the other two. For example, consider the following sentence from a college anthropology text.

> "Anthropologists . . . want to understand the rules that you know unconsciously that instruct you when to bow your head and speak reverently, when to sound smart, when to act dumb, and when to cuss like a sailor."

Here the author has added humor to informative writing. Or, an author might support a persuasive writing with information. For example, consider this sentence from the same anthropology text:

> "Anthropology has practical value in the modern world, and it is not as esoteric as many people think. . . . The value of inculcating understanding and tolerance between citizens of different nations is another practical lesson of anthropology. . . . The information that ethnographers have collected about alternative ways of being human allows us to judge the benefits against the costs of industrialization and progress. The comparative perspective of anthropology helps us to see which elements of societies are amenable to change and what the consequences of this change might be. . . ."

Here the author attempts to persuade you to believe that anthropology is a practical, day-to-day science by providing examples of how it affects your life. Finally, even writing whose sole purpose is to entertain contains information; however, because such writing exists strictly for your recreational pleasure, you do not have to explore it with as much critical thought as you do persuasive and informative writing. Thus, the remainder of this section focuses on only the latter two types of writing.

Informational Writing

Informational passages seek to educate. Usually, an author tries to present material in a way that readers will easily understand. Such writing often consists of explanations, analyses, descriptions, demonstrations, and definitions. It also includes examples, statistics, comparisons, contrasts, and expert opinions. Although it is most often found in textbooks, newspapers and magazines also include informative writing.

Persuasive Writing

An author writes a persuasive passage to bring about a change in either your opinion or your behavior. Authors change your opinion by convincing you to agree with what they think. Such writing seeks to make you believe the author's point of view. For example, an author might try to convince you that survival depends on conservation of resources. This author can try to change your behavior in two ways. First, he changes your beliefs. Then, he asks for a promise of action on your part. For example, the author might convince you that conservation is necessary. Then, you'd be asked to recycle waste products in order to conserve resources.

You find persuasive writing in educational, cultural, or historical documents. Like informative writing, it includes examples, statistics, comparisons, contrasts, and expert opinions.

WRITE TO LEARN

Choose an editorial from your school paper or local paper. After reading the editorial, write a short paragraph in which you identify what the writer would like you to believe and the question at issue. Were the purpose and question actually stated? If so, include the quote. If they were not, how did you know what the purpose and question were? Give examples of any information the author adds to back up the persuasion. Does the author attempt to use humor in order to convince you? If so, give examples.

Exercise 8.6   Answer briefly but completely.

Identify the purpose and question at issue for your thinking about the following situations.

1. Choosing a major

   Purpose _____

   Question at issue _____

2. Your grades in a class
   Purpose _____

   Question at issue _____
3. Your summer plans
   Purpose _____

   Question at issue _____

Identify the purpose for reading about the following topics:

4. An article about an upcoming election
   Purpose _____

   Question at issue _____
5. An article about AIDS research
   Purpose _____

   Question at issue _____
6. A chapter in a history text about the Vietnam War
   Purpose _____

   Question at issue _____
7. A chapter in a biology text about plant cells
   Purpose _____

   Question at issue _____

Identify the writer's purpose in writing about the following situations.

8. A writer who states "Some scientists believed that the accumulation of carbon dioxide and other human-generated gases were creating a 'greenhouse effect.' These gases, according to the theory, were preventing the escape of the sun's heat from the earth's atmosphere, causing the earth to heat up in much the same way an automobile with closed windows does on a summer day. . . . Geological records indicate that the earth goes through many cyclic changes of temperature and rainfall over time. We do not know what precise factors are most significant. . . . How much modern industrial practices have contributed is not clearly known."
   Purpose _____

   Question at issue _____
9. A writer who states, "Within a few weeks after first exposure, some HIV-infected persons develop a seven-to-fourteen-day illness with enlargement of the lymph glands, sore throat, fever, muscle aching, headache, and a skin rash that often looks like measles. HIV can be detected in circulating blood lymphocytes at this time, but tests for antibodies to HIV seldom become positive until six weeks to six months later. This early form of illness usually disappears or is so mild that it is not even remembered."
   Purpose _____

   Question at issue _____
10. A writer who states, "The relationship between the experience of past stress and current stress tolerance suggests that confidence in your ability to handle stress is an

important factor in how much tolerance you have. The greater your confidence that you can handle such threats to your adjustment as they come along, the less likely you are to experience events and changes as stressful. To put it another way, your past experience affects your cognitive evaluation of a situation."

Purpose _____

Question at issue _____

N: INTROSPECTION

The word *introspection* comes from the Latin word *introspectus,* meaning to look inward. In terms of critical thinking, introspection means using what you already know to think about and process new materials under consideration. This combination of old and new knowledge results in **inferences** and **interpretations.**

An inference can be defined as a statement or prediction about the unknown based on the known. The process of inferring involves interpreting information or occurrences to make predictions about the present or future or a guess about the past.

Making accurate predictions or educated guesses often poses problems because people who get identical information about a topic do not necessarily "see" or interpret the information in the same way. As a result, completely different predictions about what that information suggests could result. In other words, you form guesses and inferences by interpreting the information at hand in light of your background knowledge, assumptions, and point of view.

A particularly tragic example of differing inferences and interpretations using the same information involves the death of a Japanese exchange student in Baton Rouge, Louisiana, in October of 1992. Invited to a Halloween costume party, the student and his American friend attempted to find the home where a party was being held. By mistake, they went to the wrong address in a neighborhood that had recently experienced several burglaries. Since the homeowners who answered the knock were frightened, the man at the house came to the door with a gun. As the exchange student moved toward him saying, "We're here for the party," the man yelled "Freeze." The student, new to the United States and unfamiliar with that expression, continued to advance. The man inferred that only someone who intended harm would continue to move toward him. The man also inferred that since the intruder failed to "freeze," his intentions were to rob the home. Acting on his incorrect inference, the man shot the student, fatally wounding him. From the exchange student's point of view, he failed to infer that he was at risk because burglary and homicide are not societal problems in Japan. For the same reason, he did not interpret the command to freeze as a warning statement. The homeowner used his own background and new information to interpret the actions of the student as threatening. Ironically, the nonthreatening student was at risk, while the threatening homeowner was not.

Reconsider the example of the newspaper article about the basketball game on page 379. One of your favorite players often scores 20 to 30 points per game. As you read the article, you notice that he scored only 20 percent of his shots resulting in 10 points. Based on your knowledge of his past performance, you infer that he has some sort of problem—an illness, a worry, or an injury, perhaps. Someone who knew little of this player's background might read the same information and infer that he's not a very strong player. The information remains the same, but the interpretations result in very different inferences.

Exercise 8.7   Respond to the following using Sample Chapter 11, ''Personal Values, Career Planning, and Success with People at Work'' as a source.

1. Refer to pp. 519-520, "What Management Employees Can Expect from the Company." You are interviewing with XYZ company. What questions should you ask to ensure that XYZ adheres to basic obligations to employees?

_____

_____

_____

_____

2. Refer to pp. 522-524, "Developing Trust with the Boss." What are the implications of failure to meet each condition?

_____

_____

_____

_____

3. Refer to pp. 533-535, "Another Look: Which Corporate Culture Fits You?" What are the implications of the traits in terms of the four business cultures they represent?

_____

_____

_____

_____

D: *DECISION*

Fish, or cut bait.

—American proverb

You gathered the information you needed. You identified your purpose and questions. You analyzed your interpretations and inferences. Now it's time to make a decision and do it—in the words of the American proverb: to fish or to cut bait!

Since all critical thinking is done for a purpose, it must come to an end in a **conclusion** concerning the situation or a solution to the question at issue. In a way, the conclusion often brings you full circle in your thinking. You may reach some decision about the question at issue, but that decision might be to examine another question or gather more information before reaching a decision. A student who critically examines possible majors as a freshman may not reach a conclusion on the perfect major. Instead, that student may eliminate certain majors and begin the thinking process again as new courses and information become available. In some cases, two people begin with the same purpose and question and use the same information, but their individual points of view, assumptions, and inferences lead them to different decisions. For example, rational people armed with the same information about the death penalty often come to separate and different conclusions.

Whenever you reach conclusions, **implications,** or **consequences,** follow. Conclusions and implications/consequences are analogous to causes and effects. They form chain reactions; that is, a conclusion sets into motion a series of possible outcomes, or implications, and given outcomes, or consequences. For example, the implications and consequences of living in an apartment rather than at home or in a residence hall might include the need for transportation to and from your institution, the cost of turning on utilities, monthly bills, and cooking for yourself. Problems occur when conclusions are reached with little or no consideration of possible implications and probable consequences. Perhaps you rented an apartment within walking distance from the campus because you don't own a car, and your city provides no public transportation system. However, you failed to think about the need for transportation to a supermarket so that you could cook for yourself. Thus, reaching a conclusion or solving a problem requires that you carefully consider the implications and consequences of each available alternative before making a final decision.

Think again about the report of the basketball game. You had a purpose—to locate information—and a question at issue—who won the game. After reading the article, you found the information that answered your question. You might make inferences, but no decision needs to be made based on your original question. In other words, while you were thinking, you were not thinking critically.

Have you ever heard the phrase, "He met his Waterloo?" It means that the person in question suffered a crushing defeat. The etymology of the phrase alludes to the critical battle at Waterloo in which Napoleon Bonaparte lost the war to Prussia and, thus, lost his title as Emperor of France. Napoleon probably carefully considered his options and weighed the possible implications of victory or defeat before choosing to attack at Waterloo. Changing his mind might have changed the outcome of the war and its consequences on his career.

The outcome of most decisions can be rethought. Even decisions that appear monumental in scope can be altered. For example, perhaps you decided to live off campus because it offered you more privacy, more independence, and a change from living at home or on campus. However, you discovered your expenses were greater, you hated walking to campus in bad weather, you didn't like to cook for yourself, and you got lonely. At this point, you might feel compelled to stick to your decision. But, why? If you made a decision that isn't working, what's a better choice—being miserable or rethinking the situation and making another decision?

The notion of assessing and rethinking is, for some people, a new idea. Some people think that once you decide, you stick with that decision, no matter what. Assessing a decision gives you the power and the freedom to change your mind, your situation, and your life.

DECISION-MAKING PROCEDURES

It's been said that the only exercise some people get is jumping to conclusions, sidestepping responsibility, and pushing their luck. These same people exercise this way because they do not think critically. Hence, the decisions they make often involve hasty leaps, tricky stepping, and what they would probably call bad luck. You, the critical thinker, can label these conclusions as what they really are—faulty. You recognize that without a decision-making process, logical conclusions are difficult to make. You know the importance of considering assumptions, point of view, information, concepts, purpose, and the central question at issue in decision making. You also understand the importance of knowing about ways of thinking; having several plans for weighing implications; reaching a final conclusion; and assessing the consequences. In this process, **informal dialogues, balance sheets,** and **criteria matrices** are tools that can help you reach your final inference, your conclusion.

Informal Dialogue

Informal dialogue refutes the suggestion that the people who talk their heads off aren't losing much. That's because informal dialogue involves your talking about your possible decision and its implications both to others and to yourself. Speaking with others just makes sense. The old adage "Two heads are better than one" comes into play. Informal dialogue with others allows you to explore new points of view, acquire new information, and hear what others see as the implications of various issues. Placing possible solutions on the worksheet found in Table 8.3 provides you with an active way to see possibilities concretely.

How can you carry on a dialogue with yourself? You do so through **brainstorming.** Here you list on a piece of paper as many possible solutions as you can. List unbelievable, ridiculous, or even unacceptable solutions. Write any and all suggestions you can create, and try not to evaluate or edit any ideas until you've exhausted yourself on possible solutions. Brainstorming in this way releases you from tunnel vision and allows you to entertain ideas that could lead to a worthwhile and workable solution. Once you've completed your list, then you need to evaluate the information and add promising possibilities to your possible solutions worksheet. Evaluation questions appear in Table 8.4.

Many of the options you list on your worksheet will be unworkable due to the amount of money, time, or risk they involve. Eliminate these from your list. Doing so allows you to further reduce a long list into a more manageable size.

Table 8.3   Possible Solutions Worksheet

Possible Solutions Worksheet

Problem to Solve/Decision to Make _____

Possible Solutions	Positive Implications	Negative Implications

Table 8.4	Questions for Evaluating Brainstorming Activities

1. How does each possibility measure up?
2. Which possibility seems most workable and worthwhile?
3. What possibility has the best chance to succeed?
4. How risky is each possibility?
5. Which possibility seems most preferable?

Adapted from Pokras, S. (1995). *Team problem solving: Solving problems systematically.* Menlo Park, Calif. Crisp Publications.

Table 8.5	Balance Sheet for Making a Decision

PROJECTED GAINS FOR SELF	PROJECTED LOSSES FOR SELF
PROJECTED GAINS FOR OTHERS	PROJECTED LOSSES FOR OTHERS
PROJECTED SELF-APPROVAL	PROJECTED SELF-DISAPPROVAL
PROJECTED APPROVAL FOR OTHERS	PROJECTED DISAPPROVAL FROM OTHERS

Balance Sheet

According to Janis and Mann (1977), a balance sheet (see Table 8.5) of pluses and minuses helps you logically weigh your available options. They found that balance sheet users regretted their choices less often and were more likely to stick to their decisions. To create a balance sheet, you record projected gains and losses for yourself; projected gains and losses for others; projected self-approval or self-disapproval; and projected approval or disapproval of others.

While the balance sheet gives you only your odds, it's value lies in making explicit the possible implications involved in the options you are weighing. What do you stand to gain? What might you lose in the bargain? The decision remains yours. You determine how much risk you're willing to take or the level of safety you want to maintain.

Exercise 8.8   List below a situation in which you need to make a decision. Assess the situation as objectively as possible. Then assess from another point of view. (You may ask someone to provide this for you.) Generate and list three possible options. Then, on separate sheets of paper, create a balance sheet to explore each possibility. Identify the type of conflict each option involves. Then choose the option you plan to pursue.

1. a. SITUATION: _____

    _____

   b. YOUR ASSESSMENT: _____

    _____

    _____

   c. SECOND ASSESSMENT: _____

    _____

    _____

   d. OPTION 1: _____

   e. OPTION 2: _____

   f. OPTION 3: _____

   g. CONFLICT IN OPTION 1: _____

   h. CONFLICT IN OPTION 2: _____

   i. CONFLICT IN OPTION 3: _____

   j. WRITE BALANCE SHEET ON SEPARATE PAPER.

   k. DECISION: _____

Criteria Matrix

Much like a balance sheet, a criteria matrix allows you to see options and evaluate them. Here, however, you identify beforehand the standards, or criteria, you will use for evaluation and the scale by which you will evaluate them. Criteria usually include those aspects of the decision which seem most important to you. For example, if you were deciding whether to purchase school insurance, you might use *cost, level of risk,* and *effect of illness on your coursework* as possible criteria. Scales for ratings include + or –, grades—*A, B,* or *C* or *A, C,* or *F,* and numeric scales like 1 to 3, 1 to 5, or 1 to 10.

To complete a criteria matrix (see Table 8.6), you list possible solutions in the left-hand column of the matrix. Then you list criteria across the top; remember to abbreviate, if necessary. Next, you need to rate your possibilities against each criteria. If you use a numeric scale, add up each row to get the score for each possibility.

ENACTING YOUR DECISIONS

Consider the role of the explorer. Explorers venture into the unknown—sometimes damned if they do, and sometimes damned if they don't.

You can and you can't
You shall and you shan't;
You will and you won't
You'll be damned if you do,
And you'll be damned if you don't.

—LORENZO DOW

Nineteenth Century American Evangelist

Table 8.6   Criteria Matrix

Rating Scale:

Problem to be Solved/Decision to be Made: _____

Alternative Solutions	Evaluation Criteria	Summary Rating

Adapted from Pokras, S. (1995). *Team problem solving: Solving problems systematically.* Menlo Park, Calif.: Crisp Publications.

Enacting a decision requires the same sort of risk taking. It also mandates commitment and effort. Table 8.7 gives you some tips for putting your decisions into motion.

APPLYING STANDARDS TO THINKING

A **standard** is another word for a flag—a piece of colored fabric that serves as a symbol or signaling device. Flags express victory, honor, loyalty, hope, pride, and many other messages about a person or a group

Table 8.7   Tips for Enacting Decisions

1. Set a reasonable deadline for enacting your decision. Doing so gives you a target to aim for.

2. Think of your decision positively instead of negatively. You, like others, probably tend to think in major concepts. Sometimes your mind overlooks the small details. A decision *not* to score less than a *C* on any test in the semester sounds like a good one. However, instead of stating your goal negatively (''I do not want to score less than a *C* on any test in the semester''), a positive way to think about that choice would be to say ''I intend to score a *C* or better on every test in the semester.''

3. Make your decisions dependent on only you. Forming a study group the week before the final exam seems like a good goal . . . unless everyone gets sick or otherwise fails to show up. If you depend on others for success on the test, you may be disappointed with the results.

4. Use others for support. This seems like a contradiction of the previous suggestion; however, there is a difference. While not making a decision contingent on others, you should use others only for help and assistance. This kind of network provides you with information, advice, and friendship.

5. Visualize success. Once you make a choice, do you find yourself constantly doubting your decision? Do you picture the worst possible outcome? Most people tend to mentally replay their personal errors and mistakes until they've rehearsed them well enough that they happen again and again. If you tend to replay images of your past mistakes, you may also be rehearsing images of future mistakes. You can avoid some problems by visualizing and rehearsing the success of your decision rather than its failure.

6. Become aware of self-sabotage; instead, set yourself up for success. What do you do to shortchange your decisions? If you decide to study, do you put yourself in situations (dorm room, student center, kitchen, etc.) in which you might be unable to concentrate? What could you do to set yourself up for success? Organize your study area? Choose a quiet location? Unplug the telephone?

of people. The symbols a person or country chooses to use on a flag tells a lot about how a person or country thinks and believes as well as what it values.

Standard is also another word for the criterion or rule against which you judge or measure success. Like the standard that is synonymous with flag, a standard expresses messages about what you think and what you value. To paraphrase Crane, you may not always get to choose the situations in which you must think critically, but you can set the standards by which you will judge your success in thinking in whatever situations you encounter. These standards help you focus, govern, and guide the thinking process. They provide benchmarks to assist you in assessing or evaluating the effectiveness of your thinking. Just as someone who paints as a hobby differs from an artist whose paintings hang in the Louvre, a thinker who thinks without standards differs from one who applies standards to evaluate thinking.

Classroom Types

By Val Cheatham

$2 \times (4+3)$	$\dfrac{4 \times 2}{3}$	$3+(4-2)$	$\dfrac{3 \times 2}{4}$	$4 \times (3+2)$
$\dfrac{3 \times 4}{2}$	$\dfrac{2 \times 3}{4}$	$2-(4+3)$	$3-(4+2)$	$4 \times (3-2)$
$3-2 \times 4$	$2+2$	$\dfrac{2 \times 2}{3+3}$	$3+2-4$	$3-3$
$\dfrac{2+2}{4}$	$3 \times 2+4$	$3 \times (2+4)$	$\dfrac{4-3}{2}$	$\dfrac{3+4}{2}$
$4-2$	$2 \times 3+4$	$(2+2)=4$	$3-2$	$\dfrac{3+2}{4}$
		$\dfrac{3 \times 4}{2}$		

"Now that we all know how to set up the equation, who can tell me the correct answer?"

Although every standard theoretically applies to each aspect of thinking, the use or lack of use of some standards in conjunction with particular components affects the outcome of thinking more directly. For example, clarity of information affects all aspects of thinking from your information to your analysis of your assumptions to your identification of implications and consequences. However, some standards are less applicable in terms of other aspects of thinking. For instance, the standards of fairness and consistency impact question and purpose less than they affect point of view or information. Table 8.8 compares MIND components to applicable standards.

WRITE TO LEARN

On a separate sheet of paper, or in your journal, list the standards you will use to judge your success in college. How do they differ, if at all, from the standards you used to judge your success in high school or on a job.

CLARITY

If you've ever thought you understood a lecture, only to find out later

Table 8.8 Comparison of MIND Components to Applicable Standards

	Clarity	Accuracy Precision Specificity	Relevance Significance	Depth Breadth Complete-ness	Fair Consistency	Logic Justifibilty
MATERIALS						
information	X	X	X	X	X	X
assumptions	X				X	X
point of view	X			X	X	X
INQUIRY						
purpose	X	X	X			X
questions	X	X	X		X	X
INTROSPECTION						
inferences/ implications	X	X	X	X	X	x
DECISION						
conclusions	X	X	X	X	X	X
implications	X	X	X	X	X	X
consequences	X	X	X	X	X	X

that you were completely off base, you've experienced a lack of understanding. But what causes such misunderstandings? Was the professor unclear in giving information or was your thinking unclear? Whatever the case, **clarity,** or clearness, of thought forms the first standard against which you judge thinking. If you fail to express or understand a situation, idea, or assumption clearly, you cannot apply the other standards effectively. For example, although businesses spend billions of dollars on advertising each year, some ads backfire as the result of lack of clarity in language. Translating American ad slogans into foreign languages is particularly tricky. When advertisers tried to translate Coca-cola in phonetic Chinese symbols, they used the symbols for "Co" "Ca" "Co" "La." Unluckily, that means "Bite the wax tadpole." When General Motors introduced the Chevrolet Nova in Latin America, they discovered that the Spanish translation of nova is "doesn't go." In both cases, lack of clarity resulted in great misunderstandings. Clarity, then, forms the foundation for evaluation of thought because it assesses understanding. And, without understanding, no further thinking can occur.

While the concept of clarity—clearness or transparency of thought and language—seems obvious, applying the standard is often difficult. In situations where you can verbally discuss or question the clarity of information, you can paraphrase what you think you understand and ask for confirmation of meaning. For example, perhaps your math instructor says, "A convex *n*-gon is an *n*-sided polygon with the property that a straight line segment between any two points of the polygon is entirely within the polygon." Your response might be, "So, a triangle would be a convex *n*-gon because you can draw a line from any point to any other point inside the triangle and it remains in the triangle. But, a crescent is not a convex *n*-gon because a line from one tip to the other would be outside the shape." If your instructor agrees with your translation, you know that you clearly understand the information. In asking questions for clarity, you might try prefacing the information you don't understand with information you do understand. For example, using the information on the convex *n*-gon, you might say, "I understand that an *n*-sided polygon can be called a convex *n*-gon, but I don't understand what you mean about the line segment property." Expressing information this way gives your instructor a place to start in clarifying information.

In analyzing information for clarity, you should look for one or more of the following: concrete examples, vocabulary and ideas that you understand, or metaphors or analogies. Although you can't always ask for confirmation, putting information in your own words—either in written or verbal form—often helps you attain clarity. You can also look words up in a dictionary or use a thesaurus for clarification of meaning. Finally, you can look for a variety of other resources on the topic, which may express the information in a way that is more clear to you.

ACCURACY, PRECISION, AND SPECIFICITY

What are you afraid of? Whatever it is, there is probably a term that exactly defines your fear. Such fears are called phobias and research shows that the average person possesses three phobias. Over 150 words have been coined to express our fears. Do you faint at the sight of blood? Perhaps you have hematophobia, or fear of the sight of blood. Do you dislike confinement in small spaces? You might have claustrophobia, or fear of enclosed spaces. You could even suffer from dromophobia (fear of crossing streets), telephonophobia (fear of using the telephone), or even verbaphobia (fear of words). Whatever the case, there is a term that specifies the concept you fear in accurate and precise terms.

Once you satisfy the standard of clarity, you analyze your thoughts in terms, **accuracy, precision,** and **specificity.** Accuracy refers to correctness, while precision concerns exactness. Specificity suggests a limiting of details so that you exclude particulars to identify a single item. To further illustrate these concepts, imagine that you must take two science courses for your major, and you need to decide which course to take this term. You look in the catalog and notice that freshman-level science courses consist of two courses in each of the following: biology, chemistry, physics, and astronomy. At this point, any choice you make about science would be accurate. However, in reading the catalog more closely, you see that one science must be biological and one science must be physical. To follow the directions in the catalog precisely, you would not be able to take both courses in biology. You could, however, choose one biology and one chemistry. To make sure that you enter the beginning-level course for your first science class, you sign up for Biology 101. That is the specific course that you are choosing. You limited which course in biology you wanted to the first-semester freshman course and excluded the rest. There will be no doubt in the registrar's mind which biology course you want.

RELEVANCE AND SIGNIFICANCE

Imagine that you went on a cruise that, unluckily, ran into an unexpected hurricane. Your ship begins to sink. Not knowing what will happen, you race around the ship gathering supplies. You find the following items: a flashlight and some batteries, a short-wave radio, a chest full of money, a case of canned food, ten gallons of water, a gun, another passenger, and a raincoat. You realize that you will only be able to carry three items on the two-person lifeboat. Which three will you choose? As you make your decisions, you face questions of **relevance** and **significance.**

Relevance, as indicated previously in this chapter, means to be connected to something else. Significance refers to importance. The distinction between them lies in the application of the terms. For example, suppose you and your roommate want to choose a cable TV package for this term. As an incentive for buying, one package offers an extra channel featuring children's programing for free if you enroll in the next week. Since the programs on that channel fail to interest either of you, the free channel is not relevant to your decision. As you look at the other features and cost of the cable packages, you notice that the two packages under consideration differ by $10.00 a month or $120.00 a year. You choose the cheaper package. That information was not only relevant in your decision making, it became an important or significant factor in your decision.

BREADTH, DEPTH, AND COMPLETENESS

What do you see in the following figure? This image, called Necker's Cube, combines an unstable figure with an illusory figure. In an unstable figure, contradictory cues affect depth perception making it difficult to determine which part of the figure is closer to you. In this case, when you look once one side appears closer. Look again, and the other side appears closer. To be an illusory figure, you see things that are not actually there. In most figures, lines and shapes form the image with paper and space forming the background. Here you see a complete geometric figure even though no lines form it. You used your background knowledge to "fill in" the spaces and create a full image.

In many ways, this figure depicts the roles of **breadth, depth,** and **completeness** in thinking. As you make decisions or think about issues, you must also consider the amount and quality of the information you have. Just as you can look at the image in more than one way, breadth suggests that you consider more than one viewpoint, kind of information, implication, or other aspect of thinking. Depth considers the level of complexity of the thought much like this three-dimensional image is more complex than a two-dimensional figure. Completeness requires that you have all of the information to form a comprehensive picture—either from the information itself or combined with your own background knowledge.

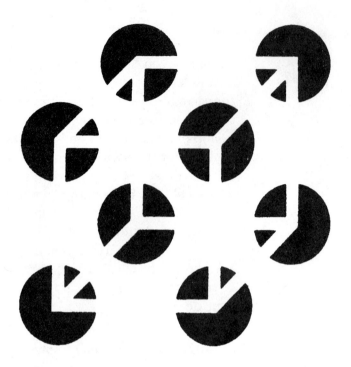

Choice of a particular college or university provides an example for examining these standards. For example, if you wanted to attend an institution that allows you to major in international business and gives you an opportunity to participate in an internship in South America, you would not want to consider just one institution and its program. That would not give you a broad base with which to make a decision. At the same time, reading just the catalog information about the courses would not afford the same depth that you would gain from visiting the institution and talking with the faculty. And finally, before you make a decision, you would need to have all of the information about each college or university that you are considering in order to have information that is complete enough to make a decision.

FAIRNESS AND CONSISTENCY

The standards of **fairness** and **consistency** help you examine the ways in which thinking is done as well as the quality of the thinking. Comparisons help you determine fairness and consistency in information. A variety of different sources often provides a more balanced and fair view. Thus, if you have three treatments of the same information by three different individuals, similarities help you pinpoint consistencies and fair, unbiased coverage of the topic. Or, within a single document, you look for biased language or incompatible information in order to assess fairness and consistency.

For example, suppose you want your friend to be elected as student body president. But, as chairman of the group that schedules debates in the student union, you neglect to give information about the upcoming debate to the strongest opponent. You did not treat the information fairly and may have manipulated the outcome of the election. Consistency suggests that you apply the same criteria all of the time. In the case of the election, if you gave each candidate ten minutes to speak, followed by five minutes for questions, you would need to treat each candidate in the same way to be both fair and consistent.

LOGIC AND JUSTIFIABILITY

A professor at a local college was noted for his practical approach to life. He always insisted that there were logical and justifiable explanations for everything. Naturally, his friends were surprised to see that he carried a lucky rabbit's foot keychain. "Why do you use that?" one of them asked. "Surely you don't believe that old superstition that a rabbit's foot brings good luck." "Of course I don't believe it," growled the professor, "but I understand that it's supposed to work whether you believe it or not." "Just remember," said his friend, "it didn't bring much luck to the rabbit."

Logic and **justifiability** form two final standards against which to judge thought. Logic suggests that thinking or problem solving follows a line of reasoning that others can understand. In other words, it makes sense. You begin with a problem and, after looking at the information and your interpretation of it, you choose a decision that makes sense. In the case of the professor, his decision to hang on to a rabbit's foot does not actually make sense. In fact, from the rabbit's point of view, it's not justifiable at all—it certainly didn't work for the rabbit. Thus, beyond just knowing that something makes sense, you need to be able to list the reasons so that others can follow your thought processes in decision making.

Exercise 8.9   Create a chart with the following headings at the top: High degree of comfort, Rationale, Low degree of comfort, Rationale, Strategies for change. List the standards for assessing components of MIND vertically on the left. Using your favorite course as the subject of your consideration, complete the chart as follows: In column 1, check the standards you feel most comfortable using in this subject. Describe why you feel comfortable using these in column 2. In column 3, check which of the standards you feel least comfortable using in this subject. Describe why you feel uncomfortable using these in column 4. For each standard checked in column 4, identify a strategy for increasing your level of comfort in column 5.

Create a second chart using your least favorite course as the subject of your consideration. What accounts for similarities and differences between the charts?

Exercise 8.10   Reread the introduction to Sample Chapter 12, ``The Industrial Revolution and Its Impact on European Society.'' Then answer the questions below as a way of using MIND to identify information from a text.

1. What are your assumptions about the Industrial Revolution?

   _____

   _____

   _____

   _____

2. What is your point of view as you read/learn about the Industrial Revolution?

   _____

   _____

   _____

   _____

3. What concepts pertaining to the Industrial Revolution are discussed in this introduction? List them below, one concept per line.

   _____

   _____

   _____

   _____

   _____

   _____

   _____

   _____

   _____

   _____

4. Beside each concept listed in your answer to the preceding question, identify information to support it.

5. a. What is the author's purpose for including this introduction?

   _____

   _____

   b. What is your purpose for reading it?

   _____

   _____

   _____

   _____

6. a. What is the question at issue for the author?

   _____

   b. What is the question at issue for you?

   _____

   _____

   _____

   _____

7. a. What inferences can you make about the Industrial Revolution?

   _____

   _____

   _____

   _____

   b. What inferences can you make about the topics discussed in this chapter?

   _____

   _____

   _____

   _____

8. What ultimate conclusion do you make about the Industrial Revolution?

   _____

   _____

   _____

   _____

9. What are implications of that conclusion?

   _____

   _____

   _____

10. What consequences have resulted from the Industrial Revolution?

   _____

   _____

   _____

   _____

Exercise 8.11   Read the sample short story ``Strange Inventions.'' Then answer the following questions.

1. From what point of view does John Muir write this story?

_____

_____

_____

_____

2. Suppose Muir had written about his life when he was fifteen years old. How might his account of his life change? What would account for this change?

_____

_____

_____

_____

3. Suppose Muir had written about his life when he was fifteen years old. How might his description of his father change? What would account for this change?

_____

_____

_____

_____

4. Identify three examples of bias in "Strange Inventions." What accounts for this bias?

_____

_____

_____

_____

5. Should a young Muir have written this story, would there also be bias? If so, what would account for this?

_____

_____

_____

_____

6. Identify three examples of euphemistic or loaded language in this story.

_____

_____

_____

_____

7. Identify five concepts in this story. List them below, one per line. Then identify information to support these concepts.

_____

_____

_____

_____

_____

_____

_____

_____

_____

_____

GROUP LEARNING ACTIVITY
STEREOTYPES: DEBUNKING ARCHIE BUNKER

Archie Bunker, a character in TV's "All in the Family," was known for branding people and behavior. Uncritical thinkers—like Archie—often think in stereotypes. These are typical images or conceptions held by members of a specific group or applied to a person, group, or idea. Like Archie, you probably believe some form of stereotypes. That's because you've never examined these ideas to find why you hold them.

Application

What stereotypes do you hold? What stereotypes might apply to you?
    Determine how each person in your group defines each person in the following pairs. What does each one do? How would he/she or they act? What facts and opinions apply to each one? How does the concept of relevance apply to each one? Discuss your responses and conclusions with the group.

1. College Student/Retiree
2. Employer/Employee
3. American/Foreigner
4. Gang Member/Police
5. Priest/Atheist
6. Kindergarten Teacher/Professor
7. Two-Year-Old Child/Adult
8. Democrat/Republican
9. Men/Women
10. Vietnam Veteran/Desert Shield Veteran

Application

How do stereotypes impact your ability to think critically? What examples could debunk these stereotypes? How does this activity change the way you think about these groups and yourself?

CHAPTER SUMMARY

1. Critical thinking involves examination of materials (information, concepts, assumptions, point of view), establishing purposes and asking questions through inquiry, introspection to make inferences and interpretations, and making and enacting a decision (conclusion about the issue based on implications and consequences).

2. Evaluating information involves determining relevance, checking credibility, identifying facts, evaluating opinions, noting expert opinions, and recognizing propaganda and bias.

3. The critical thinker also needs to recognize the reader's as well as the author's purposes in both informational and persuasive writing.

4. Introspection concerns logical reasoning such as deductive and inductive processes and illogical reasoning identified by recognizing both fallacies in deductive reasoning and illogical inductive reasoning.

5. Decision-making procedures include informal dialogues, balance sheets, and criteria matrices.

6. Critical thinking mandates the application of standards such as clarity, accuracy, precision, specificity, relevance, significance, breadth, depth, completeness, fairness, consistency, logic, and justifiability.

CHAPTER REVIEW

TERMS

Terms appear in the order in which they occurred in chapter.

critical thinking
MIND
information
concepts
assumptions
point of view
relevance
credibility
facts
primary sources
secondary sources
weasel words
opinions
definitional
    assumption
expert opinions
bias
propaganda
euphemisms
loaded words
purpose
questions
inferences
interpretations
conclusion
implications
consequences
informal dialogues
balance sheets
criteria matrices
brainstorming
standard
clarity
accuracy
(*terms continued*)

1. List three of the courses in which you are now enrolled. For each course, what do you think it means for you to think like a professional in that field? For example, how would a mathematician think? How do assignments in each course contribute, or fail to contribute, to your ability to think like a professional in the field?

     _____

     _____

     _____

     _____

     _____

     _____

2. What does it mean to discipline and control your thinking? Is discipline and control the same for every subject or does it differ by topic? Explain your point of view.

     _____

     _____

     _____

     _____

     _____

     _____

3. Reread the section on introspection. Using the text from that section, identify one example of a concept and one example of information related to that concept.

     _____

     _____

     _____

     _____

     _____

     _____

4. Imagine that you could discuss your ability to think critically with three of the following individuals: your parents or guardians, your best friend, your first-grade teacher, your employer, your favorite high school teacher, one of your current professors. For each individual that you choose, give two examples of each person's assumptions about you. How does each person's point of view

TERMS

precision
specificity
relevance
significance
breadth
depth
completeness
fairness
consistency
logic
justifiability

affect those assumptions? Use the following chart to record your answers

INDIVIDUAL	PERSPECTIVE	ASSUMPTIONS

5. Consider one of your academic goals (e.g., to complete an undergraduate degree, to make a 3.0 (*B*) average at the end of this term, to complete a lab assignment in chemistry). State your goal. Then describe how each step of MIND can help you achieve that goal.

GOAL _____

M _____

I _____

N _____

D _____

6. You have a job in the Admissions Department at your college. One of your assignments is to call prospective students and provide them with information about your institution. What three concepts do you think are most important for a new student to know about postsecondary education? What one assumption might you need to refute about your institution? What question about your institution should new students ask?

IMPORTANT CONCEPTS _____

_____

INCORRECT ASSUMPTIONS _____

_____

QUESTIONS _____

_____

7. Choose one of your textbooks and turn to Chapter 3. Respond to the following based on the content of that chapter:
Identify three to five concepts that appear to be most important to the understanding of the content. How did you make this determination? What assumptions do you have about the content of this chapter? What questions might you have about the content?

_____

_____

_____

_____

_____

8. It has been said that thinking is essentially interesting while memorization is essentially uninteresting. Why would this be so? How might using the MIND approach result in more interesting thinking about a topic?

_____

_____

_____

_____

9. List three inferences you made about your college in terms of your major. How do you interpret these inferences in terms of your ability to get a job after you complete your coursework?

_____

_____

_____

_____

10. Using a separate sheet of paper, respond to the following questionnaire on nutrition:
    A. Identify the categories of food as described in the food pyramid.
    B. Describe how your eating habits and patterns have changed since entering college.
    C. Describe a typical breakfast meal that you regularly eat.
    D. Describe a typical lunch or dinner that you regularly eat.
    E. Describe the snacks you regularly eat.

    Using the questionnaire and your responses, identify three concepts important to the subject of nutrition. Identify two assumptions you make about nutrition. Define your point of view. Other than completion of an assignment, what might be your purpose for completing the questionnaire? What questions do you have as a result of your responses? How do you interpret the results of the questionnaire? How might those results impact a decision to maintain or alter current eating habits? In what ways could you assess your thinking process on this issue?

_____

_____

_____

_____

_____

_____

11. In terms of grades in the courses you take, how could you use the standards described in this chapter to evaluate your progress in a course?

_____

_____

_____

_____

12. Courts often hear cases in which homicide is said to be justified. In terms of law, how are the concepts of justice and justifiability alike? How are they different? What would be an example of justifiable homicide? How would justice be served in this case?

_____

_____

_____

_____

_____

REFERENCES

Anderson, R.C., and Pitchert, J.W. (1978). Recall of previously unrecallable information following a shift in perspective. *Journal of Verbal Learning and Verbal Behavior, 17:* 1-12.

Owen, D. (1990). The Best Teacher I Ever Had. *Life, 13, 70.*

Paul, R.W. (1990). Critical thinking: What every person needs to survive in a rapidly changing world. Rohnert Park: Center for Critical Thinking and Moral Critique.

ANSWER FOR ANALYSIS FIGURE

No. Because you are looking at concentric circles, *not* a spiral.

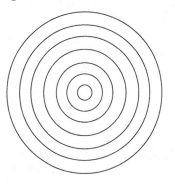

Vocabulary Development   Connotation: Know What I Mean?

An elderly woman watched MTV for a long time. She turned to her son and asked, "But what does it all mean?" College coursework and life exposes you to a variety of situations, people, and ideas. Appearances are often deceiving, and things are not always what they seem. You, too, may find yourself wondering just what everything means.

Postsecondary education helps you refine your ability to analyze and evaluate experience and find meaning. Words, too, represent a variety of situations, people, and ideas. Your ability to think critically about their meanings, both in connotation and denotation, helps you understand the courses you take, as well as life in general.

Jim Varney, star of such movies as "Ernest Goes to Camp" and "Ernest's Christmas," first created the character of Ernest P. Worrell for an amusement park commercial. A country bumpkin, Ernest constantly harasses an off-screen character named Vern with the phrase, "Know what I mean, Vern?" Vocabulary development is a constant analysis to discover the answer to "Know what I mean?" in college coursework.

Words actually have two meanings. The first is the denotation—the literal, or dictionary definition. The second is the connotation. This includes the way a word is understood and used by the text or lecturer, as well as your own understanding of what a word means. You derive these implied meanings from hearing, reading, speaking, writing, and experiencing the word in everyday life. For example, a sociology class might study labor unions. The denotation of *labor union* would be "an organization of wage earners designed to improve the economic interests and general working conditions of its members." Your experiences might provide you with your own connotations. If your experiences were good, you might define a labor union as a benevolent group that works for the common good and supports its members. If your experiences were not favorable, (for example, your family's company was financially ruined by a union strike), you might think of a labor union as a ruthless group that destroys companies and the people associated with it.

The words an author or lecturer chooses and uses provide insights into what they really mean—both in literal meaning and implied connotations. The words you use in responding to class discussions or writing assignments similarly require the listener or reader to know what you mean. Vocabulary development occurs when you critically consider connotation as well as denotation in listening, reading, speaking, and writing.

Activity 1

For each of the following taken from an anthropology chapter entitled "Culture: The Ideas and Products People Adopt and Create," list your connotation for the boldface words or phrases. Then, using a dictionary, provide the word's denotation. Contrast your connotation and the word's definition.

Derek Freeman, another ethnographer who studied the Samoan culture between 1940 and 1967, reported evidence that contradicted Mean's findings
(Freeman, 1983). Contrary to Mead's report, the Samoan **adolescents** that
Freeman describes are aggressive, **impulsive,** status-hungry, violent, and sexu-
ally "hung up."

1. **adolescents**

    Connotation _____

    _____

    Denotation _____

    _____

    Contrast _____

    _____

2. **impulsive**

    Connotation _____

    _____

    Denotation _____

    _____

    Contrast _____

    _____

In his Inaugural Address, George Bush suggested what he hoped to be the
values of his Presidency," a **summons** back to the **patrician** values of restraint
and responsibility.

3. **summons**

    Connotation _____

    _____

    Denotation _____

    _____

    Contrast _____

    _____

4. **patrician**

    Connotation _____

    _____

    Denotation _____

    _____

    Contrast _____

    _____

The youth movement of the 1960s, the Hare Krishna religious **sect,** and the **Amish** are examples of countercultures. The theme of the youth movement of the sixties was that success and materialism were misguided goals for individuals in society. Love, peace and sharing was the suggested alternative. The **"hippies"** (as they were called) who flourished in such communities as Haight-Ashbury in San Francisco and the East Village in New York have virtually disappeared.

5. **sect**

Connotation _____

_____

Denotation _____

_____

Contrast _____

_____

6. **Amish**

Connotation _____

_____

Denotation _____

_____

Contrast _____

_____

7. **"hippies"**

Connotation _____

_____

Denotation _____

_____

Contrast _____

_____

Activity 2

On a separate sheet of paper, describe how the differences between your connotations and the word's denotation changed your understanding of the word's meaning? Give one example and explain.

CHAPTER 9

Making Your Way through the Maze: Library and Research Skills

OBJECTIVES

By the end of this chapter you should be able to do the following:

1. Describe ways in which a librarian can assist you in developing library and research skills.

2. Compare and contrast different ways in which libraries may be organized.

3. Create a working bibliography and identify research skills.

4. Compare general references, specialized content references, and computerized references.

5. Identify the steps in the research process.

CHAPTER MAP

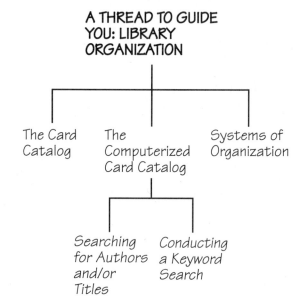

SOMEONE TO ASSIST YOU: THE LIBRARIAN

A THREAD TO GUIDE YOU: LIBRARY ORGANIZATION

The Card Catalog

The Computerized Card Catalog

Systems of Organization

Searching for Authors and/or Titles

Conducting a Keyword Search

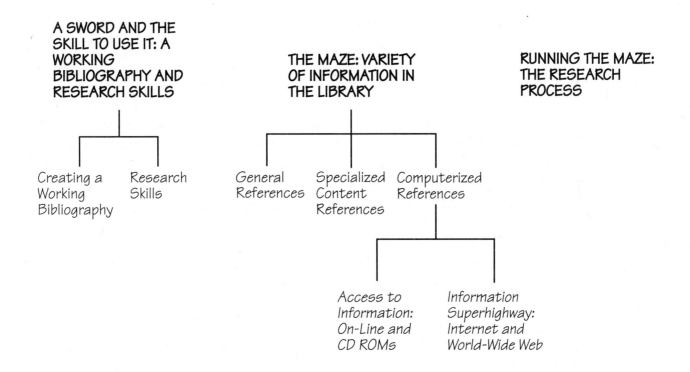

A Greek myth tells how the Minotaur, a creature with a man's body and a bull's head, was imprisoned in a maze by King Minos of Crete. The Minotaur, the strongest creature of the time, was fed seven young men and seven young women each year. A young prince named Theseus posed as one of the young men so he could kill the Minotaur. He took with him a sword given to him by his father. He also carried a ball of thread given to him by Ariadne, daughter of Minos. He used the thread to help him mark his way. After a systematic search, he found the Minotaur and killed it with his sword. Then, using the thread as a guide, he returned to freedom.

If you have ever spent time trying to find information in a library, you probably know how Theseus felt. You, too, were trapped in a maze, facing what seemed to be dead ends. You needed what Theseus had— someone to assist you, a thread to help you find information and guide you through a library's maze of materials, and a sword and the skill to use it.

SOMEONE TO ASSIST YOU: THE LIBRARIAN

If you are confused by a library's maze of information, you need the assistance of someone like Ariadne to help you find your way in the library. That person is the librarian or librarian assistant.

A librarian or a librarian assistant is one of the most helpful people you can know on campus. Asking politely for assistance and remembering to thank the librarian for help pay off. The librarian knows what sources of information and services the library offers. The librarian can direct you to ones you may overlook. Librarians also know about materials and services of other libraries. Often they can help you secure materials from them through an **interlibrary loan.**

You don't always have to go to the library in person in order to get assistance. If you need a quick answer to a simple question (e.g., verification of a reference, correct spelling of a word, availability of a particular book), a phone call to the library often gets you the help you need. Some libraries also provide reference assistance by e-mail.

Complex questions require more time from both you and the librarian. Libraries, like other departments, often have peak time periods at which every student on campus appears to be working on papers or requiring other library assistance. To be sure a librarian has a block of time to devote to your needs, schedule a reference interview or appointment. This enables the librarian to provide you with undivided attention, and it gives you an opportunity to fully explain the requirements of your project (e.g., the nature of your topic, your approach to the topic, the kinds of references you've already examined, suggestions from your instructor, and so on). This is a better approach than asking, "Do you have any books on . . . ?"

Librarians spend years learning about a wide variety of reference materials. Trained to aid students who are looking for specific information, librarians are much more than clerical people who keep up with the library's inventory. Librarians are more like travel agents who guide you in your library search. Perhaps the most valuable travel advice librarians offer concerns the way your campus library is organized.

Exercise 9.1   Provide the following information about your campus library:

1. Library's hours.

_____

_____

_____

2. Policy on overdue books.

_____

_____

_____

3. The titles of five books found in the ready reference section.

_____

_____

_____

4. The titles of three indices.

_____

5. The titles of three computerized indices.

6. The location of current and bound periodicals.

7. Available media services.

8. The location of a map of the library holdings.

9. The location of the card catalog or computerized card catalog.

10. The name of your librarian.

11. The location of the microfiche reader.

12. The location of general collection books.

A THREAD TO GUIDE YOU: LIBRARY ORGANIZATION

The thread that marks your way through the maze of library information is the **card catalog.** Your library uses the **Library of Congress (LC)** or the **Dewey decimal** system to help you locate what you need. Libraries create and use their own variations of the card catalog and these location systems. That's not a problem for you, however. You need only know the general framework of the system your library uses. For example, the LC system of classification is the Library of Congress system of subject headings. A book is classified by its subject(s) and then assigned a call number—a location number. The card catalog provides an organized inventory of the library's information to help you locate what you need quickly and easily. Such inventories are stored either in files or in a computerized **database.** Because the catalog is crucial to finding materials, libraries usually place the files or computer terminals in the front or center of the library.

THE CARD CATALOG

Catalogs kept in files require you to manually search for information. Sets of drawers contain cards, at least one for each book in the library. Drawers are labeled on the outside, much like encyclopedias, to tell you what they contain. Cards, filed alphabetically, help you find what you need. Three cards for each **nonfiction** publication in the library are made before the book is shelved: the **author card** or **main entry card,** the **subject card,** and the **title card.** The catalog usually contains only title and author cards for **fiction.**

Each card provides information about the author, publisher, contents, and **call number** of the book. Each type of card gives this information in a different order (see Figure 9.1). Author information includes the author's name (last name first) followed by the dates of the author's birth and death. Publishing facts tell who published the book and when and where it was published. Content information consists of the number of pages, if there are maps and illustrations, a brief description of the contents, and cross-references.

At the bottom of a card, there are two distinct kinds of references. Those numbered with arabic numerals list the subjects of the book; these are subjects taken from the Library of Congress List of Subject Headings. A book may fall into several categories and each of these will be listed. There will be a card for each of the subject headings. One book may have as many subject cards as necessary to cover its content. The value of subject references on a library card is that they lead a researcher to the appropriate subject headings for his or her topic.

References listed with uppercase Roman numerals are additional cards found in the author/title catalogue. These are tracings, and their primary function is to facilitate catalogue maintenance. (If a book is withdrawn from the collection, they enable the librarian to locate the complete card set for the item.)

Figure 9.1   Example of Dewey Decimal Author, Title, and Subject Cards

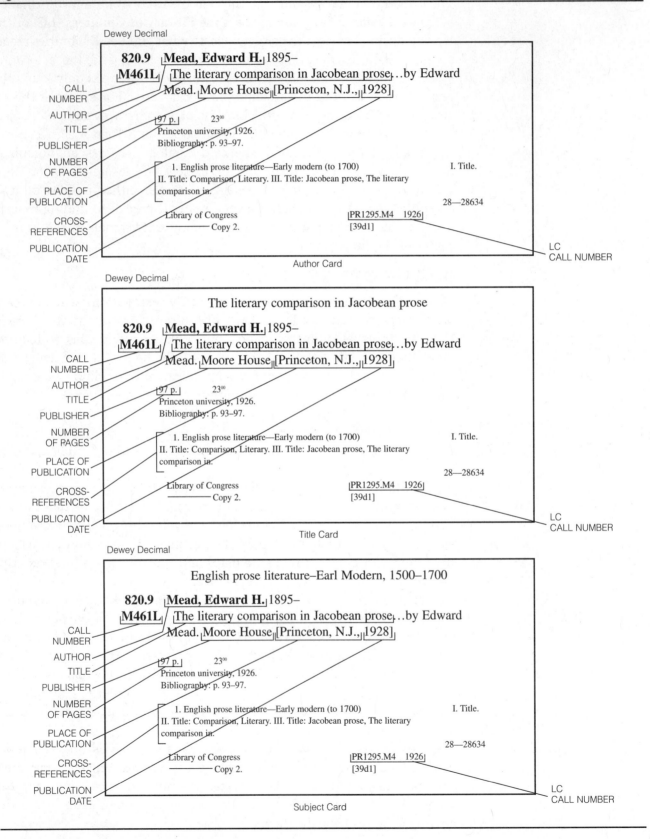

Cross references are a part of the catalogue mechanism. There are two major types: *see* and *see also*. *See* references lead the researcher from an incorrect heading to a correct heading. If, for example, one looked up "gladness," one would find a card reading "see cheerfulness." Pursuing this happy subject further, when one had found the card for "cheerfulness," one would read "see also happiness, optimism." Although current cataloging practice uses pseudonyms, there are *see* cards in the author/ title catalogue directing the researcher from a pseudonym to the author's real name, for example, "Eliot, George" see "Evans, Marian."

The call number, formed from either the Dewey decimal or the Library of Congress system, reflects content, author's name, and publication date. It is found in the upper left corner of each catalog card and on the spine or cover of each publication. The call number not only indicates where the material is kept in the library but also identifies how your library is organized.

Searching by subject is an effective way to locate information as long as you search by the right descriptors. The Library of Congress publishes a special book that lists the specific terms it uses to define subjects. Your librarian can help you locate this book and provide suggestions about its use.

To save space, some libraries store their card listings on **microfiche.** Microfiche, one of many types of **microforms,** is a piece of photographic film usually 4 by 6 inches. Such film is kept in files similar to those containing cards. However, one piece of film actually holds dozens of cards, greatly reduced in size. To read it, you enlarge the print with a machine called a **microfiche reader.** Like other microforms, a microfiche card catalog saves space, is cheaper to produce, and can be updated quickly.

THE COMPUTERIZED CARD CATALOG

In many libraries, the card catalog has been replaced either partially or entirely by an on-line catalog accessible through a computer terminal. A computerized card catalog allows you to find information more quickly because the computer does the work for you. It searches all entries for the author, subject, or title you need. Sometimes such a system uses specialized subject headings. A list of these is kept in a manual near the computer terminal. Some libraries develop their own catalog systems, but many others alter ready-made software to fit their collections. The examples in this text are from NOTIS, a widely used system developed at Northwestern University.

The features and commands for differing on-line systems vary. The commands are the symbols and/or terms that are used to access information (see Figure 9.2). Figures 9.3 through 9.5 show sample screens from the NOTIS system.

Figure 9.2   Commands for Retrieving Information Using NOTIS

Author search	a = author's name; last name first
Title search	t = exact title of the publication; ignore *a*, *an*, and *the* if they are the first word in a title
Subject search	s = appropriate subject heading
Keyword search	k = important ideas or concepts

Figure 9.3   Introductory Screen

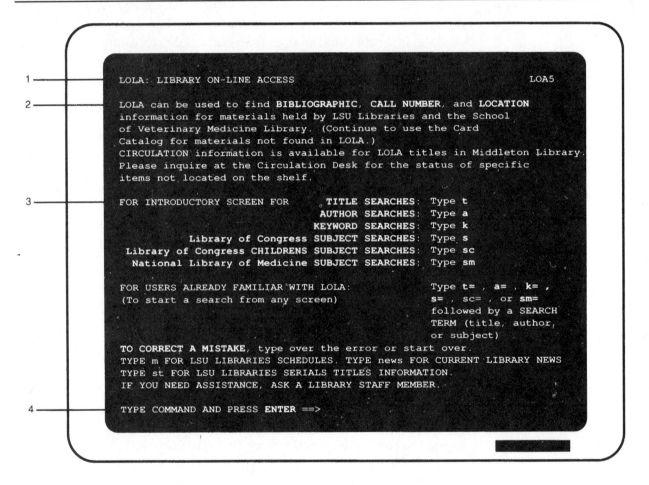

```
LOLA: LIBRARY ON-LINE ACCESS                                    LOA5

LOLA can be used to find BIBLIOGRAPHIC, CALL NUMBER, and LOCATION
information for materials held by LSU Libraries and the School
of Veterinary Medicine Library. (Continue to use the Card
Catalog for materials not found in LOLA.)
CIRCULATION information is available for LOLA titles in Middleton Library.
Please inquire at the Circulation Desk for the status of specific
items not located on the shelf.

FOR INTRODUCTORY SCREEN FOR        TITLE SEARCHES: Type t
                                  AUTHOR SEARCHES: Type a
                                 KEYWORD SEARCHES: Type k
           Library of Congress SUBJECT SEARCHES: Type s
   Library of Congress CHILDRENS SUBJECT SEARCHES: Type sc
     National Library of Medicine SUBJECT SEARCHES: Type sm

FOR USERS ALREADY FAMILIAR WITH LOLA:            Type t= , a= , k= ,
(To start a search from any screen)              s= , sc= , or sm=
                                                 followed by a SEARCH
                                                 TERM (title, author,
                                                 or subject)
TO CORRECT A MISTAKE, type over the error or start over.
TYPE m FOR LSU LIBRARIES SCHEDULES. TYPE news FOR CURRENT LIBRARY NEWS
TYPE st FOR LSU LIBRARIES SERIALS TITLES INFORMATION.
IF YOU NEED ASSISTANCE, ASK A LIBRARY STAFF MEMBER.

TYPE COMMAND AND PRESS ENTER ==>
```

1. Acronym used for Library On-Line Access.
2. Introductory information provides general data about the system. Since this is necessarily brief, libraries often provide more comprehensive written instructions.
3. List the kinds of searches available on the system and the commands needed to find materials by author, title, subject or keyword.
4. Information needed to access the database.

Figure 9.4   Subject and Title Index Screen

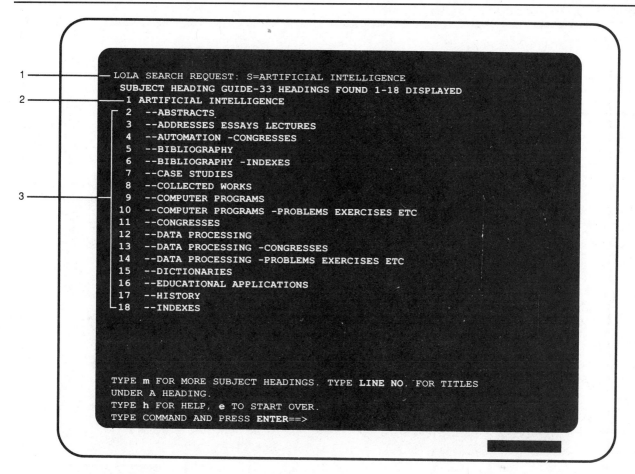

```
— LOLA SEARCH REQUEST: S=ARTIFICIAL INTELLIGENCE
   SUBJECT HEADING GUIDE-33 HEADINGS FOUND 1-18 DISPLAYED
   1 ARTIFICIAL INTELLIGENCE
   2   --ABSTRACTS
   3   --ADDRESSES ESSAYS LECTURES
   4   --AUTOMATION -CONGRESSES
   5   --BIBLIOGRAPHY
   6   --BIBLIOGRAPHY -INDEXES
   7   --CASE STUDIES
   8   --COLLECTED WORKS
   9   --COMPUTER PROGRAMS
   10  --COMPUTER PROGRAMS -PROBLEMS EXERCISES ETC
   11  --CONGRESSES
   12  --DATA PROCESSING
   13  --DATA PROCESSING -CONGRESSES
   14  --DATA PROCESSING -PROBLEMS EXERCISES ETC
   15  --DICTIONARIES
   16  --EDUCATIONAL APPLICATIONS
   17  --HISTORY
   18  --INDEXES




   TYPE m FOR MORE SUBJECT HEADINGS. TYPE LINE NO. FOR TITLES
   UNDER A HEADING.
   TYPE h FOR HELP, e TO START OVER.
   TYPE COMMAND AND PRESS ENTER==>
```

1. Number 1 entered to go from subject heading guide to the subject title index
   Number 7 selected to go to the bibliographic record screen
   Number 11 selected to go to the bibliographic record screen
2. Example of a reference to a government publication. Call number is a SuDocs number. GP, dodd indicates that the book is in the documents collection.
3. Both MD and midl indicate that book is in the Middleton Library.

Searching for Authors and/or Titles

Although you don't have to be a computer whiz to use a computerized database, exact spelling is essential. While some databases allow you to abbreviate or omit words or parts of words, you need to follow standardized rules for doing so. Table 9.1 supplies some of those rules.

Conducting a Keyword Search

A keyword search is different from searching for a specific author or title. You perform a keyword search for one of two reasons: when you have incomplete or uncertain information about an author or title or when you are unsure of the correct subject heading or when the most appropriate subject heading is not included in the database.

Keyword searches are executed the same way as title, author, and subject searches. When the search is completed, what you have is every

Figure 9.5   Author and Title Index Screen

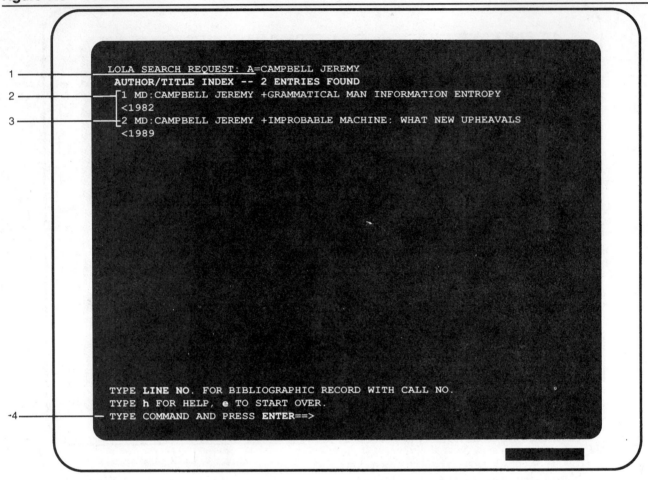

```
LOLA SEARCH REQUEST: A=CAMPBELL JEREMY
 AUTHOR/TITLE INDEX -- 2 ENTRIES FOUND
 1 MD:CAMPBELL JEREMY +GRAMMATICAL MAN INFORMATION ENTROPY
 <1982
 2 MD:CAMPBELL JEREMY +IMPROBABLE MACHINE: WHAT NEW UPHEAVALS
 <1989




 TYPE LINE NO. FOR BIBLIOGRAPHIC RECORD WITH CALL NO.
 TYPE h FOR HELP, e TO START OVER.
 TYPE COMMAND AND PRESS ENTER==>
```

1. Command entered into the system to access this screen.
2. Numbers 1–2. List of book titles available in the database under the author's name.
3. Number entered to access the complete bibliographic record for the book, *The Improbable Machine* by Jeremy Campbell.
4. Instructions needed to enter the database.

record in the database that contains the key word. Figure 9.6 shows a partial listing of what you might get if you type the command "k = dog." Because keyword searches retrieve so much information, it is important that you carefully select your key words. Doing so limits the number of entries you must read to find the information you seek. Table 9.2 provides you with some suggestions for limiting your keyword search.

WRITE TO LEARN

A friend of yours is not in this class but is taking a course in which he must write a term paper. On a separate sheet of paper, explain to him how to use a card catalog or a computerized database, whichever your college library has.

Table 9.1   Rules for Abbreviating Reference Titles

• Abbreviate from right to left. For example, *Dictionary of Recreational Education* becomes *Dictionary of Recreational Ed.*
• Use standard abbreviations, for example, *Psych* for psychology and *J* for journal.
• Omit *a, an,* and *the* (and foreign language equivalents) from titles and begin the search command with the first word that follows the article.
• Enter initials, acronyms, abbreviations, numbers, and dates exactly as they appear in the title. For example, if you are looking for the book *100 Ways to Manage Time Better,* type *100 Ways to Manage Time Better,* not *One Hundred Ways to Manage Time Better.*
• Type two dashes between the primary subject heading and all subdivisions.
• To avoid confusion and save time in searches, avoid using common last names without first names or initials.

Figure 9.6   Partial Listing for "k = dog"

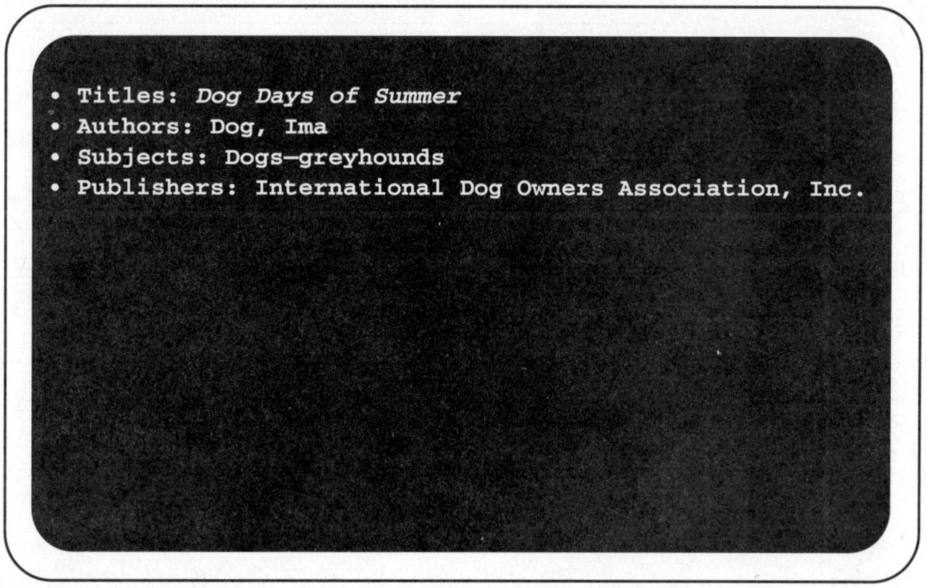

```
• Titles: Dog Days of Summer
• Authors: Dog, Ima
• Subjects: Dogs—greyhounds
• Publishers: International Dog Owners Association, Inc.
```

Table 9.2   Suggestions for Limiting Your Keyword Search

• Omit *a, an,* and *the* (and foreign language equivalents) from titles and begin the search command with the first word that follows the article.
• Avoid common words such as *and, by, from, for, in, not, of, or, same, to,* and *with.* These words are so common the computer cannot search for them and may actually stop the search.
• Avoid broad, general words such as *geography* and *music.*

1. Which of the following books are in your library? List call numbers and dates of publication for each one.
   The Chinese Welfare System—John E. Dixon

   _____

   Early American Furniture—Morton Yamon

   _____

   Challenges in Mental Retardation—Geimar Dybward

   _____

   Law and the Jungle—Harvey Ellsworth Newbranch

   _____

   A General Income Tax Analyzer—John Bossons

   _____

2. Who wrote *One Man's America*?

   _____

3. List the call numbers of each of the following subjects: architecture, music, education, computer science, and psychology.

   _____

   _____

4. How many books does your library hold under the listing *pineapple*? What types of books (that is, fiction, nonfiction, reference, and so on) are included under this listing?

   _____

   _____

5. List three books that your library has on nuclear energy.

   _____

   _____

6. List three periodicals that are found on microfiche or microfilm in your library.

   _____

   _____

7. Photocopy the title page from one article found on microfiche or microfilm.
8. Do your library holdings include ERIC documents? If so, what are they used for?

   _____

   _____

9. On separate sheets of paper, copy, one author, one title, and one subject card or screen and label their parts.
10. Identify three daily newspapers to which your library subscribes.

   _____

   _____

SYSTEMS OF ORGANIZATION

Libraries use the Library of Congress and/or the Dewey decimal systems to organize nonfiction materials. The numbers in these systems form the call number of the material and indicate where the material is shelved.

Many large research and university libraries use the LC system. Its advantages over the Dewey decimal system include its precision and capability for expansion. A combination of capital letters and numbers classify and identify books. The first letter indicates the general topic (see Table 9.3). The second letter represents a subject of that topic. The numbers further specify the subject. A second line identifies the book's author and edition.

Some libraries use an older but just as effective system of classifying materials called the Dewey decimal system. This method classifies materials into ten major categories (see Table 9.3). Its cll numbers also are written in two lines. The top line is the Dewey decimal classification number (three digits with decimals indicating more specific classifications). The bottom line identifies the book's author and edition.

Table 9.3   Comparison of the Dewey Decimal and Library of Congress Systems

Subject	Dewey Decimal	Library of Congress
General works	000	A
Philosophy and psychology	100	B
Religion	200	BL-BX
History	900	C-E
Geography	910	G
Social science	300	H
Political science	320, 350	J
Law	340	K
Education	370	L
Music	780	M
Fine arts	700	N
Language	400	P
Literature	800	P
Pure science	500	Q
Medicine	610	R
Agriculture	630	S
Applied science and technology	600	T
Military science	355	U
Naval science	359	V
Bibliography	010	Z

A SWORD AND THE SKILL TO USE IT: A WORKING BIBLIOGRAPHY AND RESEARCH SKILLS

To reach his goal of killing the Minotaur, Theseus needed a weapon and the skill to use it. In meeting your goal of finding information within the library, you also need a weapon—a **working bibliography**—and the skill to use it—research skills.

CREATING A WORKING BIBLIOGRAPHY

A working bibliography consists of a list of materials found on a topic after a survey of the card catalog. To compile this list, you record the titles, authors, dates of publication, and call numbers of materials that seem relevant to your topic and worth your consideration (see Table 9.4). Writing each item of this list on an index card provides a permanent record of possible references.

Another way to develop a working bibliography is through the use of a computer search of special databases. Such a search generally requires the assistance of the librarian or other staff member in identifying the most appropriate database and explaining necessary procedures for its use. The computer printout serves the same purpose as the self-made notebook of references. The computer search has two advan-

Table 9.4   Checklist for Judging the Relevance of References

1. Who is the author? Do you know anything about the author's reputation?

2. If you cannot judge the author's qualifications or reputation, does the author have more than one publication on this topic?

3. If you cannot judge the author's qualifications, depth of writing experience, or reputation, what is the reputation of the publisher?

4. When was the material published? Is information of this time period relevant to your research?

5. Does the material contain a bibliography?

6. Does the material contain appendices?

7. Does the material contain illustrations?

8. Was this publication considered worthy of reprinting?

9. Have you seen other publications reference this publication?

10. If a book, has the information in it been updated through the publication of subsequent editions?

tages over the self-prepared working bibliography. First, it identifies references you may overlook. Second, it takes you less time and effort to find possible sources of information. The major disadvantage of computer searches is cost. Unless you consider time equal to money, the self-made working bibliography is free compared to the fees charged for computer searches. Rates vary from one database service to another. Rates also vary within services depending on the time of day or day of the week.

RESEARCH SKILLS

After acquiring your working bibliography, you are ready to begin searching for and evaluating materials. First, you locate the references on the shelves. Then, you survey the pertinent features of the material. Next, you skim or scan these features to decide if the material fits your needs. Skimming and scanning speed the process of selecting or eliminating materials. Skimming is a means of quickly understanding what a publication is generally about, its main idea. Scanning helps you find specific details. In evaluating the relevance of material, you use your skimming and scanning skills at the same time (see Table 9.5). Finally, you note information or eliminate unsuitable materials.

After you survey materials and decide that you want to use information contained in them in your paper, take notes, or make photocopies of the information for later use. Whatever method you choose, it's important to reference your notes or photocopies with complete bibliographical information (title, author, publisher, place and date of publication, volume or issue number, and page numbers) for later identification.

If you only need a small amount of information, notetaking is sufficient (see Table 9.6). If you need a larger amount or complex graphics, photocopying may be more useful. You need to be aware that laws limit the number of photocopies made from a single source. However, for educational research purposes, the laws allow single copies to be made of a small percentage of the total material.

Notes consist of two basic types: **direct quotes** and summaries or paraphrases of main ideas and specific details (see Figure 9.7). Direct quotes are exactly what an author says about a topic. They leave no room for your opinion or thoughts. A **summary** or a **paraphrase,** likewise, contains an unbiased version of what the author said. This version, however, is written in your own words. It is your attempt to condense and clarify information.

You record a direct quote exactly as it is written and note its original source. You identify a direct quote as such by using quotation marks to set it apart from other statements. When a quote contains information that you think is unnecessary or unimportant, you may omit it only if you indicate that you are doing so. You show this omission by placing an

---

Table 9.5 Important Features to Survey in Evaluating Books

1. Survey the title page and copyright page (usually found on the back of the title page) to answer:

   a. What is the complete title of this material?

   b. Who wrote the material?

   c. What is the author's title and professional affiliation?

   d. What occupation, position, titles, education, experience, and so forth qualifies this author to write on this topic?

   e. Is this material collected from other sources?

   f. If so, who edited the collection?

   g. Who is the publisher of the material?

   h. When and where was the material published?

   i. Have there been other editions or revisions?

2. Scan the table of contents to determine:

   a. How is the book organized?

   b. Are topics important to you covered and how many pages are devoted to them?

   c. How does the coverage in this material compare with other references?

3. Scan the preface or introduction to discover:

   a. What is the author's point of view?

   b. Why did the author write this material?

   c. What information is covered in the material?

   d. Does the author's experience and scholarship seem sufficient for a thorough discussion of the topic?

   e. What method of research or data collection was used—personal opinions, personal experience, interviews, library research, surveys, clinical experiments, or other?

   f. To what audience is this material addressed?

---

ellipsis, three dots (. . .), where the missing information normally would appear.

Summaries or paraphrases state main ideas and supporting details or examples in your own words. They include specific details that are new or important points or concepts. Van Dijk and Kintch (1978) identified five basic rules essential to summarization. Table 9.7 lists these as steps—with slight variations—for you to follow in summarizing or paraphrasing information.

Table 9.5 Important Features to Survey in Evaluating Books (cont.)

4. Scan the bibliography, a listing of references used in the material, to answer:

    a. Does the author give primary sources (the actual words of an identified person, a historical document, a literary work, and so on) rather than secondary sources (other authors' descriptions of the original events)?

    b. Does the length of the bibliography indicate the scholarship of the author?

    c. Does the bibliography contain references you can use to further research your topic?

    d. Does the bibliography include articles by other authorities in the field besides the author?

5. Scan the index (an alphabetical listing of important topics included in the material) to answer:

    a. Are topics important to you covered?

    b. How many pages are devoted to them?

6. Scan, then skim, important terms in the materials' glossary (a small dictionary of terms used in the material) to decide:

    a. Do terms have specialized definitions?

    b. Are terms defined clearly and completely?

    c. Do the meanings of terms provide new insights into the topic?

Table 9.6 Steps in Taking Research Notes

1. Use note cards or regular-sized pieces of paper to record important information.

2. Write all notes about one topic on the same piece of paper or note card. If you need additional space, be sure to keep notes on the same topic together.

3. Write notes using a standard format.

4. If taking notes on large amounts of information, use the same shorthand system you use when taking notes in class (see Chapter 4).

5. Cross-reference information.

Figure 9.7   Examples of Direct Quotes and Summaries or Paraphrases

Intact Text

Most messages are sent with signals. Animals use singing, growling, chirping, roaring, and other sounds to warn and attract others. Baboons display their huge canine teeth to threaten one another. Dogs and other animals raise their hackles to intimidate; some apes pound their chests. Animals also use gestures to attract mates. Dances, feather displays. and other signals convey mating intentions.

Sloshberg, W. and NesSmith, W. (1983). <u>Contemporary American Society: An Introduction to the Social Sciences</u> St. Paul, MN: West Publishers, p. 65.

Direct Quote

"Animals use singing, growling, chirping, roaring and other sounds to warn and attract others. Animals also use gestures to attract mates."

Sloshberg, W. and NesSmith, W. (1983). <u>Contemporary American Society: An Introduction to the Social Sciences</u> St. Paul, MN: West Publishers, p. 65.

Summary/Paraphrase

Animals use sounds and gestures as signals to warn and attract other animals

Sloshberg, W. and NesSmith, W. (1983). <u>Contemporary American Society: An Introduction to the Social Sciences</u> St. Paul, MN: West Publishers, p. 65.

Table 9.7	Steps in Writing Summaries or Paraphrases

1. Delete unimportant information.

2. Delete repeated information.

3. Group similar objects and concepts; find an identifying word for this group. (For example, group *pears, bananas, apples,* and *peaches* as *fruit.*)

4. Write important details in your own words.

5. Locate the topic sentence of the passage.

6. Once you locate the topic sentence, restate it in your own words. If you cannot locate the topic sentence, compose your own.

Exercise 9.3   Use Sample Chapter, ``Personal Values, Career Planning, and Success with People at Work,'' to identify two pieces of information that you could use as direct quotes. Then summarize or paraphrase this same information.

Exercise 9.4   In the space provided below, use the rules in Table 9.7 to write a summary or paraphrase of any one of the case situations in Sample Chapter 13, "An Invitation to Computers."

_____

_____

_____

_____

_____

_____

_____

_____

_____

_____

_____

_____

_____

_____

_____

_____

_____

WRITE TO LEARN

On a separate sheet of paper, compare and contrast the characteristics of a working bibliography and the bibliography that should be included with your final draft.

THE MAZE: VARIETY OF INFORMATION IN THE LIBRARY

To many students, the **stacks** in the library resemble the Minotaur's maze. In the past, knowing your way through the stacks was sufficient for doing library research. However, modern libraries reflect the ever-increasing influx of knowledge, both in the size and formats of their collections. Although materials in the stacks remain a major part of today's libraries, a variety of other collections and sources provide you with innumerable references.

GENERAL REFERENCES

General references are vast in number and scope. Because of their utility to large numbers of students, they need to be kept available. Most libraries store these books in **ready reference.** They keep others in a reserved section of the library. Libraries either do not allow such books to be checked out or check them out only for limited periods of time.

"Medieval history . . . on a bearing of N37°E go 400 feet, then S15°E 175 feet."

Reserve books are books that are temporarily removed from the stacks at the request of faculty member. This is done to ensure that a book is not checked out for a long period of time, making it unavailable as a reference for their students.

General **periodical indices** do for journals what the card catalog does for other materials. They list authors, titles, and subjects of articles in many periodicals. They also include cross-references. The *Reader's Guide to Periodical Literature* is a common index of general and nontechnical journals and magazines. An alphabetical listing includes authors and subjects of articles. Entries provide information for finding specific articles (see Figure 9.8).

Accurate research often depends on knowing exactly what is meant by the words that describe the topic. A library's holdings usually include two general sources about word meanings. The first source is the

Figure 9.8   Example of *Reader's Guide* Entry

Marketing

See also

Booksellers and bookselling

Market group to launch book coupon drive. *Publ Wkly* 230:19 Ag 8 '86

MPBA research explores independent bookstore customer. *Publ Wkly* 230:48 S 26 '86

The power of positive marketing [Guideposts home Bible study program marketed by mail] E. Bence. *Publ Wkly* 230:43–4 O 3 '86

Preservation

See Books—Conservation and restoration.

Prices

U.S. book title output and average prices. 1983–1985. C. B. Grannis. il *Publ Wkly* 230:89–92 O 3 '86

Statistics

Best sellers

Paperback books

Royalties

Talking books

Textbooks

The yestermorrow of the book [reprint from January 1972 issue] M. McLuhan. il *UNESCO Cour* 39:50-1 My/Je '86

Advertising

Giveaways, gimmicks and gizmos [children's book promotions] A. M. Martin. il *Publ Wkly* 230:164-6 Jl 25 '86.

Mine the midlist [promoting trade novels] K. Ray. por *Publ Wkly* 230:76 Ag 15 '86

SUBJECT

ARTICLE TITLE

VOLUME NUMBER

MONTH/DATE/YEAR

CROSS-REFERENCE

PERIODICAL

ILLUSTRATIONS

AUTHOR

Care

See Books—Conservation and restoration

Censorship

See Censorship

Collectors and collecting

See also

Libraries. Private

Oliver Optic (William T. Adams): nineteenth-century novelist's books are collectible. D. E. Matter and R. M. Matter. il *Hobbies* 91:52–4 S '86

Conservation and restoration

Rescuing old papers [deacidification] S. Budiansky. il *U S News World Rep* 101:84 S 22 '86

Dedications

See Dedications (in books)

Figure 9.8   Example of *Reader's Guide* Entry *continued*

Exhibitions
See Book exhibits

Export-import trade
Beyond the 10% tariff [tariff on books exported to Canada] P. Yaffe. por *Publ Wkly* 230:76 Ag 1 '86

Canada's writers oppose 'free trade' talks [trade with U.S.] P. Adams. *Publ Wkly* 230:98 Jl 25 '86

Eight firms win against California importer [copyright infringement lawsuit against J. B. Stark] M. Yen. *Publ Wkly* 230:14 Ag 1 '86

Selling books in China. J. Chan. il *Publ Wkly* 230:23–6 Ag 8 '86

U.S. exports, imports, UNESCO reports. C. B. Grannis. il *Publ Wkly* 230:96–8 S 19 '86

Illustration
See Illustration

Manufacture
See Book industries

SOURCE: *Reader's Guide to Periodical Literature* © 1986 by the H. W. Wilson Company. Material reproduced by permission of the publisher.

---

unabridged dictionary, the most comprehensive general dictionary found in a library. It lists all words used in the English language, including obsolete words, scientific terms, and proper names. Definitions include word histories, quotations, related terms, and other information. A **thesaurus** provides a second general source for finding words. It identifies synonyms, antonyms, and related words for specific headings. Like a dictionary, this aids you in finding other key words that identify your topic.

Some types of information cannot be put in book form. The **vertical file** or **clipping file** holds materials of this type. These include pamphlets, newspaper and magazine clippings, pictures, circulars, and bulletins. Such materials are stored in large manila folders or envelopes. The envelopes are arranged alphabetically by subject in a vertical file cabinet.

Almanacs or **yearbooks** provide information about government, industry, politics, commerce, world events, sports, and almost any other topic. Updated yearly, they contain statistical, tabular, and general information.

The most logical sources of current information are daily and/or weekly newspapers. Current issues of local, state, and national papers are shelved or displayed racks in your library. Some libraries also display newspapers from other countries. Newspapers may or may not be indexed. This causes no problems, however. If you find the date of a particular event in any **newspaper index,** other papers probably carried reports of that event the same day. Examples of such indices include *Facts on File* (weekly summaries of world news), the *New York Times Index* (summaries of *New York Times* articles), and the *Wall Street Journal Today* (a yearly list of its financial and business articles).

Atlases and **gazetteers** provide geographical information. An atlas contains a collection of topographical, climatic, geological, economic, and political maps. These maps are arranged alphabetically according to region. Atlases often include gazetteers, which are general dictionaries of geographical names. A gazetteer lists names of places, seas, mountains, and so on. Entries cover pronunciation, classification, population, height, length, area, and points of interest.

Books of quotations identify well-known or important statements by general topic and by their sources. *Bartlett's Familiar Quotations* indexes information by subject and author.

General biographical indices or dictionaries report information about the lives of important people. Facts include birth and death dates, nationality, profession, accomplishments, and other personal and professional information. Examples of such dictionaries include *Who's Who in America, Who Was Who in America,* and *Current Biography. Who's Who in America,* updated every other year, contains information about notable living Americans. *Who Was Who in America,* includes information on important deceased Americans. Published since 1940, each year's volume of *Current Biography* contains an illustrated description and a short biography about living important world figures.

Government documents are materials published by municipal, state, and federal governmental agencies. They include detailed information on governmental policies and procedures as well as almost any other topic. Because of the volume and variety of publications, identifying the agency that publishes the one you need poses a problem. Writing to your representative or senator or the Government Printing Office aids in finding the proper department and the publication you need. In addition, some libraries possess a collection of government documents. *The U.S. Government Organization Manual* and the *Monthly Catalog of United States Government Publications* index federal government publications.

Exercise 9.5   Match each reference with its corresponding phrase.

_____ 1. Periodical

a. Temporarily removed from stacks at instructor's request.

_____ 2. *Reader's Guide*

b. Index of general and nontechnical journals and magazines

_____ 3. Reserve books

c. Materials in reduced format

_____ 4. Microforms
_____ 5. Vertical file
_____ 6. Newspaper
_____ 7. Gazetteer
_____ 8. Almanac
_____ 9. *Who Was Who in America?*
_____ 10. Newspaper index

d. Dictionary of geographical names
e. Index of the most up-to-date information
f. Clipping file
g. Contains biography of Martin Luther King
h. Current events published annually
i. Provides the most up-to-date information
j. Magazine or journal

Exercise 9.6   Answer the following questions using references in your campus library. Indicate the title of the reference that you used to locate the answer.

1. Which city is farther north: Duluth, Minnesota, or Toronto, Canada? Which city is farther south: Tijuana, Mexico, or Houston, Texas?

_____

_____

Reference type: _____

2. What lines from Dorothy Parker's *Resumé* describe her feelings about suicide?

_____

_____

Reference type: _____

3. On what day in October 1987 did the stock market suffer a 508-point drop?

_____

_____

_____

Reference type: _____

4. What was the leading cause of death among Americans in 1985?

_____

_____

Reference type: _____

5. List three synonyms for *ghat.*

_____

_____

Reference type: _____

_____

_____

6. What magazine in August 1987 contained the article "God and Money"? Who wrote the article?

_____

_____

Reference type: _____

7. What is the title of the microfiche that has the ERIC Document Reproduction Service number 136189?

_____

_____

Reference type: _____

8. Who said, "The cruelest lies are often told in silence"?

_____

Reference type: _____

9. Define *paparazzi.*

_____

_____

Reference type: _____

10. Who was Clarence Darrow?

_____

_____

Reference type: _____

SPECIALIZED CONTENT REFERENCES

The sources of general and specific information you'll use depend upon your interests and the courses you are taking. You need not be familiar with every publication your library owns, but you need to know how to find the information for your particular course.

Specialized content reference books list and briefly describe various sources on a particular subject. Two such references many libraries keep on ready reference are A. J. Walford's *Guide to Reference Material* and Eugene P. Sheehy's *Guide to Reference Books,* both published by the American Library Association. *Guide to Reference Material* consists of three volumes. Volume 1 deals with science and technology; volume 2 concerns social and historical sciences, as well as philosophy and religion; and volume 3 includes generalities, languages, the arts, and literature. *Guide to Reference Books* is a one-volume index of general references, humanities, social sciences, history and area studies, and pure and applied science. Another guide that is briefer and less costly than library sources is

Reference Books: A Brief Guide, published by Enoch Pratt Free Library (400 Cathedral Street, Baltimore, MD 21201). Every four or five years, Enoch Pratt Free Library updates this helpful 180-page booklet. With it, you have a personal reference book at your fingertips.

WRITE TO LEARN

On a separate sheet of paper, identify the general reference that would be of most use to you in your chosen major. Explain your choice.

COMPUTERIZED REFERENCES

In today's libraries, many references no longer physically exist anywhere. The use of stand-alone and on-line computers revolutionized access to information. Instead of painstakingly copying bibliographic information, you often can download the references you want and print the results. Instead of searching for a specific piece of information through mountains of books, you can search electronic texts. Instead of using the resources of only your library, you can use on-line access to search libraries and research facilities across the country and around the world.

Access to Information: On-line and CD-ROMs

Computers allow you to use and search information electronically. On-line access provides you with information from another computer at a remote site—either somewhere else on your campus, within your college system, in another state, or even in another country. The information you search usually consists of a database (collections of information such as phone lists, bibliographic references, summaries of articles) from which you can extract specific pieces.

Libraries subscribe to database services and provide on-line access to science, social science, and humanities databases. Such databases include indices and abstracts; full-text materials; collections of raw data; and directories to other information.

You search a database via a terminal at the library or a microcomputer with a modem. You choose key words for your search with the use of special thesauruses that accompany the databases. You may be able to access some databases yourself; however, you may need to make an appointment with a librarian to use other databases.

On-line searches benefit you as a researcher in a number of ways. First, they save you time and effort. They also provide access to information other than that available in your campus's or college system's holdings. Information obtained through on-line searches is often more current than that derived from print formats.

Although on-line searching has many advantages, it does have a few flaws. First, on-line searches involve some expense. Thus, you must weigh the worth of your time against the amount of money you want to spend. Second, the logic of database searching sometimes fails because of the ambiguity of the English language. Thus, if you want to search for information on Apple computers and use only the key word *apple,* you'll probably get information on fruits as well as on computers. Your librarian can help you select key word and qualifiers (e.g., *and, or, not*) so that you locate the information you need while excluding irrelevant topics. Third, while databases may provide you with the latest information, they often do not include older references and materials.

Databases are also available on stand-alone computers that use CD-ROM drives to access information. Because a CD stores much less data than mainframe computers, separate databases are stored on single CDs or, in some cases, collections of CDs. In addition to databases, CDs also store other types of information including visual and auditory data. With new information pressed on CDs all the time, the array of multimedia materials available in these formats ranges from three-dimensional models of molecules, which can be rotated to show different perspectives, to full texts of the classics of literature. Your librarian can show you what CDs are available at your library and instruct you in their use.

Information Superhighway: Internet and World Wide Web

During the 1960s, the U.S. Department of Defense created a special system of computers to connect key locations in case of nuclear or other disaster. What made the system special was that there really was no system. There was no hub, no central switching location, and no governing authority to administer the system. Instead, the computers formed an interconnected network through which information traveled, more or less independently, from sender to receiver. In the 1960s and 1970s, some colleges and universities, as well as government research labs, also joined the network. As time went on, other countries joined, making it an international network. During the mid 1980s, the National Science Foundation (NSF) built the data lines to form a backbone for the network, and in 1992, the NSF lifted commercial restrictions. This made the **Internet** available to virtually anyone with a computer and modem access and created an information superhighway with millions of users and a theoretically unlimited source of information.

The Internet continues to be a worldwide nonsystem. Nobody controls or owns the Internet. The only thing constant about it is its lack of constancy. Information on the Internet is in a constant state of change as knowledge expands and explodes. Information on the Internet, then, is more up-to-date than other sources that require commercial publication and distribution. You can access information on the Internet through your campus library, computer center or other department, or through a commercial on-line service.

In terms of references, the Internet taps into the holdings and bibliographies of a number of large university libraries. For example, the University of Minnesota offers a comprehensive list of libraries accessible through Gopher, a special browsing service it created for Internet users around the world. However, the Internet represents literally millions of computers around the world. As such, it provides instant access to a variety of information from books in electronic form to displays of art, from advice to discussion groups, and from research in Australia to literature from France. It also provides standard references such as the *Concise Oxford Dictionary, Oxford Dictionary of Familiar Quotations, the Encyclopedia Britannica,* and *Roget's Thesaurus.* Your library or computer center can show you how to get on the information superhighway.

The World Wide Web (WWW) opened a new phase in the development of worldwide communication. In this subset of the Internet system, Web software allows for integration of sound, video clips, fancy text markings, and other types of information through **hypertext** or **hypermedia links.** Hypertext links show up as highlighted key words on the computer screen. Like menus, these key words form doorways to additional text information. Hypermedia links provide multimedia information. For example, in accessing the text of a famous speech, you might also be able to watch a video clip of the speech being given. Your campus library or computer center can help you gain access to the Web.

Exercise 9.7   Choose one of the following topics. Go to your college library or use the Internet or World Wide Web to find three references on this topic. List these references in the spaces below. Evaluate them using the criteria in Table 9.5.

Topics
1. Ozone layer
2. Landscape architecture
3. Music composition
4. Presidential elections
5. American history
6. Medical technology
7. Nuclear weapons
8. Forestry
9. Economic recession
10. Industrial Revolution

Reference 1

_____
_____
_____
_____
_____
_____
_____
_____
_____
_____
_____
_____
_____
_____
_____
_____
_____
_____
_____
_____
_____
_____
_____
_____
_____
_____

Reference 2

_____
_____
_____
_____
_____
_____

Reference 3

_____

_____

_____

_____

_____

_____

_____

_____

_____

_____

RUNNING THE MAZE: THE RESEARCH PROCESS

To know you've found the most information you possibly can, you need to look at every resource alternative. Because of the overwhelming size of this task, it sometimes helps to know where you're going and where you've been. The flowchart in Figure 9.9 looks much like the maze Theseus faced. With someone to assist you (the librarian), a thread to guide you in locating information (library organization), and a sword and the skill to use it (a working bibliography and research skills), you, too, can run the maze and kill the Minotaur.

Figure 9.9 A Flowchart of Library Information

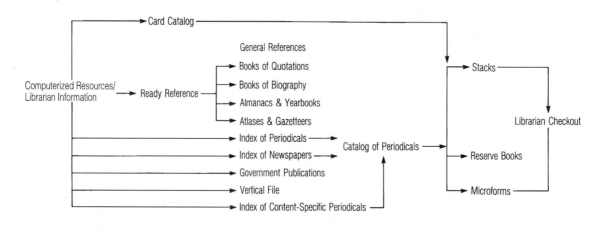

Exercise 9.8   Using the directions for charting found in Table 6.6, create a chart that compares and contrasts the information found in the three references in Exercise 9.7.

GROUP LEARNING ACTIVITY
APPROACHING LIBRARY RESEARCH

Just as you can take different routes to get to a specific location, you can use different routes to approach library research. These approaches do not have to be used exclusively. You can choose to use one as a starting point until you have enough information to try something else. The following eight standard approaches often are suggested (Morse, 1975).

Bibliographic. This approach is the most basic. A bibliography is a list of all materials consulted in your search for information. References all relate to the topic in some way, although that relationships can differ. Thus, the result of a bibliographic approach is an annotated list of books, articles, and other related materials.

Biographical. Biographies concern people—their lives and accomplishments. Thus, if a particular person is associated with a topic, the story of that person's life may be an appropriate starting point for the context of your paper. Although this approach is not suitable for all topics, it is appropriate for some.

Chronological. Chronological order concerns the time line of events associated with your topic. This approach is particularly suitable for historical events, current events, and other topics that have a beginning, middle, and, sometimes, end.

Geographical. Sometimes you want to know where or in what locations an event occurred. In this approach, you use a map to focus on specific areas, locations, or countries.

Linguistic. Linguistics refers to the study of language. This approach focuses on definition of key words and ideas as the basis for beginning research. Other words or terms in the definition, or the etymology of the word, can be a springboard to other references. The meanings you find help you clearly define your topic and the words you intend to research.

Practical. The sequence or order of a process can be the focus of your research. This method is particularly appropriate for "how to do it" topics that focus on the step by step progression of an action or idea.

Statistical. Some topics are best described by data. Here, you search for information that tells you how many, how much, who, where, and why in numerical terms. This collection of facts forms the basis for analysis and interpretation of information to form new conclusions.

Theoretical. Sometimes exact answers to life's questions are not available. In those cases, the theories that answer those questions suffice. These can be compared, contrasted, or related in other ways.

Application

As a group, complete the following activity and compare your results.

1. The group as a whole should select one of the following topics: AIDS research and treatment, automobiles, the brain, gymnastics, voting rights, or war veterans of the twentieth century.

2. Each group member should select one of the eight approaches described above. No two group members should use the same approach.

3. Each group member should find and annotate five references for that topic and approach.

4. As a group, compare the information you located.

CHAPTER SUMMARY

1. The librarian assists your research by identifying appropriate sources and services.

2. Understanding the organizational system that your library uses helps you locate materials efficiently. The card catalog is a file or computerized database that indexes nonfiction library holdings by author, title, and subject, and fiction holdings by author and title. Two classification systems are used to identify library holdings: the numerically based Dewey decimal system and the alphabetically based Library of Congress system.

3. A working bibliography, created through a systematic search of the card catalog or a computer search, provides you with a list of possible research references. Searching, evaluating, and recording information from reference sources requires skills in skimming, scanning, and notetaking.

4. Modern libraries contain a variety of materials for both general, content-specific, and computerized research purposes. General references include unabridged dictionaries, thesauruses, vertical files, almanacs, yearbooks, atlases, gazetteers, biographies, books of quotations, government documents, and indices to magazines and newspapers. The specific subject references you need depend on your interests and coursework. You use indices to content-specific sources to find them. Computerized references can be found through on-line or CD ROM sources or through Internet or World Wide Web access.

TERMS

Terms appear in the order in which they occurred in the chapter.

interlibrary loan
card catalog
Library of Congress
    (LC) system
Dewey decimal
    system
database
nonfiction
author card
main entry card
subject card
title card
fiction
call number
cross references
micofiche
microforms
microfiche reader
working
    bibliography
direct quotes
summary
paraphrase
ellipsis
ready reference
reserve books
periodical indices
unabridged
    dictionary
thesaurus
vertical file
clipping file
almanacs
    (terms continued)

CHAPTER REVIEW

Answer briefly but completely.

1. Compare and contrast the role of Ariadne with that of the librarian. Be specific.

   _____

   _____

   _____

   _____

2. What is the purpose of a call number?

   _____

   _____

   _____

   _____

3. Contrast the advantages of microfiche with its disadvantages.

   _____

   _____

   _____

   _____

4. You plan to write a research paper on music in the 1920s. List three key words you might use to access this information in your library's database.

   _____

   _____

   _____

   _____

5. Contrast the Dewey decimal system with the Library of Congress system. Which system does your library use?

   _____

   _____

   _____

   _____

TERMS

yearbooks
newspaper index
atlases
gazetteers
government
    documents
hypertext
hypermedia links

6. When might you use direct quotes instead of summaries? Why?

_____

_____

_____

_____

7. Using the microfiche or microfilm in your library, copy the front page of the *New York Times* on the day you were born.

8. How do skimming and scanning aid you in researching a paper?

_____

_____

_____

_____

9. Identify two of each of the following found in your library:

    a. general references and their call numbers

    _____

    _____

    b. general biographical indices

    _____

    _____

10. Compare and contrast the use of Internet with that of the World Wide Web.

_____

_____

_____

_____

REFERENCES

Morse, G. W. (1975). *Concise guide to library research* (2d ed.). New York: Fleet Academic Editions.

Van Dijk, T. A., and Kintch, W. (1978). Cognitive psychology and discourse: Recalling and summarizing stories. In W. V. Dressler (Ed.), *Trends in text linguistics*. New York: DeGruyter.

Vocabulary Development   Ready References for Words: Dictionary, Glossary, and Thesaurus

". . . 98, 99, 100! Here I come, ready, prepared, anticipated, girded, on the alert, provided for—or not."

SOURCE: Use by permission of Frank Hauser.

Like Roget, you, too, need to be ready, prepared, apt, and all set to seek whatever your college coursework has hidden. Luckily for you, three references found in all libraries—the dictionary, the glossary, and the thesaurus—are ready for your use in learning the meaning of unfamiliar terms.

Using the Dictionary. What do you do when you see a word you don't know? Most students define words by looking them up in the dictionary. After all, for years parents and teachers have said, "You don't know how to spell that word? You don't know what it means? Well, look it up!" Using the dictionary, then, becomes second nature to you. This often-used method works best when you know how to use the dictionary effectively.

To find word entries quickly in the dictionary, use the **guide words** at the top of each page. They indicate the words that appear between them. Arranged in alphabetical order, definitions contain much more than correct spellings, pronunciations, and meanings.

A dictionary **entry** follows a general format (see Figure 1). First, the word is spelled and divided into syllables. Second, the word's phonetic pronunciation is

Figure 1   Example of a Dictionary Entry

library (lī′brer′ē) *n., pl.* -les [< L. *liber.*book] **1.** a collection of books, etc. **2.** a room or building for, or an institution in charge of, such a collection

SOURCE: Reprinted with permission from *Webster's New World Dictionary of the American Language.* Copyright © 1982 by Simon & Schuster. All rights reserved.

given. (A key to phonetic symbols usually appears at the bottom of the page.) Next appears an abbreviation of the word's part of speech followed by its **etymology.** This is the word's origin or history and tells how or why the word became a word. The word's definition comes after the etymology. Usually the longest and most often used part of the entry, the definition is the word's meaning(s). If the word has several different and distinct meanings, these are numbered separately. Some entries also include **synonyms** (words with the same meaning) and/or **antonyms** (words with the opposite meaning). Finally, the entry shows the **derivations** of the word and their parts of speech. Derivations are words formed from the entry word. Although entry formats vary slightly from one dictionary to another, their general consistency allows you to use a variety of dictionaries easily.

Resorting to a dictionary is not always the best solution. First, because many words have specialized meanings, you may have difficulty locating the meaning you need. By the time you find the one you need, you may forget why you needed it. This break in concentration leads to a loss of understanding. This increases study time and decreases study efficiency. Thus, glossary usage, context, and structural analysis are alternatives for understanding.

Using a Glossary. When a glossary is included in a textbook, it stands as your greatest resource in understanding the language of the course. An entry in this dictionary-like listing of words generally consists of only the term and its course-specific definition (see Figure 2). Examining the glossary before the beginning of a course provides you with an introduction to the language of the course. Referring to the glossary during reading requires less time than using a dictionary. It also assures that you get the correct meaning for the content of the course. Reviewing glossary entries before exams helps you determine which words and concepts require further study.

Using a Thesaurus. Once you have a sense of what a word means, using a thesaurus provides you with other words with similar meanings (synonyms). First compiled by Peter Mark Roget in 1852, a thesaurus is a collection of words that enhances vocabulary development.

As in a dictionary, the information found in a thesaurus entry varies (see Figure 3). A thesaurus entry is less complicated than a dictionary entry. It omits a word's pronunciation, etymology, and derivations. Consistently, however, entries contain a word's part of speech, synonyms and related words or phrases, and cross-references. Some also include antonyms.

Figure 2   Example of a Glossary

Interpreter A high-level language translator that evaluates and translates a program one statement at a time; used extensively on microcomputer systems because it takes up less primary storage than a compiler.

Interrecord gap (IRG) A space that separates records stored on magnetic tape; allows the tape drive to regain speed during processing.

Interrupt A condition or event that temporarily suspends normal processing operations.

Inverted structure A structure that indexes a simple file by specific record attributes.

K (kilobyte) A symbol used to denote 1,024 (2^{10}) storage units (1,024 bytes) when referring to a computer's primary storage capacity; often rounded to 1,000 bytes.

Key The unique identifier or field of a record; used to sort records for processing or to locate specific records within a file.

Keypunch A keyboard device that punches holes in a card to represent data.

Keypunch operator Person who uses a keypunch machine to transfer data from source documents to punched cards.

Label A name written beside a programming instruction that acts as an identifier for that instruction; also, in spreadsheets, information used to describe some aspect of the spreadsheet.

Large-scale Integration (LSI) Method by which circuits containing thousands of electronic components are densely packed on a single silicon chip.

Laser printer A type of nonimpact printer that combines laser beams and electrophotographic technology to form images on paper.

Laser storage system A secondary storage device using laser technology to encode data onto a metallic surface; usually used for mass storage.

Librarian The person responsible for classifying, cataloging, and maintaining the files and programs stored on cards, tapes, disks, and diskettes, and all other storage media in a computer library.

Librarian program Software that manages the storage and use of library programs by maintaining a directory of programs in the system library and appropriate procedures for additions and deletions.

Light pen A pen-shaped object with a photoelectric cell at its end; used to draw lines on a visual display screen.

Linear structure A data structure in which the records in a computer file are arranged sequentially in a specified order.

Link A transmission channel that connects nodes.

Linkage editor A subprogram of the operating system that links the object program from the system residence device to primary storage.

LISP (LISt Processing) A high-level programming language commonly used in artificial intelligence research and in the processing of lists of elements.

Local system Peripherals connected directly to the CPU.

Logical file The combination of data needed to meet a user's needs.

Figure 2   Continued

Logo An education-oriented, procedure-oriented, interactive programming language designed to allow anyone to begin programming and communicating with computers quickly.

Loop A structure that allows a specified sequence of instructions to be executed repeatedly as long as stated conditions remain constant.

Figure 3   Examples of Various Thesaurus Entries

Gratitude

Nouns—gratitude, gratefulness, thankfulness; indebtedness; acknowledgement, recognition, thanksgiving; thanks, praise; paean, *Te Deum,* WORSHIP, grace; thank-offering; requital.

Verbs—be grateful, thank; give, render, return, offer, *or* tender thanks; acknowledge, requite; thank *or* bless one's [lucky] stars.

Adjectives—grateful, thankful, appreciative, obliged, beholden, indebted to, under obligation.

Interjections—thanks! much obliged! thank you! thank Heaven! Heaven be praised! thanks a million! *gracias! merci!*

Antonyms, see INGRATITUDE.

rumble, *n.* roll, hollow roar, reverberation. See LOUDNESS.

rumble, *v.* boom, thunder, roll (RESONANCE, LOUDNESS).

rumble *verb*

1. To make a continuous deep, reverberating sound: *heard the convoy rumbling in the distance.* **Syns**: boom, growl, grumble, roll.

2. MUTTER.

rumble *noun* MUTTER.

Thesauruses use the same labels for parts of speech as dictionaries. Again, these labels tell how a word functions in language. Because many words can be used as more than one part of speech, a thesaurus lists synonyms for each function. Thus, when looking for words in a thesaurus, you need to know how a word is to be used in a sentence.

Because it would be redundant to reprint every term associated with each entry, an entry sometimes includes cross-references. Found at the end of an entry, these either begin with the words "See also" or are written in all caps. Cross-references direct you to other entries that contain additional synonyms or to antonyms.

Choosing Ready References. A glossary is your first and best choice for determining the meaning of the terms you encounter because their meanings are specific to your course of study. Nonetheless, a personal dictionary and thesaurus are imperative for continued vocabulary development. Contrary to popular opinion, all dictionaries and thesauruses are not alike. Most are abridged versions containing a limited number of entries. When determining what to purchase, you need to base your choice on more than size alone. Indeed, large unabridged dictionaries would be inappropriate for everyday use but would be the best choice for an extensive etymology search. How, then, do you decide which reference book you need? Table 1 provides guidelines for your selection.

Table 1   Guidelines for Purchasing a Dictionary and Thesaurus

Dictionary

1. What size is the dictionary? Will you use it at home or in class? If you plan to use the dictionary at home, it can be larger than if you will be carrying it to class each day.

2. How many total entries are included? Within the limits of size manageability, the more entries, the better.

3. What is the copyright date of the dictionary? More up-to-date dictionaries contain new words that older dictionaries do not contain.

4. What is the quality of the entries given? Contrast the entries of several dictionaries to determine which would best fit your needs.

5. Is the type clear and easy to read?

6. Does the dictionary include a clear guide to aid you in using information contained in it? Skim it to determine how easy it is to use.

7. What additional information is included in the dictionary? Many contain such features as a periodic table, sections on punctuation and language usage, lists of foreign words or spellings, and a table of weights and measures. The components you need depend on how you plan to use your dictionary.

Thesaurus

1. Are entries listed alphabetically or by subject? Thesauruses with an alphabetical format are easier to use.

Table 1	Guidelines for Purchasing a Dictionary and Thesaurus *continued*

2. How many total entries are included? Within the limits of size manageability, the more entries, the better.

3. Are cross-references included? Cross-references are necessary in helping you locate the exact synonym you need.

4. Does the entry include antonyms when possible? Thesauruses with antonyms are helpful because sometimes you need a word that means the opposite of a word you know.

5. Is the type clear and easy to read?

6. Does the thesaurus include a clear guide to aid you in using information contained in it? Skim it to determine how easy it is to use.

Activity

I. Define each of the following words using a dictionary. Then define them using the glossary in Figure 2. Using a thesaurus, find three to five words that would generally be considered synonyms of these words. Compare the glossary, dictionary, and thesaurus meanings. What differences do you find?

1. *interpreter*

Dictionary: _____

Glossary: _____

Thesaurus: _____

Comparison: _____

2. *key*

Dictionary: _____

Glossary: _____

Thesaurus: _____

Comparison: _____

3. *label*

Dictionary: _____

_____

Glossary: _____

_____

Thesaurus: _____

_____

Comparison: _____

_____

_____

4. *link*

Dictionary: _____

_____

Glossary: _____

_____

Thesaurus: _____

_____

Comparison: _____

_____

_____

5. *loop*

Dictionary: _____

_____

Glossary: _____

_____

Thesaurus: _____

_____

Comparison: _____

_____

_____

II. How does using these references as combined sources affect your vocabulary development?

Writing the Research Paper

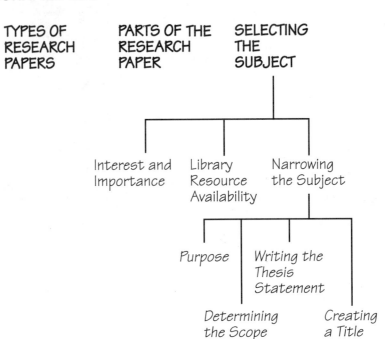

OBJECTIVES

By the end of this chapter you should be able to do the following:

1. Compare and contrast types of research papers.

2. Identify different parts of the research paper.

3. Select research paper subjects.

4. Synthesize sources using outlines or charts.

5. Describe the process involved in writing a paper.

6. Identify why writing schedules are needed and how to set a writing schedule.

7. Identify suggestions for presenting the content of your paper or other information to a group.

CHAPTER MAP

TYPES OF RESEARCH PAPERS

PARTS OF THE RESEARCH PAPER

SELECTING THE SUBJECT

Interest and Importance

Library Resource Availability

Narrowing the Subject

Purpose

Writing the Thesis Statement

Determining the Scope

Creating a Title

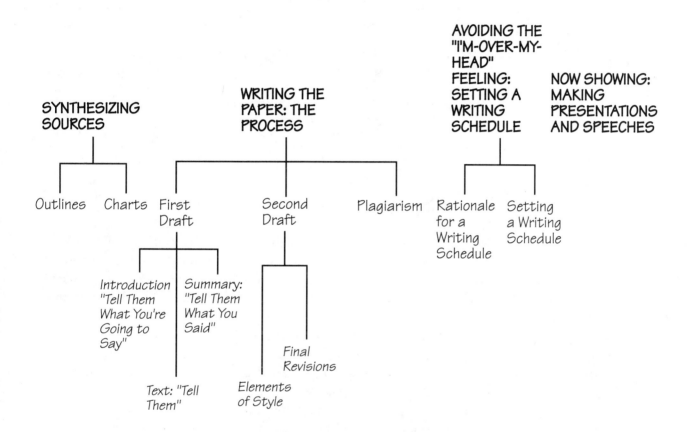

The deadline would strike In exactly twenty-one days. I had to start writing. The next morning, a beauteous one in June, I woke up, washed my face and brushed my teeth in a hurry, made a pot of coffee, tightened the sash on my bathrobe, snapped my typewriter out of its case, carefully placed it on the kitchen table, unwrapped the pack of bond paper I had purchased the day before, retrieved my notes from the floor where they were stacked tidily in manila folders . . . opened the first folder, put the top sheet of paper in the typewriter, looked at it, put my head on the keys, wrapped my arms around its base, and cried. If I had known then how many times, during the next fifteen years, I would have the same feeling—the I'm-over-my-head-and-this-time-they're-going-to-catch-me feeling—I might have become a receptionist in a carpeted law office and married the first partner in a three-piece suit who asked me. But I didn't know. I thought, if I get through this, it'll be over.

—BETTY ROLLIN

SOURCE: Reprinted with permission from *Am I Getting Paid for This?* by Betty Rollin. Little, Brown and Company, Publishers.

No matter if your assignment comes from an editor or an instructor, the "I'm-over-my-head-and-this-time-they're-going-to-catch-me feeling" often prevails. Unlike Betty Rollin, you may have no clear idea of what's involved in researching and writing a paper. Perhaps the writing process confuses and frustrates you. If so, you—like Betty Rollin—probably feel like crying.

Writing a paper is much like cooking. If a chef follows the recipe, everything goes as planned. If the chef leaves something out or fails to follow directions, the recipe is ruined. A paper has a recipe, too. As with cooking, leaving out a part of the paper or a step in the writing process results in a paper that's not all you hoped it would be.

The recipe for your paper depends on the type of paper you need to write and the parts you plan to include. It also consists of other key ingredients and steps for you to follow. These help you find where you are in the process and what you need to do next. You complete four steps when writing a paper: selecting a topic, narrowing your subject, gathering information, and actually writing the paper.

TYPES OF RESEARCH PAPERS

There are almost as many types of papers as there are types of food. Instructors often assign **themes** or **essays, reports,** and **research papers** or **term papers.** Themes require little or no research. Somewhat short in length, they usually contain your personal opinions about a single topic. Other kinds of papers vary in length and purpose. Reports narrate or describe something that you have experienced firsthand. They sometimes include information that you derive from the accounts of others. Research papers are required assignments, written as a culmination or synthesis of a course's content. They often require supporting research. Called term papers by some instructors, research papers involve much library work. They focus on either part or all of a course's content or a related topic.

PARTS OF THE RESEARCH PAPER

Regardless of the purpose or topic, all research papers include the same basic parts: the title page, body of the paper, and **bibliography,** in that order. In addition, they often contain a table of contents, an **abstract,** and **appendices** (see Figure 10.1).

The title page lists the paper's title, your name, the course and the instructor for whom the paper is written, and the date. Second is the body of the paper. It contains the introduction of the topic, synthesis of information, and summary or conclusions. Third, your paper includes a list of references, sometimes called a bibliography.

Whether or not your paper contains additional information depends on the options your instructor wants and the scope of the paper. The first optional item is a table of contents, often used in papers that are lengthy or segmented. An abstract—a second optional element—briefly summarizes the content of your paper. Both the table of contents and abstract follow the title page. A final optional element consists of appendices that contain supplementary material (for example, illustrations, figures, charts). These are placed at the end of your paper.

"A fill-in-the-blank research paper is a unique idea, but. . . ."

Figure 10.1   Parts of a Research Paper

TITLE

The State of Education:
Comparisons between Louisiana
and Maryland

Henry Brandt

Professor Miles Jeffrey
Education 4443
Trends in Education
Spring 1984

SAMPLE PAGE FROM BODY

Population Characteristics

The population of Maryland is comparable to that of Louisiana (4,265,000 VS. 4,362,000), although Maryland is much more densely populated than Louisiana (431.2 persons per square mile VS. 97.1 per square mile). Louisiana is 68.7% urban as compared to Maryland's urban population of 80.3%. Louisiana's racial make-up is 69.2% white, 29.4% black, and 1.4% other. Only two other states have black populations higher than Louisiana. The racial make-up of Maryland is 74.9% white, 22.7% black, and 2.4% other. (Feist, 1983; American Almanac, 1983).

    Maryland's physical density and urban atmosphere would seem to be advantageous for its residents. This would facilitate accessibility to formal educational resources (i.e. libraries and schools). In addition, opportunities for participating in non-school educational/cultural activities (i.e., museums, plays, concerts, exhibitions, etc.) would be increased.

History

Louisiana was first visited by Spanish explorers in 1530 but was claimed for France in 1682. French control of the state

ABSTRACT

ABSTRACT

The State of Education:
Comparisons between Louisiana
and Maryland

Henry Brandt

    The purpose of this paper is to provide a descriptive examination of factors relating to education in the states of Louisiana and Maryland.

    The context of the situation in each state will be developed through a discussion of population characteristics, state history, political history, economic trends, and readership data.

    The scope of this paper focuses on the following aspects of the educational system in each state: enrollment, public elementary and secondary schools, private elementary and secondary schools, teachers, adult literacy, and post-secondary institutions.

APPENDIX

APPENDIX A. Readership Data

	LOUISIANA	MARYLAND
Newsweek (7/30/83)		
Subscriptions	55,025	60,000
Single Copy Sales	2.933	4.535
Total	57,958	65,535
Time (7/30/83)		
Subscriptions	53,700	79,036
Single Copy Sales	3,542	3,216
Total	56,242	82,252
U.S. News and World Report (7/30/83)		
Subscriptions	39,162	44,775
Single Copy Sales	924	1,644
Total	40,086	46,419
Sports Illustrated (7/30/83)		
Subscriptions	62,741	58,149
Single Copy Sales	1,391	2,126
Total	64,132	60,275
House Beautiful (7/30/83)		
Subscriptions	18,725	19,048
Single Copy Sales	4.600	5,016
Total	23,326	24,064
Reader's Digest (6/30/83)		
Subscriptions	244,603	286,333
Single Copy Sales	15,235	10,333
Total	232,538	296,666

Figure 10.1   Parts of a Research Paper *continued*

TABLE OF CONTENTS

TABLE OF CONTENTS

Population Characteristics	1
History	3
Politics	6
Economics	9
Readership	11
Education	12
Enrollment	12
Public Elementary and Secondary Schools	14
Private Elementary and Secondary Schools	15
Teachers	16
Adult Literacy	18
Post-secondary Institutions	20
Appendices	
A. Readership	21
B. Teacher Salaries	22
Bibliography	23

REFERENCES

BIBLIOGRAPHY

Ashworth, J., (1980). *Education in Louisiana*. Baton Rouge, Louisiana; University Press.

Craig, F.J. (ed.). (1983). *American Almanac* Boston: Ginn Co.

Feist, J.T., (1983). *General Education Facts and Figures* New York: Holt.

Jones, E.M. (1982). "Maryland's Push for Better Education." *Journal of General Education, 21*, pp. 192–193.

Stoll, E.P., & Bradley, A.C. (1984). *Readership Data for Popular Magazines*. New York: Hill & Smith.

SELECTING THE SUBJECT

A chef's library contains many specialized cookbooks. For example, when planning to bake a cake, the chef selects a cookbook containing cake recipes. The choice of a specific recipe depends on the ingredients on hand, the amount of preparation time involved, the number it will serve, and so on. The subject of your paper, much like a specialized cookbook, is the general area that you plan to research. Your instructor sometimes assigns specific topics. If this is the case, your job is to find information on that topic and write about it. If not, your job is more difficult. You then choose a subject from either a list of subjects supplied by the instructor or from your own research. Subject selection depends on your interest, the importance of the subject, and the availability of resources.

INTEREST AND IMPORTANCE

The subject you choose needs to be one of interest or importance to you, the course content, and your audience. Because writing a paper requires much work, you stand a better chance of doing a good job if you care about the subject that you select. The subject of your paper also should be relevant to the course. Finally, the content of your paper needs to meet the demands of your audience, whether that be your instructor, your peers, or others.

Finding a subject that relates to you, the course, and your audience requires effort. By scanning your text's index or table of contents, you can identify topics that interest you or appeal to your audience. Skimming your notes or class handouts also helps you pinpoint likely subjects. Talking with your instructor or classmates is a third means of finding possible areas of research. Finally, subject areas surface through vicarious and direct experiences. These include books, magazines, television, newspaper accounts, travel, and work.

LIBRARY RESOURCE AVAILABILITY

The availability of library resources is a second consideration in subject selection. Consulting the card catalog helps you determine if your library owns books or other references on your subject. Computer access to on-line information on the topic also may be an option. If your library contains limited information or if on-line information is not readily available, choosing another subject may be advisable. In addition, checking the location of such resources helps you determine the availability of those references to you. If the ones you want are checked out or are otherwise unavailable, again you may need to find another subject.

NARROWING THE SUBJECT

Narrowing your subject into a manageable topic is much like a chef deciding what kind of cake to bake. Because you can't write about every aspect of a subject, you need to decide specifically what you plan to cover. The narrower the topic, the better your chance of covering it.

Purpose

Establishing the purpose of a paper aids you in narrowing the subject. Purposes are sometimes set by instructors; however, you often must set them yourself. Determining the purpose helps you determine the type of information you need to collect (see Table 10.1).

To identify your purpose, you ask questions about the subject. Asking "Who?" elicits information describing a person or a group. Asking "What?" requires you to find information defining a process, an event, a place, or an object. Asking "Why?" involves your finding information that explains the importance of the person or group, a process, an event, a place, an object, or the relationships among these. Asking "When?"

Table 10.1   Identifying Research Purposes

If Your Purpose is to . . .	You Collect . . .
define or describe,	details, characteristics, features, qualities, relationships.
compare/contrast,	similarities and differences.
analyze,	factors or elements that comprise the totality of the topic.
explain or interpret,	reasons, causes, effects, data.
persuade,	facts that support or refute an argument.
chronicle,	sequence, process, or history.
relate,	spatial or geographical associations or patterns.
infer,	evidence to make predictions or conclusions.

''*I don't think that's what your instructor meant by reducing the scope of your paper.*''

helps you pinpoint the time frame you want to cover. Asking "How?" helps you focus on process.

Determining the Scope

Once you identify your purpose, you determine the **scope** of your paper. This refers to the general size and specification of your topic. The scope of your topic needs to be neither too broad nor too specific but "just right."

Figure 10.2   Example of Progressively Limiting a Subject's Scope

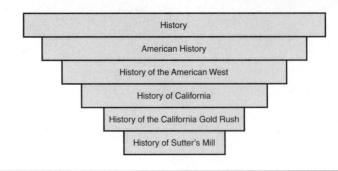

Your paper reflects its scope. Its contents, too, must be neither too broad nor too specific but "just right."

Scope involves setting limits on the amount of information covered and the number of details included. It also depends on your expertise, the amount of time you have to spend on the topic, and the type of paper you are writing. Once you determine your scope, you refrain from exceeding these limits. You set these limits by progressively narrowing your topic until it becomes a manageable size (see Figure 10.2). In doing so, you move from general to specific. Encyclopedias and textbooks do this when they divide information into sections or chapters. You can use these as guides when setting the scope of your paper.

Exercise 10.1   Using Sample Chapter 11, 12, and 13 as possible sources, go to your campus library and locate two additional sources that pertain to one of the following broad topics or another related topic of your choice. Skim the references to help you narrow the scope to a workable topic.

1. Working Conditions
2. Employee Responsibilities
3. Industrial Revolution
4. Women and Children in Industry

SUBJECT _____

Subtopic _____

Subtopic _____

Subtopic _____

Workable topic _____

Writing the Thesis Statement

The scope of a paper's contents often determines the **thesis statement.** Because it defines the limits of your research, the thesis statement guides and controls your research, your writing, and—later—your audience. The thesis statement of your paper is much like a topic sentence in a paragraph. It states your paper's purpose and your major assertions or conclusions. You write your thesis statement in the form of a complete, declarative sentence. It restates your title or topic, states major assertions or conclusions (not minor details, illustrations, quotations), and establishes the purpose of your research.

For example, suppose you are researching the topic "Rising Health Costs for Big Businesses" to analyze results of increases in the cost of health care. You assert that the rising cost of health care results in lower dividends for stockholders. Based on this, your topic sentence could be: "The rising cost of health care for employees threatens to wipe out many companies' profits."

Creating a Title

Like the thesis statement, your title identifies the contents of your paper. Also, it needs to appeal to your readers, spark their interest in your topic, and motivate them to read your paper. Often, your narrowed topic serves as the title of your paper. On the other hand, composing the thesis statement sometimes helps you form a more appropriate title. Such titles are precise and state your topic in a few key words. Wordy, overly cute, or fancy titles often detract from the seriousness of your research. Finally, it really doesn't matter if you title your paper before or after you write it. Sometimes you find through research or **synthesis** (concise, unified compilation of ideas) a title that perfectly fits your paper. Until then, your thesis statement serves as your composition guide. A good title is worth the wait.

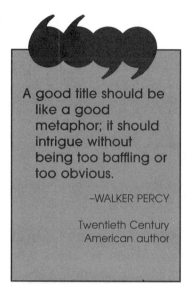

A good title should be like a good metaphor; it should intrigue without being too baffling or too obvious.

–WALKER PERCY

Twentieth Century American author

The title comes last.

–TENNESSEE WILLIAMS

Twentieth Century American author

Exercise 10.2 Given the following topics, major assertions or conclusions, and purposes of research, construct a thesis statement for each topic.

1. *Topic:* The American Presidential Election of 1864
   Major assertions: Out of their desire for an end to the Civil War, many leading Republicans refused to support Abraham Lincoln in his bid for renomination to the presidency.
   Purpose of research: To analyze the political scene.

   Thesis statement: _____

   _____

2. *Topic:* Choosing a Personal Computer
Major assertions: Choosing a personal computer is based on the software you want to use, the amount of money you have to spend, and the recommendations you receive from other users.
Purpose of research: To compare and contrast features of MacIntosh and IBM personal computers.
Thesis statement: _____

_____

3. *Topic:* Increasing Unemployment Rates in Urban Poverty Areas
Major assertions: Unemployment rates in urban poverty areas have increased in the past five years.
Purpose of research: To analyze reasons for the increase in unemployment rates in urban poverty areas.
Thesis statement: _____

_____

4. *Topic:* Quality of Health Care in Public Health Facilities
Major assertions: Patient care in public health facilities is of a lower standard than that in private facilities.
Purpose of research: To compare health care in public and private institutions.
Thesis statement: _____

_____

5. *Topic:* The Origin of the Universe
Major assertions: One of the fundamental problems in astronomy is to develop a theory describing the origin of the universe.
Purpose of research: To analyze various theories describing how the universe was formed.
Thesis statement: _____

_____

6. *Topic:* U.S. Space Program's Unmanned Interplanetary Missions
Major assertions: Unmanned interplanetary missions are a major component of the U.S. space program. This is based on the fact that they began with the program's inception and continue today.
Purpose of research: To chronicle the history of the U.S. space program's unmanned interplanetary missions.
Thesis statement: _____

_____

7. *Topic:* Comparing the Netherlands and My Home State
Major assertions: The terrain of the Netherlands varies from low and flat to hilly.
Purpose of research: To compare the Netherlands with my state.

Thesis statement: _____

_____

8. *Topic:* Cable Television: The Pros and Cons
   Major assertions: The local cable television company celebrated its tenth anniversary with the usual insincere promises of expansions and breakthroughs.
   Purpose of research: To analyze propaganda techniques used in advertisements to persuade people to subscribe to cable television.

   Thesis statement: _____

   _____

9. *Topic:* Rebuilding the Statue of Liberty
   Major assertions: The rebuilding of the Statue of Liberty was financed through contributions of patriotic Americans.
   Purpose of research: To list the sources of contributions for the refurbishing of the Statue of Liberty.

   Thesis statement: _____

   _____

10. *Topic:* UFOs: Sightings as Proof
    Major assertions: Since 1947, reports of UFOs have been increasing. Large numbers of sightings in varied locations prove their existence.
    Purpose of research: To persuade the reader to believe in UFOs.

    Thesis statement: _____

    _____

SYNTHESIZING SOURCES

It's a great feeling. You have completed your research. You have taken your last note. No more searching through stacks of books and articles for information. You have everything you need. All you have to do is combine the information and write the paper.

For some people, the moment of elation over completing their research turns to one of dread. Like Betty Rollin, they suddenly have that "I'm-over-my-head-and-this-time-they're-going-to-catch-me" feeling. You, too, may experience these "what-do-I-do-now" feelings when you begin the actual writing process.

As in identifying and collecting research information, your thesis statement guides the process of writing your paper. It reminds you of the original purpose of your research and the limits you set for its scope. Knowing your purpose and limits helps you organize the information you've collected. Outlining and charting major sections provides you with the means of establishing the framework for the development of your topic.

OUTLINES

Outlining—organizing information in a sequence—is the first step in synthesis. Because research usually is collected from a variety of sources at different times, information may seem disjointed and isolated. Thus, in completing an outline, you first review your notes. This helps you become familiar with what they contain.

The second stage of outlining—determining relevance—depends on how well you know what your references contain. Now you judge their importance to your paper. One way to do this is to randomly list important terms and concepts necessary to the understanding of your topic. Next, determine the relative importance of each term and concept. You do this by making inferences about the relationships between common themes found in your research and your paper's purpose. These themes become the main headings or subheadings of your outline, depending upon their complexity. If the remaining terms and concepts further develop your topic, they become supporting details. You omit unnecessary information. You probably won't need all the information you collected in your research. That doesn't mean that you wasted your time. The information you gathered helped you refine your understanding in order to define the limits of relevance.

The third stage of outlining begins the charting process in synthesis. Once you identify the main headings and subheadings you wish to include, you search for information on these themes in your different sources.

CHARTS

As discussed in Chapter 6, charts help you identify and categorize information. As you write your research paper, they aid you in comparing themes from various sources.

To construct a synthesis chart for writing (see Figure 10.3), you first list horizontally the sources you plan to use as references. Then, you list vertically the themes you've identified. Third, you construct a grid by drawing lines between each theme and each source. Now, you determine if the source contains information about a specific theme and briefly note that information. Fifth, you look at your chart to categorize sources based on likenesses and differences of information contained in them. This helps you to see patterns and relationships. Finally, you use the chart to write your paper.

Figure 10.3   Example of Synthesis Chart, Sources, and Resulting Paper

SOURCE 1

INTRODUCTION

The hardware of the computer is the physical devices that comprise the computer system: the central processing unit, the input devices, the output devices, and the storage devices. Basically, hardware includes all parts of the computer that are tangible. Hardware is *not* operating systems, concepts, or programs (these are software). Hardware consists of only those parts of the computer that one could reach out and touch.

THE CENTRAL PROCESSING UNIT

The **central processing unit**, or **CPU**, is the essence of the computer's hardware. It is the "brain" of the computer. It tells the other parts of the computer what to do; it decides what to do with the instructions that the programmer gives it; and it ensures that the tasks assigned to it are properly carried out.

The CPU is composed of three separate units—the control unit, the arithmetic/logic unit, and the primary storage unit (Figure 2-1). The **control unit** is, quite literally, in control of the operations. It reads the actual instructions and tells the other computer parts what to do. The control unit directs the appropriate input device to send the necessary data. It keeps track of what parts of the program have already been executed and which ones are left to be done. Finally, it controls the execution of the specific instructions, collects the output, and sends the output to the designated output device.

The **arithmetic/logic unit (ALU)** is the computer's own personal mathematician. It executes all arithmetic and logic statements. Logic statements aren't quite so straightforward as arithmetic statements, but they are equally easy to understand. A logic statement is a statement that makes a comparison and then does something based on the result. For example, if today is Friday, then pick up paycheck and go to the bank; if not, don't. Obviously, this isn't quite the type of logic statement that the computer would work with, but the idea is the same. More likely, the computer would want to know: If this is the end of the input data, then make the calculations and output the results. If not, read the rest of the input. Arithmetic and logic operations are the only type of instructions that the ALU can execute. But when you think about it, you will realize that almost everything you want the computer to do is either an arithmetic or logic problem. The only noticeable exceptions are reading input and printing output. (These are controlled by the control unit.)

The **primary storage unit** is in charge of storing data and programs in the computer's internal memory. It is very important to distinguish this internal memory, called primary storage, from external memory, called auxiliary storage. The primary storage unit is a part of the actual internal hardware of the computer. Without the primary storage unit, the computer could not work because it would not be able to store the programs. Auxiliary storage is not necessary for the computer to function; it is not part of its internal hardware. The CPU can access only primary storage; information between primary and auxiliary storage is transferred through electrical lines.

Most current primary storage hardware consists of **semiconductors** which have their memory circuitry on silicon chips. The data are stored in **bit cells**, located on the chips, which can be in either an "on" or an "off" state. Each cell holds a BInary digiT (bit). The cells are arranged so that they can be written to or read from as needed.

CENTRAL PROCESSING UNIT (CPU)
Acts as the "brain" of the computer.

CONTROL UNIT
Controls the execution of programs.

ARITHMETIC/LOGIC UNIT (ALU)
Executes mathematical and logic statements.

PRIMARY STORAGE UNIT
The computer's internal memory.

SEMICONDUCTOR
A type of primary storage that stores data in bit cells located on silicon chips.

Figure 10.3   Source 1 Continued

Basically, the primary storage unit holds the program that is being exe- cuted, as well as its input, output, and intermediate results of any calcula- tions. When a program is entered into the computer, the control unit sends the program to the primary storage unit. The control unit then re- trieves one line at a time from the primary storage unit. Therefore, the pri- mary storage unit acts somewhat like a shelf upon which statements, in- structions, and results are placed when they aren't being read by the control unit.

All three parts of the central processing unit work together to enable the computer to function. Together they are often called the "computer proper" because in some microcomputers, they *are* the computer. In any computer, the CPU is the central core.

Computers derive most of their amazing power from three features; speed, accuracy, and memory. Generally, computer speed is expressed as the time required to perform one operation. The following units of time apply:

BIT CELL
Used in semiconductors; stores data by designating each cell as "on" or "off."

UNIT	SYMBOL	FRACTIONS OF A SECOND	
Millisecond	ms	one-thousandth	(1/1,000)
Microsecond	μs	one-millionth	(1/1,000,000)
Nanosecond	ns	one-billionth	(1/1,000,000,000)
Picosecond	ps	one-trillionth	(1/1,000,000,000,000)

Today's computers can complete computations in a matter of **nanose- conds.**

A nanosecond is one-billionth of a second. The best way to compre- hend just how small a nanosecond is to compare it visually with one second. In the computer, computations are made electrically. The speed of electricity is approximately the speed of light. Thus, in one second the electricity used for computations will travel 186,000 miles. In one nano- second that electricity will travel 11.8 inches.

NANOSECOND
One-billionth of a second.

MORE ON INTERNAL STORAGE
Storage Locations and Addresses

When the CPU stores programs, input data, and output, it does not do so randomly. These items are stored in specific memory locations that can then be accessed by their addresses to retrieve their contents.

To process information, the CPU's control unit must first locate in stor- age each instruction and piece of data. Computer storage can be com- pared with a large array of mailboxes. Each mailbox is a specific location and can hold one item of information. Since each location in storage has a distinct address, stored-program instructions can locate particular items by giving their addresses.

Suppose, for instance, the computer is instructed to calculate an em- ployee's salary by subtracting TOTAL TAX from his or her GROSS PAY.

SOURCE 1

Figure 10.3   Continued

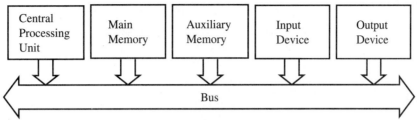

Fig. 3–1. The hardware components of a computer system.

- *Main memory.* The data that the computer is manipulating and the program that it is executing are both stored in main memory. In many respects, main memory serves as the computer's scratch pad or blackboard.

- *Input and output devices.* Input and output devices convert data between the binary codes that computers use and forms suitable for human use—such as pictures, sounds, and printed text.

- *Auxiliary memory.* Auxiliary memory is used for long-term storage of data files and program libraries. If main memory is the computer's scratch pad, auxiliary memory is its filing cabinet.

For large computers, the central processor and main memory usually occupy one centrally located cabinet, around which are arranged the input, output, and auxiliary memory devices. For this reason, the input, output, and auxiliary memory devices are often called *peripherals.* In small computers, however, some or all of the "peripherals" may be installed in the same cabinet as the central processor and main memory.

The Central Processing Unit

The central processing unit is *the* essential component of a computer because it is the part that executes the program. Other components—such as auxiliary memory, input and output devices, or even main memory—can sometimes be omitted. But without a central processor, there is no computer.

Not surprisingly, in view of the job it has to do, the central processor is the most complex part of a computer. This is why the development of the microprocessor, a central processor on a single silicon chip, was such an important advance. Microprocessors make it possible to buy the complex central processor as a single, inexpensive component, instead of having to build it out of thousands of individual transistors and integrated circuits.

The central processor is itself made up of two components—*the arithmetic-logic unit,* which does the calculations, and the *control unit,* which coordinates the activities of the entire computer.

The arithmetic-logic unit
The arithmetic-logic unit performs the same jobs for a computer that a pocket calculator performs for a human being. It can perform arithmetical operations, comparisons, and logical operations.

Arithmetical operations. The arithmetic-logic unit adds, subtracts, multiplies, and divides. On some computers, only addition and subtraction are built into the arithmetic-logic unit. Such machines need programs to tell them how to multiply and divide.

Comparisons. The arithmetic-logic unit can determine such things as whether two alphabetic characters are the same or whether one number is less than, equal to, or greater than another. The results of these comparisons are made available to the control unit, which can use them to determine which instruction to execute next. Under the control of its program, the computer can "decide" what action to take next depending on the input it has received and on the outcome of previous calculations.

Figure 10.3   Continued (*Source 2*)

This decision-making capability allows a computer to be far more responsive to its user's requests than is possible with most other machines. Indeed, one reason computers are often installed in machines such as household appliances is to endow these machines with some of the computer's flexibility and responsiveness.

Logical operations. Sometimes we want to use complicated criteria to determine the action a computer will take. For example, we may ask a computer to print the names of every employee of a company who has been with the company more than ten years *and* who makes less than twenty thousand dollars *and* who has not had a raise in the last three years.

In general, such criteria consist of simple conditions (such as "the employee has been with the company more than ten years") joined by *and, or,* or *not.* Given whether each of the simple conditions is true or false for a particular individual, the program must calculate whether or not the overall criterion is satisfied. To simplify this kind of calculation, the arithmetic/logic unit provides *logical operations,* which correspond to the English words *and, or,* and *not.*

The control unit

The control unit fetches instructions one by one from main memory. Like everything stored in memory, instructions are represented by binary codes. The control unit decodes each instruction, then sends the necessary control signals to other units (such as the arithmetic-logic unit or a peripheral device) to get the instruction carried out.

The control unit is said to work in a *fetch-execute cycle* because it fetches each instruction from main memory and then executes the instruction. When an instruction has been executed, the control unit fetches the next instruction, executes it, and so on. (To speed things up, some computers fetch the next instruction while the previous instruction is being executed.)

It's important to realize that no matter how complex or subtle the job is that the program is doing, the control unit is still working in a simple, repetitive cycle—fetching and executing instructions, one after another. Herein lies the real power of programming: A machine that works in a very simple, repetitive cycle can nevertheless exhibit very complicated behavior by following suitable instructions. People who sneer that a computer can only do what it is told to do completely miss this point.

Computer Memory

Memory is the part of the computer that stores information for later use. Most computers have both *main memory* and *auxiliary memory.* Main memory is sometimes referred to as *main storage, primary memory,* or *primary storage.* In the past, because of the widespread use of the now-obsolete magnetic-core technology, main memory was often called *core.* Auxiliary memory is sometimes referred to as *auxiliary storage, secondary memory, secondary storage,* or *mass storage.*

Main memory

A computer's main memory is divided into a large number of individual *memory locations,* each of which can hold a certain amount of data. Each location has an *address,* which the central processor uses to designate which location to store data in or retrieve data from. We can picture a computer's memory as an array of post-office boxes, each having a unique address and containing an item of data.

Access to data stored in main memory is very fast. The time required to store a data item in main memory or to recall an item from main memory is measured in billionths of a second. Main memory also allows

Figure 10.3   Continued

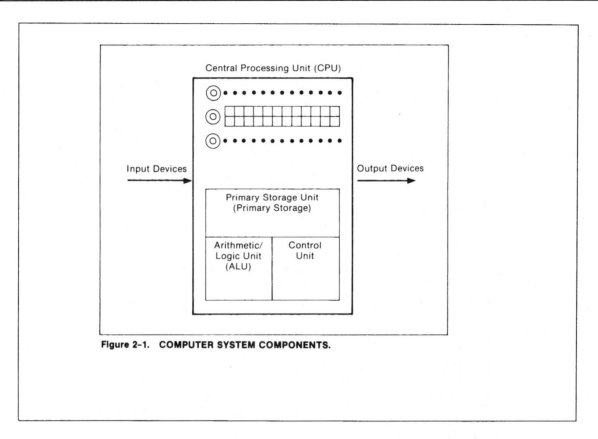

Figure 2-1. **COMPUTER SYSTEM COMPONENTS.**

Figure 10.3 Continued

The Central Processing Unit

The **central processing unit (CPU)** is the heart of the computer system. It is composed of three units: the control unit, the arithmetic/logic unit (ALU), and the primary storage unit. Each unit performs its own unique functions.

The **control unit**, as its name implies, controls what is happening in the CPU. It does not process or store data; rather, it directs the sequence of operations. The control unit retrieves one instruction at a time from the storage unit. It interprets the instruction and sends the necessary signals to the ALU and storage unit for the instruction to be carried out. This process is repeated until all the instructions have been executed.

Another function of the control unit is to communicate with the input device in order to transfer program instructions and data into storage. Similarly, it communicates with the output device to transfer results from storage to the output device.

The **arithmetic/logic unit (ALU)** handles the execution of all arithmetic computations. It does not store data; it merely performs the necessary calculations. Functions performed by the ALU include arithmetic operations (addition, subtraction, multiplication, and division) and comparisons. Since the bulk of computer processing involves calculations or comparisons, the capabilities of a computer often depend upon the capabilities of the ALU.

The **primary storage unit (internal storage** or **main storage)** holds all the instructions and data necessary for processing. These are transferred from an input device to the primary storage unit, where they are held until needed for processing. Data that are being processed and intermediate results from ALU calculations are also held in primary storage. After all processing is completed, the control unit directs the final results to be transferred to an output device.

A **microprocessor** is the CPU of a microcomputer. It performs arithmetic operations and control functions, much as the CPU of a large computer does; however, a microprocessor fits on a single silicon chip the size of a nailhead (see Figure 2-2).

CENTRAL PROCESSING UNIT The heart of a computer system, consisting of three components.

CONTROL UNIT The part of the CPU that directs operations.

ARITHMETIC/ LOGIC UNIT The part of the CPU that executes arithmetic computations and comparisons.

PRIMARY STORAGE Part of storage inside the CPU.

The CPU in Operation

Let us examine a simple problem. Assume we want the computer to add two numbers and print the result. The following series of steps demonstrates the flow of program instructions and data through the CPU.

Step A: The control unit directs an input device to transfer program instructions to primary storage. (As will be shown later, some data and instructions may be stored outside of the CPU and transferred to primary storage when needed.) Since this is a simple problem, there may be only two instructions—one to add and one to print.

Step B: The control unit examines the first instruction and interprets it as addition.

Step C: The control unit sends an electronic signal for the data (the two numbers) to be brought into primary storage from an input device, or for data already in primary storage to be transferred to the ALU.

Figure 10.3   Continued

Step D: The ALU performs the necessary calculation (addition).

Step E: The results are transferred back to the primary storage unit.

Steps B through E: These steps are repeated until all instructions are executed. (In this simplified example, steps B through E are not repeated.)

Step F: The control unit signals the primary storage unit to transfer the results to an output device to be printed.

"It looks like Coach Henson's been using my terminal again."

Figure 10.3

Synthesis Chart:

Topic: Central Processing Unit

	BRENAN/MANDELL	HOPPER/MANDELL	GRAHAM
CONTROL UNIT			
DIRECTS PROCESSES	X	X	X
Retrieves instructions	X	X	X
Interprets instructions	X	X	X
Sends instructions	X	X	X
COMMUNICATES W/INPUT & OUTPUT	X		
Reads input		X	
Prints output		X	
DECISION-MAKING CAPABILITY			X
USES BINARY CODES			X
EXECUTES "FETCH, EXECUTE CYCLES"			X
ARITHMETIC LOGIC UNIT			
PERFORMS ARITHMETICAL CALCULATIONS	X	X	X
COMPARES INFORMATION	X		X
$<,>,=$			X
CARRIES OUT LOGICAL OPERATIONS		X	X
"and," "or," "not"			X
DEFINITION OF LOGIC STATEMENT		X	
PRIMARY STORAGE			
SAME AS INTERNAL OR MAIN STORAGE	X	X	
FUNCTIONS OF PRIMARY STORAGE	X	X	
Holds program being executed	X	X	
Holds results	X	X	
PRIMARY STORAGE HARDWARE		X	

Paper:

The Central Processing Unit

A computer's central processing unit consists of three components: the control unit, the arithmetic logic unit, and primary storage.

In general, the control unit directs the computer's processes by retrieving instructions from storage, interpreting and sending instructions back to storage (Brenan and Mandell, 1984; Graham, 1983; and Hopper and Mandell, 1984). These form "fetch-execute" cycles (Graham 1983). It also communicates with input and output devices by reading input and printing output (Hopper and Mandell, 1984). The control unit utilizes binary codes and has decision-making capability (Graham, 1983).

The second component of the central processing unit is the arithmetic logic unit (ALU). As its name suggests, the ALU performs arithmetical calculations (Brenan and Mandell, 1984; Graham, 1983; and Hopper and Mandell, 1984). It also compares information (Brenan and Mandell, 1984; Graham, 1983) by determining if one piece of information is equal to, greater than, or less than another piece of information (Graham,

1983). The ALU also carries out logical operations (Graham, 1983; Hopper and Mandell, 1984). A logic statement is "a statement that makes a comparison and then does something about it based on the results" (Hopper and Mandell, 1984).

Primary storage (also called internal or main storage) is a final component of the central processing unit. It holds both the program being executed and the results of processing (Brenan and Mandell, 1984; Hopper and Mandell, 1984). Here data is stored as binary digits (bits) in the computer's hardware (Hopper and Mandell, 1984).

WRITING THE PAPER: THE PROCESS

> What is written without effort is in general read without pleasure.
>
> —SAMUEL JOHNSON
>
> Eighteenth Century English Author

The effort you put into writing a research paper shows in the quality of what you've written. Often *how* you write your paper is graded as much as *what* you write in your paper. It pays, then, to spend whatever effort and time is necessary to master the two main steps of the writing process: writing the first draft and revising it in the second draft. Your final version, the product of your effort, will deserve the grade it receives.

FIRST DRAFT

Your first writing effort is often called a **rough draft,** and with good reason. Its goal is simply to get your ideas on paper. As Jackie Collins once said, "If you want to be a writer, stop talking about it and sit down and write!" No one reads your first draft but you. To some extent, you write without worrying about neatness. However, writing only on the front of your paper or using a word processor aids you in later constructing your second draft.

The flow of words forms your most important consideration. Because your objective is to sketch your paper, you might try following the advice given to speakers. In the introductory paragraph, "Tell them what you're going to say." In the text, "Tell them." And, in the summary, "Tell them what you said." Although this seems redundant, most papers take this form.

Although you should keep the basic format of introduction-body-summary in mind, many writers find starting and completing a paper to be the hardest parts. Because your thesis statement guides your writing, sections need not be written in a set order. As you write the body of your paper, you may think of the perfect beginning or ending for it. Otherwise, you may stare at a blank page for a very long time.

Introduction: "Tell Them What You're Going to Say"

In telling your audience what you're going to say, you set the stage for the rest of your paper. The introduction informs readers of your paper's general content and tells them why they will want to read your paper. The introduction lets you be creative, an important trait in capturing an audience's attention. A new approach, perfect example, or clever phrase won't always come easily. You need to keep an open mind and a patient outlook in searching for ideas.

By getting your readers' interest, you motivate them to continue reading. Briefly summarizing your most important sources provides a background for your specific subject. The reader then sees how your paper relates to a larger context of information. Interest also may be elicited by focusing the reader's attention on a particularly relevant or surprising aspect of your topic. This could be a question, generalization, viewpoint, definition, quotation, problem, conflict, or other pertinent factor. A related way to motivate the reader is to note the significance of your research. Here you tell the contribution (answers to questions, facts that support a generalization or viewpoint, new insights) that your paper proposes to make.

In telling your readers what you're going to say, you want to familiarize them with your topic. Your thesis statement tells them your purpose and plan for your paper. A summary of the main headings to be discussed in the paper expands the thesis statement. It provides a preview of important ideas.

Text: "Tell Them"

The bulk of your paper consists of the text. Here you provide a detailed synthesis of your information. When you synthesize information, you identify patterns and relationships among supporting details found through charting. Thus, the end result of your research is a concise, unified combination of ideas, rather than a summary or collection of facts.

Your most important consideration in writing the text of your paper is its organization. How you order the points you make in your text depends on your purpose and the research you collect. Several patterns of organization are possible (see Table 10.2). Once again, you rely on your inferential skills to determine which pattern best fits your paper. Following an organizational pattern helps you include all the information you've identified for a specific point. It also makes corrections in the second draft easier.

No matter what your topic and organizational pattern are, your paper needs to conform to a research paper format, which includes **footnotes** or **endnotes** with an accompanying bibliography or **parenthetical references** with an accompanying list of references. Rules for making these notations depend on the style that your instructor requires or that

Table 10.2   Organizational Patterns

Inductive/Deductive (specific to general/general to specific)
Hierarchical (most to least or least to most)
Chronological (time order)
Sequential (process order)
Part to Whole/Whole to Part
Spatial (top to bottom, left to right, etc.)
Categorization
Alphabetical
Comparison/Contrast
Problem-Solution
Cause-Effect

you choose. Specific books describe and provide examples for your reference. Table 10.3 identifies some of the most common **style manuals** for different content areas.

Summary: "Tell Them What You Said"

The summary paragraph(s) provides closure for the text of your paper. It is especially important in lengthy papers. In the summary paragraph(s), you restate your thesis and the purpose of the research. In addition, you highlight the major points that supported your topic. You indicate the relationship between headings and how these prove the points you've made. You also identify the need for further research. You raise new questions or speculate on information or conclusions in your paper.

SECOND DRAFT

Have you ever talked with a friend, left, and then thought of a forgotten detail, an omitted point, or a perfect example, and thought, "I wish I'd said that." Your second draft gives you that chance. Allowing some time between writing the first draft and starting the second lets your ideas gel. Thus, when you begin to revise your paper, you have a fresh perspective.

One way to revise your first draft involves scissors and tape. Instead of rewriting, you simply cut apart sentences, paragraphs, or sections, and tape them in the order you desire. This patchwork manuscript forms the basis for writing your final draft.

Using a personal computer for writing your rough draft decreases the time it takes for revisions. Word processing programs allow you to change sentence or paragraph order, style, spelling, and punctuation without having to retype the entire manuscript. Some programs even check your grammar and writing style.

Two drawbacks hinder the use of word processing programs. Luckily, they are not insurmountable ones. First, using a word processor takes some skill. Learning a word processing program involves time and practice. When planning to use a word processor, you need to allow time for learning the program. Second, word processing requires access to personal computers. If you do not own a computer, one may be available through local computer rental agencies or your institution's computer center.

Elements of Style

Regardless of the subject of your research, to write a well organized, readable paper, you must remember the three elements of style: conciseness, clarity, and cohesion. Each is easier if you consider order when compiling your first draft. These elements demand much of your writing ability.

First, conciseness demands brevity. If you've got something to say, you need to say it clearly and quickly without omitting important details. Adding extra details detracts from the quality of your paper. Undue padding contributes nothing to your topic.

Table 10.3   Style Manuals for Various Content Areas

American Mathematical Society. *A Manual for Authors of Mathematical Papers,* 7th ed. Providence, R.I.: American Mathematical Society, 1990.

American Psychological Association. *Publication Manual of the American Psychological Association,* 4th ed. Washington, D.C.: American Psychological Association, 1988.

A Uniform System of Citation, 13th ed. Cambridge, Mass.: Harvard Law Review Association, 1991.

The Chicago Manual of Style, 14th ed. Chicago: Univ. of Chicago Press, 1993.

Geowriting: A Guide to Writing, Editing, and Printing in Earth Science. Alexandria, Va.: American Geological Institute, 1984.

Council of Biology Editors. Style Manual Committee. *CBE Style Manual: A Guide for Authors, Editors, and Publishers in the Biological Sciences,* 5th ed. Bethesda, Md.: Council of Biology Editors, 1983.

Day, Robert A. *How to Write and Publish a Scientific Paper,* 3d ed. Phoenix, Ariz.: Oryx Press, 1988.

Dodd, Janet S., ed. *The ACS Style Guide: A Manual for Authors and Editors.* Washington, D.C.: American Chemical Society, 1986.

Garner, Diane L., and Smith, Diane H. *The Complete Guide to Citing Government Documents: A Manual for Writers and Librarians.* Bethesda, Md.: Congressional Information Service, 1984.

Gibaldi, Joseph, and Achtert, Walter S. *MLA Handbook for Writers of Research Papers,* 2d ed. New York: Modern Language Association, 1988.

Huth, Edward J., M.D. *How to Write and Publish Papers in the Medical Sciences.* 2nd ed. Philadelphia: ISI Press, 1987.

International Steering Committee of Medical Editors. ``Uniform Requirements for Manuscripts Submitted to Biomedical Journals.'' *Annals of Internal Medicine* 90: 95–99, 1982.

Michaelson, Herbert B. *How to Write and Publish Engineering Papers and Reports,* 2d ed. Philadelphia: ISI Press, 1986.

Rosnow, R. L. & Rosnow, M. *Writing Papers in Psychology.* Belmont, CA: Wadsworth, 1992.

Skillin, Marjorie E., and Gay, Robert M., eds. *Words into Type,* 3d ed. Englewood Cliffs, N.J.: Prentice-Hall, 1986.

Society of Mining Engineers. *Author's Guide.* Littleton, Colo.: Society of Mining Engineers/AIME, 1983. Includes supplement entitled ``Suggestions to Authors of Papers Intended for Society of Mining Engineers Publications.''

Steffens, H. J. & Dickerson, M. J. *Writers Guide: History.* Lexington, MA: D.C. Heath, 1987.

Table 10.3   Style Manuals for Various Content Areas *continued*

U.S. Department of the Interior. Bureau of Reclamation. *Style Guide for Technical Publications.* Denver: Bureau of Reclamation, 1989.

U.S. Geological Survey. *Suggestions to Authors of Reports of the United States Geological Survey,* 6th ed. Washington, D.C.: Government Printing Office, 1991.

U.S. Government Printing Office. *Style Manual.* Washington, D.C.: GPO, 1984.

Note: More recent editions of these manuals may be available upon request of their publisher.

Second, clarity means writing clearly and logically to clarify vague or complex information. It also involves rewriting stilted sentences and omitting trite expressions.

Clarity relates to coherence, or cohesion, the "glue" that holds your paper together. The topic and summary sentences of paragraphs or sections and transition words build coherence. They help the parts of your paper "stick together."

Writing a research paper, or any paper, is difficult. Some students choose to take composition courses to improve their skills. Others use style manuals to develop better writing styles. Table 10.4 lists such manuals on writing style.

Final Revisions

Final revisions consist of editing, rewriting, and polishing your second draft into the final draft. You reread, looking for both structural and grammatical errors. You check the paper's structure by looking at organization and transition. You look at your choice of words and use of details and examples. To check for grammatical errors, you inspect words, sentences, and paragraphs for mistakes in spelling, punctuation, etc.

When you select a book to read, does its cover affect your choice? What about the size of the print? Do you consider how well it's packaged? Just as these external factors color your perception about a book, they affect the way your instructor perceives your paper. Your final draft needs to be a revised copy, as error-free as possible. Papers that are neatly written in ink or neatly formatted and printed out receive higher grades than those typed without care. Margins should be wide enough for your instructor's comments. However, they should not be so wide that your instructor suspects that you're padding your work. Your final draft should include a title page, body, references, and any other elements required by your instructor. Table 10.5 is a checklist for locating errors that need correcting.

I think of being a child in my family at the dinner table, with seven kids and hubbub and parents distracted by worries and responsibilities. Before I would say anything at the table, before I would approach my parents, I would plan what I wanted to say. I'd map out the narrative, sharpen the details, add color, plan momentum. This way I could hold their attention. This way I became a writer.

—PEGGY NOONAN

Twentieth Century American Author

Table 10.4   Guide to General Manuals of Writing Style

Standard Handbooks of Composition

Baker, S. *The Complete Stylist and Handbook.* New York: Harper, 1984.

Elsbree, et al. *Heath Handbook of Composition,* 10th ed. Lexington, Mass.: Heath, 1981.

Gefvert, C. J. *The Confident Writer: A Norton Handbook.* New York: W. W. Norton, 1988.

Hodges, J. C., and Whitten, M. E. *Harbrace College Handbook,* 10th ed. New York: Harcourt Brace Jovanovich, 1990.

Kirszner, L. G. and Mandell, S. R. *The Holt Handbook.* New York: CBS College Publishing, 1986.

Leggett, G. C., Mead, D., and Charvat, W. *Prentice-Hall Handbook for Writers,* 8th ed. Englewood Cliffs, N.J.: Prentice-Hall, 1988.

McCrimmon, J. M. *Writing with a Purpose: Short Edition.* Boston: Houghton Mifflin, 1988.

Neeld, E. C. *Writing Brief,* 2d ed. Glenview, Ill.: Scott, Foresman, 1986.

Guides to Writing Style

Chicago Guide to Preparing Electronic Manuscripts. Chicago: University of Chicago Press, 1986.

Chicago Manual of Style, 14th ed. Chicago: University of Chicago Press, 1993.

Eastman, R. M. *Style: Writing as the Discovery of Outlook,* 2d ed. New York: Oxford University Press, 1978.

Elbow, P. *Writing with Power: Techniques for Mastering the Writing Process.* New York: Oxford University Press, 1981.

Howell, John Bruce. *Style Manuals of the English-Speaking World: A Guide.* Phoenix, Ariz.: Oryx Press, 1983.

Strunk, W., Jr., and White, E. B. *The Elements of Style,* 3d ed. New York: Macmillan, 1982.

Turabian, K. L. *A Manual of Style for Writers of Term Papers, Theses, and Dissertations,* 5th ed. Chicago: University of Chicago Press, 1987.

U.S. Government Printing Office Style Manual, rev. ed. Washington, D.C.: Government Printing Office, 1984.

Walker, Mellisa. *Writing Research Papers: A Norton Guide.* New York and London: W. W. Norton & Company, 1984.

Webster's Standard American Style Manual. Springfield, Mass.: Merriam-Webster, 1985.

Weidenborner, Stephen, and Domenick Caruso. *Writing Research Papers: A Guide to the Process.* New York: St. Martin's Press, 1982.

Williams, N. M. *Style: Ten Lessons in Clarity and Grace.* Glenview, Ill.: Scott, Foresman, 1989.

Table 10.5   Checklist for Revisions

	Revise	Leave as is
1. Structure		
a. Appropriate title	_____	_____
b. Thesis statement	_____	_____
• Purpose		
• Audience appeal		
c. Introductory paragraph(s)	_____	_____
d. Logically organized text	_____	_____
e. Supporting research or examples	_____	_____
f. Summary or concluding paragraph(s)	_____	_____
2. Grammar		
a. Spelling	_____	_____
b. Sentences (complete? run-ons?)	_____	_____
c. Punctuation	_____	_____
d. Paragraphs (indented? topic and summary sentences?)	_____	_____
e. Tense (past, present, future)	_____	_____
f. Subject-verb agreement	_____	_____
3. Style		
a. Conciseness	_____	_____
b. Clarity	_____	_____
c. Cohesion (transition)	_____	_____
d. Word choice	_____	_____
e. Format of footnotes and bibliography (as required by style book of choice)	_____	_____
4. References		
a. Identification of direct quotes or other referenced information	_____	_____
b. Complete citations	_____	_____
c. Relevancy	_____	_____
d. Objectivity	_____	_____
e. Author's qualifications	_____	_____
f. Primary sources	_____	_____
g. Secondary sources	_____	_____
h. Adequate number of references	_____	_____
i. References from a variety of sources	_____	_____
5. Form		
a. Title page	_____	_____
b. Table of contents	_____	_____
c. Abstract	_____	_____
d. Bibliography or references	_____	_____
e. Appendices	_____	_____

Exercise 10.3   On a separate sheet of paper, revise the following paper according to the standards indicated in the checklist in Table 10.5.

Countries and Their Constitutions

A constitution is a statement which outlines the basic principals of formal organizations. Such organizations include countries, political associations, and private groups. A constitution can be written or unwritten. It sets up the way the organization will function in terms of rules and purposes, etc

The first kind of American Constitution was a document called the Articles of Confederation. It granted freedoms to each state, but this document was inadequate for governing the country. The new country of america faced many problems left unresolved by the Articles. The document did not contain means for getting states to work together. It lacked provisions for an executive branch and a national court system. The Articles of Confederation made no allowances for regulating trade among states. No means for getting taxes.

At first statesman such as George Washington and Alexander Hamilton planned to meet to rewrite the Articles into a stronger document but then they decided to write the Constitution of the United States. A Constitutional Convention got together in 1787. Twelve of the thirteen colonies attended.

Only Rhode Island didn't. George Washington was president of the convention.

Fifty-five men attended the convention, but only thirty-nine signed the Constitution. The ones that did not sign disagreed with some of the things it said. But just because these men signed it, it did not represent the wishes of American yet. It had to be voted on and approved by nine states. This kind of approval was called ratification. People who liked the Constitution and supported it were called Federalists. Those that opposed it were Anti-Federalists. These groups formed the basis of the first political parties in the U.S.

The Constitution consist of the preamble, seven articles, and twenty-six amendments. The preamble a short introduction which explains the overall purposes of the Constitutuion. The Constituion established a federal government which divided power between the states and the national government.

The first three articles establish the branches of the government. So there are three branches of the national govenment. Including the executive, legislative, and the judicial. The executive branch enforces the laws made by the legislative

branch which are explained by the judicial branch. The fifth article provides for future amendments or changes in the Constitutuion. The sixth article concerns the national debt. The fourth article tell how states will relate to each other. The last article tells how the constitution was to be ratified.

After the Constitution was ratified. It was amended by a document called the Bill of Rights. These were the first ten amendments to the Constitutuion. They protect citizens from unfair governmental acts. In all there have been twenty-six additions or amendments to the Constitutions covering everything from individual freedoms to voting procedures. Everyone agrees that the American Constitution is the best document for running a country.

Exercise 10.4   On a separate sheet of paper, construct a synthesis chart and write a paper comparing and contrasting information found in the following sources.

Biological, Psychological, and Sociological Aspects of Aging

Aging occurs in three ways: biological, psychological, and sociological.

BIOLOGICAL ASPECTS OF AGING. There are various views about how the body ages (Birren 1986):

1. *Tissue organ deficiency.* Tissues and organs of the body may become diseased, so that the body becomes debilitated. This view is too limiting and does not address the issue of whether the diseased tissues/organs cause aging or are the result of aging. Also, there is considerable variability between people regarding the rate at which these tissues/organs alter with time.
2. *Hardening of the arteries.* This view emphasizes that as individuals age, their arteries become clogged, preventing the blood from taking oxygen and nutrients to the vital organs of the body. Decline in alertness, for example, would be explained as a consequence of inadequate oxygen to the brain. This focus also has limitations because changes in the blood vessels are currently viewed as an avoidable condition.
3. *Endocrine gland malfunction.* Another biological view of aging suggests that it is tied to the breakdown of the endocrine glands (including thyroid, pancreas, gonads, adrenals). However, researchers have discovered that hormone levels, by themselves, do not have inevitable predictable effects on the body.
4. *Immunity system changes.* Another aspect of aging suggests that "the debilitated older person may not only come to forget events, names, and familiar faces, but may also gradually lose the biological memory necessary to recognize and fight previously encountered viruses and 'unfriendly' proteins" (Birren 1986, 271). However, lower forms of life without specialized immune systems also show characteristics of aging. Hence, the breakdown of an immune system does not automatically lead to aging.
5. *Genetic diseases.* Longevity is an inherited trait. While diet, exercise, and lack of stress all play a role in avoiding disease and living a long time, individuals whose parents and grandparents have lived a long time are more likely to have a similar lifespan than are those whose ancestors died relatively early.

These biological changes emphasize that although the body does alter with time, it does so in different degrees and at different rates. Hence, any statement that a person will experience a specific biological decline at a specific age must be considered tentative.

PSYCHOLOGICAL THEORIES OF AGING. In studying aging, psychologists look at changes in the speed of behavior, and changes in perception, memory, and depression.

1. *Speed of behavior.* As an individual ages, so it is assumed, it takes longer to register incoming information, process it, and act. But the degree to which there is slowing of behavior, and whether this change is inevitable, are controversial. In some cases, with extensive and concerted effort to master a specific task, speed of response can increase.
2. *Perception.* Perception, both visual and auditory, may change with age. Our eyes and ears are not immune to generalized decline. However, independent of disease (glaucoma, cataracts), visual perceptual functioning may remain substantially intact. The ability to hear higher tones, and every syllable of what someone is saying, generally declines with age. The psychological effect of such loss may be the development of mild paranoia. The elderly may assume others are talking about them.
3. *Memory.* Short-term memory functions also decline with age. The elderly take slightly longer to retrieve information.

▼   LIVING SOCIOLOGY   ▼

In our society, mistakes in memory on the part of the elderly are labeled differently than similar mistakes on the part of young people. If a young person forgets something, we say that he or she simply forgot. If an old person forgets something, we say that he or she is old. The way our society regards "memory mistakes" is another illustration of its prejudice against the elderly.

(Sociology, continuing)

SOCIOLOGY SOURCE

4. *Depression.* Depression is the most common psychological complaint of the elderly. Feelings of hopelessness, worthlessness, and despair characterize depression. Depression can be mild, lasting a few days; or debilitating, requiring hospitalization. The causes of depression may be physiological (brain cell degeneration) or cultural (social changes in the person's life, such as loss of spouse, job, or children). Treatment may involve taking medication and increasing their involvement in meaningful relationships, social positions, and roles.

Psychological variables influence biological outcomes. For example, feelings of not being in control of one's life circumstance or of feeling helpless or hopeless have been correlated with an increase in reported physical symptoms (Pennebaker et al. 1977).

SOCIOLOGICAL ASPECTS OF AGING. The concept of social aging refers to the arbitrary social definitions of what is appropriate or expected of people at various ages. Definition of the situation and status-role connections become important in discussing how individuals age sociologically.

If people define themselves as old (Thomas and Thomas 1928), the consequences of their doing so are to limit what they do. People who define themselves as too old to be a romantic lover, a hang-glider flyer, or a race-track driver tend to avoid these roles. Others may also define the elderly as persons who should engage in certain behaviors (play canasta) and not others (use a skateboard).

The status a person is in implies certain role behaviors. People whose status is elderly (that is, elderly people) are expected to act certain ways. Although some elderly people like to skydive and some young people like to play canasta, age tends to limit the range of behavior considered appropriate. A 10-year-old can be a member of a neighborhood skateboard group, a cub scout, and a fourth grader. A 16-year-old can be a driver, an 18-year-old a voter, a 21-year-old a legal alcohol drinker, and a 65-year-old a retiree. Each age status provides eligibility for some roles and closes eligibility for other roles. An 18-year-old cannot be a grandparent and a 90-year-old cannot compete in the Olympics.

One consequence of accepting social definitions of status positions is to restrict people into interactions in subgroups with others who approve of their role choices. The young and the old keep to themselves (have a disproportionate level of interaction within their own groups) because their peers approve of their role behavior.

Aging brings new statuses. Although there are various status paths, a typical one involves being a child, teenager, spouse, parent, empty nester, grandparent, retiree, and widow or widower. Other statuses some assume along the way are divorced person, single parent, and stepparent.

The culture an individual lives in defines the value of that person. In our youth-oriented culture, the elderly are more likely to feel devalued. "Evidence indicates that young adults view the life circumstances of older adults more negatively than do older adults themselves. Hence, the young regard aging as moving from, rather than toward, an ideal state" (Birren 1986, 277). Sociologists suggest that as people adopt statuses that have traditionally been associated with being old, they inadvertently adopt the values associated with those statuses. For example, because the retired are stereotyped as being bored, some people may adopt those feelings once they assume the status. Sometimes the elderly are subjected to worse treatment than negative social reflections. They are abused (see the feature on the next page).

▼ GERONTOLOGICAL THEORIES OF AGING

Gerontology is the study of the process of aging and of the elderly. Social gerontology focuses on the social changes that occur as individuals age. Five general theories of aging follow.

Disengagement Theory

The earliest and most controversial theory of aging, disengagement theory, was developed by Cumming and Henry (1961). They took the view that as people age and move toward death they gradually disengage from all social attachments, obligations, and activities. The researchers viewed the process as natural and emphasized that the process of withdrawal was functional both for society and the elderly.

Reaction to the theory was immediate and negative. The theory (as originally proposed) did not

(Sociology, continuing)

acknowledge that individuals in different cultures vary in how much they "disengage." Indeed, in some cultures, the elderly stay very much involved in social relationships and in society. In addition, many people in our society do not typically disengage. We discuss one such group, the centenarians, later in this chapter.

Exchange Theory

Dowd (1980) argues from an exchange theory perspective that the elderly withdraw because they have nothing to offer other people as an incentive to interact with them (the elderly). Young people are generally not interested in interacting with the elderly because they (the young) look to peers for companionship. Corporations also tend to favor young rather than old employees. Exchange theory says that the elderly are usually forced into a lower devalued social position because they have nothing of value to offer society.

This theory is flawed because the elderly do offer skills others regard as rewarding. For example, grandparents provide invaluable child care for their children and grandchildren. The elderly as workers also have shown themselves to be responsible and productive.

Exercise 10.4   Continued

▬▬ Aging—Will You Still Need Me When I'm 64?

Some years ago, students at Long Beach City College in California elected Pearl Taylor their spring festival queen. Ms. Taylor had everything necessary to win: looks, intelligence, personality, and campus-wide popularity. At about the same time, citizens of Raleigh, North Carolina, elected Isabella Cannon as their mayor.

Question: What's so remarkable about these events?

Not too much really, except that Pearl was 90 years old when elected, and Isabella was 73 (Barrow & Smith, 1979). Both are part of the graying of America. Currently, some 30 million Americans are over the age of 65. By the year 2020, some 50 million persons, or *1 out of every* 5, will be 65 years of age or older. These figures make the elderly the fastest-growing segment of society. Understandably, psychologists have become increasingly interested in aging.

Question: What is life like for the aged?

There are large variations in aging. Most of us have known elderly individuals at both extremes: those who are active, healthy, and satisfied and whose minds are clear and alert; and those who are confused, childlike, dependent, or senile. Despite such variations, some generalizations can be made.

Aging   Biological aging is a gradual process that begins quite early in life. Peak functioning in most physical capacities reaches a maximum by about 25 to 30 years of age. Thereafter, gradual declines occur in muscular strength, flexibility, circulatory efficiency, speed of response, sensory acuity, and other functions.

Question: So people are "over the hill" by 30?

Hardly! Prime abilities come at different ages for different activities. Peak performances for professional football and baseball players usually occur in the mid-20s; for professional bowlers, the mid-30s; for artists and musicians, the 50s; and for politicians, philosophers, business or industrial leaders and others, the early 60s.

For those who are still young, the prospect of aging physically may be the greatest threat of old age (see Highlight 4-2). However, it is wrong to believe that most elderly people are sickly, infirm, or senile. Only about 5 percent of those over 65 years old are in nursing homes. As for the possibility of a mental slide, physician Alex Comfort (1976) comments, "The human brain does not shrink, wilt, perish, or deteriorate with age. It normally continues to function well through as many as 9 decades." As a **gerontologist** (jer-ON-TOL-o-jist: one who studies aging), Comfort estimates that only 25 percent of the disability of old people is medically based. The remaining 75 percent is social, political, and cultural.

Comfort's view is backed by studies of the intellectual capacities of aging individuals. Little overall decline occurs in intelligence test scores with aging. Although it is true that **fluid abilities** (those requiring speed or rapid learning) may decline, **crystallized abilities,** such as vocabulary and stored-up knowledge, actually improve—at least into the 70s (Baltes & Schaie, 1974). The general intellectual decline attributed to old age is largely a myth.

Biological aging Physiological changes that accompany increasing age and alter a variety of physical and psychological functions.

Maximum life span The biologically determined maximum number of years humans could live under optimal conditions.

Life expectancy The average number of years a person of a given sex, race, and nationality can expect to live.

Gerontologist One who scientifically studies aging and its effects.

Fluid abilities Innate abilities based on perceptual, motor, or intellectual speed and flexibility; abilities that are not based on prior intentional learning.

(Psychology, continuing)

132   Essentials of Psychology

Crystalized abilities Abilities that a person has intentionally acquired in the past and has practiced to a high level of mastery; accumulated knowledge and skills.

Disengagement theory of aging Theory stating that as people age it is normal and desirable for them to withdraw from society and from roles they held earlier.

Activity theory Theory of aging stating that the best adjustment to aging occurs for individuals who remain active mentally, socially, and physically.

Ageism Discrimination or prejudice based on a person's age.

Critical Thinking Exercise

In Japan, aging is seen as positive, and growing older brings increased status and respect. Is this an example of ageism?

Answer

Yes it is. Even when the elderly are revered, they are being prejudged on the basis of age (Kimmel, 1988). Also, giving higher status to the elderly relegates the young to lower status—another instance of ageism.

Question: What kind of person adjusts most successfully to aging?

Activity and Disengagement   Two principal theories have been proposed to explain successful adjustment to the physical and social changes of aging. **Disengagement theory** assumes that it is normal and desirable for people to withdraw from society as they age (Cumming & Henry, 1961). According to this theory, elderly persons welcome disengagement since it relieves them of roles and responsibilities they have become less able to fulfill. Likewise, society benefits from disengagement as younger persons with new energy and skills fill positions vacated by aging individuals.

Certainly we have all known people who disengaged from society as they grew older. Nevertheless, disengagement theory can be criticized for describing successful aging as a retreat. While disengagement may be common, it is not necessarily ideal.

Question: What does the second theory say?

A second view of optimal aging is provided by **activity theory,** a sort of "use-it-or-lose-it" view that assumes activity is the essence of life for people of all ages. Activity theory predicts that people who remain active physically, mentally, and socially will adjust better to aging (Havighurst, 1961).

Proponents of activity theory believe that aging persons should maintain the activities of their earlier years for as long as possible. If a person is forced to give up particular roles or activities, it is recommended that these activities or roles be replaced with others. In so doing, the aging person is able to maintain a better self-image, greater satisfaction, and more social support—resulting in more successful aging.

Question: Which theory is correct?

The majority of studies on aging support the *activity theory*, although there have been exceptions (Barrow & Smith, 1979). At the same time, some people do seek disengagement, so neither theory is absolutely "correct." Actually, successful aging probably requires a combination of activity and disengagement. For example, one researcher found that the elderly tend to disengage from activities that are no longer satisfying while maintaining those that are (Brown, 1974). In the final analysis, it seems that life satisfaction in old age depends mainly on how much time we spend doing things we find meaningful (Horn & Meer, 1987) (Fig. 4-9).

Ageism   In one way or another you have encountered ageism. **Ageism** refers to discrimination or prejudice on the basis of age. It applies to people of all ages and can oppress the young as well as the old. For instance, a person applying for a job may just as likely be told, "You're too young," as "You're too old." In most Western nations, ageism tends to have a negative impact on older individuals. Usually, it is expressed as an aversion, hatred, or rejection of the elderly. As Alex Comfort (1976) points out, the concept of "oldness" is often used to expel people from useful work. According to Comfort, retirement is frequently just another name for dismissal and unemployment.

Another facet of ageism is stereotyping of the aged. Popular stereotypes of the "dirty old man," "meddling old woman," "senile old fool," and the like, help perpetuate the myths underlying ageism. Contrast such images to those associated with youthfulness: The young are perceived as fresh, whole, attractive, energetic, active, emerging, appealing, and so forth. Even positive stereotypes can be a problem. If older people are perceived as financially well-off, wise, or experienced, it can blind others to the real problems of the elderly (Gatz & Pearson, 1988). The important point, then, is to realize that there is a tremendous diversity among the elderly—ranging from the infirm and senile, to aerobic-dancing grandmothers.

(Psychology, continuing)

| Highlight 4-2 | Biological Aging—How Long Is a Lifetime? |

Whatever the biological causes of aging, humans seem to grow, mature, age, and die within a set time. The length of our lives is limited by a boundary called the **maximum life span.** Humans, like other animals, appear to live a limited number of years, even under the best of circumstances. Estimates of the average human life span place it around 95 to 110 years (Botwinick, 1984).

For most people, **life expectancy** (the actual number of years the average person lives) is shorter than a life span. In the 1800s the average life expectancy was 36 years. Now, average life expectancy for American males is 72 years and for females it is 79 years. With improved health care, life expectancy should move even closer to the maximum life span.

At present there is no known way to extend the human life span. On the other hand, there is every

reason to believe that life expectancy can be increased. If you would personally like to add to a new, higher average, here are some deceptively simple rules for living a long life (Coni et al., 1984):

1. Do not smoke.
2. Use alcohol in moderation or not at all.
3. Avoid becoming overweight.
4. If you suffer from high blood pressure, have it treated.
5. Remain socially and economically active in retirement.
6. Exercise regularly throughout life.

To this we can add: Get married (married persons live longer), learn to manage stress, and choose long-lived parents!

Question: What can be done about ageism?

One of the best ways to combat ageism is to counter stereotypes with facts. For example, studies show that in many occupations older workers perform better at jobs requiring *both* speed and skill (Giniger et al., 1983). Gradual slowing with age is a reality. But often, it is countered by experience, skill, or expertise (Schaie, 1988). One study, for example, showed that older typists responded slower on reaction-time tests than younger typists. Nevertheless, there was no difference in the actual typing speeds of younger and older typists (Salthouse, 1987).

Taking a broader view, Bernice Neugarten (1971) examined the lives of 200 people between the ages of 70 and 79. Neugarten found that 75 percent of these people were satisfied with their lives after retirement. Neugarten's findings also refuted other myths about aging.

Countering Myths About Aging

1. Old persons generally do not become isolated and neglected by their families. Most *prefer* to live apart from their children.
2. Old persons are rarely placed in mental hospitals by uncaring children.
3. Old persons who live alone are not necessarily lonely or desolate.
4. Few elderly persons ever show signs of senility or mental decay, and few ever become mentally ill.

In short, most of the elderly studied by Neugarten were integrated, active, and psychologically healthy. Findings such as these call for an end to the forced obsolescence of the elderly. As a group, older people represent a valuable source of skill, knowledge, and energy that we can no longer afford to cast aside. As we face the challenges of this planet's uncertain future, we need all the help we can get!

Living will A written declaration stating that a person prefers not to have his or her life artificially prolonged in the event of a terminal illness.

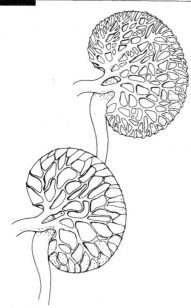

As the heart pumps less blood into an organ, the capillary trees within that organ recede, leaving some of the cells without nourishment. Exercise promotes maintenance, and even growth, of capillaries.

cardiac index: the cardiac output per square meter of body surface area. The **cardiac output** is the quantity of blood pumped into the aorta each minute. Cardiac output is responsible for transport of substances to and from the tissues; it changes markedly with body size.

vital capacity: the maximum volume of air that can be inhaled into or exhaled from the lungs.

Aging of Systems

The aging of cells is reflected by changes in the organs they are a part of. The most visible changes take place in the skin. As people age, wrinkles increase, partly because of a loss of elasticity and of the fat that lies under the skin. Scars accumulate from many small cuts and roughen the skin's texture. Exposure to sun, wind, and cold hastens wrinkling.

Less visible, but much more important to nutrition, are the changes that take place in the digestive system. The gums deteriorate, causing loss of teeth; gum disease afflicts 90 percent of the population in the decade after age 65. The senses of taste and smell diminish, reducing the pleasure of eating. The stomach's secretions of hydrochloric acid and enzymes decrease, as do the secretions of digestive juices by the pancreas and small intestine, impairing the digestive process. The digestive tract muscles weaken with reduced use, so that pressure in the large intestine causes the outpocketings of diverticulosis. Constipation becomes a problem.

The liver is somewhat different. Liver cells regenerate themselves throughout life, but even with good nutrition, fat gradually infiltrates the liver, reducing its work output. The pancreatic cells become less responsive to high blood glucose levels, and the body's cells become resistant to insulin, so that it takes more to make them respond.

The heart and blood vessels age similarly. All organs and tissues depend on the circulation of nutrients and oxygen, so degenerative changes in the cardiovascular system critically affect all other systems. The decrease in blood flow through the kidneys makes them gradually less efficient at removing wastes and maintaining the blood's normal composition. As the heart pumps blood less forcefully, the capillary trees of the kidneys diminish in size; some kidney cells die. This degenerative process can be retarded by regular exercising, which ensures that an ample volume of blood is pumped into the kidneys, keeping the capillaries open.

The body's systems age at different rates and to different extents. In a lifetime, nerve conduction velocity appears to be affected least and lung function most, with other functions between the extremes:

- Nerve conduction velocity and cellular enzyme activities decline about 15 percent.
- Cardiac index falls 30 percent.
- Vital capacity and renal blood flow decrease by 50 percent.
- Maximum breathing capacity, maximum work rate, and maximum oxygen uptake fall by 60 to 70 percent.[1]

Like the body's organ systems, the skeletal system is subject to change with the passage of time. Bone-building and bone-dismantling cells are constantly remodeling this structure, but after 40, bone loss becomes more rapid than bone building. The result is osteoporosis—a disease that afflicts close to half of all people over 65. Arthritis, a painful swelling of the joints, is another problem that troubles many people as they grow older. During movement, the bones must rub against each other at the joints. The ends are protected from wear by cartilage and by small sacs of fluid that act as a lubricant. With age, the ends of the bones become pitted or eroded as a result of wear and the loss of cartilage and fluid. The cause of arthritis is unknown, but it afflicts millions around the world and is a major problem of the elderly.

Exercise 10.5 Using Sample Chapters 11, 12, and 13 as possible sources in addition to sources at your campus library, create a synthesis chart and paper that addresses one of the following topics: Working Conditions, Employee Responsibilities, Industrial Revolution, Women and Children in Industry, or another topic of your choice that integrates the content of two or more sample chapters.

> **WRITE TO LEARN**
>
> On a separate sheet of paper, explain how the old saying, ``Making a silk purse out of a sow's ear'' is analogous to writing a research paper.

PLAGIARISM

Plagiarism (see Chapter 1) is stealing another person's work and presenting it as your own. Plagiarism comes in two forms: unintentional and intentional. Unintentional, or accidental, plagiarism occurs through inaccurate notetaking or through incorrect citation of references. Intentional plagiarism is deliberate, premeditated theft of published information. Intentional plagiarism also includes getting a paper from a friend or "term paper service." The article reprinted in Excerpt 10.1 describes the hazards of buying term papers.

When you plagiarize, you run the risk of disciplinary action. You avoid plagiarism by carefully noting and documenting reference materials.

Excerpt 10.1 Buying a Term Paper Could Turn Out to Be the First Step to Academic Bankruptcy

"Tired of typing? Is your research wretched? When term paper trauma sets in, call us! 15,483 papers to choose from. All subjects from Anthropology to Zoology. Call Researchers to the Rescue now! 555-3211."

The end of the semester. It's 3:00 in the morning. You've already gone through two pots of coffee and a box and a half of cookies. Your eyes are bloodshot. You've been staring at that blank sheet of paper so long you've memorized the number of lines.

Worst of all, you still don't know what you're going to write for your Econ paper.

When academic deadlines have you stressed out, an ad like the one above could have you dialing in desperation. But, beware! Before you send up an S.O.S. to "Researchers to the Rescue," consider what happened to Suzy B.

"I went to an organization that advertised in the classified section of the campus paper," she confessed. "Since I had a paper due on one of Shakespeare's plays, which is a pretty universal topic, I figured they could whip out a great essay. At $10 a page, it was worth its weight in gold for the amount of aggravation it saved me. It was worth gold until I until I showed it to a friend of mine who went to the same place last semester and found parts of her paper in mine!"

Although Suzy's lack of originality went unnoticed, her story points out one of the major hazards of buying a term paper. The biggest risk, of course, is getting caught at what clearly is cheating. We'll deal with that biggie in a moment, but it's not the only risk. Another is being accused of plagiarism.

For instance, let's say the one paper you choose out of the fifteen written on Shakespeare was submitted to your prof by another student last semester. Your professor might spot this repeat or even discover your paper contains a few lines of famous criticism copied verbatim.

Other things can go wrong. You always run the risk that the style of a purchased paper will clash with the rest of your semester's work. When you suddenly start sounding like Hemingway, your professor will notice. And you might find that you can do a better job yourself.

"Often the papers aren't that good," one student pointed out. "The companies that write these papers don't know the focus of the course or the teacher's expectations. I paid $120 for a 10-pager and only got a C+."

Which brings up another issue: cost. Any paper longer than a few pages is a costly investment for a questionable return. At $10-$12 a page, wouldn't it be better to do the research yourself and spend the money on the finer things in life?

The biggest hazard, of course, is getting caught. One university alone reported fifteen cases last year. If you do get caught, the price is a lot more than just a slap on the hand.

Robert Brooks, Associate Dean of Students at the University of Massachusetts, warns, "Not only is it in violation of our code of student conduct, but in Massachusetts it is a statutory offense to sell plagiarized goods, punishable by fine and imprisonment."

Care to know the procedure you'll go through if you're caught plagiarizing? Robert Mannes, Dean for Student Life at the University of Southern California, says that the faculty member who teaches the course the student is enrolled in makes the initial decision. "For a paper that doesn't count as a major portion of the course grade, the student will usually receive an 'F' for the paper alone, particularly if it's a first offense. However, if the paper is more heavily weighted in the course, if it is a student's second offense or if the degree of plagiarism is severe, then the student will usually receive an 'F' in the course and go before a review board."

Proving plagiarism, Mannes continues, can be tough. "If we're not sure if a paper has been plagiarized, we'll compare it to the catalog from one of these organizations. In one case, the student didn't even change the title of the paper!"

Okay, okay. So you're smart enough to change the title. What else can happen?

At the University of Arizona, a charge of plagiarism is also worked out as much as possible between faculty member and student. However, if the case does go through a formal committee hearing (profs and peers present), several things can happen.

According to Dean Glenn Smith, Administrator of the Code of Academic Integrity, "the student can be suspended for a semester or more, expelled from the university altogether, have an academic dishonesty clause placed on his transcripts or be refused a degree from that particular department."

While writing a paper on the imagery and style of Shakespearean tragedy might take a lot of effort on your part, the alternative of buying a paper can take a lot more out of you. Getting caught will not only contribute to the decline of that GPA you worked so hard for, but will cause a lot of embarrassment. It may also bias the teacher against the rest of the work you do in that class.

And, in the end, you have to live with the fact that you compromised your integrity by taking credit for someone else's work.

The risks are real. So, even if it takes two typewriter ribbons, three pots of coffee and forsaking your cherished sleep, work until you rip your hair out and write your own paper.

AVOIDING THE "I'M-OVER-MY-HEAD" FEELING: SETTING A WRITING SCHEDULE

All authors experience the "I'm-over-my-head-and-this-time-they're-going-to-catch-me" feeling. Knowing what's involved in writing a paper helps you avoid the writer's block that comes with this feeling. Table 10.6 outlines the writing process.

Once you know the process of writing a research paper, you realize that you cannot write a paper in a day or a week. Avoiding the "I'm-over-my-head-and-this-time-they're-going-to-catch-me" feeling involves scheduling enough time to complete the writing process. Setting specific objectives and completion dates helps you budget time and make the best use of resources.

Table 10.6   Steps in Writing a Research Paper

1. Identify type of paper
   a. Theme or essay
   b. Report
   c. Term paper
   d. Research paper
2. Determine format of paper
   a. Title page
   b. Table of contents
   c. Abstract
   d. Body
   e. References
   f. Appendices
3. Select subject
   a. Identify interest and importance of topic
   b. Estimate availability of library resources
4. Narrow subject into manageable topic
   a. Establish purpose of paper
   b. Set scope of paper
      • Write thesis statement
      • Select title
5. Gather sources
   a. Library research
   b. Observation
   c. Interviews
   d. Personal experience
   e. Personal inferences

6. Evaluate sources
   a. Determine primary sources versus secondary sources
   b. Judge relevancy
   c. Estimate objectivity and bias
   d. Evaluate author's qualifications
7. Avoid plagiarism
8. Synthesize sources
   a. Outline
   b. Chart
   c. Revise thesis statement and/or title
9. Write first (rough) draft
   a. Introduction
   b. Text
      • Determine organizational pattern
      • Select style manual
   c. Summary
10. Write second draft
    a. Check style
    b. Make final revisions

RATIONALE FOR A WRITING SCHEDULE

You need a writing schedule for several reasons. First, research takes time in what is probably a full schedule of academic, personal, and perhaps work commitments. Without a time line for beginning, continuing, and completing your research, your paper may not reflect the quality of work you wish.

Second, the resources you need may not be readily available. Interlibrary loans help you obtain materials that are not part of the library's holdings. If a book you need is checked out, you can ask the library to request that it be returned as soon as possible. Copy machines may be out of order, preventing you from obtaining information for later study. Whatever the case, you need to plan for such delays.

Finally, you need time to reflect on the information you gather. This time gives you opportunities to consider your information in different ways and get fresh perspectives. Such reflection helps you determine the commonalities of your ideas and your organizational structure.

SETTING A WRITING SCHEDULE

Suppose that on the first day of class your instructor says that a research paper will be due at mid-term. Your first task in completing this assignment would be to set a writing schedule. Table 10.7 lists the steps in setting a schedule.

You need to modify the steps according to your own research and writing strengths or weaknesses. If you are familiar with your library's holdings and your subject, you may complete your task more quickly. If you lack such background information, your task will probably take more time. If writing comes easily to you, you may not require as much time. On the other hand, if writing is difficult for you, you need to budget extra time.

In most procedures, you begin at the beginning. Here you begin at both the beginning and the end. You begin at the beginning by setting your schedule as soon as a research paper is assigned. You begin at the end by plotting the activities you need to complete in relationship to the paper's final due date.

WRITE TO LEARN

Consider Excerpt 10.1. On a separate sheet of paper or in your journal, describe the hazards of buying term papers. Identify other implications of buying term papers.

Table 10.7   Setting a Writing Schedule

Using your term calendar, mark the following dates:

1. Due date for the paper.

2. If the paper needs to be typed, identify a completion date for getting your final draft to a word processor, whether you or someone else is typing the paper. You may need to call a word processor and reserve time if your final due date is close to midterm, finals, or other busy time in the term. Determine how the length of your paper will affect the time it will take to be typed.

3. Your personal due date for the final draft. Leave ample time for typing or rewriting your draft.

4. Your personal due date for completing a rough draft. The rough draft should be completed approximately ten days to two weeks before the final due date.

5. Due date for completing your research. Allow time to evaluate and synthesize your sources before beginning your rough draft. Your research should be completed approximately two-and-a-half to three weeks before the due date.

6. Due date for beginning your research. This should be the day the research paper is assigned. Within the first week, you should determine the type and format of the paper, select a subject, and narrow your subject into a manageable topic.

NOW SHOWING: MAKING PRESENTATIONS AND SPEECHES

The only thing we have to fear is fear itself.

— FRANKLIN DELANO ROOSEVELT

Twentieth Century U.S. President

How do you feel about giving a speech or presentation in a class? If the idea of making a speech strikes a bit of fear in your heart, you're not alone. Most people rank giving speeches as being almost as frightening as being physically assaulted or as the prospect of surgery. Although the context of Roosevelt's statement was World War II, it applies to giving speeches today.

The content of your paper, with some modifications, forms the basis of your speech or presentation. As in any good paper, your speech should begin with an introduction that tells the audience what you intend to tell them. The text of your paper forms the body of your speech. Your summary and conclusions tell the audience what you said.

The careful work you invested in your research paper forms a solid foundation that allows you to make presentations and speeches with confidence. For most people, speechmaking is a learned skill that improves with practice. The development of a good speech, like the development of a good paper, involves a number of steps, which require time and effort. If you follow the practical suggestions for making speeches and presentations listed in Table 10.8 you will have nothing to fear when you make your next speech in class.

WRITE TO LEARN

On a separate sheet of paper or in your journal, describe how preparing for a presentation is like writing a research paper. How is it different?

Exercise 10.6   Convert one of the following into a format suitable for a two-minute presentation: ``Countries and Their Constitutions'' from Exercise 10.3, ``Buying a Term Paper Could Turn Out to Be the First Step to Academic Bankruptcy'' in Excerpt 10.1, or the paper you wrote in Exercise 10.4 or 10.5.

Exercise 10.7   Read the sample short story, ``Strange Inventions'' by John Muir. Find three books in your campus library about Muir. Create a synthesis chart that combines information from these books and information in this story. Then write a three-page biography of Muir. Be prepared to present this information in class.

Table 10.8   Suggestions for Making Speeches and Presentations

Before giving a speech or presentation, you should . . .

1. **Identify with your audience.** Although the content of your paper dictates the content of your speech to some degree, the tone of your speech should match that of the audience in terms of vocabulary and background knowledge. Avoid using jargon, or specialized or technical vocabulary. Use examples you think apply to the audience or that bridge the gap between your knowledge level and theirs. As others in the class give their presentations, listen and watch carefully to determine how it feels to be in the audience, what appeals to members of the audience, and what fails to appeal to them. Consider involving the audience by asking a question or using a short activity.

2. **Structure your content.** The organization of a speech or presentation must be clear, obvious, and simple because the listening audience has no way to see the overall structure of information or visually review what you've said.

Table 10.8 Suggestions for Making Speeches and Presentations (Continued)

3. **Recreate your information.** Although you may need to turn in your speech for credit, you need to modify its form to facilitate presentation. At the very least, you might want to enlarge the print size of your speech, highlight important points, or note ideas to emphasize. Some people transfer main points of their speech to note cards or create concept maps to organize ideas graphically.

4. **Show them what you're going to tell them.** The saying ``one picture is worth a thousand words,'' applies to presentations as well as art. Diagrams, photos, models, and actual items add interest because they give the audience something to see as well as hear. Some individuals use overhead transparencies so they can face the audience as they provide text and graphic information. Today's speechmakers often create electronic presentations with computer graphics and multimedia or presentation software. Your campus media center or computer center can help you devise visuals to accompany your speeches and presentations. Whatever visuals you choose, they should be eye catching as well as accurate, legible from the back of the room, clear, simple, and neat.

5. **Practice.** Although some people believe practice makes perfect, practice actually makes permanent. The way you rehearse contributes to your final performance; thus, visualize yourself doing well. Envisioning worst-case scenarios often becomes a self-fulfilling prophecy because you rehearse them so often and so well. As you begin rehearsing your speech, practice it aloud to check for inadvertent tongue twisters and other aspects of verbal style. Verbal rehearsals also help in timing because you read silently more quickly than you speak. Gain familiarity with the manuscript, but don't over-rehearse.

6. **Play it again.** If possible, videotape or audiotape your speech. Review and critique your performance. If equipment is unavailable, ask a supportive friend to listen to your speech—preferably in a location similar to the one in which you will give your presentation. Have that person sit in different areas of the room to check for volume of speech and visibility of visuals.

Before giving a speech or presentation, you should . . .

7. **Dress for the part.** Just as a neatly printed paper makes a better impression than a hand-written copy, presentations made in appropriate attire set the tone for your speech. Your appearance should contribute to the effectiveness of your speech, not detract from it. Choose something a little more formal than what you might normally wear to class. Select a ``lucky'' item of clothing or one that you enjoy wearing.

When giving a speech or presentation, you should . . .

1. **Wait a minute.** Don't start your speech until you reach the speaker's stand and feel ready. Pause, survey notes, mentally review opening. Take a deep breath. If audience is quiet and prepared to listen, begin.

Table 10.8   Suggestions for Making Speeches and Presentations (Continued)

2. **Be yourself.** Don't affect an unnatural style. Show your interest and enthusiasm in your topic.

3. **Get a head start.** Learn your first sentence or two cold so you don't hesitate.

4. **Get a grip.** Attribute initial nervousness to eustress (positive adrenaline that gives you a boost to do your best) rather than distress (negative stress that leads to panic). Check your self-talk and replace it, if necessary, with positive affirmations. Take a deep breath. Speak slowly and at a volume loud enough to be heard. Keep in mind that the audience is with, not against, you. After all, one of them will be speaking next.

5. **Look 'em over.** Look directly at a person each time you make a point as if you were really talking to that individual. Make eye contact with individuals in the audience as you speak.

6. **Watch your watch.** End your speech in a timely manner.

7. **End it all.** Provide a finish for your speech. Summarize your main points, draw conclusions based on the content, use a particularly relevant quotation, or conclude your speech in some other definite manner.

After giving a speech or presentation, you should . . .

1. **Reward yourself.** You did it! Savor your successful conclusion. Mentally replay what went well. Congratulate yourself for your preparation, practice, and presentation.

2. **Critique your performance.** Critique, rather than criticize, your performance. Analyze what went right as well as what went wrong. Make written notes for future reference.

GROUP LEARNING ACTIVITY
NOTETAKING AS A CAUSE OF UNINTENTIONAL PLAGIARISM

Although the consequences of intentional and unintentional plagiarism are the same, their causes differ greatly. Intentional plagiarism has deceit as its purpose. But could people accidentally copy information and plagiarize without realizing it? Yes, it is easier than you think. The following group exercise (Nienhuis, 1989) can be used to demonstrate how unintentional plagiarism might occur.

1. Divide the group into two parts.

2. Individually, group members should go to the campus library and observe other students taking notes. Observe the methods that students use most often in taking notes from reference materials.

3. Compare observations in the group. Did you see students looking back and forth between the reference source and their paper? Did they seem to look at the source, write, look at the source, and write again? Did it appear as if they were copying almost directly from the text?

4. Half of the study group should take notes from the "The Great Irish Famine" from page 000 of Sample Chapter 12 as described in Step 3. The other half of the group should take notes on the same material in the following manner. Put pencils and pens down and read without taking notes. Mentally summarize information that you think is important. Close the book and summarize on paper without looking back at the source. Open the book and check what you've written against the original source. Add quotation marks around direct quotes that you recalled. Note bibliographic citations.

Application

Compare the notes taken according to each of the two methods. Use the following questions as springboards for group discussion. What differences can you find? What do you think accounts for the differences? How would these differences be manifested if the material were more difficult? Less difficult?

Application

The two subgroups should exchange notes. Underline any phrases or sentences in the notes that are uncited direct quotations from the passage. Compare results.

CHAPTER SUMMARY

1. Instructors usually assign themes or essays, reports, and research papers or term papers.

2. A research paper includes a title page, table of contents, abstract, body, references, and appendices.

3. Selecting the subject depends on its interest and importance and the availability of library resources.

4. Narrowing the subject is done by determining the purpose of the paper. The scope determines the thesis statement and title.

5. Outlining and charting are used to organize information for synthesis.

6. The first draft of your paper includes an introduction, the text of the paper, and a summary.

7. Your second draft should follow an established style. Revisions occur until the paper is error-free.

8. To complete your paper, you first set a writing schedule and then follow the steps in the writing process.

9. Effective presentations rely on principles of speech-making as well as well-written content.

CHAPTER REVIEW

Answer briefly but completely.

1. Complete the following analogy:
   reports : narration :: research papers :: _____

   _____

2. On what factors do you base the decision to include a table of contents, abstract, and/or appendices?

   _____

   _____

   _____

3. Your instructor has asked you to write a paper on any aspect of environmental pollution. Identify a topic that would be of interest to you and your classmates. Explain the factors on which you based your topic selection. Then narrow this topic into one of suitable scope.

   _____

   _____

   _____

   _____

   _____

   _____

4. Complete the following analogy:
   topic sentence : _____ :: thesis statement : research paper

   _____

5. Contrast outlines and charts as methods for synthesizing sources of information. Which method do you prefer? Why?

   _____

   _____

   _____

TERMS

Terms appear in the order in which they occurred in chapter.

themes
essays
reports
research papers
term papers
bibliography
abstract
appendices
scope
thesis statement
synthesis
rough draft
footnotes
endnotes
parenthetical
   references
style manuals
plagiarism

6.   Reread the quotation by Samuel Johnson on page 000. Use this quote to write the point you would make in an argument in favor of writing first and second drafts and for using word processing programs.

_____

_____

_____

7.   Complete the following analogy: plagiarism : _____ :: grand theft auto : cars

_____

8.   Examine Table 10.6. How would you modify the steps shown here to accommodate your research and writing strengths and weaknesses?

_____

_____

_____

9.   How does a writing schedule help you avoid procrastination?

_____

_____

_____

10.   Review the specific suggestions for giving a speech or presentation found in Table 10.8. To what aspect of giving speeches do they relate?

_____

_____

_____

REFERENCES

Nienhuis, T. (1989). Curing plagiarism with a note-taking exercise. *College Teaching* 37(3): 100.

Yelon, S., and Massa, M. (1990). Heuristics for creating examples. In R. A. Neff and M. Weimer (Eds.), *Teaching college: Collected readings for the new instructor.* Madison, WI: Magna Publications.

Vocabulary Development   Figurative Language: Just Like Home

You can only analyze and measure knowledge and experience against what you already know. If you don't have prerequisite knowledge, you must get a sense of how an experience is like something else you already know. Because authors are well-acquainted with their subjects, they can draw comparisons between a subject's features and features of some other, more common, concept or process. They often use figurative speech to make such comparisons. In writing a paper, your role is that of an author. You must inform your reader—who may or may not be familiar with your subject. Figurative language helps you refine your own thoughts about a concept and facilitates communication with your reader.

Analogies, it is true, decide nothing, but they can make one feel more at home.

—SIGMUND FREUD

Twentieth Century Psychologist

The problem with a new idea is often your unfamiliarity with it. You may not understand the processes involved. You might lack the terms to describe those processes. Everything seems strange. In short, you just don't know what the new idea is like. And that is the solution to your dilemma. In order to learn new information, you must link it to something you do know. You have to figure out what the new information is like.

The authors of your textbooks and the instructors in your classrooms also want you to know what new information is like. They often describe new and unfamiliar concepts by relating them to common items and processes with which you are familiar. Such comparisons often take the form of figures of speech: similes, metaphors, symbols, and analogies. Like Freud, they know that these can help you feel more at home with unfamiliar subject matter.

Similes and metaphors. Similes and metaphors are figures of speech that state or imply that two unlike ideas are comparable. At first glance, the two ideas may seem so totally different that they could have nothing in common. However, a closer look reveals a basic relationship between them.

The words *like* or *as* signal the use of a simile. For example, in describing an atom, you might describe the movement of electrons around a nucleus as being "like planets around the sun." Thus, if you know how a solar system moves, you know that the parts of an atom move in a similar fashion.

In a metaphor, one idea is described as if were another, but without the use of *like* or *as* to serve as a link between the disparate items. For example, a biology professor might describe glucose as the gasoline that powers the human engine.

That means that glucose performs the same function in the body as gasoline performs in a car.

Symbols. Symbols are like metaphors and similes with one major difference. Similes and metaphors name both ideas being compared. In symbolism, the comparison between two ideas became so well-known that one part of the comparison is no longer used. Thus, you are given one idea. You must infer the other. For example, the sentence "A rainbow is like a promise of better times for the coalition" would be a simile. "A rainbow is a promise of better times" is a metaphor. A rainbow alone symbolizes a promise of better times.

Symbols are based on background knowledge and experiences. In general, they are universally understood due to years of association between the symbol and the object it represents; however, symbols mean different things in different cultures. The flag that inspires patriotism in one country evokes little sentiment in another. A symbol's meaning also varies according to context. Symbols in one time and place (for example, *X* as in "*X* marks the spot", "X-tra Savings," size XXXL, and so on) may have a different meaning in another time and place.

Analogies. An analogy is a kind of expanded simile. Instead of comparing items as a whole, analogies compare specific features of a concept, process, person, place, or thing. For example, suppose you need to understand the relationship between a *secondary trait* (a characteristic that affects personality only under certain conditions) and *personality*. You might think of this concept as being like a knock that you get in your engine when you forget to add oil. This comparison is clarified by an analogy: A secondary trait is to personality as a knock is to a car's engine. The order of the ideas expressed in the analogy is important. Analogies can show any kind of relationship. These include synonyms, antonyms, parts to whole, age or size, or object to use.

Using figurative language in writing. Just as authors and faculty use figurative language to make you feel at home with an idea, you, too, can use such language to help the reader feel at home with the concepts in your research paper.

Your own understanding of the topic increases as you think of clear and appropriate examples. The metaphor, simile, symbol, or analogy you choose should include the following characteristics described by Yelon and Massa (1990):

- **Accuracy.** The ideas being compared should be similar in definition, composition, function, or description. The comparison should be believable and realistic.

- **Clarity.** Whenever possible, use words, images, or actions that are observable and evoke sensory images. The connection between the example and the topic should be emphasized so that the reader easily grasps the relationship.

- **Brevity.** Examples need to be short enough so that their connection to the topic is not lost.

Activity

Following the guidelines presented in this section, use figurative language in creating an example to explain each of the following paragraphs.

1. Simple sequence is one of the four major logic patterns in computer programming. In simple sequence, the computer executes one statement after the other in the order in which they are listed in the program.

    EXAMPLE _____

    _____

    _____

2. In exploitation, one person or party controls the "rules" for access to rewards while keeping the second party or person naive or helpless concerning such access.

    EXAMPLE _____

    _____

    _____

3. The vascular, or blood circulatory, system is a closed system of vessels through which blood flows continuously in a figure eight, with the heart serving as a pump at the crossover point. As the blood circulates through the system, it picks up and delivers materials as needed.

    EXAMPLE _____

    _____

    _____

4. Pinocytosis involves a large area of the cell membrane, which actively engulfs liquids and "swallows" them into the cell. Occasionally, an entire protein can enter the body this way.

    EXAMPLE _____

    _____

    _____

5. The concept of nuclear reactions emerged following research into atomic structure in the 1920s. In fusion reactions, nuclei merge to create a larger nucleus representing a new chemical element. In fission reactions, a single nucleus splits into two or more smaller nuclei.

    EXAMPLE _____

    _____

    _____

Sample Chapter 11

Personal Values, Career Planning, and Success with People at Work

PERSONAL VALUES, CAREER PLANNING, AND SUCCESS WITH PEOPLE AT WORK

This chapter answers several all-important questions:

- What are the four key components of career planning?

- How can goal planning be kept realistic?

- What are some broad questions to ask yourself in regard to career planning?

- Where can you look for occupational information useful in career planning?

- What is value clarification, and how can it help you develop a good career plan?

- What do organizations expect from their managers?

- What can managers reasonably expect from their companies?

- Why is the clarification of expectations an important step to becoming successful?

- How can you become an effective subordinate by managing your manager?

- How can you better manage yourself, your time, and your tasks?

The answers to these and other questions are coming up next in chapter 19....

CHAPTER 19

If you've read this entire book so far, you will recognize that getting meaningful work accomplished through the efforts of others is a complex business. We hope you now better understand more about human relationships and their effects on people at work.

Managerial leadership is not a job designed for everyone. Directing the work efforts of other employees can be frustrating and difficult. Nevertheless, people feel a great sense of satisfaction when they accomplish organizational work in the spirit of cooperation and teamwork.

There are all kinds of managers: some are highly successful, some are dismal failures, and most are somewhere in between. Since you have had the good sense to select our book as a guide to your study of human relations, we assume that you are a person of discriminating taste and impeccable judgment. You, we suspect, will be satisfied with nothing less than becoming highly successful!

A few key ideas can help you achieve this, and we'll share them with you in the following pages. These ideas are based on our studies of highly successful managers whom we've worked with and observed over the past twenty-five years or so. The highly successful manager has learned to manage his or her career. That manager has learned to do the following:

- Develop clear career plans
- Clarify expectations on the job
- Manage not only subordinates but also bosses
- Manage himself or herself

▼ KEY IDEA 1: CAREER PLANNING

- Having clear, appropriate goals is a prerequisite for job success.

Knowing where you're going, or at least having a pretty good idea of where you'd like to be, puts you way ahead of most people. Most people spend more time planning their annual two-week vacations than they do planning their careers.

Career planning is particularly important because it leads to goal-directed behaviors. In other words, the more conscious one is of one's own goals, the more direct and efficient the pursuit of those goals will be. We have used the terms *goals* and *goal direction* many times in this book. Having clear objectives is a prerequisite to success in most careers. But for goals to effectively guide one, they must also mesh with one's self-appraisal and with the realities of the management job one seeks.

- Career planning has four components:
  Goal selection
  Self-evaluation
  Vision
  Occupational information

Career planning has four components: *goals, self-evaluation, vision,* and *occupational information* (see figure 19.1). To develop an effective career plan for yourself, all four elements must be considered very carefully. To set personal goals without considering the nature of the job market or, for that matter, the nature of one's own personality can lead to considerable frustration and disappointment.

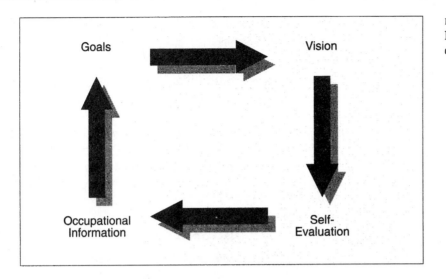

FIGURE **19.1**
Four key components of career planning.

Developing Personal Goals: Start with a Dream List

For many people, writing down specific goals is an unfamiliar process. Yet without tangible objectives, keeping direction in one's life can be difficult. What do you really want to get out of life?

Goals should be based on what is realistically attainable. But before we focus on those realistic goals, it can be fun—and useful—to do some personal brainstorming. Take a piece of paper and write down virtually *everything you ever* want to accomplish, be, or have. Typically, people begin by listing such things as a new Mercedes, a yacht, a few million dollars, and some other tangible items. But keep writing far beyond that. Try filling up several sheets of paper with lists of all kinds of things you would like to accomplish or have in your life. Be sure to include the intangible also: such things as harmonious family relationships, sense of satisfaction at work, spirituality, the esteem of others, and so forth. Keep on writing until you can think of nothing more to put down. Don't be overly critical at this point—write it *all* down.

■ Personal brainstorming can help sort out goals.

If you are like most people, you will find that some conflicts exist among the goals you have listed. Frequently, people say that they would like to be major corporate executives, yet somewhere else on their goal "dream lists" they speak of spending a great deal of time with their families. Likewise, some people want to be rich and famous but also seek quiet and privacy.

Obviously, reality poses some limitations on our dream lists. By listing all of these things, however, one can begin to recognize where potential conflicts among different objectives emerge. Then the process becomes one of selecting objectives that have the highest priority.

As you review your dream list, consider which goals are related to your career. If you are like most people, you will have many career

■ Career planning starts with some key questions.

goals—although some will conflict with others. To help focus further, ask yourself these questions:

- What type of work do I prefer?
- What type of organization would I like to work for?
- What type of position do I prefer (research, line, staff, governmental, industrial)?
- What kind of monetary and noneconomic reward balance do I want from working?
- What kinds of things do I find particularly satisfying in work (accomplishing a difficult task, solving problems, interacting with others, creating something new)?

Conducting a Self-Appraisal

In the process of career planning, one must reflect in considerable depth. Some of the broad questions we posed in the preceding paragraphs can also provide some insights into what you would like to get out of your life. But self-evaluation goes even further than that.

■ One's personal values justify the goals and objectives one sets.

A critical activity for people is to identify and clarify in some way their personal *values*. A personal *value* can be defined as an idea of something that is intrinsically (in and of itself) desirable to you. Values, once clarified and accepted as your own, provide the justification for the goals and objectives you set.

What people say they value most can be divided into eight broad categories (although exceptions could be made to these):

1. Career success (achievement and satisfaction on the job)
2. Family
3. Social life
4. Health and vigor
5. Financial stability or independence
6. Leisure (a comfortable life)
7. Spiritual development
8. Personal development (mental ability, physical skills, and so on)

■ Value clarification is not an easy process.

The process of identifying basic values is not an easy one. Many people feel frustrated when asked to identify core values. In part, this may be because we typically experience value conflicts—our behaviors do not always jibe with what we say we value. Many people say their families are of the greatest importance to them, yet research has shown that fathers spend only about seven minutes a week talking, one-on-one, with each child in their family. Likewise, our relationships with our spouses may be highly valued, yet studies show that the average couple spends only twenty minutes a week with each other, alone, communicating.

Value conflicts are normal. Yet the people who enjoy the greatest life satisfaction work constantly to bring their behaviors into line with their values. The goal-setting process we discussed earlier gains impact when we include value clarifying, too. If you were to spend a few hours carefully defining and describing your core values, you could return to the brainstormed list of goals and sort them out quickly. If, for example, you determine that health and vigor is a *major* value for you, you may decide that the goal of being a top executive in a pressure-packed, stressful industry may *not* be all that is desirable for you.

Just how important is value clarification? In their best-selling book *In Search of Excellence,* Tom Peters and Robert Waterman devote considerable space to describing or illustrating how values affect the "excellent" companies they studied. The points they make about organizational values can readily be applied to personal values. At one point, they summarize:

> Let us suppose that we were asked for one all-purpose bit of advice for management, one truth that we were able to distill from the excellent companies researched. We might be tempted to reply, "Figure out your value system. Decide what your company *stands for.* What does your enterprise do that gives everyone the most pride? Put yourself out ten or twenty years in the future: What would you look back on with the greatest satisfaction?[1]

In the book *Successful Self-Management,* Paul Timm recommends a three-step process for value clarifying:

1. *Name the value.* Call it whatever you like; for example, *financial security, family solidarity, professional excellence, freedom.*

    ■ A three-step process for value clarification.

2. *Describe what that value means to you.* Write this description in the present tense as if you have already achieved it. For example, the value you call physical fitness may be described this way: "I jog one thousand miles a year. I play golf at least twice a month. I feel good and maintain appropriate weight and blood cholesterol level. I get enough sleep and do not let stress grind me down. I am generally optimistic. I am active in many sports." Even if you don't yet accomplish all these things, write them in the present tense. They then become *affirmations*—statements of where you are going.

3. *Write out the value-aligning activities or goals needed to become congruent with your value.* If you see jogging twelve hundred miles a year as a definition of physical fitness, a value-aligning activity will be to jog one hundred miles a month, or an average of twenty-five miles a week. If financial freedom is a value, your value-aligning activities may include a plan for getting out of debt.[2]

The process of value clarification is a powerful one and should be taken seriously. When we take the time and effort to do this, we begin the process of creating a vision.

Creating a Vision

Successful managers and leaders focus their thinking and their people on worthy goals for the future. A vision, in its simplest form, is a view of the future. While the definition is simple, the concept is profound. Wise people have known about the power of the mind—the power of thought—since ancient times. The prophet and teacher Solomon said, "Without a vision, the people perish!" In his book *The Greatest Secret in the World,* Og Mandino said the "greatest secret" is that "we become what we think about most of the time."[3]

Researchers know that vision is a key ingredient in most success recipes. In their extensive study of leadership strategies, Warren Bennis and Burt Nanus found vision to be the first key element associated with the success of the leaders they interviewed.[4]

Vision gives a sense of direction to individuals and to organizations. In turn, it can be formalized in written plans or *mission statements,* which are statements that explain the purpose for which, or reason, an organization exists.

Gathering Occupational Information

■ Where can one find career-planning information?

The fourth side of the career-planning square we have described deals with gathering information about possible opportunities. Many good books are available on career planning that may suggest to you some areas for employment that you had not previously considered.

■ Some people are likely to end up in careers that don't even exist yet.

Become aware of as many possible alternatives as you can. Many people end up in careers they never considered initially. In fact, many attractive careers didn't even exist a few years ago. Rapidly developing technology, as well as specialization within professional fields, have created new and frequently attractive opportunities. Keep abreast of changes and new opportunities by being professionally alert. If your field is business management, read the business magazines and newspapers regularly.

If you're not certain about what field you'd like to work in, spend a few hours in a good university library reading professional magazines from a wide variety of areas. Look for the specialty magazines, such as *Advertising Age* and *Sales and Marketing Management,* as well as publications in engineering, electronics, retailing, and the like.

Keep your mind open, your ear to the ground, your shoulder to the wheel, and your nose to the grindstone. (Do all this, and you'll be a great contortionist!) But seriously, and old clichés aside, it does make sense to be open to a wide variety of career possibilities.

▼ KEY IDEA 2: CLARIFYING EXPECTATIONS

■ Why is clarifying expectations so important?

One theme of this book is the importance of creating better understanding among people by clarifying expectations. Theory X managers miss many opportunities to help subordinates grow because of their unclarified and generally pessimistic expectations of others. Likewise, communicators or motivators who fail to clarify what arouses interest in others operate in a hit-and-miss fashion. The result frequently is wheel spinning and unproductive management.

Successful managers spend time and effort in clarifying what is expected of them as well as what is expected of the organization.

What Organizations Expect of Management Employees

Typically, when people begin new jobs, some uncertainties are involved. The level of uncertainty is especially high for the recent graduate who is going into his or her first full-time employment. Both the new employee and the organization must first come to agreement about what each expects from the other. Typically, companies expect the following kinds of things from their management employees.

REPRESENTATION OF THE COMPANY

Management employees at all levels, be they first-line supervisors or top-level executives, are expected to represent their company on and off the job. We all represent the organizations to which we belong. The people we meet socially, in community activities, as neighbors, or within the scope of our business dealings develop an impression of our company based on our behavior. If we come across as being shifty or suspicious, others may well question the ethics of our corporation. If we are aboveboard, honest, optimistic, and direct about our organization, we reflect a more positive image in the eyes of our friends and neighbors.

Even minor conflicts of interest or seemingly inconsistent behavior can hurt the organization. A few years ago, Lee Iacocca, as head of Chrysler Corporation, was aggressively selling people on the need to buy American automobiles while publicly expressing his preference for Cuban cigars. The contradiction was not lost on one U.S. tobacco manufacturer, who complained in a letter to a national news magazine.

More recently, President George Bush was pictured fishing from a boat powered by a Yamaha outboard. A little thing? Perhaps. But with the increasing competition with Japan, it sent a mixed message.

Managers expect their people to behave in ways that reflect positively on the company. They expect people to avoid activities or behaviors that might compromise or embarrass the organization in the eyes of the public. Although public relations (PR) is often a specialized function within an organization, in a very real sense, all employees are involved in PR. The public judges a company by the people it keeps.

■ The public judges a company by the people it keeps.

A DESIRE FOR SUCCESS

Companies expect their employees to truly want to be successful. Few organizations want to hire people who have negative self-images or severe reservations as to what they can accomplish.

past successes are not enough. The ongoing desire to be successful within the organization is a very positive characteristic.

We once had lunch with a highly successful young executive who had formed a small conglomerate with his two brothers. Their growth rate had been highly impressive—all three had become self-made millionaires while still in their twenties. In our conversation, this individual identified his desire to be successful as a key to their organization's growth. All three brothers sincerely wanted their organization to be successful. There was no questioning of each other's desire. Each knew that the other two were working just as hard as he to make the corporation go. Organizational success was the first priority. In fact, this businessman made the point that if he were suddenly given three hundred dollars for some advice or service, he would immediately, and without hesitation, give each of his brothers one hundred dollars. An "all for one and one for all" philosophy guided their business decisions.

■ Companies want managers who want to succeed as an organization.

A tightly knit family corporation is fairly unique, but the point here is that these men had a true desire to succeed *as an organization,* not just as individuals. This is one key to becoming a highly successful manager.

A PROFESSIONAL BUSINESS APPEARANCE

Corporations expect their employees to dress and groom themselves in a way that reflects positively on the company. Many major corporations require men and women to wear business suits and to avoid grooming habits that are too far out of the mainstream of society. Although "dressing for success" may not be stressed too heavily in some companies, few organizations would be satisfied with management representatives who are excessively sloppy or poorly groomed.

The key word here is *appropriateness.* In some organizations and in some industries, casual dress is normal and accepted. Top male executives in the building materials business in Florida wear casual slacks and knit shirts for example.

In rural Saskatchewan or Montana, in Boston, in San Francisco, in Toronto, footwear, outerwear, and accessories are as local as the dialect.

In his series of books on dressing for success, John T. Molloy asserts that people will have a better chance to do a better job at a higher salary if they learn to use clothing as a business tool, beginning with the initial job interview.[5] One should not believe, however, that dress alone can overshadow the importance of proper education and personal development. We would never think to suggest that dress alone could, as Molloy states, "put a boob in the board room," but, as Molloy concludes, "incorrect dress can definitely keep an intelligent, able man out." Such guidelines as to what is appropriate business appearance should be regarded as just that: *guidelines.* People don't need to look like clones.

■ "Dress-for-success" advocates see clothing as a business tool.

TIME SPENT ON THE JOB

Most companies expect their employees to spend a certain amount of time on the job each day. Normally, workers are expected at work at a certain time, and they are also expected to remain there until quitting time. Employees who habitually show up late for work or leave early create the impression of doing less than their fair share. This negative impression may be difficult to overcome, even if the employee is quite successful. Some individuals in sales, for example, accomplish a great deal of work in a short period of time. They meet their company objectives while only working a few hours a day in active sales. Nevertheless, they are regarded with some suspicion. The question is, "If they can attain company objectives working half a day, how much could they do if they worked a full eight-hour day?"

■ People who work short hours are seen as doing less than their share.

The old adage of "An honest day's work for an honest day's pay" still makes sense to most employers. Highly successful managers are typically generous with the time and effort they give to the organization. Clockwatchers seldom succeed.

SOME CREATIVITY

Most organizations expect their management employees to be creative. Creativity here does not necessarily mean coming up with a brand-new concept or idea that changes the entire direction of the corporation. It can, however, mean using ingenuity and initiative to do work in different, more productive, or more effective ways. We have talked throughout this book about the importance of motivating employees to participate in the creative process of doing the work of the organization more effectively. Good managers use creativity. They are not bound to "the way we've always done it" but constantly look for a better way, a more creative way of accomplishing the organization's work.

■ Managers are expected to be somewhat creative in solving organizational problems.

A LONG-TERM COMMITMENT

Perhaps one of the most frustrating experiences for a company is to recruit and hire a potentially valuable team member, only to have that person quit after a few months on the job. Recruiting, training and employee development are costly processes for most organizations. Few employees carry their own weight immediately on joining an organization. The training period costs the company far more than the immediate return that those employees can make to the organization's profitability.

■ Managers should make a long-term commitment to their organizations.

Organizations often spend forty thousand, fifty thousand, or even one hundred thousand dollars on extensive training of employees. Training is very expensive. Ethically, employees are bound to stay with a company at least until they are contributing members of the organization. Don't take a job with a company if you don't intend to give it your best shot for a reasonable period of time.

CUSTOMER SERVICE[6]

Regardless of your job title, position in an organization, or experience, *your number-one task* will *always* be to attract, satisfy, and preserve "customers." And *everyone has customers.*

For many of us, these are easy to identify. They buy something from us. But some people will say, "I don't work directly with customers." Before you accept this idea, take a closer look at just who exactly your customers are.

In organizations, customers take two forms, *internal* and *external.* *Internal* customers are those people, departments, or organizations served by what we do. The only person who might have no internal customers is the individual who works completely alone. For the rest of us, internal customers are a fact of life.

For example, a word processing clerk or copy center worker within a company serves other workers' document-handling needs. A personnel office worker serves employees' needs for benefits information, management's needs for staffing, and company legal people's needs for handling various government paperwork requirements.

As individuals, we all have at least one internal customer: our boss; as managers, we also have internal customers in the form of the people we supervise. They rely on us to meet their needs.

External customers are those people or departments who are the end users of our organization's product or services. This is, of course, the traditional use of the term *customer.*

Arguably, the key to your success is your ability to meet and exceed customer expectations.

What Companies Do Not Expect from a New Manager

■ New employees are not expected to know it all.

Organizations *do not* expect a new employee to know it all. Clearly, new employees do not have a basis for making all the right decisions and performing all the right actions. This is why expensive employee development programs are provided in all major organizations.

By the same token, new employees are not typically expected to produce immediate or profitable results for the company. As we've said, most organizations take a loss in productivity initially on hiring new employees. They hope to regain that initial loss by developing productive contributors to the organization as time goes on, but immediate results are seldom expected.

Having a realistic understanding of these expectations up-front can help avoid problems later. You must also have a realistic picture of what you as an employee can expect from your company.

What Management Employees Can Expect from the Company

Clarifying expectations is a two-way street. Not only must employees understand what is expected of them, but the organization's leaders must understand what employees normally expect from the company. Basic obligations to employees normally include the following.

OPENNESS AND HONESTY IN THE RECRUITING PROCESS

Organizations have an obligation to tell potential employees what the company is all about. The individual being recruited should have an understanding of the company's management philosophy and the nature of the products or services provided by the company, as well as clear statements about what the company expects from its employees. Getting this information during the recruiting process should be the responsibility of both the applicant, who should seek it out, and the potential employers, who should readily provide it.

- Companies should give applicants a clear picture of the organization before hiring them.

APPROPRIATE AND ADEQUATE TRAINING

Organizations need to provide both their new employees and current employees with the training necessary for them to skillfully complete the tasks to which they've been assigned. Training is not and should not be regarded as a fringe benefit; it is at the heart of the managerial process.

- Training is at the heart of the management process.

REASONABLE COMPENSATION AND BENEFITS

Organizations have an obligation to provide fair and equitable compensation, as well as reasonable benefit plans.

■ Employees have a right to know how they are doing.

PERFORMANCE REVIEWS AND PERIODIC RAISES
In addition to receiving pay and benefits, employees have a right to know how well they are doing. The performance review, discussed earlier as a motivational technique, is widely expected in industry. People who perform well also expect to receive additional compensation. An individual who produces more is worth more to the organization and therefore should be paid more.

A GOOD WORKING ENVIRONMENT
Corporations have an obligation to provide a safe, healthy, and reasonably pleasant working environment for their employees. Although some tasks must be performed under less-than-desirable conditions, employees who do difficult, dangerous, or unpleasant work should receive additional compensation.

▼ KEY IDEA 3: MANAGING YOUR BOSS

Nearly everybody has a boss. People at all levels in the organization report to someone else; even the top executive reports to stockholders and the public. Yet, from university classroom lectures to the slick paperbacks we find in bookstores, people have focused on how to develop your "management style" by successfully directing those *beneath* you. Little attention has been paid to the other side of the issue: establishing your career based on your ability to manage *those who formally manage you.*

■ Little attention has been paid to the important art of managing your manager.

Norman C. Hill and Paul H. Thompson wrote an article entitled "Managing Your Manager: The Effective Subordinate." In it, they suggested a number of ideas that can be useful as we try to become highly successful managers.

Building initially on the idea of expectation clarification that we have already discussed, they suggest some specific areas where understandings need to be established. We've paraphrased a number of their ideas in this section.[7]

Resolving Key Issues

In the traditional role, bosses give orders and subordinates carry them out. Many individuals expect the manager to define the job, make assignments, and then check to see that the work is completed. When the boss doesn't behave in this manner, frustration arises. The worker becomes confused. This confusion usually arises because people have different expectations about job roles that lead to tension, conflict, missed deadlines, and turnover.

■ Sit down with your boss and talk things out.

One way to avoid some of these kinds of problems is to sit down with your boss and talk things out. One successful manager described doing this: "Whenever I get a new boss, I sit down with him and ask him to make his expectations explicit. We try to list not my job activities, but the main purposes of my job. To do that, we continue each statement of activity with 'in order to ...' and try to complete the sentence. By recording my job purposes, we get a clear picture of what I should be accomplishing; and that's what counts—results."

This approach works very well for the individual, but most bosses are not able (or willing) to be nearly that clear about their expectations. In most cases, communication between superiors and subordinates is an ongoing process. Most issues are not resolved in a one-shot conversation.

You can excel in your organization by taking the initiative to resolve certain issues with your boss directly. This will be an ongoing process. The kinds of things that need to be discussed include (1) the content of your job, (2) the degree to which you should take initiative on your job, (3) how to keep the boss informed, and (4) how to ask for help.

- Repeated conversations are often required.

CLARIFYING JOB CONTENT

Reach an agreement on your responsibilities. Having a clearly written job description is more useful in some companies than in others. If, for example, your company is experiencing unusual growth or a rapidly changing environment, job descriptions may be less useful. In other words, people need to be able to react to changes and be flexible.

- Job descriptions often need to be flexible.

TAKING INITIATIVE

One manager describes a good subordinate as one who "thinks of the things I would do before I do them. What this means is that he or she tries to adopt my perspective and look at things from my position in the organization."

Some employees think that just reporting back their efforts, even though those efforts may not have succeeded, is enough. But good intentions are no substitute for what the boss needs. The message in this is that individuals need to take initiative on the job. But the degree of initiative taken needs to be talked out with your boss. Some bosses may be threatened by subordinates who anticipate their desires; others welcome the enterprise of such employees.

- Just reporting back may not be enough.

KEEPING THE BOSS INFORMED

Keeping the boss informed is closely tied to taking initiative, but some aspects deserve separate consideration. Subordinates need to learn how to keep the boss advised on *appropriate* matters. But don't overdo it and report everything. One rule of thumb is to let the boss know about the *progress* being made on a particular project and to avoid reporting all the *activities* engaged in to achieve those results.

- Don't overdo your reporting to the boss; report progress, not activities.

Managers need to have negative information as well as positive. Subordinates often like to "cover their tracks." To be a successful manager, don't hesitate to bring *needed* negative and positive information to your boss.

- Tell the boss the bad news, too—when he or she needs to know.

ASKING FOR HELP

Some bosses want to be deeply involved in a project, and they use requests for help as an opportunity to teach their subordinates.

Others only want to see the final product and do not want to be bothered with frequent questions.

A bank manager presented his views on the issue: "Some subordinates will take an assignment, work as hard on it as possible, then come back to you when they get stuck or when it is completed. Other people start coming back to you to do their work for them. People in the second group don't do very well in our bank."

Asking for help too often can undermine the boss's confidence in you. When you're stuck, seek out the help of more experienced people on your own level first.

Also consider the amount of risk involved in a situation. A promising young accountant described his strategy on seeking advice from the boss: "My boss had high expectations from me when he hired me, and I believe I have lived up to them. To ensure that I would perform successfully, I adopted a strategy of taking risks—not gambles, but calculated risks. If a decision involved a high level of risk, I would consult with my boss. However, if a job was not overly risky or of crucial importance, I would do as much of it on my own as I could and not waste my boss's time with the details. I assumed it was important to look out for my boss's welfare, not just my own. If I could make him look good or make his job easier and less time-consuming, then it would benefit me as well. However, when I made a decision that turned out to be a mistake, I told my boss about it and didn't try to cover my errors."

This suggests some important guidelines for deciding when to go to the boss for help and when to handle a situation alone:

- Take risks, not gambles (and recognize the differences between the two).
- Handle the details, but keep the manager informed.
- Check with the boss on decisions that will affect work units outside the department.
- Give the boss a recommendation each time he or she asks for an analysis of a project.
- Ask for an appointment only when you are prepared to suggest some action that should be taken.

Developing Trust with the Boss

Four conditions are necessary for subordinate-superior trust to develop: accessibility, availability, predictability, and loyalty. Let's look at each briefly.

ACCESSIBILITY
An accessible person takes in ideas easily and gives them out freely. If two people are going to develop a productive relationship, they must respect each other's ideas and give those ideas careful thought and consideration. A subordinate who does not respect the boss's ideas will never be trusted and will not obtain needed help to develop his or her own ideas. You don't have to agree, just be respectful of each other's point of view.

Margin notes:

- Asking for help too often can undermine your boss's confidence in you.

- Guidelines for when to go to the boss for help.

- Four conditions for trust are as follows:
  Accessibility
  Availability
  Predictability
  Loyalty

AVAILABILITY

The subordinate should be attentive and available physically, mentally, and emotionally when the manager is under pressure and needs support.

Don't become upset because the help you may need from the boss is not immediately there. Instead, take an attitude such as the following: "I know you're under a lot of pressure right now trying to complete high-priority projects. This project I'm working on is less important, so I am quite willing to let it wait for a while. In addition, if I can be of help on any of your projects, just let me know. I'm willing to pitch in and help in any way I can."

PREDICTABILITY

Predictability means the handling of delicate administrative circumstances with good judgment and thoroughness. If subordinates have been given appropriate assignments—ones that allow them to develop their personal skills—they will acquire the ability to handle even sensitive situations. However, if a subordinate lacks sensitivity or interpersonal skills and jeopardizes relationships with customers, in the future this subordinate will not be trusted and thus will be of much less value to the boss.

Predictability also means reliability in reaching important deadlines and doing work of high quality. Managers don't like to be let down. Surprises or failures to meet deadlines embarrass them, make them look bad, and do not help build manager-subordinate trust.

■ Embarrassing surprises do not help build trust.

LOYALTY

Personal loyalty to one's boss and to one's subordinate is important. A manager is not likely to trust a subordinate with important information if he or she fears that the information might be used to further the subordinate's own interests at the manager's expense.

But loyalty must also be considered in a broader context. Sometimes loyalty to an immediate supervisor conflicts with loyalty to the organization or to society. What is good for the boss is not always good for the organization and vice versa. When such potential conflicts arise, your personal ethics enter in. One highly regarded middle manager described his strategy: "I'm not a 'yes' man. I know the importance of speaking up and saying what's on my mind. I also know that other people in the organization may have a better perspective than I do. So I follow this rule of thumb: I argue forcefully *one* time for my position. If my boss then does not accept my recommendation, I try to make his decision an effective one through my support and commitment. That is, of course, unless I feel a conflict with my personal values."

■ Loyalty does not mean always saying yes.

Once again, we suggest being up-front with managers. The relationship between two individuals in a superior-subordinate relationship is critical, and mutual expectations must be achieved if the individual is to become a valued subordinate. Herein lies the key to becoming a highly successful manager.

To recap some key thoughts, certain issues should be evident to any worker, regardless of organizational level:

- Very few bosses will do all that is necessary to clarify expectations in a superior-subordinate relationship.
- Most managers will respond favorably to a discussion of the manager-subordinate relationship. However, managers have varying styles, so an individual is well-advised to find out how the boss is *likely* to respond.

▼ KEY IDEA 4: MANAGING YOURSELF

Ultimately, success is a "do-it-yourself" project.

We have talked about the importance of clarifying expectations, creating your personal vision, and finding career-planning information. All of these actions will help you decide what kind of organization—if any—you would best work in.

Regardless of where you work, *how* you work is equally important. And of all the resources you work with, *time* is your most valuable.

Identifying Time-Saving Techniques

- Leaders pay lip service to time management but fail to help others be productive with time.

It's ironic that some managers pay lip service to time management (after all, "time is money," they are quick to say) but fail to help subordinates be productive with their time. Indeed, the manager may be the employees' worst enemy when it comes to using time.

R. Alec Mackenzie begins his book *The Time Trap* by identifying examples of a few exceptional people who have used time-saving techniques well. Among them, he cites the following:

- A company leader who cut his staff meetings in half and began sticking to an agenda. Immediately, the participants began to accomplish better results in less time.
- An Eastern school superintendent [who] discourages reverse delegation. When someone sends in a problem he thinks should have been handled at a lower level, he returns it with a note asking, "Why are you sending this to me?" If he allows himself to get involved in the daily decisions, he won't have time to manage.
- A Dutch manager [who] does not say yes when his subordinates call to ask if they can come in with a problem. After determining ... the problem is not an emergency, he says, "Give me ten minutes (or whatever time he needs) to complete the task I am doing. Then I will come to your office." This saves times, he says, because if he sits down in his own office, the *visitor* is [in] control. If he goes to the subordinate's office, he says, "I'm in control because I can leave at my time."
- Another businessman [who] got tired of a caller who wasted his time on the telephone. One call came at a particularly bad moment. The manager hung up on *himself*. Of course, the caller

assumed the fault was the phone company's—no one would ever think a person would do that to himself.[8]

Supervisors can and should develop time-saving techniques that show others they value time. We need to be *constantly jealous* of our time as well as our subordinates' and co-workers' time. Consistent awareness of time doesn't mean you become a slave to the clock. Quite the contrary. It means you more productively use your time so that you can have more leisure as well as better results.

Working with people can be particularly time-consuming. And working with people is a central task of managers. People are time consumers. And most people are time wasters—to some extent. We need to develop a sensitivity to others that tells us when to spend more time with people and when to cut back.

■ We need to be constantly jealous of our own and others' time.

Time and Task Management Tools and Skills[9]

The best tool for making the most of your time is a planner system. Bookstores and office supply stores are well stocked with a wide variety of planners, to-do list forms, and calendars. While formats differ, the purpose is the same: to help you get organized and better spend your daily 86,400 seconds.

A planner needn't be elaborate or expensive. Some people succumb to the status symbolism of certain planners, but any appropriately designed planner can tremendously boost your power to be productive.

A planner needs five things to make it work for you:

1. A place to list and assign priorities to tasks. (We'll show you how to develop a priority task list in just a moment.)
2. A place to record notes and follow-up information.
3. A place for goals and values. Having these incorporated into your planning tool is a powerful way to make sure they are realized.
4. A place for frequently referred-to information, especially addresses, phone numbers, perhaps birthdays, and so forth.
5. Flexibility to meet your needs.

Some people resist planning. Some say they don't like to feel bound by a plan—they want to stay "flexible." Others claim to do all their planning in their heads. And more than a few simply don't see the value to planning. They live by wandering around.

Time management experts claim that as a general rule, spending only 5 percent of the day planning can help managers achieve 95 percent of their goals. Planning prevents managers from doing the wrong things the wrong way at the wrong time, and it forces them to answer the question, 'What really needs to be accomplished?'

Planning is a good idea because it is always best to perform activities sequentially rather than simultaneously. In fact, we *can't* do things simultaneously and do them well. The idea behind time management is determining *how to do things sequentially.*

The Nuts and Bolts of Time and Task Management

Devote a minimum of ten to fifteen minutes a day solely to planning. Use a planner system you like. Then apply the steps described below, and you will see a significant increase in your personal effectiveness. First-time users of a planner report immediate productivity increases of 25 percent or more!

STEP 1. DEVELOP A PRIORITY TASK LIST FOR EACH DAY

Prioritizing tasks helps us sort them out, determine which need to be attacked first and which can be saved for later.

Here's how: List the specific tasks you want or need to spend your time on for a particular day. Using your own shorthand, list the items you wish to accomplish. It might read something like this: "Complete the XYZ report, get stamps, attend Billy's softball game, eat more fish, keep date with Chris."

At this stage, don't be overly concerned with the *importance* of the items; just get in the habit of listing *all* nonroutine tasks that you want to accomplish that day. Don't bother listing all those tasks you do automatically (e.g., brushing teeth, doing the dishes, waiting on customers).

STEP 2. ASSIGN A LETTER PRIORITY TO EACH ITEM ON YOUR LIST

Use A, B, C, or a star and place the letter A next to items that *must* be done. These are critical to you, though you alone determine whether they are critical or not based on your values and goals. Tasks required either by outside forces (e.g., your boss) or internal ones (e.g., a strong personal commitment) will normally receive an A priority. Be careful not to assign A's to *every* task. Giving everything an A defeats the purpose of prioritizing.

Using the letter B to indicate *should-do* items. These tasks aren't quite as critical as the A tasks, yet it is worth spending time to achieve them.

The letter C is for *could-do* items. These tasks are worth listing and thinking about—and, if you complete your A's and B's, worth doing.

A star indicates an item that is *urgent*—something that *must* be done and done *now*. It is both important and vital and must be done right away. Occasionally, such a job occurs during a workday (i.e., a crisis). When you add starred items to your list, drop whatever else you're doing, even an A item, and complete the starred tasks first.

Use a star very sparingly. Normally, urgent tasks are not factored into your dedicated planning time. They pop up and scream "do me now!" Be careful, however, to determine that an item really *is* important before you bump the rest of your plan to squeeze it in. Just because something makes a lot of noise doesn't necessarily mean that it must be done instantly. Don't let a false urgency override an important task you've planned.

STEP 3. ASSIGN A NUMBER TO YOUR TASK

Your plan of attack can be further sharpened by assigning a number to each task. Some people, however, see little value in numbering tasks once the priority letter has been assigned. You can decide what works best for you.

The best use of the numbering system is as a chronological indicator. Ask, "Which task should I do first?" If you have a meeting at two in the afternoon and it's an A item, the meeting may not be A-1 simply because other priorities must be attended to earlier in the day.

STEP 4. USE COMPLETION SYMBOLS: THE PAYOFF

After you complete the tasks listed in your planner, you deserve a reward. This reward takes the form of a completion symbol.

Here are several completion symbols:

- (✔) The check mark symbol indicates that a task has been completed. That should feel good. Many people prefer to make their check marks in red as a reminder of how productive they have been.

- (→) A second symbol, an arrow, is used when a task needs to be rescheduled. Perhaps a meeting has been cancelled or an appointment changed, or the task simply could not be completed because you were wrapped up in another matter.

IMPORTANT: Whenever you use the arrow, be sure to reschedule the task to another day in the planner. Using the arrow and rescheduling the task for another day earns you the right to forget that task for awhile. You'll be reminded of it automatically on the new day on which you scheduled it. And it'll be there when you do your daily personal planning.

(O) A third symbol often used is a circle placed in the margin to the left of the completion symbol column to indicate that the task has been delegated to someone else.

It may be that you've asked your spouse to pick up a book of stamps on the way home from work or assigned a child to clean out the garage. Or it may be a more formal kind of delegation, in which you've asked a colleague or subordinate to complete a task. If several people are reporting to you, you may want to use the circle centered with the initial of the person to whom the task has been delegated. When the task has been completed, you should then place a check mark in the "completed" column.

(X) A fourth symbol is an X, to indicate that a task has been deleted. It may mean that you blew it, and it just didn't get done, or it may mean that you've reconsidered and determined that this task simply isn't worth doing. Remember, you are in charge. If you schedule a task but later decide it really isn't what you want to do— so be it. You X it out.

Incorporating Goals and Values in Your Daily Planning

Your priority task list should provide an overview of your daily activities. But how do these activities tie in with your long-term values and goals?

For most people, they don't. And that's why people often fail to achieve what's really important to them. The challenge is to *make your daily activities consistent with your goals and values.*

The best planner system is more than just a calendar. It should have a place to record your core values and goals.

While planning your daily priority tasks, make sure that the goals and values you previously articulated for yourself are evident. It is very important to refer to them. The more often these are reviewed, the more likely they will become a part of your being. Your daily plan should reflect "the big picture" described in your value clarifying efforts.

BLOCKING OUT TIME WASTERS

Writing down tasks and prioritizing them helps avoid one time waster: lack of focus. This is an internal time waster. External time wasters are another problem. Primarily, these are forces that interrupt you from working your plan. Telephone calls, impromptu meetings, visits from workers, and excessive amounts of junk mail pose interruptions.

■ Don't get so well organized that you can't take some time for others.

There is no foolproof formula to use when such interruptions arise. Indeed, an interruption now, although aggravating, may clarify a worker's task or solidify a relationship that will prevent more serious problems down the road. Let's hope we never become so perfectly organized that we cannot take unplanned time to help another person in need. One of the fastest ways to create employee resentment is to give the impression of being too busy to be accessible. Here is where the *art* of managing comes into play. There are no scientific ways to teach people sensitivity to the needs of others. There are times when you'll need to waste a little time. And there are times to avoid such distractions.

Disruptive incoming mail is easy to handle. When in doubt, throw it out. Rather than let reports, memos, letters, and ads pile up on your desk, ask these questions: "What would happen if I threw this out?" "Will I need to refer to this later?" "Will someone else keep a file copy if, by some chance, I do need to see it?"

■ Handle each piece of mail only once.

Don't let paperwork pile up. Handle each piece of incoming mail only once. Look at it, decide what to do with it, and get it out of sight. Either

■ file it,
■ respond to it,
■ pass it on to someone else, or
■ throw it away.

People are trickier to deal with than mail. If you determine that someone is wasting your time, be up front about it. Simply say, in a matter-of-fact tone (don't sound accusing or sarcastic):

■ Be candid with those who try to waste your time.

■ "Tom, I'd like to talk with you more about that issue, but I have some other work I need to do first," or
■ "Carmelita, I think I understand what you are saying. Can we pursue this more after I've had a chance to think through a few ideas?" or

- (When the interrupter is a telephone caller) "I have someone else here with me. Can we talk this out later?"

Once the interruption is set aside, you can determine whether the issue is worth following up on. If you are concerned, you can initiate contact. If not, you can use selective forgetfulness to let the matter drop.

Delegating to Save Time

A leader's willingness and ability to delegate effectively will have an important bearing on his or her time use. Simply stated, the more we can delegate, the more time we'll have for other activities.

Be aware of your attitudes toward delegation, when you should delegate, your understanding of subordinate attitudes toward accepting delegation, and your skills at assigning tasks. Let's take a closer look at these criteria:

WHY SOME MANAGERS HESITATE TO DELEGATE

Delegating work to others always involves some risk. Sometimes the job doesn't get done as well as you'd like—or doesn't get done at all. A few bad experiences with delegated tasks "dropping between the cracks," and a supervisor can easily become gun-shy. But most managers have no choice. Some work *must* be delegated.

If you are overly hesitant about delegating, your behavior may stem from one of these common reasons supervisors don't delegate:

- *I-can-do-it-myself reasoning.* Sure, you probably can do virtually anything you ask others to do. That's not the issue. The real question isn't whether or not you *can* do it. It's a matter of whether or not you *should*. Is doing it yourself a productive use of your time? If not, delegate.

- *Lack of confidence in subordinates.* If you are hesitant to delegate work to others because you think they'll foul up the job, your problem goes much deeper. Either you are insufficiently aware of what your people can do, or you have failed to provide proper and sufficient training or development opportunities. Your supervisory task here is not to avoid delegating but to *increase* delegating until you find out the limitations of your workers. Then work to upgrade employee capabilities through training and job enrichment.

- *Fear of not getting credit and recognition.* We all like to get credit for our efforts. And to some extent, we fear that someone else—perhaps someone we see as a competitor—will get the honor and glory for a job well done. In reality, supervisors can and should get full credit for the productivity of their entire work section. Top management recognizes that supervisors don't do all the work alone. That's not their job! The supervisor's job is to get meaningful work accomplished *through the efforts of others*. The talent to do so is highly valued. As someone said, "There are no limits to what can be accomplished when we don't care who gets the credit."

> - Most supervisors have no choice. Work *must* be delegated.

- *Lack of time, skills, or both at turning work over to others.* Sometimes it seems to take more time to delegate than to do the work yourself. But that is a short-range viewpoint. You could spend quite a bit of time teaching a secretary how to handle routine incoming correspondence initially. But eventually, that secretary will be able to handle what had been a significant time-eating task.

You can spend time and effort now. Or you can keep on spending it forever. It's your choice.

WHY YOU MAY NOT DELEGATE

Most of us have hesitations about delegating in some cases. But if these hang-ups apply to you consistently, you'll have considerable difficulty in being a good supervisor.

To be an effective delegator, a supervisor must be willing to do the following:

- Entrust others with responsibilities.
- Give subordinates the freedom necessary to carry out expanded tasks.
- Spend the time to bring people along from easy to more complex tasks.
- Let subordinates participate increasingly in decisions that affect them.

In short, an effective, time-conscious supervisor *must* delegate in order to strengthen the organization. Without delegation, people are limited to accomplishing only what they can do in a limited time, before exhaustion sets in. With delegation, opportunities for accomplishment are almost unlimited.

HOW DELEGATION CAN SOMETIMES GO WRONG

The most common reasons that delegation sometimes fails to produce the desired results follow, with some suggestions for overcoming the problems.

- *Supervisors fail to keep the communication channels open.* Look for feedback about delegated jobs. Create a climate where the worker can ask you for clarifying instructions or periodically check on how he or she is doing.
- *Supervisors fail to allow for mistakes.* Workers will make mistakes when doing delegated work. Allow for these. Don't jump all over the worker or make him or her feel inadequate. Let him or her learn from the inevitable—and forgiven—mistakes.
- *Supervisors fail to follow up on delegated tasks.* Periodic checking to keep up-to-date on a job conveys a sense of continued interest and also provides communication opportunities.
- *Supervisors fail to delegate enough authority to complete the task.* If you ask one of your workers to research a particular problem that involves interviewing other workers, for example, be sure those other employees know that the interviews are authorized. Often a memo announcing that employee X has been given

such-and-such a task and asking others to cooperate will suffice.

- *Supervisors don't delegate clearly.* Be sure the expected results or outcome is understood by both boss and worker. Specify the nature of the finished product. Do you want a written report or an oral briefing? Should the worker review parts shortages for the entire year or just for the third quarter? Be specific.

In this chapter, we've stressed the importance of career planning, clarifying organizational and personal expectations, managing the manager, and managing one's own time and tasks. As a closing thought, we encourage you to *now take charge!* You can indeed find a rewarding career in people management and create the skills needed to be *human-relations smart.* Applying the principles we've discussed in this book, you can magnify your efforts and make this a better place for all of us to live and work.

▼ Summary of Key Ideas

- The highly successful manager learns to develop clear career plans, clarify job expectations, manage both subordinates and superiors, and manage himself or herself.
- The four components of career planning are goals, self-evaluation (value clarification), vision, and occupational information.
- Clarifying one's expectations requires understanding what organizations do and do not expect of managers as well as what managers can expect from companies.
- The art of managing one's superior is often overlooked in management texts but is nonetheless important for successful people at work.
- Managing upward requires that one understands job responsibilities, takes the initiative, keeps the boss informed, asks for help when needed, and, above all, develops trust with the boss.
- The four conditions for establishing trust with one's boss involve accessibility, availability, predictability, and loyalty.
- Managing your own time and tasks is critical to overall success.
- Prioritizing tasks, writing "to-do" lists, delegating, and accepting responsibility for the use of your most precious resource, time, will make a huge difference in your success.
- Success is a "do-it-yourself" project.
- The highly successful manager recognizes the significance of a manager's role, applies human relations principles, and is willing to take charge.

▼ Key Terms, Concepts, and Names

A-B-C tasks   Career planning
Availability of subordinate   Creativity on the job
   to manager   Dream list

Dress for success
Goal selection
Job expectations
Long-term commitment
Managing your manager
Noneconomic rewards
Occupational information

Predictability
Priority task list
Self-appraisal
Superior-subordinate trust
Value-aligning activities
Value clarification

▼ QUESTIONS AND EXERCISES

1. What do you expect from your employer (present or future)? Discuss these expectations with a manager. How realistic have you been?

2. Try developing a dream list (as suggested in this chapter). Get as many of your personal goals, wants, or desires as possible down on paper. Do this as a free-flowing, brainstorming activity. Don't be critical or particularly selective at first. Then review what you've written, to identify conflicting items. Determine a priority of goals from this, and then boil the list down to ten long-range and ten short-range objectives.

3. List five sources of occupational information that may be useful to your career planning.

4. How can a person show others that he or she values time?

5. What are some ways to reduce clutter and get organized?

6. How does the A-B-C system work to help organize time?

7. What are some common excuses people offer for not delegating enough?

8. How can a person be a more effective delegator?

9. Answer the introductory questions at the beginning of this chapter.

▼ NOTES

1. Thomas J. Peters and Robert H. Waterman, *In Search of Excellence: Lessons from America's Best-Run Companies* (New York: Harper and Row, 1982), p. 279.

2. For details on value planning, see Paul R. Timm, *Successful Self-Management* (Los Altos, Calif.: Crisp Publications, 1987).

3. Og Mandino, *The Greatest Secret in the World* (New York: Bantam Books), 1982.

4. Warren Bennis and Burt Nanus, *Leaders: The Strategies for Taking Charge* (New York: Harper and Row, 1985), p. 27.

5. John T. Molloy, *Dress for Success* (New York: Warner Books, 1976).

6. Paul R. Timm, *50 Simple Things You Can Do to Save Your Customers* (Hawthorne, N.J.: Career Press, 1992), pp. 2–3.

7. Norman C. Hill and Paul H. Thompson, "Managing Your Manager: The Effective Subordinate," *Exchange* (Fall-Winter 1978).

8. R. Alec Mackenzie, *The Time Trap*. (New York: McGraw-Hill, 1972).

9. Adapted from Paul R. Timm, *Recharge Your Career and Your Life* (Los Altos, Calif.: Crisp Publications, 1990), pp. 124–31.

ANOTHER LOOK: WHICH CORPORATE CULTURE FITS YOU?

"Academy" or "fortress"? "Baseball team" or "club"?

According to one management scholar, those four descriptions of corporate culture are more than mere fodder for gossip around the water cooler. Understanding the culture you work in—and knowing whether it matches your career personality—can affect how far or how easily you scurry up the management ranks.

"We've taught managers how to assess their own abilities but not how to match those with the right company," says Jeffrey Sonnenfeld, director of Emory University's Center for Leadership and Career Change who is researching career paths in different corporate cultures.

A risk-taker, for instance, will thrive at a baseball-team company but fall flat on his face at an academy. But take note, a team player who craves security won't last at a baseball team, says Mr. Sonnenfeld, who is also a professor at Emory.

Analyzing a company's corporate culture doesn't guarantee landing a job or a promotion, career experts and managers agree. But it can illuminate why achievements and a sense of belonging come easier in some settings than in others.

Academies.   For the steady climber who wants to thoroughly master each new job and make one company his or her career home, Mr. Sonnenfeld recommends the academy. There, new recruits are invariably young college graduates who are steered through a myriad of specialized jobs.

A classic academy is International Business Machines Corp., where every manager spends at least 40 hours each year in management-training school, with 32 hours devoted to people management.

IBM identifies fast-trackers early on and "carefully grooms them to become expert in a particular function," Mr. Sonnenfeld says. "They'll tell you they're IBMers first and foremost but then add they're an IBMer who cares about data-entry systems or applications technology."

Donald Laidlaw, IBM's director of executive resources and management development and a 37-year veteran of the company, calls himself "an IBM personnel executive." He joined IBM right after college as a sales trainee, then moved from marketing to personnel, mastering 11 jobs at 10 locations. "You don't move ahead until you perform where you are," he says.

Clubs   While managers in academies must stand out to move ahead, "those in clubs must strive to fit in," says Mr. Sonnenfeld, describing his second grouping.

"What counts isn't individual achievement but seniority, commitment and doing things for the good of the group," he says. "If you like quick upward mobility and notoriety, clubs aren't for you."

And unlike academies, clubs groom managers as generalists, with initiation beginning at an entry-level job. At **United Parcel Service of America,** Inc., chief executive John W. Rogers and his management committee began their careers as clerks, drivers and management trainees. Instead of becoming narrow specialists, they learned a little of everything from distribution to marketing as they crisscrossed their way up the corporate ladder.

The chief executive, a 32-year UPS veteran, still does his own photocopying, eats lunch in the cafeteria alongside packagers and junior managers, and shares a secretary. "When decisions have to be made, we get everyone's opinion, and the company feels like a family to a lot of us," says John Tranfo, a staff vice president who will soon be celebrating his 40th year at UPS. "In management, we have hardly any turnover," he adds.

Baseball Teams   Baseball-team companies, which include accounting and law firms, consulting, advertising and software development, are a different breed entirely. Entrepreneurial in style, baseball teams seek out talent of all ages and experience and reward them by what they produce.

"They don't care how committed you'll be tomorrow," says Mr. Sonnenfeld.

ANOTHER LOOK: WHICH CORPORATE CULTURE FITS YOU? *continued*

"They want cutting-edge results today. And they don't train their employees; either you come in with skills or develop them quickly on the job."

Managers at baseball-team companies perceive themselves as free agents, much like professional athletes. If one company doesn't give them the freedom or rewards they think they deserve, they'll leave for a company that does—or form their own.

Such was the case with Bruce Wasserstein and Joseph Perella, two young investment-banking wizards who made mergers and acquisitions Wall Street's most lucrative business. **First Boston** Corp. paid them more than the firm's top executives. Yet last year they quit to form their own company, **Wasserstein Perella** & Co., because they felt the profits they were producing shouldn't be used to subsidize money-losing operations, like securities trading.

"It took me less than an hour to decide to go with them," says George Hornig, a former First Boston colleague who is now managing director and chief operating officer of Wasserstein Perella. But like most baseball-team managers, he also can't predict where he'll work in the future. "Beyond five years it starts to cloud in my crystal ball," he says.

After working as a consultant at **Booz, Allen & Hamilton** Inc. and as an executive at **Time** Inc.,

Sandra Kresch concludes that "Booz Allen's baseball team meritocracy works better for me. At Time, (where the culture is clubby) who you knew seemed more important than anything you did, and that didn't fit my style." Ms. Kresch is now an independent consultant.

Fortresses   If baseball-team companies value inventiveness, fortresses are concerned with survival. Many fortresses are academies, clubs or baseball teams that have failed in the marketplace and are struggling to reverse their fortunes. Others, including retailing and natural-resources companies, are in a perpetual boom-and-bust cycle.

Fortresses can't promise job security or reward people simply on the basis of how well they perform. The most competent fortress manager may find himself suddenly out of a job when the business he oversees is sold or restructured.

Yet for those who relish the challenge of a turnaround, fortresses can be exciting. "I like the fact that there's adrenaline flowing, because you're doing an overhaul, not just a refining, and you have the chance to really create something," says Bruce McKinnon, senior vice president of **Microbrand Wireless Cable** of New York. In the past six years, he's worked at three other cable-television companies, recruited to each as

"a portable warlord to help them back on track," he says.

Managers who crave security and conviviality may not be able to tolerate fortresses. "No one likes to be told they're overweight, but when you're doing a turnaround you're usually putting everyone on a diet," says Mr. McKinnon. "I elicit strong emotions from subordinates."

Blends and Transitions   Of course, many companies can't be neatly categorized in any one way. Many have a blend of corporate cultures. Within **General Electric** Co., the Kidder Peabody unit and the NBC unit both have baseball-team qualities. But GE's aerospace division operates more like a club, the electronics division is like an academy and the home-appliance unit is a fortress. "All four cells are there," Mr. Sonnenfeld says.

Still other companies are in transition. **Apple Computer** Co. started out as a baseball team but is becoming an academy as it matures. And with deregulation, banks—once the clubbiest of employers—are fast evolving into baseball teams.

Managers of **Chemical Bank** Corp. can no longer count on lifelong employment there or working with people out of the same mold, says Pat Cook, a former senior vice president at the bank. Today, "the old club members who played by all the rules are being outpaced by new hotshots from Wall

ANOTHER LOOK *continued*

Street" recruited to combat competition and takeover tremors, she adds. "There's been a massive plate shifting."

COMPARING BUSINESS CULTURES

The four categories of corporate cultures—Academies, Clubs, Baseball Teams and Fortresses—in general appear to attract certain personalities. Based on surveys of 125 Harvard Business School graduates from the class of 1974, these are some of the traits found within managers who gravitated to a particular corporate culture.

ACADEMIES

- had parents who valued self-reliance but put less emphasis on honesty and consideration
- tend to be less religious
- graduated business school with high grades
- had more problems with subordinates in their first 10 years of work

CLUBS

- had parents who emphasized honesty and consideration
- had a lower regard for hard work and self-reliance
- tend to be more religious
- care more about health, family and security and less about future income and autonomy
- are less likely to have substantial equity in their companies

BASEBALL TEAMS

- described their fathers as unpredictable
- generally had more problems planning their careers in the first 10 years after business school, and worked for more companies during that period than classmates did
- priorities include personal growth and future income
- value security less than others

FORTRESSES

- had parents who valued curiosity
- were helped strongly by mentors in the first year out of school
- are less concerned than others with feelings of belonging, professional growth and future income
- experienced problems in career planning, on-the-job decisions and job implementation

SOURCE: Jeffrey Sonnenfeld and Carol Hymowitz, "Which Corporate Culture Fits You?" *Wall Street Journal* (July 17, 1989), p. B-1.

ANOTHER LOOK: CHOOSING TO BE A TOP PERFORMER

Our success in life is determined by the choices we make. You are going to be making choices that will determine your success as you learn to manage yourself and others. To be effective in making proper choices, you must understand the difference between reacting and responding.

If *react* and *respond* sound like the same things to you, let me explain the difference. You go to the doctor, who gives you a prescription and tells you to come back the next day. When you go back, if he looks worried and tells you he needs to change the prescription because your body is "reacting" to the medicine, you're probably going to be concerned.

On the other hand, if he tells you your body is "responding" to the medicine, you're going to smile because you know you're on your way to recovery. So, to react is negative and to respond is positive—the choice is yours! It's a fact that you can't tailormake the situations in life, but you can tailormake the attitudes to fit those situations before they arise.

RESPOND FOR A BETTER TOMORROW

Now, there are some things you simply are not going to change. If you were born white, you're going to stay white. If you were born black, you're going to stay black. I don't care how much thought you give it, you're not going to add a single cubit to your height. You're not going to change when you were born, where you were born, how you were born or to whom you were born. As a matter of fact, you're not going to change one single whisper that's taken place in the yesterdays of your life.

Tomorrow is a different subject. Regardless of your past, your tomorrow is a clean slate. You can choose what you want to write on that slate. You make that choice each time you decide to respond to negative events or react to those negative events. As a manager, when your employees act in a rude, thoughtless, and inconsiderate manner and are impossible to deal with, please understand you can still choose to respond or react. Your choice will play a major role in your relationship with your people.

Obviously, this doesn't mean that to lead others, you must be "perfect" and never blow your cool. That's not only unrealistic, it is impossible and maybe even undesirable. After all, managers are people, too, and our employees need to know we are human and have feelings. On balance, however, we need to be careful that we choose to respond far more often than we choose to react, and that when we react it is under control and is to the action the person took and not to the employee personally.

My friend, Fred Smith, one of the truly outstanding consultants and management experts in America, gives us some helpful advice on this matter in his excellent book *You and Your Network*. Fred says that when others deal with us in a dogmatic or even in a mean and vicious way, it doesn't necessarily mean they want to hurt us. It could mean, and generally does, that they are acting that way because they are hurting.

If you will remember that every obnoxious act is a cry for help, you are way ahead of the game. Recognizing and accepting this fact makes it much easier for us to take a calmer, more level-headed approach to our functions as managers and as people.

IT'S UP TO YOU

All of life is a series of choices, and what you choose to give life today will determine what life will give you tomorrow. You can choose to get drunk tonight, but when you do, you have chosen to feel miserable tomorrow. You can choose to light up a cigarette today, but when you do you have chosen to die 14 minutes early.

You can choose to eat properly today, and when you do, you have chosen to be healthier tomorrow. You can choose to be overweight, or you can choose to be the right weight. You can choose to be happy or you can choose to be sad....

When a young person chooses to sit up late at night

ANOTHER LOOK *continued*

watching television or socializing, he has chosen to be sleepy in class the next day and, consequently, absorb less of the information he needs to know in order to be successful in the competitive world in which he lives. When we choose to be mean, nasty, and ornery to other people, we have chosen to be treated in a mean, nasty, and ornery fashion by others. By the same token, when we choose to be thoughtful and considerate of others, we've chosen to be treated in a thoughtful and considerate manner.

This list is endless, but the message is the same: *You are free to choose, but the choices you make today will determine what you will have, be, and do in the tomorrows of your life.* You can choose to take the necessary steps to help you succeed as a manager, or you can choose to ignore the experience of successful managers and take the consequences for you and your employees.

We must teach our employees that they are responsible for their attitudes and their conduct and that in life, every choice we make, whether it is good or bad has consequences! Once those consequences are thoroughly understood, it's easier to make the right choice.

THE CHOICE IS YOURS

I choose to respond for one simple reason. I don't have, need, or want ulcers, high blood pressure, a heart problem, or any of the negative consequences that go with reacting. I have chosen to respond to negative situations in life instead of reacting to those situations. Even if this does not benefit anyone else, I'm persuaded that it is the best thing I can do for me. When it's the best thing for me, then obviously that puts me in a far better position to do my work, which basically is designed to help other people.

Once I was in Kansas City for a lengthy four-hour recording session. I finished at one and had a three o'clock flight to Dallas. We packed and made a mad dash for the airport.

When we arrived, the ticket agent looked at me, smiled and said, "The three o'clock flight to Dallas has been canceled."

To this I enthusiastically responded, "Fantastic."

"Yes," said the agent, "but the next flight doesn't leave until 6:05."

To that I smiled and responded, "Fantastic."

The woman looked at me in complete shock and said, "I'm really puzzled. Why would you say 'fantastic' when I've just told you that you have a four-hour wait in the airport?"

I smilingly said, "Ma'am, it's really very simple. I have never had a chance to spend four hours in the airport in Kansas City, Missouri. Why do you realize that at this moment there are literally tens of millions of people on the face of this earth who not only are cold but also hungry?

"Here I am in a beautiful facility, and even though it's cold outside, it's comfortable inside. Down the corridor is a nice little coffee shop. I'm going to go there, relax for a few minutes and enjoy a cup of coffee. Then I've got some extremely important work to do. And here I am in one of the nicest buildings in the whole area. It's easily the biggest, most comfortable, rent-free office I've ever had at my disposal. Fantastic."

As a practical matter, I do not know anyone who works for that airline. From the chairman of the board to a single one. However, it is their airline, and if they choose to do so, they can cancel my flight. But they can't cancel my day! It's mine. God Himself gave it to me with written instructions on how I am to use it. He told me to "rejoice and be glad in it."

That, my friend, is exactly the same position you are in. When you respond, you are making real progress toward living a healthier, happier life and developing effective, efficient, and happy employees.

Yes, your past is important, but as important as it is, according to Dr. Tony Campolo, it is not nearly as important to your present as the way you see your future. Ralph Waldo Emerson was right when he said that what lies behind you and what lies before you pale in significance when you learn to

ANOTHER LOOK: CHOOSING TO BE A TOP PERFORMER *continued*

respond and not react to life's daily challenges.

It's been said before and it will be said again: You cannot change the past, but your future is spotless. You can write on it what you will. In order to do so, however, you need to learn to respond to the positive and the negative.

Fortunately, you have far more control than you realize. For example, all of us have on occasion been guilty of saying, "He/She makes me so mad!" That simply is not so. As a wise man said, you can't stir the soup unless there's some soup in the pot to stir. Nobody can make you act mad unless there is already some mad in you. Mad reactions are *learned*

behaviors and consequently they can be *unlearned*.

You can watch a person go about his or her daily activities for days or weeks and learn a great deal about him. However, you can watch a person under adverse circumstances for five minutes and see whether he has learned to respond or react. Actually, you can learn more about him a few minutes under trying conditions than you can in days of just watching him involved in daily activities.

Your response or reaction to negative reveals what's inside of you. It exposes your heart and shows the kind of person you really are. The problem is that most people have a tendency to

react instead of respond. They have a tendency to blame everything and everybody for the difficulties and reversals in life.

Most of us have a tendency to blame somebody else for our difficulties, but keep appropriate credit for our success to ourselves. What about you? Do you respond to the negative and make it better, or do you react to the negative and make it worse? To be a Top Performer, you must make the proper choices.

SOURCE: Zig Ziglar, "Choosing to Be a Top Performer," *Executive Excellence* (April 1987). Reprinted with permission of *Executive Excellence,* © 1987.

A CASE IN POINT: BRIDGET GOES BANANAS

As a typist, Bridget was incredible. She seemed to turn out error-free work at an amazing pace. Her attention to detail was admired by all who used her services. She seldom committed even a minor typo.

Last month, Bridget became supervisor over the executive word processing center. It is her first management experience. But already some problems have surfaced. Leslie, a typist with four years experience, went over Bridget's head to complain to Alice Benson, administrative manager, about the "unbelievable nit-picking."

"I can't seem to do anything right, according to Bridget," complained Leslie. "She

checks everything I type! She's driving me nuts, not to mention the fact that my output has slowed down dramatically. Just yesterday, Phil Underwood, that new VP of marketing, made a wisecrack about cobwebs growing on his report before he could get it out of typing."

When Alice asked about Leslie's concerns, Bridget flew off the handle. "We're supposed to be the best typing pool in the company. After all, we type for the top people. The work has to be *perfect!*" She was almost screaming. Then she slumped down in a chair in Alice's office.

A CASE IN POINT *continued*

"Alice, I'm going nuts up there. None of my people seems to care about the quality of the work the way I do. I've been working till nine or ten every night checking work and just trying to keep up. I'm about convinced that being a supervisor just isn't worth it."

QUESTIONS

1. What seems to be a driving need in Bridget's work?

2. If you were Alice, what would you suggest to Bridget?

SOURCE: Paul Timm, *Supervision* (St. Paul: West Publishing, 1992), p. 417. Reprinted by permission. Copyright © 1992 by West Publishing Company. All rights reserved.

▼ A CASE IN POINT: GEORGE LANDEN'S SHORT CAREER

After only eight months on the job, George Landen was looking for a way out. Not that he was incompetent: He had graduated near the top of his M.B.A. class at a leading business school, had been heavily recruited, and had finally accepted a position with a major accounting firm. A successful career had seemed the inevitable next step.

But Landen's short career in public accounting had been more painful than successful. When asked what had gone wrong, Landen shrugged his shoulders. "I guess it's the work itself," he sighed. "You can't get into depth on any problem. Deadlines are so tight that all your work ends up being pretty superficial. I guess that's what they want, but it drives me crazy."

Questioned about his performance, Landen's fellow workers told a different story.

Said one, "Landen's technical competence is impeccable, but he's too quiet—he keeps to himself. It's almost impossible for him to handle his clients and colleagues effectively. If he could break out of his shell, things might be different. But as it is now, I'm afraid that the management wouldn't be the least bit sorry to see him go."

QUESTIONS

1. What problems seem to be at the root of Landen's situation?

2. If you were Landen's manager and wanted to help him stay with the company, what advice would you give him?

SOURCE: Adapted from Gene W. Dalton and Paul H. Thompson, *Novations: Strategies for Career Management* (Glenview, Ill.: Scott, Foresman, 1986), p. 20. Copyright © 1986 by Gene W. Dalton and Paul H. Thompson. Reprinted by permission Scott, Foresman and Company.

Supplementary Article

Wacky Ways to Make a Living

Bad movies, bronzed frogs and straw houses are all needs some entrepreneur has filled

Condensed from KIWANIS
CHARLES DOWNEY

WHEN JIM McCABE burned out as a psychologist, he and his attorney wife, Jane, decided to start a business. The McCabes love movies, so it seemed natural to open a video-rental store. Since most stores in their area rented the same films, they checked catalogues to see what else was available. These contained many listings for unusual films, some of which could only be described as "bombs." The entrepreneurial duo liked such off-the-wall offerings and figured others would too.

When they opened Video Vault in Alexandria, Va., they stocked movie oddities alongside the usual Hollywood fare and adopted the slogan "Guaranteed Worst Movies in Town." Customers flocked in for cinematic stinkers such as *The Incredibly Strange Creatures Who Stopped Living and Became Mixed-Up Zombies* and one of Jim McCabe's all-time personal favorites, *Faster, Pussycat! Kill! Kill!*

Now the McCabes rent films throughout the United States via a toll-free telephone number and do about $500,000 worth of business yearly. "We found a niche and outmaneuvered the competition," says Jim McCabe. "The small operator has to make himself a little bit different."

In business, the usual formula for starting a successful product or service is just that basic: find a need and fill it. But you never know how—or when—a need will present itself. Many times, an entrepreneur just stumbles into what people want. At other times, the need stumbles squarely into the entrepreneur.

Consider Finders Company of Clear Lake Shores, Texas. When Joe Davis worked in a graphic-arts studio in Chicago, he noticed that artists and photographers constantly were seeking hard-to-find props. Clients who wanted eye-catching ads demanded unusual items, such as World War II British fighter planes. *Why not become a professional finder,* Davis thought. He formed Finders Company with his wife, Suzanne, and sold his skills at an hourly fee, usually to advertising agencies.

One of Davis's most unusual calls came from someone who wanted to track down a cargo boat loaded with whiskey that had sunk in the Missouri River in 1887. Davis compared old and new maps and noticed that the course of the river had changed. He found the sunken boat, 20 feet beneath a farmer's cornfield.

Davis has also located the soundtracks of all the World Series games played by the Chicago Cubs. An ecology group requested a number of skulls for an Earth Day display, and Davis obtained them from various sources in Mexico.

When a restaurant opened in an old bank, the owner decided he wanted infamous bank robber Willie Sutton for the occasion. Finders went through Sutton's prison records and looked up family members. When the Davises finally found Sutton, he was living inconspicuously in an average neighborhood.

SOMETIMES the inspiration for filling an unmet need comes through hunches or even dreams. Such a revelation visited Gay Balfour when he and his wife, Judy, were struggling with a marina business in Cortez, Colo. Around town, he had seen a truck-borne vacuum used to clean out sewage systems. In his dream, Balfour saw the vacuum-on-wheels sucking prairie dogs from their holes.

Prairie dogs are a nuisance for ranchers, because cows and horses often step into their holes and break legs. Moreover, the creatures are hard to capture in their tunnels. Poison and traps aren't good options because other animals can be harmed.

Balfour named his new business Dog-Gone and made a few minor alterations to the truck, including installing six inches of padding inside the vacuum tank. He now travels to rodent-infested fields and, for $800 to $1000 a day, sucks the varmints from their holes and releases them at other locations.

Airports soon learned of his service. So Balfour now travels to 13 states to clear prairie dogs from grass runways. Inquiries about vacuuming rabbits have come from Australia.

MATTS MYHRMAN, a former professor, left teaching in 1990, unsure of what he wanted to do. He loved research, so when he heard about a man building houses of straw, he sought more details. He learned that houses with walls made of bales of straw were built around the turn of the century in Nebraska, where materials were scarce on the treeless plains. Many such houses were still standing.

It was an idea whose time had come again. Straw is an excellent insulator and is inexpensive; the house goes up quickly and can be built by the homeowner.

Myhrman and his wife, Judy Knox, founded Out on Bale Unlimited in Tucson, Ariz., to build the houses. They now give seminars on the technique and have an education center for straw-built construction. The hardest part about building the homes has been satisfying code officials, who find little on the books about straw homes.

SOMETIMES a product is useful beyond its original purpose. Bron-Shoe of Columbus, Ohio, specialized in bronzing baby shoes, but business sagged when couples began having fewer babies. The owners soon learned that people had other objects to bronze—odd things like umbilical cords, body casts, bras, all the clipping tools of a deceased barber, and a dead pet frog. They began filling those needs, and business boomed.

FRED WELLBORN, an avid golfer and owner of a paint-supply business, learned that he was not alone in preferring to golf on lush-looking greens. So he put his paint-making skills to work and developed a non-polluting grass paint for lawns, golf courses and real-estate agents. The result: Green-Graphics Green, a New Mexico firm whose customers include golf courses and baseball stadiums as well as countries such as Israel.

MARGE CARLSON specializes in whistling gospel music and gives 30 to 40 concerts a year. She is also owner of Artistry in Whistling in Fullerton, Calif., the only school she knows of in the United States that teaches whistling. Carlson discovered that children with reading or learning difficulties can bolster their self-confidence by learning something they can do well.

STEVE RAINES belonged to a Texas snake club, and he couldn't help but notice how many people gathered around to watch when rattlesnakes were handled. So he formed Texas State Diamond Hunters to perform snake skits for nightclubs, fairs and other groups. In one skit, a handler puts a balloon into his mouth and moves just close enough to a rattler for the creature to strike and pop the balloon. In another, a handler slips into a sleeping bag that is then filled with rattlers. The handler must wriggle out—very slowly.

"When you're in a sleeping bag with a pile of wriggling rattlers, they think you're just another snake," says Diamond Hunters handler Cassandra Luchak. In 20 years, Raines has had only two serious bites.

RON CRISP was a private investigator who was tiring fast of his bread-and-butter clients—lawyers. One day on vacation he decided to use his tracking skills to locate his first girlfriend, from 1955. It took only 48 hours, and the experience was as sweet as honey.

Crisp told friends about his vacation and received immediate orders to find other lost loves. Thus, Old Flame Finders of Long Beach, Calif., was launched and now handles about 200 cases yearly at $250 to $500 per old flame.

In a world of such businesses, there just might be a place for *your* next idea.

Sample Chapter 12

The Industrial Revolution and Its Impact on European Society

C H A P T E R   2 1

The Industrial Revolution and Its Impact on European Society

The French Revolution dramatically and quickly altered the political structure of France while the Napoleonic conquests spread many of the revolutionary principles in an equally rapid and stunning fashion to other parts of Europe. During the late eighteenth and early nineteenth centuries, another revolution—an industrial one—was transforming the economic and social structure of Europe, although in a less dramatic and rapid fashion.

The use of machinery to produce goods, one of the characteristics of the Industrial Revolution, was not entirely new. Beginning in the Middle Ages, Europeans had developed innovative tools that harnessed the power of wind and water to manufacture articles for consumption. Wind and water power, however, were neither sufficient nor reliable enough to create a self-sustaining system of manufacturing. Most products were still made by hand. The period of the Industrial Revolution witnessed a quantum leap in industrial production. New sources of energy and power, especially coal and steam, replaced wind and water to create labor-saving machines that dramatically decreased the use of human and animal labor and, at the same time, increased the level of productivity. In turn, power machinery called for new ways of organizing human labor in order to maximize the benefits and profits from the new machines; factories replaced shop and home workrooms. During the Industrial Revolution, Europe experienced a shift from a traditional, labor-intensive economy based on agriculture and handicrafts to a more capital-intensive economy based on manufacturing by machines, specialized labor, and industrial factories.

Although the Industrial Revolution took decades to spread, it was truly revolutionary in the way it fundamentally changed Europeans, their society, their relationship to other peoples, and the world itself. The development of large factories encouraged mass movements of people from the countryside to urban areas where impersonal coexistence replaced the traditional intimacy of rural life. Higher levels of productivity led to a search for new sources of raw materials, new consumption patterns, and a revolution in transportation that allowed raw materials and finished products to be moved quickly around the world. The creation of a wealthy industrial middle class and a huge industrial working class (or proletariat) substantially transformed traditional social relationships. Finally, the Industrial Revolution fundamentally altered how the Western world related to nature, ultimately creating an environmental crisis that in the twentieth century has finally been recognized as a danger to human existence itself

The Industrial Revolution in Great Britain

Although the Industrial Revolution evolved out of antecedents that occurred over a long period of time, historians generally agree that it had its beginnings in Britain in the second half of the eighteenth century. By 1850, the Industrial Revolution had made Great Britain the wealthiest country in the world; by that time it had also spread to the European continent and the New World. By the end of the nineteenth century, both Germany and the United States would surpass Britain in industrial production.

Origins

A number of factors or conditions coalesced in Britain to produce the first Industrial Revolution. One of these was the agricultural revolution of the eighteenth century. The changes in the methods of farming and stock breeding that characterized this agricultural transformation led to a significant increase in food production. British agriculture could now feed more people at lower prices with less labor. Unlike the rest of Europe, even ordinary British families did not have to use most of their income to buy food, giving them the potential to purchase manufactured goods. At the same time, a rapid growth of population in the second half of the eighteenth century provided a pool of surplus labor for the new factories of the emerging British industry. Rural workers in cottage industries also provided a potential labor force for industrial enterprises.

Britain had a ready supply of capital for investment in the new industrial machines and the factories that were needed to house them. In addition to profits from trade and cottage industry, Britain possessed an effective central bank and well-developed, flexible credit facilities. Nowhere in Europe were people so accustomed to using paper instruments to facilitate capital transactions. Many early factory owners were merchants and entrepreneurs who had profited from eighteenth-century cottage industry. Of 110 cotton spinning mills in operation in the area known as the Midlands between 1769 and 1800, 62 were established by hosiers, drapers, mercers, and others involved in some fashion in the cottage textile industry. But capital alone is only part of the story. Britain had a fair number of individuals who were interested in making profits if the opportunity presented itself (see the box on p. 707). The British were a people, as one historian has said, "fascinated by wealth and commerce, collectively and individually." These early industrial entrepreneurs faced considerable financial hazards, however. Fortunes were made and easily lost. The structure of early firms was

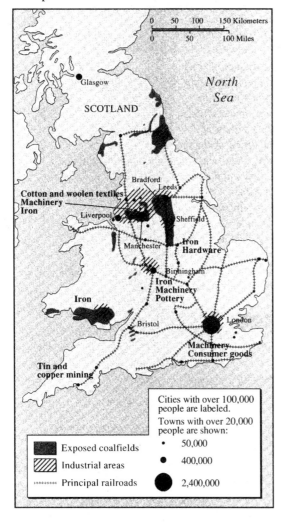

▼ Map 21.1 Britain in the Industrial Revolution.

0   50   100   150 Kilometers
0   50   100 Miles

Glasgow

North Sea

SCOTLAND

Bradford
Leeds

Cotton and woolen textiles
Machinery
Iron

Liverpool

Sheffield

Manchester

Iron
Hardware

Birmingham

Iron
Machinery
Pottery

Iron

Bristol

London

Machinery
Consumer goods

Tin and copper mining

Cities with over 100,000 people are labeled.

Towns with over 20,000 people are shown:

•   50,000

●   400,000

● 2,400,000

▮ Exposed coalfields

▨ Industrial areas

┈┈┈ Principal railroads

≽ The Traits of the British Industrial Entrepreneur ≼

Richard Arkwright (1732–1792), inventor of a spinning frame and founder of cotton factories, was a good example of the successful entrepreneur in the early Industrial Revolution in Britain. In this selection, Edward Baines, who wrote The History of the Cotton Manufacture in Great Britain *in 1835, discusses the traits that explain the success of Arkwright and presumably other British entrepreneurs.*

Edward Baines, *The History of the Cotton Manufacture in Great Britain*

Richard Arkwright rose by the force of his natural talents from a very humble condition in society. He was born at Preston on the 23rd of December, 1732, of poor parents: being the youngest of thirteen children, his parents could only afford to give him an education of the humblest kind, and he was scarcely able to write. He was brought up to the trade of a barber at Kirkham and Preston, and established himself in that business at Bolton in the year 1760. Having become possessed of a chemical process for dyeing human hair, which in that day (when wigs were universal) was of considerable value, he travelled about collecting hair, and again disposing of it when dyed. In 1761, he married a wife from Leigh, and the connexions he thus formed in that town are supposed to have afterwards brought him acquainted with Highs's experiments in making spinning machines. He himself manifested a strong bent for experiments in mathematics, which he is stated to have followed with so much devotedness as to have neglected his business and injured his circumstances. His natural disposition was ardent, enterprising, and stubbornly persevering: his mind was as coarse as it was bold and active, and his manners were rough and unpleasing. . . .

The most marked traits in the character of Arkwright were his wonderful ardour, energy, and perseverance. He commonly laboured in his multifarious concerns from five o'clock in the morning till nine at night; and when considerably more than fifty years of age,—feeling that the defects of his education placed him under great difficulty and inconvenience in conducting his correspondence, and in the general management of his business,—he encroached upon his sleep, in order to gain an hour each day to learn English grammar, and another hour to improve his writing and orthography [spelling]! He was impatient of whatever interfered with his favorite pursuits; and the fact is too strikingly characteristic not to be mentioned, that he separated from his wife not many years after their marriage, because she, convinced that he would starve his family [because of the impractical nature of his schemes], broke some of his experimental models of machinery. Arkwright was a severe economist of time; and, that he might not waste a moment, he generally travelled with four horses, and at a very rapid speed. His concerns in Derbyshire, Lancashire, and Scotland were so extensive and numerous, as to [show] at once his astonishing power of transacting business and his all-grasping spirit. In many of these he had partners, but he generally managed in such a way, that, whoever lost, he himself was a gainer.

open and fluid. An individual or family proprietorship was the usual mode of operation, but entrepreneurs also brought in friends to help them. They just as easily jettisoned them. John Marshall, who made money in flax spinning, threw out his partners: "As they could neither of them be of any further use, I released them from the firm and took the whole upon myself."[1]

Britain was richly supplied with important mineral resources, such as coal and iron ore, needed in the manufacturing process. Britain was also a small country, and the relatively short distances made transportation readily accessible. In addition to nature's provision of abundant rivers, from the mid-seventeenth century onward, both private and public investment poured into the construction of new roads, bridges, and, beginning in the 1750s and 1760s, canals. By 1780, roads, rivers, and canals linked the major industrial centers of the North, the Midlands, London, and the Atlantic. Unlike the continental countries, Britain had no internal customs barriers to hinder domestic trade.

Britain's government also played a significant role in the process of industrialization. Parliament added to the favorable business climate by providing a stable government and passing laws that protected private property. Moreover, Britain was remarkable for the freedom it provided for private enterprise. It placed fewer restrictions on private entrepreneurs than any other European state.

Finally, a supply of markets gave British industrialists a ready outlet for their manufactured goods. British exports quadrupled from 1660 to 1760. In the course of its eighteenth-century wars and conquests, Great Britain had developed a vast colonial empire at the expense of its leading continental rivals, the Dutch Republic and France. Britain also possessed a well-developed merchant marine that was able to transport goods to any place in the world. A crucial factor in Britain's successful industrialization was the ability to produce cheaply those articles most in demand abroad. And the best markets abroad were not in Europe, where countries protected their own incipient industries, but in the Americas, Africa, and the Far East, where people wanted sturdy, inexpensive clothes rather than costly, highly finished, luxury items. Britain's machine-produced textiles fulfilled that demand. Nor should we overlook the British domestic market. Britain had the highest standard of living in Europe and a rapidly growing population. As Daniel Defoe noted already in 1728:

> For the rest, we see their Houses and Lodgings tolerably furnished, at least stuff'd well with useful and necessary household Goods: Even those we call poor People, Journey-men, working and Pains-taking People do thus; they lye warm, live in Plenty, work hard, and [need] know no Want.

These are the People that carry off the Gross of your Consumption; 'tis for these your Markets are kept open late on Saturday nights; because they usually receive their Week's Wages late ... in a Word, these are the Life of our whole Commerce, and all by their Multitude: Their Numbers are not Hundreds or Thousands, or Hundreds of Thousands, but Millions; ... by their Wages they are able to live plentifully, and it is by their expensive, generous, free way of living, that the Home Consumption is rais'd to such a Bulk, as well of our own, as of foreign Production.[2]

This demand from both domestic and foreign markets and the inability of the old system to fulfill it led entrepreneurs to seek and accept the new methods of manufacturing that a series of inventions provided. In so doing, these individuals produced the Industrial Revolution.

Technological Changes and New Forms of Industrial Organization

In the 1770s and 1780s, the cotton textile industry took the first major step toward the Industrial Revolution with the creation of the modern factory.

THE COTTON INDUSTRY Already in the eighteenth century, Great Britain had surged ahead in the production of cheap cotton goods using the traditional methods of cottage industry. The development of the flying shuttle had sped the process of weaving on a loom and enabled weavers to double their output. This, however, created shortages of yarn until James Hargreaves's spinning jenny, perfected by 1768, allowed spinners to produce yarn in greater quantities. Richard Arkwright's water frame spinning machine, powered by water or horse, and Samuel Crompton's so-called mule, which combined aspects of the water frame and spinning jenny, increased yarn production even more. Edmund Cartwright's power loom, invented in 1787, allowed the weaving of cloth to catch up with the spinning of yarn. Even then, early power looms were grossly inefficient, enabling cottage, hand-loom weavers to continue to prosper, at least until the mid-1820s. After that they were gradually replaced by the new machines. In 1813, there were 2,400 power looms in operation in Great Britain; they numbered 14,150 in 1820, 100,000 in 1833, and 250,000 by 1850. In the 1820s, there were still 250,000 hand-loom weavers in Britain; by 1860, only 3,000 were left.

The water frame, Crompton's mule, and power looms presented new opportunities to entrepreneurs. It was much more efficient to bring workers to the machines and organize their labor collectively in factories located next to rivers and streams, the sources of power for many of these early machines, than to leave the workers dispersed in their cottages. The concentration of labor in the new factories also brought the laborers and their families to live in the new towns that rapidly grew up around the factories.

The early devices used to speed up the processes of spinning and weaving were the products of weavers and spinners, in effect, of craftsmen tinkerers. But the subsequent expansion of the cotton industry and the ongoing demand for even more cotton goods created additional pressure for new and more complicated technology. The invention that pushed the cotton industry to even greater heights of productivity was the steam engine.

THE STEAM ENGINE   The invention of the steam engine played a major role in the Industrial Revolution. It revolutionized the production of cotton goods and caused the factory system to spread to other areas of production, thereby creating whole new industries. The steam engine secured the triumph of the Industrial Revolution.

As in much of the Industrial Revolution, one kind of change forced other changes. In many ways the steam engine was the result of the need for more efficient pumps to eliminate water seepage from deep mines. Deep coal mines were in turn the result of Britain's need and desire to find new sources of energy to replace wood. By the early eighteenth century, the British were acutely aware of a growing shortage of timber, used in heating, building homes and ships, and in enormous quantities to produce the charcoal utilized in the smelting of iron ore to produce pig iron. At the beginning of the eighteenth century, the discovery of new processes for smelting iron ore with coal and coke (see the next section) led to

more intensive mining of coal by digging deeper and deeper mines. But as mines were dug below the water table, they filled with water. An early solution to the problem was the use of mechanical pumps powered by horses walking in circles. In one coal mine in Warwickshire, for example, 500 horses were used to lift the water from the mine, bucket by bucket. The need for more efficient pumps led Thomas Newcomen to develop a steam pump or, as it was called, an "atmospheric engine" that was first used in 1712. While better than horses, it still proved inefficient.

In the 1760s, a Scottish engineer, James Watt (1736–1819), was asked to repair a Newcomen engine. Instead he added a separate condenser and steam pump and transformed Newcomen's machine into a genuine steam engine. Power was derived not from air pressure as in Newcomen's atmospheric engine, but from steam itself. Much more efficient, Watt's engine could pump water three times as quickly. Initially, it possessed one major liability, however; as a contemporary noted in 1778: "the vast consumption of fuel in these engines is an immense drawback on the profit of our mines, for every fire-engine of magnitude consumes £3000 worth of coals per annum. This heavy tax amounts almost to a prohibition."[3] As steam engines were made more efficient, however, they also became cheaper to use.

In 1782, James Watt enlarged the possibilities of the steam engine when he developed a rotary engine that could turn a shaft and thus drive machinery. Steam power could now be applied to spinning and weaving cotton, and before long cotton mills using steam engines were multiplying across Britain. By 1850, seven-eighths of the power available to the cotton industry for all of Britain came from steam. Since steam engines were fired by coal, they did not need to be located near rivers; entrepreneurs now had greater flexibility in their choice of location.

The new boost given to cotton textile production by technological changes became readily apparent. In 1760, Britain had imported 2.5 million pounds of raw cotton, which was farmed out to cottage industries. All work was done by hand either in workers' homes or in the small shops of master weavers. In 1787, the British imported 22 million pounds of cotton; most of it was spun on machines, some powered by water in large mills. By 1840, 366 million pounds of cotton—now Britain's most important product in value—were imported. By 1840, although there were still some hand-loom weavers, most cotton industry employees worked in factories. The price of yarn was but one-twentieth of what it had been. The cheapest labor in India could not compete in quality or quantity with Britain. British cotton goods sold everywhere in the world. And in Britain itself, cheap cotton cloth made it possible for millions of poor people to wear undergarments, long a preserve of the rich who alone could afford the underwear made with expensive linen cloth. New work clothing that was tough, comfortable to the skin, and yet cheap and easily washable became common. Even the rich liked the colorful patterns of cotton prints and their light weight for summer use.

The steam engine proved invaluable to Britain's Industrial Revolution. In 1800, engines were generating 10,000 horsepower; by 1850, 500,000 in stationary engines and 790,000 in mobile engines, the last largely in locomotives (see A Revolution in Transportation later in this chapter). Unlike horses, the steam engine was a tireless source of power and depended for fuel on a substance—namely, coal—that seemed then to be unlimited in quantity. The popular saying that "Steam is an Englishman" had real significance by 1850. The steam engine also replaced waterpower in such places as flour and sugar mills. Just as the need for more coal had helped lead to the steam engine, so the success of the steam engine led to a need for more coal and an expansion in coal production; between 1815 and 1850, the output of coal quadrupled. In turn, new processes using coal furthered the development of an iron industry.

THE IRON INDUSTRY The British iron industry was radically transformed during the Industrial Revolution. Britain had large resources of iron ore, but at the beginning of the eighteenth century, the basic process of producing iron had altered little since the Middle Ages and still depended heavily on charcoal. In the early eighteenth century, new methods of smelting iron ore to produce cast iron were devised based on the use of coke derived from coal. A better quality of iron was still not possible, however, until the 1780s when Henry Cort developed a system called puddling, in which coke was used to burn away impurities in pig iron and produce an iron of high quality. A boom then ensued in the British iron industry. In 1740, Britain produced 17,000 tons of iron; in the 1780s, almost 70,000 tons; by the 1840s, over 2 million tons; and by 1852, almost 3 million tons, more than the rest of the world combined.

The development of the iron industry was in many ways a response to the demands for the new machines. The high-quality wrought iron produced by the Cort process made it the most widely used metal until the production of cheaper steel in the 1860s. The growing supply of less costly metal encouraged the growth of machinery in other industries, most noticeably in new means of transportation.

A REVOLUTION IN TRANSPORTATION The eighteenth century had witnessed an expansion of transportation facilities in Britain as entrepreneurs realized the need for more efficient means of moving resources and goods. Turnpike trusts provided new roads, and between 1760 and 1830 a network of canals was built. Both roads and canals were soon overtaken by a new form of transportation that dazzled people with its promise. To many economic historians, railroads were the "most important single factor in promoting European economic progress in the 1830s and 1840s." Again, Britain was the leader in the revolution.

The beginnings of railways can be found in mining operations in Germany as early as 1500 and in British coal mines after 1600 where small handcarts filled with coal were pushed along parallel wooden rails. The rails reduced friction, enabling horses to haul more substantial loads. By 1700, some entrepreneurs began to replace wooden rails with cast-iron rails, and by the early nineteenth century, railways—still dependent on horsepower —were common in British mining and industrial districts. The development of the steam engine brought a radical transformation to railways.

In 1804, Richard Trevithick pioneered the first steam-powered locomotive on an industrial rail-line in south Wales. It pulled ten tons of ore and seventy people at five miles per hour. Better locomotives soon followed. Those engines built by George Stephenson and his son proved superior, and it was in their workshops in Newcastle upon Tyne that the locomotives for the first modern railways in Britain were built. George Stephenson's *Rocket* was used on the first public railway line, which opened in 1830, extending thirty-two miles from Liverpool to Manchester. *Rocket* sped along at sixteen miles per hour. Within twenty years, locomotives had reached fifty miles per hour, an incredible speed to contemporary passengers. During the same period, new companies were formed to build additional railroads as the infant industry proved to be not only technically but financially successful. In 1840, Britain had almost 2,000 miles of railroads; by 1850, 6,000 miles of railroad track crisscrossed much of the country.

The railroad contributed significantly to the success and maturing of the Industrial Revolution. The demands of railroads for coal and iron furthered the growth of those industries. British supremacy in civil and mechanical engineering, so evident after 1840, was in large part based upon the skills acquired in railway building. The huge capital demands necessary for railway construction encouraged a whole new group of middle-class investors to plough their money into joint-stock companies (see Limitations to Industrialization later in this chapter). Railway construction created new job opportunities, especially for farm laborers and peasants who had long been accustomed to finding work outside their local villages. Perhaps most importantly, a cheaper and faster means of transportation had a rippling effect on the growth of an industrial economy. By reducing the price of goods, larger markets were created; increased sales meant more factories and more machinery, thereby reinforcing the self-sustaining aspect of the Industrial Revolution that marked a fundamental break with the traditional European economy. The great productivity of the Industrial Revolution enabled entrepreneurs to reinvest their profits in new capital equipment, further expanding the productive capacity of the economy. Continuous, even rapid, self-sustaining economic growth

came to be seen as a fundamental characteristic of the new industrial economy.

The railroad was the perfect symbol of this aspect of the Industrial Revolution. The ability to transport goods and people at dramatic speeds also provided visible confirmation of a new sense of power. When railway engineers pierced mountains with tunnels and spanned chasms with breathtaking bridges, contemporaries experienced a sense of power over nature not felt before in Western civilization.

THE INDUSTRIAL FACTORY   Initially the product of the new cotton industry, the factory became the chief means of organizing labor for the new machines. As the workplace shifted from the artisan's shop and the peasant's cottage to the factory, the latter was not viewed as just a larger work unit. Employers hired workers who no longer owned the means of production but simply provided the hands to run the machines. Wages formed the basis of their economic relationship, but discipline formed the foundation of their functional relationship.

From its beginning, the factory system demanded a new type of discipline from its employees. Factory owners could not afford to let their expensive machinery stand idle. Workers were forced to work regular hours and in shifts to keep the machines producing at a steady pace for maximum output. This represented a massive adjustment for early factory laborers.

Pre-industrial workers were not accustomed to a "timed" format. Agricultural laborers had always kept irregular hours; hectic work at harvest time might be followed by periods of inactivity. Even in the burgeoning cottage industry of the eighteenth century, weavers and spinners who worked at home might fulfill their weekly quotas by working around the clock for two or three days, followed by a leisurely pace until the next week's demands forced another work spurt.

Factory owners, therefore, faced a formidable task. They had to create a system of work discipline in which employees became accustomed to working regular, unvarying hours during which they performed a set number of tasks over and over again as efficiently as possible. One early industrialist said that his aim was "to make such

❧ *Discipline in the New Factories* ❧

Workers in the new factories of the Industrial Revolution had been accustomed to a life-style free of overseers. Unlike the cottages, where workers spun thread and wove cloth in their own rhythm and time, the factories demanded a new, rigorous discipline geared to the requirements of the machines. This selection is taken from a set of rules for a factory in Berlin in 1844. They were typical of company rules everywhere the factory system had been established.

The Foundry and Engineering Works of the Royal Overseas Trading Company, Factory Rules

In every large works, and in the co-ordination of any large number of workmen, good order and harmony must be looked upon as the fundamentals of success, and therefore the following rules shall be strictly observed.

1. The normal working day begins at all seasons at 6 A.M. precisely and ends, after the usual break of half an hour for breakfast, an hour for dinner and half an hour for tea, at 7 P.M., and it shall be strictly observed. . . .

   Workers arriving 2 minutes late shall lose half an hour's wages; whoever is more than 2 minutes late may not start work until after the next break, or at least shall lose his wages until then. Any disputes about the correct time shall be settled by the clock mounted above the gatekeeper's lodge. . . .

3. No workman, whether employed by time or piece, may leave before the end of the working day, without having first received permission from the overseer and having given his name to the gatekeeper. Omission of these two actions shall lead to a fine of ten silver groschen [pennies] payable to the sick fund.

4. Repeated irregular arrival at work shall lead to dismissal. This shall also apply to those who are found idling by an official or overseer, and refused to obey their order to resume work. . . .

6. No worker may leave his place of work otherwise than for reasons connected with his work.

7. All conversation with fellow-workers is prohibited; if any worker requires information about his work, he must turn to the overseer, or to the particular fellow-worker designated for the purpose.

8. Smoking in the workshops or in the yard is prohibited during working hours; anyone caught smoking shall be fined five silver groschen for the sick fund for every such offence. . . .

10. Natural functions must be performed at the appropriate places, and whoever is found soiling walls, fences, squares, etc., and similarly, whoever is found washing his face and hands in the workshop and not in the places assigned for the purpose, shall be fined five silver groschen for the sick fund. . . .

12. It goes without saying that all overseers and officials of the firm shall be obeyed without question, and shall be treated with due deference. Disobedience will be punished by dismissal.

13. Immediate dismissal shall also be the fate of anyone found drunk in any of the workshops. . . .

14. Every workman is obliged to report to his superiors any acts of dishonesty or embezzlement on the part of his fellow workmen. If he omits to do so, and it is shown after subsequent discovery of a misdemeanour that he knew about it at the time, he shall be liable to be taken to court as an accessory after the fact and the wage due to him shall be retained as punishment.

machines of the men as cannot err." Such work, of course, tended to be repetitive and boring, and factory owners resorted to tough methods to accomplish their goals. Factory regulations were minute and detailed (see the previous box). Adult workers were fined for a wide variety of minor infractions, such as being a few minutes late for work, and dismissed for more serious misdoings, especially drunkenness. The latter was viewed as particularly offensive because it set a bad example for younger workers and also courted disaster in the midst of dangerous machinery. Employers found that dismissals and fines worked well for adult employees; in a time when great population growth had produced large numbers of unskilled workers, dismissal meant disaster. Children were less likely to understand the implications of dismissal so they were sometimes disciplined more directly—by beating.

The efforts of factory owners in the early Industrial Revolution to impose a new set of values were frequently reinforced by the new evangelical churches. Methodism, in particular, emphasized that people reborn in Christ must forgo immoderation and follow a disciplined path. Laziness and wasteful habits were sinful. The acceptance of hardship in this life paved the way for the joys of the next. Evangelical values paralleled the efforts of the new factory owners to instill their own middle-class values of hard work, discipline, and thrift upon laborers. In one crucial sense, the early industrialists proved successful. As the nineteenth century progressed, the second and third generations of workers came to view a regular working week as a natural way of life. It was, of course, an attitude that made possible Britain's incredible economic growth in that century.

The Great Exhibition: Britain in 1851

In 1851, the British organized the world's first industrial fair. It was housed at Kensington in London in the Crystal Palace, an enormous structure made entirely of glass and iron, a tribute to British engineering skills. Covering nineteen acres, the Crystal Palace contained 100,000 exhibits that showed the wide variety of products created by the Industrial Revolution. Six million people visited the fair in six months. While most of them were Britons, who had traveled to London by train, foreign visitors were also prominent. The Great Exhibition displayed Britain's wealth to the world; it was a gigantic symbol of British success. Even trees were brought inside the Crystal Palace as a visible symbol of how the Industrial Revolution had achieved human domination over nature. Prince Albert, Queen Victoria's husband, expressed the sentiments of the age when he described the exhibition as a sign that "man is approaching a more complete fulfillment of that great and sacred mission which he has to perform in this world . . . to conquer nature to his use." Not content with that, however, he also connected British success to divine will: "In promoting [the progress of the human race], we are accomplishing the will of the great and blessed God."[4]

By the year of the Great Exhibition, Great Britain had become the world's first and richest industrial nation. Britain was the "workshop, banker, and trader of the world." It produced one-half of the world's coal and manufactured goods; its cotton industry alone in 1851 was equal in size to the industries of all other European countries combined. The quantity of goods produced was growing at three times the rate it had achieved in 1780. No doubt, Britain's certainty about its mission in the world in the nineteenth century was grounded in its incredible material success story.

 ## The Spread of Industrialization

Beginning first in Great Britain, industrialization spread to the continental countries of Europe and the United States at different times and speeds during the nineteenth century. First to be industrialized on the Continent were Belgium, France, and the German states and in North America, the new nation of the United States. Not until after 1850 did the Industrial Revolution spread to the rest of Europe and other parts of the world.

Limitations to Industrialization

In 1815, Belgium, France, and the German states were still largely agrarian. During the eighteenth century, some of the continental countries had experienced developments similar to those of Britain. They, too, had achieved population growth, made agricultural improvements, expanded their cottage industries, and witnessed growth in foreign trade. But while Britain's economy began to move in new industrial directions in the 1770s and 1780s, continental countries lagged behind because they did not share some of the advantages that had made Britain's Industrial Revolution possible. Lack of good roads and problems with river transit made transportation difficult. Toll stations on important rivers and customs barriers along state boundaries increased the costs and prices of goods. Guild restrictions were also more prevalent, creating restrictions that pioneer industrialists in Britain did not have to face. Finally, continental entrepreneurs who tended to adhere to traditional patterns of business life, such as a dislike of competition, a high regard for family security coupled with an unwillingness to take risks in investment, and an excessive worship of thriftiness, were generally less enterprising than their British counterparts.

One additional factor also affected most of the Continent between 1790 and 1812: the upheavals associated with the wars of the French revolutionary and Napoleonic eras. Disruption of regular communications between Britain and the Continent made it difficult for continental countries to keep up with the new British technology. Moreover, the wars wreaked havoc with trade, caused much physical destruction and loss of manpower, weakened currencies, and led to political and social instability. Napoleon's Continental System helped to ruin a number of hitherto prosperous ports. The elimination of European markets for British textiles did temporarily revive the woolen industry in France and Belgium and stimulated textile manufacturing along the Rhine and in Silesia. After 1815, however, when cheap British goods again flooded European markets, the European textile industry suffered.

In the long run, the revolutionary and Napoleonic wars created an additional obstacle to rapid industrialization by widening the gap between British and continental industrial machinery. By 1815, after Napoleon had finally been defeated and normal communication between Britain and the Continent had been restored, British industrial equipment had grown larger and become more expensive. As a result, self-financed family enterprises were either unable or unwilling to raise the amount of capital necessary to modernize by investing in the latest equipment. Instead, most entrepreneurs in France, Belgium, and Germany initially chose to invest in used machines and less productive mills. Consequently, industrialization on the Continent faced numerous hurdles, and as it proceeded in earnest after 1815, it did so along lines that were somewhat different from Britain's.

Lack of technical knowledge was initially a major obstacle to industrialization. But the continental countries possessed an advantage here; they could simply borrow British techniques and practices. Of course, the British tried to prevent that. Until 1825, British artisans were prohibited from leaving the country; until 1842, the export of important machinery and machine parts, especially for textile production, was forbidden. Nevertheless, the British were not able to control this situation by legislation. Already by 1825, there were at least 2,000 skilled British mechanics on the Continent, and British equipment, whether legally or illegally, was also being sold abroad.

Although many Britons who went abroad to sell their skills were simply skilled mechanics, a number of them were accomplished entrepreneurs who had managerial as well as technical skills. John Cockerill, for example, was an aggressive businessman who established a highly profitable industrial plant at Seraing near Liège in southern Belgium in 1817. Encouraged by the Belgian government, Cockerill thought nothing of pirating the innovations of other British industrialists to further his own factories. Aware of their importance, British technicians abroad were often contentious and arrogant, arousing the anger of continental industrialists. Fritz Harkort, who initiated the engineering industry in Germany, once exclaimed that he could scarcely wait for Germans to be trained "so that the Englishmen could all be whipped out: we

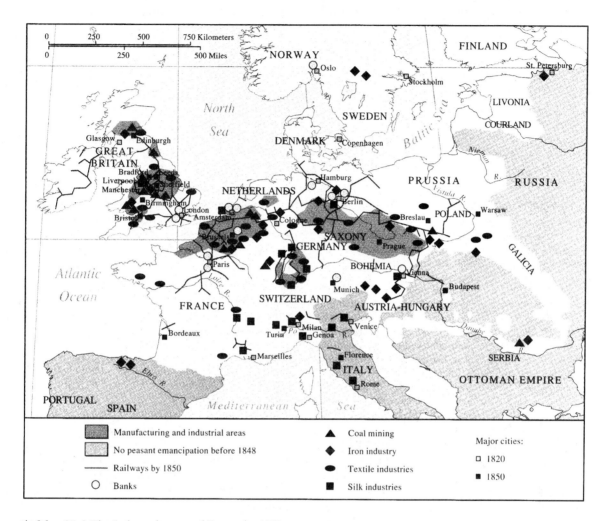

Map 21.2 The Industrialization of Europe by 1850.

must even now tread softly with them, for they're only too quick to speak of quitting if one does so little as not look at them in a friendly fashion."[5]

Gradually, the Continent achieved technological independence as local people learned all the skills their British teachers had to offer. By the 1840s, a new generation of skilled mechanics from Belgium and France was spreading their knowledge east and south, playing the same role that the British had earlier. More importantly, however, continental countries, especially France

and the German states, began to establish a wide range of technical schools to train engineers and mechanics.

That government played an important role in this regard brings us to a second difference between British and continental industrialization. Governments in most of the continental countries were accustomed to playing a significant role in economic affairs. Furthering the development of industrialization was a logical extension of that attitude. Hence, governments provided for the costs of technical education; awarded grants to inventors and foreign entrepreneurs; exempted foreign industrial equipment from import duties; and, in some places, even financed factories. Of equal, if not greater importance in the long run, governments actively bore much of the cost of building roads and canals, deepening and widening river channels, and constructing railroads. By 1850, a network of iron rails had spread across Europe, although only Germany and Belgium had completed major parts of their systems by that time. Although European markets did not feel the real impact of the railroad until after 1850, railroad construction itself in the 1830s and 1840s gave great impetus to the metalworking and engineering industries.

Governments on the Continent also used tariffs to further industrialization. After 1815, cheap British goods flooded continental markets. The French responded with high tariffs to protect their fledgling industries. The most systematic exposition for the use of tariffs, however, was made by a German writer, Friedrich List (1789–1846), who emigrated to America and returned to Germany as a United States consul. In his *National System of Political Economy*, written in 1844, List advocated a rapid and large-scale program of industrialization as the surest path to develop a nation's strength. To assure that path to industrialization, he felt that a nation must use protective tariffs. If countries followed the British policy of free trade, then cheaper British goods would inundate national markets and destroy infant industries before they had a chance to grow. Germany, he insisted, could not compete with Britain without protective tariffs.

A third significant difference between British and continental industrialization was the role of the joint-stock investment bank on the Continent. Such banks mobilized the savings of thousands of small and large investors, creating a supply of capital that could then be ploughed back into industry. Previously, continental banks had been mostly merchant or private banks, but in the 1830s two Belgian banks, the Société Générale and the Banque de Belgique, took a new approach. By accepting savings from many depositors, they developed large capital resources that they invested on a large scale in railroads,

mining, and heavy industry. These investments were especially important to the Belgian coal industry, which became the largest on the Continent in the 1840s. Shareholders in these joint-stock corporations had limited liability; they could only be held responsible for the amount of their investment.

Similar institutions emerged in France and German-speaking lands as well in the 1850s with the establishment of the Crédit Mobilier in France, the Darmstadt Bank in Germany, and the Kreditanstalt in Austria. They, too, took in savings of small investors and bought shares in the new industries. The French consul in Leipzig noted their significance: "every town and state [in Germany]," he pointed out, "however small it may be, wants its bank and its Crédit Mobilier." These investments proved invaluable to continental industrialization. By starting with less expensive machines, the British had been able to industrialize largely through the private capital of successful individuals who reinvested their profits. On the Continent advanced industrial machines necessitated large amounts of capital; joint-stock industrial banks provided it.

Centers of Continental Industrialization

The Industrial Revolution on the Continent occurred in three major centers between 1815 and 1850—Belgium, France, and the German states. Here, too, cotton played an important role, although it was not as significant as heavy industry. France was the continental leader in the manufacture of cotton goods but still lagged far behind Great Britain. In 1849, France used 64,000 tons of raw cotton, Belgium, 11,000, and Germany, 20,000, while Britain utilized 286,000 tons. Continental cotton factories were older, used less efficient machines, and had less productive labor. In general, continental technology in the cotton industry was a generation behind Great Britain. But that is not the whole story. With its cheap coal and scarce water, Belgium gravitated toward the use of the steam engine as the major source of power and invested in the new machines. By the mid-1840s, Belgium had the most modern cotton-manufacturing system on the Continent.

The development of cotton manufacturing on the Continent and in Britain differed in two significant ways. Unlike Britain, where cotton manufacturing was mostly centered in Lancashire (in northwestern England) and the Glasgow area, cotton mills in France, Germany, and to a lesser degree, Belgium, were dispersed through many regions. Noticeable, too, was the mixture of old and new. The old techniques of the cottage system, such as the use of hand looms, held on much longer. In the French district of Normandy, for example, in 1849 eighty-three mills were still driven by hand or animal power.

As traditional methods persisted alongside the new methods in cotton manufacturing, the new steam engine came to be used primarily in mining and metallurgy on the Continent rather than in textile manufacturing. At first, almost all of the steam engines on the Continent came from Britain; not until the 1820s was a domestic machine industry developed.

In Britain, the Industrial Revolution had been built upon the cotton industry; on the Continent, the iron and coal of heavy industry led the way. As in textiles, however, heavy industry on the Continent before 1850 was a mixture of old and new. The adoption of new techniques, such as coke-smelted iron and puddling furnaces, coincided with the expansion of old-type charcoal blast furnaces. Before 1850, Germany lagged significantly behind both Belgium and France in heavy industry, and most German iron manufacturing remained based on old techniques. Not until the 1840s was coke-blast iron produced in the Rhineland. At that time, no one had yet realized the treasure of coal buried in the Ruhr valley. A German official wrote in 1852, "It is clearly not to be expected that Germany will ever be able to reach the level of production of coal and iron currently attained in England. This is implicit in our far more limited resource endowment." Little did he realize that although the industrial development of continental Europe was about a generation behind Britain at mid-century, after 1850 an incredibly rapid growth in continental industry would demonstrate that Britain was not, after all, destined to remain the world's greatest industrial nation.

The Industrial Revolution in the United States

In 1800, the United States was an agrarian society. There were no cities over 100,000, and six out of every seven American workers were farmers. By 1860, however, the population had grown from 5 to 30 million people, larger than Great Britain. Almost half of them lived west of the Appalachian Mountains. The number of states had more than doubled, from sixteen to thirty-four, and nine American cities had over 100,000 in population. Only 50 percent of American workers were farmers. From 1800 to the eve of the Civil War, the United States had experienced an industrial revolution and the urbanization that accompanied it.

The initial application of machinery to production was accomplished—as in continental Europe—by borrowing from Great Britain. A British immigrant, Samuel Slater, established the first textile factory using water-powered spinning machines in Rhode Island in 1790. By 1813, factories with power looms copied from British versions were being established. Soon thereafter, however, Americans began to equal or surpass British technical inventions. The Harpers Ferry arsenal, for example, built muskets with interchangeable parts. Because all the individual parts of a musket were identical (e.g., all triggers were the same), the final product could be put together quickly and easily; this enabled Americans to avoid the more costly system in which skilled craftsmen fitted together individual parts made separately. The so-called American system reduced costs and revolutionized production by saving labor, important to a society that had few skilled artisans.

Unlike Britain, the United States was a large country. The lack of a good system of internal transportation seemed to limit American economic development by making the transport of goods prohibitively expensive. This was gradually remedied, however. Thousands of miles of roads and canals were built linking east and west. The steamboat facilitated transportation on the Great Lakes, Atlantic coastal waters, and rivers. It was especially important to the Mississippi valley; by 1860, a thousand steamboats plied that river (see

⇉ "S–t–e–a–m–boat a–coming'!" ⇇

Steamboats and railroads were crucial elements in a transportation revolution that enabled industrialists to expand markets by shipping goods cheaply and efficiently. At the same time, these marvels of technology aroused a sense of power and excitement that was an important aspect of the triumph of industrialization. The American novelist Mark Twain captured this sense of excitement in this selection from Life on the Mississippi.

Mark Twain, *Life on the Mississippi*

After all these years I can picture that old time to myself now, just as it was then: the white town drowsing in the sunshine of a summer's morning; the streets empty, or pretty nearly so; one or two clerks sitting in front of the Water street stores, with their splint-bottomed chairs tilted back against the walls, chins on breasts, hats slouched over their faces, asleep; . . . two or three lonely little freight piles scattered about the "levee"; a pile of "skids" on the slope of the stone-paved wharf, and the fragrant town drunkard asleep in the shadow of them; . . . the great Mississippi, the majestic, the magnificent Mississippi, rolling its mile-wide along, shining in the sun; the dense forest away on the other side; the "point" above the town, and the "point" below, bounding the river-glimpse and turning it into a sort of sea, and withal a very still and brilliant and lonely one. Presently a film of dark smoke appears above on those remote "points"; instantly a negro drayman, famous for his quick eye and prodigious voice, lifts up to cry, "S–t–e–a–m–boat a–coming'!" and the scene changes! The town drunkard stirs, the clerks wake up, a furious clatter of drays follows, every house and store pours out a human contribution, and all in a twinkling the dead town [Hannibal, Missouri] is alive and moving. Drays, carts, men, boys, all go hurrying from many quarters to a common center, the wharf. Assembled there, the people fasten their eyes upon the coming boat as upon a wonder they are seeing for the first time. And the boat is rather a handsome sight, too. She is long and sharp and trim and pretty; she has two tall, fancy-topped chimneys, with a gilded device of some kind swung between them; a fanciful pilot-house, all glass and "gin-ger bread," perched on top of the "texas" deck behind them; the paddle-boxes are gorgeous with a picture or with gilded rays above the boat's name; the boiler deck, the hurricane deck, and the texas deck are fenced and ornamented with clean white railings; there is a flag gallantly flying from the jack-staff; the furnace doors are open and the fires glaring bravely; the upper decks are black with passengers; the captain stands by the big bell, calm, imposing, the envy of all; great volumes of the blackest smoke are rolling and tumbling out of the chimneys—a husbanded grandeur created with a bit of pitch pine just before arriving at a town; the crew are grouped on the forecastle; the broad stage is run far out over the port bow, and an envied deck-hand stands picturesquely on the end of it with a coil of rope in his hand; the pent steam is screaming through the gauge-cocks; the captain lifts his hand, a bell rings, the wheels stop; then they turn back, churning the water to foam, and the steam is at rest. Then such a scramble as there is to get aboard, and to get ashore, and to take in freight and to discharge freight, all at one and the same time; and such a yelling and cursing as the mates facilitate it all with! Ten minutes later the steamer is under way again, with no flag on the jack-staff and no black smoke issuing from the chimneys. After ten more minutes the town is dead again, and the town drunkard asleep by the skids once more.

related box). Most important of all in the development of an American transportation system was the railroad. Beginning with 100 miles in 1830, by 1860 there were over 27,000 miles of railroad track covering the United States. This transportation revolution turned the United States into a single massive market for the manufactured goods of the Northeast, the early center of American industrialization.

Labor for the growing number of factories in this area came primarily from rural New England. The United States did not possess a large number of craftsmen, but it did have a rapidly expanding farm population; its size in the Northeast soon outstripped the available farmland. While some of this excess population, especially men, went west, others, mostly women, found work in the new textile and shoe factories of New England. Indeed, women made up more than 80 percent of the laboring force in the large textile factories. In Massachusetts mill towns, company boarding houses provided rooms for large numbers of young women who worked for several years before marriage. Outside Massachusetts, factory owners sought entire families including children to work in their mills; one mill owner ran this advertisement in a newspaper in Utica, New York: "Wanted: A few sober and industrious families of at least five children each, over the age of eight years, are wanted at the Cotton Factory in Whitestown. Widows with large families would do well to attend this notice." When a decline in rural births threatened to dry up this labor pool in the 1830s and 1840s, European immigrants, especially poor and unskilled Irish, English, Scottish, and Welsh, appeared in large numbers to replace American women and children in the factories.

Women, children, and these immigrants had one thing in common as employees; they were largely unskilled laborers. Unskilled labor pushed American industrialization into a capital-intensive pattern. Factory owners invested heavily in machines that could produce in quantity at the hands of untrained workers. In Britain, the pace of mechanization was never as rapid because Britain's supply of skilled craftsmen made it more profitable to pursue a labor-intensive economy.

By 1860, the United States was well on its way to being an industrial nation. In the Northeast, the most industrialized section of the country, per capita income was 40 percent higher than the national average. Diets, it has been argued, were better and more varied; machine-made clothing was more abundant. Industrialization did not necessarily lessen economic disparities, however. Despite a growing belief in a myth of social mobility based upon equality of economic opportunity, the reality was that the richest 10 percent of the population in the cities held 70 to 80 percent of the wealth compared to 50 percent in 1800. Nevertheless, American historians generally argue that while the rich got richer, the poor, as a result of experiencing an increase in their purchasing power, did not get poorer.

 ## The Social Impact of the Industrial Revolution

Eventually, the Industrial Revolution revolutionized the social life of Europe and the world. Although much of Europe remained bound by its traditional ways, already in the first half of the nineteenth century, the social impact of the Industrial Revolution was being felt and future avenues of growth were becoming apparent. Vast changes in the number of people and where they lived were already dramatically evident.

Population Growth

Population increases had already begun in the eighteenth century, but they became dramatic in the nineteenth century. They were also easier to discern because record keeping became more accurate. Governments in the nineteenth century began to take periodic censuses and systematically collect precise data on births, deaths, and marriages. In Britain, for example, the first census was taken in 1801, and a systematic registration of births, deaths, and marriages was begun in 1836. In 1750, the total European population stood at an estimated 140 million; by 1800, it had increased to 187 million and by 1850 to 266 million, almost twice its 1750 level.

This population explosion cannot be explained by a higher birthrate for birthrates were declining after 1790. Between 1790 and 1850, Germany's birthrate dropped from 40 per thousand to 36.1; Great Britain's from 35.4 to 32.6, and France's from 32.5 to 26.7. The key to the expansion of population was the decline in death rates evident throughout Europe. Historians now believe that two major causes explain this decline. There was a drop in the number of deaths from famines, epidemics, and war. Major epidemic diseases, in particular, such as plague and smallpox declined noticeably, although small-scale epidemics continued. The ordinary death rate also declined as a general increase in the food supply, already evident in the agricultural revolution of Britain in the late eighteenth century, spread to more areas. More food enabled a greater number of people to be better fed and therefore more resistant to disease. Famine largely disappeared from western Europe, although there were dramatic exceptions in isolated areas, Ireland being the most significant.

In those areas where industrialization proceeded in the nineteenth century, the composition of the population also changed. By 1850, the proportion of the active population involved in manufacturing, mining, or building had risen to 48 percent in Britain, 37 percent in Belgium, and 27 percent in France. But the actual areas of industrialization in 1850 were minimal, being concentrated in northern and central England, northern France, Belgium, and sections of western and eastern Germany. As one author has commented, "they were islands in an agricultural sea."

This minimal industrialization, in light of the growing population, meant severe congestion in the countryside where a growing population divided the same amount of land into ever-smaller plots and also created an ever-larger mass of landless peasants. Overpopulation, especially noticeable in parts of France, northern Spain, southern Germany, Sweden, and Ireland, magnified the already existing problem of rural poverty. In Ireland, it produced the century's greatest catastrophe.

Ireland was one of the most backward and oppressed areas in western Europe. The predominantly Catholic peasant population rented land from mostly absentee British Protestant landlords whose primary concern was collecting their rents. Irish peasants lived in mud hovels in desperate poverty. The cultivation of the potato, a nutritious and relatively easy food to grow that produced three times as much food per acre as grain, gave Irish peasants a basic staple that enabled them to survive and even expand in numbers. As only an acre or two of potatoes was sufficient to feed a family, Irish men and women married earlier than elsewhere and started having children earlier as well. This led to significant growth in the population. Between 1781 and 1845, the Irish population doubled from 4 to 8 million. Probably half of this population depended on the potato for survival. In the summer of 1845, the potato crop in Ireland was struck by blight due to a fungus that turned the potatoes black. Between 1845 and 1851, the Great Famine decimated the Irish population (see the accompanying box). Over 1 million died of starvation and disease while almost 2 million emigrated to the United States and Britain. Of all the European nations, only Ireland had a declining population in the nineteenth century. But other countries, too, faced problems of dire poverty and declining standards of living as their populations exploded. Some historians, in fact, have argued that without industrialization and the improvements it brought in the standard of living, other countries might have faced "Irish disasters."

The flight of so many Irish to America reminds us that the traditional safety valve for overpopulation has always been emigration. Between 1821 and 1850, the number of emigrants from Europe averaged about 110,000 a year. Most of these emigrants came from places like Ireland and southern Germany, where peasant life had been reduced to marginal existence. Times of agrarian crisis resulted in great waves of emigration. Bad harvests in Europe in 1846–1847 (such as the catastrophe in Ireland) produced massive numbers of emigrants. In addition to the estimated 1,600,000 from Ireland, for example, 935,000 people left Germany between 1847 and 1854. More often than emigration, however, the rural masses sought a solution to their poverty by moving to towns and cities within their own

⮞ *The Great Irish Famine* ⮜

The Great Irish Famine was one of the nineteenth century's worst natural catastrophes. Overly dependent on a single crop, the Irish were decimated by the potato blight. In this selection, an Irish nationalist reported what he had witnessed in Galway in 1847.

John Mitchel, *The Last Conquest of Ireland*
In the depth of winter we travelled to Galway, through the very centre of that fertile island, and saw sights that will never wholly leave the eyes that beheld them—cowering wretches, almost naked in the savage weather, prowling in turnip-fields, and endeavouring to grub up roots which had been left, but running to hide as the mail-coach rolled by;—very large fields where small farms had been "consolidated," showing dark bars of fresh mould running through them where the ditches had been levelled;—groups and families, sitting or wandering on the high-road, with failing steps and dim patient eyes, gazing hopelessly into infinite darkness; before them, around them, above them, nothing but darkness and despair;—parties of tall brawny men, once the flower of Meath and Galway, stalking by with a fierce but vacant scowl; as if they knew that all this ought not to be, but knew not whom to blame, saw none whom they could rend in their wrath; . . . . Around those farmhouses which were still inhabited were to be seen hardly any stacks of grain; the poor-rate collector, the rent agent, the county-cess collector had carried it off; and sometimes I could see in front of the cottages little children leaning against a fence when the sun shone out—for they could not stand—their limbs fleshless, their bodies half naked, their faces bloated yet wrinkled, and of a pale greenish hue,—children who would never, it was too plain, grow up to be men and women.

countries to find work. It should not astonish us then that the first half of the nineteenth century was a period of rapid urbanization.

Urbanization

Although the Western world would not become a predominantly urban society until the twentieth century, cities and towns had already grown dramatically in the first half of the nineteenth century, a phenomenon related to industrialization. Cities had traditionally been centers for princely courts, government and military offices, churches, and commerce. By 1850, especially in Great Britain and Belgium, they were rapidly becoming places for manufacturing and industry. With the steam engine, entrepreneurs could locate their manufacturing plants in urban centers where they had ready access to transportation facilities and unemployed people from the country looking for work.

In 1800, Great Britain had one major city, London, with a population of 1 million, and six cities between 50,000 and 100,000. Fifty years later, London's population had swelled to 2,363,000 while there were nine cities over 100,000 and eighteen cities with populations between 50,000 and 100,000. All together, these twenty-eight cities accounted for 5.7 million or one-fifth of the total British population. When the populations of cities under 50,000 are added to this total, we realize that over 50 percent of the British population lived in towns and cities by 1850. Britain was forced to become a food importer rather than exporter as the number of people involved in agriculture declined to 20 percent of the population.

Urban populations also grew on the Continent, but less dramatically. Paris had 547,000 inhabitants in 1800, but only two other French cities had populations of 100,000: Lyons and Marseilles. In 1851, Paris had grown to 1 million while Lyons and Marseilles were still under 200,000. German and Austrian lands had only three cities with over 100,000 inhabitants (Vienna had 247,000) in 1800; fifty years later, there were only five while Vienna had grown to 440,000. As these figures show, urbanization did not proceed as rapidly here as in Britain; of course, neither had industrialization. Even in Belgium, the most heavily industrialized country on the Continent, almost 50 percent of the male work force was still engaged in agriculture by mid-century.

URBAN LIVING CONDITIONS IN THE EARLY INDUSTRIAL REVOLUTION   The dramatic growth of cities in the first half of the nineteenth century produced miserable living conditions for many of the inhabitants. Of course, this had been true for centuries in European cities, but the rapid urbanization associated with the Industrial Revolution intensified the problems in the first half of the nineteenth century and made these wretched conditions all the more apparent. City authorities of whatever kind either felt little responsibility for these conditions or more frequently did not have the skills to cope with the complex, new problems associated with such rapidly growing populations. City authorities might also often be factory owners who possessed little or no tradition of public service or public responsibility.

Wealthy, middle-class inhabitants, as usual, insulated themselves as best they could, often living in suburbs or the outer ring of the city where they could have individual houses and gardens. In the inner ring of the city stood the small row houses, some with gardens, of the artisans and lower middle class. Finally, located in the center of most industrial towns were the row houses of the industrial workers. This report on working-class housing in the British city of Birmingham in 1843 gives an idea of the general conditions they faced:

> The courts [of working-class row houses] are extremely numerous; . . . a very large portion of the poorer classes of the inhabitants reside in them. . . . The courts vary in the number of the houses which they contain, from four to twenty, and most of these houses are three stories high, and built, as it is termed, back to back. There is a

wash-house, an ash-pit, and a privy at the end, or on one side of the court, and not unfrequently one or more pigsties and heaps of manure. Generally speaking, the privies in the old courts are in a most filthy condition. Many which we have inspected were in a state which renders it impossible for us to conceive how they could be used; they were without doors and overflowing with filth.

The people who lived in such houses were actually the fortunate; the truly unfortunate were those forced to live in cellars. As one reformer asked, "how can a hole underground of from 12 to 15 feet square admit of ventilation so as to fit it for a human habitation?" Rooms were not large and were frequently overcrowded, as this government report of 1838 revealed: "I entered several of the tenements. In one of them, on the ground floor, I found six persons occupying a very small room, two in bed, ill with fever. In the room above this were two more persons in one bed ill with fever." Another report said: "There were 63 families where there were at least five persons to one bed; and there were some in which even six were packed in one bed, lying at the top and bottom—children and adults."[6]

Sanitary conditions in these towns were appalling. Due to the lack of municipal direction, sewers and open drains were common on city streets: "In the centre of this street is a gutter, into which potato parings, the refuse of animal and vegetable matters of all kinds, the dirty water from the washing of clothes and of the houses, are all poured, and there they stagnate and putrefy."[7] Unable to deal with human excrement, cities in the new industrial era smelled horrible and were extraordinarily unhealthy. Towns and cities were fundamentally death traps. As deaths outnumbered births in most large cities in the first half of the nineteenth century, only a constant influx of people from the country kept them alive and growing.

Adding to the deterioration of urban life was the adulteration of food. Consumers were defrauded in a variety of ways: alum was added to make bread look white and hence more expensive; beer and milk were watered down; and red lead despite its poisonous qualities was substituted for pepper. The government refused to intervene; a parliamentary committee stated that "more benefit is likely to result from the effects of a free competition . . . than can be expected to result from any regulations." It was not until 1875 that an effective Food and Drugs Act was passed in Britain.

Our knowledge of the pathetic conditions in the early industrial cities is largely derived from an abundance of social investigations. Such investigations began in France in the 1820s. In Britain the Poor Law Commissioners produced detailed reports. The investigators were often struck by the physically and morally debilitating effects of urban industrial life on the poor. They observed, for example, that young working-class men were considerably shorter and scrawnier than the sons of middle-class families and much more subject to disease. They were especially alarmed by what they considered the moral consequences of such living conditions: prostitution, crime, and sexual immoralities, all of which they saw as the effect of such squalid lives.

To many of the well-to-do middle classes, this situation presented a clear danger to society. Were not these masses of workers, sunk in crime, disease, and immorality, a potential threat to their own well-being? Might not the masses be organized and used by unscrupulous demagogues to overthrow the established order? One of the most eloquent British reformers of the 1830s and 1840s, James Kay-Shuttleworth, described them as "volcanic elements, by whose explosive violence the structure of society may be destroyed." Another observer spoke more contemptuously in 1850:

> They live precisely like brutes, to gratify . . . the appetites of their uncultivated bodies, and then die, to go they have never thought, cared, or wondered whither. . . . Brought up in the darkness of barbarism, they have no idea that it is possible for them to attain any higher condition; they are not even sentient enough to desire to change their situation. . . . they eat, drink, breed, work and die; and . . . the richer and more intelligent classes are obliged to guard them with police.[8]

Some observers were less arrogant, however, and wondered if the workers could be held responsible for their fate.

One of the best of a new breed of urban reformers was Edwin Chadwick (1800–1890). With a background in law, Chadwick became obsessed with eliminating the poverty and squalor of the metropolitan areas. He became a civil servant and was soon appointed to a number of government investigatory commissions. As secretary of the Poor Law Commission, he initiated a passionate search for detailed facts about the living conditions of the working classes. After three years of investigation, Chadwick summarized the results in his *Report on the Condition of the Labouring Population of Great Britain*, published in 1842. In it he concluded that "the various forms of epidemic, endemic, and other disease" were directly caused by the "atmospheric impurities produced by decomposing animal and vegetable substances, by damp and filth, and close overcrowded dwellings [prevailing] amongst the population in every part of the kingdom." Such conditions, he argued, could be eliminated. As to the means: "The primary and most important measures, and at the same time the most practicable, and within the recognized province of public administration, are drainage, the removal of all refuse of habitations, streets, and roads, and the improvement of the supplies of water."[9] In other words, Chadwick was advocating a system of modern sanitary reforms consisting of efficient sewers and a supply of piped water. Six years after his report and largely due to his efforts, Britain's first Public Health Act created a National Board of Health empowered to form local boards that would establish modern sanitary systems.

New Social Classes: The Industrial Middle Class

The rise of industrial capitalism produced a new middle-class group. The bourgeois or middle class was not new; it had existed since the emergence of cities in the Middle Ages. Originally, the bourgeois was the burgher or town dweller, whether active as a merchant, official, artisan, lawyer, or man of letters, who enjoyed a special set of rights from the charter of his town. As wealthy townspeople bought land, the original meaning of the word *bourgeois* became lost, and the term came to include people involved in commerce, industry, and banking as well as professionals, such as lawyers, teachers, physicians, and government officials at varying levels. At the lower end of the economic scale were master craftsmen and shopkeepers.

Lest we make the industrial middle class too much of an abstraction, we need to look at who the new industrial entrepreneurs actually were. These were the people who constructed the factories, purchased the machines, and figured out where the markets were. Their qualities included resourcefulness, single-mindedness, resolution, initiative, vision, ambition, and often, of course, greed. As Jedediah Strutt, the cotton manufacturer said, "Getting of money . . . is the main business of the life of men."

But this was not an easy task. The early industrial entrepreneurs were called upon to superintend an enormous array of functions that are handled today by teams of managers; they raised capital, determined markets, set company objectives, organized the factory and its labor, and trained supervisors who could act for them. The opportunities for making money were great, but the risks were also tremendous. The cotton trade, for example, which was so important to the early Industrial Revolution, was intensely competitive. Only through constant expansion could one feel secure, so early entrepreneurs reinvested most of their initial profits. Fear of bankruptcy was constant, especially among small firms. Furthermore, most early industrial enterprises were small. Even by the 1840s, only 10 percent of British industrial firms employed more than 5,000 workers; 43 percent had fewer than 100 workers. As entrepreneurs went bankrupt, new people could enter the race for profits, especially since the initial outlay was not gigantic. In 1816, only one mill in five in the important industrial city of Manchester was in the hands of its original owners.

The social origins of industrial entrepreneurs were incredibly diverse. Many of the most successful came from a mercantile background. Three London merchants, for example, founded a successful ironworks in Wales that owned eight steam engines and employed 5,000 men. In Britain, land and domestic industry were often inter-

dependent. Joshua Fielden, for example, acquired sufficient capital to establish a factory by running a family sheep farm while working looms in the farmhouse. Intelligent, clever, and ambitious apprentices who had learned their trades well could also strike it rich. William Radcliffe's family engaged in agriculture and spinning and weaving at home; he learned quickly how to succeed:

> Availing myself of the improvements that came out while I was in my teens . . . with my little savings and a practical knowledge of every process from the cotton bag to the piece of cloth . . . I was ready to commence business for myself and by the year 1789 I was well established and employed many hands both in spinning and weaving as a master manufacturer.[10]

By 1801, Radcliffe was operating a factory employing 1,000 workers.

Members of dissenting religious minorities were often prominent among the early industrial leaders of Britain. The Darbys and Lloyds who were iron manufacturers, the Barclays and Lloyds who were bankers, and the Trumans and Perkins who were brewers were all Quakers. These were expensive trades and depended upon the financial support that co-religionists in religious minorities provided for each other. Most historians believe that a major reason members of these religious minorities were so prominent in business was that they lacked other opportunities. Legally excluded from many public offices, they directed their ambitions into the new industrial capitalism.

It is interesting to note that in Britain in particular aristocrats also became entrepreneurs. The Lambtons in Northumberland, the Curwens in Cumberland, the Norfolks in Yorkshire, and the Dudleys in Staffordshire all invested in mining enterprises. This close relationship between land and industry helped Britain to assume the leadership role in the early Industrial Revolution.

By 1850, in Britain at least, the kind of traditional entrepreneurship that had created the Industrial Revolution was declining and being replaced by a new business aristocracy. This new generation of entrepreneurs stemmed from the professional and industrial middle classes, especially as sons inherited the successful businesses established by their fathers. It must not be forgotten, however, that even after 1850 a large number of small businesses existed in Britain and some were still founded by people from humble backgrounds. Indeed, the age of large-scale corporate capitalism did not begin until the 1890s.

Increasingly, the new industrial entrepreneurs—the bankers and owners of factories and mines—came to amass much wealth and play an important role alongside the traditional landed elites of their societies. The Industrial Revolution began at a time when the pre-industrial agrarian world was still largely dominated by landed elites. As the new bourgeoisie bought great estates and acquired social respectability, they also sought political power, and in the course of the nineteenth century, their wealthiest members would merge with those old elites.

New Social Classes: The Industrial Workers

At the same time the members of the industrial middle class were seeking to reduce the barriers between themselves and the landed elite, they also were trying to separate themselves from the laboring classes below them. The working class was actually a mixture of different groups in the first half of the nineteenth century. In the course of the nineteenth century, factory workers would form an industrial proletariat, but in the first half of that century, they by no means constituted a majority of the working class in any major city, even in Britain. According to the 1851 census in Britain, while there were 1.8 million agricultural laborers and 1 million domestic servants, there were only 811,000 workers in the cotton and woolen industries. Even one-third of these were still working in small workshops or in their own homes.

Within the cities, artisans or craftsmen remained the largest group of urban workers during the first half of the nineteenth century. They worked in numerous small industries, such as shoemaking, glovemaking, bookbinding, printing, and bricklaying. Some craftsmen formed a kind of aristocracy of labor, especially those employed in such luxury trades as coachbuilding and clockmaking who earned higher wages than others. Artisans were not factory workers; they were traditionally organized in guilds where they passed on their skills to apprentices. But guilds were increasingly losing their power, especially in industrialized countries. Fearful of losing out to the new factories that could produce goods more cheaply, artisans tended to support movements against industrialization. Industrialists welcomed the decline of skilled craftsmen, as one perceptive old tailor realized in telling his life story:

> It is upwards of 30 years since I first went to work at the tailoring trade in London. . . . I continued working for the honourable trade and belonging to the Society [for tailors] for about 15 years. My weekly earnings then averaged £1 16s. a week while I was at work, and for several years I was seldom out of work . . . no one could have been happier than I was. . . . But then, with my sight defective . . . I could get no employment at the honourable trade, and that was the ruin of me entirely; for working there, of course, I got "scratched" from the trade society, and so lost all hope of being provided for by them in my helplessness. The workshop . . . was about seven feet square, and so low, that as you [sat] on the floor you could touch the ceiling with the tip of your finger. In this place seven of us worked. [The master] paid little more than half the regular wages, and employed such men as myself—only those who couldn't get anything better to do. . . . I don't think my wages there averaged above 12s a week. . . . I am convinced I lost my eyesight by working in that cheap shop. . . . It is by the ruin of such men as me that these masters are enabled to undersell the better shops. . . . That's the way, sir, the cheap clothes is produced, by making blind beggars of the workmen, like myself, and throwing us on the parish in our old age.[11]

Servants also formed another large group of urban workers, especially in major cities like London and Paris. Many were women from the countryside who became utterly dependent upon their upper and middle-class employers.

WORKING CONDITIONS FOR THE INDUSTRIAL WORKING CLASS Industrial workers were not the largest working-class group in the first half of the nineteenth century, but they soon would be, and

⇒ *Child Labor: Discipline in the Textile Mills* ⇐

Child labor was certainly not new, but in the early Industrial Revolution it was exploited more systematically. These selections are taken from the Report of Sadler's Committee, which was commissioned in 1832 to inquire into the condition of child factory workers.

How They Kept the Children Awake

It is a very frequent thing at Mr. Marshall's [at Shrewsbury] where the least children were employed (for there were plenty working at six years of age), for Mr. Horseman to start the mill earlier in the morning than he formerly did; and provided a child should be drowsy, the overlooker walks round the room with a stick in his hand, and he touches that child on the shoulder, and says, "Come here." In a corner of the room there is an iron cistern; it is filled with water; he takes this boy, and takes him up by the legs, and dips him over head in the cistern, and sends him to work for the remainder of the day. . . .

What means were taken to keep the children to their work?—Sometimes they would tap them over the head, or nip them over the nose, or give them a pinch of snuff, or throw water in their faces, or pull them off where they were, and job them about to keep them waking.

The Sadistic Overlooker

Samuel Downe, age 29, factory worker living near Leeds; at the age of about ten began work at Mr. Marshall's mill at Shrewsbury, where the customary hours when work was brisk were generally 5 A.M. to 8 P.M., sometimes from 5:30 A.M. to 8 or 9:

What means were taken to keep the children awake and vigilant, especially at the termination of such a day's labour as you have described?—There was generally a blow or a box, or a tap with a strap, or sometimes the hand.

Have you yourself been strapped?—Yes, most severely, till I could not bear to sit upon a chair without having pillows, and through that I left. I was strapped both on my own legs, and then I was put upon a man's back, and then strapped and buckled with two straps to an iron pillar, and flogged, and all by one overlooker; after that he took a piece of tow, and twisted it in the shape of a cord, and put it in my mouth, and tied it behind my head.

He gagged you?—Yes; and then he ordered me to run round a part of the machinery where he was overlooker, and he stood at one end, and every time I came there he struck me with a stick, which I believe was an ash plant, and which he generally carried in his hand, and sometimes he hit me, and sometimes he did not; and one of the men in the room came and begged me off, and that he let me go, and not beat me any more, and consequently he did.

You have been beaten with extraordinary severity?—Yes, I was beaten so that I had not power to cry at all, or hardly speak at one time. What age were you at that time?—Between 10 and 11.

it is appropriate to look at the working conditions they faced. The pathetic living conditions of the industrial working classes were matched by equally wretched working conditions. We have already observed the psychological traumas workers experienced from their employers' efforts to break old pre-industrial work patterns and create a well-disciplined labor force. But what were the physical conditions of the factories?

Unquestionably, in the early decades of the Industrial Revolution, "places of work," as early factories were called, were dreadful. Work hours ranged from twelve to sixteen hours a day, six days a week, with a half hour for lunch and

≽ *Child Labor: The Mines* ≼

After examining conditions in British coal mines, a government official commented that "the hardest labour in the worst room in the worst-conducted factory is less hard, less cruel, and less demoralizing than the labour in the best of coal-mines." Yet it was not until 1842 that legislation was passed eliminating the labor of boys under ten from the mines. This selection is taken from a government report on the mines in Lancashire.

The Black Holes of Worsley

Examination of Thomas Gibson and George Bryan, witnesses from the coal mines at Worsley:

Have you worked from a boy in a coal mine?—(Both) Yes.

What had you to do then?—Thrutching the basket and drawing. It is done by little boys; one draws the basket and the other pushes it behind. Is that hard labour?—Yes, very hard labour.

For how many hours a day did you work?—Nearly nine hours regularly; sometimes twelve; I have worked about thirteen. We used to go in at six in the morning, and took a bit of bread and cheese in our pocket, and stopped two or three minutes; and some days nothing at all to eat.

How was it that sometimes you had nothing to eat?—We were over-burdened. I had only a mother, and she had nothing to give me. I was sometimes half starved. . . .

Do they work in the same way now exactly?—Yes, they do; they have nothing more than a bit of bread and cheese in their pocket, and sometimes can't eat it all, owing to the dust and damp and badness of air; and sometimes it is as hot as an oven; sometimes I have seen it so hot as to melt a candle.

What are the usual wages of a boy of eight?—They used to get 3d or 4d a day. Now a man's wages is divided into eight eighths; and when a boy is eight years old he gets one of those eighths; at eleven, two eighths; at thirteen, three eighths; at fifteen, four eighths; at twenty, man's wages.

What are the wages of a man?—About 15s if he is in full employment, but often not more than 10s, and out of that he has to get his tools and candles. He consumes about four candles in nine hours' work, in some places six; 6d per pound, and twenty-four candles to the pound.

Were you ever beaten as a child?—Yes, many a score of times; both kicks and thumps.

Are many girls employed in the pits?—Yes, a vast of those. They do the same kind of work as the boys till they get above 14 years of age, when they get the wages of half a man, and never get more, and continue at the same work for many years.

Did they ever fight together?—Yes, many days together. Both boys and girls; sometimes they are very loving with one another.

dinner. There was no security of employment and no minimum wage. The worst conditions were in the cotton mills where temperatures were especially debilitating. One report noted that "in the cotton-spinning work, these creatures are kept, fourteen hours in each day, locked up, summer and winter, in a heat of from eighty to eighty-four degrees." Mills were also dirty, dusty, and unhealthy:

Not only is there not a breath of sweet air in these truly infernal scenes, but . . . there is the abominable and pernicious stink of the gas to assist in the murderous effects of the heat. In addition to the noxious effluvia of the gas, mixed with the steam, there are the dust, and what is called cotton-flyings or fuz, which the unfortunate creatures have to inhale; and . . . the notorious fact is that well constituted men are rendered old and past labour at forty years of age, and that children are rendered decrepit and deformed, and thousands upon thousands of them slaughtered by consumptions, before they arrive at the age of sixteen.[12]

Thus ran a report on working conditions in the cotton industry in 1824.

Conditions in the coal mines were also harsh. The introduction of steam power meant only that steam-powered engines mechanically lifted coal to the top. Inside the mines, men still bore the burden of digging the coal out while horses, mules, women, and children hauled coal carts on rails to the lift. Dangers abounded in coal mines; cave-ins, explosions, and gas fumes (called "bad air") were a way of life. The cramped conditions—tunnels often did not exceed three or four feet in height—and constant dampness in the mines resulted in deformed bodies and ruined lungs.

Both children and women were employed in large numbers in early factories and mines. Children had been an important part of the family economy in pre-industrial times, working in the fields or carding and spinning wool at home with the growth of cottage industry. In the Industrial Revolution, however, child labor was exploited more than ever and in a considerably more systematic fashion (see the boxes on child labor). The owners of cotton factories appreciated certain features of child labor. Children had an especially delicate touch as spinners of cotton. Their smaller size made it easier for them to move under machines to gather loose cotton. Moreover, children were more easily broken to factory work. Above all, children represented a cheap supply of labor. In 1821, 49 percent of the British people were under twenty years of age. Hence, children made up a particularly abundant supply of labor, and they were paid only about one-sixth or one-third of what a man was paid. In the cotton factories in 1838, children under eighteen made up 29 percent of the total work force; children as young as seven worked twelve to fifteen hours per day six days a week in cotton mills.

Especially terrible in the early Industrial Revolution was the use of so-called pauper apprentices. These were orphans or children abandoned by their parents who had wound up in the care of local parishes. To save on their upkeep, parish officials found it convenient to apprentice them to factory owners looking for a cheap source of labor. These children worked long hours under strict discipline and received inadequate food and recreation; many became deformed from being kept too long in unusual positions. Although economic liberals and some industrialists were against all state intervention in economic matters, Parliament eventually remedied some of the worst ills of child abuse in factories and mines (see Efforts at Change: Reformers and Government later in this chapter). The legislation of the 1830s and 1840s, however, primarily affected child labor in textile factories and mines. It did not touch the use of children in small workshops or the nonfactory trades that were not protected. As these trades were in competition with the new factories, conditions there were often even worse. Pottery works, for example, were not investigated until the 1860s when it was found that 17 percent of the workers were under eleven years of age. One investigator reported what he found:

> The boys were kept in constant motion throughout the day, each carrying from thirty to fifty dozen of moulds into the stoves, and remaining . . . long enough to take the dried earthenware away. The distance thus run by a boy in the course of a day . . . was estimated at seven miles. From the very nature of this exhausting occupation children were rendered pale, weak and unhealthy. In the depth of winter, with the thermometer in the open air sometimes below zero, boys, with little clothing but rags, might be seen running to and fro on errands or to their dinners with the perspiration on their foreheads, "after labouring for hours like little slaves." The inevitable result of such transitions of temperature were consumption, asthma, and acute inflammation.[13]

Little wonder that child labor legislation enacted in 1864 included pottery works.

By 1830, women and children made up two-thirds of the cotton industry's labor. However, as the number of children employed declined under the Factory Act of 1833, their places were taken by women, who came to dominate the labor forces of the early factories. Women made up 50 percent of the labor force in textile (cotton and woolen) factories before 1870. They were mostly unskilled labor and were paid half or less of what men received. Excessive working hours for women were outlawed in 1844, but only in textile factories and mines; not until 1867 were they outlawed in craft workshops.

The employment of children and women in large part represents a continuation of a pre-industrial kinship pattern. Cottage industry had always involved the efforts of the entire family, and it seemed perfectly natural to continue this pattern. Men migrating from the countryside to industrial towns and cities took their wives and children with them into the factory or into the mines. Of 136 employees in Robert Peel's factory at Bury in 1801, 95 belonged to twenty-six families. The impetus for this family work often came from the family itself. The factory owner Jedediah Strutt was opposed to child labor under ten but was forced by parents to take children as young as seven.

The employment of large numbers of women in factories did not produce a significant transformation in female working patterns, as was once assumed. Studies of urban households in France and Britain, for example, have revealed that throughout the nineteenth century traditional types of female labor still predominated in the women's work world. In 1851, fully 40 percent of the female work force in Britain consisted of domestic servants. In France, the largest group of female workers, 40 percent, worked in agriculture. In addition, only 20 percent of female workers labored in Britain's factories, only 10 percent in France. Regional and local studies have also found that most of the workers were single women. Few married women worked outside their homes.

The Factory Acts that limited the work hours of children and women also began to break up the traditional kinship pattern of work and led to a new pattern based on a separation of work and home. Men came to be regarded as responsible for the primary work obligations while women assumed daily control of the family and performed low-paying jobs such as laundry work that could be done in the home. Domestic industry made it possible for women to continue their contributions to family survival.

Historians have also reminded us that if the treatment of children in the mines and factories seems particularly cruel and harsh, contemporary treatment of children in general was often brutal. Beatings, for example, had long been regarded, even by dedicated churchmen and churchwomen, as the best way to discipline children.

Standards of Living

One of the most heated debates on the Industrial Revolution concerns the standard of living. Most historians assume that in the long run the Industrial Revolution increased living standards dramatically in the form of higher per capita incomes and greater consumer choices. But did the first generation of industrial workers experience a decline in their living standards and suffer unnecessarily? Some historians have argued that early industrialization required huge profits to be reinvested in new and ever more expensive equipment; thus, to make the requisite profits, industrialists had to keep wages low. Others have questioned that argument, pointing out that initial investments in early machinery were not necessarily large nor did they need to be. What certainly did occur in the first half of the nineteenth century was a widening gap between rich and poor. One estimate, based on income tax returns in Britain, is that the wealthiest 1 percent of the population increased its share of the national product from 25 percent in 1801 to 35 percent in 1848.

Wages, prices, and consumption patterns are some of the criteria used for measuring the standard of living. Between 1780 and 1850, as far as we can determine from the available evidence, both wages and prices fluctuated widely. Most historians believe that during the Napoleonic wars the increase in prices outstripped wages. Between 1815 and 1830, a price fall was accompanied by a slight increase in wages. But from 1830 to the late 1840s, real wages seem to have improved although regional variations make generalizations dangerous.

When we look at consumption patterns, we find that in Britain in 1850 tea, sugar, and coffee were still semiluxuries consumed primarily by the upper and middle classes and better-off artisans. Meat consumption per capita was less in 1840 than in 1780. On the other hand, a mass market had developed in the cheap cotton goods so important to the Industrial Revolution. As a final note on the question of the standard of living, some historians who take a positive view of the early Industrial Revolution have questioned what would have happened to Britain's growing population without the Industrial Revolution. Would it have gone the way of Ireland's in the Great Hunger of the mid-nineteenth century? No one really knows.

No doubt the periodic crises of overproduction that haunted industrialization from its beginnings caused even further economic hardship. Short-term economic depressions brought high unemployment and increased social tensions. Unemployment figures could be astronomical. During one of these economic depressions in 1842, for example, 60 percent of the factory employees in Bolton were laid off. Cyclical depressions were particularly devastating in towns whose prosperity rested on one industry.

Overall we can say that some evidence exists for an increase in real wages for the working classes between 1790 and 1850, especially in the 1840s. But can standards of living be assessed only in terms of prices, wages, and consumption patterns? No doubt those meant little to people who faced dreadful housing, adulterated food, public health hazards, and the psychological traumas associated with a complete change in work habits and way of life. The real gainers in the early Industrial Revolution were the middle and upper classes—and some skilled workers whose jobs were not eliminated by the new machines. But industrial workers themselves would have to wait until the second half of the nineteenth century until they reaped the benefits of industrialization.

Efforts at Change: The Workers

Before long, workers looked to the formation of labor organizations to gain decent wages and working conditions. The British government, re-

acting against the radicalism of the French revolutionary working classes, had passed a series of Combination Acts in 1799 and 1800 outlawing associations of workers. The legislation failed to prevent the formation of trade unions, however. Similar to the craft societies of earlier times, these new associations were formed by skilled workers in a number of new industries, including the cotton spinners, ironworkers, coal miners, and shipwrights. These unions served two purposes. One was to preserve their own workers' position by limiting entry into their trade; another was to gain benefits from the employers. These early trade unions had limited goals. They favored a working-class struggle against employers, but only to win improvements for the members of their own trades.

Some trade unions were even willing to strike to gain their goals. Bitter strikes were carried out by hand-loom weavers in Glasgow in 1813, cotton spinners in Manchester in 1818, and miners in Northumberland and Durham in 1810. Such blatant illegal activity caused Parliament to repeal the Combination Acts in 1824, accepting the argument of some members that the acts themselves had so alienated workers that they had formed unions. Unions were now tolerated, but other legislation enabled authorities to keep close watch over their activities.

In the 1820s and 1830s, the union movement began to focus on the creation of national unions. One of the leaders in this effort was a well-known cotton magnate and social reformer, Robert Owen (1771–1858). Owen came to believe in the creation of voluntary associations that would demonstrate to others the benefits of cooperative rather than competitive living. Although Owen's program was not directed specifically to trade unionists, his ideas had great appeal to some of their leaders. Under Owen's direction, plans emerged for a Grand National Consolidated Trades Union, which was formed in February 1834. As a national federation of trade unions, its primary purpose was to coordinate a general strike for the eight-hour working day. Rhetoric, however, soon outpaced reality, and by the summer of the same year, the lack of real working-class support led to its total collapse. Afterward, the union movement reverted to trade unions for individual crafts. The largest and most successful was the Amalgamated Society of Engineers, formed in 1850. Its provision of generous unemployment benefits in return for a small weekly payment was precisely the kind of practical gains these trade unions sought. Larger goals would have to wait.

Trade unionism was not the only type of collective action by workers in the early decades of the Industrial Revolution. The Luddites were skilled craftsmen in the Midlands and northern England who in 1812 attacked the machines that they believed threatened their livelihoods. These attacks failed to stop the industrial mechanization of Britain and have been viewed as utterly naive. Some historians, however, have also seen them as an intense eruption of feeling against unrestrained industrial capitalism. The inability of 12,000 troops to find the culprits provides stunning evidence of the local support they received in their areas.

A much more meaningful expression of the attempts of British workers to improve their condition developed in the movement known as Chartism. It was the first "important political movement of working men organized during the nineteenth century." Its aim was to achieve political democracy. A People's Charter drawn up in 1838 demanded universal male suffrage, payment for members of Parliament, and annual sessions of Parliament (see the following box). Two national petitions incorporating these points, affixed with millions of signatures, were presented to Parliament in 1839 and 1842. Both were rejected by the members of Parliament who were not at all ready for political democracy. As one member said, universal suffrage would be "fatal to all the purposes for which government exists" and was "utterly incompatible with the very existence of civilization." After 1843, Chartism as a movement had largely played itself out. It had never really posed a serious threat to the British establishment, but it had not been a total failure either. Its true significance stemmed from its ability to arouse and organize millions of working-class men and women, to give them a sense of working-class consciousness that they had not really possessed before. This political education of working people was important to

the ultimate acceptance of all the points of the People's Charter in the future.

Efforts at Change: Reformers and Government

Efforts to improve the worst conditions of the industrial factory system also came from outside the ranks of the working classes. From its beginning, the Industrial Revolution had drawn much criticism. Romantic poets like William Wordsworth (see Chapter 22) decried the destruction of the natural world:

> I grieve, when on the darker side
> Of this great change I look; and there behold
> Such outrage done to nature as compels
> The indignant power to justify herself.

Reform-minded individuals, be they factory owners who felt twinges of Christian conscience or social reformers in Parliament, campaigned against the evils of the industrial factory, especially condemning the abuse of children. One hoped for the day "that these little ones should once more see the rising and setting of the sun."

As it became apparent that the increase in wealth generated by the Industrial Revolution was accompanied by ever-increasing numbers of poor people, more and more efforts were made to document and deal with the problems. As reports from civic-minded citizens and parliamentary commissions intensified and demonstrated the extent of poverty, degradation, and suffering, the reform efforts began to succeed.

Their first success was a series of Factory Acts passed between 1802 and 1819 that limited labor for children between the ages of nine and sixteen to twelve hours a day; the employment of children under nine years old was forbidden. Moreover, the laws stipulated that children were to receive instruction in reading and arithmetic during working hours. But these acts applied only to cotton mills, not to factories or mines where some of the worst abuses were taking place. Just as important, no provision was made for enforcing the acts through a system of inspection.

In the reform-minded decades of the 1830s and 1840s, new legislation was passed. The Fac-

❧ *The Political Demands of the Chartist Movement* ☙

In the late 1830s and early 1840s, working-class protest centered on achieving a clear set of political goals, particularly universal male suffrage, as the means to achieve economic and social improvements. This selection is taken from one of the national petitions presented to Parliament by the Chartist movement. Although the petition failed, Chartism helped to arouse and organize millions of workers.

National Petition (1839)

To the Honourable the Commons of the United Kingdom of Great Britain and Ireland, in Parliament assembled, the Petition of the undersigned, their suffering countrymen, HUMBLY SHEWETH,—

The energies of a mighty kingdom have been wasted in building up the power of selfish and ignorant men, and its resources squandered for their aggrandisement. The good of a part has been advanced at the sacrifice of the good of the nation. The few have governed for the interest of the few, while the interests of the many have been sottishly neglected, or insolently . . . trampled upon. . . . We come before your honourable house to tell you, with all humility, that this state of things must not be permitted to continue. That it cannot long continue, without very seriously endangering the stability of the throne, and the peace of the kingdom, and that if, by God's help, and all lawful and constitutional appliances, an end can be put to it, we are fully resolved that it shall speedily come to an end. . . . Required, as we are universally, to support and obey the laws, nature and reason entitle us to demand that in the making of the laws the universal voice shall be implicitly listened to. We perform the duties of freemen; we must have the privileges of freemen. Therefore, we demand universal suffrage. The suffrage, to be exempt from the corruption of the wealthy and the violence of the powerful, must be secret. . . . To public safety, as well as public confidence, frequent elections are essential. Therefore, we demand annual parliaments. With power to choose, and freedom in choosing, the range of our choice must be unrestricted. We are compelled, by the existing laws, to take for our representatives men who are incapable of appreciating our difficulties, or have little sympathy with them; merchants who have retired from trade and no longer feel its harassings; proprietors of land who are alike ignorant of its evils and its cure; lawyers by whom the notoriety of the senate is courted only as a means of obtaining notice in the courts. . . . We demand that in the future election of members of your . . . house, the approbation of the constituency shall be the sole qualification, and that to every representative so chosen, shall be assigned out of the public taxes, a fair and adequate remuneration for the time which he is called upon to devote to the public service. . . . Universal suffrage will, and it alone can, bring true and lasting peace to the nation; we firmly believe that it will also bring prosperity. May it therefore please your honourable house, to take this our petition into your most serious consideration, and to use your utmost endeavours, by all constitutional means, to have a law passed, granting to every male of lawful age, sane mind, and unconvicted of crime, the right of voting for members of parliament, and directing all future elections of members of parliament to be in the way of secret ballot, and ordaining that the duration of parliament, so chosen, shall in no case exceed one year, and abolishing all property qualifications in the members, and providing for their due remuneration while in attendance on their parliamentary duties.

tory Act of 1833 strengthened earlier labor legislation. All textile factories were now included. Children between nine and thirteen could work only eight hours a day; those between thirteen and eighteen, twelve hours. Inspection was to be enforced. Another piece of legislation in 1833 required that children between nine and thirteen have at least two hours of elementary education during the working day. In 1847, the Ten Hours Act reduced the work day for children between thirteen and eighteen to ten hours. Women were also now included in the ten-hour limitation. In 1842, a Coal Mines Act eliminated the employment of boys under ten and women in mines. Eventually, men too would benefit from the move to restrict factory hours.

The Industrial Revolution became one of the major forces of change in the nineteenth century as it led Western civilization into the industrial era that has characterized the modern world. Beginning in Britain, its spread to the Continent and the new American nation ensured its growth and domination of the Western world.

The Industrial Revolution seemed to prove to Europeans the underlying assumption of the Scientific Revolution of the seventeenth century— that human beings were capable of dominating nature. By rationally manipulating the material environment for human benefit, people could create new levels of material prosperity and produce machines not dreamed of in their wildest imaginings. Lost in the excitement of the Industrial Revolution were the voices that pointed to the dehumanization of the work force and the alienation from one's work, one's associates, one's self, and the natural world.

The Industrial Revolution also transformed the social world of Europe. The creation of an industrial proletariat produced a whole new force for change. The development of a wealthy industrial middle class presented a challenge to the long-term hegemony of landed wealth. While that wealth had been threatened by the fortunes of commerce, it had never been overturned. But the new bourgeoisie was more demanding and eventually in some places, this new industrial bourgeoisie came to play a larger role in the affairs of state.

NOTES

1. Quoted in W. Gorden Rimmer, *Marshall's of Leeds, Flax-Spinners 1788–1886* (Cambridge, 1960), p. 40.
2. Daniel Defoe, *A Plan of the English Commerce* (Oxford, 1928), pp. 76–77.
3. Quoted in David Landes, *The Unbound Prometheus: Technological Change and Industrial Development in Western Europe from 1750 to the Present* (Cambridge, 1969), pp. 99–100.
4. Quoted in Albert Tucker, *A History of English Civilization* (New York, 1972), p. 583.
5. Quoted in Landes, *The Unbound Prometheus*, pp. 149–50.
6. Quotations can be found in E. Royston Pike, *Human Documents of the Industrial Revolution in Britain* (London, 1966), pp. (in order of quotations) 320, 313, 314, 343.
7. Ibid., p. 315.
8. Quoted in A. J. Donajgrodzi, ed., *Social Control in Nineteenth Century Britain* (London, 1977), p. 141.
9. Quoted in Pike, *Human Documents of the Industrial Revolution in Britain*, pp. 343–44.
10. Quoted in Eric J. Evans, *The Forging of the Modern State: Early Industrial Britain, 1783–1870* (London, 1983), p. 113.
11. Henry Mayhew, *London Labour and the London Poor* (London, 1851), 1:342–43.
12. Quoted in Pike, *Human Documents of the Industrial Revolution in Britain*, pp. 60–61.
13. Quoted in Evans, *The Forging of the Modern State*, p. 124.

SUGGESTIONS FOR FURTHER READING

The well-written work by D. Landes, *The Unbound Prometheus: Technological Change and Industrial Development in Western Europe from 1750 to the Present* (Cambridge, 1969) is still the best introduction to the Industrial Revolution. Although more technical, also of value are C. Trebilcock, *The Industrialization of the Continental Powers, 1780–1914* (London, 1981); and S. Pollard, *Peaceful Conquest: The Industrialization of Europe, 1760–1970* (Oxford, 1981). There is a good collection of essays in P. Mathias and J. A. Davis, eds., *The First Industrial Revolutions* (Oxford, 1989). A volume in the Fontana Economic History of Europe edited by C. M. Cipolla, *The Industrial Revolution* (London, 1973) is also valuable. Although older and dated, T. S. Ashton, *The Industrial Revolution, 1760–1830* (New York, 1948), still provides an interesting introduction to the Industrial Revolution in Britain. Much better, however, are P. Mathias, *The First Industrial Nation: An Economic History of Britain, 1700–1914*, 2d ed. (New York, 1983); R. Floud and D. McCloskey, eds., *The Economic History of Britain since 1700* (New York, 1981); and P. Deane, *The First Industrial Revolution* (Cambridge, 1965). For a discussion of the areas in Europe that lagged behind in the industrialization process, see I. T. Behrend and G. Rankl, *The European Periphery and Industrialization, 1780–1914* (Cambridge, 1982).

Given the importance of Great Britain in the Industrial Revolution, a number of books are available for placing the Industrial Revolution in Britain into a broader context. See E. J. Evans, *The Forging of the Modern State: Early Industrial Britain, 1783–1870* (London, 1983); S. Checkland, *British Public Policy, 1776–1939: An Economic, Social and Political Perspective* (Cambridge, 1983); H. Perkin, *The Origins of Modern English Society, 1780–1880* (London, 1969); and E. J. Hobsbawm, *Industry and Empire* (London, 1968).

The early industrialization of the United States is examined in P. Temin, *Causal Factors in American Economic Growth in the Nineteenth Century* (London, 1975); and D. C. North, *The Economic Growth of the United States, 1790–1860* (New York, 1961), although the latter's stress on the importance of regional specialization to economic growth has been questioned. G. R. Taylor, *The Transportation Revolution, 1815–60* (New York, 1951) examines the importance of transportation in American industrialization. On the economic ties between Great Britain and the United States, see D. Jeremy, *Transatlantic Industrial Revolution: The Diffusion of Textile Technology between Britain and America, 1790–1830* (Cambridge, Mass., 1981).

A general discussion of population growth in Europe can be found in T. McKeown, *The Modern Rise of Population* (London, 1976), although it has been criticized for its emphasis on nutrition and hygiene as the two major causes of that growth. For an examination of urban growth, see the older but classic work of A. F. Weber, *The Growth of Cities in the Nineteenth Century: A Study in Statistics* (Ithaca, N.Y., 1963); and the more recent work by A. R. Sutcliffe, *Towards the Planned City: Germany, Britain, the United States and France, 1780–1914* (Oxford, 1981). C. Woodham Smith, *The Great Hunger* (New York, 1962) is a well-written account of the great Irish tragedy. Many of the works cited above have much information on the social impact of the Industrial Revolution, but additional material is available in C. Morazé, *The Triumph of the Middle Classes* (London, 1966); F. Crouzet, *The First Industrialists: The Problems of Origins* (Cambridge, 1985), on British entrepreneurs; E. P. Thompson, *The Making of the English Working Class* (New York, 1964); and E. Gauldie, *Cruel Habitations, A History of Working-Class Housing, 1790–1918* (London,

1974). G. Himmelfarb, *The Idea of Poverty: England in the Early Industrial Age* (New York, 1984) traces the concepts of poverty and poor from the mid-eighteenth century to the mid-nineteenth century. A valuable work on female labor patterns is L. A. Tilly and J. W. Scott, *Women, Work, and Family* (New York, 1978).

Supplementary Article

Are Americans Working Too Hard?

Source: Excerpt from *Being God's Partner* by Jeffrey K. Salkin, Jewish Lights Publishing, 1994, $19.85 plus $3.50 s/h. P.O. Box 237 Woodstock, Vermont 05091. Permission granted by Jewish Lights Publishing.

FOR MANY AMERICANS, work is now the emotional and spiritual center of life. Professionals labor an average of almost 44 hours a week. Some fields, such as law, finance and medicine, often require employees to work twice that much. Factory employees in the United States work 430 more hours annually—the equivalent of 2½ months—than their German counterparts.

Writer John Updike was right when he said, "We may live well, but that cannot ease the suspicion that we no longer live nobly." I hear this on the ball field from other parents. I hear it in my study. I meet many who are burned out from work, who are disillusioned with their professions. We seem spiritually damaged by the pernicious cycle of working, wanting and having as ends in themselves.

Workaholism and its handmaidens, careerism and materialism, aren't only social issues—they are religious issues. As Diane Fassel wrote in *Working Ourselves to Death*, "Work is god for the compulsive worker, and nothing gets in the way of this god." Work becomes an end in itself, a way to escape from family, the inner life, the world.

All genuine religions are concerned with the shattering of false gods. How can we break the false gods of career?

• First, remember the most profound revolution in religious thinking: the Sabbath. Whether one celebrates it on Friday, Saturday or Sunday, its spiritual reality goes beyond ritual. It is the ultimate statement that the world does not own us, that we are made for rest and holiness as surely as we are made for ambition.

• Second, don't sacrifice your family on the altar of career. The journey up the ladder to success has brought us much wealth. But it has also devalued the traditional role of the parent as nurturer and teacher.

In the Yiddish song *"Mayn Yingele"* ("My Little One"), a father sings to his sleeping child:

I have a son, a little son,
A boy completely fine.
Whenever I see him, it seems to me
That all the world is mine.
But seldom, seldom do I see
My child awake and bright.

I only see him when he sleeps;
I'm only home at night.
It's early when I leave for work;
When I return, it's late.
Unknown to me is my own flesh,
Unknown is my child's face.
When I come home so wearily
In the darkness after day,
My pale wife exclaims to me:
"You should have seen our child play."
I stand beside his little bed;
I look and try to hear.
In his dream he moves his lips:
"Why isn't Papa here?"

That song was written in 1887. Today, Papa and Mama are no longer in the sweatshops, but the anguish of the parent who has impaled himself on the sword of ambition has not changed. It has merely changed addresses.

• Third, don't judge yourself by what you do, but by the meaning you bring to it. Many people have transformed dull work into a true vocation—into a place where they hear the voice of something deeper and higher. At the funeral I performed for a woman who worked in a lingerie store, her co-workers warmly eulogized her for the compassion and sensitivity she showed toward customers who had been mastectomy patients.

When my family moved from Pennsylvania to New York, the boss of the moving crew told me: "Moving is hard for most people. They are nervous about going to a new community and about strangers packing their most precious possessions. I think God wants me to treat my customers with love and make them feel that I care about their lives." Like so many anonymous people, this man was a messenger of God.

We never know what we do in our work that will be remembered, that will be holy. It has nothing to do with our job titles. It has everything to do with the faith, vision and love that we bring to it.

Rabbi Jeffrey K. Salkin is the spiritual leader of Central Synagogue of Nassau County in Rockville Centre, N.Y.

Sample Chapter 13

An Invitation
to Computers

Reprinted by permission of *Understanding Computers, 3E* by Grace Murray Hopper and Steven L. Mandell. Copyright 1990 by West Publishing Company. All rights reserved.

INTRODUCTION

Do you drive a car? Almost certainly you do. If not, it is almost certain that you will learn to drive in the near future. For most people, the ability to drive is considered a necessity, a key to survival in modern society. After all, there are now more than 50 million cars on the road in the United States.

Before you could be licensed to drive, you had to learn some basics about how cars are built and how they work. You also had to learn about traffic rules and safety. As a beginner, you probably completed a training program called "driver education."

In today's **information society,** knowledge about computers is as important to personal and career success as knowledge about automobiles is to personal transportation. An information society consists of a working and living environment in which the majority of people depend on information generated by computers. This information is necessary for successful performance on the job and in everyday life.

Consider: Some 20 million computers already are being used in the United States. Soon, the number of computers in use will approach the number of automobiles on the road. As this happens, an understanding of computers and their functions has become just as important as basic knowledge about cars. This book is designed to be your starting point for the building of computer knowledge. In effect, the course in which you use this book is the equivalent of the driver education program that helped put you behind the wheel of a car.

THE COMPUTER ITSELF

Computers are all around you. You depend on computers. It makes sense, therefore, to know just what a computer is and what it does.

A **computer** is a device that processes electricity to perform certain functions. These characteristics or functions define a computer:

- A computer is an electronic device. This means a computer can accept and react to signals represented by electrical currents.
- A computer can perform a basic set of operational functions. These include arithmetic and comparisons. In other words, a computer can perform addition, subtraction, multiplication, and division; it can also compare two values and select processing functions on the basis of the results of each comparison.
- A computer can represent and store information in the form of electrical signals recorded on electronic and magnetic media.
- A computer can store sets of instructions known as **programs** and can carry out complete sets of instructions without human intervention.
- A computer has the ability to accept instructions or information as **input** and to deliver results, or **output,** in a form that is useful to people.

Computer processing functions are illustrated in Figure 1-1.

OUTLINE

Introduction
The Computer Itself
Computers In Your World
Volume Computation
The Industrial Revolution: Expanding Computational Horizons
Case Situation: The 1890 Census
Transaction Processing
Case Situation: Complex Payrolls
Supporting the War Effort
Information Collection and Reference
Management Information Systems
Student Program Planning
The Computer Age
Batch Processing and Its Problems
The Information Age
Case Situation: Putting Random Access to Work
Conclusion—Summary Points
Review Questions
Discussion Questions
Profile—Lady Ada Augusta, countess of Lovelace
Profile—John von Neumann
Issue—Who's in Control?
Countdown to Computing—A Time Line

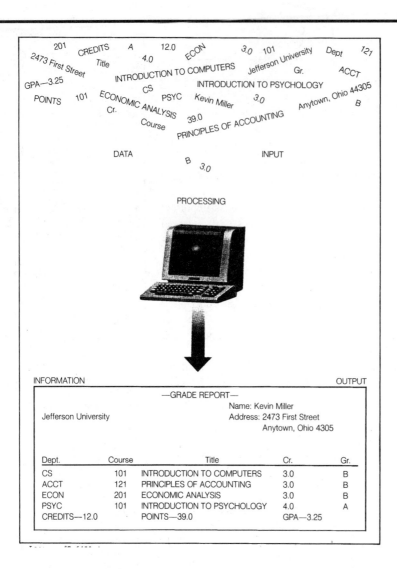

FIGURE 1.1. *Computers accept input, process data, and deliver and store meaningful information.*

COMPUTERS IN YOUR WORLD

Every major technology answers some human need or desire. The automobile provided a better, faster, cleaner method of personal transportation than the horse and buggy. The computer has provided a series of tools and conveniences that have changed living and working conditions. The following list highlights just a few of the impacts that computers have had on you and on society as a whole:

● Computers help to start your car and keep it running. Fuel-injection systems in modern engines are controlled by tiny **microprocessors,** complete computers built on glasslike chips smaller than one of your fingernails. Microprocessors also control engine emissions (smog), brakes, and suspension.

● In homes, computers serve people by controlling microwave and other ovens, laundry equipment, heating and air conditioning, and security systems (burglar alarms).

- In factories, computers assist in the design and manufacture of products.
- In schools and colleges, computers assist with registration, grade reporting, and actual instruction.
- When you make purchases at supermarkets, department stores, or fast-food restaurants, the **transactions** are recorded on computers. A transaction is a basic act of doing business. Each transaction involves an exchange of items or services of equal value, such as the receipt of a hamburger in exchange for cash. After transactions are recorded, the computers help businesses to order replacements for the items you purchase.
- Computers collect information about transactions, people, and organizations. This information is organized for convenient use. Of course, people have always collected and used information; that's why mountains of paper are crammed into file drawers. Computers gather and control more information—and they make it available in less time—than was previously possible. For example, consider the information required by just one organization, the Internal Revenue Service (IRS). This one agency collects the great majority of the money received by the federal government. To do this, the IRS operates a series of computer centers that handle and coordinate use of information about more than 110 million workers.
- For scientists, engineers, and technicians, computers provide the capacity for **number crunching,** or the ability to perform large volumes of calculations rapidly and reliably—at rates of tens of millions of computations per second.

These examples identify three major needs that computers meet:

- Volume computation
- Transaction processing
- Information collection and reference.

The remainder of this chapter looks at the history of these needs and at the development of equipment and methods to help solve the problems.

Volume Computation

Computation demands grew as people gathered in large villages and then built cities because, with growth, trading activities increased. This trend goes back thousands of years.

The Chinese enhanced number-crunching capabilities with the **abacus,** a device that enabled people to compute by manipulating strings of beads. However, the picture changes quickly as volumes mount and complications are added. Cooking and selling a single hamburger, for example, presents no special problems. The order is placed; the food is delivered, money is collected. The transaction is complete. Now, repeat this sequence a billion times. Keeping records of transactions can become extremely complex if you work in the headquarters of McDonald's and are involved in billions of hamburger transactions.

CASE SITUATION: Complex Payrolls _____

Transaction activities grew both in volume and complexity with the growth of American industry. For example, volumes of payroll transactions mounted as the work force grew toward a level of 50 million. Complexity was added when the Social Security system went into operation on January 1, 1936.

Payroll is a special kind of transaction. Workers, in effect, sell their time and skills in exchange for the money they need to live. Until 1935, computing payroll transactions was relatively simple: The worker's hourly pay rate was multiplied by the number of hours worked; the result was the worker's earnings, or wages.

After January 1, 1936, employers had to deduct Social Security taxes from workers' pay. Outwardly, the job didn't seem difficult. A worker's earnings had to be computed to determine the Social Security tax—at that time, 1 percent of gross earnings. This amount was deducted from the worker's pay. The employer added an additional 1 percent and set up an account for each employee. The withheld tax and the employer contribution were paid periodically to the government. No individual procedure was very complex, but the net effect was dramatic: The payroll processing workload expanded by more than 1,000 percent.

Other types of business transactions also became more complex. Many state and local agencies introduced sales taxes on business transactions. Again, transaction processing volumes and complexity multiplied.

To keep up with exploding processing volumes, businesses turned to punched card accounting machines, running up monthly bills of tens of millions of dollars for rental of this equipment. The idea: Transaction data items could be punched into cards and processed in a series of steps, called a **system,** to produce the information files and documents that businesses were required to generate. Dr. Hollerith's principle turned out to be a workable solution for the new information processing requirements of business organizations. Punched cards allowed data items to be captured once, at the time transactions were recorded. After that, cards could be reprocessed in a sequence of operations that generated checks, invoices, and other transaction documents.

The acceptance of punched cards in the business community can be demonstrated dramatically: Punched cards were made from the same basic paper stock as milk cartons. During the precomputer era when punched card machines dominated the data processing scene, more paper stock was used for cards than for milk cartons.

Supporting the War Effort

Transaction volumes grew rapidly as the country prepared for and was drawn into World War II. Some 10 million men and women were inducted into the armed forces. Each of these people became the focus of transactions for training information, work assignments, pay, medical care, and other needs. Wartime commitments to the development and production of weapons and materials also overloaded the country's data processing capacities. In addition, scientific and engineering projects connected with new weapons systems presented unprecedented number-crunching workloads.

In effect, the war effort gave birth to the modern electronics industry. Radar was developed as a means of identifying and tracking aircraft. Battlefield communication requirements led to the development of portable electronic radios, called "walkie-talkies." Massive calculation capabilities were needed to support new aircraft and artillery developments.

The ancient Egyptians encountered problems with record-keeping volumes when they began to receive full shiploads of goods from Mediterranean ports. They recorded information on clay tablets, then on papyrus, an early form of paper made from woven reeds. The Egyptians invented **double-entry book-keeping,** a technique in which entries with positive and negative values are balanced to verify accuracy. This method is still used by modern accounting and computer systems.

During the seventeenth century, a young Frenchman encountered a problem involving volumes of computations. His name was Blaise Pascal. His father was a tax collector. To ease his father's burden, Pascal invented one of the first mechanical calculators. Pascal's contribution was acknowledged during the 1970s, when an advanced computer language based on modern, structured methods of programming was named in his honor.

The Industrial Revolution: Expanding Computational Horizons

Through the eighteenth and nineteenth centuries, the **Industrial Revolution** promoted increased commerce and rapid growth of cities. During this period, methods of mass production were developed and factories were built in order to meet the demands of growing populations.

To keep pace, eighteenth- and nineteenth-century inventors developed a series of important information processing machines and mathematical methods:

● Charles Babbage invented a series of mathematical processing machines, including one called the **difference engine.** The machine could add, subtract, multiply, and divide.

● Lady Ada Augusta, countess of Lovelace, was a friend of Babbage and a skilled mathematician. She developed techniques for use of one of Babbage's machines that became forerunners of modern computer programming. Lady Ada's main contribution was the concept that information processing systems could be built from a series of procedures that completed standard computational sequences. This principle, known as **looping,** has become a mainstay for use of computers in business and for many scientific applications.

● Another British mathematician, George Boole, developed a system of algebra based on a series of logic and comparison functions. **Boolean algebra** became an important element in the design of computer processors.

● Continuing needs for keeping up with demands for computation led to the development of adding machines, calculators, and the cash register. The cash register led to major changes in the retail sale of goods to consumers. Previously, stores had separate areas for selling and for handling cash. Cash registers made it possible to handle cash at the point of sale and thus led to the growth of retail stores and chains.

Ultimately, the job of keeping track of people themselves led to the main breakthrough in computation tools that preceded development of computers.

PROFILE
LADY ADA AUGUSTA, COUNTESS OF LOVELACE

Lady Ada Augusta, countess of Lovelace, did not lead the kind of life typical of most aristocratic English women during the early 1800s. The daughter of the romantic English poet, Lord Byron, Lady Ada contributed significantly to modern-day programming concepts.

The countess first became involved with the theoretical concepts of computers when she translated a paper on Charles Babbage's analytical engine. The analytical engine was a device designed to perform mathematical calculations automatically from coded card instructions. In 1842, at the age of 27, Lady Ada began working with Babbage.

During the first year of this association, several of her ideas were incorporated into the design of the analytical engine. The most significant idea was what is now called the loop concept. In her studies, Lady Ada noticed that the same sequence of instructions often had to be repeated for different data when a single calculation was being performed. She concluded that one set of instruction cards could be used if there was a way to loop back to those instructions. A calculation then could be made with only a fraction of the original effort.

Lady Ada is now considered to be the first programmer because of her insight into the dynamics of the programming process. A high-level programming language used mostly by the government was named Ada in honor of her achievements.

C A S E   S I T U A T I O N : The 1890 Census _____

Between 1880 and 1920, some 40 million immigrants came to the United States from Europe. These hordes of people provided the talent and the strength to build America into a world-class power. Population growth outpaced the ability of the U.S. Bureau of Census to prepare the reports required by the nation's laws. A complete **census,** or count and analysis of population, is required every 10 years.

In 1880, the population of the United States was approximately 40 million. The census count for 1880 was done manually. This involved endless copying and checking of information. When the work was done, the resulting reports were of limited value: Figures for 1880 weren't completed until mid 1887.

To deal with this problem, the Census Bureau hired a mathematician, Dr. Herman Hollerith. Hollerith set out to find a way to record information items so they could be entered only once, then reused in further tallies and analyses. He built machines that punched holes in cards to represent census numbers. Other machines could read and count the **punched cards,** which could be used repeatedly for different calculations. In this way, Hollerith mechanized information processing, and society gained a tool that could handle the exploding volumes of computation needed to support increasing numbers of transactions. Figure 1-2 shows the format and coding for a punched card.

TRANSACTION PROCESSING

A single transaction is no problem. The customer selects an item (or service). The seller delivers. The customer pays. At this level, things are simple, easy. Engineering efforts in the history of the world—at least up to that point—occurred with the Manhattan Project, which led to the development of the atomic bomb.

To meet these demands, a number of university laboratories and special scientific facilities were instructed to devise practical electronic computers. Consider: At the beginning of the war, the most powerful data processing machines available processed up to 100 cards per minute to deliver relatively simple calculations. Immediately after the war, the first commercial computer, UNIVAC I, could perform up to 2,000 computations per second. Some 40 years after the war, computer manufacturers were delivering systems with capacities for up to *80 million calculations per second.*

Some key events related to the development of computers and to increases in the power of computers are described in the accompanying time line. The main point here is that electronics, communications, and computing technologies were developed in answer to growing demands by society and its business organizations. People needed more computation capabilities than they could get out of existing equipment. Scientists and engineers were challenged to produce greater capacities; the computer was a solution to a pressing problem.

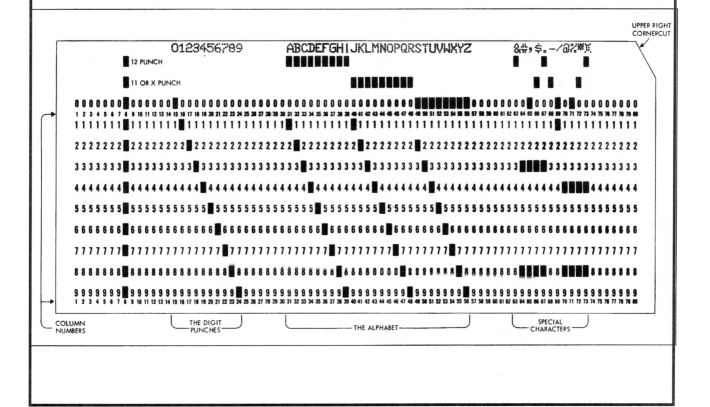

COUNTDOWN TO COMPUTING—A Time Line

1823	The difference engine, a mechanical calculator with capabilities for addition, subtraction, multiplication, and division is introduced by Charles Babbage.
1843	Lady Ada Augusta, countess of Lovelace, introduces the concept of automatic repetition of standard computation sequences, an idea that proves to be a forerunner of "looping," an important computer programming technique.
1854	George Boole introduces a system for algebraic processing of logical functions. Boolean algebra becomes the basis for computer processor design.
1887	The first punched card data processing machine is built by Dr. Herman Hollerith.
1937	Professor Howard Aiken begins work at Harvard University on a practical electromechanical calculator. The project results in development of the Mark I, the first practical, large-scale electromechanical calculator.
1939	John Vincent Atanasoff and Clifford Berry develop the Atanasoff-Berry Computer, the ABC. This is the first device to use electronics for digital processing.
1945	A paper published by Dr. John von Neumann of Princeton describes EDVAC (Electronic Discrete Variable Automatic Computer). With this paper, von Neumann proposes a processing design, or architecture, that dominates the computer field for more than 40 years. The design is built around a single, central processor that ensures the sequential execution of all commands under control of stored programs.
1946	A practical computer applying von Neumann architecture, ENIAC (Electronic Numerical Integrator and Computer), is developed at the University of Pennsylvania by a team of 50 headed by J. Presper Eckert and John Mauchly. ENIAC weighs 30 tons, is two stories high, and occupies some 15,000 square feet of space. ENIAC is used by the Army for ballistics computations.
1947	The first computer "bug" is identified and named by Grace Murray Hopper, who discovers that a dead moth has short-circuited a unit of the Mark I calculator.
1948	Thomas J. Watson, Sr., president of IBM, orders development of an ENIAC-like system called the Selective Sequence Electronic Calculator (SSEC). IBM's commitment is said to be a result of a snub by Professor Aiken at the dedication of the Mark I system, for which IBM provided financial support.
1949	Maurice Wilkes of Cambridge University, England, builds EDSAC (Electronic Delay Storage Automatic Computer). This is the first operational computer that uses stored programs. Wilkes is a former student of Eckert and Mauchley at the Moore School, University of Pennsylvania. His computer applies the principles introduced in von Neumann's EDVAC paper.
1950	A working model of von Neumann's EDVAC is completed. This marks the first use of digital mathematics by an electronic computer.
1951	Eckert and Mauchly's UNIVAC I (UNIVersal Automatic Computer) is delivered by Remington Rand to the U.S. Census Bureau. UNIVAC I can perform up to 2,000 computations per second.
1953	The first magnetic tape drive, the IBM Model 726, is introduced as an alternative to punched card storage. Storage capacity is 100 characters per inch and processing capacity is 75 inches per second.

COUNTDOWN TO COMPUTING—A Time Line

1954	The first compiler programming language, FORTRAN (FORmula TRANslator), is developed by John Bakus of IBM. Compiler languages make it possible to program computers in terms that are meaningful to people. This is the first step toward user-friendly design of computers.
1956	The term "artificial intelligence" is introduced by John McCarthy of Dartmouth College. McCarthy and Marvin Minsky of MIT are organizers of the Dartmouth Conference, which deals with the potential for artificial intelligence applications.
1958	The first fully transistorized computer, the CDC 1604, is built at Control Data Corporation by Seymour Cray.
1959	The concept for the integrated circuit is developed through the work of Jack Kilby of Texas Instruments and Robert Noyce of Fairchild Semiconductor. The integrated circuit is to play a major role in the reduction of computer equipment sizes and costs. COBOL (COmmon Business-Oriented Language), a major, high-level programming tool for business applications, is introduced. COBOL is based on a technique developed by Grace Murray Hopper, known as FlowMatic. COBOL development is sponsored by CODASYL (COmmittee on DAta SYstems Languages). A compiler technique developed by Hopper makes it possible to use the same COBOL instructions on multiple makes and models of computers. SABRE, the first computerized airline reservation system, is introduced by American Airlines.
1960	General use of transistors makes possible lower-cost, smaller computers. This is known as the second generation of computers, in contrast with first-generation systems that used vacuum tubes in their processors. The first automated check processing system for banks is announced by the Bank of America and General Electric.
1963	The first ultra-large-scale computer—a supercomputer—is shipped to the Lawrence Livermore National Laboratories by Control Data.
1964	IBM introduces a computer line of unprecedented popularity, System/360. The introduction highlights the arrival of the third generation of computers, marked by use of integrated circuits for both processing and main memory components.
1965	BASIC (Beginner's All-purpose Symbolic Instruction Code), a language designed for ease of student training, is introduced by Thomas Kurtz and John Kemeny of Dartmouth. BASIC will become the most widely used programming language for microcomputers when they are developed. The first minicomputers are marketed by Digital Equipment Corporation. These midsized computers make full computing capabilities available to smaller companies, expanding the market for computers and increasing the number of them in use.
1966	The first hand-held electronic calculator is introduced by Texas Instruments.
1967	Intel (Integrated Electronics) Corporation, a pioneer in microprocessors, is formed by Gordon Moore and Robert Noyce specifically for development and marketing of microprocessors.
1968	Intel introduces its first microprocessor, the 4004. The microprocessor becomes the basis for development of fourth-generation computer equipment and also for the design of microcomputers.

COUNTDOWN TO COMPUTING—A Time Line

1971	Intel markets its 4004 microchip in production quantities. The availability of a computer on a chip spurs development of smaller computers and opens the way for development of the microcomputer.
	   The floppy disk is introduced for use with input devices for the IBM System/370.
	   Pascal, a language that implements advanced, structured programming methods, is introduced by Niklaus Wirth of Switzerland.

1975	The Cray-1, first of a major family of supercomputers, is introduced. Microsoft Corporation, a major developer of software for the fledgling microcomputer industry, is founded by Bill Gates and Paul Allen. One of the first products is a BASIC compiler for microcomputers.
1977	The Apple II computer, the first fully assembled, commercially marketed desktop computer, is introduced by Apple Computer, founded by teenagers Steve Jobs and Steve Wozniak. Digital Research markets the first generally accepted operating system for microcomputers, CP/M (Control Program/Microcomputers).
1978	Visicalc, the first successful electronic spreadsheet application package for microcomputers, is introduced by Dan Bricklin and Bob Frankston.
1979	WordStar, the first commercially successful word processing application package for microcomputers, is introduced by Micropro International.
1980	The Winchester disk, a disk drive using a rigid metal platter, is introduced by Shugart Associates. Winchester disks have 30 times more data storage capacity than the floppy disks of the day. Also, access times are about one-tenth of those available with floppy disks.
1981	IBM introduces its Personal Computer, which dominates the microcomputer field and moves rapidly to a shipping rate of more than 1 million units per month. Microsoft's MS-DOS becomes the operating system standard for the IBM PC and for microcomputers generally. Osborne Computers introduces the first portable computer.
1983	Lotus Corporation introduces Lotus 1-2-3, which becomes the most popular spreadsheet application package. Lotus's founder, Mitch Kapor, is responsible for development of the program. The first microcomputer built for touch-screen input, the HP-150, is introduced by Hewlett-Packard.
1985	Manufacturers announce work in process on a memory chip with a capacity of 1 million bits.
1988	Multiprocessor computers begin to come to market. These units represent the first processor design advance since von Neumann architecture was described in 1945. The new computers use multiple processors in parallel to increase capacity over von Neumann's single-processor design.
1989	Designs for neuron computers with processor circuits patterned on the human nervous system are announced. Work moves ahead quickly on design of superconductor circuits, which eliminate most of the resistance of electrical conductors. The technology shows promise for faster computers that dissipate far less heat than present systems.

INFORMATION COLLECTION AND REFERENCE

Transaction processing generates information. Information, in turn, is a necessity of life for modern organizations and their managers. One of the great discoveries that has resulted from application of computers is the recognition of the value of information files. Initially, these files were considered merely to be necessities for and by-products of transaction processing. Eventually, the information itself became a major value for the use of computers. Computers added value to information because of their ability to organize facts and develop reports that were meaningful to decisions that businesspeople had to make. To illustrate, consider two typical applications:

- Management information systems for businesses
- Student program planning in colleges and universities.

Management Information Systems

As an everyday example, consider the operation of a fast-food chain specializing in hamburgers and related menu items.

At one of these restaurants, you ask for a hamburger, an order of fries, and a soft drink. For each item you order, the counterperson presses a single key on the sales register, which is actually a miniature computer linked into a large computer network.

For each food-item entry, the computer refers to its information files. The computer displays and/or prints descriptions and prices for all ordered entries. Under some systems, the order is also printed in the kitchen and used by the cooks to prepare the items. Under other systems, the food is precooked; thecounterperson simply picks up the ordered item and uses the register listing to collect what you owe.

So far, the computer has served as a simple transaction processing tool. The computer tallies the value of customer purchases and controls the collection of cash. But such transaction processing, once the main purpose of computers, is now just the tip of the iceberg. Much greater value results from the collection of information into usable files.

Consider what happens when you place a food-and-drink order. Besides recording the individual transaction, the computer tallies information on items sold. That is, the computer reports on the number of sales for each menu item. Further processing relates these sales figures to the supplies on hand in each restaurant. From this information, managers determine how many hamburger patties, rolls, and bags of fries each restaurant will need. In effect, when you order a hamburger and fries, information on your transaction leads automatically to the purchase of supplies that will be used to serve the customers who follow.

The computer also records the time of each sale. This information lets managers know business volumes on an hour-by-hour basis in each restaurant. Managers can then use this information to plan the working hours for employees. Finally, sales information accumulated in computers also determines whether each restaurant is delivering a profit and, if so, how much.

When computers were introduced to businesses, transaction processing was regarded as the main end product. In other words, computers were paperwork generators that produced orders, invoices (bills), and checks. Eventually, greater value was discovered in the **information resources** accumulated by computers. The term *information resources* refers to the information files that have become an asset, or valuable possession, of a computer-using organization. Information resources are now considered an asset equivalent to a company's cash or inventory.

Student Program Planning

Suppose you knew nothing about the procedures—and roadblocks—encountered in course selection and student registration at a large college or university. From a vantage point of inexperience, the process might look simple. The course catalog has thousands of listings. An individual student may want to take three to five courses during any given quarter or semester. What's the big deal?

Problems arise because of the volume and complexity of registration activities on a typical campus. Even computer systems become swamped when 10,000 to perhaps 30,000 students are to be registered over a period of a few days. Procedures are complicated when that many students have to devise programs that include prerequisites for many courses and that meet graduation requirements. Also, payment of student fees, arrangements for student aid or loans, and other factors add complexity.

Thus, the major value of a computer on a campus lies in its maintenance of information files on students, courses, faculty, graduation requirements, financial information, and other elements. These files make the process of serving student needs more manageable than if the information resources did not exist.

When student registration is supported by a computer system, countless problems are handled automatically. For example, when a course request is entered, the computer correlates information on the student and the course. If course prerequisites exist, the computer matches the requirements against the student record. Student progress is also monitored and courses needed to complete a major or to qualify for graduation are reported. If a student's grade point average is slipping, the individual can be referred for counseling.

In short, use of information resources in an educational institution helps to guide students rather than simply ensure them seats in classrooms.

THE COMPUTER AGE

The first computer system delivered for commercial use—a UNIVAC I—was, fittingly, delivered to the U.S. Bureau of Census for computation of data on the 1950 population count. Thus, the same problem that led to the development and sale of billions of dollars' worth of punched card equipment also prompted the first practical application for computers.

Deliveries of large-scale computers began in the early 1950s. Within a decade, more than 10,000 computers had been shipped to business and government organizations, as well as to universities. From the early 1950s through the mid 1960s, computers were mainly used for the same kinds of transaction processing that had been handled by punched card machines.

P R O F I L E
JOHN VON NEUMANN

John von Neumann made a contribution to the electronic digital computer that can be likened to the importance of the internal combustion engine for the automobile. Indeed, the concept of the von Neumann gate, or von Neumann architecture, proved to be a key building block in the development and manufacture of tens of millions of computers.

Von Neumann was an advanced mathematician who came to the United States as a refugee from Nazi Germany. He became a scholar in residence at Princeton University's Institute of Advanced Studies along with another renowned refugee from Nazism, Albert Einstein.

In 1945, some of the last remaining obstacles to the design of a practical electronic computer were being tackled by leading mathematicians and scientists. The main problem centered around how to set up a computer with operating instruction sequences, or programs. The first operational computer used extensive plugboards and electrical switches as its programming method.

This was impractical because the procedure was so time-consuming and prone to errors. Each time a job was to be run, all of the plugs and switches had to be set manually from scratch. While switches were being manipulated, extremely expensive equipment sat idle. The solution envisioned by von Neumann was to store sets of programs electronically within the computer. These recorded programs would be repeatable and would avoid the frustration of trying to set hundreds of plugs and switches manually to run each application.

In 1945, von Neumann published a paper on a computer system he was developing, called EDVAC (Electronic Discrete Variable Automatic Computer). Von Neumann proposed a method for storing instructions within a computer's electronic circuits. His design called for executing the programs and processing items of data in preset sequences through a single, central processor, which has been referred to as the von Neumann gate or von Neumann architecture. This design dominated the computer field from its inception. The first alternate designs, involving use of multiple, parallel processors, were introduced in the late 1980s.

Batch Processing and Its Problems

Handling transactions involved processing of groups of individual records. Each record was brought into the computer, updated, then output. For example, a payroll program might update information on thousands of individual employees. But it could be extremely difficult to apply payroll information to the analysis of operating costs and projected profits.

During the transaction processing years, emphasis was on **unit record** processing and maintenance. A unit record, in this sense, was a collection of data items about one entity. For example, each employee's earnings record was separate from every other individual earnings record. Groups of unit records were processed as individual elements within **batch processing** systems. That is, each time an application was run on a computer, the complete file of unit records had to be processed, in sequence, from beginning to end. This is because the unit records existed in **sequential files** that were set up in a fixed order.

At first, unit records were stored in large decks of punched cards. Individual files might occupy thousands of cards housed in endless rows of file cabinets. Later, sequential files of unit records were recorded on **magnetic tape.** This increased the speeds and capacities for batch transaction processing, but the basic limitations of sequential processing were not affected. It was impossible to correlate information from batch files to derive management information.

The need to organize records in sequential files made it impossible to use computers for direct support of business operations. This is because of the way sequential files have to be used: The entire set of records has to be processed each time any reference is made to the file. For example, it was impossible to use a computer to record sales information on individual purchases in department stores, supermarkets, or fast-food restaurants. With the needed information in sequential files, it would have been necessary to process tens of thousands of records to support each transaction. The only effective way to use sequential files was to process information in batches, separately from the handling of transactions.

Computers could not be brought into the mainstream of operations for businesses and other organizations until a major breakthrough made possible **random access** storage and retrieval of information. The ability to record and retrieve individual records from massive files was the major factor in creating information resources. In turn, random access proved to be the breakthrough that made it possible for America, which led the way in the use of computers, to become an information society.

THE INFORMATION AGE

Random access storage was made possible with the invention of the **magnetic disk drive.** The idea was to break out of the limits of sequential storage and processing, limits imposed by recording information on cards or magnetic tape. The magnetic disk device uses an entirely different approach. Storage is on a flat, round platter that resembles a phonograph record. Recording is in a series of circular patterns around the hub of the disk. Like a phonograph record, the random access disk rotates when it is in use. A magnetic recording and reading device, called the **read/write head,** then moves back and forth across the surface of the disk in order to find unit records on individual recording paths, or **tracks.** The impact on the potential application of computers to support of human and business needs was dramatic.

CASE SITUATION: Putting Random Access to Work

One of the first uses of random access disk devices involved wholesale operations such as auto parts distributors. In a typical application situation, a distributor might stock supplies of some 50,000 separate parts for sale to independent garages or to people repairing their own cars.

Keeping up with sales and stocks for so many parts involves a tremendous amount of paperwork. Auto parts distributors adopted computer techniques early in the computer age, but these applications were limited to historic processing of information on a batch basis. Historic processing meant simply that transactions had to be carried out under traditional, pencil-and-paper methods. Salespeople checked inventories by looking in the stock bins. Ordered items were delivered on the spot, supported by handwritten invoices to document the transactions. Copies of these invoices then were used to record information into computer files that kept track of stocks of parts and also followed up for collection of bills from customers. The problem was that the power of computers could not be applied directly to the mainstream operation of the business. Computers were limited to historic, after-the-fact information processing.

The ability to find and handle individual records changed all that. Random access computers were designed to include files with records of customer information, credit information, and product information. The records for products included descriptions, prices, quantities in stock, and stock levels at which each item should be reordered. With this kind of information support, salespeople could serve their customers directly from computer workstations. Salespeople no longer needed to wander through the warehouse looking at bins to see if items were in stock. Order information was entered into the computer, which responded with an entry on the customer invoice. At the same time, the computer reduced the record of the amount of stock on hand for the item to reflect the sale.

With this approach, computers became a tool for direct, mainstream management of business operations. It was said that an information system of this type could **model** the condition of a business. That is, the current realities of business conditions were reflected in computer-stored files. The information age had dawned.

CONCLUSION

Computers have become part of the living and working environment for the great majority of citizens in this information age. Computers are technological tools people use to solve problems that they identify. People identify problems and figure out solutions; computers help to implement those solutions. Computers are sophisticated tools, but their value and the results they deliver depend on the imagination and skill applied by people. The remainder of this book is designed to provide the knowledge and understanding that will qualify you to move into your future as an information worker or, perhaps, as a computer professional.

DISCUSSION QUESTIONS

1. How and why are the skills of driving a car compared with the ability to understand the value of information and the operation of computers?
2. How did the size of populations and the volumes of transactions lead to requirements for increased computation capabilities?
3. Why did the advent of payroll deductions for Social Security create bottlenecks in the processing of business information?
4. How did the development of random access processing lead to the advent of the information age?

Who's in control?

Do computer systems take on a life and a *will* of their own once they are built and programmed by people? Will computers become the masters of the people who develop them?

These questions have fascinated a wide range of people, including science fiction enthusiasts, military planners, and millions of average citizens. Best-sellerdom and box-office success have been conferred on books and movies that conjure up images of world-class destruction brought on by computers that break their "fail-safe" *traces* and run out of control

Computer scientists, military leaders, and business managers have *discounted* these images as fantasies—entertainment that has little to do with reality. Still, the image of Dr. Strangelove, the mad scientist, continues to exist in the consciences and concerns of millions of people. Fictitious stories about "accidental" wars resulting in *wholesale* death continue to capture the human imagination.

Fantasy?

There was no fantasy to the real-life dread of Russian missiles on ships off the coast of Cuba. Nor was there any fantasy behind the confrontation between the United States and the Soviet Union over the *measures* and countermeasures conceived to deal with what became known as the Cuban Missile Crisis.

There was no fantasy about the situation in 1985 when Korean Airlines Flight 007, bound from Alaska to Hong Kong, was shot down on the basis of data generated by the Soviet Union's computer-controlled air defense system. There certainly was no fantasy for the families of more than 300 dead passengers and crew members.

Nor was there fantasy involved in the incident in 1988 during which an American frigate shot down an Iranian airliner mistaken for a military attack plane.

The embarrassing overlaps between science fiction and computer-involved errors have not let the underlying issue go away: Is there a real danger that computers can run amok and become instruments for destruction and misery?

The issue is at the heart of development of military defense systems that have been called "doomsday machines." The situation: A hostile nation launches a missile attack in an effort to cripple another country. The attacker apparently believes that a sneak attack could begin and end World War III in an hour or less. As a deterrent, defense systems are designed to convince prospective enemies that such an attack would assure their own doom. The idea. A radar detection network would *issue* a warning while enemy attack missiles were still en route. The commander-in-chief would issue an order activating a retaliatory mechanism. Thousands of missiles would be *fired* at enemy targets or would intercept in-transit missiles. Thus the enemy that launched a sneak attack could bring about its own doom.

In the name of defense, trillions of dollars have been spent on systems designed for destruction. The question cannot be avoided: Are world leaders wise enough to avoid unleashing the potential "overkill" possible in a world *replete* with weapons of atomic and chemical warfare?

The main hope; People, as a general rule, love life. Fear of death is universal. the *point* has been reached at which fears raised by scenarios of destruction have become the main deterrents to global war. The human race is being preserved by its own natural, healthy fears. People may not possess the innate wisdom to develop a purely fail-safe network of computers and death-dealing machinery. Therefore, if people are to remain in control of human destiny, their ability to conjure up images of catastrophe represents a hope for the future of humanity. Fallibility, once recognized, can be a strong guide toward safe, secure controls over instruments with massive potential for destruction.

What does all this have to do with the study of computers and computer systems?

Failure probability, justifiably, has become a major area of concern and serious study. For example, it is known that a complex system with 1,000 components, each 99.9 percent reliable, has a 50 percent probability of failure at any given time. The rule of thumb: Anything that can fail will. These failures have different sets of consequences.

Many systems developed to serve societies in an information age are complex and have the potential to fail. consequences for many of these failures fall far short of mass destruction. But *power* failures in metropolitan areas and other real examples do have serious, potentially uncomfortable consequences. On the other hand, a breakdown of an electronic ignition system in a car or the automatic control of a microwave oven can be merely a minor inconvenience.

The point: In the development and use of any automatic devices, an awareness of and healthy respect for the consequences of failure can provide the margin needed to increase the probability of success. Part of the planning for development and use of any computer system should include creation of scenarios that picture potential failures. This process has been called "constructive worrying." It should not be discredited, but should be recognized for its potential for assuring safe, productive use of computers—at all levels.

Sample Short Story

Strange Inventions

From *The Story of My Boyhood and Youth* by John Muir. Reprinted by permission of the publisher, Houghton Mifflin Company.

I think it was in my fifteenth year that I began to relish good literature with enthusiasm, and smack my lips over favorite lines, but there was desperately little time for reading, even in the winter evenings— only a few stolen minutes now and then. Father's strict rule was, straight to bed immediately after family worship, which in winter was usually over by eight o'clock. I was in the habit of lingering in the kitchen with a book and candle after the rest of the family had retired, and considered myself fortunate if I got five minutes' reading before Father noticed the light and ordered me to bed; an order that of course I immediately obeyed. But night after night I tried to steal minutes in the same lingering way, and how keenly precious those minutes were, few nowadays can know. Father failed perhaps two or three times in a whole winter to notice my light for nearly ten minutes, magnificent golden blocks of time, long to be remembered like holidays or geological periods. One evening when I was reading church history Father was particularly irritable, and called out with hope-killing emphasis, "*John, go to bed!* Must I give you a separate order every night to get you to go to bed? Now, I will have no irregularity in the family; you *must* go when the rest go, and without my having to tell you." Then, as an afterthought, as if judging that his words and tone of voice were too severe for so pardonable an offense as reading a religious book, he unwarily added: "If you *will* read, get up in the morning and read. You may get up in the morning as early as you like."

That night I went to bed wishing with all my heart and soul that somebody or something might call me out of sleep to avail myself of this wonderful indulgence; and next morning to my joyful surprise I awoke before Father called me. A boy sleeps soundly after working all day in the snowy woods, but that frosty morning I sprang out of bed as if called by a trumpet blast, rushed downstairs, scarce feeling my chilblains, enormously eager to see how much time I had won; and when I held up my candle to a little clock that stood on a bracket in the kitchen I found that it was only one o'clock. I had gained five hours, almost half a day! "Five hours to myself!" I said, "five huge, solid hours!" I can hardly think of any other event in my life, any discovery I ever made that gave birth to joy so transportingly glorious as the possession of these five frosty hours.

In the glad, tumultuous excitement of so much suddenly acquired time-wealth, I hardly knew what to do with it. I first thought of going on with my reading, but the zero weather would make a fire necessary, and it occurred to me that Father might object to the cost of firewood that took time to chop. Therefore, I prudently decided to go down cellar, and begin work on a model of a self-setting sawmill I had invented. Next morning I managed to get up at the same gloriously early hour, and though the temperature of the cellar was a little below the freezing point, and my light was only a tallow candle, the mill work went joyfully on. There were a few tools in a corner of the cellar—a vise, files, a hammer, chisels, etc., that Father had brought from Scotland, but no saw excepting a coarse crooked one that was unfit for sawing dry hickory or oak. So I made a fine-tooth saw suitable for my work out of a strip of steel that had formed part of an old-fashioned corset; that cut the hardest wood smoothly. I also made my own bradawls, punches, and a pair of compasses, out of wire and old files.

My workshop was immediately under Father's bed, and the filing and tapping in making cogwheels, journals, cams, etc., must, no doubt, have annoyed him, but with the permission he had granted in his mind, and doubtless hoping that I would soon tire of getting up at one o'clock, he impatiently waited about two weeks before saying a word. I did not vary more than five minutes from one o'clock all winter, nor did I feel any bad effects whatever, nor did I think at all about the subject as to whether so little sleep might be in any way injurious; it was a grand triumph of will power over cold and common comfort and work-weariness in abruptly cutting down my ten hours' allowance of sleep to five. I simply felt that I was rich beyond anything I could have dreamed of or hoped for. . . .

Father, as was customary in Scotland, gave thanks and asked a blessing before meals, not merely as a matter of form and decent Christian manners, for he regarded food as a gift derived directly from the hands of the Father in Heaven. Therefore every meal to him was a sacrament requiring conduct and attitude of mind not unlike that befitting the Lord's Supper. No idle word was allowed to be spoken at our table, much less any laughing or fun or storytelling. When we were at the breakfast table, about two weeks after the great golden time-discovery, Father cleared his throat preliminary, as we all knew, to saying something considered important. I feared that it was to be on the subject of my early rising, and dreaded the withdrawal of the permission he had granted on account of the noise I made, but still hoping that, as he had given his word that I might get up as early as I wished, he would as a Scotchman stand to it, even though it was given in an unguarded moment and taken in a sense unreasonably far-reaching. The solemn sacramental silence was broken by the dreaded question:

"John, what time is it when you get up in the morning?"

"About one o'clock," I replied in a low, meek, guilty tone of voice.

"And what kind of a time is that, getting up in the middle of the night and disturbing the whole family?"

I simply reminded him of the permission he had freely granted me to get up as early as I wished.

"I *know* it," he said, in an almost agonized tone of voice, "I *know* I gave you that miserable permission, but I never imagined that you would get up in the middle of the night."

To this I cautiously made no reply, but continued to listen for the heavenly one o'clock call, and it never failed.

After completing my self-setting sawmill I dammed one of the streams in the meadow and put the mill in operation. This invention was speedily followed by a lot of others—water wheels, curious doorlocks and latches, thermometers, hygrometers, pyrometers, clocks, a barometer, an automatic contrivance for feeding the horses at any required hour, a lamplighter and firelighter, early-or-late-rising machine, and so forth.

After the sawmill was proved and discharged from my mind, I happened to think it would be a fine thing to make a timekeeper which would tell the day of the week and the day of the month, as well as strike like a common clock and point out the hours; also to have an attachment whereby it could be connected with a bedstead to set me on my feet at any hour in the morning; also to start fires, light lamps, etc. I had learned the time laws of the pendulum from a book, but with this exception I knew nothing of timekeepers, for I had never seen the inside of any sort of clock or watch. After long brooding, the novel clock was at length completed in my mind, and was tried and found to be durable and to work well and look well before I had begun to build it in wood. I carried small parts of it in my pocket to whittle at when I was out at work on the farm, using every spare or stolen moment within reach without Father's knowing anything about it. In the middle of summer, when harvesting was in progress, the novel time machine was nearly completed. It was hidden upstairs in a spare bedroom where some tools were kept. I did the making and mending on the farm, but one day at noon, when I happened to be away, Father went upstairs for a hammer or something and discovered the mysterious machine back of the bedstead. My sister Margaret saw him on his knees examining it, and at the first opportunity whispered in my ear, "John, Father saw that thing you're making upstairs." None of the family knew what I was doing, but they knew very well that all such work was frowned on by Father, and kindly warned me of any danger that threatened my plans. The fine invention seemed doomed to destruction before its time ticking commenced, though I thought it handsome, had so long carried it in my mind, and like the nest of Burns' wee mousie it had cost me mony a weary whittling nibble. When we were at dinner several days after the sad discovery, Father began to clear his throat to speak, and I feared the doom of martyrdom was about to be pronounced on my grand clock.

"John," he inquired, "what is that thing you are making upstairs?"

I replied in desperation that I didn't know what to call it.

"What! You mean to say you don't know what you are trying to do?"

"Oh, yes," I said, "I know very well what I am doing."

"What, then, is the thing for?"

"It's for a lot of things," I replied, "but getting people up early in the morning is one of the main things it is intended for; therefore it might perhaps be called an early-rising machine."

After getting up so extravagantly early all the last memorable winter, to make a machine for getting up perhaps still earlier seemed so ridiculous that he very nearly laughed. But after controlling himself and getting command of a sufficiently solemn face and voice he said severely, "Do you not think it is very wrong to waste your time on such nonsense?"

"No," I said meekly. "I don't think I'm doing any wrong."

"Well," he replied. "I assure you I do, and if you were only half as zealous in the study of religion as you are in contriving and whittling these useless, nonsensical things, it would be infinitely better for you. I want you to be like Paul, who said that he desired to know nothing among men but Christ and Him crucified."

To this I made no reply, gloomily believing my fine machine was to be burned, but still taking what comfort I could in realizing that anyhow I had enjoyed inventing and making it.

After a few days, finding that nothing more was to be said, and that Father after all had not had the heart to destroy it, all necessity for secrecy being ended, I finished it in the half-hours that we had at noon and set it in the parlor between two chairs, hung moraine boulders that had come from the direction of Lake Superior on it for weights, and set it running. We were then hauling grain into the barn. Father at this period devoted himself entirely to the Bible and did no farm work whatever. The clock had a good loud tick, and when he heard it strike, one of my sisters told me that he left his study, went to the parlor, got down on his knees and carefully examined the machinery, which was all in plain sight, not being enclosed in a case. This he did repeatedly, and evidently seemed a little proud of my ability to invent and whittle such a thing, though careful to give no encouragement for anything more of the kind in future.

But somehow it seemed impossible to stop. Inventing and whittling faster than ever, I made another hickory clock, shaped like a scythe to symbolize the scythe of Father Time. The pendulum is a bunch of arrows symbolizing the flight of time. It hangs on a leafless mossy oak snag showing the effect of time, and on the snath is written, "All flesh is grass." This, especially the inscription, rather pleased Father, and, of course, Mother and all my sisters and brothers admired it. Like the first it indicates the days of the week and month, starts fires and beds at any given hour and minute, and, though made more than fifty years ago, is still a good timekeeper.

My mind still running on clocks, I invented a big one like a town clock with four dials, with the time-figures so large they could be read by all our immediate neighbors as well as ourselves when at work in the fields, and on the side next the house the days of the week and month were indicated. It was to be placed on the peak of the barn roof. But just as it was all but finished, Father stopped me, saying that it would bring too many people around the barn. I then asked permission to put it on the top of a black oak tree near the house. Studying the larger main branches, I thought I could secure a sufficiently rigid foundation for it, while the trimmed sprays and leaves would conceal the angles of the cabin required to shelter the works from the weather, and the two-second pendulum, fourteen feet long, could be snugly encased on the side of the trunk. Nothing about the grand, useful timekeeper, I argued, would disfigure the tree, for it would look something like a big hawk's nest. "But that," he objected, "would draw still bigger bothersome trampling crowds about the place, for who ever heard of anything so queer as a big clock on the top of a tree?" So I had to lay aside its big wheels and cams and rest content with the pleasure of inventing it, and looking at it in my mind and listening to the deep solemn throbbing of its long two-second pendulum with its two old axes back-to-back for the bob.

One of my inventions was a large thermometer made of an iron rod, about three feet long and five eighths of an inch in diameter, that had formed part of a wagon box. The expansion and contraction of this rod was multiplied by a series of levers made of strips of hoop iron. The pressure of the rod against the levers was kept constant by a small counterweight, so that the slightest change in the length of the rod was instantly shown on a dial about three feet wide multiplied about thirty-two thousand times. The zero point was gained by packing the rod in wet snow. The scale was so large that the big black hand on the white-painted dial could be seen distinctly and the temperature read while we were plowing in the field below the house. The extremes of heat and cold caused the hand to make several revolutions. The number of these revolutions was indicated on a small dial marked on the larger one. This thermometer was fastened on the side of the house, and was so sensitive that when anyone approached it within four or five feet the heat radiated from the observer's body caused the hand of the dial to move so fast that the motion was plainly visible, and when he stepped back, the hand moved slowly back to its normal position. It was regarded as a great wonder by the neighbors and even by my own all-Bible father.

Glossary

A

abilities   power to do some special thing; skill

abstract   a brief statement of main ideas of an article, book, etc.; a summary

academic action   suspension from the university after a period of extended probation

academic code of student conduct   the academic standards for your university

academic probation   goes into effect if a student's cumulative grade average is ten quality points below a 2.0 or C average

accuracy   refers to correctness

acronyms   words created from the first letter or the first few letters of the items on a list

acrostics   phrases or sentences created from the first letter or first few letters of items on a list

active listening   conscious control of the listening process through preplanned strategies

adult   one of the three inner dialogue voices, the one who thinks analytically and solves problems rationally

almanacs   annual publications which include calendars, weather forecasts, and other useful tabular information

analysis   a stage of critical thinking that requires an examination of information by breaking it into parts

antonym   a word that has the opposite meaning of another

appeals   the right to contest academic disciplinary actions

appendices   additions at the end of a book or document; supplements

application   a stage of critical thinking that requires using information concerning the process, idea, and theory, etc. appropriately to accomplish what is required

aptitude test   an examination which predicts future performance in a given activity

aptitudes   natural tendencies or talents

assumption   an inference made with the use of given facts and global knowledge

atlas   a book of maps

auditory practice   repeating aloud information that you are trying to remember or discussing it with another student

aural   acquiring information through reading and writing

author card   a catalog card filed under the author's last name which contains other bibliographical information

B

background knowledge what you know about a topic

balance sheets a mechanism that helps you logically weigh your available options

bar graph a graphic in which bars indicate the frequency of data; shows quantitative comparisons; a histogram

behavior modification a technique to change behavior by systematically rewarding desirable behavior and either ignoring or punishing undesirable behavior

bias an opinion before there is a reason for it; prejudice

bibliography a list of books or articles consulted or referred to by an author in the preparation of a manuscript

brain dominance the side of your brain that influences your thinking the most

brainstorming a method of dialoging with yourself in which you list as many possible solutions as you can

breadth suggests that you look at more than one viewpoint, kind of information, implication, or other aspect of thinking

burnout physical or mental exhaustion of a person's supply of energy, ambition, or ideas

C

call number a classification number assigned to library material to indicate its location in the library

card catalog an alphabetical listing with one or more cards for each item

cartographer one who draws maps or charts; a mapmaker

cause/effect in a communication, a stated or implied association between some outcome and the condition which brought it about

chapter maps provide verbal information in the context of a visual arrangement of ideas; show relationships among concepts and express an author's patterns of thought

charts information arranged by rows and columns; also called tables

child one of the three inner dialogue voices, the part of you that wants to have fun

chronology arrangement of data according to group features

chunks groups of information that are clustered together in order to remember through association

circle graph a graphic that shows how a whole unit is divided into parts

clarity clearness of thought; the first standard against which you judge thinking

clipping file vertical file; source of print materials which have not been published in book form

closure the condition of being ended, finished, or concluded; the process by which incomplete figures, ideas, or situations tend to be completed mentally or perceived as complete

college catalog a book describing the services, curricula, courses, faculty, and other information pertaining to a post-secondary institution

comparison/contrast the organization of information for placing like or unlike ideas, situations, or characters together

completeness requires that you have all of the information to form a comprehensive picture

comprehensive tests examinations that cover all materials presented in class over the course of an entire term

concepts connected and organized networks or webs of information

conclusions decisions, judgments, or opinions reached by reasoning or inferring

consequences a series of given outcomes

consistency reliability of information in both spoken and written forms

coping meeting or encountering success in overcoming problems or difficulties

coping mechanisms strategies which help you manage stress more effectively

cramming studying rapidly under pressure for an examination; usually done at the last minute instead of over time

creativity ultimate form of synthesis; taking all available information, creating hypotheses, drawing conclusions, and coming up with a new idea or product

credibility evaluating whether or not information is fact or opinion

credit hour the quantitative measure of recognition given to a course, usually based on the number of times a course meets in one week of a regular semester

criteria matrices mechanisms that allow you to see options and evaluate them

critical thinking thinking logically about information, people, and choices in order to make reasonable, informed decisions about learning, relationships, and life

critic one of three inner dialogue voices, the part of you that denounces you

cross-references information which refers from one item, passage, or text to another

curricula the total program of studies of a school

curve of forgetting a line diagram which shows the relationship between recall of information without review and the amount of time since the material's presentation; also called the Ebbinghaus Curve

D

data base collection of data arranged for ease of retrieval, especially by a computer

definition a type of context clue in which punctuation marks that indicate that the meaning of an unknown word follows directly

definitional assumption concluding that everyone defines qualitative words the same way you do

denial a defense mechanism that involves pretending that a problem doesn't exist or isn't important

depth consideration of the level of complexity of the thought

derivations the use of affixes to build new words from a root or base word, often with a change in the part of speech of the word

Dewey decimal system library classification scheme which divides all knowledge into ten major groups by subject, each of which can be subdivided infinitely

diagram plan, drawing, figure or combination thereof made to show clearly a thing or how it works

direct quote showing a person's exact words

distractions diversions which cause a turning away from the focus of attention

distress a type of stress that hurts your performance

distributed practice a method of developing a skill by setting task or time limits (practicing a specified amount of time or information each day) rather than attempting to cram much practice into a small period of time; spaced study

disuse release of information that is seldom used from memory

E

ellipsis the omission of a word or phrase shown by a series of marks (. . .)

endnotes a form of footnotes which occurs at the end of a book or document

(dictionary) entry a term listed alphabetically, usually in boldface, in a dictionary

enumeration/sequence placement of information in a systematic organizational pattern according to time or rank

ESL students students whose native languages aren't English and who are enrolled in a program for learning English language skills (English as a Second Language)

essay a brief paper expressing opinion about a single topic; theme

etymology the study of the origins of words

euphemisms words or phrases used to soften the reality of negative statements or to disguise the truth

eustress the type of stress that energizes you and drives you to be your best

evaluation judgement, the highest level of thinking; requires being able to recall, translate, interpret, apply, analyze, and synthesize to judge and evaluate effectively

expert opinions   judgments of those who have knowledge and skill in particular subjects

exploration   evaluation of oneself and one's career possibilities

external motivation   behavior directed toward satisfaction through anticipated rewards or punishment

F

fact   information based on direct evidence, a statement of truth

fairness   unbiased coverage of a topic

fantasy   belief that one can have any career

feature analysis table   a table analyzing characteristics rather than amounts; a quality table

fiction   one of two types of writing; not based on fact or truth; written to entertain

flowchart   a drawing which shows the steps in a complicated process

footnotes   notes at the bottom of a page about something on the page

free elective   a course which is not specified in a degree program

full-time student   student carrying enough credit hours during a term to be considered as having a complete load of coursework

G

gazetteer   dictionary or index of geographical terms

general reference maps   maps which give general geographic information

government documents   library holdings consisting of material published by U.S. government agencies

grade point average (GPA)   average of numerical values assigned to course grades

graphics   drawings or reproductions of drawings, maps, pictures, graphs, etc.

graphs   diagrams or charts in which various data is presented through differing lengths of bars (bar graphs), dots connected to form lines (line graphs), or pie-shaped wedges to form circles (pie or circle graphs; symbolic representations of information that show quantitative comparisons between two or more kinds of information

guide words   words that appear at the top of each page in a dictionary to aid in locating entries quickly

H

histogram   a graphic in which bars indicate the frequency of data; shows quantitative comparisons; a bar graph

Hypermedia links   key words to multimedia information

Hypertext   like menus; key words that form doorways to additional text information

hypothesis   an educated guess; an idea of what will happen next in a particular situation or of what the consequences of a given action will be

I

idea or concept map a method of notetaking or processing notes; a diagram, similar to a flow chart, which shows relationships between and among concepts

implications a series of possible outcomes

inductive outline a process in which you reduce information from major concepts to specific main ideas

inferences statements or predictions about the unknown based on the known

informal dialogues conversations which allow you to explore new points of view, acquire new information, and hear what others see as the implications of various issues

information knowledge which comes from the data you acquire from life—what you see, hear, smell, taste, touch, feel, read, or experience

information matrices tables, pictures, or diagrams of information; charts

interest inventory an informal checklist for exploring preferences for a given activity

interests feelings of wanting to know, see, do, own, share in, or take part in

interference memory loss caused by the process of conflicting information

interlibrary loan a method by which one library borrows an item from the holdings of another library

internal motivation self-directed incentives for behavior

interpretation the ability to explain events through a knowledge of the connections that exist among ideas

intramural sports athletic events other than varsity competition involving members of the same school, college, or organization

introduction/summary placement of information for the purpose of initiating or ending a discussion of a topic

J

justifiability a rationale based on a list of logically supportive reasons

K

key a list of words or phrases giving an explanation of symbols and/or abbreviations used on a map; a legend

kinesthetic acquiring information through the use of physical experiences

kinesthetic perception the drawings made from words or phrases that appeal to the senses; physical imagery; mnemonigraphs

L

lecture patterns   the organizational pattern of a lecture (similar to text patterns)

left brain   cognitive processing of information in sequential, linear, logical ways

legend   a list of words or phrases giving an explanation of symbols and/or abbreviations used on a map

Library of Congress (LC) system   a method of classifying publications using letters and numerals which allows for infinite expansion

line graphs   graphics used to show quantitative trends for one or more items over time

loaded words   words or phrases that make people, issues, and things appear worse than they might really be

logic   a form of thinking or problem solving that follows a line of reasoning that others can understand

logical inference   a conclusion that cannot be avoided; for example, if a=b and b=c, then a=c

long-term goal   an objective which requires a lengthy time committment

long-term memory   permanent memory; last stage of memory processing

M

main entry card   the full catalog record of an item in the library's collection, often the author card

mantras   relaxing words repeated in a meditative manner

map   a two-dimensional graphic of a specific location

meditation   a form of relaxation, it involves narrowing your conscious mind until anxiety wanes

microfiche   a microfilm sheet containing rows of written or printed pages in reduced form

microfiche reader   a device which makes any microform large enough to be easily read

microforms   consist of microfiche, microfilm, ultrafiche; reduced forms of books, journals, articles, etc.

MIND   an acronym that helps you systematically work through the process of critical thinking

mnemonigraph   the drawings made from words or phrases that appeal to the senses; kinesthetic perception; physical imagery

multisensory   the combination of two or more senses (sensory preferences)

Myers-Briggs Type Indicator (MBTI)   an evaluation of personality types, based on the work of Carl Jung

N

need   something that is needed or desired

newspaper index   an index to selected daily/weekly published newspapers

non-comprehensive   describes examinations that do not cover all materials presented in class over the course of an entire term; examinations covering only a specific amount of material

non sequitur   a conclusion or statement that makes no sense; not supported by facts or preceding information

nonfiction   prose based upon fact; written to explain, argue, or describe rather than to entertain

note-taking outline   outline made before reading a chapter as preview for the lecture

O

objective test   a type of test in which a student selects an answer from several choices provided by the instructor; included among these are multiple choice, true/false, matching and some fill-in-the-blank

opinion   a judgement or viewpoint

outlining   a formal or informal pattern of ideas

overlearning   overlapping study of information to reinforce initial learning

P

paraphrase   a summary; contains an unbiased version of what the author said

parenthetical references   statements which help explain or qualify information

parody   copy of series works or phrases through satire or burlesque

part-time student   student carrying less than the minimum number of credit hours to be considered full-time

peer pressure   a controlling mechanism that regulates group membership through conformity and loss of personal freedom

perception   reception of information that is understood in memory

periodical indicies   alphabetical listings, journals and magazines that list the authors, titles, and subjects of articles in periodicals

personality   your personal preferences based on the Myers-Briggs Type Indicator or other instrument

perspective   point of view

pictorial graphs   graphics that use symbols to show quantitative amounts; symbol graphs

plagiarism   an idea, expression, plot, etc. taken from another and used as one's own

point of view   the position from which one looks at something

precision   refers to exactness

previewing surveying to get the main idea about something that will be read later

primary source original documents or first-person accounts of an event

prime study time the time of day or night when a student is most mentally alert for learning and remembering information

procrastination the act or habit of putting tasks off until later

projection defense mechanism in which the blame for a problem is placed on someone or something else

propaganda tells only one side of an issue to make you believe only that particular viewpoint

psychoactive drugs drugs that lead to psychological dependence, the feeling that you need a drug to stay "normal" or "happy"

puns use of words or phrases to suggest more than one meaning

purpose intention for reading

Q

quality points numerical value assigned to each letter grade from "A" to "F" when given as the final grade in a course; used to calculate grade point average

quality table a table analyzing characteristics rather than amounts; a feature analysis table

questions ways to set purpose in thinking and reading

R

rationalize defense mechanism which offers acceptable excuses in place of the real ones

ready reference books held in reserve by a library for patrons to use only while they remain in the library

realistic period career development stage consisting of exploration, crystallization, and specification

recall the lowest level of understanding; requires little more than auditory or visual memory skills

reception receiving information into short-term memory without understanding

recitation silent, oral, or written repetition of information to increase recall

registration the part of memory consisting of reception, perception, and selection; first stage of memory processing

relevance; relevancy the state of being applicable, appropriate, pertinent, useful, etc.

report a formal written presentation of facts

repression defense mechanism in which the cause of stress is blocked from memory

research paper a lengthy, well documented written presentation

reserve books books held in a special area of the library that can be checked out only for designated periods of time

rewards recompense for something that you do or say

right brain cognitive processing which synthesizes rather than analyzes, it uses holistic, perceptual understanding

rough draft an author's first attempt at writing a particular manuscript

S

scale of distance a representation of size or space on maps; indicates the relationship between the distance of one place shown on a map and this distance in actuality

scan reading quickly to find specific information; reading for specific answers

schedule a written or printed statement of fixed times or appointments; a timetable

scope range of application

secondary source second-person accounts of an event

selection a deliberate processing of information into memory or a deliberate disregard of it

self-talk the dialogue inside your mind as your think to yourself about how to act or feel about a situation

semantic practice writing or diagramming information that you are trying to remember

sensory preferences concern the way or ways in which you like to acquire information

short-term goals an objective which requires a brief time commitment

short-term memory immediate or brief memory; second stage of memory processing

significance refers to importance

skim reading quickly to find main ideas

spaced study a method of learning which requires setting task or time limits (practicing a specified amount of time or information each day) rather than attempting to cram much practice into a small period of time; distributed practice

special purpose maps maps which highlight some specific natural or man-made feature; a thematic map

specification period final career decision

specificity a limiting of details so that you exclude particulars to identify a single item

stacks shelves in the library for holding books and journals

standard the criteria against which you judge thinking

stress a physical or emotional factor that causes tension; anxiety

style   the mix of attributes that defines you

style manual   reference for the preparation of a manuscript

subject card   filed under the subject of the material, this card contains the full catalog record of an item in the library's collection

subject development   the organization of information for discussing a topic and its related details

subjective   describes tests that require you to supply the answers in your own words

subjective tests   type of exam in which students must provide an original written answer; included among these are essay and some fill-in-the-blank questions

summary   a condensed statement or paragraph that contains only the essential ideas of a longer statement, paragraph, or passage

symbol graphs   graphics which uses symbols to show quantitative amounts; pictorial graphs

symbols   an idea or concept that stands for or suggests another idea or concept by means of association or relationship

synonym   a word which has a similar meaning to that of another word

synthesis   the combination of parts or elements into a whole

T

tables   systematic listings of information in rows and columns

tentative period   one's realization that some careers are inappropriate goals while others are more appropriate goals

term papers   lengthy, well documented written presentations of information

terms   specialized or technical vocabulary in a specific subject

test   an examination; a way of evaluating how well a student has mastered the material presented in class or in the textbook. These examinations may be comprehensive or non-comprehensive. There are two types of questions that may appear on a test, objective and subjective.

text labeling   strategy which helps you identify relationships and summarize information

text marking   strategy which involves finding important information and highlighting or underlining it

text structure   the way in which a written text is presented (outline, headings, sub-headings, etc.)

thematic maps   maps which highlight some specific natural or man-made feature; special purpose maps

theme   a brief paper expressing opinion about a single topic; essay

thesaurus   book of synonyms and sometimes antonyms

thesis statement   similar to a topic sentence, this sentence contains the main idea to be covered in a paper

time lines graphic outlines of sequenced information; a chronology of important dates or events

time management a system for scheduling commitments efficiently

title card filed under the title of the material, this card contains the full catalog record of an item in the library's collection

transition words terms that signal the identity and flow of a lecture's pattern

translation the ability to convert information into your own words while retaining the essence of the idea

trends changes in direction over time

U

unabridged dictionary a dictionary whose number of entries have not been limited or reduced

V

values that which is of worth/importance to an individual

verbatim information information that you must remember word for word—exactly as it was written or said

vertical file clipping file; source of print materials which have not been published in book form

visual acquiring information through the use of visual perception

visual practice silently reading information that you are trying to remember

visualization uses imagination to put positive messages into action

W

weasel words words that show the possibility of other options and lack exactness

working bibliography a list of the books or articles consulted or referred to by an author as the rough draft is written

working memory part of memory where information is processed; limited in size; third stage of memory processing

Y

yearbooks published yearly, this book contains a summary or review of facts

Index

Page numbers appearing in italic type refer to figures, tables, exercises, etc.

A

Abilities used in setting goals, 63
Abstracts, 463, *464*
Academic actions, 23, 25
Academic classification, *16*
Academic disciplines, *49*
Academic freedom, 65–66
Academic policies and regulations, 15, *16*
Academic probation. *See* Probation
Academic standards, *16*, 27–28
Accuracy in critical thinking, *394*, 396
Achieving goals, 69–73
Acronyms as memory aids, 318–19
Acrostics as memory aids, 318–19
Admissions information in catalog, *16*
Adult as inner role in self-talk, 66, *67*
Adult students, 34
Alcohol, use of, 141–42, *142*
Alienation, ways to decrease, 33–37
Almanacs, 437
Analogies, *506*
Anxiety
   about coursework, 122–23
   test, 145–50
Appeals, student, 28, 31–32
Appendices, 463, *464*
Applied courses, *49*
Aptitudes used in setting goals, 62
Aptitude tests, 62
Association in memory processing, 315–21, *317*
Assumptions
   in critical thinking, 364, 375–76, 384–85
Atlases, 438
Auditory practice as memory aid, 323
Aural preference, impact on effective learning, 5, 7, *10*
Author cards, 419, *420*
Averages, grade point. *See* Grade point averages

B

Background knowledge
   effect on inferences and interpretations, 384–85
   use to maximize learning, 222–24
   in vocabulary development, *217–19*
Balance sheets as decision-making tools, 389, *389*
Bar graphs, 280, *281*, *282*, *283–84*
Behavior modification, 72–73, 324
Believing goals, 66–69
Bias, evaluating, 369–71, *372*
Bibliographies
   creating working, 428–29
   in research papers, 463, *465*
Bloom's taxonomy of thinking, *310*
Body language in the classroom, 30
Brain dominance
   applied to time management, 57, 59, *60*
   attributes and applications to learning, 11, *12*
   graphics and, 265, 267
   in vocabulary development, *306–7*
Brainstorming in decision making, 388, *389*
Breadth in critical thinking, *394*, 398
Burnout, ways to avoid, 91–92
Bursar's office, *19*

C

Calendar(s), academic, *16*
Call numbers, 419, *420*, 421
Campus involvement, types, 38–44
Campus services. *See* services, campus
Card catalogs
   computerized, 421–24, *422–25*
   manual file, 419–21
Career decisions
   campus offices offering assistance, *19*, 62
   and choice of major, 100

Cartographers, 293
Catalogs, card. *See* Card catalogs
Catalogs, college, 15, *16–17*
Cause/effect
    as lecture pattern, 185, *186*
    as text pattern, 242, *243*
CD-ROM searches, 441–42
Chapter maps to show relations
    among concepts, 175–77, *177–79*
Chart(s), 269–79, *280*
    steps in making, *279*
    to synthesize research information,
    472, *473–80*
    vs. graphs, 290
Cheating, 27–28, *494–95*
Child as inner role in self-talk, 66, *67*
Chronology, time line as, 276
Circle graphs, *286*, 286–87, *288*
Clarity in critical thinking, *394*,
    394–95
Classroom interactions
    with classmates, 39–40
    with instructors, 29–30
Clipping files, 437
Code(s) of student conduct, aca-
    demic, 28
College catalogs. *See* Catalogs,
    college
College community. *See* Higher
    education
Communication
    in the classroom, 30, 39–40
    with instructors, 30–31
    in study groups, 40–41
Commuting students, 36–37
Comparison/contrast
    as lecture pattern, 185, *186*
    as text pattern, 242, *242*
Completeness in critical thinking,
    394, 398
Composition, standard handbooks
    of, *486*
Computerized card catalogs, 421–24,
    422–25
Conceiving goals, 61–66
Concept maps. *See* Idea maps
Concept(s), 364
Conclusions in critical thinking,
    386–89, 391
Confidence, ways to increase, 69,
    121–24, *123*

Consequences, considering
    in reaching decisions, 386–89, 391
Consistency in critical thinking, *394*,
    398–99
Coping mechanisms for stress, defen-
    sive (negative), 118–19, 121, *121*
Coping strategies for stress, positive,
    121–24, *122–23*
Cornell system of notetaking, 205–6,
    206
Costs of higher education, ways to
    meet, 38
Course descriptions, *16*
Courseloads, full- *vs.* part-time, *17*
Course numbers, *17*
Courses, choosing, 99–100
Cramming, 327
Creativity in right-brain processing, *12*
Credibility in critical thinking, 366–67
Credit hours, use in computing GPA
    of, 23
Credit(s), transfer, *17*, 34
Crisis situations affecting studies,
    132–33, *133–34*
Criteria matrices as decision-making
    tools, 391, *391*
Critical thinking, 360–412. *See also*
    components of MIND process
Critic as inner role in self-talk, 66, *67*
Criticism by instructors, 30
Cross references on library cards, 421
Cumulative averages. *See* Grade point
    averages
Curve of forgetting, 191

D
Database searches, 441–42
Databases of library collections, 419
Deadlines, tips for meeting, *60*
Dean of students, *19*
Decision(s)
    in critical thinking, 386–92
    enacting, 391–92, *392*
    procedures in making, 387–89, *389*,
    391, *391*
Degree requirements, *16*
Denial as response to stress, 119,
    121, *121*
Depth in critical thinking, *394*, 398
Dewey decimal system, 419, *420*,
    427, *427*

Diagrams, 267–69
Dictionaries
  in library research, 437
  use and choice of, *452–53, 456–57*
Diet to reduce stress, 135, *137*
Disabilities, students with, 37
Distractions
  effect on listening, 184–85
  tips on handling, 83–84
Distress, 117
Distributed practice as memory aid,
  323–24
Disuse, effect on memory of, 327–28
Diversity, 33–38
  effect on point of view, 377–78
  of values in college, 65–66
"Drop," defined, *17*
Drugs, recreational, 140–42, *141–44*

E
Electives, *17*, 99–100
Employment, on-campus, 41
Enumeration/sequence
  as lecture pattern, 185, *186*
  as text pattern, *239*, 240, *241*
ESL (English as a second language)
  students, 35–36
Essay exams. *See under* Exams
Essays, 462
Euphemisms, 371
Eustress, 117
Evaluation of goals, 71
Exams
  comprehensive v.
    noncomprehensive, 330
  essay
    sample question and responses,
      /b336/B, 335–37
    steps in taking, *335*
  final, 348
  general suggestions for preparing
    for and taking, 329–32
  learning from returned, 146, *147,*
    148–49
  makeup, 150
  objective
    described and illustrated, 329, *330*
    POSSE study plan for, 338, *338–39*
    preparing for and taking, 337–46
  open-book, 347, *347*
  specialized, 347–48

  steps in taking, *331*
  stress concerning, 145–46, 148–50
  subjective
    described and illustrated, 329, *330*
    PORPE study plan for, 332,
      333–34
    preparing for and taking, 332–37
  take-home, *347*, 347–48
Exercise to reduce stress, 140
Experience, learning by, 5, 7, *10*
Expulsion for academic dishonesty, 28
Extracurricular activities, *17*
Extraversion (E), 3, *6, 58*

F
Facts, identifying
  in critical thinking, 367–68
Faculty. *See* Instructors
Fairness in critical thinking, *394,*
  398–99
Fear
  in relations with classmates, 40
  of speaking in class, 30
Feature analysis table(s), 270, *270*
Feeling (F), 3–4, *7, 58*
Financial aid, *19*, 38
Flowcharts, 273, *274–75*
  steps in creating, *279*
Forgetting, 327–28
Fraternities, 44
Freshmen, *17*
Full-time status, *17*, 96–97

G
Gazetteers, 438
Geographic maps, 291–94, *293–95*
  general reference, 292, *293*, 294
  special purpose or thematic,
    292–94, *294*
Glossaries, *453–56*
Goals, 61–145
  conceiving, believing, and
    achieving, 61–73
  later evaluation of, 71
  long-term *vs.* short-term, 70, 89
  setting, 61–66, 70–71
  techniques for implementing, 75–85
Government documents, 438
Grade point averages (GPAs), 23,
  24, 25
Grading systems, 23

Graphics, 262–307. *See also* specific types
Graphs, 280–90. *See also* specific types
  steps in analyzing, *281*
  steps in creating, 290
  types, 280
  vs. charts, 290
Greek groups, 44

H

Hearing, learning by, 5, 7, *10*
Hierarchy of needs (Maslow), 64, *65*
Higher education, 1–53
  assimilation into community of, 32–44
  rights and responsibilities within, 15–32
  student as citizen in, 2–14
Highlighting. *See* Text marking
Histograms, 280
Honesty, academic, 27–28, 494, *494–95*
Humanities courses, *49*
Hypermedia links, 443
Hypertext links, 443

I

Idea maps, 296–99, *297–302*
  branching, *299*
  steps in constructing, *301*
  structure patterns and corresponding elements in, 297, *297*
  types of structures, *300*
  web, *298*
Imagery as memory aid, 317–18, *318*
Implementing goals, 75–85
Implications, considering, 386–89, 391
Incomplete (I) grades, 31, 150
Inductive outline(s), 236, *237–38*
Inferences in critical thinking, 384–85
Informal dialogues as decision-making tools, 387–88
Information, evaluation and use in critical thinking of, 345–72, *372*
Information processing. *See* Memory
Information superhighway, 442–43
Inquiry in critical thinking, 378–82
Instructors
  interactions with, 29–30, 31

maximizing student understanding of, 189, 192–94, *195–96*
  student choice of preferred, 98–99
Interest groups on campus, 43
Interests used in setting goals, 63–64
Interest tests, 64
Interference
  effect on memory, 327–28
  study breaks to avoid, 324
Interlibrary loan(s), 416
Internet, the, 442–43
Interpretations in critical thinking, 384–85
Intramural sports, 44
Introduction/summary
  lecture pattern, 185, *186*
  text pattern, 237–38, *239–40*
Introspection in critical thinking, 384–85
Introversion (I), 3, *6, 58*
Intuition (N), 3–4, *6, 58*

J

Job placement office, *20*
Jobs on campus, 41
Judging (J), 3–4, *7, 58*
Juniors, *17*
Justifiability in critical thinking, *394, 399*

K

Keys
  in line graphs, 285
  in maps, 292, 294, *294*
Kinesthetic perception as memory aid, 318
Kinesthetic preference, impact on effective learning of, 5, 7, *10*

L

Labeling main ideas, 233–35. *See also* Text labeling
Learning (resource) center, *20*
Learning style(s), 2–11, *12*
  brain dominance, 11, *12*
  MBTI personality types, 3–4, *6–7*
  sensory preferences, 5, 7, *10*
Lectures
  following patterns to understand, 185–86, *186*

maximizing understanding of, *195–96*

notetaking according to type, 197–98

Left-brain dominance. *See* Brain dominance

Legends

in line graphs, 285

in maps, 292, 294, *294*

Liberal education, 32

Librarians, assistance provided by, 416–17

Libraries

finding information in, 434–43

organization of, 419–27

standard research methods in, 446, *447–48*

Library and research skills, 414–58

Library of Congress (LC) system, 419, 427, *427*

Line graphs, 285, *285*

LISAN plan for notetaking, *212–13*

Listening and notetaking skills, 164–219

Listening in class, 177–96

identifying important information, 185–86, 189

levels, *179, 182*

maintaining concentration, 184–85

recall of previous lectures to assist in, 190–91

Loaded words to sway beliefs, 371

Location as memory aid, 319–20

Logical links as memory aids, 317

Logic in critical thinking, *394*, 399

Long-term memory (LTM), 316, 327–28

LTM (long-term memory), 316, 327–28

M

Main entry cards, 419

Main ideas

finding in text, 233–35

using inductive outline to discover, 236, *237–38*

Major(s), choosing, 99–100

Makeup exams, 150

Making up work to improve grades, 31

Maps, 291–99, *300–302*. *See also* specific types

Marks used in grading, 23

Maslow's hierarchy of needs, motivation based on, 72, *73*

Materials in critical thinking, 363–78

MBTI (Myers-Briggs Type Indicator)

personality types, 3–4, *6–7*

applied to time management, 57, *58*

Measurability of goals, 70

Media

taking notes from lecture, 207–8

use in lectures, 198, *199*

Meditation to reduce stress, 130, *130–31*

Memory, 308–59

association in, 316–21

cognitive interview to stimulate, *349*

depth of processing, 310–12

effects of practice on, 323–27

factors in forgetting, 327–28

long-term (LTM), 316

overlearning for, 326, *326*

registration in, 313–14

short-term (STM), 314

stages in, 312–16

working, 315

Metaphors, *505*

Microfiche, library catalogs on, 421

MIND process. *See also* individual steps

applied to standards of thinking, *394*

in critical thinking, 362–63, *363*

Minority students, 33–34

Mnemonic devices, 316–21

Mnemonigraph, 318

Motivation, 72–73, *73*

Multisensory approach to learning, 7

Myers-Briggs Type Indicator (MBTI)

personality types, 3–4, *6–7*

applied to time management, 57, *58*

N

Natural sciences courses, *49*

Needs, personal

use in setting goals, 64–65

Newspaper indices, 437–38

Nontraditional students, 33–38. *See also* specific types

Notetaking, 201–10

constructing outlines before class, *173*

Cornell system of, 205–6, *206*
criteria for evaluation, *211*
developing a personal system, 202, *202–4*
LISAN plan, *212–13*
for research, 429–30, *431–33*
taping and borrowing in, 208–10
Notetaking and listening skills, 164–219
Nutrition to reduce stress, 135, *137*

O
Objective exams. *See under* Exams
Objectivity in critical thinking, 369
Off-campus resources, 37
Office hours, instructors', 31
Offices, campus, *19–20. See also* specific offices
Older adult students, 34
On-line searches, 441–42
Opinions, evaluating, 368–69
Organization
    of class material by student, 197–98
    of information
        background knowledge used in, 266
        in memory processing, 315
        through outlining, 207, *208*
    of the library, 419–27, *427*
    patterns in research papers, *482*
    skills for commuting students, 37
    spatial
        for study time, 85
        tips, *60*
Outlining
    inductive, 236
    in lecture notes, 207, *208*
    to synthesize research information, 472
    through text previewing, 173, *173–74,* 175
Overlearning to reinforce information, 326, *326*

P
Paraphrases in notetaking, 429–30, *432–33*
Part-time status, *17,* 96–97
Passive notetaking, 208–10
Peer pressure as motivation for achieving goals, 73

Perceiving (P), 3–4, *7, 58*
Perception in memory processing, 313
Periodical indices, 435, *436–37*
Pictorial graphs, 282, *284*
Pie charts, *286,* 286–87, *288*
Placement offices, *19–20*
Plagiarism, unintentional *vs.* intentional, 27–28, 494, *494–95*
Point of view
    in critical thinking, 364, 377–78
    effect on inferences and interpretations, 384–85
PORPE study plan for subjective exams, 332, *333–34*
Positive thinking as coping strategy for stress, 121–24
POSSE study plan for objective exams, 338, *338–39*
Postsecondary education. *See* Higher education
Practice as memory aid, 323–27
Precision in critical thinking, *394,* 396
Predictions in critical reading, 380
Prerequisites, *17*
Presentations, suggestions for making, 498–99, *499–501*
Previewing
    to aid memory, 324
    before class, 166–77
    in SQ3R process, 222–24
    steps in, *167*
Primary sources, 367
Probation
    for academic dishonesty, 28
    for poor grades, 23
Procrastination, avoiding, 86–95
Professors. *See* Instructors
Projection as response to stress, 121, *121*
Propaganda, 370–71, *372*
Psychoactive drugs, use and abuse of, 140–42, *141–44*
Punishment as motivation, 73

Q
Qualitative terms, 369, 376
Quality points in computing GPA, 23
Quality table(s), 270, *271*
Quantitative terms, 368
Quarter system, *17*
Questioning as Step 2 in SQ3R, 225

Questions
    as aids to critical reading, *225, 380*
    evaluating use in SQ3R, 247
    guidelines for classroom, 30
Quotes, direct
    in notetaking, 429–30, *432*

R
Rationalization as response to stress,
    121, *121*
Reader's Guide to Periodical Literature,
    435, *436–37*
Reading
    improving comprehension in, *248*
    purposes for, *379, 379–80*
    as Step 3 in SQ3R, 225–42, *226, 243*
    strategies for groups, *250*
Reading/writing preference, impact
    on effective learning of, 5, 7, *10*
Recall of previous lectures, 190–91
Reception in memory processing, 313
Recitation as memory aid, 325
Reciting as Step 4 in SQ3R, 247, *248*
Reentry students, 37–38
Reference lists in research papers,
    463, *465*
References
    checklist for choosing relevant, *428*
    computerized, 441–43
    evaluating, *430–31*
    general, 435, 437–38
    parenthetical, 482–83
    with special content, 440–41
Registrar's office, *20*
Registration, college, 34
Registration of information in
    memory processing, 313–14
Rehearsal in memory processing, 315
Relaxation to reduce stress, *129,*
    129–30, *131–32*
Relevance in critical thinking, 365,
    394, 396–97
Repression as response to stress,
    119, *121*
Research and library skills, 414–58
Research methods to begin projects,
    428–30, *431–33, 446, 447–48*
Research paper(s), 460–506
    body of text, 482–83
    first draft, 481–83
    introductions, 481–82

narrowing subjects, 466–69
organizational patterns, *482*
parts, 462–63, *464–65*
purpose, 466, *467*
scope, 467–68, *468*
second and final drafts,
    483–85, 487
selecting subjects, 465–69
steps in writing, *496*
summaries, 483
synthesizing sources for, 471–72,
    473–80
thesis statements, 469
titles, 469
types, 462–63
writing process, 481–95
writing schedules for, 496–97, *498*
Reserve books, 435
Residency, *17*
Rest to reduce stress, 139–40
Retention in the institution, 38–39
Returning adult students, 34
Reviewing as Step 5 in SQ3R, 249
Revisions to research papers, 485,
    487, *488*
Rewards for achieving goals, 72–73
Right-brain dominance. *See* Brain
    dominance

S
Scales of distance in maps, 292–93
Scanning, 429
Schedule(s). *See also* Time
    management
    choosing a workable, 97–98
    daily, 79–80
    maintaining balance in, 103–4
    term, 75–76, *76*
    weekly, 78–79, *79*
    for writing research papers,
        496–97, *498*
Scholarships, applying for, 38
Sciences, natural, *49*
Sciences, social, *49*
Searches
    database, 441–42
    on-line and CD-ROM, 441–42
    using computerized library catalog,
        423–24, *423–25*
Secondary sources, 367–68
See references on library cards, 421

Selection in memory processing, 313–14, 315

Self-talk
  to build confidence, 66, *67*, 122–24, *123*
  to counter distractions, 185

Semantic practice as memory aid, 323

Semester system, *17*

Seniors, *17*

Sensing (S), 3, *6, 58*

Sensory preferences
  impact on effective learning, 5, 7, *10*
  use in time management, 59

Service organizations on campus, 43–44

Services, campus, 15, *19–20*, 33–35, 37

Shorthand system for notes, *203–4*

Short-term memory (STM), 314

Sight, learning by, 5, 7, *10*

Significance in critical thinking, *394*, 396–97

Similes, *505*

Skimming, 429

Small group learning, 40

Social organizations on campus, 44

Social sciences courses, *49*

Sophomores, *17*

Sororities, 44

Sources, primary *vs.* secondary, 367–68

Spaced study as memory aid, 323–24

Special interest groups on campus, 43

Specificity in critical thinking, *394*, 396

Speeches, suggestions for making, 498–99, *499–501*

SQ3R plan, 220–60. *See also* individual steps
  steps in, *223*

Standards
  for achievement, 23
  for critical thinking, 392–99
  for honesty, 27–28

STM (short-term memory), 314

Stress, 114–63
  common sources, *118–19*
  concerning exams, 145–50
  definitions, causes, and symptoms, 114–33, *134*
  physical and psychological signs, *120*
  positive coping strategies, 121–24, *122–23*

unhelpful responses, 118–19, 121, *121*
  ways to reduce, 35, 135, *137*, 139–40

Student services, 15, *16, 19*

Study groups
  to enhance memory in learning, 325–26
  establishing, 40–41, *42–43, 106*
  reading strategies for, *250*

Study partners to enhance memory in learning, 325–26

Study skills
  after-class reading and evaluation, 210, *211*
  assistance at learning center, *20*
  impact of learning style, *10, 12*
  notetaking, 201–10
  previewing text before class, 166–77
  students' organization of class material, 197–98
  using returned exams to improve, 146, *147*

Study time, prime, 83–85

Style manuals, *484–86*

Subject cards, 419, *420*

Subject development/definition
  lecture pattern, 185, *186*
  text pattern, *239*, 239–40, *241*

Subjective exams. *See under* Exams

Substance use and abuse, 140–42, *141–44*

"Suitcase" students. *See* Commuting students

Summaries in notetaking, 429–30, *432–33*

Surveying as Step 1 in SQ3R process, 222–24

Suspension from institution, 23, 25, 28

Syllabus, *17*

Symbol graphs, 282, *284*

Symbols, *506*
  in maps, 292, 294

T

Tables
  steps in creating, *279*
  steps in reading, *271*
  uses and types, 269–70, *270–71, 273*

Technical courses, *49*

Terminology, college, *17, 48–49*

Term papers, 462–63
  buying, *494–95*

Test anxiety, controlling, 145–50
Tests. *See* Exams
Test taking, 308–59
    general skills, 330, *331*
    using returned exams to improve, 146, *147*
Test-wiseness, 342–46
Text
    identifying structure of, 236–40, *239–42, 242, 243*
    relation to lectures, 197–98
    SQ3R plan for systematic reading, 222–60
Text labeling, 228, *232, 232–35, 234–35*
Text marking
    in careful reading, 226–28, *229–31, 232, 232*
    evaluation of, 247
Themes, 462
Thesauruses, 437, *453, 455–57*
Thesis statement(s), 469
Thinking critically, 360–412. *See also* components of MIND process
Thinking (T), 3–4, *7, 58*
Time line(s), 275–76, *276–79*
Time management, 54–112
    avoiding procrastination, 86–95
    maintaining balance in schedule, 103–4
    for nontraditional students, 34, 36–37
    over a term, weekly, daily, 75–80
    scheduling classes for maximum learning, 97–98
    scheduling future and present semesters, 96–101
    use of learning style in, 57–59, *60*
    use of spare minutes, *85*
Title cards, 419
Transcript(s), *17,* 28, 34
Transfer credits, *17*
Transition words in understanding lectures, 186, *186*
Tuition and fees, *16*
Tutoring, *20*

U
Underlining. *See* Text marking

V
Values used in setting goals, 65–66
Vertical files, 437
Visualization
    to help individual believe in ability, 67–68, *68*
    to reduce stress, 128–30
Visual practice as memory aid, 323
Visual preference, impact on effective learning of, 5, 7, *10*
Vocabulary development
    analyzing words structurally for meaning, *157–62*
    brain dominance in, *306–7*
    connotation *vs.* denotation, *410*
    describing college courses and disciplines, *48–51*
    dictionary, glossary, and thesaurus use, *452–57*
    learning terminology for specific courses, *110–11*
    use of figurative language, *505–6*
    using background knowledge in, *217–19*
    using clues from context, *254–56*
    using word histories for meaning, *355–56*
Vocational interest tests, 64

W
"Weasel words" to limit factual statements, 368
Wellness, maintaining physical and psychological, 134–42, *143–44*
W-grade, 23
Withdrawal as response to stress, 118–19, 121, *121*
"Withdraw," defined, *17*
Word games as memory aids, 320–21
Word maps, 298–99, *302*
Working memory, 315
World Wide Web (WWW) computer network, 442–43
Writing
    elements of style, *483, 485*
    style manuals, *486*
    types and purposes, 381–82

Y
Yearbooks, 437